New England families, genealogical and memorial; a record of the achievements of her people in...the founding of a nation

American Historical Society

BIBLIOLIFE

NEW ENGLAND FAMILIES

GENEALOGICAL AND MEMORIAL

A Record of the Achievements of Her People in the Making of Commonwealths and the

Founding of a Nation

———————

COMPILED UNDER THE EDITORIAL SUPERVISION OF

WILLIAM RICHARD CUTTER, A M

Historian of the New England Historic-Genealogical Society Massachusetts

WILFRED HAROLD MUNRO, L. H. D.

Professor of History, Brown University Presi-
dent of Rhode Island Historical Society, ex-
Governor Society of Colonial Wars Rhode
Island

GUY POTTER BENTON, D D., LL D

President of the University of Vermont Secretary and Treasurer National Association of
State Universities, Elector of the Hall of
Fame, Author of The Real College ' Vermont

SAMUEL HART, D D, D C L

Dean of Berkeley Divinity School, President
of Connecticut Historical Society Connecticut

AUGUSTUS FREEDOM MOULTON, A M.

Ex-President and Historian Maine Society,
Sons of the American Revolution, Member of
Board of Overseers Bowdoin College; Member
of Council, Maine Society of the Colonial Wars,
Member of Standing Committee Maine His-
torical Society Maine.

JOHN REYNOLDS TOTTEN

Editor of "New York Genealogical and Bio-
graphical Record " New York

———————

ILLUSTRATED

———————

THE AMERICAN HISTORICAL SOCIETY (Inc)

NEW YORK   BOSTON   CHICAGO

1916

Both justice and decency require that we should bestow on our forefathers an honorable remembrance—*Thucydides*

BIOGRAPHICAL

ENCYCLOPEDIA OF BIOGRAPHY

RHODES, Marcus Arnold,

Manufacturer

The Rhodes family has been a continuous one in Massachusetts for more than two hundred and seventy-five years, members of which in succeeding generations have given a good account of themselves in the business and social life of the communities in which they have abided, rising to useful and substantial citizenship, and as well to responsible public trust This article is to particularly treat of the branch of this family to which belonged the late Marcus Morton Rhodes, of Taunton, Massachusetts, one of the highly honored and respected citizens of that community, and who was the head of a family which has figured so conspicuously in the business history of that city, the father of sons whose careers have been marked in industrial, moral and social circles, and whose generous deeds and good citizenship are universally conceded and commended The ancestral line of this branch of this family, from the first American ancestor, which follows, is given in chronological order, the Roman numerals indicating the generations

(I) Henry Rhodes, born in 1608, in England, is of record at Lynn, Massachusetts, in 1640, where he was an ironmonger, residing on the east side of the Saugus river, and some of his descendants still reside in that section He married Elizabeth ———, and his family comprised children, as follows Eleazer, born in February, 1641, Samuel, February, 1643, married, in 1684 Abigail Coates, Joseph, January, 1645, married,

in 1674, Jane Coates; Joshua, April, 1648, married, in 1678, Ann Graves, Josiah, mentioned below, Jonathan, May, 1654, and Elizabeth, 1657

(II) Josiah Rhodes, son of Henry and Elizabeth Rhodes, was born in April, 1651, and married, in 1673, Elizabeth Coates, and to this union were born children as follows Henry, 1674, Elizabeth, 1676, Mary, 1677, died in infancy, John, 1679, died in infancy, Josiah, Jr, 1681, Eleazer, July 8, 1683, John (2), March 22, 1685, Mary (2), March 26, 1687, and Jonathan, September 18, 1692

(III) Eleazer Rhodes, son of Josiah and Elizabeth (Coates) Rhodes, was born July 8, 1683, and married, November 21, 1710, Jemima Preble, and to this union were born children John, September 9, 1711, Jemima, December 19, 1712, Eleazer, Jr, January 16, 1714-15, Stephen, mentioned below; Josiah, 1718; Mary (Lynn vital records say Sarah), August 24, 1719, Joseph, September 8, 1721, Benjamin, 1723; Elizabeth, May 26, 1726, Samuel, April 24, 1728, Joshua, August 19, 1730, and Mary, April 14, 1733 Eleazer Rhodes removed with his family to Stoughtonham, about 1720, and was constable in that town in 1725-26, and there died in 1742, his widow being administratrix of his estate

(IV) Stephen Rhodes, son of Eleazer and Jemima (Preble) Rhodes, was born February 1, 1716-17, in Lynn, Massachusetts, and married (intentions published October 25, 1740) Deliverance Walcot, who was born November 15, 1724, daughter of William Walcot, of Attleboro, Massachusetts Their children were Stephen, Jr, mentioned below,

3

Daniel, Simeon, and Deliverance The father died January 23, 1792, and the mother September 4, 1804

(V) Stephen (2) Rhodes, son of Stephen (1) and Deliverance (Walcot) Rhodes, married, January 18, 1764, Mary Boyden, who was born May 11, 1744, of Walpole, Massachusetts, and their children were Millie, who married a Mr Plimpton, Mary, born August 24, 1767, married Jesse Pratt, Aaron, who married Mary Wilkinson, and Stephen, mentioned below. Stephen Rhodes, Jr, died in 1770, inventory of his estate being taken by John Boyden He is of record as having enlisted in February, 1760, for service in the French and Indian War His widow married for her second husband, on November 24, 1775, Asa Morse

(VI) Stephen (3) Rhodes, son of Stephen (2) and Mary (Boyden) Rhodes, was born October 17, 1769, and married (first) Anna (Daniels) Carpenter, who was born March 27, 1763, daughter of Francis Daniels, and widow of Nehemiah Carpenter, of Foxboro, Massachusetts The children born of this union were: Achsah, April 14, 1793, died October 30, 1795, Stephen, mentioned below, Susan, born May 10, 1797, married Ira Fairbanks, and died in 1864, Anna, July 5, 1799, married John Corey, Mary, March 20, 1804, married Ira French Stephen (3) Rhodes married (second) March 20, 1815, Polly Carpenter, and she died April 9, 1839, the mother of the following children Catherine, born March 12, 1816, who married William Payson, Maria, November 1, 1817, who married Stephen Coleman, Martha, December 4, 1819, who married William Hitchcock, Elizabeth C, May 20, 1824, who married a Mr Greene, and Sarah, January 9, 1828, who died January 3, 1839

(VII) Stephen (4) Rhodes, son of Stephen (3) and Anna (Daniels-Carpenter)

Rhodes, was born March 15, 1795 He was for many years connected with the straw hat industry, prominently identified with Foxboro's industrial history. In 1835, with his family, he removed to Taunton, Massachusetts, and there went into the tack manufacturing business, under the firm name of S Rhodes & Son, his son, Marcus M Rhodes, being connected with him in this enterprise They were among the first promoters of the industry that subsequently caused Taunton to be widely noted as the home of tack making The business was established at Brittanniaville, the original site being that of the present plant of the Reed & Barton Company, occupying a part of the same building with the original silverware concern Both concerns grew and prospered, and as a consequence the Rhodes works had to seek new quarters, establishing itself on Union street Mr Rhodes died in Taunton, October 24, 1874 On January 1, 1817, he married Betsey Bird, who was born July 10, 1795, daughter of Elijah and Sarah (Pratt) Bird, of Foxboro, Massachusetts (see Bird VI and Pratt VI) To this union were born the following children 1 Lavinia, born October 17, 1817 2 Lucretia M, born September 2, 1819, died November 21, 1878 3 Marcus Morton, mentioned below 4 Stephen Holbrook, born November 7, 1825, married Elizabeth M Godfrey, he was for many years prominent in the affairs of Taunton, where he was a member of the Board of Aldermen, and mayor of the city, later becoming president of the John Hancock Insurance Company, of Boston 5 Mary Bird, born April 30, 1829. 6 John Corey, born October 10, 1831; married (first) Sarah B. Perrigo, and (second) Caroline M Jewett, he was for many years a prominent manufacturer in New Bedford, Massachusetts, where he passed

4

away, July 15, 1916 7 Almira Elizabeth, born February 3, 1835 8 Ellen
Frances, born December 30, 1839

(VIII) Marcus Morton Rhodes, son of
Stephen (4) and Betsey (Bird) Rhodes,
was born January 22, 1822, in Foxboro,
Massachusetts, and acquired his education in the common schools of Franklin,
Foxboro and Taunton, and at the high
school and Bristol Academy, of Taunton
After leaving school, he entered the tack
factory of his father, where he familiar-
ized himself with the details of the trade
of making tacks and nails At the age
of twenty-one years he was taken into
partnership with his father, becoming a
member of the firm of S Rhodes & Son
In the middle fifties the business was
transferred to the Taunton Tack Company, and Marcus M Rhodes then
started a new enterprise the Dighton
Manufacturing Company, engaged in the
manufacture of tacks, of which he was
agent and treasurer A foible of feminine
fashion which prevailed at that time gave
a field for the making of hoop skirt trim-
mings, which were a side line with the
manufacture of tacks This plant was in
lower Dighton opposite Berkley, on the
Taunton river In 1872, Mr Rhodes
established himself in the button manufacturing industry with which he was
prominently identified throughout the remainder of his long and active life. Up
to that time the shoe industry flourished
in this part of Massachusetts, it being the
day of the small shoe shops, which were
scattered through the country in this
section, but there had been a handicap as
a result of the necessity of importing all
the shoe buttons from the foreign countries, France supplying most of them.
Realizing the commercial value of a machine that would turn out this line of
buttons, Mr Rhodes, who had an in-
genious inventive faculty, set to work in

this direction A button works had been
started in Connecticut, with an American
designed machine, but the device had
many imperfections, which rendered the
enterprise a failure, and it had been abandoned Mr Rhodes was more fortunate,
the machine he invented for the purpose
of making shoe buttons from *papier-
mache* proved a success, and thereby the
first successful shoe button manufactory
in this country was established by him,
under the firm name of M M Rhodes &
Sons Shoe hooks and other accessories
were also manufactured for the trade by
this new concern, which grew and prospered from the beginning, under the
direction of Mr Rhodes His sons were
associated with him in the business, which
was incorporated under the laws of Massachusetts, in 1888, as the M M Rhodes
& Sons Company, of which he became
president, continuing in that capacity until his death

Aside from his manufacturing enterprises, Mr Rhodes always displayed an
active interest in civic affairs He was
one of the leading townsmen at the time
the town government of Taunton was
abandoned and he had no opposition for
a place on the original City Council,
when the city form of government was
created, in 1865 At this time Taunton
was also considering the establishing of
a water works system, and the following
year Mr Rhodes was elected a member
of the board of water commissioners, by
which board the present water system
was established He served for three
years in this capacity, declining a re-
election In his younger days he was
connected with the old Taunton Volunteer Fire Department, of which he was a
member, and for several years was captain of the old "Union Company, No 1,"
a hand-tub, with a history earned under
Mr Rhodes' captaincy that was credit-

able for efficiency, and which was situated at a station at the foot of Union street, in the vicinity of the home he occupied for many years on Cedar street Besides these offices, he was for many years a member of the board of directors of the Taunton National Bank, and of the Taunton-New Bedford Copper Company

Mr Rhodes was always held in high esteem in the community. He was of a kind-hearted, benevolent disposition, his benefactors being many and of the sort that carried no ostentation in the giving "He was," as a close friend said, in speaking of his death, "a man who was always looking for an opportunity to do a kind act for somebody" He found these even to the last months of his life, and there are many who have special occasion to mourn him personally, by the loss of a benefactor   Mr Rhodes had lived during the administration of all but the first four United States presidents He had watched the growth of this country from the days when the Ohio Valley was the frontier in the West, as the population spread by degrees to the Pacific, and increased from less than ten million people to over one hundred million   To the very last day of his life he was blessed with an intellect that was unclouded by any infirmities that often follow advanced age, and his memory of the improvements and advancements made in various lines during his recollections made him a particularly interesting conversationalist, especially when he talked of his impressions of the advance that man had made in procuring conveniences and methods for improved living conditions during the marvelously developing nine decades of history over which his life had extended. Mr Rhodes devoted his personal attention to his business affairs until within

a few months of his death, visiting the factory every day until the infirmities of age became more marked

On November 11, 1845, Mr Rhodes was united in marriage to Rowena A Williams, who was born November 16, 1825 She was the daughter of George W and Rowena C (Wilbur) Williams, the former of whom died in Taunton, August 19, 1858, aged sixty-nine years, and the latter July 23, 1892, in the eighty-eighth year of her age   To Mr and Mrs Rhodes were born three sons, namely 1 Charles Marcus, born October 6, 1846, married Annie B Haskins, and they reside in Taunton   2 George Holbrook, mentioned below 3 Albert Clinton, born April 9, 1857, married Cora E Dyer, and they reside at Clifton Springs, New York

Mr Rhodes passed away at his home on Cedar street, Taunton, Massachusetts, March 23, 1916, in the ninety-fifth year of his age   He was a member of no fraternal organizations, but for many years and until its dissolution was connected with the Trinitarian Society   He was an active member of the Old Colony Historical Society   In political faith he was first an old line Whig, and upon the formation of the Republican party, in 1856, he became identified with the latter political party   He was the last survivor of Taunton's original City Council, of which body he was a member in 1865, in which year the city government was established   The Taunton "Gazette," of March 23, 1916, in speaking of the death of Mr Rhodes, editorially, said

Taunton loses one of its grand old men in the passing of Mr Marcus M Rhodes   A leading manufacturer, a useful and honorable citizen, his many years of active life placed him in close touch with all the elements working to build up the city, and his influence and his moral and financial support were always found quietly con-

cerned in every worth-while movement His later years, going far beyond the span of life usually allotted to man, were spent in enjoying that quiet repose which is all the more enjoyable when it is compassed by the wholesome and united respect of one's fellow citizens, as in the case of Mr Rhodes

(IX) George Holbrook Rhodes, second son of Marcus Morton and Rowena A (Williams) Rhodes, was born August 11, 1848, in Taunton, Massachusetts His educational training was acquired in the public schools of his native town, graduating from the high school, in 1866, the year following the incorporation of Taunton as a city After leaving school he entered the factory of his father, and in 1872, when his father organized the firm of M M Rhodes & Sons, he was admitted to partnership In 1888, when the concern was incorporated as the M M Rhodes & Sons Company, Mr Rhodes was elected treasurer of the corporation, which official position he continued to hold until his death In political faith Mr Rhodes was a staunch Republican, and served his native city as a member of the Common Council from 1877 to 1886, inclusive, during which service he was for the last four years president of that body He was president of the City Council at the time the high school building was erected, and by virtue of his office as president of the Council was also a trustee of the public library, and a member of the school committee Mr. Rhodes never sought any other public office although he was on various occasions solicited to become a candidate for various public positions, but always declined, preferring to give his undivided attention to his business interests He was a director of the Taunton National Bank, a trustee of the Taunton Savings Bank and a trustee of Morton Hospital for a number of years, in all of which

capacities he gave valued and efficient service

Mr Rhodes was an active and prominent member of the Masonic fraternity, having attained the highest degree in that organization, having been elevated to the thirty-third degree, September 21, 1897 He was a member and past worshipful master of Charles H Titus Lodge, Ancient Free and Accepted Masons, of Taunton; a member of Keystone Chapter, Royal Arch Masons, of Foxboro, Massachusetts; a member and past eminent commander of St John's Commandery, Knights Templar, of Providence, Rhode Island, and a member of the Massachusetts Consistory, thirty-second degree, of Boston He was one of the trustees of the Masonic Education and Charity Trust of the Grand Lodge of Massachusetts, elected in December, 1895, to serve eight years, and reelected in 1902 for another term of eight years He was also treasurer of the Taunton Masonic Corporation While not holding office in the institution, Mr Rhodes was for many years very actively interested in Wheaton Seminary, and the present Wheaton College, at Norton, Massachusetts For a period of twelve years he officiated as marshal of the commencement exercises, officiating at these exercises in that capacity in June preceding his demise, and during all these years was a steadfast worker in its interests When the Young Men's Christian Association was organized in Taunton, Mr Rhodes was made treasurer of the association, and was actively interested in the work of this organization

On September 10, 1874, Mr Rhodes married (first) Louisa L Bassett, who was born October 10, 1846, daughter of Charles J H and Nancy L (Gibbs) Bassett of Taunton Massachusetts (see Bassett VIII) To Mr and Mrs Rhodes

7

were born children as follows   1. Helen
Holbrook, born August 13, 1877, mar-
ried, June 4, 1901, Ralph F Barker, of
Taunton, she passed away June 5, 1915,
the mother of the following children:
Anson, born March 21, 1902, Humphrey,
June 20, 1905, and George Holbrook,
June 5, 1915   2 Nancy Bassett, born
January 20, 1880, who became the second
wife of Ralph E Barker, on February 10,
1917   3 Marcus Arnold, mentioned be-
low   The mother of these children
passed away March 30, 1902, and Mr
Rhodes married (second) October 15,
1913, Mary E Van Patten, of Auburn,
New York, who survives him

Mr Rhodes passed away October 19,
1916, at Poland Springs, Maine, whence
he had gone in hopes of regaining his
broken health his death being a severe
shock to his wide circle of friends and
acquaintances   As a man and citizen,
Mr Rhodes was noted for his uniform
courtesy, democratic manners and personal integrity   Few men could be less
pretentious and yet dignified, and none
commanded greater respect   He was a
forcible, energetic and progressive man
in his ideas and purposes, and succeeded
to the prestige of his family which has
conducted one of Taunton's leading industries for many years   His usefulness
as a citizen extended far outside his business career into spheres of active benefi-
cence   His many and substantial acts
of real charity were seldom known except to the recipients   There was neither
ostentation nor show in his make-up, but
rather a marked antipathy for pretense
and deceit   Nowhere in New England
can there be found a family that for more
than half a century has occupied a
higher position in the industrial, financial and social life of their community
than this Rhodes family in Taunton   Mr
Rhodes' greatest pleasure may be said to

have been found in his home and family,
where were displayed a devotion and an
indulgence rarely witnessed

(X) Marcus Arnold Rhodes, only son
of George Holbrook and Louisa I (Bassett) Rhodes, was born in Taunton, Massachusetts, July 17, 1881   His educational training was obtained in the public
and high schools of his native city, and
after graduating from the high school, he
entered Amherst College, from which he
was graduated in 1903 with the degree of
Bachelor of Arts   He then took a special
course at Harvard University, graduating therefrom with the degree of Master
of Arts in 1905   During the following
three years he was engaged in teaching
at Deerfield Academy   In 1908, Mr
Rhodes became associated with the M
M Rhodes & Sons Company, and upon
the death of his father, in 1916, succeeded
him as treasurer of the corporation   In
political faith Mr Rhodes is an independent Republican, and is now (1917) serving on his second three year term as a
member of the school committee   Fraternally, he is a member of the Masonic
organization, holding membership in
Ionic Lodge, Ancient Free and Accepted
Masons, and St. Mark's Chapter, Royal
Arch Masons, of Taunton, and is also a
member of Alpha Delta Phi college fraternity   Socially, he is a member of the
Winthrop Club, of Taunton   Like his
father, Mr Rhodes is an active and
valued member of the Broadway Trinitarian Congregational Church, of which
he has served as deacon for several years,
and as superintendent of the Sunday
school for a number of years

On September 1 1908, Mr Rhodes was
united in marriage to Ruth L Bangs,
daughter of Frank W and Elmina (Tisdale) Bangs, of Greenfield, Massachusetts, and this union has been blessed
with four children, namely   Louisa Bas-

set', born February 12, 1910, Stephen
Holbrook, February 25, 1911, Rowena
Lincoln, July 6, 1914, and Marcus Arnold,
Jr , March 20, 1917

(The Bird Line).

The Bird family is of long and honorable standing in Massachusetts, having
been settled there early in the settling of
this country, being referred to by historians as an industrious people, modest and
retiring in disposition

(I) Thomas Bird, the founder of this
family in America, was born in England,
in 1613 He came to New England at an
early period, locating at Dorchester, Massachusetts, where he joined the church,
in 1642, on its reorganization under the
distinguished Rev Richard Mather He
was a tanner by trade, which occupation
he followed in Dorchester, and lived on
what was called Humphrey street He
was bailiff in 1654 He died June 8, 1667,
aged fifty-four years His widow, Ann,
died August 21, 1673 They were the
parents of six children

(II) John Bird, the second son of
Thomas and Ann Bird was born at Dorchester, March 11, 1641, and died August
2, 1732 He married Elizabeth Williams
who was born in Taunton, in 1644, and
died at Dorchester, October 20, 1724, aged
seventy-seven years She was the daughter of Richard and Frances (Dighton)
Williams, her father being one of the first
settlers of Taunton, Massachusetts John
Bird and his wife were the parents of
eleven children

(III) Samuel Bird, sixth child of John
and Elizabeth (Williams) Bird, was born
in Dorchester, April 14, 1680, and married, May 16, 1704 Sarah Clapp, who was
born March 24, 1686 He died March 20,
1740, in Stoughton, Massachusetts, where
his estate inventoried 1,731 pounds, 5
shillings and 10 pence They were the
parents of nine children

(IV) Samuel (2) Bird, youngest child
of Samuel (1) and Sarah (Clapp) Bird,
was born July 27, 1726 He lived in
Stoughton, Massachusetts, where he was
married April 13, 1748, by Rev Jonathan Bowman, to Anna Atherton, who
was born at Dorchester, Massachusetts,
daughter of Humphrey Atherton

(V) Elijah Bird, son of Samuel (2)
and Anna (Atherton) Bird, was born at
Sharon, Massachusetts, June 9, 1753, and
married, December 12, 1777, Sarah Pratt
of Stoughton Massachusetts, daughter of
Captain Josiah and Abigail (Williams)
Pratt (see Pratt VI) Elijah Bird, of
Stoughtonham, was a soldier in the Revolutionary War, serving as a private in
Captain Robert Swan's company, Colonel
Benjamin Gill's regiment, marched December 19, 1776, service six days, at Castle
Island, company raised from Milton,
Stoughton and Stoughtonham, he was
also corporal in Captain Theophilus Wilder's company, Colonel Dike's regiment,
return of men in service from December
30, 1776, to March 1, 1777 He died at
Foxboro, Massachusetts, November 20,
1821, and his wife died October 12, 1821,
aged sixty-nine years

(VI) Betsey Bird, daughter of Elijah
and Sarah (Pratt) Bird, was born in Foxboro, Massachusetts July 10, 1795, and
married there January 1, 1817, Stephen
Rhodes of that town (see Rhodes VII)

(The Pratt Line)

The Pratt family has been noted for
integrity and capacity, and members of it
have played important parts in the early
history of New England, as well as in
more recent generations

(I) Matthew Pratt, of Weymouth, Massachusetts, a freeman of May, 1640, and
who died there, August 29, 1672, was
among the earliest settlers of that town,
where he was frequently selectman, and
appears to have been one of the most

prominent men in the Colony He married Elizabeth Bates, and their children were Thomas, Matthew, Jr., John Samuel, Joseph, Elizabeth, and Mary.

(II) Samuel Pratt, son of Matthew and Elizabeth (Bates) Pratt, was born in Weymouth, and married there, in 1660, Hannah Rogers, who died in 1715 He died in 1678 Their children were Judith, John, Hannah, Mary, Samuel, Jr., Experience and Ebenezer

(III) Samuel (2) Pratt son of Samuel (1) and Hannah (Rogers) Pratt was born at Weymouth, November 15, 1670 He married Patience Church, and their children were Judith, Samuel, Josiah, Jonathan Benjamin, Peter, Paul, Hannah, and Patience Samuel Pratt removed to Taunton, Massachusetts shortly after the birth of his daughter, Judith, in 1695, where he became a man of considerable prominence owning a large estate in the latter town where he died August 11, 1728

(IV) Josiah Pratt, son of Samuel (2) and Patience (Church) Pratt, was born in Taunton, Massachusetts, about 1797 and married, November 22 1716 in Norton, Massachusetts, Sarah Jones, of Taunton, who died March 2, 1723 He married (second) May 20 1725, Tabitha Smith, who died January 16 1772 He died about 1745

(V) Captain Josiah (2) Pratt, son of Josiah (1) and Sarah (Jones) Pratt, was born in Norton Massachusetts, February 14, 1719-20 The intentions of his marriage to Abigail Williams was published in Norton, September 17, 1743 She was born in Norton, May 2, 1723 daughter of Benjamin and Elizabeth (Dean) Williams, of Norton Captain Josiah Pratt was a soldier in the Revolution serving as captain of a Stoughtonham company, Colonel Gill's regiment, which marched to Roxbury on an alarm, March

4, 1776 He died at Foxboro, Massachusetts, February 8, 1800, aged eighty years His wife, Abigail, died June 2, 1814, aged ninety-one years

(VI) Sarah Pratt, daughter of Captain Josiah (2) and Abigail (Williams) Pratt, was born at Foxboro Massachusetts in 1753 She married, December 12, 1777, Elijah Bird, of Foxboro (see Bird V)

TOLMAN, Fred Sawin,

Founder of the Tolman Print.

The Tolman coat-of-arms is described as follows Sable a martlet argent between three ducal crowns or The crest Two arms in armour embowed wielding a battle ax, all proper This is the only Tolman armorial, and according to the rule followed by American families of English descent belongs to the Tolman family in this country The Tolman family in England dates back to ancient times.

(I) Thomas Tolman the immigrant ancestor, was born in England, about 1608, and according to family tradition came to Dorchester, Massachusetts, with the first colonists there, in the ship 'Mary and John" in 1630, and that he owned land extending from the salt water to the Dedham line He certainly settled very early in Dorchester, and not only had land there but in the present towns of Stoughton Canton and Sharon His name is mentioned first in the Dorchester records of October 31, 1639, as follows "It is ordered that Goodman Tolman's house be appointed for the receiving of any goods that shall be brought in whereof the owner is not known " He signed the church covenant of 1636, was admitted a freeman of the colony, May 13, 1640. He located near Pine Neck, now called Port Norfolk, his house being within one hundred feet of Pine Neck creek on the west side and within two hundred feet on

10

the north side, the creek being shaped like an elbow at this point Some of his homestead was at last accounts still in the possession of his lineal descendants. The house in which his son Thomas afterward lived, between what ,is now Ashmont street and Washington street, was probably built by him and has remained in the family He was a wheelwright, and a man of substance and prominence He held various town offices in Dorchester His first wife was Sarah, his second Katherine, who died November 7, 1677 He died June 8, 1690, in his eighty-second year His will was dated October 29, 1688 proved February 5, 1691-92, bequeathing to his eldest son Thomas, daughters Sarah Leadbetter, Rebecca Tucker, Ruth Royall, Hannah Lyon and Mary Collins, son, John Tolman, James Tucker, husband of Rebecca, to pay a certain sum to Isaac Royall's (Ryall) two eldest daughters, Ruth and Mary Royall Children of Thomas Tolman 1 Thomas, born 1633, John, mentioned below, Sarah, married Henry Leadbetter, Rebecca, married James Tucker, Ruth, married Isaac Royall, Hannah, born August 27 1642, married (first) George Lyon and (second) William Baker, Mary, married —— Collins, of Lynn

(II) John Tolman, son of Thomas Tolman, was born about 1635 He was admitted a freeman in 1678 He married (first) Elizabeth Collins, daughter of John Collins, of Lynn She died October 7, 1690, and he married (second) June 15, 1692, Mary Paul, widow, who died August 25, 1720 He was a selectman of Dorchester, in 1693-94-95 He died January 1, 1724-25 Children Elizabeth, born December 14, 1667, John, April 8, 1671, Joseph, September 6, 1674, Benjamin mentioned below, Henry, March 13, 1678-79, Ann, April 1, 1681, Ebenezer, March 27, 1683, Ruth, July 1, 1685, William September 2, 1687

(III) Benjamin Tolman, son of John Tolman, was born at Dorchester, December 6, 1676 In 1709 he removed from his native town and settled in Scituate, Massachusetts He married, August 4, 1709, Elizabeth Palmer, daughter of Bezaleel Palmer They lived a quarter of a mile southeast of Church Hill Children born at Scituate Benjamin, March 28 1710, Samuel, October 22, 1711, Elizabeth, November 5, 1713 Joseph, mentioned below, William January 12, 1716, Elisha November 20, 1718

(IV) Captain Joseph Tolman, son of Benjamin Tolman, was born in Scituate September 6, 1715 He married there, May 22, 1738, Mary Turner, daughter of Squire Turner, the lawyer Children born in Scituate Hannah, baptized September 29 1740, Samuel, baptized January 29 1743-44 died young Mary, baptized November 3, 1745, Elizabeth, baptized November 8, 1747, Joseph, baptized October 28, 1750, John, mentioned below.

(V) John (2) Tolman, son of Captain Joseph Tolman, was born in 1750, and died in Scituate, June 3 1831, aged eighty-one years He married (second) April 8, 1784, at Scituate, Dorothy Hall, daughter of Dr Hall His sons removed to Boston Children John, mentioned below; Molly, lived at Marshfield; Benjamin, Hewett

(VI) John (3) Tolman son of John (2) Tolman, was born in Marshfield or Scituate, September 3, 1777 He married, October 13, 1802 or 1803, Averick Everson (see Everson IV) She was born October 13, 1782 daughter of Levi and Eunice (Briggs) Everson They lived at Pembroke and Abington Children, born at Pembroke William Cushing born July 2, 1804 Moses September 26, 1805. died September 28, 1805, John, mentioned below, Aaron, June 26, 1808, died June 26 1808, Eliza West June 24, 1809, Eunice Briggs, July 28, 1815, married, May 7, 1835, Turner Sampson, Sardis, June 14,

1819, Byron, August 23, 1824, Averick September 16, 1828

(VII) John (4) Tolman, son of John (3) Tolman was born at Pembroke, March 27, 1807 He married, November 28, 1833, Eliza Russell Sawin, born at Bridgewater, November 18, 1811, daughter of Dr Daniel and Hannah (Barrell) Sawin (see Sawin VII) Children, born at Hanson Daniel Sawin, mentioned below, Eliza, born 1839, died September 3, 1841, Charles December 11, 1846; and George

(VIII) Daniel Sawin Tolman, son of John (4) Tolman, was born in Hanson, August 21, 1834, and died at Brockton He settled on a farm in Stoughton, removing later to North Bridgewater, where he engaged in the men's furnishing business in partnership with his brother, Charles Their store was at the corner of Main and Green streets, and for many years the firm of Tolman Brothers enjoyed an extensive business and a high reputation for square dealing and reliable goods He married, at Stoughton, Eliza F Monk (see Monk V) Children Fred Sawin, mentioned below, Harry C, who has been for many years manager of the business office of the Tolman Print in Boston, Carrie, died at the age of eighteen years

(IX) Fred Sawin Tolman, son of Daniel Sawin Tolman, was born December 9, 1856, in Stoughton, on the homestead, which was located near the famous old Swann tavern In his boyhood he came with his parents to Brockton, then to North Bridgewater He attended the public schools of Stoughton and Brockton and was graduated from the Brockton High School He started in his business career as clerk in the store of Tolman Brothers, but in 1875 left the employ of his father to engage in the printing business on his own account In a little shop, at the rear of his father's store, he started

with a capital of $35, with a plant costing $30 84, the bill for these goods, which he bought of Joseph Watson, of Boston, Mr Tolman preserved and treasured all his life At that time card printing was popular and it was adapted to his meagre type fonts and hand press An advertisement in the "Youth's Companion,' costing him $10, brought in the first week $60 worth of work and put his business on a sound basis He soon added to his plant and before long had to secure larger quarters To move and enlarge his plant was another strain on his resources, but a loan from W W Cross tided him over and he never forgot the kindness of Mr Cross, though the amount was only $125, but Mr Tolman in speaking of the transaction always explained that Mr Cross had to his credit many other similar transactions, giving timely aid to young men needing capital to get on their feet He remained in his second office in the old Gazette Building at the corner of Main and Ward streets about a year, removing in 1876 to the Holbrook Building on the present site of Hotel Keswick, where he remained until 1887, when he moved his plant to the old fire engine house on East Elm street When he went there he occupied about 3,800 square feet of space, but from time to time he rented more room until he had doubled the area

From July 25, 1876, to September 19 1877, Frederick B Howard, who was later associated with Mr Tolman in real estate deals of large magnitude, was his partner in the printing business In 1876 the firm employed one printer, doing the rest of the work with their own hands In 1899 Mr Tolman had a force of thirteen printers, in 1892, twenty-seven, in 1895, thirty-eight and at the time of his death more than one hundred and twenty-five Considering the size of the city and that his business was confined to job printing, his business record was phenomenal He made a specialty of town orders and secured business in all parts of the country.

In 1899 he moved to the present location of the Tolman Print, in the Howard-Tolman Building, occupying at first 15,000 feet of space Though the plant has doubled in size since that time, Mr Tolman had good reason to be proud of this modern office in a new building of which he was half-owner He then had two cylinder presses and sixteen job presses He manufactured his own electricity for his printing office and the rest of the building, and made use of a building on Church street for a stockroom and power plant At the time it was built the Howard-Tolman Building was one of the finest in the city

The Tolman Print takes rank with the best equipped, most efficient and successful job printing plants in the country Mr Tolman was the originator of the shoe carton label In the old days shoes were shipped in sacks and boxes When the shoe carton or paper box for each pair of shoes came into use, he designed the labels and developed an enormous business, finding customers in every country where shoes are manufactured His Brockton fair posters have been marvels of the printer's art and he secured the poster work for innumerable fairs and horse shows throughout the country

During the last fifteen years of his life he occupied a beautiful residence on Arlington street, Brockton It was one of the garden spots of the section The grounds were arranged according to Mr Tolman's own artistic taste and were extremely attractive His flowers and shrubs were second to none The interior of his home also gave evidence of his exceptional taste and love of the beautiful

He was an important factor in the development of the great institution, known as the Brockton Fair When an art exhibit was an annual feature in the big exhibition hall, he had charge of it He was active in promoting the horse show feature that attracted exhibitors from every part of the country He was a member of the Commercial Club of Brockton, vice-president and director of the Brockton Agricultural Society, member of the Merchants' and Manufacturers' Club, the Algonquin Club of Boston, director of the Home National Bank of Brockton He was made a Mason in Paul Revere Lodge, in 1886, and was later a member of Satucket Chapter, Royal Arch Masons, Bay State Commandery, Knights Templar, and the Massachusetts Consistory He was also a member of the Odd Fellows, and the New England Order of Protection, of the Thorny Lea Golf Club and the Brockton Country Club He was fond of all out-door life He occupied a summer home at Monument Beach on Buzzard's Bay and loved yachting He was often on the golf links His flowers and horses were his most cherished possessions

He was a man of sterling integrity, exceptional ability, generous impulses and cultivated mind One of the most prominent shoe manufacturers of Brockton said of him "Although not engaged in the manufacture of shoes, Mr Tolman was closely identified with the industry and some of the credit for the growth of Brockton's leading industry properly belongs to him In the publicity work no man took a more conspicuous or more honorable part It was Mr Tolman who led in the preparation of shoe catalogues, original labels, striking designs and in developing this side of the business to the high plane on which it now rests Personally a man of parts, a magnetic and most agreeable personality, he was a good friend and an agreeable companion We shall miss him and his death will be felt " He died July 1, 1914

He married, December 25, 1877, Isabelle A Brett, daughter of Henry A Brett (see Brett VII). Children 1 Mabelle Foster, born July 17, 1879, married George B Holland, of Taunton, Massachusetts 2 Blanche, born February 2, 1882, unmarried 3 Fred Harold, born February 7, 1886, married Rosamond Smith, of Brockton, and they have one daughter, Virginia Pauline, born November 21, 1915, in Brockton 4 Daniel Sawin, born December 23, 1892

(The Everson Line)

(I) Richard Everson, the first of the family in this country as far as known, was born as early as 1675, and with John Eversor, presumably a brother of about the same age, settled in Plymouth, Massachusetts, before 1700 They were in what is now Plympton, formerly part of Plymouth, and entitled to vote in 1708 Richard was one of the petitioners living in the north part of Plymouth, who petitioned in 1717 for the incorporation of the town of Kingston His wife Elizabeth died February 16, 1716 Children by wife Elizabeth, born at Plymouth Richard, mentioned below, Ephraim, born September 1, 1702, Ebenezer, April 14, 1705, Benjamin, January 26, 1716

(II) Richard (2) Everson, son of Richard (1) Everson, was born in Plymouth colony and town, November 10, 1700 He married, March 31, 1718, Penelope Bumpus, of Middleborough Among their children was Richard, mentioned below

(III) Richard (3) Everson, son of Richard (2) Everson, was born about 1725, and settled in Kingston, also formerly part of Plymouth He married, October 30, 1750, Averick (Churchill) Standish, widow of Ebenezer Standish, and daughter of Isaac and Susanna (Leach) Churchill Children, born in Kingston Samuel, September 22, 1751, Levi, mentioned below, Martha, March 1, 1757, Susannah, July 22, 1759, died May, 1761

(IV) Levi Everson, son of Richard (3) Everson, was born March 26, 1754 He married, July 17, 1777, at Halifax, Eunice Briggs, of that town He was then of Kingston He was drowned from the North river bridge, April 5, 1800, aged forty-six years He was a soldier in the Revolution, enlisting as a private in Captain Jesse Barlow's company, stationed at Plymouth to defend the sea coast He was also in Captain Seth Stower's company, Colonel Robinson's regiment. Children, born at Kingston Levi Eunice, November 25, 1780, Averick, October 13, 1782, married John Tolman (see Tolman VI), Abigail, August 14, 1784, Sylvanus, June 27, 1786, died August 15, 1872; Charlotte, January, 1788, Samuel, February 1, 1790, Richard, November 23, 1791, Martha, October 8, 1793, Clarissa, October 18, 1795, Dulcina, May 12, 1797; Barnabas, December 14, 1798

(The Monk Line)

The original settlers of the Monk family in this country were Christopher, George and Elias Monk, presumably brothers, who came to Boston about 1675 Christopher Monk had children born from 1686 to 1700 in Boston—Susan, Mary, Christopher, Thomas and Ebenezer George Monk was a vintner in Boston at the Blue Anchor, married Lucy (Gardner) Turner, widow of John Turner, and had sons George, born 1683, William, 1686, his will gives a clue to the English home of the family and the name of his father, the estate being formerly owned by his father, William Monk, and located at Navestock, four miles from Rumford, England, in County Essex

14

(I) Elias Monk, the third of the pioneers, doubtless a son of William Monk, of Navestock, England, was born before 1670 He served in Captain Withington's company in the expedition against Canada in 1690 He was surveyor of highways in Dorchester in 1703 Monk's meadow in what is now Canton was mentioned in records as early as 1704 He leased two hundred acres there, March 4, 1703-04, for £6 for 219 years After the death of his wife Hope, he married Abigail Puffer, widow of James Puffer. In 1726 he deeded land to Elias Monk, Jr, his son, and in 1727 to sons, Elias and George He died May 29, 1743 The names of his sons George and Christopher furnish evidence that the other two immigrants were his brothers Children Mary, born 1691, George, born at Dorchester, May 1, 1696; Elias, mentioned below; Christopher, May 10, 1702, Freelove, May 2, 1704; Abigail, May 5 1708 Elizabeth, June 15, 1711

(II) Elias (2) Monk, son of Elias (1) Monk, was born before 1700 He married, May 5, 1725, Susanna Blackman He settled in the southeast part of Stoughton in 1720, died there in 1750 Children Eliphalet, born March 18, 1725-26, at Dorchester, born at Stoughton Abigail, Elias, married (first) May 5, 1744, Elizabeth Buck, of Bridgewater, (second) May 5, 1752, Elizabeth Wright, of Bridgewater, Christopher, born January 14, 1732-33, George, mentioned below; William, born November 2, 1739, soldier in the French and Indian War, fought in the battle of the Plains of Abraham in the taking of Quebec

(III) George Monk, Jr (so-called probably to distinguish him from his Uncle George), son of Elias (2) Monk, was born at Stoughton, February 10, 1734 He was a soldier in the Revolution from Stoughton, a corporal in Captain William Brigg's

company of minute-men on the Lexington Alarm, April 19, 1775, sergeant in the same company, Colonel Joseph Read's regiment, from May to September, 1775, also sergeant in Captain Simeon Leach's company, Colonel Benjamin Gill's regiment, in 1776 He married, February 10, 1762, Sarah Hixon Children, born at Stoughton Jeremiah, January 11, 1763, soldier in the Revolution, George, Jr, January 15, 1764, soldier in the Revolution Freelove, August 1, 1766, Nathan, March 12, 1769, Jacob, mentioned below

(IV) Jacob Monk, son of George Monk, was born at Stoughton, March 9, 1773, and died at the age of sixty-seven He was a man of large physique and presence, quiet, capable and of sterling qualities He married, May 29, 1796, Milly Randall, of Easton Colony railroad Children, born in Stoughton Nathan, born April 9, 1797, George Randall, mentioned below; Stillman, Jacob, Almira, married Isaac Blanchard, Eliza, died unmarried; Caroline married Charles Stone

(V) George Randall Monk, son of Jacob Monk, was born March 23, 1799, at Stoughton He was educated in the public schools of his native town In 1825 he became a manufacturer of boots and shoes in Stoughton and continued for a period of ten years He then engaged in business in West Troy, New York, but was injured by a fall that caused paralysis of both legs and he was obliged to retire from active life permanently He died at Stoughton, October 9, 1843 He married Sarah Capen, daughter of Deacon Elisha and Milly (Gay) Capen It is related that from flax raised on her father's farm, Milly Gay made the yarn, wove the cloth and sold enough homespun to buy her wedding dress Her father, Timothy Gay was a minute-man in the Revolution, serving in the defenses at

15

Roxbury Children of George R Monk
1 George E 2 Elisha Capen, born April
25, 1828, manufacturer of shoes in Stoughton, one of the founders of Greeley,
Colorado, where he was part owner of a
store, went to the Massachusetts Legislature in 1856 and to the State Senate in
1866-67, married, January 13, 1851, Sally
B French, and had children Bertha,
George and Eunice C 3 Harriet, married Ephraim W Littlefield 4. Adelia
A, married (first) W H Curtis, and (second) A A Lane 5 Eliza F, married
Daniel Sawin Tolman (see Tolman VIII).

(The Sawin Line)

(I) Robert Sawin, the progenitor of the
Sawin family of America, lived in Boxford, County Suffolk, England, and died
there in 1651. In December following
John Sawin, then in New England, sold
the homestead in Boxford to Samuel
Groome, shipwright, of Langham, England, reserving the rights of his brother's
wife and agreeing also to give a deed from
his own wife, if necessary, to complete
the title

(II) John Sawin, the immigrant ancestor, son of Robert Sawin, settled in Watertown, Massachusetts, where he was living,
May 26, 1652, when he was admitted freeman, but he was in this country as early
as April, 1650, when he was a witness,
and he was mentioned in the will of Edward Skinner, of Cambridge, in 1641.
John Sawin was a cordwainer by trade
and occupied a house owned by his
father-in-law on the west side of School
street, Watertown, about halfway between the present Belmont and Auburn
streets By the help of his father-in-law
he became the owner in 1653 of the home-
stall on which he lived and of a farm at
Watertown Farms, now Weston, near
the Sudbury line (now Wayland) on the
south side of the Sudbury road, having

the Cowpen farm to the eastward In
1664 and 1672 he was a selectman of
Watertown He married, about April,
1652, Abigail Manning, daughter of
George (commonly written Munning or
Munnings at that time, whence the name
of his son Munnings Sawin) She em-
barked with her parents and elder sister
Elizabeth at Ipswich, England, in April,
1634, then seventeen years old, after her
husband died she seems to have lived
with her son John She died after 1667
Children John, born April 16, 1653,
Munning, mentioned below, Thomas,
September 27, 1657, ancestor of the
Natick Sawins

(III) Munning Sawin, son of John
Sawin, was born at Watertown, April 4,
1655, and died November 8, 1722 He
was a prominent citizen of Watertown
His homestead was between the old
graveyard and Mount Auburn on the
south side of the Cambridge road as far
southeast as the swamp, being lots one to
four with part of Lot 5 He was clerk
of the writs in 1691, selectman, 1691-94,
treasurer, 1703-04, town clerk, 1705-07.
He was the best penman in town and did
a large share of the town business for
thirty years He married, December,
1681, Sarah Stone Children, born at
Watertown Sarah, 1684, Abigail, 1686,
John, 1689, Joseph, mentioned below,
Mary, 1694-95, George, 1697, settled at
Willington, Connecticut; Deborah, 1702,
married George Fairbanks, Elizabeth,
1705; Judith, 1707, Mercy, 1710, died
1711.

(IV) Joseph Sawin, son of Munning
Sawin, was born in Watertown, in 1691-
92 He married, in 1714, Lydia Paine,
born 1681 He settled in Braintree Children, born at Braintree Joseph, 1715,
Lydia, 1717, Munning, 1717; Eliphalet,
mentioned below.

(V) Captain Eliphalet Sawin, son of

16

Joseph Sawin, was born in Braintree, in 1722, and died in 1801, leaving a large estate He removed to what is now the town of Randolph He served in the Revolutionary War as captain of minutemen in Colonel Benjamin Lincoln's regiment on the Lexington Alarm; and again for four days in June, 1776 He was captain of the third company in Colonel Ebenezer Thayer's regiment, Fifth Suffolk County, commissioned July 17, 1777, also captain in Colonel William McIntosh's regiment from March 25 to April 7, 1778, serving at Roxbury (See p 848, vol XIII, Massachusetts Soldiers and Sailors of the Revolutionary War)

Eliphalet Sawin married (first) Rachel Thayer, a descendant of John Alden, who came in the ' Mayflower," through Ruth Alden, Sarah Bass, and Shadrach Thayer, her father Eliphalet Sawin married (second) Sarah ——— He and his sons were remarkable for their great physical strength He owned and operated a saw mill Children, born at Braintree Rachel, married Isaac Thayer, Sarah, baptized in 1754, lived at Randolph; Shadrach, married Dorothy Thayer; Susan, born 1755, Naomi, baptized 1759, Amasa, Eliphalet, mentioned below

(VI) Eliphalet (2) Sawin, son of Eliphalet (1) Sawin, was born about 1750 He married Eunice Wild Among their children was Daniel, mentioned below

(VII) Dr Daniel Sawin, son of Eliphalet (2) Sawin, was born in Randolph, April 30, 1786 He married (first) Hannah Barrell, November 18, 1810, in Bridgewater She died November 2, 1816, aged twenty-six years He married (second) April 1, 1820, Deborah Cushman, of Hanson They lived in East Bridgewater, where Dr Daniel Sawin died April 29, 1822 Children, born at Bridgewater Eliza Russell, November 18, 1811, married, November 28, 1833, John

Tolman (see Tolman VII), Hannah, January 1, 1814, Daniel C, 1821

(The Brett Line)

(I) William Brett, immigrant ancestor, was born in England and came from County Kent in 1640. He was one of the founders and original proprietors of Bridgewater, Massachusetts, and deputy from the date of incorporation in 1656 to 1661 His son William and many of his descendants in later generations have also served in the Legislature He was elder of the church and often preached when the pastor was absent He died December 17, 1681, aged sixty-three years By wife Margaret he had children William, Elihu, Nathaniel, Hannah.

(II) Nathaniel Brett, son of William Brett, married, in 1683, Sarah Hayward, daughter of John Hayward He was deacon of the church and for several years town clerk He died November 19, 1740 Children, born at Bridgewater Alice, January 29, 1686, Seth, mentioned below, Mehitable, August 12, 1692, Sarah, January 28, 1695; Hannah, October 18, 1699, William, April 26, 1702, Nathaniel, November 3, 1704

(III) Seth Brett, son of Nathaniel Brett, was born February 24, 1688 He married, in 1712, Sarah Alden, daughter of Isaac and Mehitable (Allen) Alden, granddaughter of Joseph and Mary (Simmons) Alden, and great-granddaughter of John and Priscilla (Mullins) Alden, who came in the "Mayflower" Mr Brett died of smallpox, January 11, 1722 Children, born at Bridgewater Samuel, mentioned below, Silas, February 28, 1716, minister of Berkley, Sarah, March 3, 1718, Simeon, Seth, April 13, 1722.

(IV) Samuel Brett, son of Seth Brett, was born at Bridgewater, August 22, 1714 He married, in 1737, Hannah Packard, daughter of David and Hannah

ENCYCLOPEDIA OF BIOGRAPHY

(Ames) Packard, and a direct descendant in the fourth generation of Samuel Packard, who came from Windham, England, and settled in Hingham, Massachusetts, later in Bridgewater. Mr. Brett was an early settler in the north parish of Bridgewater, where he died in 1807.

(V) William (2) Brett, son of Samuel Brett, was born at Bridgewater, April 7, 1758. He married (first) in 1782, Molly Allen, daughter of Ezra Allen. She died and he married (second) August 27, 1801, Betty Phillips. Children, born at Bridgewater: Susanna, May 1, 1784, Zenas, mentioned below. William, January 7, 1787, Cyrus, October 18, 1789, Sally, April 19, 1792, Polly, August 30, 1794, Phebe. Children by second wife: Asa, born 1802, Mary, September 24, 1803, Betsey, September, 1805, Almira, February, 1807.

(VI) Zenas Brett, son of William (2) Brett, was born July 31, 1785, and died October 6, 1868. He was a general merchant in North Bridgewater, and a prominent citizen. He married (first) June 27, 1813, Sibbil French, daughter of Captain William French, of Stoughton. She died September 22, 1834. He married (second) November 28, 1836, Almira Packard, daughter of John and Martha (French) Packard, and a direct descendant in the seventh generation of Samuel Packard. Children, by first wife, born at North Bridgewater: William French, July 13, 1816, Mary Allen, August 13, 1818, died young, Zenas Franklin, October 20, 1822, Sibbil Alma, October 23, 1824, Henry Allen, mentioned below. Children by second wife: Mary Ellen, born June 18, 1838, Charles Edward, July 29, 1839, Cordelia Almira, May 25, 1841, Sarah Adelaide, November 22, 1843; George Elmer, May 24, 1849, died in infancy.

(VII) Henry Allen Brett, son of Zenas Brett, was born at North Bridgewater,

April 4, 1830. He married, November 9, 1851, Hannah Foster Gibbs, daughter of Thomas Foster Gibbs, of Bridgewater. He was educated in the public schools of North Bridgewater, the Loomis Academy, the Adelphian Academy and the Blanchard Academy at Pembroke, New Hampshire, from which he graduated at the age of fourteen years. He entered the employ of his elder brother's firm, Brett & Kingman, in North Bridgewater, as a clerk and remained for some years. In 1850, when he was twenty years of age, he engaged in business in Lewiston, Maine. where he opened a retail clothing store and conducted it for a period of eight years. Then he established a general store at Wareham, Massachusetts, and for another period of eight years continued in business there with substantial success, making a host of friends, who presented him with a unique testimonial of their regard at the time he sold his store. A hammered silver pitcher made of silver coins contributed for the purpose by a large number of persons made a souvenir that he cherished greatly. He returned to his native town, where he engaged in business as a general merchant. To the ordinary departments of dry goods and hardware, he added a department of tailoring and dressmaking, and from February 15, 1860, until he retired in 1880, his store was one of the most profitable and popular in that town. Afterward he spent a year in Chicago in the employ of the Witherbee Hill Clothing Company on Clark street, and a year in the employ of the Sydney Packard Clothing house at Springfield, Massachusetts. He lived for a year or two in Brockton, Middleborough and Sandwich, then returned to business in the employ of the Howard & Caldwell Clothing Company of Brockton, and continued with that concern to the end of his life.

18

At the time he had completed fifty years in business, his associates honored him with a banquet and gave him as a souvenir an elegant easy-chair. He died at Brockton, and was buried in Union Cemetery. He was a member of Social Harmony Lodge, Ancient Free and Accepted Masons, of Wareham; Scituate Chapter, Royal Arch Masons, Brockton Council, Royal and Select Masters, Bay State Commandery, Knights Templar, of Brockton.

He married, November 9, 1851, Hannah Foster Gibbs, born at Sandwich in 1834, daughter of Thomas Foster and Patience (Coan) Gibbs (see Gibbs VI). She died July 5, 1889, aged fifty-five years, and was buried in Union Cemetery, Brockton. Children: William Frank, born September 13, 1852, resides in Dorchester, Massachusetts; Isabelle Alma, born December 30, 1854, married Fred Sawin Tolman (see Tolman IX); Allen Foster, resides in Brockton, Massachusetts; Harry Meade, born January 20, 1862, died May 21, 1865; Edith, died in infancy.

(The Gibbs Line)

(I) Thomas Gibbs, the immigrant ancestor of the Cape Cod family of this surname, was an early settler in the town of Sandwich. His name was on the list of men able to bear arms in 1643. He had a brother, Samuel Gibbs, who also settled in Sandwich, and had a son Samuel born there June 22, 1649, and a daughter Sarah, born April 18, 1652. Thomas Gibbs was one of the proprietors of Sandwich and died there before April 14, 1693, when his estate was divided among his sons John, Thomas and Samuel, making provision also for his widow. Children, born at Sandwich: Thomas, March 23 or 25, 1636, Samuel, June 22, 1639 or 1649, John, mentioned below; Sarah, April 11, 1652; Job and Bethia, twins, April 15

1655; Mary, August 12, 1657. The dates in Savage's dictionary differ somewhat from those in "Pope's Pioneers of Massachusetts."

(II) John Gibbs, son of Thomas Gibbs, was born at Sandwich, September 12, 1644 (or 1634?) He married —— ——. Children, born at Sandwich: John, April 27, 1676; Barnabas, June 24, 1684, and others.

(III) Sylvanus Gibbs, of the Sandwich family, was born as early as 1700, and is believed to be son of John Gibbs, but his birth is not recorded. His name appears on the list of heads of families in Sandwich in 1730, as prepared by Rev. Benjamin Fessenden (See Vol 13, New England General Register, p 13.)

(V) Sylvanus (2) Gibbs, grandson of Sylvanus (1) Gibbs, was born as early as 1750. He was a soldier in the Revolution, in Captain Joseph Palmer's company, from Sandwich, Colonel John Cushing's regiment, in a Rhode Island campaign in 1776. Roll dated at Falmouth. He was sergeant in Captain Ward Swift's company, Colonel Freeman's regiment, in the fall of 1778, second lieutenant in the Eighth Company, Colonel Freeman's regiment (first Barnstable county regiment) in 1779, commissioned April 21. (See p. 389, Vol VI, Massachusetts Soldiers and Sailors in the Revolution)

He married (first) August 25, 1774, Katy Toby. He married (second) Hannah —— ——. Children of first wife, born in Sandwich: Hannah, June 20, 1777; Joanna, October 12, 1779; Sylvanus and Benjamin, twins, January 27, 1782. Children by second wife Hannah: Nathan B., September 27, 1783, died March 10, 1849; Katy Toby, March 3, 1785, married William Swift; Alfred, November 3, 1786; Ebenezer, August 11, 1788; Clarissa, March 19, 1790; Thomas Foster, mentioned below, Caroline, October 1, 1793, Joseph, December 21, 1795, Experience, January 18, 1797, Alexander, May 12, 1799, Joanna, August 12, 1803

(VI) Thomas Foster Gibbs, son of Sylvanus (2) Gibbs, was born May 28, 1792, and died February 4, 1860 He married Patience Coan Children, born at Sandwich Joanna J, born 1821, married, October 28, 1845, Charles Dillingham, Nancy I, born 1823, married at Bridgewater, August 14, 1845, Charles J H Bassett, cashier of the Taunton Bank, of Taunton, Hannah Foster, born 1834, married Henry Allen Brett (see Brett VII).

BASSETT, Thomas Borden,

Business Man.

The family bearing the name of Bassett is one among the oldest in America, having had a continuous existence in the Commonwealth of Massachusetts since the earliest settlement of this country, and where it has had a record of prominence and eminent respectability

(I) William Bassett, the emigrant ancestor and founder of this family in this country, was born about 1590 According to the records he married (first) Cecil Licht, and (second) in 1611, in Leyden, Holland, Margaret Oldham As there is no further record of the second wife the supposition is that she died soon after William Bassett left Delft Haven in the ship "Speedwell," July 22, 1620, and went to Southampton, England, with other Pilgrims There the "Mayflower" was waiting for them, and after the company was divided between the two vessels they set sail for America, August 5, 1620. The "Speedwell" was found to be leaking, and both vessels put into Dartmouth for repairs Both vessels set sail again on August 21st, and the "Speedwell" again

began leaking Those passengers on the "Speedwell" that could be accommodated on the "Mayflower" were taken aboard the latter, and Robert Cushman and family, William Bassett and others, about twenty in all, returned to London Early in November, 1621, the ship "Fortune," a vessel of about fifty-five tons burden, and a new ship, arrived at Plymouth, Massachusetts, from England, with thirty-five passengers, among whom were William Bassett and Robert Cushman Whether William Bassett's third wife, Elizabeth Tilden, came with him or not, has never been established, as she is not mentioned until 1627, when William and wife Elizabeth, and children, William, Jr, and Elizabeth, were included in the record of the division of cattle at Plymouth, Massachusetts William Bassett was elected deputy assistant to the governor in 1640, 1643, 1644, 1645 and 1648, from Duxbury, Massachusetts, where he had gone in 1637 and made a settlement with others He became one of the original proprietors of Bridgewater, Massachusetts, where he settled in about 1650, this town being incorporated in 1656 He was a large landholder, and one of the wealthiest of the colony, only four in Plymouth paying a larger tax than he, in 1633 He must have been an educated man, as he possessed a large library He had become a freeman of the colony in 1633, and in 1637 he was a volunteer in the company raised to assist Massachusetts and Connecticut in the Pequot War He was also a member of the committee of the town of Duxbury to lay out the bounds and to decide on the fitness of persons applying to become residents He was representative to the Old Colony Court for a period of six years He died in Bridgewater, Massachusetts, in May, 1667 His children were: William, mentioned below, Elizabeth, who married Thomas Burgess;

Nathaniel, who settled first in Marshfield, and in 1684 in Yarmouth; Joseph, who remained on the paternal homestead at Bridgewater, Sarah, who married Peregrine White, of Marshfield, the first white child born of English parents at Cape Cod Harbor, in November, 1620, Jane, Ruth, born in 1632, who married John Sprague, and perhaps others

(II) William (2) Bassett, son of William (1) and Elizabeth (Tilden) Bassett, was born in 1624, and died in 1670. He married Mary Burt

(III) William (3) Bassett, son of William (2) and Mary (Burt) Bassett, was born in 1656, and died in 1721 He married, in 1675, Rachel Willison

(IV) William (4) Bassett, son of William (3) and Rachel (Willison) Bassett, married, in 1709, Abigail Bourne

(V) John Bassett, son of William (4) and Abigail (Bourne) Bassett, lived in Rochester, Massachusetts, where the births of his twelve children are of record His wife's Christian name was Mary He died May 17, 1781 His children were Aurelia, born in 1743, Bethsheba, 1744, Benjamin, 1746, Mary, 1747, Emma, 1749, Peter, 1752, Desire, 1754, Sarah, 1756, Newcomb, 1757, Thomas, mentioned below, Meltiah, 1761, and Abigail, 1763

(VI) Thomas Bassett, son of John and Mary Bassett, was born in Rochester, Massachusetts, June 19, 1759, where he died February 24, 1833 On January 7, 1781, he married Lydia Mendall, of that town, who was born March 19, 1760 To them were born children as follows Newcomb, born in 1781, Anselm, mentioned below, Samuel, 1786, Abner, 1788, who married Harriet B. Spaulding, of Norwich, Connecticut, Thomas, Jr, and Lydia, twins, 1790, John, 1793, who married Laura Wing, of Marion, Massachusetts, Stephen, 1798, who married Abigail

Mendall; and Ezra, 1800, who married Keziah Russell.

(VII) Anselm Bassett, son of Thomas and Lydia (Mendall) Bassett, was born in the town of Rochester, Massachusetts, April 29, 1784 He was prepared for college under the tuition of Hon. Tristam Burgess, who was then preceptor of the Rochester Academy, and entered Brown University in 1799, being the youngest member of his class, graduating therefrom in 1803 Upon leaving college he was engaged in teaching school in his native town, and also took up the study of law in the office of Abraham Holmes He was admitted to the bar in January, 1808, and immediately engaged in the practice of his profession, locating at Narraguagus, in what was then called the district of Maine In 1809, he removed to Columbus, Maine, where he practiced successfully for a period of about three years, when, on account of business being prostrated as a result of the war with Great Britain, he returned to Rochester, his native town Here he married Rosalinda Holmes, daughter of Abraham Holmes, with whom he had studied law, and soon thereafter settled at Head of Westport, Massachusetts, where for about twenty years he continued the practice of his chosen profession with a marked degree of success In 1849 was formed what was long the well-known and successful law firm of Bassett & Reed After a long and most successful practice at the bar covering a period of over fifty-five years, on June 1, 1863, Mr Bassett withdrew from this partnership and determined to relinquish the duties of his profession At the time of his retirement he was the oldest practitioner in Bristol county, and one of the oldest in the State Although he closed his office and withdrew from the bar, he was constantly sought by his former clients, who were unwilling to rely on other advice until his could no longer be obtained

Mr Bassett always took a deep interest in public affairs, and was called upon to perform public duties In 1831 he represented his town in the State Legislature, and in 1832 was appointed registrar of probate for the county of Bristol, at which time he was required to take up his residence at Taunton, Massachusetts He continued to fill this office for a period of nineteen years, and discharged the duties thereof with distinguished promptness and faithfulness He also kept up his practice during this official period, being counselor to a large number of clients As a public official and as a lawyer, Mr Bassett enjoyed the greatest respect and esteem for his uprightness and for his pronounced kindness of heart Mr Bassett passed away September 9, 1863, in the eightieth year of his age, as a result of the natural decay of old age and without disease

After the death of his first wife, Rosalinda (Holmes) Bassett, Mr Bassett married (second) Mrs Lucy Smith, of Troy, New York The children of Anselm Bassett, all born to the first marriage, were Thomas, born in 1811, died in 1835 Charles J H , mentioned below, George F H , born in 1817, died in 1820, Cynthia C H , 1821, and Elizabeth M , 1824

Mrs Rosalinda (Holmes) Bassett was a direct descendant in the sixth generation from William Holmes, who was an inhabitant of Scituate, Massachusetts, as early as 1646, and a freeman of the colony in 1658, later removing to Marshfield, where he died in 1678 William Holmes was descended from a long and distinguished line of ancestry in England, tracing back in direct line to John Holmes, who was a captain in the army of William the Conqueror, in 1066 Mrs Bassett's line of descent from William Holmes, the

founder of the family in this country, is through Abraham and his wife, Elizabeth (Arnold) Holmes, of Rochester, he dying there in 1722; Experience Holmes, who died in 1715, aged thirty-three years, and his wife, Patience (Nichols) Holmes, Experience (2) Holmes and his wife, Hannah (Sampson) Holmes, and Hon Abraham Holmes and Bethiah (Nye) Holmes, of Rochester, the former of whom was a distinguished lawyer of the State of Massachusetts

(VIII) Charles Jarvis Holmes Bassett, son of Anselm and Rosalinda (Holmes) Bassett, was born July 10, 1814, in the town of Westport, Massachusetts, where his educational training was begun For a time he lived with his uncle, Hon Charles Jarvis Holmes, in Rochester, Massachusetts, where he also attended school. Taking up the study of law, he was admitted to the bar of Bristol county, but did not engage in practice He became cashier of the Taunton National Bank, and later filled the same position in the Hanover National Bank, of New York City, but was recalled to the Taunton Bank, of which he became president, a position he held for some years Mr Bassett was interested in religious affairs, and was a member of the Congregational church

He married (first) January 20, 1840, Emeline Deane Seabury, who was born in Taunton, Massachusetts, October 2, 1817, daughter of John Westgate Seabury She passed away April 1, 1842, the mother of three children, as follows Sarah S , born in 1840, who died in Taunton, married Erastus Morse, of Taunton , John S and Charles A (twins), born April 1, 1842, the former of whom married Marianna C Perry, of Taunton, and the latter is mentioned below Mr Bassett married (second) August 14, 1845, Nancy L Gibbs, who was born in Sand-

wich, Massachusetts, February 28, 1823, and who at the time of her marriage was living in Bridgewater, Massachusetts She died May 12, 1848, the mother of the following children   Louisa L , born in 1846, who married George H Rhodes, of Taunton , Isabel, born in 1848, died in infancy On December 25, 1850, Mr Bassett married (third) Martha B French, of Pawtucket, Rhode Island, who was born June 2, 1825, daughter of Squire and Betsey (Bucklin) French (see French VI) To this union were born children as follows   Henry F , born September 23, 1851, who married Emma C Jackson, of Taunton , Rufus W , mentioned below , Martha E , born in 1855, who died in 1881 , Mary R , born in 1858, who married Colonel Henry Pierce, of Pawtucket, Rhode Island, she a widow, residing in Taunton , George F H , born in 1862, died at the age of thirty years, and Susie A , born in 1864

(IX) Charles A Bassett, son of Charles J H and Emeline Deane (Seabury) Bassett, was born April 1, 1842, in Taunton, Massachusetts, in which city he acquired his educational training by attendance at the public and high schools At the age of seventeen years he entered a dry goods store, where he remained a clerk for about one year, when he accepted a position as clerk in the Taunton National Bank, of which is father was an official, and here he remained for a period of four years, being the youngest employee of that institution Through the influence of the late Hon John S Brayton, at the age of twenty-one years he went to Fall River, Massachusetts, where he was connected with the First National Bank of that city for a period of thirteen years, soon rising to the position of cashier In February, 1877, he was elected to the position of treasurer of the Fall River Savings Bank, and continued

to fill that position up to the time of his death, covering a period of nearly forty years   Mr Bassett had the reputation of being one of the ablest savings bank officials in Massachusetts, and his counsel was widely sought by banking men   Up to the time of his death he was one of the two surviving charter members of King Philip Lodge, Ancient Free and Accepted Masons, of Fall River, which celebrated the fiftieth anniversary of its founding in January, 1916 He was also a member of Fall River Chapter, Royal Arch Masons Mr Bassett was connected with the First Congregational Church of Fall River Of a quiet and retiring disposition he had little inclination for political or social affairs, being strictly interested and entirely occupied in his attention to the duties of the bank, which under his control has become one of the largest and strongest savings institutions in New England Mr Bassett saw the Fall River Savings Bank deposits increase from $4,-000,000 to $10,000,000, during his official connections therewith   He was for a number of years a member of the Board of Sinking Fund Commissioners of Fall River, giving the city valuable services in this connection

On June 15, 1870, Mr Bassett was united in marriage to Mary L Hooper, daughter of the late Dr Foster Hooper, one of the leading physicians of Fall River, who died October 18, 1870 To Mr and Mrs Bassett was born one daughter, Mary Hooper, who married George H Waring a cloth broker, of Fall River, and they are the parents of four children, namely   Seabury Bassett, born March 26, 1900 , Margaret, April 27, 1902 , Janice July 25, 1903, and Mary Hooper, July 7 1910

Mr Bassett passed away at his home on Rock street, Fall River, Massachusetts, on January 23, 1916, in the seventy-

23

fourth year of his age, honored and respected in the community with the financial institutions of which he had so long and honorably been connected.

(IX) Rufus W. Bassett, son of Charles J. H. and Martha B. (French) Bassett, was born July 22, 1853, in Taunton, Massachusetts. His educational training was acquired in the schools of his native city, including the high school. After leaving school he entered the office of the Eagle Cotton Company, of Taunton, where he was employed for several years, which position he resigned to accept the position of bookkeeper of the Troy Cotton and Woolen Manufactory, of Fall River, Massachusetts, to which city he then removed. After serving some years in this capacity, during which time he had acquired a thorough and comprehensive knowledge of the cotton manufacturing industry, he opened an office in Fall River as a cotton and cloth broker, later associating himself with Nathan Durfee, under the firm name of Bassett & Durfee, in a partnership, which was continued with marked success up to the time of the death of Mr. Bassett. This well-known firm did a large and extensive business, being the representatives of the American Printing Company in the purchase of goods in this market, and in this capacity frequently took over very large consignments of cloth for this well-known concern. Mr. Bassett's recognized business ability and insight in financial affairs brought him into close touch with the industrial and financial institutions of Fall River, and he served for a number of years as a director in the Metacomet National Bank, the Fall River Electric Light Company, and the Richard Borden Manufacturing Company.

Of robust stature, in early manhood Mr. Bassett was fond of athletics, and as an amateur played right field and first base with the Fall River baseball team, a semi-professional organization. When he first located in Fall River he served for a time in Company M, Massachusetts Volunteer Militia, of which he was a charter member. He was also a consistent member of the First Congregational Church of Fall River. In political faith Mr. Bassett was a stalwart adherent of the principles of the Republican party, in the councils of which party he was a prominent and influential factor, being called upon to fill various offices of honor and responsibility, the duties of which he administered with ability and faithfulness. He was a member of the Common Council of the city of Fall River in 1887 and 1889, and of the Board of Aldermen from Ward Eight, in 1890-91. On June 4, 1902, Governor W. Murray Crane appointed him to the Board of Police Commissioners of the city for a three years' term, and on June 19, 1903, he was appointed chairman of the board by Governor John L. Bates. At the expiration of his term, Governor William L. Douglas, a Democrat, was in office, and James Tansey was appointed to succeed him. On May 22, 1907, Mr. Bassett was again appointed to the board by Governor Curtis Guild, Jr., and in June, 1908, was again appointed chairman of the board, his term to expire the first Monday in June, 1910. Mr. Bassett also served as a trustee of the Public Library from 1891 to February 4, 1901, when he resigned to accept the police commissionership. He was again appointed a trustee, March 31, 1906, resigning June 19, 1908. He was also a member of the Old Colony Historical Society.

Mr. Bassett passed away at his home on High street, Fall River, July 26, 1909, at the age of fifty-six years, his death being an irreparable loss to the community where he was so well and favorably known, as well as to a large circle of friends. Possessed of a most genial

24

nature, even temperament and obliging disposition, he was deservingly popular in the highest sense, having hosts of friends who regarded him as a gentleman of ability, strictest integrity and incorruptible character, and was recognized by all classes as a useful and valuable citizen

On September 13, 1882, Mr Bassett was united in marriage to Harriet Minerva Borden, who was born June 15, 1856, daughter of the late Colonel Thomas J and Mary E (Hill) Borden, of Fall River, Massachusetts Mrs. Bassett passed away October 16, 1904, the mother of the following children Thomas Borden, mentioned below, Frederick Waterman, born April 23, 1885, who died September 26, 1904; Margaret, born January 26, 1888, who married, September 7, 1912, Samuel T Hubbard, Jr, of Yonkers, New York, and they have two children, namely Harriet Borden and Mary Hustis, Charles French, born April 5, 1891, who died December 26, 1891, and Constance, born January 19, 1896

(X) Thomas Borden Bassett, eldest son of the late Rufus W and Harriet Minerva (Borden) Bassett, was born August 24, 1883, in Fall River, Massachusetts After acquiring his early educational training in the public schools of his native city, including the B M C Durfee High School, he was prepared for college at Browne & Nichols Preparatory School, Boston, from which he entered Harvard University, graduating therefrom in the class of 1905, with the degree of Bachelor of Arts After spending a short time in a stock brokerage office in Boston, he returned to Fall River, where he entered the office of Nathan Durfee, cotton and cloth broker of that city, and former partner of his father, with whom he continued until 1912, when Mr Durfee retired from business, and Mr Bassett, in company with Frank T Albro, under

the firm name of Bassett & Albro, took up the business Mr Bassett is unmarried

(The French Line)

For two hundred and seventy-five years the French family has been prominently identified with the history of the Commonwealth of Massachusetts And across the water the French family is one ancient and historic, claiming its origin from Rollo, Duke of Normandy, who, himself, was a Norseman viking, but who settled in France, and in A D 910, formally adopted the Christian religion and was baptized, taking the name of Robert, Count of Paris, who was his godfather In direct line from Rollo descended Sir Theoples French (or Freyn), who went with William the Conqueror, to England, and fought at the battle of Hastings Thus was the first branch of the French family planted in England

(I) John French, the first of the name in this country, in the branch of the family here considered, was a native of England, where he was born in 1612 He is first of record at Braintree, Massachusetts, where he had lands granted to him February 24, 1639-40 He was admitted to the church in the adjoining town of Dorchester, January 27, 1642 He became a freeman, May 29, 1639 and was active and prominent among the early settlers

(II) John (2) French, son of John (1) French, was born February 28 1641 About 1676 he removed to Rehoboth, Massachusetts, from Northampton, being accompanied by his wife, who was a daughter of John Kingsley, and children John Thomas, Samuel, and Jonathan, the first three of whom took the oath of allegiance, February 8, 1679, besides three daughters Mary, wife of Samuel Stebbins, Hannah, wife of Francis Keet; and Elizabeth, wife of Samuel Pomeroy The father died February 1, 1697

(III) John (3) French, son of John (2) French, married, November 22, 1678, Hannah (Savage says Mary) Palmer. Mr French lived with his grandfather Kingsley His children, of Rehoboth town record, were Hannah, born October 19, 1679; John, April 13, 1681, Mary, March 15, 1683-84, Elizabeth, January 19, 1684-85, Martha, March 28, 1688, Samuel, March 30, 1690, Jonathan, November 17, 1693, Thomas, September 6, 1696, and Ephraim, mentioned below.

(IV) Deacon Ephraim French, son of John (3) French, was born January 22, 1698-99, and died April 24, 1796. He married, August 13, 1726, Bethiah Dean, of Taunton, Massachusetts, and their children, of Rehoboth town record, were Elkanah, born November 9, 1727, Bethiah, April 7, 1731. Ephraim, April 25, 1734, James, March 25, 1737, Luce, January 19, 1741-42, and John, mentioned below

(V) John (4) French, son of Deacon Ephraim French, was born February 25, 1746-47, and married in Rehoboth, Massachusetts, the Rev Ephraim Hyde officiating. June 4, 1770, Lydia Allen, who was born October 24, 1750, in Rehoboth, daughter of Stephen and Amie (Wheaton) Allen, and to this union were born the following children: Lydia, born October 27, 1771 Otis, April 23, 1773, Belle, January 14, 1775, Olive, March 30, 1777, John, January 20, 1779, died young, Squire, mentioned below; Bethiah, November 11, 1782, Benjamin, September 15, 1784, Cyrell, March 24, 1786, died in infancy, Amie, October 13, 1787, and Cyrell (2), born March 30, 1790. John French, of Rehoboth, was a private in Colonel Nathaniel Carpenter's regiment, Captain Isaac Burr's company, which marched on an alarm, April 19, 1775, service eight days

(VI) Squire French, son of John (4)

and Lydia (Allen) French, was born in Rehoboth, Massachusetts, January 26, 1781, and married Betsey Bucklin (intentions published in the town of Seekonk, September 30, 1821). She was the daughter of David and Dorcas (Waterman) Bucklin, and granddaughter of David and Elizabeth (Arnold) Bucklin Their children were George Arnold, born in 1822, married, November 26, 1844, Betsey O'Brien, Martha B born June 2, 1825, married, December 23, 1850, Charles J H Bassett (see Bassett VIII); Ellen, born in 1835, married, December 20, 1854, Henry L Dana

---

HARTSHORN, George Trumbull,

Chemist, Musician

The Hartshorn family is of ancient English lineage The surname was taken from a parish of this name in Litchfield diocese, Derbyshire, and the parish, it is believed, was so named, from its geographical resemblance to a hart's horn The family was well established, as the records show, as early as the thirteenth century Henry de Hertishorn and others of the family are mentioned in Derbyshire The Hartshorn coat-of-arms is described Three bucks' heads, and the crest is a buck's head The design obviously refers to the significance of the name The family is one of long standing in this country and one of achievement. The name has been a continuous one in the old home town of Reading, Massachusetts, and in that region of country since early in the seventeenth century, and some years ago some of the land of the original settlers was still in the family name; and in different fields of effort not a few of the name have been men of achievement and of large means During the struggle of the Colonies for independence the family was well represented in the field, the names of Benjamin, James, Jeremiah, John, Jonathan, Thomas and William appearing on the rolls as from Reading

(I) Thomas Hartshorn, founder of the family in this country, and ancestor of all of the name, was born in England, in 1614, according to his deposition, April 3, 1654, that he was aged about forty years. He settled in Reading, Massachusetts, took the freeman's oath, May 10 1648, and was a prominent and influential citizen, serving as selectman and in other offices of trust. He died about May, 1683, and his inventory was dated May 18 that year. His will was dated October 26, 1681, and proved June 16, 1683, bequeathing to sons Benjamin and Thomas, daughter Susannah and wife Sarah. His other children must have received their shares previously. His first wife Susannah died March 18, 1660. His second wife Hannah was received from the church in Ipswich, April 6, 1663. She died July 20, 1673, and he married (third) Sarah Lamson widow of William Lamson, of Ipswich. Children: Thomas, born October 30, 1646, died young, Thomas, September 30, 1648, John, May 6, 1650, Joseph, July 2, 1652, Benjamin, mentioned below, Jonathan, August 20, 1656, David, 1657, Susannah, March 2, 1659, Timothy, February 3, 1661; Mary, August 19, 1672

(II) Benjamin Hartshorn, fifth son of Thomas and Susannah Hartshorn, was born April 18, 1654, in Reading, and made his home in that town, where he died May 3, 1694. He married (first) February 28, 1681, Mary, daughter of George Thompson, born April 19, 1664, died October 26, 1682. He married (second) November 6, 1684, Elizabeth, daughter of John and Elizabeth (Osgood) Brown. Children: Mary, born and died 1682; Benjamin, mentioned below; Elizabeth, December

20, 1686, Hannah, February 10, 1689, Jonathan, November 10, 1690, Susannah, March 21, 1692

(III) Benjamin (2) Hartshorn, eldest child of Benjamin (1) and Elizabeth (Brown) Hartshorn, was born September 16, 1685, in Reading, and lived in that town. He married there, April 2, 1716, Elizabeth, daughter of Sergeant James and Rebecca Boutwell, born October 9, 1687. Children: Benjamin, mentioned below, Jonathan 1721, Elizabeth, January 18 1724, James May 17, 1727

(IV) Benjamin (3) Hartshorn, eldest child of Benjamin (2) and Elizabeth (Boutwell) Hartshorn, was born March 4, 1720, in Reading, and was a resident of that town. He married, February 24, 1742, Mary, daughter of Jonathan and Sarah (Burnap) Swain, born October 23, 1724, in Reading. Children: Benjamin, born July 4, 1744, Mary October 15, 1746, died young, James, May 19 1750, William, November 26, 1753, Jonathan August 30, 1756, Jeremiah, mentioned below, Mary, October 5, 1765, Samuel, July 25, 1768

(V) Jeremiah Hartshorn, fifth son of Benjamin (3) and Mary (Swain) Hartshorn, was born November 15, 1760, in Reading, and lived in Foxboro, Massachusetts. He married about 1781, Rebecca Richardson, and the records of Foxboro show the following children. Sally, born November 15, 1782 Jeremiah, August 28, 1784, Eunice, September 5, 1786, Jesse, mentioned below; Harvey, May 25, 1795. The following were baptized August 16 1801. Jeremiah, Harvey, Rebecca, Sally and Eunice

(VI) Jesse Hartshorn, second son of Jeremiah and Rebecca (Richardson) Hartshorn, was born May 17, 1789, in Foxboro, Massachusetts. In 1807 he went to Taunton, Massachusetts, where he secured employment with the Green Mill

ENCYCLOPEDIA OF BIOGRAPHY

Company, owned by the Shepard family, who were pioneers in the cotton manufacturing business in that place In 1813, in association with Robert Dean and some others, Mr Hartshorn formed a company and built a mill in the east part of Taunton, of which he became superintendent and agent In 1819 he built and equipped a mill at Falls of Tarboro, North Carolina, and later built and organized other mills at various places, including Pawtucket and Blackstone, Rhode Island, and Humphreysville and New London, Connecticut About 1813 he returned to Taunton, and was employed by Crocker, Richardson & Company until their failure in 1837 Three years later he took a lease of the cotton and paper mills at Westville, where he continued five years In 1846 he entered the service of William Mason & Company, as superintendent of their machine works, remaining until 1851, when he retired from that position In the early years of the nineteenth century, before his removal to Taunton, Mr Hartshorn served as selectman of the town of Foxboro He died at Taunton, April 2, 1868 He married Priscilla, daughter of Abizer Dean, born April 5 1791, died January 14, 1885 Children Charles Warren, born October 8, 1814 died March 31, 1893, Mary Leonard, April 25 1818, died April, 1885, George Franklin, mentioned below, Martha E, December 31, 1830, died June 8, 1900

(VII) George Franklin Hartshorn, second son of Jesse and Priscilla (Dean) Hartshorn, was born September 27, 1826, in Taunton He was educated at the Bristol Academy, which he attended from 1836 to 1843 In the latter year he entered the employ of Bates, Turner & Company, importers and jobbers in Boston, Massachusetts, but remained with them only a year, in 1846 going to New York City as a clerk in the commission house of William F

Mott, Jr He went to Worcester, Massachusetts, in 1848, where he was engaged as cashier of the Central Bank until 1856 Mr Hartshorn was one of the first manufacturers of machine-made envelopes in the country, buying the patent of the inventor He resigned his cashiership to engage in this business, but was reappointed to it in 1859 and served until 1862, retaining his interest in the envelope business, which grew to large proportions until 1865 In 1867 he left Worcester, and resided in Taunton until 1873, then in Quincy until 1878, in Cambridge until 1885, and from that date up to the time of his death in 1901, in Taunton He married, July 18, 1855, Isabella Frink, daughter of George Augustus Trumbull, of Worcester, Massachusetts (see Trumbull, VII)

(VIII) George Trumbull Hartshorn, only son of George Franklin and Isabella Frink (Trumbull) Hartshorn was born October 20, 1860, in Worcester, Massachusetts He was educated at Adams Academy, Quincy, Massachusetts, and at Harvard University, always taking a high rank as a scholar, particularly in chemistry, in which he was deeply interested After graduating he was for some time an instructor in the chemistry department of the university At the close of his term as a college instructor, Mr Hartshorn went to Taunton, making his home with his parents, and followed the profession of an analytical chemist his work being as much a pleasure as a profitable undertaking He was also deeply interested in music, was a splendid performer on the violin-cello, and his home was always regarded as one of the central points in musical and social life in Taunton Some years later, owing to the illness of his father, the consequent cares of the management of a large estate engrossed the larger portion of his time, and this he

28

continued to look after until within a few years of his death. He purchased the ancestral acres on Dean street and there fitted up for himself and family a beautiful country place, amply adequate for all the enjoyments of life, but which he himself was destined only to enjoy for a short time. Mr Hartshorn was actively interested in social life in Taunton and prominent in it. Up to 1895 he had been secretary of the Segregansett Country Club from its formation, and had a lively part in making it the success that it proved to be. A gentleman, a scholar, a hearty, whole-souled friend, a good husband and father, who found his greatest pleasures in a quiet studious home life, and in the entertainment of his friends with unstinted hospitality, his death was sincerely mourned by a large circle. This event occurred August 22, 1905, at his home on Dean street. He married Alice Roberts, of Cambridge, who survives him with her son, George Deane, born April 3, 1894.

(The Trumbull Line)

(I) John Trumbull, a cooper, came from Newcastle-on-Tyne to New England, and settled in Rowley, Massachusetts, in 1640. He was in Roxbury as early as 1639, and was a member of the Apostle John Eliot's church. He shortly removed, however, to Rowley, and his homestead was in the heart of that village, fronting on the common. He taught the first school in the town, was a freeman, May 13, 1640, selectman in 1650 and 1652, town clerk 1654 to 1656, and died in 1657. He was buried May 18 of that year. He married in England, in 1635, Eleanor Chandler and brought his wife and a son John with him. Her name appears in the New England records as Ellen. She died about 1648-49, and he married (second) in August, 1650, Ann, widow of Michael Hopkinson, of Rowley. She survived

him and married (third) March 1, 1658, Richard Swan, as his second wife. She died in Rowley and was buried April 5, 1678. Children of first wife: John, Hannah, born December 14, 1640, Judah, April 3, 1643, Ruth, February 23, 1645, Joseph, mentioned below. Children of second marriage: Abigail, born October 13, 1651, Mary, April 7, 1654.

(II) Joseph Trumbull, son of John and Eleanor or Ellen (Chandler) Trumbull, was born March 19, 1647, in Rowley, and removed to Suffield, Connecticut, in 1670. During King Philip's War he was forced to leave the settlement, but returned in 1676; was a freeman in 1681, and one of the few qualified voters at the first town meeting of Suffield. His homestead was on the Connecticut river, near those of his brother Judah, and brother-in-law, Edward Smith. He died August 15, 1684. He married, before May 10, 1669, Hannah, daughter of Hugh Smith, of Rowley, who died in East Windsor, Connecticut, October 5, 1689. Children: John, mentioned below, Hannah, born June 8, 1673, Mary March 28, 1675, Joseph, January 16, 1678, Ammi, August 1, 1681, Benoni, August 20, 1684.

(III) John (2) Trumbull, eldest child of Joseph and Hannah (Smith) Trumbull, was born November 27, 1670, in Rowley, and was a small child when his parents settled permanently in Suffield. In 1694 he settled in Enfield, Connecticut, but four years later was again in Suffield. He married in the latter town, September 3, 1696, Elizabeth, daughter of David and Elizabeth (Filley) Winchell, of Suffield, born December 9, 1675, in Windsor, Connecticut, died January 3, 1751, in Suffield. Children Elizabeth, April 30, 1699, Mary, December 2, 1701, Joseph, March 14, 1704, died 1706, Abigail, May 27, 1706; Joseph, mentioned below, Mercy, November 2, 1710,

John, 1715, was the first member of the Congregational church at Watertown, Connecticut

(IV) Joseph (2) Trumbull, eldest surviving son of John (2) and Elizabeth (Winchell) Trumbull, was born May 13, 1708, in Suffield, and died in June, 1761, on the paternal homestead, which he received from his father by deed in 1743 This deed also included other lands, for all of which the son paid five hundred pounds, the father reserving twenty-two acres of the homestead for his own use He married Obedience Belden, who survived him, and married (second) in 1764, James Sheppard, of Hartford She died in 1804 Children Elizabeth, born May 3 1739, Joseph, mentioned below

(V) Joseph (3) Trumbull, only son of Joseph (2) and Obedience (Belden) Trumbull, was born October 12, 1756, in Suffield, and settled in Petersham, Massachusetts, whence he removed about 1803 to Worcester, same State He was a physician and apothecary, but paid little attention to the practice of his profession He often went to Europe, and spent much time in London A very talented man, with high artistic and literary genius, a keen wit, his society was much prized by those who knew him He was a member of the Cordon Bleu, a social club of Worcester For seventeen years he was confined to a chair with gout, but retained his serenity and cheerfulness of manner throughout He died at his residence on Trumbull Square, Worcester, March 2, 1824 During his long confinement he painted a portrait of himself, representing the Devil holding a hot coal on his toe He also wrote a poetical will, in which he remembered all of his friends and associates He married, February 14, 1786, at Worcester (the first marriage at the Second Church of that city), Eliza-

beth, youngest daughter of Timothy and Sarah (Chandler) Paine, of Worcester

(VI) George Augustus Trumbull, only son of Joseph (3) and Elizabeth (Paine) Trumbull, was born January 23, 1792, at Worcester, and was engaged there in business as a book publisher, from 1819 to 1823 He was associated with William Manning, in the publication of the "Massachusetts Spy," one of the oldest newspapers in the State On the incorporation of the Central Bank in 1829, he became its cashier, and thus continued until 1836, when he resigned to accept a similar position with the Citizen's Bank of Worcester, where he continued to 1858, when failing health compelled him to resign In 1865 his golden wedding was celebrated at the mansion on Trumbull Square, Worcester, which he inherited from his father There he died August 17, 1868

He married, September 20, 1815, at Greenfield, Massachusetts, Louisa Clapp, born September 24, 1798, in that town, daughter of Caleb and Elizabeth (Stone) Clapp, of Greenfield (see Clapp VIII) Children Elizabeth, born August 31, 1816, married William S Lincoln, George Clapp, March 1, 1818, engaged in business in Worcester and Boston, Caroline Burling, June 24, 1820, married Francis Blake, Louisa Jane, October 12, 1822, married Henry Lea, Sarah Paine, August 26, 1824, married John C Ripley, Joseph, September 22, 1826, John, July 31, 1828, died young, Charles Perkins, September 12, 1830, Susan, March 20, 1832, Isabella Frink, mentioned below, Mary Abbot, February 2, 1837

(VII) Isabella Frink Trumbull, sixth daughter of George Augustus and Louisa (Clapp) Trumbull, was born May 20, 1834, in Worcester, and was married July 18, 1855, to George Franklin Hartshorn, of Taunton (see Hartshorn VII)

(The Clapp Line)

The surname Clapp had its origin in the proper or personal name of Osgod Clapa, a Danish noble in the court of King Canute (1017-36) The site of his country place was known afterward as Clapham, County Surrey, The spelling in the early records varies from Clapa to the present form, Clapp The ancient seat of the family in England is at Salcombe in Devonshire, where important estates were held for centuries by this family Their coat-of-arms First and fourth three battleaxes, second sable a griffin passant argent; third sable an eagle with two heads displayed with a border engrailed argent A common coat-of-arms in general use by the family in America as well as in England Vaire gules and argent a quarter azure charged with the sun or Crest A pike naiant proper Motto— *Fais ce que Dois advienne que pourra* The American branches of this family are descended from six immigrants, brothers and cousins, who settled in Dorchester, Massachusetts, whence they and their descendants have scattered to all parts of the country

(I) Nicholas Clapp, progenitor of the family, lived at Venn Ottery, Devonshire, England Three of his sons and one daughter (wife of his nephew, Edward Clapp), came to America His brother, William Clapp, lived at Salcombe Regis, England, and besides his son Edward, another son, Roger Clapp, immigrated to America and settled at Dorchester The printed family genealogy gives the name of Richard instead of Nicholas Children Thomas, born 1597, Ambrose, lived and died in England, Richard, remained in England, Prudence, came to New England, married her cousin, Edward Clapp; Nicholas, mentioned below, John, came to Dorchester

(II) Nicholas (2) Clapp, ancestor of

this branch of the family, and the fourth son of Nicholas (1) Clapp, of England, was born in Dorchester, England, in 1612, and came to America with his brother Thomas, probably arriving at Dorchester, Massachusetts, in 1633 His name is on the records of the town in 1634, he held many town offices of responsibility, was much respected by those who knew him, and was a deacon of the church In September, 1653, he served as a juror at a special court held relative to disputed matters connected with the Lynn Iron Works His home was in the north part of Dorchester, on the west side of what is now Boston street a little south of Five Corners, and he owned land in various places. He died suddenly, while working in his barn, November 24, 1679 In 1849 several of his descendants erected a marble gravestone over his grave in the old cemetery near Stoughton street His sons, Nathaniel and Ebenezer, were administrators of his estate, but both died before the final settlement, and in 1716 Noah was appointed to complete it Nicholas Clapp married (first) his cousin, Sarah Clapp, sister of Captain Roger Clapp, daughter of William Clapp, of Salcombe Regis He married (second) Abigail, widow of Robert Sharp, of Brookline, Massachusetts Children by first wife, born in Dorchester. Sarah, December 31, 1637, Nathaniel, mentioned below; Ebenezer, 1643; Hannah, 1646 By second wife Noah, July 15, 1667; Sarah, December, 1670

(III) Nathaniel Clapp, son of Nicholas (2) and Sarah '(Clapp) Clapp, was born September 15, 1640, in Dorchester, Massachusetts, and was a well-to-do man, much respected in the town In 1671 he served as one of the town constables The following is found in the Dorchester church records "May 16th, 1707, Mr. Nathaniel Clap, a choice man, rested in the Lord and was interred May 17th." His house was very likely on the land which makes the western angle of the place known as Five Corners in Dorchester, now junction of Boston, Cottage and Pond streets His autograph is in a book printed in London in 1623, containing two sermons by "William Whately, Preacher of the Word of God in Banburie;" his brother Ebenezer, his sister Sarah, and son Nathaniel all signed their names in this book at different dates His will was dated April 22, 1707, and in it he mentioned his wife and children He married, March 31, 1668, Elizabeth, daughter of Lawrence Smith She died September 19, 1722 (September 12, according to the gravestone) Children, born in Dorchester Nathaniel, born January 20, 1669, John, mentioned below, Jonathan, August 31, 1673, Elizabeth, May 22, 1676; Ebenezer October 25, 1678; Mehetable, August 30, 1684, died February 20, 1685.

(IV) John Clapp, second son of Nathaniel and Elizabeth (Smith) Clapp, was born April 7, 1671, in Dorchester, and removed after 1693 to Sudbury, Massachusetts, where he was a deacon of the church and an influential citizen, and died November 26, 1735. He married in Dorchester, November 26, 1698, Silence Foster, born there April 4, 1677, daughter of James and Mary (Capen) Foster Children John, mentioned below, Thankful, born October 6, 1706; Nathaniel, September 10, 1709, Elizabeth, married Peter Noyes, a deacon of Sudbury

(V) John (2) Clapp, eldest child of John (1) and Silence (Foster) Clapp, born March 21, 1700, in Sudbury, where he lived, and was a man of much ability, a student of philosophy, astronomy, mathematics and divinity He died April 12, 1788, in Sudbury He married, March 17, 1724, Abigail, daughter of Daniel and

Abigail (Flint) Estabrook of Lexington, baptized there September 27, 1702 Children Beulah, born January 1, 1724, Joel, mentioned below, Jerusha, May 14, 1728, Asahel, March 12, 1730, Ann February 9, 1732, Mary, November 18, 1733, John, December 24, 1735, Silas, September 17, 1737, Daniel, October 10, 1739, Samuel, died December 11, 1755

(VI) Joel Clapp, eldest son of John (2) and Abigail (Estabrook) Clapp, was born July 2, 1726, in Sudbury, Massachusetts, and lived in Hardwick, that State, and subsequently in Ashburnham He was a soldier of the French war, and at the time of his death in 1770 owned eighty acres of land in Ashburnham, Massachusetts which came to him as the heir or a soldier who served against the French in 1690 The identity of this ancestor has not been established He married, October 17, 1749, Elizabeth, fourth daughter of Jonas and Harriet (Johnson) Burke, of Sudbury Children John, born January 29, 1751, died 1752, Caleb, mentioned below, and Jonathan (twins), February 9, 1752, Catherine, September 6, 1753, John, November 9, 1755, Abigail, December 6, 1757

(VII) Caleb Clapp, second son of Joel and Elizabeth (Burke) Clapp, was born February 9, 1752, in Hardwick, and was one of the patriots of the Revolution, participating in the battle of Bunker Hill In August, 1775, he was sergeant-major of Colonel Doolittle's regiment, and in 1776 was ensign in the Twenty-fifth Massachusetts Regiment, in which he was successively promoted lieutenant and captain He served until the close of the struggle, and was one of the founders of the Order of the Cincinnati In want of male line his membership descended to his nephew, George Clapp Trumbull, of Cambridge, Massachusetts His diary of the military operations in New York during the years 1776-77 was published in the "New York Historical Magazine," volume 23 He represented Greenfield in the Massachusetts Legislature, 1797, and in subsequent years, and died there June 5, 1812 He married in Rutland, Massachusetts, March 17, 1782, Elizabeth, eldest daughter of Captain John and Lucy (Fletcher) Stone, born July 8, 1758, died September 14, 1843 Children Joel John, born November 15, 1783, in Rutland, Harriet, June 5, 1785, Daniel, April 1, 1787; Lucy Stone, March 9, 1789, in Hardwick, Isabel Frink, June 22, 1791, Eliza, July 1, 1793, in Greenfield, Susanna, August 29, 1795, Louisa, mentioned below, Elizabeth, October 19, 1801

(VIII) Louisa Clapp, sixth daughter of Caleb and Elizabeth (Stone) Clapp, was born September 24 1798, in Greenfield, and became the wife of George Augustus Trumbull, of Worcester (see Trumbull VI)

(The Cogswell Line)

(I) John Cogswell was born in Westbury, Leigh, Wiltshire, England, in 1592, son of Edward and Alice Cogswell, of ancient and honorable lineage He and his wife resided in Westbury until 1635, when they sailed for New England in the ill-fated ship "Angel Gabriel," which was wrecked off the Maine coast, August 15, 1635, the passengers of which were washed ashore at Pemaquid, Maine He was the third settler in that part of Ipswich, now the town of Essex, and was admitted a freeman, March 3, 1636 He was a farmer in America, but in England was a woolen manufacturer, and the English Cogswells at Westbury still own and operate woolen mills there, or did until recently He married, in England, September 10, 1615, Elizabeth, daughter of Rev William and Phillip Thompson Her father was vicar of the parish Chil-

dren A daughter, resided in London, Mary, married, 1649, Godfrey Armitage, William, mentioned below; John, baptized July 25, 1622; Hannah, married, 1652, Deacon Cornelius Waldo, Abigail, married Thomas Clark, Edward, born 1629; Sarah, married, 1663, Simon Tuttle; Elizabeth, married, July 31, 1657, Nathaniel Masterson

(II) William Cogswell, eldest son of John and Elizabeth (Thompson) Cogswell, was born in England, baptized at Westbury, Wiltshire, in March, 1619, and died December 15, 1700 He settled in Chebacco (Essex), was a leading citizen, often moderator and selectman, and gave the land for the first meeting house site His will is dated August 5, 1696. He married, in 1649, Susanna Hawkes, born 1633, in Charlestown, Massachusetts, daughter of Adam and Anne (Hutchinson) Hawkes Children Elizabeth, born 1650, Hester, August 24, 1655, married Samuel Bishop Susanna and Ann (twins), January 5, 1657, William, December 4, 1659, Jonathan, April 26, 1661, Edmund, died May 15 1680, John, mentioned below, Adam, born January 12, 1667; Sarah, February 3, 1668

(III) Lieutenant John (2) Cogswell, fourth son of William and Susanna (Hawkes) Cogswell, was born May 12, 1665, in Chebacco, and died 1710 He married Hannah Goodhue, born July 4, 1673, died December 25, 1742, daughter of Deacon William and Hannah (Dane) Goodhue She married (second) in 1713, Lieutenant Thomas Perley Children Hannah, born March 27, 1693, William, mentioned below; Susanna, March 10, 1696, John, December 2, 1699, Francis, March 26, 1701; Elizabeth, married, October 20, 1717, Colonel Joseph Blancy Margaret; Nathaniel, born January 19 1707, Bethia, Joseph, died 1728

(IV) William (2) Cogswell, eldest son

33

of Lieutenant John (2) and Hannah
(Goodhue) Cogswell, was born September 24, 1694, at Chebacco, and died February 19, 1762 He built the old Cogswell mansion, which has remained to the present day in the possession of the family He married (first) September 24, 1719, Mary Cogswell, born 1699, died June 16, 1734, (second) March 13, 1735, Elizabeth (Wade) Appleton, who died December 13 1783, daughter of Captain Thomas Wade, and widow of Benjamin Appleton Children of first marriage Ebenezer, born June 13, 1720, John, February 23, 1722, Mary, September 15, 1723, Jonathan, May 9, 1725, Jacob, mentioned below, Lucy, June 28, 1728, Sarah, February 5 1729, William, May, 1731 By second marriage Hannah, baptized June 7, 1737, William, born March 5, 1740, died young, Susanna, April 19, 1741, died young, Samuel, March 15, 1742, Susanna, July 9, 1743, William, May 31, 1745

(V) Jacob Cogswell, fourth son of William (2) and Mary (Cogswell) Cogswell, was born May 18, 1727, in Chebacco Parish, and lived there, where he died December 1, 1805 He married (intentions published February 2, 1748) Elizabeth Eveleth, baptized November 10, 1728, in Ipswich, daughter of James and Elizabeth (Cogswell) Eveleth Children William, mentioned below, Francis, born August 8, 1768, Jacob, May 21, 1770 There were probably others, the last two only are on the vital records of Ipswich

(VI) William (3) Cogswell, son of Jacob and Elizabeth (Eveleth) Cogswell was born about 1766, in Chebacco, lived there, and was lost in a hurricane in 1792 at St Martins, West Indies He married, February 12, 1791, Mary Smith, probably the Mary Smith baptized October 18, 1767, in Ipswich, daughter of John and Mary (Work) Smith

(VII) Daniel Cogswell, only child of William (3) and Mary (Smith) Cogswell, was born August 31, 1792 in Chebacco, where he made his home, and died March 31, 1863 He married (first) February 14, 1822, Sarah Cogswell, born September 22, 1793, in Chebacco, daughter of Benjamin and Abigail (Choate) Cogswell, died May 8, 1825 He married (second) in November, 1828, Eunice Smith, born August 10, 1803, in Ipswich, died September 7, 1829, daughter of Samuel and Hannah (Choate) Smith. He married (third) May 21, 1833, Mercy Davis Randall, born 1807, baptized at the second church of Ipswich, September 1, 1816, died August 14, 1849 She was a daughter of Caleb and Lucy (Caldwell) Randall The only child of the first marriage died in infancy There was a daughter of the second marriage, Eunice Smith Cogswell, born 1829, died 1845. Children of the third marriage Mercy, baptized August 24, 1834, William, August 22, 1836, Daniel Albert, July 11, 1838, George, baptized March 15, 1841, died one week later, Lucy, mentioned below, Alice, January 5, 1845, Charles Howard, February 6, 1848

(VIII) Lucy Cogswell, third daughter of Daniel Cogswell, and child of his third wife, Mercy Davis (Randall) Cogswell, was born January 3, 1842, in Ipswich, and was married, June 15, 1864, to George B Roberts, of Cambridge George B Roberts was a son of Thomas J. Roberts, who is said to have been a native of New Hampshire, and settled in Boston when a young man There he was engaged in contracting and building, and after some years moved to Ipswich, Massachusetts, where his home continued until his death in 1876 He was the builder of the Boston City Hall and many other public structures He married, in Boston, Massachusetts, Rachel Sargeant, a native of

1233852

that town, who died in Ipswich in 1883 They had children George B , mentioned below, Edwin, now deceased, Sarah Elizabeth, wife of Walter Purlett, of Ipswich

George B Roberts, eldest child of Thomas J and Rachel (Sargeant) Roberts, was born December 12, 1833, in Boston, and died August 3, 1916, at Marblehead Neck, Massachusetts He was educated in the schools of Boston Early in life he was connected with the dry goods business in Boston, and in New York About the time of the Civil War, in which he served, enlisting from Salem, Massachusetts, he located in Cambridge, Massachusetts, where he was one of the pioneer steam boiler manufacturers and an original member of the old Cambridge firm of Kendall & Roberts Iron Company, and when he left this company he organized the Roberts Iron Works Company of Cambridgeport, of which he was president He retired from active business about five years prior to his death, when he was succeeded by his eldest son, Daniel C Roberts. He was a resident of Cambridge for fifty years George B Roberts served in the Union army during the Civil War, enlisting May 23, 1861, in Company G, First Regiment Massachusetts Infantry, and was honorably discharged for disability, December 20, 1862, with the rank of corporal Children of Mr and Mrs Roberts Daniel Cogswell, born December 25, 1865; Alice, mentioned below ; Frances Willett, January 14, 1871, George Newman, December 17, 1874, Edith, June 13, 1878 ; Ernest Bemis, December 9, 1879

(IX) Alice Roberts, eldest daughter of George B and Lucy (Cogswell) Roberts, was born June 19, 1868, in Ipswich, and became the wife of George Trumbull Hartshorn, of Taunton, Massachusetts (see Hartshorn VIII)

COPELAND, Horatio Franklin, M D ,
Physician, Surgeon

Lawrence Copeland, the immigrant ancestor, was born in Scotland, according to family tradition, in 1599 Copeland is an ancient Scotch surname and the seat of the family has been in Dumfriesshire since 1400 or earlier It is believed that he had served in the Scotch army against Cromwell and that he was with the Scotch prisoners that Cromwell sent to New England after the battle of Worcester At any rate he was living in Braintree late in 1651, and died there December 30, 1699, aged one hundred years, according to various testimony, including the town records, Marshall's diary and others He married, December 12, 1651, Lydia Townsend But if he were born in 1599 he was over fifty at the time of this marriage, and seventy-five years old when his youngest child was born Hence it is believed that Lydia was not his first wife and that the family tradition that he brought his wife with him receives support, but there is no record of her If his wife came with him, he doubtless came not from Scotland, not a prisoner of war, but an English settler from England Little is known about him, and his name but seldom appears in the records He was doubtless a quiet kind of a farmer His wife died January 8, 1688 Children by wife Lydia Thomas, born October 3, 1652, Thomas, 2d, February 8, 1655, William, mentioned below , John, February 10, 1659, Lydia, May 31, 1661 , Ephraim, January 17, 1665, Hannah, February 25, 1668, Richard, July 11, 1672, Abigail, 1674

(II) William Copeland, son of Lawrence Copeland, was born at Braintree November 15, 1656, and died there in 1716 He married, April 13, 1694, Mary (Bass) Webb, widow of Christopher Webb, Jr ,

35

ENCYCLOPEDIA OF BIOGRAPHY

and daughter of John and Ruth (Alden) Webb, granddaughter of John and Priscilla (Mullins) Alden, who came in the "Mayflower," and are celebrated in the poem of Longfellow, entitled the "Courtship of Miles Standish." All the Copelands descended from William and Mary are therefore eligible to the Society of Mayflower Descendants. Mary Bass was also descended from Samuel Bass, of Braintree and Boston, a deacon of the church and a deputy to the General Court, who died December 30, 1694, aged ninety-four years, then the progenitors of one hundred and sixty-two persons, we are told. Copeland remained in his native town, he was one of the dissenters from the vote of the town to pay the minister his full salary of eighty pounds, half in money, half in farm produce, March 2, 1690-91. He was elected fence viewer in 1696; signed the agreement to pay the expenses of defending the title of the proprietors of Braintree to their lands, January 10, 1697-98. Children, born at Braintree: William, March 7, 1695; Ephraim, February 1, 1697; Ebenezer, February 16, 1698; Jonathan, mentioned below; David, April 18, 1704; Joseph, May 18, 1706; Benjamin, October 5, 1708; Moses, May 28, 1710; Mary, May 28, 1713.

(III) Jonathan Copeland, son of William Copeland, was born at Braintree, August 31, 1701; married, in 1723, Betty Snell, born 1705, daughter of Thomas Snell, and granddaughter of Thomas Snell, who came from England and settled in Bridgewater about 1665. Jonathan Copeland settled in West Bridgewater, and died there in his ninetieth year, 1790. Children: Abigail, born in 1724; Betty, 1726; Jonathan, 1728; Mary, 1731; Joseph, 1734; Hannah, 1737; Elijah, mentioned below; Daniel, 1741; Sarah, 1745; Ebenezer, 1746; Betty, 2d, 1750.

(IV) Elijah Copeland, son of Jonathan

Copeland, was born in 1739, married, in 1765, Rhoda Snell, born 1743, daughter of Josiah Snell, granddaughter of Josiah Snell, and great-granddaughter of Thomas Snell, the immigrant, mentioned above. Elijah Copeland located in what is now the town of Easton, and died there at the age of seventy-eight years. He was a soldier in the Revolution in Captain Keith's company from Easton on a Rhode Island alarm and again for three months, beginning December 30, 1777, with his company in Rhode Island. He also turned out with the militia on Rhode Island alarms in 1780 and 1781, and in that year probably witnessed the reception to Washington and Rochambeau. He and his wife were buried in what is known as the Elijah Copeland graveyard, south of the old Copeland homestead on Bay Road, opposite Beaver street, Easton. He died September 8, 1817; his wife Rhoda died October 5, 1825 aged eighty-two years. Children: Elijah, born in 1766, moved to Weston, Massachusetts; Josiah, mentioned below; Luther, born 1770, moved to Vermont, a daughter, born January 12, 1775, died January 25, 1775; Calvin, born March 17, 1776, died September 14, 1778; Rhoda, born March 18, 1778, married (first) February 20, 1837, Aaron Gay, and (second) June 14, 1848, Eleazer Keith; Abigail, born June 10, 1781, married, June 16, 1803, James Guild; Martin, born January 16, 1784, died June 2, 1814; Molly, born September 5, 1786, married Leonard Dunbar.

(V) Josiah Copeland, son of Elijah Copeland, was born in Easton, in 1768, and resided in that town and Bridgewater. He was active and enterprising. For many years he was a manufacturer in South Easton, sometimes with and sometimes without partners, operating a saw mill, an oil mill, a forge and yarn mill. From 1811 to 1816 he was a selectman of

36

Easton He died there December 14, 1852, at the age of eighty-four years. He married, September 11, 1794, Susanna Hayward, who died at Easton, May 5, 1859, aged eighty-five years Children Horatio, mentioned below, Hiram, born September 9, 1798, married a Miss Copeland, Susannah H, born July 21, 1800, a school teacher, never married.

(VI) Horatio Copeland, son of Josiah Copeland, was born at Easton, March 5, 1796 He was also a leading citizen of his native town a manufacturer having mills there and also put into operation cotton gins in the south In 1836 he bought the general store of the Reed estate, Easton, and kept it until a few years before he died He was a soldier in the War of 1812, in Captain Isaac Lothrop's company, Lieutenant-Colonel Towne's regiment of light infantry, and was on duty in September and October at Boston harbor in 1814 From 1839 to 1843 he was a selectman of Easton, in March, 1859 he was appointed postmaster at South Easton, the third postmaster of that village and held the office until 1861, when he was succeeded by his son George, who continued in the office for fifty years He died at South Easton, December 2, 1865, and was buried in Easton He married, May 16, 1834, Delia Maria (Nye) Howard, who was born April 14, 1804, daughter of Samuel and Mary (Polly) Nye (see Nye XV), widow of Thomas Howard She died at Easton, January 26, 1878, and was also buried in Easton Children, born at South Easton Sarah Frances, born June 5, 1835, died August 27, 1845; George, mentioned below, Josiah, born September 5, 1838, died in Colorado in 1859, Horatio Franklin, mentioned below

(VII) George Copeland, son of Horatio Copeland, was born in Easton, Janu-

ary 5, 1837 He was a moulder by trade From 1859 to 1882 he was a grocer at South Easton, and from 1861 to 1910 the postmaster In 1873 he was representative to the General Court, and from 1882 to 1905 a selectman He is a member of Paul Revere Lodge, Free and Accepted Masons, of Brockton Chapter, Royal Arch Masons, and of Old Colony Commandery, Knights Templar, of Abington He married, June 30, 1868, Harriet Augusta Kimball, of Easton Children Marion Augusta, born March 1, 1871, who married Clifton G Brown, D M D, of Cambridge, George Hubert, born June 15, 1875, of South Easton, Ethel Helene, born February 7, 1877, married George H Briggs, of Dorchester

(VII) Dr Horatio Franklin Copeland, son of Horatio Copeland, was born November 15, 1842, in Easton He attended the district schools of his native town, and prepared for college in the old Thetford Academy in Vermont Omitting a college course, as was customary for medical students in his day, he began to study medicine under the instruction of Dr Caleb Swan, of Easton, afterward entering the Harvard Medical School, from which he was graduated in 1865 with the degree of Doctor of Medicine He was immediately appointed acting assistant surgeon in the army and assigned in charge of the post hospital at Bermuda Hundred, Virginia, and of an isolation hospital for the smallpox cases, and went on duty there in January, 1865 His experience in the army was not only of great value to the men who came under his care and treatment, but proved extremely important and useful to him after he began his private practice in Abington, in what is now Whitman, where he has continued to the present time Throughout his long career as a physician and surgeon, Dr Copeland has been a student and investigator, keeping pace with the progress in medical research The esteem in which he is held by his fellow-practitioners was shown at the annual meeting, June 15, 1915, of the Hatherly Medical Club, of which he is a member, when to mark the fiftieth anniversary of the beginning of his practice in Abington, he was given a silver loving cup In the same year, the Plymouth District Medical Society, of which he has been a prominent member for many years, tendered a reception and banquet at the rooms of the Commercial Club, in Brockton, to him and other veterans of the society—Dr Copeland, Dr Edward Cowles, of Plymouth; Dr Calvin Pratt, of Bridgewater; Dr A Elliott Paine, of Brockton, and Dr Durgin, of Boston, all of whom had rounded out a half century of active practice in their profession The occasion was unique and extremely pleasant in every detail

His extensive practice is perhaps the best testimonial of his skill and qualifications as a physician, it hardly needs the commendation of his associates in the medical profession to afford support to the statement that he ranks among the best in the county But on both these occasions the testimony of other physicians was most kind and complimentary to Dr Copeland

Not alone as a successful physician, eminent in his chosen profession and distinguished by the unusual length of his service to mankind, but as a highly useful citizen in other relations of life, has the career of Dr Copeland been exceptional He has been for many years a trustee of the Whitman Savings Bank, and a director of the Whitman National Bank, in both of which his judgment is highly respected by his associates In town affairs he possesses and has often felt called upon to exert a determining in-

fluence He is a Republican, but has never accepted public office In religion he is a liberal Congregationalist It is superfluous to say that he is interested in the veterans of the Civil War, for every veteran in this section is his personal friend He is a member of David A Russell Post, No 78, Grand Army of the Republic, of Whitman

His circle of friends throughout the county is particularly large in Masonic circles He was made a Mason in Rising Star Lodge, of Stoughton, many years ago, and is now a member of Puritan Lodge, of Whitman, also of Pilgrim Chapter, Royal Arch Masons, of Abington; of Abington Council, Royal and Select Masters, of which he was one of the charter members and of which he was the presiding officer for four years He is also a past eminent commander of Old Colony Commandery, Knights Templar, of Abington

Dr Copeland is one of two surviving members of a remarkable social organization formed in Boston in 1870 by twelve well known citizens of Plymouth county, known as the United Twelve It was then decided that no other members should be added Annually since then the club has held a dinner with places set for twelve, but year by year the number of vacant chairs has increased, and at the end of forty-seven years Dr Copeland and Mr B S Bryant, of Marshfield, are the only survivors, but they continue as before to dine once a year at a table set for a dozen The other members were: William L Read, first president; Daniel Lovering, vice-president; Samuel N Dyer, secretary; Newton M Reed, of Abington; Edward P Reed, of Abington; Frank A Hobart, of South Braintree; Henry Hobart, of East Bridgewater; Charles C. Bryant, of Brockton; Bradley S Bryant, Amos S

ENCYCLOPEDIA OF BIOGRAPHY

Stetson, of Whitman, and Hosea F Whidden, of Whitman

Dr Copeland has made fishing and hunting his principal recreations He is a member of the Massachusetts Medical Society and the American Medical Association, of which he is a member of the auxiliary legislative committee   Dr Copeland is unmarried

(The Nye Line)

The surname Nye, according to the genealogy, appears first in the middle of the thirteenth century in the Sjelland section of Denmark, and in Danish the word signifies new or newcomer, when used as a preface   It was not adopted as a surname until after the family settled in England   The Nye coat-of-arms is described   Azure a crescent argent. Crest   Two horns couped counter-charged, azure and argent

(I) Lave, a Dane to whom the line is traced in the genealogy, was son of a descendant of Harold Blautand, who died in 985, through a daughter who married one of the most famous of the Swedish medieval heroes, Styrbiorn, son of Olaf, King of Sweden   He became prominent, and in 1316 was Bishop of Roskilde

(II) Sven was heir of Svenem in 1346

(III) Marten was declared heir of Sven in 1363 in Tudse.

(IV) Nils was mentioned, in 1418, as owning land in Tudse

(V) Sertolf was mentioned, in 1466, as son of Nils, and he had sons, James and Randolf. The son James fought a duel and was obliged to flee to England and was accompanied by his brother

(VI) Randolf Nye, son of Sertolf, settled in Sussex, England, in 1527, and held land in Uckfield

(VII) William Nye, son of Randolf Nye, married Agnes, daughter of Ralph

Tregian, of County Hereford, he studied for the ministry and became rector of Ballance-Horned before his father died

(VIII) Ralph Nye, son of William Nye, inherited his father's estate in Uckfield and Ballance, in 1556, married, June 18, 1556, Margaret Merynge, of St Mary, Woolchurch Children   Thomas, mentioned below, Edmundus, buried in Somersetshire, March 9, 1594; Ralph, married, August 30, 1584, Joan Wilkshire, Anne, married, August 6, 1616, Nicholas Stuart, Mary, married, April 24, 1621, John Banister

(IX) Thomas Nye, son of Ralph Nye, married, September 6, 1583, at St Andrew, Hubbard, Katherine Poulsden, of Horley, County Surrey He sold to his wife's brother, William Poulsden, a tenement builded with a croft adjoining, containing sixteen acres and a half in Bidlenden, County Kent, for which he received an annuity of four shillings Children   Henry, graduate of Oxford, 1611, vicar of Cobham, County Surrey, and rector of Clapham, County Sussex; Philip, graduate of Oxford, 1619, rector of St Michael's, Cornhill and Acton, Middlesex, a celebrated preacher of Cromwell's day, John, and Thomas, mentioned below

(X) Thomas (2) Nye, son of Thomas (1) Nye, was a haberdasher of Bidlenden, County Kent, married, June 10, 1619, Agnes Nye, aged thirty-nine years, widow of Henry Nye He granted land to his youngest son Thomas, in Bidlenden, July 4, 1637, and in the deed stated   "My eldest son Benjamin, having gone to New England." Children   Benjamin, mentioned below, Thomas, born September 16, 1623, married Margaret Webster, and left descendants at Bidlenden

(XI) Benjamin Nye, son of Thomas (2) Nye, was born May 4 1620, at Bid-

39

lenden, England, and came in the ship "Abigail," to Lynn, Massachusetts, in 1635, locating in Sandwich two years later. His name is on the list of men in Sandwich able to bear arms in 1643; he contributed to the cost of building a mill there in 1654 and a meeting house in 1656. He took the oath of fidelity in 1657. He was supervisor of highways there in 1655, grand juror in 1658 and later, constable in 1661 and 1673; collector of taxes in 1674. He received, in 1669, twelve acres of land from the town for building his mill at the little pond and had other similar grants later. He was given permission by vote of the town to build a fulling mill on Spring Hill river, August 8, 1675, and it is said that the ruins of his old mill may still be seen there. He married, in Sandwich, October 19, 1640, Katherine Tupper, daughter of Rev. Thomas Tupper. Children: Mary, married Jacob Burgess; John; Ebenezer; Jonathan, born November 29, 1649; Mercy, April 4, 1652; Caleb; Nathan mentioned below; Benjamin, killed March 26, 1676, by Indians.

(XII) Nathan Nye, son of Benjamin Nye, lived at Sandwich, and took the oath of fidelity there in 1678. His will was dated September 18, 1741, and proved May 13, 1747. Children born at Sandwich: Reuben, February 28, 1686-87; Temperance, August 7, 1689; Thankful, August 11, 1691; Content, September 25, 1693; Jemima, February 20, 1695; Lemuel mentioned below; Deborah April 28, 1700; Maria, April 2, 1702; Caleb, June 28 1704; Nathan, September 28, 1708.

(XIII) Lemuel Nye, son of Nathan Nye, was born at Sandwich, March 21 1698-99, lived and died there. His will is dated July 22, 1762, and proved March 18, 1763. Children, mentioned in will: Samuel, mentioned below; Lot; Lemuel,

born 1733; Mercy, Mary, Sarah, Thankful.

(XIV) Samuel Nye, son of Lemuel Nye, was born in Sandwich; married there, February 25, 1767, Mercy Bourne, born June 24, 1727, daughter of Jonathan and Hannah Bourne. Children, born at Sandwich: Anna, born August 16, 1768, lived to the age of ninety-one years; Nathan, August 8, 1770; Isaac, September 11, 1772; Andrew, Mercy, September 8, 1778; Samuel, mentioned below; Braddock, August 25, 1784; Maria, August 25, 1787; Sarah, November 18, 1789; John.

(XV) Samuel (2) Nye, son of Samuel (1) Nye, was born at Sandwich, November 18, 1780. He lived at Nantucket, and later at Wareham, dying at the latter place, November 3, 1858. He married, in 1801, Mary Snow, who was born January 24, 1778, and died at Easton, April 25, 1869. Children: 1 Thomas S, born March 30, 1802, married four times. 2 Delia Maria, born April 14, 1804, married (first) Thomas Howard, and (second) Horatio Copeland (see Copeland VI). 3 Andrew S, born at Nantucket, March 18 1806, married Lucinda H. Leonard. 4 Mary, born June 19, 1809, married Nathaniel Jones. 5 Susan, born May 19, 1812, married (first) George Patterson and (second) George W Esten. 6 Margaret H, born November 25, 1815, married James Holmes. 7 Harriet Newell, born December 10, 1819, died January 29 1844 at Wareham, unmarried. 8 Almira (or Myra) Snow, born February 22 1823, married Thomas Mitchell.

CRANE, Joshua Eddy,

Educator, Librarian

From the best information at hand it appears that between the years 1635 and 1640 John Samuel and Jaspar Crane came to Massachusetts, John making a home in that part of Boston now Brookline, Samuel in Dorchester, and Jaspar removing about 1639 to New Haven, Connecticut, whether they were brothers or not is yet an open question. John Crane was in Boston as early as January 8, 1637.

(II) John Crane was succeeded by Henry Crane, born about 1621, probably in England. He married (first) Tabitha, daughter of Stephen Kinsley, settled in Braintree, and left a large line of descendants. Without evidence to the contrary it may be reasonably supposed that Samuel was the father of this Henry. Samuel Crane is mentioned in the Braintree records, 1640, as one of several elected to administer town affairs, among them Stephen Kinsley, this the first association in these records of the names Kinsley and Crane. In 1654 Stephen Kinsley (who was at Mount Wollaston, Massachusetts, in 1639) and his sons-in-law, Anthony Gulliver and Henry Crane, were settled on adjacent farms in that part of Dorchester which was later incorporated as Milton. Henry Crane was in main a husbandman. He was one of the selectmen of Milton in 1679, 1680 and 1681, and was one of the trustees of the first meeting house built in the town. His wife Tabitha died shortly after 1681, and he married (second) about 1683, Elizabeth, surname unknown, who survived him. His children were: Benjamin, mentioned below; John, mentioned below; Stephen married (first) Mary Denison, (second) Comfort, widow of Samuel Belcher, of Braintree; Henry, Elizabeth, born 1663, married (first) Eleazer Gilbert, of Taunton, (second) George Townsend of that same town; Ebenezer, born 1665, married Mary Tolman, Mary, born 1666, married Samuel Hackett, of Taunton; Mercy, 1668, Samuel, 1669, Anna C, 1687, who re-

moved to Taunton. Henry Crane died in Milton, March 21, 1709.

It should have been stated ere this that according to Mr. Ellery Bicknell Crane, the Cranes of England are classed among the families belonging to the county of Suffolk. Though numerous families bearing the name have been found residents of other counties in Great Britain, it is among the records of Suffolk county that we find delineated the long roll of aristocratic landholders in a line of succession from father to son covering a period of time marked by hundreds of years. Here their estates are to be found recorded for nearly three hundred years. It will be observed that some of the immediate posterity of Henry Crane located in Taunton, and the towns of Dighton, Berkley and Norton also became the places of residence of their descendants.

(III) Benjamin Crane, son of Henry Crane, born about 1656, was a member of Captain Johnson's company in King Philip's War and was severely wounded in the battle of Narragansett Swamp, December 19, 1675. His death occurred October 13, 1721. Many of the Crane family of Berkley were his descendants.

(III) John (2) Crane, son of Henry Crane, born November 30, 1658, in Dorchester, married, December 13, 1686, Hannah, daughter of James and Hannah Leonard, of Taunton, and there became a settler, but in 1698 had sold his place in Taunton and with his brother Benjamin in that year bought of the heirs of Jonathan Briggs a farm of three hundred acres in the South Purchase of Taunton, now Berkley, which in a few years was divided in two portions by the two brothers. John Crane died August 5, 1716, and his wife died October 24, 1760. Children: Henry, Gershom, Zipporah, Tabitha, John.

(IV) Gershom Crane, son of John (2)

41

and Hannah (Leonard) Crane, born September 3, 1692, married, February 27, 1716, Susanna Whitmarsh, daughter of Samuel Whitmarsh, then of Dighton It was at his house that the first meeting of the town of Berkley was held and of which he was the moderator in 1735 He died June 23, 1787 His wife, Susanna, died September 11, 1770 Their children were Abiah, born 1716, Abel, 1718, Ebenezer, 1720; Hannah, 1722, Elisha, mentioned below, Gershom, 1728, died 1732, John, 1731, married Rachel Terry and was a resident of Norton, and his son, Rev John Crane, D D, born 1756, was the minister of Northbridge and died in 1836, Gershom, 1735; Jonathan, 1737, was graduated at Harvard College in 1762, married Mary, daughter of Colonel Josiah Edson, 1770, and practiced his profession of medicine in Bridgewater, his son, Daniel Crane, was graduated at Brown University in 1796

(V) Elisha Crane, son of Gershom and Susanna (Whitmarsh) Crane, born December 25 1724, married Thankful Axtell, daughter of Daniel Axtell of Berkley, January 15 1774, and lived at the home of Daniel Axtell which was established in 1710 in the town of Dighton, now Berkley Their children were: Betsey, born 1775, married Benjamin Hathaway, 1801; Susannah 1776, married, 1802, Christopher Paull; Daniel 1777, died 1805; Polly, 1779, married, in 1806, Dean Burt, Barzillai, mentioned below Elisha Crane died November 20, 1807 Thankful (Axtell) Crane died January 22, 1832

(VI) Barzillai Crane, son of Elisha and Thankful (Axtell) Crane, born February 24 1783, married (first) January 22, 1810, Lydia Eddy, daughter of Captain Joshua Eddy and his wife Lydia (Paddock) Eddy, of Middleboro, and lived in Berkley Children Charlotte Maria, born 1811 died 1818, Susanna W, 1815,

married Samuel Breck, Elisha, 1817, died 1843, a physician, unmarried; Charlotte M, 1820, died 1841, Joshua Eddy, mentioned below, Irene Lazell, 1826, married Dr Thomas Nichols; Lydia, 1829, died 1833, Morton Eddy, 1831, died 1857, unmarried Lydia (Eddy) Crane died February 10, 1842 Barzillai Crane married (second) in 1844, Eliza Tobey, daughter of Apollos and Hannah (Crane) Tobey, of Berkley He died June 15, 1851 Eliza (Tobey) Crane, born October 29 1801, died December 9, 1882

Mrs Lydia (Eddy) Crane, wife of Barzillai Crane, was born December 23, 1787, daughter of Captain Joshua and Lydia (Paddock) Eddy, Joshua Eddy being a direct descendant of Samuel Eddy, who was the son of William Eddy, A M vicar of St Dunstan's Church, Cranbrook, County Kent, England, and his wife, Mary (Fosten) Eddy Samuel Eddy came from Boxted, County Suffolk, England, to America in the ship "Handmaid," in 1630, settling in Plymouth, where he purchased property in 1631 From this Samuel Eddy and his wife Elizabeth the descent of Lydia Eddy is through Obadiah and his wife Bennet, Samuel (2) and his wife Melatiah (Pratt), Zechariah and his wife Mercy (Morton), and Captain Joshua Eddy and his wife Lydia (Paddock).

Captain Joshua Eddy saw much hard service in the Revolution He entered the service, enlisting in 1775, in Captain Benson's company, Colonel Cotton's regiment, was at Roxbury, Massachusetts, during the siege of Boston, and at the battle of Breed's (Bunker) Hill In 1776 he was lieutenant in Colonel Marshall's regiment and went to Castle Island He was in the retreat from Ticonderoga and was at Saratoga at the surrender of General Burgoyne He then went to New Jersey, was in winter quarters with General Washington, and was at the battle of Monmouth After the close of the war he was extensively engaged in various kinds of business He was a man of unusual energy For many years he was a deacon in the church of his community He died in 1833

(VII) Joshua Eddy Crane, son of Barzillai and Lydia (Eddy) Crane, was born July 9, 1823, in the town of Berkley, Massachusetts and acquired his education in both the public and private schools of his native town Desiring to enter business he, at sixteen years of age, began preparation for it in the office of a commission merchant in New York City Later, in 1844, he was at Bridgewater with his uncle, Morton Eddy, who retired from the firm in 1848 Thereafter while in active business the concern was conducted by Mr Crane A man of ability, good judgment, one successful in the management of his own business affairs, Mr Crane was soon found by his fellow citizens to possess the qualities required in the same, and as a conservative public man was often sought and long continued in public official service He cast his first vote in 1844 for the candidates of the Liberty party, having been present at the organization of that party at Boston He soon became active politically in local affairs He was a delegate to the Worcester convention, at which Judge Charles Allen presided, and at which was organized the Republican party in Massachusetts For many years he was chairman of the Republican town committee of Bridgewater, and also a member of the State Republican Committee In 1857 he was a representative for the town in the General Court On the breaking out of the Civil War, in 1861, when party lines were almost obliterated, he was chosen senator from the South Plymouth district, and in the following year was almost

unanimously again elected to that body, the Democrats making no nomination against him While in the Senate he had the honor of taking part in the election of Hon Charles Sumner to the United States Senate from Massachusetts In the Senate he served on the committees on claims and on mercantile affairs and insurance He was town clerk of Bridgewater for several years, from 1855 to 1858 inclusive, and in 1873 and 1874 For more than thirty years he was in various capacities connected with the Plymouth County Agricultural Society, and for a number of years was treasurer and member of the board of trustees of that society On the occasion of the celebration of the fiftieth anniversary, September 30, 1869, he delivered the historical address For a dozen and more years he served as chairman of the board of trustees of the State Workhouse at Bridgewater, and for twenty and more years was a trustee of the Bridgewater Academy, and was active in the erection of the present school building For upward of twenty-five years Mr Crane was a correspondent for the newspapers of the vicinity writing many sketches of interest to those of antiquarian tastes He prepared the sketch of the town of Bridgewater contained in the "History of Plymouth County," published in 1884 His religious faith was that of the Central Square Congregational Church in Bridgewater of which he was a member, and he was chairman of the building committee at the time of the erection of the present church edifice

On January 9, 1849, Mr Crane married Lucy Ann Reed, born September 25, 1825, daughter of the late Quincy and Lucy (Loud) Reed, of Weymouth, Massachusetts, and their children were Joshua Eddy, mentioned below, Charles Reed, born 1852, Lucy Reed, 1854, died 1856;

43

Morton Eddy, 1857, of Washington, D.
C., Henry Lovell, January 31, 1860, died
March 16, 1905, Anna Howe, 1862, married Charles A. Drew, M. D., Edward
Appleton, 1865, died 1887 Joshua E.
Crane died in Bridgewater, August 5,
1888, Lucy Ann (Reed) Crane died September 24, 1898

Quincy Reed, the father of Mrs Crane,
descended from William Reade, who
settled in Weymouth in 1635, from whom
his descent is through Thomas Reed and
his wife Sarah (Bicknell); John Reed
and his wife Sarah (Whitmarsh), John
Reed (2) and his wife Mary (Bate) and
Ezra Reed and his wife Mary (Lovell)

(VIII) Joshua Eddy (2) Crane, son of
Joshua Eddy (1) and Lucy Ann (Reed)
Crane, was born October 1, 1850, in
Bridgewater, Massachusetts, and there
educated in the public schools of the place
and at the Bridgewater Academy, then
under the instruction of Mr Horace M.
Willard He furthered his studies at
Brown University, from which he was
graduated in 1872 Mr Crane was preceptor of Bridgewater Academy, 1873-75;
principal of the English preparatory department of the Syrian Protestant College, Beirut, Syria, 1876-79, subsequently
was employed as private tutor, and was
in charge of the Latin classes of Albany
Academy, Albany, New York, until 1884,
when he became librarian of the Young
Men's Association of Albany In 1887 he
accepted the position of associate principal of the Portland Latin School in
Portland, Maine, and in 1890 resumed his
former position at the library, from which
he withdrew in 1892 He became librarian of the Public Library of Taunton in
1895 He is an officer of the Old Colony
Historical Society, and of the Old Bridgewater Historical Society

Mr Crane married, January 1, 1884,
Katharine Perkins, daughter of Henry

and Amelia Bartlett (Sherman) Perkins,
of Bridgewater (see Perkins VIII)
Their daughter is Clara Whitney Crane
(Radcliffe, 1914)

(The Perkins Line)

(I) Abraham Perkins, one of the first
settlers of Hampton, New Hampshire,
was made a freeman, May 13, 1640 He
was a man of good education, was much
employed in the service of the town, and
died August 31, 1683, at the age of seventy-two His widow Mary died May
29, 1706, at the age of eighty-eight The
will of Abraham Perkins, dated August
22, 1683, and probated September 18,
1683, contains the names of his wife and
sons Jonathan, Humphrey, James, Luke
and David To the last two were given
five shillings each, as they had already
received their share The names of the
children of Abraham Perkins were
Mary, Abraham, Luke, Humphrey, died
young, James, died young, Timothy, died
young, James, Jonathan, David, Abigail,
Timothy, Sarah and Humphrey

(II) David Perkins, son of Abraham
and Mary Perkins, born February 28,
1653, settled in Beverly about 1675, and
in 1688 became a resident of Bridgewater,
in that part of the town which became
the South Precinct In 1694 he built the
first mill at the site of the iron works of
Messrs Lazell, Perkins & Company,
known afterwards as the Bridgewater
Iron Company, and was engaged in the
occupation of blacksmith He was the
first representative of the town in the
General Court at Boston after the union
of the colonies of Plymouth and Massachusetts, in 1692, and also served in this
capacity in 1694, and from 1704 to 1707
inclusive. His death occurred October 1,
1736 He married, in 1676, Elizabeth
Brown, born October 17, 1654, died July
14, 1735, daughter of Francis Brown, of

Beverly In his will of June 17, 1736, he names his sons David, Abraham, Thomas, sole executor, and Nathan, deceased, and grandchildren David and Jonathan, children of his son David, and Nathan, Timothy, James, Solomon, Martha and Silence, children of Nathan His children were Mary, David, Nathan and Thomas, who resided in Bridgewater, and Abraham, who became a settler in Kingston, Rhode Island, and died in 1746

(III) Thomas Perkins, son of David and Elizabeth (Brown) Perkins, born May 8, 1688, in Bridgewater, lived near the site of the present iron works, and died June 5, 1761 He married, February 20, 1717, Mary Washburn, supposed to be the daughter of James and Mary (Bowden) Washburn, of Bridgewater, died April 23, 1750 Children Mary, born 1718, married, 1742, Josiah Hayward; Hepzibah, 1720, married, 1746, Elezer Carver, Thomas, 1722, married, 1748, Mary Pratt; Charles, 1724, died 1726, Ebenezer, mentioned below; Francis, 1729, married, 1762, Susanna Waterman

(IV) Ebenezer Perkins, son of Thomas and Mary (Washburn) Perkins, born April 20, 1727, died May 31, 1770 He married, February 28, 1751, Experience Holmes Children Ebenezer, mentioned below, Mary, born 1753; Holmes, 1757, Hepzibah, 1759, Susanna, 1764, Nancy, 1769, married Rufus Leach

(V) Ebenezer (2) Perkins, eldest child of Ebenezer (1) and Experience (Holmes) Perkins, born 1752, died 1823, was a patriot in the war of the Revolution The records of Massachusetts give the following:

Ebenezer Perkins, of Bridgewater, private, Capt James Allen's company, Col Simeon Cary's regiment, pay abstract for mileage dated, "Camp near New York, Aug 9, 1776," mileage for 251 miles allowed the said Perkins, private; also

Capt Nathaniel Packard's company, Col Thomas Carpenter's regiment, entered service July 25, 1778, discharged Sept 9, 1778—service one month and sixteen days, at Rhode Island Roll sworn to at Plymouth Was also among the descriptive list of men raised in Plymouth county in 1779 to serve in the Continental army, aged twenty-seven years, stature six feet, complexion dark Engaged for town of Bridgewater, reported delivered to Capt L Bailey Was also private, Capt L Bailey's company, Colonel Bailey's (2) regiment, entered service July 25, 1779, discharged April 25, 1780, term nine months. Was also among a descriptive list of men raised to reinforce the Continental army for the term of six months, agreeable to resolve of June 5, 1780, returned as received of Justin Ely, commissioner, by Brig. Gen. John Glover, at Springfield, Aug. 2, 1780, aged twenty-eight years, stature six feet, complexion dark, engaged for town of Bridgewater, arrived at Springfield July 31, 1780, marched to camp August 2, 1780, under command of Lieut. Benjamin Pike. Was also among the list of men raised for the six months' service and returned by Brigadier General Paterson as having passed muster in a return dated October 25, 1780, was commissioned corporal Pay roll for six months' men raised by the town of Bridgewater for service in the Continental army at West Point during 1780, marched July 12, 1780, discharged January 13, 1781, service six months and thirteen days, including travel (240 miles) home

Ebenezer Perkins married, in 1782, Mary Pratt, daughter of Solomon and Mary (Keith) Pratt, died in 1849 Children · Ebenezer, born 1783, died 1784; Mary K , 1784, died 1786, Daniel, 1786; Thomas, 1788, Solomon, mentioned below, Aaron, 1792, Ornan, 1794, Minerva, 1796, Ebenezer, 1798, Simeon, 1801; Mary K , 1802; Ozias, 1804

(VI) Solomon Perkins, son of Ebenezer and Mary (Pratt) Perkins, born May 16, 1790, lived in Bridgewater, and died there February 26, 1880. He was long engaged as a foundryman in the works of Messrs Lazell, Perkins & Company He married, in Bridgewater, February 14, 1813, Clarissa Robinson, daughter of Dyer and Abigail (Stetson) Robinson,

45

died October 12, 1859 Children: Henry, mentioned below; Charles Robinson, born 1816, William Franklin, 1818, George Sproat, 1820, Ebenezer, 1826, Mary K. and Martha H. (twins), 1828; Alfred Holmes, 1830

(VII) Henry Perkins, eldest child of Solomon and Clarissa (Robinson) Perkins, was born April 25, 1814, in Bridgewater, and died March 24, 1901 In the maternal line of descent he was a grandson of Dyer Robinson, of Bridgewater, a forgeman in the iron works of Messrs Lazell, Perkins & Company, and was a nephew of Increase, Dyer, Gad and Jacob Robinson, long associated with the iron works in Bridgewater, and of Charles and Enoch Robinson, of the Old Colony Iron Works of Taunton Mr Perkins received his early training in the public schools of his native place and at Bridgewater Academy, and at an early age entered upon the occupation of an iron worker and foundryman with employment at Bridgewater, Swanzey and in the Hudson Valley In 1847, about the time of his marriage, Mr Perkins established an iron foundry in Bridgewater near the site of the cotton gin factory of Messrs Bates, Hyde & Company, now the Continental Gin Company factory, and soon after the period of the Civil War erected a spacious foundry and machine shop on the line of the Old Colony railroad, now the New York, New Haven & Hartford railroad, which has ever held an important place in the manufacturing establishments of the town Mr Perkins possessed a profound knowledge of the history and development of the iron industry and with the eye of an expert gave attention to every requirement of his office and to the operations and products of his foundry For many years the large annual production of pianoforte frames, the inventions of the Chickerings and

other manufacturers, included much of the workmanship of this foundry and established its reputation for the production of work of the best quality of American iron and illustrative of the perfection of the art of casting For many years also Mr Perkins was interested in the prosperity of the Eagle Cotton Gin Company of Bridgewater, which gave employment to a large number of men, and for a long period held the position of president of the company Interested in public affairs, he did not seek nor hold political office, but devoted himself to the demands of his occupation, and remained in active business life for more than sixty years. As a man of untiring energy and honorable business methods, he was enabled to achieve success in his undertakings and was respected and esteemed by those who were in his employ, and by the members of the community of which he was a benefactor He will long be remembered for his spirit of benevolence and for the qualities of heart which endeared him to his family and associates

Mr Perkins married, July 16, 1848, Amelia Bartlett Sherman, daughter of Aaron Simmons and Lydia (Whitney) Sherman, of Bridgewater. Children: Ralph, born March 26, 1849; Katharine, mentioned below, Henry, November 24, 1853, died December 12, 1854, Annie, January 24, 1855, died July 2, 1858; Clara, May 11, 1856, died May 24, 1888, Ebenezer, March 27, 1859, Charles, March 24, 1862, Amelia, June 16, 1864; Enoch, October 24, 1866, Harry K., August 11, 1868; Saba, September 7, 1869

(VIII) Katharine Perkins, daughter of Henry and Amelia Bartlett (Sherman) Perkins, born October 6, 1851, married, January 1, 1884, Joshua Eddy (2) Crane, of Bridgewater and Taunton (see Crane, VIII) They have a daughter, Clara Whitney Crane (Radcliffe, 1914).

46

RICHARDSON

And Allied Families

The origin of the name Richardson dates back centuries, and came from the name Richard, Richardson meaning son of Richard. This tradition was a matter of course, and the name has been widely spread in England, Scotland, Wales and Ireland. Among the name are found men of letters, barristers, clergymen, baronets, bishops, painters, authors, statesmen, professors, merchants and manufacturers. The different family seats bore arms, and it would be impossible to correctly give a coat-of-arms that would apply to all the different families, as few if any of the immigrants had the same.

(I) Samuel Richardson, one of the three noted Richardson brothers, who were among the earliest settlers of Woburn, Massachusetts, was baptized at West Mill County Herts, England, December 22, 1602 or 1604 and died in Woburn, Massachusetts, March 23, 1658. He was son of Thomas and Katherine (Durford) Richardson, of West Mill, who were married August 24, 1590. He was second in age of the three brothers, Ezekiel, Samuel and Thomas, the last of the three to come to New England. His wife Joanna, surname unknown, probably died in 1678. She was living as late as December 10, 1677, when she is mentioned as receiving fifty-five acres of land at a meeting of the proprietors held that date. Her will dated 20th, 4th, 1666, mentions sons John, Joseph, Samuel and Stephen, and daughters Elizabeth and Mary Mousall. Elizabeth and Mary married brothers, sons of Ralph Mousall, of Charlestown, Elizabeth marrying John, and Mary marrying Thomas. Samuel Richardson was executor of his father's will in England, dated March 4, 1630, and inherited his mother's part of his father's

estate. The will was presented at court in 1634 by Samuel Richardson. Samuel Richardson was married before he left West Mill, and two of his children were baptized there—Samuel, 1633, and Elizabeth, 1635. It was after 1635 that he and his brother Thomas sailed for New England. In 1636 he located in Charlestown. In 1640 he was one of the signers of Woburn town records. He was a selectman of Woburn, 1644-46-49-51, and his name appears on the first tax list of Woburn in 1645. He released certain lands, with his brothers, to the inhabitants of Woburn in 1644, and helped found the first church of Woburn in 1642. His estate was located on the "Richardson Row Road" of early times, and an estate known a century ago as the Job Miller estate, on present Washington street, in the present limits of the town of Winchester, was the more modern equivalent. This estate descended in a direct line from Samuel (1), to Samuel (2), thence to Jonathan (3), and thence to Jonathan (4) Richardson. The last Jonathan bequeathed it to his niece, Sarah Miller, wife of Job Miller. Jonathan Richardson (4), who was born in Woburn, had lived elsewhere during a part of his life, and returning in his latter days to Woburn, died in his native town, October 31, 1798. Job Miller that year occupied the house, which was a very old one at that time, thirty-six by eighteen feet in lateral dimensions, and two stories high. The adjoining farm contained fifty acres. The family of Samuel Richardson (2) was attacked by Indians on this place, April 10, 1676, and three of the family were killed. The father was at work on the afternoon of that day, with a young son for company, in his field. He noticed a commotion at the house, and hastening there found his wife Hannah and his son Thomas had been slain by a band of skulking Indians, so called, who after robbing some gardens of linen articles, at Cambridge, had on their retreat performed this mischief and slaughter A further search revealed the fact that his infant daughter Hannah had also been killed Her nurse had fled with her in her arms in the direction of a neighboring garrison house, and being closely pursued by the Indians, in order to save herself, she dropped the child, which the Indians dispatched The father pursued the Indians with a rallying party, and coming upon them seated beside a swamp in the woods, the party shot at them and hit one of them fatally, as the body was found afterwards in the woods, buried under leaves where his associates had laid him The fact of his being wounded was proved by traces of blood which were found in the woods from the point where he was first after he was shot, at this place the Indians left behind a bundle of linen in which was found wrapped up the scalps of one or more of their victims The Smith place represents the original estate of Job Miller Prince avenue traverses the original Samuel Richardson estate The estate of the first Samuel extended from the present tracks of the Boston & Maine railroad, near Nathaniel A Richardson's house, to the Stoneham and Winchester town line, the homestead being on the estate known to many of the present generation as the Josiah F Stone place A part of the lands now owned by Nathaniel A Richardson were included in the original estate The Miller house was built by the second Samuel, but the first Samuel is supposed to have lived on the other side of the present Washington street, and opposite the Miller place His house stood in a little valley, and disappeared before the year 1800 Children Samuel, baptized July 3, 1633, at West Mill, Herts, England, Elizabeth, May 22,

1635, at West Mill; Mary, February 25, 1638, at Charlestown, John, November 12, 1639, at Charlestown, Hannah, March 8, 1642, at Woburn, died April 8, 1642, Joseph, July 27, 1643, Samuel, May 22, 1646, Stephen mentioned below, Thomas, December 31, 1651, died September 27, 1657

(II) Stephen Richardson, fifth son of Samuel and Joanna Richardson was born August 15, 1649, in Woburn, Massachusetts, and died there March 22, 1717 He resided in Woburn, which then included Burlington, a part of Wilmington, and his land extended into Billerica which then joined Woburn In 1690 he was a freeman His will was dated August 15, 1713, and proved April 22, 1718 (see Middlesex probate records, vol 15, pp 157-163) In it he mentions as living wife Abigail, daughters Abigail Vinton and Prudence Kendall, sons Stephen, William, Francis, Timothy, Seth, Daniel and Solomon He married, January 2, 1675, at Billerica, Abigail Wyman, born 1659, died September 7, 1720, daughter of Francis and Abigail (Read) Wyman, the former of whom was one of the first settlers of Woburn and one of the largest landholders of Woburn Children Stephen, born February 20, 1676, Francis, January 19, 1678, died January 27, same year; William, mentioned below, Francis, January 15, 1681, Timothy, December 6, 1682, died January 18, 1683, Abigail, November 14, 1683, died June 21, 1720, Prudence, January 17, 1686, Timothy, January 24, 1688, Seth, January 16, 1690, Daniel, October 16, 1691, Mary, May 3, 1696, Rebecca, June 10, 1698, Solomon, March 27, 1702.

(III) William Richardson, third son of Stephen and Abigail (Wyman) Richardson, was born December 14, 1678, at Woburn, but the time of his death is not recorded He was a husbandman, and resided in Woburn until 1709 or 1710, when he removed to Charlestown End, or the present town of Stoneham, incorporated as such December 17, 1725 His land bordered on that of his brother-in-law, John Vinton, and he owned several lots in common with him On March 22, 1710, land in Charlestown was conveyed to John Vinton and William Richardson There are three other deeds dated 1700, 1709, 1712, by which land in Charlestown (east side of Spot Pond in Stoneham) was conveyed to them also On March 26, 1715, William Richardson sold land to John Vinton About 1718 he removed to Attleboro, Massachusetts On December 25, 1710, he bought land there of the proprietors His wife Rebecca is mentioned in her mother's will dated April 21, 1729 He married, September 15, 1703, at Woburn, Rebecca Vinton, born March 26, 1683, died after 1729, daughter of John and Hannah (Green) Vinton, of Woburn Children Rebecca, born August 4, 1704, died April 11, 1788, Hannah, October 28, 1706, Abigail, April 18, 1709, died November 23, 1730, William, April 17, 1712, Stephen, mentioned below, Mary, April 18, 1717, John, November 27, 1719, Joanna, September 17, 1722

(IV) Stephen (2) Richardson, second son of William and Rebecca (Vinton) Richardson, was born September 18, 1714, in the northern part of Charlestown, now Stoneham, Massachusetts, and was a child when the family removed to Attleboro There he made his home, and married, November 11, 1736, Hannah Coy, born October 2, 1718, in Beverly, Massachusetts, baptized there June 4, 1723, eldest daughter of Caleb and Mary (Wellman) Coy, of that town Children, born in Attleboro Stephen, August 6, 1737, Caleb, July 7, 1739, Daniel, mentioned below, Hannah, October 22, 1744, Elizabeth, October 16, 1747, Rebecca, April 18, 1750, Henry, 1752

(V) Daniel Richardson, third son of Stephen (2) and Hannah (Coy) Richardson, was born March 26, 1742, in Attleboro, and there made his home He married Sarah Read, born May 30, 1743, in Rehoboth, daughter of Thomas (2) and Bathsheba Read Children Sarah, born November 28, 1762, Rebecca, February 17, 1764, Daniel, mentioned below Abigail August 9, 1767, Alice, August 20, 1769, Selma, August 24, 1771, Alfred, June 27, 1780, Roxse, January 8, 1783, died October 31, 1798, Philene Septem- ber 29, 1785, Lucinda, July 12 1788

(VI) Daniel (2) Richardson, eldest son of Daniel (1) and Sarah (Read) Richardson, was born April 6, 1765, in Attleboro, and married there, January 18, 1787, Chloe Wilmarth, born August 14, 1763, in Rehoboth, daughter of Ezra and Prudence (Morse) Wilmarth Children Daniel, mentioned below, Chloe, Octo- ber 7, 1790, Stephen, September 2, 1793, Varnum, August 1, 1795, Enos, March 9, 1797

(VII) Daniel (3) Richardson, eldest child of Daniel (2) and Chloe (Wilmarth) Richardson, was born August 16, 1787, in Attleboro, and there married, May 9, 1813, Nancy Eaton, born June 3, 1791, in Middleboro, Massachusetts daughter of Nathan and Margaret Eaton, of that town (see Eaton, VI) Children Roxey, born January 3, 1814, Nancy Eaton, July 16, 1817, Daniel Augustus, mentioned be- low

(VIII) Daniel Augustus Richardson, only son of Daniel (3) and Nancy (Eaton) Richardson, was born February 11, 1822, in Attleboro, and lived at Attle- boro Falls, where he was engaged in the manufacture of buttons, in association with Daniel Evans He also engaged in agriculture, and owned land at Attleboro Falls, where he continued to reside until his death in 1903, and was buried in Mount Hope Cemetery He was married in Attleboro, October 9, 1842, by Benjamin H Davis, justice of the peace, to Ann Russell Bowen, born 1820, daughter of David and Amy (Rounds) Bowen, of that town (see Bowen, VIII) She died at Attleboro Falls, April 22 1911, and was buried beside her husband Children Anna Emilia, mentioned below, Henry Augustus, died in Taunton; Eugene Russell, resides in Providence, Mary Bowen, married Edgar Nicholson, and she died at Attleboro Falls

(IX) Anna Emilia Richardson, eldest child of Daniel Augustus and Ann Russell (Bowen) Richardson, born at Attleboro Falls, became the wife of William Price, of North Attleboro She now resides at Attleboro Falls, where she is a valuable member of society, and is devoted to the culture of uplifting influences She has a daughter, Gertrude, wife of James Dow, residing at Attleboro Falls, the mother of three children Russell Augustus, Marion Amelia and Margery Richardson Dow

(The Eaton Line)

(1) Francis Eaton came from England to Plymouth, Massachusetts, in 1620, in the "Mayflower," and signed the famous compact on board that historic vessel He was a carpenter by trade, was admitted a freeman in 1633, and March 25, 1633, was rated at nine shillings His wife Sarah, son Samuel, and infant, came with him. His wife died before 1627; Bradford says she died "in the generall sickness which was in the winter of 1620-21." He married a second wife, who died soon, and he married (third) Christian Penn, who came over in the "Ann" in 1623 He removed from Plymouth to Duxbury, where he died in the latter part of 1633 Administration on his estate was granted to Thomas Prence and John Doane, November 25, same year. In July,

1634, his widow married Francis Billington, by whom she had eight children Child of Francis Eaton by first wife Samuel mentioned below Child of second wife Rachel, born 1625 in Plymouth Child of third wife Benjamin, born about 1627, in Duxbury There were two other children, one an "ideote," and another who probably died without issue

(II) Samuel Eaton, son of Francis Eaton, was born about 1618, in England, and died at Middleborough, Massachusetts, in 1684 His father died when he was a child, and he was apprenticed, August 13, 1636, for seven years, to John Cooke, Jr He lived in Duxbury and Middleborough, and was one of the two Mayflower Pilgrims who settled in the latter place, where he was living before 1675 He was one of the purchasers of Dartmouth in 1652 and of Bridgewater In 1670 he was admitted a freeman The Eatons were not very rigid Puritans evidently, for Samuel Eaton was once admonished by the court for "mixed dancing" with Goodwife Hall He bought land at Duxbury of Love Brewster, and sold it in 1663 to Josiah Standish He married, January 10 1666, Martha Billington, daughter of Francis Billington Children Mercy, married Samuel Fuller, and Samuel, mentioned below

(III) Samuel (2) Eaton, son of Samuel (1) and Martha (Billington) Eaton, was born about 1662, and was one of the original members of the First Church of Middleborough He married Elizabeth, daughter of Rev. Samuel Fuller, first pastor of Middleborough, also of Mayflower ancestry Children, born at Middleborough Mercy, born 1695, Keziah, 1700, Elizabeth, 1701, Barnabas, mentioned below

(IV) Barnabas Eaton, son of Samuel

ENCYCLOPEDIA OF BIOGRAPHY

(2) and Elizabeth (Fuller) Eaton, was born 1703, and settled in Middleborough He married (first) Mehitable, surname unknown, (second) Mehitable Clements Children of first wife, born in Middleborough Hannah, 1732 Samuel, 1733; Mary, 1735, Sarah, 1737; Seth, 1739 Children of second wife Lot, born 1744, Mehitable, 1747, Elizabeth 1749, Ziba, 1750, Nathan, mentioned below, Wealthy, 1755, Keziah, 1757, Meribah, 1760

(V) Nathan Eaton, son of Barnabas and Mehitable (Clements) Eaton, was born August 11, 1753, in Middleborough He served in the Revolutionary War as a private in Captain Seth Turner's company, Colonel Thomas Marshall's regiment, enlisted June 15, 1776, service to November 1, 1776, four months and sixteen days, also same company and regiment, service between October 31, 1776, and July 1, 1777, one month company stationed at Hull, roll sworn to in Suffolk county, also Captain Job Pierce's company, Colonel Theophilus Cotton's (Plymouth County) regiment, pay roll for October, 1777, dated Middleborough, service of thirty days at Rhode Island, Captain Joshua White's company, Colonel Ebenezer Sprout's regiment, enlisted, September 6, 1778, discharged September 12, 1778, service six days on an alarm at Dartmouth, under same commanders marched August 1, 1780, discharged August 3, 1780, service two days, company marched to Tiverton, Rhode Island, on an alarm His entire lifetime was spent in his native town His wife bore the name of Margaret Children Hannah, born July 3, 1775, Martha, June 8, 1777, Polly, 1781, Barnabas, July 22, 1782, Ziba, March 18, 1784, Sarah, March, 1786; Mehitable, February 23, 1789; Nancy, mentioned below; Luther, October 6, 1793, Elizabeth, December 7, 1796

(VI) Nancy Eaton, seventh daughter

of Nathan and Margaret Eaton, was born June 3, 1791, in Middleborough, and became the wife of Daniel (3) Richardson, of Attleboro (see Richardson, VII)

(The Bowen Line)

(I) Richard Bowen came from Kittle Hill, Glamorganshire, Wales, to this country about 1638, and settled at Rehoboth, Massachusetts He was a son of James and Eleanor Bowen, of Llewyndwar, Pembrokeshire, Wales, and grandson of Mathias Bowen or Bowin He was a large land proprietor along the river "running under the bridge," called Bowen's Bridge, the fresh-water tributary of the Barrington river south from Seekonk He was a town officer and was admitted a freeman, June 4, 1645 He married, March 4, 1648, Esther Sutton He was buried February 4, 1674, and in his will, dated June 4, 1675, he bequeathed to his wife Elizabeth (or Esther), and children Thomas, Obediah, Richard, William, Alice Wheaton, Sarah Fuller and Ruth Leverich

(II) Thomas Bowen, son of Richard and Esther (Sutton) Bowen, was of Salem, Massachusetts, in 1648, and of New London, Connecticut, in 1657-60 He removed to Rehoboth, Massachusetts, where he died in 1663 His will, dated April 11, 1663, named his wife Elizabeth as executrix of his estate In 1669 she was the wife of Samuel Fuller, perhaps of Plymouth, Massachusetts, buried August 15, 1676, in Rehoboth In the will of Thomas Bowen he also mentioned his child Richard and his brother Obediah

(III) Dr Richard (2) Bowen, son of Thomas and Elizabeth Bowen, was born January 17, 1662, in Rehoboth, and died in 1736 As early as 1680 he was engaged in the practice of medicine in Seekonk, Massachusetts, within two miles of Providence, and for more than twenty

51

years he attended the sick there before it had any settled physician within its limits. He also educated his sons, Thomas and Jabez, to be physicians. He married, January 9, 1683, Mercye Titus, born March 17, 1665, in Rehoboth, daughter of John and Abigail (Carpenter) Titus, granddaughter of Robert and Hannah Titus, of England, where John was born. Children: Elizabeth, born November, 1684; Abiah, April 10, 1687; Thomas, mentioned below; Damaris, April 26, 1692; Jabez, October 19, 1696; Ebenezer, August 23, 1699; Urania, September 23, 1707.

(IV) Thomas (2) Bowen, eldest son of Dr. Richard (2) and Mercye (Titus) Bowen, was born August 20, 1689, in Rehoboth, and died there July 17, 1774. He married, August 10, 1710, in Rehoboth, Sarah Hunt, born October 16, 1690, in that town, daughter of Ephraim and Rebecca Hunt. Children: Sarah, born June 26, 1711; Huldah, February 16, 1713; Thomas, mentioned below; Ephraim, October 3, 1716; Oliver, February 3, 1719; Hannah, April 30, 1721; Lucy, July 3, 1723; Benjamin, March 8, 1724; Lydia, June 18, 1727; Bettey, April 1, 1729; Molly, November 8, 1731.

(V) Thomas (3) Bowen, eldest son of Thomas (2) and Sarah (Hunt) Bowen, called Thomas, Jr. in the records, was born October 3, 1714, in Rehoboth, lived in what is now Cumberland, Rhode Island, and died August 8, 1782. He married, June 18, 1735, Hepsibeth (Elizabeth) Carpenter, born March 28, 1715, in Rehoboth, daughter of Jonathan and Hannah (French) Carpenter. Children: Billee, born May 9, 1739; Bersham, March 31, 1742. Molly, November 12, 1744; Benjamin, January 27, 1747; Bettee, May 2, 1749; Thomas and Cyrell, June 23, 1752; Luce, April 23, 1755; Syrell, July 28, 1757.

(VI) Thomas (4) Bowen, fourth son of Thomas (3) and Hepsibeth (Elizabeth) (Carpenter) Bowen, was born June 23, 1752, probably in Cumberland, and was married there, February 7, 1771, to Anna (sometimes called Hannah) Rhodes, of Stonington, Connecticut, born October 20, 1755, in South Kingstown, Rhode Island, daughter of James and Anna (Crandall) Rhodes, later of Westerly, Rhode Island, and Stonington Children, recorded in Cumberland David, mentioned below; Rachel, born September 14, 1774; Huldah, September 25, 1775; Zebedon, December 13, 1777; John, April 26, 1780; Polly, April 26, 1782; Asa, March 23, 1785; James, July 20, 1787; Thomas, November 5, 1791.

(VII) David Bowen, eldest child of Thomas (4) and Anna (Rhodes) Bowen, was born December 24, 1771, in Cumberland, and lived in Attleboro. He married Amy Rounds, daughter of Hezekiah and Mary (Wheeler) Rounds, of Attleboro (see Rounds, V).

(VIII) Ann Russell Bowen, daughter of David and Amy (Rounds) Bowen, became the wife of Daniel Augustus Richardson, of Attleboro (see Richardson, VIII).

(The Rounds Line)

This surname is found among the descriptive ones, Bigge, Small, Little, Heigh, Haupt, Strong, Low, and in England it is usually spelled without the final s. A Robert Rounds is recorded in the calendar proceedings in chancery (time of Elizabeth), and the Round family were located in Kent and Oxford counties, England. The name appears at an early period in various sections of Massachusetts, but not among the pioneers. It was very strongly represented in and about Rehoboth, Massachusetts, and descendants have resided in the vicinity until the present time.

(I) The first of this name mentioned in New England archives was Philip Rounds, of Salem, Massachusetts, who died there in 1678 The inventory of his estate made June 24 of that year, placed its value at seven pounds, ten shillings and six pence He married, in November, 1671, Ann Bush

(II) John Rounds was a resident of Swansea, Massachusetts, and married Abigail Bowen, perhaps a daughter of Obadiah (2) and Abigail (Bullock) Bowen, of Swansea, born about 1678 Four children are recorded in Swansea John, born November 15, 1699, Mary, March 19, 1703, married, September 26, 1721, Ephraim Chase, David, January 28, 1706, Jabez, mentioned below There were undoubtedly several others, including Nathaniel, mentioned below

(III) Jabez Rounds, son of John and Abigail (Bowen) Rounds, born September 28, 1708, was residing in Swansea, April 26, 1733, at which date he was married in Rehoboth by Rev John Coomer to Renew Carpenter, of Rehoboth, born January 6, 1714, daughter of Jonathan and Desire (Martin) Carpenter Children, recorded in Rehoboth Isaac, born January 23, 1734, Jabez, January 8, 1736, Isabell, October 23, 1737 Abigail, January, 1740, Isaiah, January 30, 1741, Rebeckah, March 21, 1742, Sibbel, September 10, 1744, Oliver, mentioned below, Rhoda, January 26, 1750, Esther, October 8, 1752, Simeon, February 4, 1755

(IV) Oliver Rounds, fourth son of Jabez and Renew (Carpenter) Rounds, was born April 1, 1747, in Rehoboth, and was married, April 12, 1770, in Warren, Rhode Island, by Rev Jonathan Manning, to Anna Salisbury, probably a native of that town, not recorded there Children Daniel, born June 5, 1771, Sybel, May 1, 1773, Abigail, March 1, 1775, Calvin, October 3, 1776, Patience,

March 1, 1778; Spencer and Oliver (twins), February 26, 1780, Jabez, mentioned below, Spencer, October 24, 1785

(V) Jabez (2) Rounds, fourth son of Oliver and Anna (Salisbury) Rounds, was born November 20, 1782, in Warren, and lived in Providence, Rhode Island He married, April 20, 1806, Eliza Hudson, daughter of Reuben and Abigail (Sisson) Hudson, of Swansea, and granddaughter of George and Drusilla Sisson Children Jabez Sisson, mentioned below; Abby, died young, Harriet, married John Drown, and died in California, Anna Eliza, married Albert Hunter.

(VI) Jabez Sisson Rounds, son of Jabez (2) and Eliza (Hudson) Rounds, was born April 14, 1816, in Providence, and died in Taunton, Massachusetts, August 7, 1860 He was a well known merchant of Taunton, where he established the dry goods house now known as The N B Skinner Company He was also active in other enterprises, and was among the corporators of the Taunton Steamboat Company, which began with a capital of $25,000, and was also identified with the banking interests of Taunton and other lines of commercial pursuit He was among the most public-spirited citizens of his day, and died while still in the prime of manhood, at the age of forty-four years He was a man of both physical and intellectual force and a power in the development of his home city He was married in Taunton by Rev C H Brigham, May 26, 1845, to Almira B Leonard, daughter of Ezekiel B and Harriet (Ingalls) Leonard, of that town (see Leonard VII) She is still living, at the age of ninety-five years, and is quite active, taking an interest in current events, the oldest person in Taunton Her declining years are made happy by the filial attention of her daughter, Mrs Frederick Mason She was the mother of two children Fred-

53

erick, who died at the age of eighteen years, and Harriet Leonard, mentioned below.

(VII) Harriet Leonard Rounds, only daughter of Jabez Sisson and Almira B (Leonard) Rounds, became the wife of Colonel Frederick Mason, of Taunton, son of William and Harriet Augusta (Metcalf) Mason, and resides in her native city She is the mother of two children 1. Maurice Mason, who married Sarah Crossman Sprout, and died October 29, 1913, leaving two children Marguerite and William 2 Madeline, now the widow of Carlton Braybrook, and the mother of two children Bethena and Leonard

(III) Nathaniel Rounds, born about 1716-18, in Swansea, undoubtedly son of John and Abigail (Bowen) Rounds, was married, April 9, 1741, to Elizabeth Bowen, probably a daughter of Thomas and Thankful (Mason) Bowen, of Swansea The following children are recorded in Rehoboth, there were doubtless others Nathaniel, born November 26, 1749, Hezekiah, mentioned below, Anna, July 27. 1764 died 1768

(IV) Hezekiah Rounds, son of Nathaniel and Elizabeth (Bowen) Rounds, was born December 20, 1752, and lived in Attleboro He was a soldier of the Revolution, serving first as a private in Captain Elisha May's company, Colonel John Daggett's regiment, entered August 23 discharged September 2, 1778, eleven days at Rhode Island, roll sworn to at Attleboro He was also in Captain Alexander Foster's company, Colonel Isaac Dean's regiment, marched July 31, 1780, on an alarm at Tiverton, Rhode Island, discharged August 8, following, service ten days, roll sworn in Attleboro He married in Rehoboth, January 12, 1775, Mary Wheeler, born August 5, 1752, in Rehoboth, daughter of Valentine and

Sarah (Goff) Wheeler Children Rachel, born May 9, 1776, in Rehoboth, Mary, June 9, 1777, Lucinda, April 15, 1779, Mercy, February 1, 1781, died April 1, 1782, Elizabeth, February 18, 1783, Hezekiah Bowen, April 17, 1785, Rhoda, January 9, 1787, Amy, mentioned below, Nancy, March 23, 1791, Benjamin Wheeler, July 18, 1794, Enos Hiram, April 11, 1797, Marcus, March 30, 1802

(V) Amy Rounds, seventh daughter of Hezekiah and Mary (Wheeler) Rounds, was born March 9, 1789, in Attleboro, and became the wife of David Bowen, of that town (see Bowen VII).

BATES, Joseph M,

Business Man, Financier

Environment is said to be the making of a man's character for good or evil So is reflected upon a community, be it large or small, the life of an individual If the man is broad-minded, progressive and ambitious, there must follow an upbuilding that will outlast the mortal career Such a memorial has Joseph M Bates of Attleboro, Massachusetts, who passed away September 7, 1905, at the ripe age of seventy-two years, after a lifetime of unusual activity and usefulness, and after having achieved material success

Joseph M Bates was born at Wickford, in the town of North Kingston, Rhode Island, August 2, 1833, the son of Benoni Potter and Abigail Mahalia (Congdon) Bates His father was a contractor and builder, and was a native of Wisconsin After spending his childhood and early youth in his native town, receiving his educational training in the schools of North Kingston, Mr Bates started to learn the jeweler's trade in Providence, Rhode Island It was not long after that he made his first business venture in Attleboro, Massachusetts, being associ-

ated with the jewelry firm of Skinner, Viall & Company; which was located in a room over Willard Blackinton's shuttle shop on North Main street, he and his partners constituting the working force within the limits of one small room His first venture was in that well remembered year of "great and general depression," 1857, and the first year of the firm's history was not an eventful one, and business came slowly Mr Bates therefore sold out his interest and formed a new firm, that of Bates, Capron & Williams. This concern was located in a factory at Attleboro Falls, later occupied by the Gold Metal Braid Company About 1860, after two years of prosperity had followed this organization, Messrs Capron and Williams desired a change of location, and Mr Bates sold out his share in the concern to William Sherman Resuming his old place in the shuttle shop at Attleboro, Mr Bates engaged in business on his own account and enjoyed a moderately good business for three years, until 1863, when he removed to the lower story of the Steam Power Company's building During this time there were many difficulties and discouragements to be overcome, but Mr Bates bravely overcame them, climbing slowly but surely, until success finally crowned his labors During the Civil War his business increased, and in 1867 he deemed it wise to take a partner, associating himself with George M Bacon, under the firm name of Bates & Bacon, their specialty being the manufacture of rolled gold-plated bracelets In 1882 this firm introduced an innovation in Attleboro by beginning the manufacture of watch cases This venture proved a good one and became one of the most important departments of the firm's business Additional space was soon required by the growing trade, and in 1884 Mr Bates built a shop two

hundred feet long, thirty-five feet wide, and four stories high Later Mr Bacon retired from the firm, and Mr. Bates continued the business alone, under the same firm name Success was thus signally gained after a persistent following of the road to fortune, which was not an easy or phenomenally rapid one, but that he did succeed was but the more credit to him Perhaps the most striking example of Mr Bates' fine public spirit and faith in Attleboro's future was his action following the memorable fire of May 18, 1898, when sixteen jewelry firms of that town lost everything they owned, and property to the value of nearly a million dollars was totally destroyed Even men of experienced judgment not naturally pessimistic, believed that the town's great industry had received a death-blow from which it could never recover This belief was strengthened by the removal to Providence and elsewhere, soon after the fire, of a number of jewelry concerns, including some of the largest in the town Mr Bates, however, was not dismayed although he was by far the greatest individual sufferer With the least possible delay and in his usual unostentatious manner he caused to be erected near the site of the ruined shops a new factory building, larger and better than any of those that had been destroyed, and later other large buildings for the accommodations of many concerns desiring locations Another evidence of Mr Bates' public spirit was the erection of the building known as "Bates' Opera House " It was the first large hall in Attleboro, having a frontage of one hundred and sixty feet about one hundred and fifty feet deep and three stories high built of brick The theatre proper occupied the rear of the structure, and the full height of the building Mr Bates received unanimous commendation for providing the town with a structure so adequate in size and so convenient in arrangement A paragraph in the "History of Attleboro" states

The opening night, September 30, 1886, marked an era in entertainment in the town The audience was a large one, and made brilliant by the bright costumes and beautiful flowers worn by the ladies The play was of the best, "Richelieu", the company excellent, with one of our most talented and renowned actors Lawrence Barrett in the title role Throughout the entire season, which numbered some thirty-five performances, the position taken at the start was maintained and only plays of a good class were presented To preserve the rule thus established seems to be the owner's intention This theatre was an innovation in Attleboro, Massachusetts, and plentiful criticism was offered Mr Bates The need of a large audience room had long been felt This need was met and filled by this building The first floor is occupied by various stores A serious fire and a change of ownership has caused quite a radical change in the building and its management

Mr Bates was united in marriage, June 26, 1853, with Sarah Louise Gardner, who was born at Centreville, in the town of Warwick, Rhode Island, daughter of Nicholas E. and Hannah (Carr) Gardner, and to this union were born three children, as follows Charles Rudolphus, mentioned below, Mary Louise, who died unmarried, April 18, 1905, and Frank Morton, who died in Attleboro, May 19, 1916

Mr Bates was quiet and unassuming in manner, approachable, notwithstanding his great wealth, and possessed of rare good judgment which caused his advice and counsel to be sought in many matters of large importance He was deeply attached to his home and to the town, which he rarely left for more than a day or two at a time Upon the death of Willard Blackinton, in 1877, the first president of the First National Bank of Attleboro, Mr Bates became its presi-

dent, which position he ably filled until his death, covering a period of over thirty years Fraternally, he was a valued member of the Masonic organization, holding membership in Ezekiel Bates Lodge, Free and Accepted Masons, of Attleboro

Mr Bates passed away at Cottage City, where he had gone on a short vacation, in hopes that the change would improve his failing health Although not a native of Attleboro, Mr Bates was unusually public spirited and always upheld the interests of his adopted town His life story indicates that he was a man of endeavor, advancing himself by his activity to a place of prominence and trust in the community where his active business career was spent, and playing an important part in the business growth and development of that community.

Charles Rudolphus Bates, eldest son of Joseph M and Sarah Louise (Gardner) Bates, was born at Wickford, in the town of North Kingston, Rhode Island, January 10, 1856 He attended the public schools of his native town, and then after the removal of his father's family to Attleboro, the public schools of the latter town, finishing his educational training by a course at Schofield's Business College, at Providence After leaving school he was connected with his father in the firm of Bates & Bacon, manufacturing jewelers, continuing with this firm until the death of his father Later he engaged in the real estate business, having an office in the Bates Opera House building, where he continued until 1912, when he retired from active business Mr Bates died February 15, 1916, and was buried in Woodlawn Cemetery, Attleboro, Massachusetts

He married, October 19, 1877, Annie Carpenter Tinkham, daughter of Ebenezer and Adeline (Arnold) Tinkham, of Norton, Massachusetts They were the parents of two sons, Howard Tinkham, born February 26, 1878, and Joseph Morton, born February 23, 1880, who married Kate Eliza Shaw, daughter of F H Shaw, of Attleboro

ALLEN, Rodolphus N,
Bank Official.

This is one of the names most frequently met in the United States, and is represented by many distinct families Its use arises from the Christian name, which is very ancient In the roll of Battle Abbey, Fitz-Aleyne (son of Allen) appears, and the name comes down through the ages to the present Alan, constable of Scotland and Lord of Galloway and Cunningham, died in 1234 One of the first using Allen as a surname was Thomas Allen, sheriff of London in 1414 Sir John Allen was mayor of London in 1524, Sir William Allen in 1571, and Sir Thomas Alleyn in 1659 Edward Allen (1566-1626), a distinguished actor and friend of Shakespeare, and Ben Johnson, founded, in 1618, Dulwich College, with the stipulation that the master and secretary must always bear the name of Allen, and this curious condition has been easily fulfilled through the plenitude of scholars of the name There are no less than fifty-five coats-of-arms of separate and distinct families of Allen in the United Kingdom, besides twenty others of different spellings There were more than a score of emigrants of this surname, from almost as many different families, who left England before 1650 to settle in New England The name in early times was spelled Allin, Alline, Alling, Allyn, Allein and Allen, but the last is the orthography almost universally used at the present day It is found not only in the industrial but in the professional life of people who have stood for all that is noblest

and best It has been identified with the formative period of New England history, and from that region has sent out worthy representatives

(I) William Allen, by tradition a native of Wales, came to this country in 1660, and is of record at Portsmouth (Prudence Island), Rhode Island in 1638 He purchased a large tract of land, which included the subsequent village of Drownville (now West Barrington), built a house, and was resident of that place prior to 1670 Both he and his wife Elizabeth died in the year 1685 Children Mary, William, and Portsmouth, who was deputy to the General Court in 1705, Thomas of Swansea, Massachusetts, John mentioned below, Matthew, of Portsmouth, Warwick and North Kingstown, Mercy, Sarah; and Benjamin

(II) John Allen, son of William and Elizabeth Allen, born October 26 1670, moved from Prudence Island into Aquidnesett, and purchased one hundred and eighty-eight acres of land, paying for it $933 1-3, the deed being dated February, 1702 This was later the residence of Deacon George and Rev J W Allen He built his house in what has since been called the tobacco yard, a few rods below the south end of the Great Rocks He was a member of the Baptist church at Newport under Elder Wightman John Allen married Margaret Havens, and had children Thomas, mentioned below, William, born May 15, 1710, John, May 15, 1710; Mary, married a Gardiner, Phebe, married a Slocum, Elizabeth, married a Fairbanks, Jonathan, born August 6, 1717; Bathsheba, April 10, 1719 married a Johnston, Mercy, September 14, 1724 married a Card

(III) Thomas Allen, eldest child of John and Margaret (Havens) Allen, was

born about 1690, and lived in North
Kingstown, Rhode Island, with his wife,
Ann The birth records of North Kings-
town have been mutilated by the action
of time, and the dates of birth of their
first three children appear in North
Kingstown without the name having
occurred August 3, 1714 October 10,
1716, October 21, 1718 Others were
Samuel, mentioned below, a child, born
August 23, 1724, another, August 30,
1729, Christopher, October 26, 1731,
Martha, January 28, 1735, Bathsheba,
August 1, 1738

(IV) Samuel Allen eldest known son
of Thomas and Ann Allen, was born October 21, 1718, in North Kingstown, and
lived in Middletown, Rhode Island
There he married, January 16, 1745, Mary
Coggeshall, born March 27, 1720, in Middletown died March 17, 1768, daughter
of Thomas and Mary (Freeborn) Coggeshall Children, recorded in Middletown
Rowland, born October 15, 1746, Noel,
March 25, 1749, Joseph, mentioned below, John, December 2, 1753, Thomas,
September 9 1759

(V) Joseph Allen, third son of Samuel
and Mary (Coggeshall) Allen, was born
February 4, 1752, in Middletown, and
lived in that town He married, in Newport, January 21 1779 Mary Taggart,
and had the following children recorded
in Middletown Noel, mentioned below,
Samuel, born November 4, 1781, Thomas,
July 25, 1783, Mary, June 6, 1785 He
may have removed to Westport, Massachusetts, and had other children later

(VI) Noel Allen, eldest child of Joseph and Mary (Taggart) Allen, was
born May 12 1780, in Middletown and
lived in Westport, Massachusetts His
intention of marriage to Hannah Dunham is recorded there She was then a
resident of Dartmouth, and their marriage intention is also recorded in that

town, as well as the marriage, January
24, 1801 Children Christine, Eliza,
Susan, George, Margaret, Rhodolphus
Howard, mentioned below

(VII) Rhodolphus Howard Allen, son
of Noel and Hannah (Dunham) Allen,
was born January 1, 1808, in Westport,
and died in Fall River, Massachusetts, in
1891 He married, October 8, 1832, Mary
Turner Dean, born April 11, 1811, daughter of Joseph (3) and Elizabeth (Tew)
Dean, of that town (see Dean V) Children Rhodolphus W, mentioned below,
Mary Jane, born November 30, 1834, died
young, Mary Elizabeth February 16,
1837, Henry, October 9, 1839, Joseph
Dean, April 24, 1842, Albert Howard,
died young, Adelbert Howard, February
19, 1848, Louis Valentine, November 23,
1850, Ella Viola, July 1, 1853

(VIII) Rhodolphus W Allen, eldest
child of Rhodolphus Howard and Mary
Turner (Dean) Allen, was born July 21,
1833, and married November 19, 1856,
Amanda M Davis, daughter of Noah
Davis Children Iantha Amanda, born
September 10, 1857, Rodolphus N, men-
tioned below, Alton Alfred, March 10,
1861, resides in Fall River, Edith Earle,
November 13, 1871

(IX) Rodolphus N Allen, eldest son
of Rhodolphus W and Amanda M
(Davis) Allen, was born August 29, 1859
in that part of Freetown Massachusetts,
which is now in Fall River, and was educated in the schools of the last named
town He began his association with
business affairs as a clerk in a cotton
mill and subsequently entered the Massasoit-Pocasset National Bank, in which he
has risen by promotion until he now
holds the position of paying teller Mr
Allen is also treasurer of the Fall River
Cooperative Bank

He married, October 14, 1885, Annie
Brownell Smith, born May 9, 1861.

daughter of Charles Church and Sarah D (Shaw) Smith, of Fall River (see Smith IV) Children 1 Helen, born December 16, 1886, educated in the public and high schools of Fall River, and graduated from Wellesley College She also took a special course at Brown University, and was a teacher for two years at Norfolk High School, and one year a teacher at the B M C Durfee High School She married William J Simmons, of Woodard, North Carolina, and has one child Annie Catherine, born October 10, 1914. 2 Marian, born March 2, 1888, died March 9, 1888 3 Rodolphus Harold, born April 11, 1889, graduated from the Massachusetts Agricultural College, and is now inspector for the Agricultural Department of the State of Massachusetts 4 Annie, born July 12, 1894, graduated from the B M C Durfee High School and attended school in Washington, D C 5 Sarah Davenport, born May 31, 1898, a student at high school

(The Dean Line)

This is a name which has been identified with American history from a very early period, coming here from England, where the descendants have continued to reside and whence came recently to this country the family herein described It is the opinion of some writers that the name was originally derived from the Latin word, Decanus, a term applied to a Roman military officer of minor rank, commanding a force of ten men, and its English equivalent, Dean, was long ago adopted as an ecclesiastical title It is also time-honored as the title of a collegiate official. It has probably existed as a patronymic in England from the time of King Alfred the Great, tenth century, who was the first British sovereign to encourage the adoption of surnames The first of the name in America were

Rachel Dean, probably a widow, and Stephen Dean, both of whom arrived at Plymouth in the "Fortune," November, 1621 Stephen Dean erected and operated the first grist mill in the Plymouth Colony In 1637 two immigrants of this name, John and Walter Dean, brothers, came from Chard, a place of some importance, located about twelve miles from Taunton, county of Somerset. Information at hand states that they were the sons of William Dean They landed at Boston, and after spending a year in Dorchester proceeded to Taunton, Massachusetts, where they were admitted freemen, December 4, 1638 John Dean who was born about 1600, died in 1660 directed in his will that "in case there be no settled ministry in Taunton, my administrators shall have full power to sell either the whole or a part of these my housings and lands, so as my children and posterity may remove elsewhere, where they may employ God and His Ordinances."

(I) Walter Deane and his brother, John Deane, emigrated to America, and were among the earliest English settlers at Cohanet soon afterwards called Taunton, both their names appearing in the list of first or original purchasers. They "took up their farms on the West bank of the river, about one mile from the center of the present village" of Taunton Houses occupying the same lots as those erected by them, and nearly the exact sites, are to this day owned and occupied by descendants of each The road which passed their dwellings has been called Dean street to the present time Walter Dean was born between 1615 and 1620, in Chard, England, a market town, situated about ten miles from Taunton, both towns being located in an extensive and fertile valley called Taunton Deane, on the river Tone That Walter Deane was a man of influence and highly esteemed among his English neighbors at Cohanet or Taunton, in the American wilderness, is inferred from the fact that he was selectman for twenty years, representative to the General Court one year, and also a deacon of the church He was a tanner by trade He married Eleanor, daughter of Richard Strong, of Taunton, England, and sister of Elder John Strong, who came with her to America in the ship "Mary and John" in 1630 Children Joseph, mentioned below; Ezra, married Bethiah, daughter of Deacon Samuel Edson of Bridgewater, Massachusetts, Benjamin, married Sarah, daughter of Samuel Williams, of Taunton; Abigail, married Joseph Wood, and maybe others, one writer naming James, who, for a time, was at Scituate, Massachusetts, then removed to Stonington, Connecticut

(II) Deacon Joseph Dean, eldest child of Walter and Eleanor (Strong) Deane, was a cordwainer by trade, and became the first town clerk of Dighton, Massachusetts He lived at Assonet Neck and bore the title of deacon The Christian name of his wife was Mary He died January 10 1729, his wife surviving him Children Joseph, mentioned below, Samuel, James, married Mary Williams, Sarah, married Joseph Read, of Freetown; Esther

(III) Joseph (2) Dean, son of Deacon Joseph (1) and Mary Dean, was born 1688, and died August 11, 1773, in his eighty-fifth year His wife Sarah survived him, dying March 26, 1775, in her seventy-third year Children Sarah, born October 14 1724, married Captain Samuel Gilbert, of Berkley, Massachusetts; Joseph, August 7, 1726, married Priscilla Dillingham; Ebenezer, July 4, 1728, married Mary Read, of Dighton, John, June 29, 1730, died May 7, 1755, Elizabeth, May 26, 1736, married John

Babbitt, of Berkley, Benjamin, mentioned below

(IV) Benjamin Dean, youngest child of Joseph (2) and Sarah Dean, born May 26, 1736, married, December 22, 1757, Mary Turner, of that part of Freetown, Massachusetts, now Bowenville, Fall River Children John, died unmarried, lost at sea, Gamaliel, born 1762, died May 23, 1800, Sally, 1763, married Philip Hathaway, of Freetown, Benjamin, April 1, 1765, Aaron, 1766, married Elizabeth Weaver, of Freetown, Moses, 1769, died November 5, 1819, Patience 1773, died June 20, 1824, unmarried; Susan, 1774, married John Phillips, of Berkley, Samuel, married Hannah Hinds, of that part of Middleboro, now Lakeville, Massachusetts, Joseph, mentioned below, Ebenezer, married Elizabeth Chase, of Freetown

(V) Joseph (3) Dean, seventh son of Benjamin and Mary (Turner) Dean, born 1780, married Elizabeth Tew, of Berkley, daughter of Henry (3) and Abigail (Hathaway) Tew (see Tew VI) Among their children was Mary Turner, wife of Rhodolphus Howard Allen (see Allen VII)

(The Smith Line)

Among the early settlers of the town of Dartmouth, Massachusetts, were more than half a dozen bearing the surname Smith, and some of their descendants have continued to reside in that section of the State It is presumable that this family is included in that list As the State of New York made no pretense of keeping family records, it is difficult to establish the identity of the first named below

(I) Perry Smith came from Troy, New York, and located at Smith's Neck, Massachusetts where some of his children had preceded him It is probable that this was merely a return to the ancient home of the family, and that his father or grandfather had removed from Dartmouth to Troy Children Levi, mentioned below, Leonard, married Elizabeth Howland, Sylvia, married Joshua Howland, Royal, married Eunice Howland, Sarah, married Philip Allen

(II) Levi Smith, eldest son of Perry Smith born April 30, 1791, lived in the town of Dartmouth He married Lydia Slocum, born August 11, 1797 daughter of William Slocum, and granddaughter of John Slocum Children Charles Church, mentioned below, Nancy, born May 12, 1817, died March 10, 1820, Amanda Malvine, June 12, 1819, William Slocum, July 20, 1822, Levi Woodbury, May 2, 1830, Lydia Ann, December 29, 1831, died March 27, 1834

(III) Charles Church Smith, eldest child of Levi and Lydia (Slocum) Smith, was born January 6, 1815, in Dartmouth He married, December 3, 1845, Sarah Davenport Shaw, born November 19, 1826, in Tiverton, Rhode Island, daughter of Benjamin (2) and Mary Ann (Davenport) Shaw, of that town (see Shaw VII). Children Unnamed son, born and died 1854, Marian, born May, 1856, died 1861, Annie Brownell, mentioned below, Marian, April 4, 1866, married Captain Horace P Smith

(IV) Annie Brownell Smith, second daughter of Charles Church and Sarah Davenport (Shaw) Smith, was born May 9, 1861, in Little Compton, was married in Fall River, October 14, 1885, to Rodolphus N Allen, of that town (see Allen IX) She is a member of Quequechan Chapter, Daughters of the American Revolution, of Fall River, in which she has filled most of the offices, including that of regent

(The Tew Line)

(I) The Tew family of southeastern Massachusetts is descended from Rich-

ard Tew, who was a native of Maidford, Northamptonshire, England, and was a son of Henry Tew, of Maidford In 1640 Richard Tew came to New England, locating first in Portsmouth, Rhode Island, and in 1654 in Newport, where he spent the remainder of his life He died in Newport in 1673 He was a member of the Society of Friends, and had recorded upon the Friends' records his children's births He married, in England, Mary Clarke, daughter of William Clarke, of Priors Hardwick, Northamptonshire, and she died in 1687 Children Seaborn, born June 4, 1640, at sea (hence her name), married (first) January 5, 1658, Samuel Billings, and (second) Owen Higgins, Elnathan, October 15, 1644, died in 1711, married, November 3, 1664, Thomas Harris, Mary, August 12, 1647, died 1688, married, December 8, 1670, Andrew Harris, Henry, mentioned below

(II) Henry Tew, youngest child of Richard and Mary (Clarke) Tew, born 1654, in Newport, died April 28, 1718. He was a prominent man in the affairs of Rhode Island, and succeeded William Clarke as deputy governor of the colony He was a man of wealth and influence and owned a large tract of real estate, cattle, sheep, and was also a slave owner His first wife bore the name of Dorcas She died in 1694, and he married (second) Sarah, surname unknown, who died in 1718. Children Mary, born October 12, 1680, died May 2, 1752, married June 10, 1703, William Peckham, Henry, 1681 died 1731, married Ann Richmond; William, 1683, died April 5, 1718, Richard, 1684; John, mentioned below; Elizabeth, married, September 17, 1712, Edward Smith, and died 1769, Sarah, married Sylvester Sweet, Elisha, born 1691, Edward, died January 16, 1702, Dorcas, born September 26, 1696, died February 5, 1715; Paul,.

61

ENCYCLOPEDIA OF BIOGRAPHY

September, 1699, died May 24, 1711, Edward, November 1, 1703, died November 4, 1723

(III) John Tew, fourth son of Henry and Dorcas Tew, was born in Newport, and settled in the town of Dighton, Massachusetts, on property which was willed him by his father. He married Sarah Briggs, and their children, according to Dighton town records, were William, born February 13, 1724, died young, Elisha, October 15, 1725; Henry, mentioned below, William, September 12, 1731, Dorcas, March 26, 1734

(IV) Henry (2) Tew, third son of John and Sarah (Briggs) Tew, was born October 29, 1729, and married, December 5, 1753, Elizabeth Hathaway, born October 18, 1737

(V) Benjamin Tew, son of Henry (2) and Elizabeth (Hathaway) Tew, made his home in Berkley and there engaged in farming. He was quite active in the war of the Revolution and participated in that memorable conflict. He married Abigail Hathaway, born October 1, 1767, daughter of Philip and Lucy (Valentine) Hathaway. Philip Hathaway was lieutenant of the first foot company of local militia in Freetown. Benjamin Tew had children. Benjamin, died in infancy, Philip, married Silence Mason; Elizabeth, mentioned below; Mary, married, November 16, 1803, James Mason, Abigail, married, September 14, 1813, Isaac Sanford

(VI) Elizabeth, eldest daughter of Benjamin and Abigail (Hathaway) Tew, married, October 21, 1804, Joseph Dean (see Dean V)

(The Shaw Line)

(I) Anthony Shaw was early in Boston, Massachusetts, whence he removed to Portsmouth, Rhode Island, and later to Little Compton, same colony, where

he died August 21, 1705. The inventory of his estate footed £213, 12s, 2d, including a negro man valued at £30 and silver money amounting to £9. On April 20, 1665, he bought ten acres of land in Portsmouth, for £40, including a house and three hundred good boards. He married Alice, daughter of John Stonard, of Boston, where their first three children were born, namely. William, January 21, 1654, died March 10 following, William, February 24, 1655, Elizabeth, May 21, 1656. The others, born in Rhode Island, were Israel, mentioned below, Ruth, married John Cook, Grace, wife of Joseph Church

(II) Israel Shaw, third son of Anthony and Alice (Stonard) Shaw, lived in Little Compton, and married, in 1689, a daughter of Peter Tallman, of Portsmouth. Her baptismal name is not preserved. He sold two parcels of land in Portsmouth, February 11, 1707, to his brother-in-law, John Cook, of Tiverton, and in the bargain were included buildings and orchards, and a share in Hog Island. The consideration was £210, 10s. Children. William, born November 7, 1690, Mary, February 17, 1692, Anthony, mentioned below; Alice, November 17, 1695, Israel, August 28, 1697, Hannah, March 7, 1699; Jeremiah, June 6, 1700, Ruth, February 10, 1702, Peter, October 6, 1704, Elizabeth, February 7, 1706, Grace, October 20, 1707, Comfort, August 9, 1709; Deborah, July 15, 1711

(III) Anthony (2) Shaw, second son of Israel Shaw, was born January 29, 1694, in Little Compton, and died there in March, 1759. He was married, August 14, 1718, in Little Compton, by Justice Thomas Church, to Rebecca Wood, born April 17, 1696, died January, 1766, daughter of Thomas Wood. Children Benjamin, mentioned below, Mary, born February 24, 1722; Ruth, September 29, 1723,

Anthony, November 30, 1725; Elizabeth, January 10, 1728, died January, 1804, Rebecca, January 27, 1730; Arnold, November 13, 1732, Thomas, January 26, 1735; John, May 5, 1737.

(IV) Benjamin Shaw, eldest child of Anthony (2) and Rebecca (Wood) Shaw, was born October 5, 1720, in Little Compton, and died there in September, 1794 He married, 1749, Elizabeth Potter Children Sylvanus, born May 4, 1750, died October 22, 1777, Nathaniel, February 24, 1752, Rhoda, October 2, 1753, died young, Rhoda, January 1, 1756, Noah, mentioned below, Susanna, March 25, 1760, Barnabus, October 24, 1761, Benjamin, July 24, 1763; Elizabeth, October 5, 1764, Asa, March 1, 1766, Renanuel, July 21, 1768

(V) Noah Shaw, third son of Benjamin and Elizabeth (Potter) Shaw, was born February 2, 1758, in Little Compton, and died there February 8, 1844 He was a landowner, engaged in agriculture, and was a soldier of the Revolution, serving as a private, for which he was in receipt of a pension, commencing March 4, 1831 He was married (first) February 11, 1787, by Elder Peleg Burroughs, to Rhoda Palmer, born September 8, 1762, in Taunton, Massachusetts, daughter of Benjamin Palmer He married (second) Esther Potter Children Benjamin, mentioned below, Elizabeth, born October 16, 1789; Sarah, December 17, 1791, Hannah, October 30, 1793, Elizabeth, February 4, 1796, Rhoda, May 14, 1799, Anna, 1801, died in infancy; Noah and John (twins), March 25, 1804, latter died March 26, 1804 Child by second wife John, born July 21, 1806.

(VI) Benjamin (2) Shaw, eldest child of Noah and Rhoda (Palmer) Shaw, was born January 18, 1788, in Little Compton, and was married, September 28, 1823, by Rev Benjamin Peckham, to Mary Ann Daven-

port, born September 6, 1800, in Tiverton, died June 26, 1882, daughter of Jeremiah and Anna (Burroughs) Davenport, of that town (see Davenport VI) Children Rhoda A., born November 8, 1824; Sarah D, mentioned below, Esther B, November 20, 1828, Benjamin A, September 20, 1830, Mary A, January 12, 1833, James H, March 26, 1835, George W, November 6, 1840

(VII) Sarah Davenport Shaw, daughter of Benjamin (2) and Mary Ann (Davenport) Shaw, was born November 19, 1826, in Little Compton, and married, December 3, 1845, Charles Church Smith (see Smith III).

(The Davenport Line)

There were several immigrants in America in the days of its early settlement bearing this name, and the ancestry of the Connecticut branch has been traced in England for many generations

(I) Thomas Davenport was a member of the Dorchester church, November 20, 1640, was a freeman, May 18, 1642, and served the town as constable in 1670 He purchased a house and lands, November 25, 1653, and his residence was on the east slope of Mount Bowdoin, near the corner of the present Union avenue and Bowdoin street, in Dorchester He purchased additional lands, February 5, 1665 After his death, which occurred November 9, 1685, an inventory of his estate was made, amounting to £332, 16s , 8d His wife Mary joined the Dorchester church, March 8, 1644 She survived him nearly six years, dying October 4, 1691 Children Sarah, born December 28, 1643, Thomas, baptized March 2, 1645; Mary, January 21, 1649, Charles, September 7, 1652; Abigail, July 8, 1655, Mehitable, born February 14, 1657, Jonathan, mentioned below ; Ebenezer, April 26, 1661 , John, October 20, 1664.

(II) Jonathan Davenport, third son of
Thomas and Mary Davenport, was born
in 1659, and died January 11, 1729 He
married, December 1, 1680, Hannah Warren, born 1660, died January 14, 1729, in
Little Compton Children: Thomas, born
December 10, 1681, Jonathan, November
3, 1684, died October 14, 1751, Hannah,
December 23, 1686, Simeon, December
27, 1688, died December 8, 1763, Ebenezer, September 2, 1691, died August 4,
1776, John, mentioned below, Joseph,
March 25, 1696, died September 2, 1760,
Benjamin, October 6, 1698, Sarah, December 10, 1700

(III) John Davenport, fifth son of Jonathan and Hannah (Warren) Davenport,
was born January 12, 1694, in Little
Compton, and died April 20, 1741 He
married, in Little Compton, June 15,
1726, Elizabeth Taylor, born January 4,
1701, daughter of Peter and Elizabeth
Taylor Children Noah, born May 7,
1727, died March 5, 1818, Sarah, October
27, 1729, Jonathan, January 22, 1733,
John, mentioned below, Ephraim, July 2,
1736, Phebe, May 19, 1739, Mary, May
1, 1741

(IV) John (2) Davenport, third son of
John (1) and Elizabeth (Taylor) Davenport, was born January 18, 1735, in Little
Compton, and lived in Tiverton He married, in 1761, Sarah, surname unknown
Children Elizabeth, born November 16,
1761, died young, John, September 21,
1763, Taylor, August 29, 1766, Elizabeth,
December 20, 1768, Jeremiah, mentioned
below

(V) Jeremiah Davenport, youngest
child of John (2) and Sarah Davenport,
was born August 19, 1771, in Tiverton,
where he married (first) November 6,
1796, Anna Burroughs, born April 21,
1776, in Little Compton, died January 29,
1804, in Tiverton, daughter of Rev. Peleg
and Kezia (West) Burroughs He mar-

ried (second) December 29, 1806, Esther
Burroughs, sister of his first wife, born
June 26, 1786, in Tiverton Children:
Sarah, born January 7, 1798, Mary Ann,
mentioned below

(VI) Mary Ann Davenport, youngest
daughter of Jeremiah and Anna (Burroughs) Davenport, was born September
6, 1800, in Tiverton, and married, September 23, 1823, Benjamin (2) Shaw, of Little Compton (see Shaw VI)

OSBORN, James Edward,
Manufacturer, Man of Affairs

The Osborn family is of English ancestry There were several pioneers early
in New England Richard Osborne sailed
from London in 1634, in the ship "Hope-
well," and located in 1635, in Hingham,
Massachusetts, removing to New Haven,
Connecticut, in 1639, received for his
service in King Philip's War a land warrant for land near Fairfield, Connecticut,
where he settled about 1650 and lived
until 1682, moving finally to Westches-
ter county, New York William Osborne,
presumably a brother of Richard Osborne, located at Hingham, Massachusetts, of which he was a proprietor in
1635, moved to Braintree to become clerk
of the iron works, and to Boston in 1652
James Osborne settled in Springfield, and
Thomas Osborne in Charlestown before
1650

(I) Jeremiah Osborn, the immigrant
ancestor of the Osborns of Rhode Island
and Fall River, settled in Newport, Rhode
Island, where he died in 1673 He was
the schoolmaster No record has been
found to show any relationship with the
other pioneers, who were older. In fact
Jeremiah left so little about himself in
the public records that it must be presumed that he was not long in Newport
before he died Even the record of his

death was preserved only by Samuel Hubbard, who wrote, November 8, 1673 "This week two of Christ Church (called Mr Vahan's) departed, to wit, John Turner and Jeremy Osborne, schoolmaster" The name was often spelled Osband in the early records Austin found but one son, but Nathaniel Osband, who petitioned the General Court held at Newport in 1682, was doubtless another son

(II) Jeremiah (2) Osborn, son of Jeremiah (1) Osborn, was born about 1660, and died in 1709 He was an innholder in Bristol He married Mercy Davis, who died February 16, 1733, daughter of Nicholas and Sarah Davis His name appears in the records from time to time He and his wife sold to Nathaniel Byfield, of Boston, twenty-two acres at Pappasquash Neck for £25, October 9, 1696, and two days later he bought ten acres for £40 of Richard Pearce His will was dated at Bristol, July, 1708, proved April 6, 1709, making his wife Mercy executrix, and leaving her all his real and personal estate during life for the upbringing of his young children and providing that when his real estate was divided after her death his eldest son John should have a double share The inventory shows an estate of £412 3s., including a silver tankard, cup and porringer The possession of silver at this time indicated that the family had had wealth and standing The following children are recorded in the birth records of Bristol 1 Robert, born August 11, 1684, drowned at Bristol, September 2, 1685, aged one year 2 Katharine, born November 12, 1686, married at Bristol, May 24, 1708, Jonathan Woodbury 3 John, born October 12, 1689 4 Jeremiah, born July 25, 1693, died January 24, 1694, at Bristol 5 Margaret, born May 27, 1695 6 Sarah, May 11, 1701 7 Jeremiah, June 21, 1706 We

find no record of birth of the following, but other records show that they were about the same age as Jeremiah's children, yet not more than two of them could have been his and it is presumed that they were children of Nathaniel or another brother 1 Hannah, married, May 24, 1725, John Homans, at Bristol 2 Samuel, then of Newport, married (intentions dated November 27, 1736) Mary Gorham, married at Bristol, May 30, 1738 (St Michael's Church records, page 214, Arnold VIII) 3 Henry, mentioned below 4 James, married at Newport, April 17, 1728, Mary Jatinton 5 William, mentioned below 6 Esther, married at Newport, December 25, 1734, William Trott (See Trinity Church records, page 463, Arnold X) Evidently most of these moved away soon after marriage

(III) William Osborn, son of Jeremiah (2) or Nathaniel Osborn, married, June 2, 1728, Mary Cherry, and the supposition is that they are the parents of William, mentioned below

(IV) William Osborn, of the Newport and Bristol family described above, was born, according to family records, August 16, 1729 It is likely that he was son of William and Mary (Cherry) Osborn, grandson of Jeremiah or Nathaniel Osborn, and great-grandson of Jeremiah Osborn There is no doubt that he was descended from the first Jeremiah Osborn, mentioned above He came from Newport to Tiverton, Rhode Island, and lived during his minority in the family of Samuel Hicks He married in Tiverton, May 28, 1752, Elizabeth Shrieve, daughter of William Shrieve He died according to family records, October 29, 1810, his wife died about 1814

Another William Osborn died at Newport at an advanced age, January 18, 1808, according to the Trinity Church records and the newspapers This William Osborn married at Newport, January 26, 1772, Lydia Prior, and was doubtless the same William that married, September 21, 1783, Hannah Read (Rev Gardner Thurston's records, Arnold V, p 358)

Children of William and Elizabeth (Shrieve) Osborn Wilson, born at Tiverton, June 3, 1753, died about 1757, Weaver, born April 17, 1756; Elizabeth, June 8, 1758, Patience, July 17, 1761, died young, Thomas, mentioned below, William, July 18, 1769

(V) Thomas Osborn, son of William Osborn, was born at Tiverton, March 31, 1766 He was a ship cooper and farmer in Tiverton. He died there October 7, 1833 He married, in 1797, Anna Durfee born March 6, 1775, died May 23, 1845, daughter of Joseph and Abigail (Borden) Durfee, of Tiverton Children, born at Tiverton 1 William, born November 26, 1798, died at Tiverton, January 28, 1829, married Ruth Hambly 2 Thomas, born December 30, 1800, died at Tiverton, March 1, 1884, married Elizabeth S Hambly 3 Joseph, mentioned below 4 Ann, born December 4, 1805 died in 1812 5 Wilson, born April 15, 1808, died August 29, 1873, married Mary Wilson 6 Eliza Ann, born May 25, 1810, died in Fall River, August 18, 1887, married Rev Alexander Milne 7 Patience, born August 29, 1812, died in 1817 8 Weaver mentioned below 9 James Monroe, mentioned below

(VI) Judge Joseph Osborn, son of Thomas Osborn, was born in Tiverton, August 20, 1803 In early life he was a dealer in livestock He was elected judge of the Court of Common Pleas; was a delegate to the Constitutional Convention of Rhode Island in 1841, represented Tiverton in both branches of the State Legislature, was treasurer of the town for

forty-five years, and at one time served on the Board of State Charities and Correction In his later years he was prominent in the cotton industries of Fall River, a director of the Osborn Mills, one of the founders and director of the Pocasset National Bank, and president of the Fall River Savings Bank from the time of its organization in 1851 until he died He accumulated a fortune through his own industry and shrewd investments He married Eliza Gardner Children Ann Catherine, William Joseph, mentioned below, Jason Woodward, Eliza Gardner, Henry Clay

(VII) William Joseph Osborn, son of Judge Joseph Osborn, was born at Tiverton, December 3, 1836, and was educated in the public schools there, at Pierce's Academy, Middleborough, and in the Bryant & Stratton Business College, Providence He began his business career as clerk in the freight office of the Old Colony Railroad Company in Boston Three years later he accepted a position as clerk in the Fall River Savings Bank, resigning shortly afterward to engage in business on his own account in partnership with Frank A Brackett, under the firm name of Brackett & Osborn, dealers in tea and tobacco, with headquarters in Boston. After the Civil War he was in the railroad and banking business in New York City and later a stock broker, member of the Consolidated Stock Exchange In politics he was a Republican He was a member of the First Baptist Church, Pierrepont street, Brooklyn, New York. He died suddenly in New York, November 3, 1888. He was a member of various Masonic organizations.

He married, June 19, 1873, Hannah Humphrey French, daughter of Stephen L and Phebe Ann (Dwelly) French Since the death of her husband, Mrs Os-

ENCYCLOPEDIA OF BIOGRAPHY

born has resided in Fall River She was
a member of the school board of that
city in 1898, 1899 and 1900, 1902 to 1908,
finally declining reëlection She is a
member of the Baptist church Mr and
Mrs Osborn had one son, Charles
French, born May 2, 1878, graduate of
the Fall River High School and of Williams College, class of 1901, now in the
government service in the Bureau of
Commerce and Labor

(VI) Weaver Osborn, son of Thomas
Osborn, was born in Tiverton, May 23,
1815 He attended the public schools of
his native town and the seminary at Little
West Hill, South Kingstown, Rhode
Island During his boyhood he worked
on his father's farm At the age of
eighteen he was apprenticed to a blacksmith at Fairhaven From 1835 to 1843
he had a blacksmith shop in Tiverton,
then went to work in Providence From
1844 to 1848 he was employed in the shop
of Andrew Robeson, and from 1848 to
January, 1855, he was in business for
himself as a blacksmith in Tiverton His
shop was destroyed by fire in 1855, and
he removed to Fall River, where he and
his brother, James M Osborn, formed a
partnership under the firm name of W
& J M Osborn, blacksmiths, their shop
being located on land now occupied by
the Fall River post office, and continued
there until 1871 Their other interests in
various industries had become extensive
Weaver Osborn was a leader in the industrial development of the city He was
the prime mover and most active in procuring the capital for the mills built in
1872, and named for him He was a director of the Montaup Mills corporation,
now Osborn mill, No 2 He was elected
president of the Pocasset National Bank
in 1873 and held that office for many
years He was a director of the original
Pocasset Bank, and was an officer of this

institution under its State and national
charters as long as he lived At the beginning he was on the board of investment and he was the last survivor of the
original board, serving from 1873 until
he died as chairman For many years
he was also a trustee of the Citizens' Savings Bank, of Fall River He was a trustee of the State work houses at Bridgewater and Tewksbury, Massachusetts
He was also called upon to administer
many large estates

In early life he was a Whig in politics, casting his first presidential vote for
Henry Clay, but after the Republican
party was formed, he gave it his unfalter-
ing support to the end of his life He
represented Fall River and his district in
the State Senate in 1857-58-59 and again
in 1879, serving on the military committee and other important assignments He
was a representative to the General Court
in the House in 1868, 1869, 1871, 1873,
1876 and 1877 When a young man he
took an active part in military affairs and
rose to the rank of captain, serving during the Dorr Rebellion Mr Osborn's
career affords a most interesting example of the self-made man of the nineteenth
century He fought his own way in life,
saving while working at the forge, in-
vesting in textile industries, achieving
distinction in business, in banking, in
public life Resourceful, determined,
faithful to every trust, of sound common
sense and excellent judgment, year by
year his strength of character came more
and more into evidence and brought him
positions of trust and honor Of his
means he gave freely He was kindly,
sympathetic and generous in helping the
poor and suffering He was second to no
man in the confidence and love of the people of the community in which he lived

Mr Osborn married, January 7, 1837,
Patience B Dwelly, born at Tiverton,

67

May 27, 1817, died June 2, 1901, daughter of Daniel and Mary (Slade) Dwelly Both Mr and Mrs Osborn were members of the Baptist church Their children 1 Mary Slade, born February 23, 1838, was a teacher in the Morgan street school three years and in the Osborn street school twelve years, now residing in Fall River 2 Daniel Weaver, born June 7, 1840, died February 5, 1863 3 Thomas Frederick, born March 28, 1847, died May 11, 1857 4 Anna Jane, born March 3, 1853, died July 11, 1861

(VI) James Monroe Osborn, son of Thomas Osborn, was born at Tiverton, August 27, 1822 He remained with his widowed mother on the homestead for six years after his father died He received his education in the common schools of his native town In the shop of his brother, Weaver, he learned the trade of blacksmith At the age of twenty he returned to the farm, and after trying seine-fishing for an occupation, he resumed his trade in Providence, working there and in other places until 1845, when he located in Fall River For a year or more he was in the employ of John Kilburn and afterward with Kilburn & Lincoln until 1855, when he became a partner of his brother They bought the blacksmith shop of Gideon Packard, located on the site now occupied by the Fall River post office In 1859 the partners helped to build the Union Mill, the construction of which was soon followed by the erection of other cotton mills They became large owners in the granite mill, and in 1867 invested in the Merchants' Manufacturing Company They were associated with others in building the Stafford Mill By this time their textile interests had become so large that the blacksmith business was discontinued In 1871 James M Osborn was elected a director and the

first treasurer of the Slade Mill and superintended the building of the mill He and his brother were next interested in establishing the Osborn Mill Their interests extended constantly The partnership was finally dissolved in 1880, but their interests were almost identical James M Osborn was for many years a director of the Globe Yarn Mills, and of the Merchants', Osborn and Stafford companies, being president of the two former He was also a member of the board of investment of the Five Cents Savings Bank

Throughout his active life he gave his time and thought as well as his financial help to the church He became a member of the First Baptist Church of Fall River, April 2, 1843, and was dismissed in 1846 to the Second Baptist Church, of which he was a deacon from 1884 to 1896, and for many years chairman of its standing committee He served the society well in caring for its property and superintended the moving of its chapels from time to time He gave his hearty support to the temperance movement and joined in every project designed to promote better citizenship and public morals In early life he was a Whig, later a Republican, and he performed his part in public life He served as alderman of the city in 1856 and 1858, and in 1866 and 1871 in the Common Council, where his work and his influence were of substantial value to the municipality.

Mr Osborn married, August 9, 1847, Mary B Chace, who was born June 11, 1826, daughter of Nathan and Elizabeth (Buffinton) Chace, of Somerset Children 1 Anna Elizabeth, born April 5 1850, died July 1, 1850 2 Nathan Chace, born August 9, 1852, died January 28 1855 3 James Edward, mentioned below Mr Osborn died May 13, 1898, at his home, No 540 Cherry street, where

he had lived since building the house in 1859, and where his family lived after his death Interment was in Oak Grove Cemetery

(VII) James Edward Osborn, son of James Monroe Osborn, was born in Fall River, January 24, 1856 He attended the public schools there, graduating from the high school in 1872 He began his career as clerk in the office of the Merchants' Manufacturing Company, under William H Jennings, treasurer A few years later he left the Merchants' Manufacturing Company and associated himself with B F Randall in the cotton business In 1884 he purchased the interest of A B Sanford in the firm of Sanford & Covel, dealers in hardware and mill supplies, the firm name becoming Covel & Osborn The business was afterward incorporated as the Covel & Osborn Company, of which Mr Osborn was president for several years In July, 1896, Mr Osborn was elected treasurer of the American Linen Company, succeeding the late Philip D Borden, and in April, 1898, he was made treasurer of the Merchants' Manufacturing Company, succeeding Andrew Borden He is also vice-president and member of the executive committee of the Cotton Manufacturers' Association, a director of the Fall River Electric Light Company; the Merchants' Manufacturing Company; the American Linen Company; the Osborn Mills, the Ancona Company, the Granite Mills, and the Parker Mills, all of Fall River, the Warren Manufacturing Company of Warren, Rhode Island; the Newmarket Mills, of Newmarket, New Hampshire, and the Apponaug Company of Boston He is a trustee of the Citizens' Savings Bank, and of the Home for Aged People, both of Fall River In politics he is a Republican In religion he is a Congregationalist, attending the Central Church He is

a member of King Philip Lodge, Ancient Free and Accepted Masons, Fall River Chapter, Royal Arch Masons, and Godfrey de Bouillon Commandery, Knights Templar He belongs to various clubs and other social organizations

Mr Osborn married, October 12 1880, Delia S Carr, who was born December 4, 1856, daughter of William and Elizabeth V (Durfee) Carr, of Fall River, Massachusetts Children 1 Marion, born July 21, 1881, married Joseph F Sherer, president of the C I Sherer Company, and manager of its department store, Worcester, Massachusetts, and they have three children, Osborne, Jeanette and Helene Sherer 2 Helen, born September 22, 1882, died October 7, 1882 3 Elizabeth Carr, born January 28, 1889, married, November 8, 1911, Leeds Burchard, of New York, son of Dr Thomas Burchard, and they have one daughter, Hope, born April 28, 1914 Mr Burchard is now officially connected with the Covel & Osborn Company, of Fall River 4 Richard, born July 22, 1891, was graduated from Yale College, in the class of 1914, with the degree of Bachelor of Arts For a time he was associated with Dr Grenfeld in Newfoundland Upon the breaking out of the European war, he joined the hospital unit and served in France as one of the first automobile drivers in the ambulance corps Upon returning home he formed a copartnership with Frank H Towne and Edward Brayton, under the firm name of Towne, Brayton & Osborn, cotton dealers, of Fall River.

BURTON, Albert W,
Civil War Soldier, Manufacturer.

Among the oldest families of Rhode Island is that of Burton, and descendants are still found in that State and adjoining sections of others It has been identified with progress along social, moral and material lines, and has conferred lasting benefits on the communities with which associated

(I) William Burton was an inhabitant of Providence, in the section known as Mashantatack, north of the Pawtuxet river, where he died February 20, 1714 He sold a house and orchard in Warwick for thirty-five pounds deed dated February 1, 1668, and his brother-in-law, John Wickes, gave lands for life to Burton and wife May 17, 1680, the property to go to their son after their death Burton was taxed four shillings in 1687, was a grand juror in 1688, and died in 1714 His will, made March 20, 1703, with codicil dated July 8, 1713, was proved June 25, 1714, and the inventory of his property amounted to £111, 8s He married (first) Hannah Wickes daughter of John and Mary Wickes, born 1634, died before 1701, in which year he married (second) Isabel Moss, a widow The estate of the latter, was valued September 15, 1724, at £243, 1s Besides a daughter, baptismal name unknown, who married a Curbit, he had the following children Elizabeth, married, October 30, 1674, Thomas Hadger; Hannah, married Timothy Carpenter and died before 1726; Rose, married a Fowler, Ethelanna, married a Clarke, Susannah, born 1665, married (first) Samuel Gorton, and (second) Richard Harris, and died June 25, 1737; John, mentioned below.

(II) John, youngest child of William and Hannah (Wickes) Burton, was born May 2, 1667, and lived at Chestnut Hill, was executor of his father's estate, inherited all his housings and lands and residue of the estate, one-half the stock, and the remainder after death of his stepmother In 1702 he gave three shillings to aid in building a Quaker meeting house

at Mashapaug, in 1716 was deputy to the General Court During his lifetime, the section of Providence in which he lived was set off to the town of Cranston He died July 15, 1749, and left an estate valued at £2,512, 9s, 1d His will, made January 23, was proved September 2, 1749, giving homestead to the elder son, William Among items listed in the inventory were a negro man, books, silver money and plate, and bonds valued at £735, 14s, 10d His wife Mary married (second) Benjamin Searle, and died December 29, 1768

(III) John (2), junior son of John (1) and Mary Burton, was born about 1754, in what is now Cranston, is described as of Providence and Cranston (probably upon the same farm), and died in 1799 He was deputy from the former town in 1744, from the latter in 1762, and was assistant in 1766 His will disposed of £1,700 in cash legacies, besides a large amount of lands His wife, Mary, died September 9, 1768 Children, the first eight recorded in Providence John, born September 8, 1733, Joseph, September 19, 1735, Dinah, September 30, 1737, Mary, January 12, 1740; Hannah, died young; David, August 30, 1744, Caleb, October 15, 1746, Elizabeth, January 24, 1749, George, mentioned below; Rufus, November 19, 1753, Hannah

(IV) George, fifth son of John (2) and Mary Burton, was born September 11, 1751, in Cranston, and was not living February 20, 1799, when his father's will was made He inherited land by will of his grandmother He married, December 27, 1770, Hannah and Rosanna Potter, born about 1752-53, daughter of Thomas and Esther Potter Children Hannah, born July 23, 1771; Mary, June 19, 1774, George, mentioned below

(V) George (2), son of George (1) and Hannah (Potter) Burton, was born November 30 1776, in Cranston, and inherited the homestead of his grandfather, John (2) Burton, in that town, with part of the live stock, tools and books Late in life he removed to Hopkinton, Rhode Island, where he died November 5, 1846, aged eighty years That he was a man of influence is evidenced by the fact that he held town office In religion he was a Baptist, and in politics a Whig He married Tryphena Place, who died at Hopkinton, February 10, 1849 Children Ira, Elliott Lee, Potter C, George, Thomas, Nancy, Celinda

(VI) Elliott Lee, son of George and Tryphena (Place) Burton, was born October 20, 1803, at "Hopkinton City," Hopkinton, Rhode Island, and died at East Killingly, Connecticut, July 7, 1887 He received a common school education, and helped his father in the cultivation of the farm In early manhood he commenced to sell laces and notions, for a few years, and later removed to Foster, Rhode Island, where he kept a general store, selling West Indian and dry goods Here he was a road surveyor, a member of the militia, and with his wife joined the Free Will Baptist church, November 6, 1852. After his marriage he removed with his family to Killingly, Connecticut, where he found employment in the cotton factories of that town He also engaged in farming for a time, and later began the manufacturing and finishing of boots and shoes for various firms After ten years he again farmed in a small way, adding to his homestead land purchased from James Simmons, and which was sold to his son, Stephen, after his death In politics he was a Whig, being opposed to slavery, later becoming a strong supporter of Lincoln and his policies He married at Foster, June 11, 1828, Bernice, born November 8, 1806, died October 14, 1889, daughter of Sheldon and Naomi

(Randall) Williams, and a direct descendant in the sixth generation of Roger Williams Children Albert Williams, mentioned below, Louisa, died young, Laura Ann, born December 24, 1833, died September 20, 1883, Harris Olney, March 19, 1836, married, April 19, 1856, Olive S Oatley, and died October 12, 1897, Stephen Randall, July 17, 1839, married, November 26, 1884, Mary (Crowell) Williams, and died August 13, 1907, James Elliott, May 6, 1841, Elliott Franklin, December, 1842, married, January 3, 1655, Julia A Hopkins

(VII) Albert Williams, eldest child of Elliott Lee and Bernice (Williams) Burton, was born December 19, 1831, at Hopkins Mills, North Foster, Rhode Island, and died at Buttonwood, same State, July 24, 1909 Up to the age of twelve years he attended the district school, three months in summer and three in winter, and from this time until the age of sixteen attended only during the winter months He then removed with his parents to East Killingly, where he was employed in the cotton mills for six months, after which he worked on the farm of William Cook, of Gloucester, Connecticut At the age of eighteen years he shipped on board the whaler "Ocean," Captain Swift, bound for the Arctic seas They made a roundabout voyage, touching at the Azores, Sandwich Islands, Hongkong and Japan Later he made numerous trips along the Atlantic coast, spending altogether thirteen years at sea During the Civil War he enlisted at Wrentham February 20 1864, in the Fourteenth Massachusetts Battery, and saw much hard and honorable service He participated in the following battles that year Wilderness, May 5 to 7, Ny River, May 10, Spottsylvania, May 12 and 21, North Anna River, May 23 to 27, Bethesda Church, June 2,

Cold Harbor, June 4 to 12, Petersburg, June 16 to 25, Deep Bottom, July 9 to 17, Crater, July 30, Petersburg trenches, August 5 to 21; Fort Steadman, March 25 to 29, 1865, fall of Petersburg, 1865 On June 15, 1865, he was honorably discharged, and mustered out at Readville, Massachusetts During part of this time he was mate of the ship "Mary J Mifflin," carrying supplies for McClellan's army

At the close of hostilities he returned home and engaged with the jewelry manufacturing concern of H F Barrows, at North Attleboro, Massachusetts After five years spent in obtaining a thorough mastery of this trade he went to Plainville, Massachusetts, and for two years was in the employ of J D Lincoln, Tiffany & Bacon The Plainville Stock Company was organized in the spring of 1872 for the manufacture of specialties in jewelry, a number of the most prominent manufacturers in the jewelry line, among them being Albert Williams Burton, forming this corporation There were various changes in the membership from time to time, older members retiring and making way for new, but it was from the start a pronounced success, at no time more so than when Mr Burton retired, March 26, 1909, to enjoy a long merited rest from his arduous labors Mr Burton was an attendant of the Methodist church of Plainville, and gave liberally toward its support, especially to the building of the church, and donated the organ He was a member of George H Maintein Post, No 133, Grand Army of the Republic, and served as senior and junior vice-commander and as quartermaster many years

He married, at Wrentham, June 22, 1857, Mary Ellis born October 5, 1836, daughter of Edward Renouf and Susannah (Dale) Bennett, of that town (see Ben-

nett VII) Children 1 Edward Randall, born January 31, 1858, died February 6, 1858 2 Alice Williams, August 24, 1859, died April 6, 1885 3 Albert Edward, April 6, 1861, married, March 15, 1893, Nettie May Hopkins; children Wesley Hopkins, born December 29, 1893, Alice May, November 19, 1894, Lee Williams, November 12, 1895, Rubie Ellis, May 30, 1896, Ivy Dale, May 1, 1897; Helene Elliott, September 9, 1902, Beatrice Virginia, April 28, 1905 4 Maria Lincoln, May 13, 1866, married September 1, 1894, Dr Clarence Moore Noble, who died July 5, 1897, son of George and Sarah Noble, of Cooticook, Canada 5 Bernice Elliott, October 7, 1878, married, December 3, 1903, Clarence Mason Hatch; children Dorothy Williams, born August 15, 1905; Hazel Mason, December 26, 1907.

(The Bennett Line)

The Bennett family is of English origin, and its members were among the earliest emigrants to the shores of New England

(I) William Bennett, founder of the Wrentham, Massachusetts branch of the family, was born in England in 1603, and died in Manchester, Massachusetts, November 20, 1683 He was a carpenter by trade, and an early settler in Plymouth, Massachusetts, where he was taxed in 1632 He removed from Plymouth to Salem, where we find him recorded prior to 1636, he was admitted to the Salem church, June 18, 1643 In 1637 he removed to Manchester, was granted land in the four-hundred-acre grant after coming from Salem, and his name appears with sixteen others in a petition asking the "Honorable Court to give us power to erect a village at Jeffreys Creek," which later was named "Manchester" He was a freeman, and as such had a right to common lands, and became a proprietor and one of the factors in the affairs of the settlement; was a selectman of the town in 1660-65-72-76, and owned a house near the foot of Bennett's Hill, also a grist mill on the site of the old Forster Mill His wife Jane came from England at the age of sixteen years, in 1635, in the ship "Elizabeth and Ann," and died April 27, 1693 Children Moses, baptized July 2, 1643, was living in 1693, Aaron, mentioned below, Mary, baptized September 3. 1654; Ann, July 2, 1643, Deliverance, July 2, 1643.

(II) Aaron, second son of William and Jane Bennett, was baptized July 2, 1643, and died in 1709. He was a yeoman, living in Manchester, Massachusetts, and also followed fishing His will, dated December 3, 1708, was proved March 21, 1709. He married (first) prior to 1665, Hannah, surname unknown His second wife, Elizabeth, whom he married prior to 1708, was born in 1644, being the first child born in Manchester, Massachusetts Children Hannah, born March 25, 1665, was living in 1708, Jane, January 15, 1675, was living in 1708, Aaron, mentioned below; Alice, April 5, 1679, married, November 15, 1705, John Allin, of Beverly, Elizabeth, June 13, 1680, was living in 1708, married, December 11, 1700, Robert Warren, a fisherman of Manchester, Mary, January 31, 1685, was living in 1708.

(III) Captain Aaron (2) Bennett, eldest son of Aaron (1) and Hannah Bennett, was born March 25, 1677, in Manchester, and died suddenly in the same town, February 13, 1753 He was a husbandman, and owned much property in Manchester In 1696 he was captain of fishing vessels of nine tons, and for a time followed this calling, making trips to the banks and getting profitable catches, in 1712 he was an innholder He married (first) November 20, 1700, Ann Pickworth, (second) March 11, 1736, Mrs Abigail Geard-

ner, a widow of Gloucester Children, all of first marriage Elizabeth, born August 8, 1701, married, November 28, 1721, Nathaniel Lee, William, May 1, 1703, Aaron, July 6, 1705, died October 20, 1780, Luccee, June 2, 1709, married, June 4 1733, Benjamin Searles, of Marblehead; Abigail, June 15, 1713, died June 25, 1714, Moses, mentioned below, Benjamin, baptized March 22, 1719

(IV) Moses, third son of Aaron (2) and Ann (Pickworth) Bennett, was born February 25, 1715, in Manchester, resided in that town, and in 1754 followed the calling of fisherman The records state that he died in the service of the province near the Isle of Orleans in 1759 He married, at Essex, Massachusetts, February 15, 1739, Rachel Rust, of Ipswich, Massachusetts, born 1711, died in Manchester, November 8, 1787 Children Moses, mentioned below, Lucy, born April 11, 1741, died about 1765, Ruth, November 28, 1742, Rachel, November 28, 1747, married, May 7, 1772, Edward Renouf, of Marblehead, Amos, February 25, 1750, married, December 29, 1776, Elizabeth Oakes, of Danvers, Mary, May 26, 1752, married, September 17, 1772, Jacob Symmons, Joanna, March 16, 1757

(V) Moses (2), eldest child of Moses (1) and Rachel (Rust) Bennett, was born December 26 1739, in Manchester In early life he followed fishing as an occupation, and later became a cabinet maker, in which trade he continued for many years, in Manchester, this being at that time the principal industry there His sons learned the same trade He was a devout man and died "in the faith," as did also his wife He married, December 7, 1762, Anna Allen Children Anna, married, September 5, 1789 Isaac Miller, Patty, born November 8, 1766, married, August 29, 1794, Edward Morgan, Moses, October 23, 1770, Isaac, mentioned below

(VI) Isaac, youngest child of Moses

(2) and Anna (Allen) Bennett, was born January 13, 1773, in Manchester, and died November 25, 1851, at Wrentham, Massachusetts His education was the customary one for a farmer's son of that period, and at an early age he was taught the trade of cabinet making As a young man he went to Sharon, where he followed his trade, shortly after his marriage removing to Wrentham, where he settled in the "Wampum" district He leased his property and set up a shop as cabinet maker, and as his sons became old enough he admitted them into the business His shop was run by water power, and he manufactured bureaus, bedsteads, tables, cradles, finding a ready market for his products in Boston, and this industry became an important factor in the progress of the town The greater part of this output was sold to Edward Renouf, a leading furniture dealer of Boston and for whom his son Edward Renouf Bennett, was named Edward Renouf was a descendant of a noted and honored Norman family which had settled at Newburyport Massachusetts Mr Bennett was of very quiet habits and disposition, and he and his wife were faithful members of the Orthodox church He was a pronounced Democrat, and belonged to the militia He married, December 31, 1797, Elizabeth, born at Sharon, Massachusetts, January 22, 1774, died at Wrentham, February 20, 1859, daughter of Joseph and Esther (Fisher) Randall (see Randall II) Children Prudence Anarrette, born September 26, 1798, married Joseph Green Weeks, Eliza, December 19, 1799, died November, 1827; George Hawes, July 9, 1801, died September 4, 1871, married Margaret Dale, Mary Ann, April 17, 1803, died July 26, 1857, married August 10, 1823, Carl Moran Fisher, Esther Randall, February 6, 1805, married Jeremiah Cobb, Edward Renouf,

mentioned below, Charlotte, December 26, 1808, married Francis Fisher, William Steadman, June 23, 1812, died September 26, 1881, married, June 1, 1836, Matilda Barnes; Henry Albert, November 2, 1814 died December 11, 1873, married, January 8, 1838, Charlotte Potter, Eleanor Jane, November 2, 1814 (twin of Henry Albert), married Aaron G Hoyes Laura, August 28, 1816, died June 23, 1907, married, June 17, 1841, Ebenezer Hawes, Isaac Francis (called Frank Bennett), died July 13, 1897

(VII) Edward Renouf, second son of Isaac and Elizabeth (Randall) Bennett, was born October 22 1806, in Wrentham, and died there, April 9 1896 His school education was limited to attendance at the district school during the winter sessions, at the same time he was assisting his father in his business, and was later admitted to partnership After a time the firm was dissolved, and Edward R went to Norwood, where he was employed by George W Everett & Company, and ran a circular saw During the panic of 1857 this latter firm became insolvent, and Mr Bennett returned to Wrentham, after a short residence in Roxbury, and commenced farming in a small way His farm consisted of thirty acres and he raised general crops In 1870 his son, Edward P, purchased his father's property, and the elder Bennett and his wife made their home with their son. In connection with his farming Mr Bennett owned a saw mill at Wrentham which he operated during the winter months until within ten years of his death He was interested in military affairs, and was captain of the Wrentham company of militia He was of a quiet, unassuming nature, earnest religious views, a strong temperance advocate and he and his wife were members of the Orthodox church of Wrentham Politically he gave his support to the Republican party. He was married at Wrentham, by Rev. Elijah Fiske, September 21, 1830, to Susannah, born in Weymouth, February 7, 1805, died in Wrentham, November 14, 1885, daughter of John and Catherine (Childs) Dale, of Weymouth (see Dale IV). Children: Esther Dale, born June 24, 1834, died April 23, 1883, married, February 25, 1854, James Fiastus Hawes; Mary Ellis, mentioned below; Martha Randall, July 27, 1838, died August 17, 1882, married, February 18, 1855, George Albert Jenks, Charles Edward, April 2, 1841, died November 2, 1844; Herbert Franklin, January 5, 1845, married, January 10, 1866, Mary D. Atwood; Edward Payson, June 30, 1848, living in Wrentham.

(VIII) Mary Ellis, second daughter of Edward Renouf and Susannah (Dale) Bennett, was born October 5, 1836, and became the wife of Albert Williams Burton, or Plainville, Massachusetts (see Burton III).

(The Childs Line)

The name Child is derived from Hildr of the Norse mythology. Its descent from mythic to historical times can be traced in the Nebelungen Lied. In this saga childe is first used as a title for king. From the fifth to the tenth centuries, many of the kings of France prefixed the word Childe to their names, and during this time a large number of the rulers of Europe derived their appellations from the root Hildr. As the title Childe became obsolete, it was generally adopted as a surname by descendants or dependents. The original spelling was with the final "e," and many families in England still retain the old form. For the first two generations in this country it was written Child, but of late years, Childs is more frequently employed.

(I) Benjamin Child, or Childs, came from England in 1630, and settled in Roxbury, Massachusetts. In the records of that town he is stated to have been one of thirty who contributed towards the erection of the first church there. He died October 14, 1678, leaving an estate valued at £506 19s. His wife Mary was admitted to the church of Roxbury in 1658, and survived her husband. Children, born in Roxbury: Ephraim, 1654; Benjamin, mentioned below; Joshua, 1658; Mary, August 8, 1660; infant, 1662; Elizabeth, December 2, 1663; Margaret, December 21, 1665; John, January 8, 1667, died young; Mehitable, June 29, 1669; John, August 1, 1671; Joseph, December 10, 1674, died young; Joseph, June 1, 1678, died young.

(II) Benjamin (2), second son of Benjamin (1) and Mary Childs, born 1656, in Roxbury, was the inheritor of a large share of his father's property there, and died January 24, 1724. He spent his life in his native town, and lived on the homestead. He married, March 7, 1683, Grace, daughter of Deacon Edward and Grace (Bett) Morris. She was admitted to the church, June 21, 1681, and died December 10, 1723. Her father was an early settler of Woodstock, Connecticut, from 1677 to 1684 one of the selectmen of Roxbury, and during the same time a deputy to the General Court, and part of the time colonial auditor. Children, born in Roxbury: Ephraim, December 18, 1683; Benjamin, July 19, 1685; Edward, mentioned below; Grace, October 27, 1689; Mary, October 25, 1691; Ebenezer, September 7, 1693; Mehitable, January 5, 1695; William, October 14, 1697; Penuel, September 3, 1699; Richard, October 22, 1701; Thomas, November 10, 1703; Margaret, May 26, 1706.

(III) Edward, third son of Benjamin (2) and Grace (Morris) Childs, was born November 1, 1687, in Roxbury, and re-

sided on the paternal homestead there
He was a glazier and farmer, large landholder and well known He married, in
1712, Margaret Weld Children Hannah, born December 7, 1712, John, mentioned below; Eleazer, March 11, 1717,
Stephen, August 19 1719, Edward, September 13, 1821

(IV) John, eldest son of Edward and
Margaret (Weld) Childs, was born Janu-
ary 20, 1714, in Roxbury, and married,
January 26, 1742, Esther Child, born Sep-
tember 6, 1722, in Woodstock, Connecti-
cut, daughter of Ephraim and Priscilla
(Harris) Child Children Hannah, died
young, Margaret, born April 8, 1745,
Priscilla, December 20, 1748, Hannah,
January 30, 1750, Esther, March 2, 1753,
John, June 16, 1756; Stephen, August 10,
1758, Joanna, October 10, 1760, Ann,
January 22, 1762. Catherine, mentioned
below

(V) Catherine youngest child of John
and Esther (Child) Childs, born September 13, 1764, in Roxbury became the wife
of John Dale, of Roxbury (see Dale IV)

(The Dale Line)

(I) John Dale was in Salem, Massachusetts, in 1682 He probably lived in
that part of the town now Danvers, was
far from the centre and did not participate
in public affairs The records are silent
regarding his wife

(II) John (2), son of John (1) Dale,
was born November 2, 1685 in Salem Village, now Danvers, where he made his
home with wife, Abigail Children, recorded in Danvers John born September 13, 1718 Archelaus, September 17,
1720, Elizabeth, July 18, 1723, Anne,
April 19 1725, Betty, October 11, 1727;
Ebenezer, mentioned below, Timothy,
May 9, 1733, Abigail January 17, 1736

(III) Ebenezer, third son of John (2)
and Abigail Dale, was born March 7,

1731, in Danvers, where he lived and married, April 1, 1755, Rebecca Preston, sup-
posedly of the old Preston family of
Salem, which figures so little in the records as to be untraceable Children, on
Danvers records. Ebenezer, born December 5, 1755, Anna, September 27, 1757,
Thomas, August 19, 1759, Samuel, July
23, 1761, Rebecca, April 27, 1764, John,
mentioned below

(IV) John (3), youngest child of Eben-
eezer and Rebecca (Preston) Dale, was
born 1764-65, in Danvers, baptized there
August 31, 1766, lived in Roxbury, Weymouth and Wrentham, Massachusetts,
and died in the later town February 15,
1843 He was a housewright by trade
He married Catherine Childs, born September 13, 1764, in Roxbury, daughter of
John and Esther (Child) Childs, of that
town (see Childs IV), died in Wrentham
May 10, 1825 Children Catherine, born
March 25, 1796, in Roxbury Esther
Childs, April 19, 1798, in Roxbury, died
April, 1848, in Dorchester, Ann, October
30, 1800, in Roxbury, died in Wrentham
October 14, 1889, Margaret, December
3, 1802, in Weymouth married George
Hawes Bennet, and died in Wrentham
June 22, 1889, Susannah, mentioned be-
low, John Childs, February 16, 1812, in
Roxbury, married Caroline Tucker

(V) Susannah, youngest daughter of
John (3) and Catherine (Childs) Dale,
was born February 7, 1805, baptized in
July of that year in Weymouth, became
the wife of Edward R Bennett, of Wrentham, died November 14, 1885, there (see
Bennett VII)

(The Randall Line)

There are several old New England
families of this name, and the name is
scattered all over the United States,
whither it has carried enterprise, thrift
and morality Philip Randall was made

76

a freeman in Dorchester, Massachusetts, May 14, 1634, and mention of his sons, Abraham and Phillip, is found All removed to Windsor, Connecticut, where the name soon became extinct Possibly, some of the descendants returned to Dorchester They do not figure, however, on the records of that town The Boston vital records show the birth of several children of William and Elizabeth Randall in the latter part of the seventeenth century and early years of the eighteenth

(I) Thomas Randall, presumably of the Dorchester or Boston family of the name, was born in 1700, as indicated by the record of his death in Sharon, Massachusetts He married, in Roxbury, December 30, 1730, Katharine Tucker, born May 12, 1711, died November 24, 1802, in Sharon, daughter of Benjamin and Elizabeth (Williams) Tucker, of Roxbury, granddaughter of Benjamin and Ann (Payson) Tucker and great-granddaughter of Robert Tucker, of Weymouth and Milton, Massachusetts, pioneer ancestor of a large American family The Sharon records show only one child, mentioned below

(II) Joseph, son of Thomas Randall, was baptized in June, 1743, in Sharon (at least, recorded there), and died in that town, March 18, 1816 He married, January 27, 1766, in Wrentham, Massachusetts, Esther Fisher, born March 18, 1745, in that town, daughter of Daniel and Mercy Fisher, died December 5, 1799, in Sharon Their children, on Sharon records, were as follows John, born November 2, 1767, Molley, January 24, 1770, Elizabeth, mentioned below; Frances, December 30, 1775; Samuel, February 10, 1778, Esther, February 20, 1780, Thomas, March, 1782

(III) Elizabeth, second daughter of Joseph and Esther (Fisher) Randall, was

born January 22, 1774, in Sharon, and was married, December 31, 1797, to Isaac Bennett, of Wrentham (see Bennett VI).

HICKS, George Henry,
Physician

The family of Hicks, to which Dr George Henry Hicks, of Fall River, belongs, is one of the oldest and most distinguished in Southeastern Massachusetts In the early records the spelling Hix was also used For centuries the name has been an honored one in England also The ancestry has been traced in England to the year 1500

(I) John Hicks, we are told, was the father of Robert and Thomas Hicks, the latter mentioned below

(II) Thomas Hicks, son of John Hicks, died in Trotworth, England, in 1565 He married Margaret Atwood Among their children were John and Baptist, mentioned below

(III) Baptist Hicks, son of Thomas Hicks, was born in England in 1520 He married Mary Eberard, daughter of James Eberard Of their children, Baptist, Jr, died unmarried, and James is mentioned below

(IV) James Hicks, son of Baptist Hicks, married Phebe Allyn, daughter of Rev Ephraim Allyn Children, born in England John, Ephraim, Robert, mentioned below, Samuel, Thomas, James, and three daughters

(V) Robert Hicks, son of James Hicks, was born in England, in 1580, and came from his home in Southwark, County Surrey, in the ship "Fortune" to Plymouth, in 1621 One account says he was descended from Sir Ellis Hicks, who was knighted in 1356, by Edward, the Black Prince His wife Margaret, with her children, joined him two years later, coming in the ship "Ann" He drew lots at Plymouth, in 1623, for himself, wife and two children He was admitted a freeman in 1633 He died March 24, 1647 He married (first) in England, Elizabeth Morgan; (second) Margaret Winslow Children Samuel, mentioned below; Ephraim, Lydia, married Edward Bans; Phebe married George Watson

(VI) Samuel Hicks, son of Robert Hicks, was born in England, and came with his mother to Plymouth, in 1623 His name appears on the list of those able to bear arms in Plymouth, in 1643 Soon afterward he moved to the new town of Eastham, then called Nauset Afterward he was at Barnstable for a time He was formally admitted an inhabitant of Barnstable, October 3, 1662 He was one of the thirty-six purchasers of the territory that was later incorporated as the town of Dartmouth, March 7, 1652, and he made his home there in 1670 While in Eastham he was a deputy to the General Court in 1649 He owned one thirty-fourth part of the town of Dartmouth He married, in 1645, Lydia Doane, daughter of Deacon John Doane, one of the prominent pioneers of this section Children Dorcas, born February 14, 1651-52; Margaret, March 9, 1654; Thomas, mentioned below; Jacob, married Mary Farle

(VII) Thomas (2) Hicks, son of Samuel Hicks, married Mary Albro, daughter of John and Dorothy Albro He settled in Dartmouth, but moved to Portsmouth, Rhode Island He was a carpenter by trade He was admitted a freeman in 1673 He owned a share in Seaconnet and sold a quarter-share there in 1679 He died in 1698 His widow died after 1710 Children Sarah, Thomas, Samuel, mentioned below; Ephraim, Susanna, Abigail and Elizabeth In 1707, when the estate of Thomas Hicks, the father, was administered,

Thomas and Ephraim were of Rhode Island and Samuel was of Tiverton, then part of Massachusetts

(VIII) Samuel (2) Hicks, son of Thomas (2) Hicks, married, January 1, 1701-02, Susanna Anthony, daughter of Abraham and Alice (Wodell) Anthony They lived at Tiverton, where he died in 1742 His wife died before 1736 Children Samuel, mentioned below, Sarah, Alice, Leah, Susanna, Abigail, Mary

(IX) Samuel (3) Hicks, son of Samuel (2) Hicks, was born August 15, 1704 He lived first in Tiverton on land west of the highway leading from the Stone bridge to Fall River nearly opposite the stone house of the late Charles R Hicks The farm extended from the road to the shore of Mount Hope Bay They were Friends Samuel Hicks died at Tiverton, August 11, 1790 His will was dated December 17, 1788 (Book IV, p 469) He married (first) Mary Mumford, who died March 4, 1737, in her twenty-second year He married (second) Susanna Akin, who died three days before her husband It is related that the mourners returning from her burial found that Mr Hicks had died during their absence Children, born at Tiverton Thomas, August 2, 1735, Stephen, July 21, 1741, Samuel, January 10, 1742, married Patience Burrington (Dr Hicks has the original will of her father, Abraham Burrington, dated January 1, 1816, bequeathing to wife Elizabeth, brother Thomas and four sisters, Patience Hicks, Mary Durfee, Sarah and Alice Burrington; Samuel, Jr, died in 1825, Mary, born July 28, 1744, Elizabeth, March 23 1745-46, John, mentioned below, Joseph, died January 20, 1806, Ann, born February 5, 1752; George, May 7, 1755; Peace, 1757, Elihu, April 22, 1759, Susanna, May 2, 1761, Weston, June 30, 1764

(X) John (2) Hicks, son of Samuel (3)

Hicks, was born March 26, 1747-48. He was for a time a trader in Newport, Rhode Island, but returned to Tiverton, where he followed farming during the remainder of his active life. He bought of Abraham Brown and wife Abigail land in Tiverton bounded by land of Stephen Hicks and grantor, March 28, 1796 He bought a salt marsh on Hog Island, Portsmouth, adjoining land of William Borden, December 21, 1781. This deed was witnessed by Thomas Howland and Stephen Hicks Both these original deeds are now in the possession of Dr George H Hicks Another deed shows that John Hicks and his brother, Samuel, Jr, and Abraham Burrington bought of Abraham Brown and wife Abigail seventy-five acres in the Eighteenth Great Lot, first division in Tiverton, the homestead farm of Robert Burrington, late of Tiverton, deceased, being land set off to Abigail and Abraham Brown under the will of William Burrington, of Tiverton, son of Robert Burrington Witnesses Walter and Elizabeth Cook Deed dated September 23, 1776, acknowledged 1779

Both John Hicks and his wife were members of the Society of Friends, Mr Hicks being the last survivor of the Old Society In his sketch of the town of Tiverton, H W Blake says "Among the early supporters of the Tiverton meeting were Edward Wing and Elizabeth, his wife, Nathan Chase, Abraham Barker, Borden Durfee, Abigail Durfee, John Hicks, Elisha Estes, and Ann Hopkins, who was a maiden sister of Elizabeth Wing Mrs Wing was the minister for several years Mr Barker and Mr Hicks were the last of the old society These two, faithful to their earnest belief, sat alone in their house of worship many a First Day and silently worshipped God"

John Hicks married, December 7, 1803, Lydia Wing, daughter of Edward and Edith Wing, of Sandwich, Massachusetts.

She died November 8, 1828. He died August 11, 1828, aged eighty-one years, nine months Children, born at Tiverton Lydia Wing, born March 27, 1805, married John B Howland, in 1828, died August 25, 1842, John Russell, mentioned below, Susanna, born August 8, 1809, died June 9, 1821, Elizabeth, born January 2, 1812, died December 27, 1828; Mehitable, born December 26, 1813, married Charles W Howland, died January 18, 1875, aged sixty-one years, twenty-two days

(XI) John Russell Hicks, son of John (2) Hicks, was born in Tiverton, December 16, 1807 He owned and conducted a farm of forty-eight acres near the homestead, formerly known as the Cook farm He had a fine dairy and found his market in Fall River He was industrious, prudent and prosperous In religion he was a Friend, and his home was often visited by prominent Quakers on the way to and from meetings in this section In early life he was a Whig in politics, but afterward a Republican He died September 4, 1883 He married, May 6, 1832, Emma Gardner, who was born at Tiverton, January 25, 1809, died May 14, 1887, a daughter of Captain Samuel and Catherine (Borden) Gardner Catherine Gardner was a daughter of Benjamin Borden, granddaughter of Samuel Borden, and great-granddaughter of Richard Borden (see Borden). Captain Samuel Gardner was of a prominent Tiverton family, coming from Swansea, Massachusetts, and locating at Tiverton about the time of his marriage, January 1, 1795 Children of John Russell Hicks Charles Russell, born February 18, 1834, died January 22, 1901, twin of Charles Russell, born and died February 18, 1834, George Henry, mentioned below, Edward Wing born October 20, 1838, lived at Tiverton; Albert Gardner, born October 7, 1844, died the same month, John Russell, mentioned

below, Joseph L, born March 29, 1847, of
Fall River, Samuel Gardner, born July
3, 1849, lives at Westport, Massachusetts

(XII) George Henry Hicks, son of
John Russell Hicks, was born at Tiverton, December 12, 1836, died there January 8, 1901 He was a farmer in Tiverton In religion he was a Friend In
politics he was a Republican He married, January 1, 1862, Alice A Borden,
born November 16, 1842 (see Borden
VIII) Children: 1. Christopher B.,
born June 20, 1863, farmer in Fall River,
married Emily T Luther and has two
daughters, Lucy Davis and Lydia Howland 2 Lester H, born June 10, 1869,
married Alma Paquette, of Fall River,
resides in Fall River, children Milli-
cent, Milton, Alma 3 Edgar A, born
January 2, 1871, married Henrietta R
O Kendrick 4 Alice Borden, born September 21, 1879 lives with her mother
5 George Henry, mentioned below

(XII) John Russell (2) Hicks, son of
John Russell (1) Hicks, was born in
Tiverton, February 25, 1846, and died at
Tiverton He followed farming very
successfully on the homestead He was
prominent in public affairs for many
years He was a member of the town
committee and served the town in the
town council, as assessor, justice of the
peace, notary public and moderator He
represented the district in the Rhode
Island General Assembly from 1885 to
1887, 1888-89, and was State senator from
May, 1896, to January, 1900 While in
the house he was on the committee on
accounts and claims, on the committee on
special legislation, and while in the Senate was chairman of the committees on
education and on fisheries He was
elected alternate to the Republican National Convention at Minneapolis, Minnesota, in 1892, when Harrison was nominated for President Mr Hicks never
married

(XIII) Dr George Henry (2) Hicks,
son of George Henry (1) Hicks, was born
in Fall River, June 30, 1882 He attended the public schools of his native
city, and graduated from the B M C
Durfee High School in the class of 1901
He began his medical studies in the Long
Island College Hospital, from which he
was graduated in 1905 with the degree of
Doctor of Medicine He was an interne
for a year in the Fall River Hospital,
serving part of the time as assistant
house surgeon For six months he was
an interne in the Lying-in-Hospital at
Sixteenth street and Second avenue, New
York, and for another half-year in the
Children's Hospital of New York City
Since 1907 he has been in general prac-
tice in Fall River, having his office and
residence at 1973 South Main street. In
politics he is a Progressive Republican
He is a past master of Narragansett
Lodge, Ancient Free and Accepted Ma-
sons, of Fall River, and a member of Fall
River Chapter, Royal Arch Masons, of
Fall River Council, Royal and Select
Masters, of Godfrey de Bouillon Com-
mandery, Knights Templar, and of Azab
Grotto. of Fall River He is also a mem-
ber of the Alumni Association of the
Lying-in-Hospital, of the Fall River
Medical Society, the Bristol County Med-
ical Society, and the Massachusetts
Medical Society In Brayton Methodist
Church, of which he has been a member
for many years, he has been superin-
tendent of the Sunday school and is one
of the trustees He has also served as
district delegate from Fall River to the
State Sunday School Convention

He married, May 10, 1913, in Everett,
Massachusetts, Alice Hall Burton, who
was born at Chelsea, Massachusetts,
March 15, 1882, a daughter of Mark F
and Eliza Josephine (Durfee) Burton
She is descended from the Durfee family
mentioned elsewhere in this work Mark

F Burton married at Lynn, November 27, 1872, their children Harry Elton, born June 10, 1876, and Alice Hall, mentioned above

Daniel Burton, grandfather of Mrs. Hicks, had by wife Sarah Daniel Burton, born June 22, 1818, died July 17, 1872, Sarah Burton, born October 22, 1826, died January 20, 1906, Mark F, born January 18, 1830, died at Montreal, Canada, February 8, 1911, buried at Woodlawn (see above)

Stephen Durfee, father of Eliza Josephine Durfee, mentioned above, was born December 26, 1812, died January 16, 1886, his wife Sarah was born March 18, 1816, died September 20, 1906, their children: Orange N. Durfee, born May 14, 1838, Andrew B Durfee, born May 1, 1840, soldier in the Civil War, captured by Confederates at Sulphur Springs, died in Andersonville prison, Sarah Maria Durfee, born February 12, 1846, Eliza Josephine Durfee, born December 21, 1849, married Mark F Burton, mentioned above, Mary Elizabeth Durfee, born July 4, 1853

Benjamin Durfee, father of Stephen Durfee, had by wife Phebe (Borden) Durfee, the following children (family records) Stephen Durfee, born December 26, 1812, Eliza Ann Durfee, January 27, 1815; William B Durfee, January 29, 1817, Alanson Durfee, February 6, 1819, Jonathan B Durfee, May 25, 1821 (see Borden and sketch of Hon. James H. Kay), Richard Durfee, October 12, 1823, Benjamin Durfee, August 20, 1828, Adrienne Durfee, June 19, 1829, mother of Eric W Borden, Isaac B Durfee, July 16, 1832, died April 28, 1848, Ephraim Wanton Durfee, October 3, 1835, died April 5, 1861

(The Borden Line)

(I) Richard Borden, of County Kent, England, came to Boston in the ship,

"Elizabeth and Ann," in 1635, accompanied by his wife, Joan, and two children, in 1638 he settled at Portsmouth, Rhode Island He held town offices, and was a Quaker in religion His wife died July 18, 1688, he died June 25, 1671 Children Thomas, Francis Matthew, John, mentioned below; Joseph, Sarah, Samuel, Benjamin, Amy

(II) John Borden, son of Richard Borden, was born in Portsmouth, Rhode Island, September, 1648, and died June 4, 1716 He owned large tracts of land in New Jersey, Pennsylvania and Delaware as well as in Rhode Island He was often deputy to the General Court He married, December 25, 1670, Mary Earl

(III) Richard (2) Borden, son of John Borden, was born October 25, 1671, and died aged sixty years He bought two hundred acres in what is now Fall River, and became one of the wealthiest men in that section He married, in 1692, Innocent Wardell

(IV) Thomas Borden, son of Richard (2) Borden, was born December 8, 1697, and died at Tiverton, in April, 1740 He married, August 14, 1721, Mary Gifford, born October 6, 1695, daughter of Christopher and Meribah Gifford Children: Richard, born in 1722, Christopher, mentioned below, Deborah, Mary and Rebecca

(V) Christopher Borden, son of Thomas Borden, was born in Tiverton, October 10, 1726 He married, December 24, 1748, Hannah Borden, daughter of Stephen Borden, who was also a descendant of Richard Borden (1) Children, born at Tiverton Jonathan, mentioned below, Abraham, born May 1, 1770.

(VI) Jonathan Borden, son of Christopher Borden, was born May 3, 1761, at Tiverton He married, February 21, 1790, Elizabeth Bowen, who was born September 27, 1763, died July 2, 1840. Children, born at Tiverton: Hannah, born September 1, 1790; Abraham, mentioned below, Phebe, September, 1794, died September 3, 1862, married Benjamin Durfee (see Hicks and Durfee families), Thomas, September 19, 1796, Rhoda, March 21, 1798, Isaac, January 8, 1800, married Abby, daughter of William Borden, Elizabeth, November 8, 1803, married Thomas Tasker

(VII) Abraham Borden, son of Jonathan Borden, was born at Tiverton, July 20, 1792 and died at Westport, October 28, 1864 He lived in Fall River He married, January 17, 1815 Phebe Barker Children, born in Fall River Christopher, mentioned below Rhoda, born October 12, 1820, married, December 25, 1839, Abiel Davis, Marion B, December 4, 1826, married Weston Jenney, November 28, 1861, at New Bedford

(VIII) Christopher (2) Borden, son of Abraham Borden, was born October 29, 1815, at Fall River He married there, February 11, 1840, Lucy H Davis, born February 11, 1818 Children, born at Fall River 1 Jonathan, born May 15, 1841, died May 16, 1916, at Westport, married Mary M Estes, his daughter, Mary Robertson, married James H Kay, mayor of Fall River (see Kay) 2 Alice A, born November 16, 1842, married, January 1, 1862, George Henry Hicks, Sr (see Hicks) 3 Mary E, born December 7, 1844, married Isaac W Howland, of Little Compton, Rhode Island 4 Othniel, born August 24, 1846. 5 Edwin, born June 26, 1850, married Marietta Young, of Westport, Massachusetts 6 Phebe Sarah, born April 14, 1858, married Arthur Cornell, of Fall River, Massachusetts

---

PERKINS

And Allied Families

Abraham Perkins appears in 1638 as one of the first settlers of Hampton, then

in Massachusetts, now New Hampshire, in which town he was made a freeman, May 13, 1640 He was a man of good education, an excellent penman, and was much employed in town business An old family Bible still preserved among his descendants gives the births of eleven of his thirteen children He died August 31, 1683, aged about seventy-two His widow Mary died May 29, 1706, aged eighty-eight Children Mary, born September 2, 1639, Abraham, September 2, 1639, Luke, mentioned below, Humphrey, January 22, 1642, died young, James, April 11, 1644, died young, Timothy, October 5, 1646, James, October 5, 1647, Jonathan, May 30, 1650, David, February 28, 1653, Abigail, April 2, 1655, Timothy, June 26, 1657, Sarah, July 26, 1659, Humphrey, May 17, 1661

(II) Luke Perkins, second son of Abraham and Mary Perkins, was born 1641, and died March 20, 1710 As a boy of about fourteen, in 1654, he apprenticed himself with the consent of his parents to Samuel Carter, a shoemaker of Charlestown Massachusetts He married, March 9, 1663, Hannah, widow of Henry Cookery, and daughter of Robert Long, Sr She was admitted to the First Church in 1668, and died November 16, 1715 Children John, born May 10, 1664, Luke, March 14, 1665, died young, Luke, mentioned below, Henry, Elizabeth, May 15, 1670, John, April 15, 1670, Abraham, baptized 28th of 5th month, 1672, Hannah, born December 9, 1673 Mary, April 5, 1676

(III) Luke (2) Perkins, son of Luke (1) and Hannah (Long-Cookery) Perkins, was born March 18, 1667, and died in Plympton, December 27, 1748, nearly eighty-two years of age He lived in Marblehead, Beverly, Wenham, Ipswich and Plympton, and about 1714 the family moved from Ipswich to Plympton, Massachusetts Mr Perkins was a blacksmith, the first of that trade to settle in Plympton, and it is said that a lot of eighteen acres of land was deeded him at Rocky Run in Plympton, as an inducement to settle there as a blacksmith It is worthy of note that many of his descendants have been iron workers of one kind or another down to the present time He received from his uncle, David Perkins, of Bridgewater, the latter's land in Abington, one-third of the Solomon Leonard purchase and two-thirds of the John Robbins purchase Mr Perkins married, May 31, 1688, Martha, born August 16, 1664, daughter of Lot and Elizabeth (Walton) Conant, died January 2, 1754, in her ninetieth year Children John, born April 5, 1689, at Marblehead, Martha, September 19, 1691; Hannah, March 12, 1693, Luke, September 17, 1695, Mark, baptized April 30, 1699, in Beverly, Massachusetts, Josiah, mentioned below.

(IV) Deacon Josiah Perkins, son of Luke (2) and Martha (Conant) Perkins, born in 1700, died October 15, 1789, was town clerk for forty years He married (first) Deborah, daughter of Nehemiah Bennett, of Middleboro, Massachusetts He married (second) Rebecca Parker Children, all of first marriage Nathan, born 1723; William, 1724, John, 1726, Martha, 1727, Joshua, 1729; Abner, 1731, died young, Josiah, 1732, Luke, 1733, Abner, 1735, Deborah, 1737, Hannah, 1740, Zephaniah, 1742; Isaac, mentioned below

(V) Isaac Perkins, youngest child of Deacon Josiah and Deborah (Bennett) Perkins, was born 1744, in Middleboro, Massachusetts, and was a soldier of the Revolution from that town. He was a sergeant in Captain Amos Wade's (Third Middleboro) Company, of minute-men, which marched on the Lexington Alarm, and served three days He also served

under the same captain in Colonel Cotton's regiment, return dated October 7, 1775 He was a sergeant in Captain Joshua White's company, Colonel Ebenezer Sprout's regiment, which marched May 8, 1776, and was out twelve days at Howland Ferry, on an alarm Under the same commanders he served from May 6 to May 9 and from September 6 to September 12, nine days, in 1778, at Dartmouth Under the same commanders he marched August 1 and was discharged August 9, 1780, nine days at Tiverton He married Molly Shurtleff, born 1747, daughter of Barnabas and Jemima (Adams) Shurtleff, of Middleboro (see Shurtleff IV) Children Barnabas, born January 20, 1772, Temperance, July 13, 1773, Molly, March 17, 1775, Isaac, November 27, 1776, Lothrop, March 17, 1779, Josiah, mentioned below, John, November 17, 1783, Jemima, March 13, 1787.

(VI) Josiah (2) Perkins, fourth son of Isaac and Molly (Shurtleff) Perkins, was born April 15, 1781, in Middleboro, Massachusetts, and lived in that town He married, February 4, 1808, Asenath Clark, of Rochester, born June 5, 1783, daughter of Nathaniel and Bethiah (Crosby) Clark, of Middleboro (see Clark VI) Children Bethiah Crosby, born December 4, 1808; Eldridge Gerry, December 21, 1810, Molly Shurtleff, August 15, 1813, Nathaniel Clark, November 12, 1815; Isaac, September 4, 1817; Thomas Peleg Whitridge, mentioned below, Josiah, September 15, 1823, Asenath Sarah, December 4, 1826.

(VII) Thomas Peleg Whitridge Perkins, fourth son of Josiah (2) and Asenath (Clark) Perkins, was born December 11, 1820, in Middleboro, Massachusetts, where he grew to manhood, and learned the trade of blacksmith Soon after attaining his majority he located in Worcester, Massachusetts, where he continued at his trade until 1869, when he went to Fairhaven, Massachusetts, and there continued to make his home, spending his summers at Rock, in the town of Middleboro He died March 27, 1903, and was buried in the cemetery at North Rochester, Massachusetts He married (first) (intentions published May 20, 1843, in Rochester) Laura A Bennett, born October 19, 1822, daughter of John and Sarah Bennett, died April 5, 1848, at Wareham, Massachusetts, leaving no issue He married (second) December 18, 1851, Betsey W Canedy, born 1828, in Lakeville, Massachusetts, daughter of Zebulon Leonard and Olive (Bisbee) Canedy, of Middleboro (see Canedy VI) She died October 4, 1912 Children Oscar T, married Annie Lane Pratt, and resides in Fairhaven, Olive Bessie, mentioned below.

(VIII) Olive Bessie Perkins, only daughter of Thomas Peleg Whitridge and Betsey W (Canedy) Perkins, born October 21, 1855, in Rochester, Massachusetts, became the wife of Henry A Sherman, a well-known ironworker of New Bedford, in which city they reside. Mr Sherman is a son of the late Captain Charles and Lucy (Coleman) Sherman, and grandson of James and Abigail (Parker) Sherman James Sherman died December 12, 1850, in New Bedford, at the age of eighty-nine years and six months His wife died at Fairhaven, February 5, 1836, aged seventy-five years. Mrs Sherman is active in the social life of New Bedford, and is the organizer and first regent of Fort Phoenix Chapter, Daughters of the American Revolution She has represented this chapter as a delegate to the national congress in Washington She is also a member of the Founders and Patriots Society, of the Women's Club of New Bedford, and of the Young Women's Christian Association, in which she is especially active She conducts a circulating library in New Bedford, and is much interested in literary and historical pursuits

This name is found in Plymouth, Massachusetts, fourteen years after the landing of the Pilgrims, and is prominently identified with the management of affairs there for a long period In the records of Plymouth the name has various spellings, such as Shirtleff, Shirtley, Shurtlif It first appears in England as Chiercliffe, then Chyrecliffe, Shiercliffe, and finally Shirtleff A grandson of the American progenitor adopted the present form, which is generally in use by the family

(I) William Shurtleff, in his youth, came to Plymouth before 1635, from Ecclesfield, a village of Yorkshire, about five miles from Scrooby, the early gathering place of the Pilgrims before they went to Holland In this village, at a seat called Whitley Hall, resided the only family of the name that can be traced before its appearance in America By occupation William Shurtleff was a carpenter, and he appears in the Plymouth records as "surveyor of highways" and constable In 1643 he was enrolled among those required to give military service to the colony He was killed by a stroke of lightning at Marshfield, June 23, 1666. He married, October 18, 1655, Elizabeth Lettice, born about 1636, in England, daughter of Thomas and Ann Lettice She survived her husband over twenty-seven years, and died October 31, 1693, in Swansea, Massachusetts They had three sons: William, Thomas and Abiel, the last born within a few days after the death of his father.

(II) William (2) Shurtleff, son of William (1) and Elizabeth (Lettice)

Shurtleff, was born 1657, in Plymouth, and was a prominent citizen of the town, where he died February 4, 1730 He was enrolled as a freeman, May 27, 1681, and was surveyor of highways in 1684 On August 30, 1686, he was chosen to serve at the court of assistants, and was constable in 1689 He was selectman in 1692-93-94-95, 1698-99 and 1700-01, representative at the General Court in 1694, assessor in the same year, and town treasurer in 1695-96-97 and 1700 At various town meetings in 1695 he was appointed on important committees, among them one for making the province rate and one of six men to draw agreements "as may be of use to defend the Town Right on the North sid of the Towne" On December 1 of that year he was granted, with Ephraim Coole, "30 foott of land square" by the waterside, on which to build a "wharfe" In March, 1697, he was one of a committee to settle the ranges, and in September following he was chosen as one of a committee "to treat with Middlebery agents Respecting the Rainge between the towne" and certain purchasers of land In 1698 he was on a committee to call a minister, and in 1699 to care for and defend the commons. In 1700 he was made a surveyor of bounds, and from that time on the land records bear his name on every page, in establishing the location of real estate In 1701 he was called "leftenant," and in October of that year received a grant of "Meadow or Meadoish Ground" The Shurtleff House, built by him in Plymouth before 1698 at the corner of Leyden and Market streets, was removed in 1883 to the lot adjoining the Drew Block on Market street His headstone in the first burying ground of the Pilgrims on Cole's Hill bears this inscription "Here lyes ye body of Captn William Shurtleff who Decd Febry the 4th, 1729-30 in the

72d year of his age ' His wife, Susanna, was a daughter of Barnabas Lothrop, son of Rev John Lothrop, of Barnstable, and Susanna (Clark) Lothrop, granddaughter of Thomas Clark, of Plymouth (see Lothrop, III) She was born February 28, 1664, in Barnstable, and died August 9, 1726, in Plympton Children Jabez, Thomas, William, John, Susannah, Barnabas, Ichabod, Elizabeth, Mary, Sarah, Samuel, Abigail, born in Plymouth, and Nathaniel, born 1707 in Plympton

(III) Barnabas Shurtleff, fifth son of William (2) and Susanna (Lothrop) Shurtleff, married Jemima Adams

(IV) Molly Shurtleff, daughter of Barnabas and Jemima (Adams) Shurtleff, became the wife of Isaac Perkins, of Middleboro (see Perkins, V)

(The Clark Line)

(I) William Clark kept an ordinary in Salem, Massachusetts, whither he came about 1634 from England He was dead in 1647, when his wife Catherine renewed the license to conduct the tavern His inventory made in July, 1647, amounted to £587, 3s and 2d He had a son and daughter by a first wife, whose name is unknown, and four children by the second

(II) William (2) Clark, probably a son of William Clark, above named, is described as a vintner in Salem in 1660 There is no record of his wife There is little doubt that he was the father of the next mentioned

(III) John Clark, born about 1658-60, settled in Beverly, Massachusetts He married Sarah, daughter of John and Elizabeth Smith, of Salem, born October 20, 1660, settled in Rochester, Massachusetts, about 1705 There his will was made March 7, 1727 Children Sarah, born August 21, 1683, in Beverly, John, October 7, 1687, Joseph, mentioned be-

low, Catherine, baptized July 3, 1690, in
Beverly, Mary, July 2, 1693, Cornelius,
August 28, 1698; Elizabeth, November 1,
1702

(IV) Joseph Clark, according to the
will of his father the second son of John
and Sarah (Smith) Clark, born about
1688-89, lived in Rochester, Massachusetts He married, December 29, 1720,
Thankful, daughter of Andrew Stevens
Children Isaac, born September 6, 1721,
Katherine, October 17, 1723, Joseph, November 30, 1724; Thankful, August, 1727,
Nathaniel, mentioned below; Willard,
March 21, 1732; Sarah, Elizabeth, baptized September 12, 1736; Robert, June 8
1739

(V) Nathaniel Clark, third son of Joseph and Thankful (Stevens) Clark, was
born February 17, 1730, in Rochester, in
which town he lived He was a private
in Captain Jabez Cottle's company, Colonel Ebenezer Sprout's regiment, May 6
and 7, 1778, two days, on a Dartmouth
alarm His name appears in a list of
men in charge of James Hatch, muster-
master, to serve to January 1, 1779 He
fulfilled this service six months, from
July 1, 1778, to January 1, 1779, as a
private in Sergeant Elisha Ruggles' de-
tachment, stationed at Rochester and
Wareham, Massachusetts He served
with Captain Edward Hammond from
August 13 to September 13, 1779, detached to serve one month in Rhode
Island in command of Samuel Fisher He
was also in Captain Barnabas Doty's
company, Fourth Plymouth County Regiment, commanded by Lieutenant-Colonel
White, from July 30 to August 8, 1780,
nine days' service on a Rhode Island
alarm He married (intentions published
in Rochester, March 12, 1758) Bethiah
Crosby, of Yarmouth, Massachusetts,
born July 26, 1738, daughter of Theophilus and Thankful (Winslow) Crosby,

of that town (see Crosby, X) Children
Mary, born July 2, 1759, Sarah, March
21, 1762, Nathaniel, May 19, 1764, Theophilus, June 18, 1766, Bethiah, September
5, 1768, Sarah, January 27, 1770, Katherine, October 28, 1774; Joseph, February
27, 1777; Thomas, March 10, 1780,
Asenath, mentioned below

(VI) Asenath Clark, youngest child of
Nathaniel and Bethiah (Crosby) Clark,
was born June 5, 1783, in Rochester, and
was married, February 4, 1808, to Josiah
(2) Perkins, of Middleboro, Massachusetts (see Perkins, VI)

(The Canedy Line)

(I) Alexander Canedy was perhaps a
resident of Plymouth Of the Canedy
family and others of their time says
Weston, in his "History of Middleboro "
"Among the prominent families (of Lakeville) in the last century were The
Canedys, the Montgomerys, the Mc-
Cullys, the Pickenses, the Strobridges,
and the McCumbers There is a tradition, which has always been regarded as
true, that these families were of Scotch-
Irish descent, and that, as Protestants in
the North of Ireland, they joined with
William in the heroic resistance at the
siege of Londonderry and the battle of
the Boyne in 1690 For their services
they were rewarded by the British Crown
with various tracts of land in the New
England Colonies, and nearly a generation after those residing in and about
Londonderry determined to leave the
land for which they had fought and seek
a home where they would be free from
the persecutions to which they had been
so long subjected These families were
probably among those who, in 1718,
dispatched Rev. William Boyde with an
address to Governor Shute, of Massachusetts, signed by two hundred and seventeen of their number Such was their in-

telligence that of these all but seven wrote their names very plainly and applied to be allowed to emigrate to Massachusetts; the governor's reply was such that they concluded to embark for Boston It is said that some of these emigrants, after wandering about seeking in vain for a suitable home, finally came and settled in Lakeville, taking tracts of land, portions of which are still held by their descendants They brought with the their sterling integrity and love for the English Crown and for the Protestant faith." The children of Alexander Canedy and Elizabeth, his wife, were Hannah, born in 1678, married, in 1697, Fleazer Pratt, Elizabeth, 1682, Jean, 1685; William, mentioned below, Sarah, 1693; Annable, 1698, married Thomas Paine, of Freetown; John, 1703.

(II) Captain William Canedy, son of Alexander and Elizabeth Canedy, was born in 1689, and died June 23 1774, in the eighty-sixth year of his age He acquired land first in Middleboro, December 2, 1717, from Nathan Rowland He was commissioned ensign of forces to fight the French and Indians, and in 1723 in that service as a lieutenant he was intrusted with the command of a fort that, on December 25, 1723, was furiously attacked by the Indians, the siege lasting thirty days, when reinforcements arrived in sufficient numbers to raise the siege and relieve the garrison The conduct of Lieutenant Canedy on that occasion was deemed so meritorious that as a consequence he was promoted to captain in the service, and several years afterward he was commissioned captain of one of the companies in the local militia of Taunton He was commissioned a justice of the peace for the county of Bristol and probably continued in that relation through the remainder of his life His former residence in the eastern part of Taunton,

near the Berkley line, stood until a generation ago. He married Elizabeth Eaton, born July 26, 1701, daughter of Samuel Eaton.

(III) Captain William (2) Canedy, son of William (1) and Elizabeth (Eaton) Canedy, was born about 1729, in Middleboro, and was an influential man in that part of the town now Lakeville He served with distinction in the French and Indian War, and, having held a commission as captain under the Imperial government, declared that he could not be a traitor in his old age He died March 26, 1804, as the result of an accident, as he was returning home one evening on horseback, in a blinding snow-storm, the horse he was riding went under a shed and threw the rider to the ground, whereby he sustained injuries that proved fatal He married, December 6, 1753, Charity Leonard, born February 27, 1732, died October 13, 1805, daughter of Hon Elkanah Leonard, a distinguished lawyer, granddaughter of Ensign Elkanah Leonard, and great-granddaughter of Major Thomas Leonard

(IV) William (3) Canedy, son of Captain William (2) and Charity (Leonard) Canedy, was born December 15, 1757 He was a soldier in the Colonial forces during the Revolution, and served as a private in Captain Job Pearce's (Middleboro) company, Colonel Ebenezer Sprout, which marched December 9, 1776, to Tiverton on an alarm at Howland's Ferry, serving five days He married Mary Gooch Brown, born October 29, 1764, daughter of Josiah and Mary (Gooch) Brown Josiah Brown was a Revolutionary soldier, serving as a private in Captain Nathaniel Healy's company, Colonel Jonathan Holmes' regiment, which marched on a Rhode Island alarm in December, 1776 He was subsequently stationed in camp at Providence, twenty-one days, from January 21, 1777 Among their children was a son, Zebulon Leonard

(V) Zebulon Leonard Canedy, son of William (3) and Mary Gooch (Brown) Canedy, was born August 11, 1793, and married Olive Bisbee, of Middleboro (see Bisbee, VII) Children William, Elkanah W, married Nancy Shaw, of Middleboro, Salmon Snow, Betsey W mentioned below, Mary B, married William T Jenny, of Middleboro

(VI) Betsey W Canedy, daughter of Zebulon Leonard and Olive (Bisbee) Canedy, became the wife of Thomas Peleg Whitridge Perkins, of Rochester (see Perkins, VII)

(The Lothrop Line)

The Lothrop family is among the oldest of the Colonial families who settled in New England Members of this family suffered persecution and arrest for expressing and living according to their honest religious convictions and secured immunity from further molestation on their promise to leave the country Rev. John Lothrop, the American ancestor of this family, was one of those who suffered in the above mentioned manner, and his first wife died while he was in prison He was a minister in Egerton, Kent, England, and removed to London in 16. where he became pastor of a Congregational church He and forty-three members of his church were imprisoned by order of the archbishop, April 29, 1632, because they practiced the teachings of the New Testament Upon promise to leave the country they were released, and Rev John Lothrop came to New England with his family in 1634, and shortly afterward organized a church at Scituate, Massachusetts. He was admitted freeman of Plymouth Colony, 1636-37, and two years later removed with the larger

part of the membership of his church to Barnstable In Pope's "Pioneers of Massachusetts," we find "He married a second wife whose name is not on our records, who came here with him, joined the church, June 14, 1635, and survived him " He was a man of great piety and energy, and did much to further the secular as well as the spiritual welfare of the colony

(II) Barnabas Lothrop, son of Rev John Lothrop, baptized June 3, 1636, in Scituate, married, December 1, 1658, Susanna Clark, born 1642, daughter of Thomas (2) and Susanna (Ring) Clark, and granddaughter of Thomas Clark, mate of the "Mayflower" She died September 28, 1697 Thomas (2) Clark was a carpenter, and came in the ship "Ann" to Plymouth in 1623 He married, before 1631, Susanna Ring, daughter of Andrew and Mary Ring, of Plymouth Susanna, daughter of Thomas (2) and Susanna (Ring) Clark, became the wife of Barnabas Lathrop, as above noted.

(III) Susanna Lothrop, daughter of Barnabas and Susanna (Clark) Lothrop, married William (2) Shurtleff of Plymouth (see Shurtleff, II)

(The Crosby Line)

(I) John Crosby, born about 1440, died in 1502, in Stillingfleet, England, where he was a substantial citizen, living in the reign of Henry VI, Edward IV, Edward V, Richard III and Henry VII The name of his wife is unknown He had seven children

(II) Miles Crosby, youngest child of John Crosby, born about 1483, was executor of his father's will in 1502 In 1538 he lived in Shipton Parish, north of Holme-on-Spalding-Moor He had sons Thomas and William

(III) Thomas Crosby, son of Miles Crosby, born about 1510, died in 1558-59, was an archer on the muster roll of 1538 He married, about 1542, Janet, widow of John Bell, who died in 1568-69 They had four sons

(IV) Anthony Crosby, second son of Thomas and Janet Crosby, was born about 1545, and removed with his mother, after the death of his father, to Buhwith Parish, where, in 1592, he purchased one hundred acres of land at Holme-on-Spalding-Moor, in Yorkshire Subsequently he purchased a close in Wheldrake, where he died in 1599 His wife, Alice, was probably a Blanchard as she appears among other relatives to whom John Blanchard bequeathed property

(V) Thomas (2) Crosby, son of Anthony and Alice Crosby, born about 1575, in Buhwith County York, came to New England in 1641 following sons who had preceded him, and died at Rowley, Massachusetts, where he was buried May 6, 1661 He married, in Holme-on-Spalding-Moor, October 19, 1600, Jane Sotheron, baptized there March 4, 1582, daughter of William and Constance (Lambert) Sotheron She was buried in Rowley, May 2, 1662 Children Anthony, born about 1602, Thomas, 1604, William, 1606, Simon, mentioned below

(VI) Simon Crosby, son of Thomas (2) and Jane (Sotheron) Crosby, was born 1608, in England, and embarked for New England in the ship, "Susan and Ellen" April 18, 1634, with his wife Ann, aged twenty-five years, and son Thomas, aged eight weeks He was a prominent citizen of Cambridge, Massachusetts, where he was selectman in 1636 and 1638, resided at what is now Brattle Square, near the site of the old Brattle House He died in September, 1639 His widow Ann married (second) Rev William Thompson, of Braintree, before 1648, surviving her second husband, who died December 10, 1668 Children of Simon and

Ann Crosby Thomas, mentioned below, Simon, born August, 1637, in Cambridge; Joseph, February, 1639, settled in Braintree, Massachusetts, married Sarah Brackett

(VII) Thomas (3) Crosby, eldest child of Simon and Ann Crosby, was baptized February 26, 1635, at Holme-on-Spalding-Moor, and graduated at Harvard College in 1653 From 1655 to 1670 he was minister at Eastham, Massachusetts, at an annual salary of fifty pounds Though never formally ordained, he was very acceptable as a pastor to his people Subsequently he was a merchant in Harwich, Massachusetts, and died in Boston, June 12 1702, while on a visit there The inventory of his estate amounted to £1091 and 6s At one time he lived in Yarmouth, Massachusetts His widow Sarah survived him and married (second) April 8, 1703, John Miller, of Yarmouth. Children Thomas, born April 7, 1663, Simon, July 5, 1665; Sarah March 24, 1667, Joseph, mentioned below, John, December, 1670; a twin of John, died at birth, William, March 1673, Ebenezer, March 28, 1675, Increase, Ann and Mary (triplets), April 14 and 15, 1678, Eleazer, March 30, 1680

(VIII) Joseph Crosby, third son of Thomas (3) and Sarah Crosby was born January 27, 1669, in Yarmouth, Massachusetts and died May 30, 1725, in that town He married there, February 11 1693, Mehitable Miller, who died February 17, 1734 Children Theophilus, mentioned below, Joseph, born June 20, 1695, Mehitable, March 20 1697, Ann, June 6, 1699, Sarah and Margaret (twins) February 4, 1702, Lydia, July 14, 1704, Josiah, July 15, 1706; William March 12, 1710, Hannah, March 13, 1712, Barnabas, May 9, 1715

(IX) Theophilus Crosby, eldest child of Joseph and Mehitable (Miller) Crosby, was born December 31, 1693, in Yarmouth, where he lived, and married, February 14, 1723, Thankful Winslow, born about 1697, in Harwich, daughter of Kenelm (4) and Bethiah (Hall) Winslow. The early history of the Winslow family is elsewhere given in this work, including six English generations. The American immigrant in this line, Kenelm (2) Winslow, son of Edward Winslow, was born April 29, 1599, at Droitwich, County Worcester, England, and was a brother of Governor Edward Winslow, of the Plymouth Colony. Kenelm (3) Winslow was born about 1636, at Plymouth, and died November 11, 1715, at Harwich, Massachusetts. He lived in Yarmouth, and afterward in that part of Harwich which is now Brewster, Massachusetts, his homestead on the west border at a place now called West Brewster. In the records he is called colonel, planter and yeoman. He bought large tracts of wild land in what is now Rochester, Massachusetts, on which several of his children settled, and the water privilege which it included is still in possession of the family. On three occasions he rode sixty miles to Scituate to have a child baptized in the Second Church there, and was on a committee to seat the meetinghouse in Harwich, October 4, 1714. His first wife, Mercy (Worden) Winslow, daughter of Peter, Jr. and Mercy Worden, was born about 1641, and died September 22, 1688. She was buried in the Winslow graveyard at Dennis. Her headstone is of hard slate, brought from England, and the oldest in the yard. The history of Kenelm (2) Winslow, son of Edward Winslow, is given at length elsewhere in this work. Kenelm (4), son of Kenelm (3) and Mercy (Worden) Winslow, was baptized August 9, 1668, in Scituate. His wife, Bethiah (Hall) Winslow, was a daughter of Rev. Gershom and Bethiah (Bangs)

Hall, of Yarmouth, granddaughter of Edward Bangs, who came to Plymouth in 1623 in the ship "Ann." The history of Gershom Hall and his father, John Hall, is given elsewhere in this work. Children of Theophilus Crosby: Josiah, born September 22, 1724, Edmund, September 24, 1726, Thankful, May 22, 1729, Theophilus, January 31, 1733, Ann, October 4, 1735, Bethiah, mentioned below; Mary, August 2, 1742.

(X) Bethiah Crosby, third daughter of Theophilus and Thankful (Winslow) Crosby, was born July 26, 1738, in Yarmouth, and became the wife of Nathaniel Clark, of Rochester, Massachusetts (see Clark, V).

(The Bisbee Line)

This surname is spelled in the records Besbedge, Besbidge, Besbeech, Besbitch, Besberch, Bisbe, Bisbey, Bisby, but at the present time, Bisbee is the standard form.

(I) Deacon Thomas Bisbee, or Besbidge, was born in England. He was a man of wealth and position in Sandwich, England; settled in Scituate, Massachusetts, in 1635. He became prominent also at Plymouth. In the spring of 1634 he came in the ship "Hercules," John Witherly, master, sailing from Sandwich, with his wife, six children and three servants. He had certificates from Rev. Thomas Warren, rector of St. Peter's, Sandwich, and Rev. Thomas Harmon, vicar of Hedcorn, of conversion and conformity to orders and discipline of the church and had taken oaths of allegiance and supremacy. He became a member of Rev. Mr. Lothrop's church, first at Scituate, and was one of the first deacons. In 1638 he bought a house of William Palmer in Duxbury, and moved thither in 1643, was deputy to the General Court from Duxbury, grantee of Seipicon (Rochester), Massachusetts, but the grant was not accepted and Bisbee moved to Marshfield Afterward he was in Sudbury, where he settled in 1647, and died March 9, 1674 He was admitted a freeman, February 7, 1637, lived for a time at Cambridge, Massachusetts (1636), and sold land in Sudbury, October 13, 1664 His will was dated November 25, 1672, and proved April 7, 1674 Children Elisha, mentioned below; Alice, married John Bourne; Mary, married William Browne; three others came over with him, according to the ship's records

(II) Elisha Bisbee, son of Deacon Thomas Bisbee, was born probably on the estates at Hedcorn, England, and came with his father to America in 1634 In 1644 he was keeper of the ferry at Scituate, where Union Bridge was subsequently built He was a cooper by trade, and his house at the ferry was used by his son Elisha A tavern stood on the west side of the highway The Christian name of his wife was Joanna, and they had children Hopestill, born 1645; John, mentioned below; Mary 1649, Elisha, 1654; Hannah, 1656

(III) John Bisbee, son of Elisha and Joanna Bisbee, was born 1647, in Scituate, moved to Pembroke, Massachusetts where he died September 24, 1726 He married, in Marshfield, September 13, 1687, Joanna Brooks, died August 17, 1726 Children Martha, born October 13, 1688; John, September 15, 1690, Elijah, January 29, 1692, Mary, March 28, 1693, Moses, October 20 1695; Elisha, May 3, 1698; Aaron; Hopestill, mentioned below

(IV) Hopestill Bisbee, youngest child of John and Joanna (Brooks) Bisbee, was born April 16, 1702, and lived in Plympton, Massachusetts He married, November 21, 1731, Hannah Churchill, born October 23, 1707, daughter of William and Ruth (Bryant) Churchill, of Plympton (see Churchill, IV) Ruth

(Bryant) Churchill, daughter of John and Sarah Bryant, was born 1685, in Plymouth Children Abner, born June 16, 1739, Hopestill, mentioned below; Issachar, April 3, 1744, Sarah March 7, 1747, Hannah, February 20, 1752

(V) Hopestill (2) Bisbee, second son of Hopestill (1) and Hannah (Churchill) Bisbee, was born May 28, 1741, in Plympton, where he made his home until 1769, when he removed to Rochester, Massachusetts He was a private in Captain Jabez Cottle's company, Colonel Ebenezer Sprout's regiment May 6 and 7, 1778, two days, on a Dartmouth alarm He served in Captain Barnabas Doty's company, Colonel Sprout's regiment, September 5 to September 9 1778, four days, on an alarm at Dartmouth He also served in Captain Doty's company, Lieutenant-Colonel White, July 31 to August 8, 1780, nine days, on an alarm at Rhode Island He married September 4, 1766, Abigail Churchill, born May 10, 1744, daughter of Nathaniel and Mary (Curtis) Churchill, of Plympton (see Churchill V) Children: Abigail, born October 21, 1768, Hopestill, mentioned below; Josiah, September 27, 1771, Ansel, February 10, 1774, Levi March 22, 1776, Sylvester, August 14, 1778, Susannah, January 25, 1782, Hannah, November 27, 1786

(VI) Hopestill (3) Bisbee, eldest son of Hopestill (2) and Abigail (Churchill) Bisbee, was born October 11, 1769, in Plympton, and left that town before 1800 He married (intentions published in Rochester, April 10 1796) Betsey Clark Purington One child is recorded in Rochester Betsey, born January 16, 1797

(VII) Olive, daughter of Hopestill (3) and Betsey Clark (Purington) Bisbee, was born November 11, 1799, and died March 3 1886 She was married, November 7, 1816, to Zebulon Leonard Canedy, of Middleboro (see Canedy, V)

(The Churchill Line)

Elsewhere in this work is given an extended account of John Churchill, the immigrant ancestor, who came to Plymouth, Massachusetts, before 1643, and died there in 1662 Extended mention of his son William, and grandson William appears elsewhere

(IV) Hannah Churchill, daughter of William (2) and Ruth (Bryant) Churchill, born October 23, 1707, became the wife of Hopestill (1) Bisbee, of Plympton (see Bisbee, IV)

(II) Eliezer Churchill, second son of John and Hannah (Palmer) Churchill, was born April 20, 1652, in Plymouth, and was admitted a freeman in 1683 He resided on part of his father's estate at "Hobshole," in the first house built there, which he inherited He was granted thirty foot strip of land in 1709 for a warehouse His first wife's name was Mary He married (second) February 8, 1688, Mary Doty, daughter of Edward and Faith (Clark) Doty, born 1655, died December 11, 1715 Children of first marriage Hannah, born August 23, 1676, Joanna, November 25, 1678; Abigail, 1680, Eliezer, February 23, 1682, Stephen, mentioned below , Jedidiah, February 27, 1687 Children of second marriage Mary, born 1688, Elkanah, March 1, 1691, Nathan, February 16, 1693, Josiah, 1694, John, September 12, 1698

(III) Stephen Churchill, second son of Eliezer and Mary Churchill was born February 16, 1685, in Plymouth, and died in 1750 He married, in 1708, Experience, daughter of Mathias Ellis, of Sandwich, born 1687 Children Ephraim born October 13, 1709, Nathaniel, mentioned below; Mary, April 29, 1716, Stephen, August 24, 1717, Zachariah, October 30, 1718, Benjamin, August 19, 1725

(IV) Nathaniel Churchill, second son of Stephen and Experience (Ellis)

Churchill, was born December 19, 1712, in Plymouth, and married, January 2, 1734, Mary Curtis, born 1714 The children of this marriage, found of record, are Experience, born August 27, 1735, Eliezer, July 31, 1737, Mary, July 17, 1740, Nathaniel, December 13, 1742

(V) Abigail Churchill, daughter of Nathaniel and Mary (Curtis) Churchill, was born May 10, 1744, and became the wife of Hopestill (2) Bisbee, of Plympton and Rochester (see Bisbee, V)

PERRY, Charles H ,

Veterinary Surgeon.

There were several families of this name early in New England, and there seems to have been several in Sandwich, Massachusetts, at the same time In the early records of that town appears mention of a widow, Sarah Perry, supposed to have been the widow of Edmund Perry, of Devonshire, England, and four persons, supposed to be her children, namely Ezra, Edward, Margaret and Deborah

(I) Ezra Perry, born about 1630, was an early settler at Sandwich, Massachusetts, and "Freeman's History of Cape Cod" states that he was ancestor of all the Perrys of that town His son Ezra's name appears on the list of freemen, June 25, 1702, with his other sons, Edward, John and Samuel The name of Ezra Perry Sr , is on the list of those contributing to support the minister, July 17, 1657 He married, February 12, 1651, at Sandwich, Elizabeth Burge Children Edward, owned a town right in Sandwich, 1676, was a Quaker, and was fined with other Quakers; Ezra, mentioned below Deborah, born November 28, 1654, John, January 1, 1656, Samuel, March 15, 1657 Benjamin, January 15, 1670, Remembrance, January 1, 1676 The will of Ezra

Perry was dated October, 1689, proved April 18, 1690, bequeathing to wife Elizabeth and son Ezra

(II) Ezra (2) Perry, son of Ezra (1) Perry, was born February 11, 1652, at Sandwich, and died there, January 31, 1729. He owned land in Rochester, Massachusetts, devised to son Ebenezer. He married Rebecca ———. Children, born at Sandwich: Ebenezer, born November 18, 1673, married Judith Savory, and their son, Ebenezer, removed late in life to Hardwick, Massachusetts, and by his first wife was grandfather of Dr. Marshall S. Perry, of Barre (see Barre "Centennial History"), Mary, December 21, 1675, Hannah, Ezra, Samuel, Rebecca, married Jonathan Washburn, Patience, Freelove. His will was dated October 21, 1728, and proved February 10, 1729, bequeathing to wife Rebecca and children.

(III) One of the sons of Ezra (2) Perry was father of Elijah, mentioned below. A search of the available public records has failed to find the birth record of Elijah. In a census of the families of Sandwich in March, 1730, the following are reported as heads of families: Ebenezer, Timothy and Desire, Widow Perry, Abner, Benjamin, Benjamin, Jr., Samuel, Samuel, Jr., Ezra, Jr., Elisha and John Perry, all descendants of Ezra (1) Perry (See N E Register, 1859, p 30)

(IV) Elijah Perry, third in descent from Ezra (1) Perry, was born about 1700, in Sandwich, and appears to have lived there all his life. We find the record of marriage of an Elijah Perry to Hannah Damon in the First Church at Scituate, March 7, 1723 (town records, 1722) Elijah Perry, of Sandwich, bought twenty-two acres of land in Barre, Massachusetts, of Lewis and Sarah Turner, of Boston, December 1, 1757. It was part of Great Farm No 29 on the Hardwick line He was called deacon in the deed

(Book 39, p 463) He appears to have sent his son Phineas to clear the land and make a home there Another deed dated July 1, 1773, over fifteen years later, shows that Elijah Perry, then of Sandwich, for one hundred pounds and other valuable considerations conveyed to "my son Phinehas Perry," of Rutland District (Barre) land and buildings, being the place he now lives on, bought of Lewis Turner and wife He refers to deeds of part of this land to Chipman and Dennison Robinson Elijah Perry's wife did not sign the deed

(V) Phineas Perry, son of Elijah Perry, was the pioneer in Worcester county He was born at Sandwich, about 1735, and came when a young man to the place his father bought in Barre Near by in Hardwick, as we have shown above, relatives settled and others of the family appear to have been in Barre for a time One branch has been mentioned A sketch of the Perry family in the Barre "Centennial History" is very obscure and misleading It states that one branch under consideration came from Martha's Vineyard, but the absence of the name in the vital record shows that the family was not there long and probably not at all All of them were from Sandwich Phineas Perry, yeoman, bought of James Black, of Mansfield, Hampshire county, Massachusetts (so described in the deed) land in Rutland District adjoining John Wallace's place This deed was dated March 12, 1773 In the same year he received from his father, as already stated, a deed of another farm there on which he was living (Book 70, p 29; Book 71, p 127) These deeds unlocked a genealogical puzzle of some difficulty Phineas Perry married at Barre, May 15, 1760, Esther Gates Children, born at Barre Justus, born July 30, 1761; Daniel, March 17, 1763; Thomas, October 2,

1764, Hannah, March 25 1766, William, February 12, 1768 Luther, mentioned below, Lucretia and Luke twins, February 9, 1772, Calvin, April 21, 1774; Hemon, May 24, 1776, Martha, April 17, 1778; Hemon, December 31, 1780, Phineas, May 27, 1783 The will of Phineas Perry was dated July 11, 1796, bequeathing to children Calvin, Luke, Luther, Justus, Daniel, Thomas Phineas William, Hemon, Hannah, Lucretia Nye and Martha

(VI) Luther Perry, son of Phineas Perry, was born at Barre, February 14, 1770, and died there, July 2, 1845, aged seventy-six years He was a delegate to the Rutland Convention, January 6, 1801 He married, at Barre, March 15, 1801, Harriet Howes, who died there in March, 1810, aged twenty-six years, of spotted fever (church records) Children, born at Barre Harriet Howes, born April 5, 1802, died young; Charles Howes, mentioned below; Mary Bourne March 18, 1806.

(VII) Charles Howes Perry, son of Luther Perry, was born at Barre, January 18, 1804 His sister, Mary B Perry, deeded to him her share in the estate of Edmund Howes, their grandfather, April 5, 1828 Other deeds show that he was living in Phillipston in 1834, and that he was a tanner and currier by trade and his wife Mary deeded the homestead on the north side of the turnpike in Phillipston, June 28, 1837, to Jonathan Bowker, Jr Mr Perry married (first) (intention dated November 6, 1830, at Phillipston) Comfort H Bates, born September 11, 1811, died at Phillipston, March, 1834, aged twenty-four years He married (second) (intention dated April 4, 1835, at Phillipston) Mary B Peckham, of Petersham, born 1815, died 1896 Children by first wife Susan, born July 16, 1832, Comfort H, born March 10, 1834 Children by second wife Charles M, men-

tioned below; Caroline, born January 1839, married Mason Whitney; Matilda, born April 30, 1841, married J Munroe Rich, member of Company D, Thirty-sixth Regiment, Massachusetts Volunteers, Luther, born October 30, 1843, resides in Athol, Massachusetts, Mary, born March 30, 1846, married Henry H Coolidge, of Athol, Massachusetts, Anson born June 8, 1848, resides in Providence, Rhode Island, Henrietta, born April 5, 1850, died September 29, 1851, Henry H, born February 20, 1852, died August 15, 1859

(VIII) Charles M Perry, son of Charles Howes Perry, was born at Phillipston, November 9, 1837 and died at Worcester, May 22, 1897 He received his education in the public schools of his native town, and during his youth followed the trade of shoemaking there He removed to Worcester and entered the employ of N W Holden Company, grocers, as a clerk, a position he filled for a number of years Subsequently he engaged in the street sprinkling business and was among the first in this line of industry in the city of Worcester At the present time the streets are sprinkled or oiled by the municipality and the cost assessed on the abutting property At that time the sprinkling was a private enterprise and the property owners along the route paid for the service voluntarily Mr Perry and C W Clapp entered into partnership, their place of business being at the City Stock Yard, No 216 Summer street, Worcester, where they conducted a sales stable, dealing in horses and cattle A few years later Mr Clapp sold his share of the business to B W Abbott and the name of the firm was changed to B W Abbott & Company During the last twenty years of his life Mr Perry was the owner of the High Street Boarding Stables at No 59 High street, Worcester He leased the building there and conducted the business in a highly successful manner As the city population grew, his business extended and he became widely known in the community He was accounted an excellent judge of horses and was skillful in their care and training During the Civil War he served in Company H, Thirty-sixth Regiment, Massachusetts Volunteer Infantry He was a member of George H Ward Post, No 10, of Worcester In religion he was a Methodist and for many years an attendant of Grace Methodist Episcopal Church He married (first) at Phillipston, Hannah E Gilbert, born January 29, 1841, died at Hubbardston, February 1, 1866 He married (second) November 27, 1867, Ellen M Garfield, born June 4, 1839. Children by first wife Flora A, born in Phillipston, November 5, 1859, Warren born February 18, 1862, died August 18, 1864 Children by second wife Charles H, mentioned below, Lillian M, born September 30, 1874, married George H Howland, Alice, born November 26, 1877, died October 28, 1884 Mr Perry was generous, kind, painstaking and honest, and while he was a man of many cares, he was possessed of one dominant ambition and that was to see his son, Charles H, graduate from Harvard College, but the fates decreed differently, for he died May 22, 1897, while his son was taking his examinations preparatory to receiving his degree

(IX) Dr Charles H Perry, son of Charles M Perry, was born in Worcester, May 10, 1869 He received his early education in the public schools of his native city, beginning in the old "Summer Street" school, which he attended for four years, then spent a similar period of time in study at the "Thomas Street" school. Brought up under the watchful guidance of a painstaking father, who knew the full value of early training, Dr Perry knew the meaning of hard work long before his schoolboy friends, for, during many years of his grammar school training, he delivered milk to customers in the early mornings, and performed many chores after school hours, selling newspapers during the early evenings and later assisting his father in and around the stable, each successive day seeing the same routine Early in life Dr Perry's fondness for animals, and horses especially, was very marked, and at the age of twelve years he was a jockey, and during the following four years he successfully rode the celebrated "Peacock" for a private Worcester family, winning many races and taking many coveted purses of a substantial size Dr Perry's successes stimulated him as the years went on, and from private riding he engaged in driving professional race horses, continuing until he was twenty-five years of age. Then came the turning point in Dr Perry's life, through an accident to one of his fancy horses It was at a meet at the old Agricultural Fair Grounds that "Koon Kan," the pride of the lot, was overcome by sunstroke and removed from the track While watching the veterinary surgeons work, he stoutly declared that he could save the horse if allowed to, but because of his youth and non-professional knowledge of horses, at that time, he was not allowed to do so, and he then vowed to "take up medicine," the success of which is here given, and attested to, not only in Worcester, but all over the State of Massachusetts Dr Perry trained a string of fifteen or sixteen professional race horses

Dr. Perry entered the Veterinary School of Harvard University, in 1894, and graduated in the class of 1897 Immediately afterward he began to practice, opening an office at No 59 High street,

95

and resided at No 22 Wellington street His wide acquaintance among the owners of horses and stock in this section paved the way for an excellent business, and from the beginning he enjoyed a substantial patronage Two years later he moved to his present location, No 82 Park avenue In 1904 Dr Perry took a post-graduate course in the Chicago Veterinary College

Since 1894 he has been the local officer of the Massachusetts Cattle Commissioners, afterward known as the Massachusetts Cattle Bureau, and now the Department of Animal Industry The duties of this office have grown from year to year and its responsibilities have increased as the laws have been made more stringent regarding the inspection of cattle in dairies and all kinds of meat offered for sale For fourteen years Dr Perry held the office of inspector of animals in the city of Worcester At times, when epidemics attacked the animals of the city, Dr Perry's duties became extremely important to the public health and to the farmers whose stock was threatened During the recent epidemic of the foot and mouth disease, he handled a trying and difficult situation with tact, energy and efficiency, and received the commendation not only of his superior officers but of the owners of infected stock and of others whose property was saved by the prompt suppression of the disease in this section While the disease threatened, Dr Perry worked day and night to stay its progress At other times, when epidemics of lesser magnitude have appeared, his efforts have been equally prompt and thorough His work in inspecting the meat supply of the city has been an important factor in guarding the public health His office represents more than is realized by the public, for it is charged with the application of scientific knowledge to the problems of providing a healthful food supply, and to detect and stamp out diseases of all kinds among the animals

In his private practice, Dr Perry has been highly successful He has a modern hospital for the care of sick animals of all kinds, and it is equipped with the latest apparatus and appliances for surgical and medical treatment, and with a pharmacy in which the drugs and medicines are kept An inspection of his hospital shows that better provision is now made for animals than were available for human beings fifty years ago The owners of horses, cows, dogs and other domestic animals have found by experience that it is not only proper and humane to give treatment to animals in times of sickness but that it is wisdom from an economical standpoint It saves money to fight disease with modern scientific knowledge and equipment Dr Perry ranks among the foremost of his profession in this country and is widely known through the State Owing to illness diagnosed as partial paralysis (1908) Dr Perry was forced to give up night work, and is now (1917) improving nicely He is a member of the Massachusetts Veterinary Association, the American Veterinary Medical Association, the Harvard Club and other social organizations of Worcester He served as house surgeon at Harvard College during his last year, 1896-97

Dr Perry married, June 27, 1892, Mary J Newton, daughter of Seth S and Henrietta (Frary) Newton, of Greenfield, Massachusetts She was a native of Greenfield, and attended the public schools there, graduating from the Greenfield High School in the class of 1884 She entered the State Normal School in Worcester, in February, 1885, from which she was graduated in due course in 1887 She followed the profession of teaching for a number of years, having schools at Shelburne, Massachusetts, one term, at Sunderland High School, Sunderland, Massachusetts, one term, and then came to Worcester where she held a position in the Quinsigamond School for four years. Her last position as teacher was in the Salisbury Street School. She resigned shortly before the expiration of a year in order to prepare for her approaching marriage. Mrs Perry is prominent in social life. Dr and Mrs Perry are members of Plymouth Congregational Church. They are the parents of one child, Roger Newton, mentioned below.

(X) Roger Newton Perry, son of Dr Charles H Perry, was born March 12, 1894, in Worcester. He is widely known as the "Boy Florist." He attended the public schools quite irregularly, owing to sickness, but graduated from Becker's Business College in 1909. His further study was cut short and his professional career that had been planned abandoned on account of the loss of his eyesight as the result of illness. He began his flower gardens as a means of occupying his time, and as his health and sight improved he extended his gardens and operated on a commercial scale with marked success. At the present time (1917) with his eyesight fully restored and in the enjoyment of excellent health, he finds himself the owner of a substantial business and a large plant. He has also what counts most, a thorough knowledge of plants and flowers and skill in their cultivation. In a recent book Dr Woods Hutchinson cited the Worcester "Boy Florist" as an example of what courage, persistence and hope will do for the afflicted. In 1913 he took the extension course of Amherst Agricultural College. His greenhouses extend from Park avenue to Montvale road and cover an area of one acre. Half the space is devoted to the cultivation of

bulbs for which he has built substantial concrete beds. The flowers from his greenhouses stand comparison with those from the most noted conservatories of the State. He has proved a valuable assistant to his father in the management of the animal hospital and the care of its patients.

SARGENT, James Sanborn,
Business Man

James Sanborn Sargent, son of Jeremiah S Sargent, was born at Sydney, Maine, August 13, 1835, and was educated there in the public schools. In 1865 he removed to Newport, Maine, where he engaged in the hardware business and continued for a period of twenty-five years. In 1886 he bought a hardware store in Brockton, Massachusetts, and in partnership with his son, Charles L Sargent, conducted the business for five years. At the end of this time he retired on account of ill health. In 1891, accompanied by his wife, he went to California, in the hope of restoring his health, but the journey proved too much of an effort, and he died the day after arriving, in Pasadena, California, December 20, 1891. Mrs Sargent returned with the body, and the interment took place in Union Cemetery, Brockton.

Mr Sargent was well known and highly respected in the community. He was a charter member of Electric Lodge, Independent Order of Odd Fellows, of Brockton, and for, many years he was its treasurer. He was also a member of the Masonic organization. In religion he was a Universalist. Mr Sargent was a quiet, reserved and modest man, gifted with much business ability and beloved by those who came to know him well. In his home he was a most devoted husband and father. He married Caroline Wil-

ENCYCLOPEDIA OF BIOGRAPHY

liams Ring, who survives him, and resides in Brockton

Charles L. Sargent, only child of James Sanborn and Caroline Williams (Ring) Sargent, was born at Newport, Maine, January 3, 1867. He was educated in the public schools of his native town and in the Bryant & Stratton Commercial College in Boston. In 1884 he established himself in the hardware business in Natick, Massachusetts, but two years later joined his father in Brockton. Together they made a very prosperous business in the store at No 83 Main street, and when his father retired in 1891, he continued with substantial success until the end of his life. He died June 20, 1914, at his summer home, Sebasticook Cottage, at Point Independence, Onset, Massachusetts. The interment was in Union Cemetery, Brockton

For a period of nearly thirty years, during which time he was a merchant in Brockton, he took a leading place among the business men of that city, extending his business as the city grew, keeping pace with the progress and always maintaining a high standard of honor in all his dealings. His integrity was proverbial. He commanded the respect of every customer, every house with which he had business relations and his business extended to all parts of the county. He never married, but always shared his home with his mother, to whom he was greatly attached. Like his father, he was cut down in the prime of life at the time of his greatest usefulness, when his future seemed most promising. His loss to the community was severely felt. After his death, the store was sold by his mother. She resides at her old home on Warren street in Brockton

Charles L. Sargent was a member of the Commercial Club of Brockton, and was distinguished for his public spirit.

His chief recreation was yachting, and during the summer for many years he spent much of his time on the water in Buzzard's Bay

(The Ring Line)

(I) Robert Ring or Ringe, the immigrant ancestor, was born in England, in 1614, and came to this country in the ship "Bevis," in 1638. He settled soon afterward in Salisbury, Massachusetts, and was living in that town in 1640, when admitted a freeman of the colony. In the same year he shared in a division or common lands and had previously shared in an earlier division. He was engaged in fishing and planting at Ring's Island in 1642, though by trade he was a cooper. He was a taxpayer and householder in 1677, signed a petition of the inhabitants of Salisbury in 1680, and died there in 1690. His will was dated January 23, 1688, and proved March 31, 1691. By wife Elizabeth, he had children Hannah, Elizabeth, Martha, Jarvis, John, Joseph and Robert.

In later generations his descendants settled in various parts of New Hampshire and Maine, as well as Massachusetts. His son Joseph, born August 4, 1664, was a soldier participating in the capture of Casco Bay fort, was witness in court in 1692, but died before May, 1705, when his brother Jarvis was appointed to administer his estate.

Deacon Seth Ring, of the third generation, lived in Newington, New Hampshire, and had children Joseph, Benjamin, Jane, Mary, Seth and Eliphalet, was deacon of the Newington church. His descendants lived in this section and at Chichester, New Hampshire. Seth owned land in Barnstead and Portsmouth.

Iphidiah Ring, a descendant of Robert Ring or Ringe, was born in New Hampshire, probably in one of the towns near

98

Portsmouth, during the Revolutionary War His birth was not recorded, and the name of his father has not been found by the writer He made his home in Newport, Maine, and followed farming for a vocation Children Almon B , mentioned below, Joseph, Orin, Elbridge Gerry, Lucinda, Pamelia

Almon B Ring, son of Iphidiah Ring, was born in Newport, Maine, in 1810 By trade he was a stone mason and in later years a mason and contractor In politics he was a Republican, in religion a Baptist He married at Newport, Maine, Mary Tuttle, who was born in 1802, in Durham, Maine Children Mary A, born 1833, Frank W, 1835, Alfred W, 1837; Elbridge Gerry, mentioned below, Pamelia L, 1841, Charles H, 1843 The four eldest were born at Palmyra and the two youngest at Newport He died at North Newport.

Elbridge Gerry Ring, son of Almon B Ring, was born February 23, 1839, in Palmyra, and educated in the public schools He has been for many years engaged in carriage building at Bath, Maine, and Amesbury, Massachusetts His present home is at Newport, Maine. He served four years in the Civil War in Company C, First Massachusetts Heavy Artillery, and was wounded in the battle of Spottsylvania He is at the present time commander of the Grand Army Post of Newport He married, November 3, 1868, at Newport, Mary A Shaw, who was born at Augusta, Maine, September 28, 1845, daughter of John and Madama (Rowell) Shaw Children Sydney B, born December 1, 1872, a travelling salesman, married Leona H Weymouth, Jessie M, born February 13, 1876, now assistant cashier of the Newport Trust Company

Elbridge Gerry Ring, uncle of Elbridge Gerry Ring, mentioned above, and

son of Iphidiah Ring, was born at Newport, Maine, about 1803, and died in 1867 He was a shoe dealer and manufacturer of boots and shoes at Newport, where he spent all his active years and where he died He married Deborah Nye (see Nye XVI) She died at Newport Children Augusta, died in 1868, Caroline Williams, married James Sanborn Sargent (see Sargent), Josephine, born Sargent (see Sargent), Josephine, born who married Seldon Foss, and removed to Portland, Oregon, where she died

(The Nye Line)

The surname Nye, according to the genealogy, appears first in the middle of the thirteenth century in the Sjelland section of Denmark, and in Danish the word signifies new or newcomer, when used as a preface. It was not adopted as a surname until after the family settled in England The Nye coat-of-arms is described Azure a crescent argent Crest Two horns couped counterchanged, azure and argent

(I) Lave, a Dane to whom the line is traced in the Nye genealogy, was a son of a descendant of Harold Blautand, who died in 985, through a daughter who married one of the most famous of the Swedish medieval heroes, Stryibiorn, son of Olaf, King of Sweden He became prominent, and in 1316 was bishop of Boskilde

(II) Sven was heir of Svencin, descendant of Lave, in 1346

(III) Marten was declared heir of Sven in 1363

(IV) Nils was mentioned in 1418 as owning land in Tudse

(V) Bertolf, mentioned in 1466, as son of Nils, had sons, James and Randolf James fought a duel and was obliged to flee to England, whither he was accompanied by his younger brother, mentioned below

(VI) Randolph Nye settled in Sussex,

England, in 1527, and held land in Uck-field

(VII) William Nye, son of Randolph Nye, married Agnes, daughter of Ralph Tregian, of Hertfordshire, studied for the ministry and became rector of the parish church of Ballance-Horned, before his father died

(VIII) Ralph Nye, son of William Nye, inherited his father's estate in Uck-field and Ballance; married, June 18, 1556, Margaret Merynge, of St Mary's, Wollchurch Children Thomas, mentioned below, Edmundus, buried in Somersetshire, March 9, 1594, Ralph, married, August 30, 1584, Joan Wilkshire, Anne, married, August 6, 1616, Nicholas Stuart, Mary, married, April 24, 1621, John Banister

(IX) Thomas Nye, son of Ralph Nye, married, September 6, 1583, at St Andrew, Hubbard, Katherine Poulsden, of London, daughter of ——— Poulsden, of Horley, County Surrey He sold to his wife's brother, William Poulsden, a tenement builded with a croft adjoining, containing sixteen acres and a half in Bidlenden, County Kent, for which he received an annuity of four shillings Children Henry, graduate of Oxford, 1611, vicar of Cobham, County Surrey, and rector of Clapham, County Sussex, Philip, graduate of Oxford, 1619, rector of St Michael's, Cornhill and Acton, Middlesex, a celebrated preacher in Cromwell's time, John, Thomas, mentioned below

(X) Thomas (2) Nye, son of Thomas (1) Nye, was a haberdasher of Bidlenden, County Kent; married, June 10, 1619, Agnes Nye, aged thirty-nine years, widow of Henry Nye He deeded land to his youngest son Thomas in Bidlenden, July 4, 1637, stating in the conveyance, "ye eldest son Benjamin having gone to New England" Children Benjamin,

mentioned below, Thomas, born September 16, 1623, married Margaret Webster and left descendants at Bidlenden

(XI) Benjamin Nye, son of Thomas (2) Nye, was born May 4, 1620, at Bidlenden, England, and came in the ship "Abigail" to Lynn, Massachusetts, in 1635, locating in Sandwich two years later His name is on the list of men in Sandwich able to bear arms in 1643 He contributed to the cost of building a mill there in 1654, and for the fund to build the meeting house in 1656 He was surveyor of highways in 1655, took the oath of fidelity in 1657; grand juror, 1658 and later; constable in 1661 and 1675, collector of taxes in 1674 and later He received twelve acres of land from the town for building his mill at the little pond and had other grants of land later He was given permission by vote of the town to build a fulling mill on Spring Hill river, August 8, 1675, and it is said that the ruins of his old mill may still be seen there He married in Sandwich, October 19, 1640, Katherine Tupper, daughter of Rev Thomas Tupper Children Mary, married Jacob Burgess, John, Ebenezer, Jonathan, born November 29, 1649, Mercy, April 4, 1652, Caleb, Nathan, Benjamin, killed by Indians, March 26, 1676

(XII) John Nye, son of Benjamin Nye, was born at Sandwich about 1645 His will was dated July 19, 1720, and proved November 27, 1722 He and his brother bought one hundred acres in Falmouth and in 1689 were granted two hundred acres more He held various town offices in Sandwich He married Esther Shedd His wife's will was dated September 18, 1724, proved September 29, 1726 Children, born in Sandwich Benjamin, born November 24, 1673, John, November 22, 1675; Abigail, April 18, 1678; Experience, December 16, 1682, Hannah, January 19,

1685, Ebenezer, September 23, 1687, Peleg, mentioned below, Nathan, Joseph, 1694, Cornelius, 1697

(XIII) Peleg Nye, son of John Nye, was born at Sandwich, November 12, 1689, and died 1761 His will was dated November 4, and proved December 7, 1761 He married, June 26, 1717, Elizabeth Bryant Children, born in Sandwich Nathaniel, June 17, 1719, Elizabeth, May 22, 1721, Joseph, mentioned below, Abigail, March 5, 1725-26.

(XIV) Joseph Nye, son of Peleg Nye, was born at Sandwich, October 21, 1723, and died there in 1790 His will was dated January 23, and proved February 9, 1790 He married, December 23, 1756, Elizabeth Holman, of Sandwich Children, born in Sandwich Elisha, November 2, 1757, Bartlett, mentioned below, Temperance, May 3, 1762, Lemuel, October 14, 1764, Jane, 1766, Bryant, September 13, 1767, Joseph, October 30, 1771, Heman, November 23, 1773, Peleg, July 9, 1778

(XV) Bartlett Nye, son of Joseph Nye, was born at Sandwich, August 18, 1759 He was a soldier in the Revolution in Captain Job Crocker's company, of Eastham, in Colonel Nathan's regiment, July 2 to December 12, 1777, in Rhode Island; a corporal in Captain Simeon Fish's company, Colonel Freeman's regiment, September, 1779 In 1812 he was a deputy to the General Court from Fairfield, Maine, whither he moved in 1788 He died there in 1822 He married Deborah Ellis, of Sandwich She died in 1840 Children Thomas, Ellis, Bartlett, Jane, Joshua, Franklin, Sturgis, Stephen, Patty, Heman, born June 17, 1803, Dolly, married William Norvell, Sally Franklin, and Deborah

(XVI) Deborah Nye, daughter of Bartlett Nye, born at Fairfield about 1805, married Elbridge Gerry Ring (see Ring)

WHITE,

And Allied Families

On either side of the line separating the States of Massachusetts and Rhode Island, in the ancient town of Rehoboth, Massachusetts, lived the Round (often spelled Rounds) family, which was of some two hundred years record As early as 1711 the name is recorded in Rehoboth At that date, John Round, of Swansea, Massachusetts, was married to Hannah Carde, of Rehoboth, and a little later, in 1715, the marriage of Thomas Round and Sarah Thurston was recorded Still earlier the vital records of births are given in that town with the children of the family of Richard and Ann Round, namely Amy, born June 10, 1702, Anne, February 6, 1704-05, Richard, March 2, 1706-07, Hannah, January 29, 1710-11, Joanna, April 23, 1713 This family was then referred to as of Barrington and Rehoboth Thomas Round, probably in January or February, 1744-45, married Elizabeth West

(I) John Rounds (or more probably Round), the first of the branch of the family herein followed of whom we have any information, was a resident of Swansea, Massachusetts He married there, Abigail Bowen, daughter of Obediah Bowen, and among their children was Jabez, of whom further.

(II) Jabez Round, son of John and Abigail (Bowen) Rounds or Round, was born in Swansea, Massachusetts, 1708, and died March 14, 1790 He was married in Rehoboth, Massachusetts, April 26, 1733, by the Rev John Coomer, to Renew Carpenter, of Rehoboth, born June 6, 1714, died February 9, 1787, daughter of Jotham and Desire (Martin) Carpenter (see Carpenter) They were the parents of eleven children, all born in Rehoboth, among whom was Jabez, of whom further

(III) Jabez (2) Round, son of Jabez (1) and Renew (Carpenter) Round, was born in Rehoboth, Massachusetts, January 8, 1735-36, and died May 29, 1808 He was a Revolutionary soldier, served as private in Captain Simeon Cole's company, Colonel Thomas Carpenter's regiment, entered service on an alarm at Tiverton, Rhode Island, August 1, 1780, discharged August 8, 1780 He was married in Rehoboth, Massachusetts, March 6, 1760, by Elder Nathan Pearce, to Prudence Crossman, of Taunton, Massachusetts, born 1740, and died October 27, 1825 Children: Sylvester, of whom further, Betsey, born March 27, 1772; Jabez, Abner, Enos, Zena, Polly, Benjamin, Joseph, Prudence

(IV) Rev. Sylvester Round, son of Jabez (2) and Prudence (Crossman) Round, was born in Rehoboth, Massachusetts, April 10, 1762, and died October 26, 1824 In 1782-83 he became the pastor of the Six Principled Baptist church, known as the Rounds Church, in Rehoboth, of which the Rev David Round was the founder and pastor in July, 1743, and he continued as its pastor until his death He was also a Revolutionary soldier and served as a private in Captain Nathaniel Carpenter's company, Colonel Thomas Carpenter's regiment, service from July 20, 1777, one month and five days at Rhode Island, including travel to camp at Bristol, Rhode Island, and from Providence back to Rehoboth, also private in Captain Nathaniel Ide's company, Colonel Thomas Carpenter's regiment, enlisted August 13, 1779, discharged September 12, 1779, service one month, travel allowed to and from camp at Providence; company detached from militia for service at Rhode Island for four weeks under Captain Samuel Fisher, also private in Captain Joseph Wilmarth's company, Colonel Thomas Carpenter's regiment, marched July 28, 1780, discharged July 31, 1780, on an alarm at Rhode Island, company detached for six days' service and marched from Rehoboth to Tiverton, Rhode Island, and there served under General Heath He was married by Elder Nathan Pearce, October 11, 1781, to Mehitable Perry, born in Rehoboth, September 7, 1760, daughter of David and Margaret (Dyer) Perry Children: Rufus, born April 8 1783, Roxa, March 6, 1784, Mehitable, December 29, 1785, Sylvester, January 9, 1788, Betsey, of whom further, David Perry, April 14, 1792, Keziah, February 22, 1794; Deney March 7, 1797, Lydia, June 11, 1799, Emerancy, August 28, 1803

(V) Betsey Round, daughter of the Rev Sylvester and Mehitable (Perry) Round, was born in Rehoboth, Massachusetts, April 14 1790 She was married by her father to Samuel Woodward, of Taunton, Massachusetts, December 13, 1810 He was a descendant of John Woodward, who married, November 11, 1675, Sarah Crossman Israel Woodward, who may have been a brother of John Woodward, married, August 4, 1670, in Taunton, Jane Godfrey Samuel Woodward, a descendant of one of the above mentioned Woodwards, resided in Norton, Massachusetts, and there married Rebecca ———, and several of their children were born in Norton Ambrose Woodward, son of Samuel Woodward, was born in Norton Massachusetts, September 9, 1743, and died in Taunton, Massachusetts, March 28, 1828 He was a Revolutionary soldier, served as private in Captain Ichabod Leonard's Sixth Taunton Company, Colonel George Williams' regiment, service nine days, company marched to Warren, viz., Rehoboth on the alarm at Rhode Island, December 8, 1776 He was married in Taunton, Massachusetts, by George Godfrey, Esq, December 24, 1772, to Rachel Lincoln, she died January 5, 1815, in Taunton He must have married (second) Abigail ———, as she died a widow of Ambrose Woodward, April 17, 1841, aged eighty-two years Samuel Woodward, son of Samuel and Rachel (Lincoln) Woodward, was born in Taunton, Massachusetts, September 17, 1785, and died December 31, 1838 He married, in Rehoboth, Massachusetts, Betsey Round, as aforementioned, and their children, all born in Taunton, were as follows Samuel E, born July 16, 1811, Rinaldo B, April 10, 1813, Sylvester, March, 1818, Williard Francis, of whom further; Elizabeth Abby, October 17, 1828, Albert Augustus, April 16, 1833, Julia Ann, December 19, 1836 Mrs Samuel Woodward, the mother of these children, died July 4, 1876, aged eighty-six years, two months, twenty-one days

(VI) Williard Francis Woodward, son of Samuel and Betsey (Round) Woodward, was born in Taunton, Massachusetts, June 27, 1826 He learned the trade of moulder, which he followed for a number of years, and later was engaged in agricultural pursuits near the Norton line, being particularly interested in stock raising and in trading cattle He was a man of robust constitution, which was his great asset, and he was widely known for his enterprising and progressive ideas, and honored and respected for his many excellencies of character, especially for his devotion to his home and family His marriage intentions were published in Rehoboth, Massachusetts, December 29, 1847, and he married, in 1848 Julia Ann Smith, born in Rehoboth, March 16, 1826, daughter of John, Jr, and Hannah (Lewis) Smith, and their children were as follows Henry, deceased, Estelle, died in early life, Eugene, living in Attle-

boro, Emily, living in Attleboro, Julia Isabel, of whom further, Lottie Maria, now deceased, Edgar Elmer, resides at the homestead in Taunton Mr Woodward died at his home on Worcester street, Taunton, after a short illness in 1870 His remains were interred in Oakland Cemetery His widow died at the home of her daughter, Mrs Williard H White, in Attleboro, March 15, 1912, and her remains were interred beside those of her husband

(VII) Julia Isabel Woodward, daughter of Williard Francis and Julia Ann (Smith) Woodward, was born in Taunton, Massachusetts, August 19, 1857 She married, October 16, 1877, Williard H White, born in Taunton, Massachusetts, December 23, 1855, and died September 28, 1884, while in his young manhood He learned the trade of machinist and served in that capacity in the Masons Machine Shop in Taunton Mrs White, who is living at the present time (1917) is a resident of Attleboro, Massachusetts, where she is quite active in the social and civic life, holding membership in the Attleboro Woman's Club, and the Equal Suffrage League She is devoted to her home and family, which consists of two children 1 Gertrude Elma, wife of Robert Murray Bates, son of the Rev John Bates, and they have one daughter, Glenna Isabel, they reside in Attleboro 2 Ernest E, resides in Attleboro, is a jeweler, married Zulmar Dorrance Briggs Mrs Julia Isabel White is a member of Margaret Corbin Chapter, Daughters of the American Revolution, of Boston; a member of the Women's Auxiliary of the Chamber of Commerce, of Attleboro; and a member of the Ladies' Aid of the Sturdy Memorial Hospital Association, of Attleboro

Williard H White was a descendant of Nicholas White, who was a native of

103

England, and settled in Dorchester, Massachusetts, where he was made a freeman in 1643. He married there Susanna Humphrey, and they were the parents of four children. Between the years 1652 and 1655 the family moved to Taunton, where he spent the remainder of his life. Their eldest son, Nicholas White, Jr, was born in Dorchester, and later accompanied his parents to Taunton. He married, December 9, 1673, Ursula Macomber, daughter of William and Ursula Macomber, and they were the parents of seven children. Mrs White died in Norton, Massachusetts, January 18, 1727-28. Their youngest child, Thomas White, was born in Taunton, Massachusetts, where he spent his entire lifetime, and died in 1730. He married Abigail Crossman, born October 7, 1690, died January 22, 1767, daughter of John and Joanna (Thayer) Crossman, and they were the parents of eight children, among whom was John White, born in Taunton, who spent his entire life there, passing away January 26, 1806, aged ninety-four years, and was buried in the cemetery at the corner of Prospect Hill and Lothrop street, Taunton. He was one of the largest land owners in that town. He married, May 30, 1748, Mary Smith, born February 21, 1728, and lived to a ripe old age, daughter of Nicholas and Jerusha (Leonard) Smith. One of their ten children was John White, born in Taunton, Massachusetts, in 1749, and died there, February 14, 1828. He made his home near Scadding's Pond, where he owned a farm which he later sold and moved to the town of Norton, Massachusetts, but subsequently returned to Taunton. He served as a soldier in the Revolutionary War, member of Captain Oliver Soper's company, Continental Line, in 1776, and the tradition is that he was also a privateer in the Revolution. His marriage intentions were published April 26, 1777. He married Susanna (White) Pierce, daughter of George and Hannah (Bryant) White, and widow of Elisha Pierce. One of their eight children was Isaac White, born in Taunton, Massachusetts, January 30, 1785, and died there, February 5, 1863. He was a member of the Raynham company in the War of 1812. He married, August 2, 1806, Matilda Frasier, born in Raynham, September 6, 1788, and died in Taunton, November 9, 1869. One of their twelve children was Kingman White, born in Taunton, Massachusetts, May 8, 1809, spent his life there, and died January 11, 1863. He married, April 8, 1841. Polly Elma Leonard, who died November 16, 1876. They were the parents of seven children. Emeline, born August 10, 1842, died September 7, 1842; Oliver Allen, February 7, 1844, now deceased; Ira Alden, December 8, 1845, died February 18, 1866; Etson Holbrook, twin of Ira Alden, both Civil War soldiers and now deceased; Matilda Jane, born August 22, 1850, married Warner Alden, of Middleboro, he now deceased; Warren Clifford, born March 21, 1853, died June 6, 1854; and Williard Horace, born December 23, 1855, aforementioned as the husband of Julia Isabel Woodward.

(The Carpenter Line)

(I) William Carpenter, pioneer ancestor of the line herein followed, was born in England in 1605. He came to America in the ship "Bevis" in 1638. He was admitted freeman of Weymouth, May 13, 1640, was representative of Weymouth in 1641, 1643, and from the town of Rehoboth in 1645, constable in 1641. He was admitted as an inhabitant of Rehoboth, March 28, 1645. Governor Bradford, who married his cousin, Alice, manifested great friendship for William Carpenter and favored him in all his measures in the Plymouth Court. The town records of Rehoboth commenced in 1643. The territory of the town included what is now called Attleboro, Seekonk, a part of Cumberland, Swansea and East Providence. Many of the Carpenter residents of these towns are treated as being residents of the old town of Rehoboth, though they may have resided in some one of the other towns. He served as one of the proprietors and town clerk from 1643 until 1649. In 1645 William Carpenter, with others, was chosen to look after the interests of the town, and again in the same year William Carpenter was chosen, with others, to hear and decide on grievances in regard to the division of land by lots. In 1647 he was chosen as one of the directors of the town, also again in 1655. In 1653 his name was written William Carpenter, Sr., for the first time. The first settlement of the colony of Rehoboth consisted of fifty-eight members from Weymouth, who drew lots in the division of lands, June 31, 1644, and William Carpenter's name in that division stands number ten. The houses of the colony were built in a semi-circle around Seekonk Common, and opened toward Seekonk river. This semi-circle was called "The Ring of the Town." At a meeting of the proprietors in 1644 it was voted that nine men should be chosen to order the prudential affairs of the plantation and that they should have the power to dispose of the lands in lots of twelve, eight or six acres, "as in their discretion they think the quality of the estate of the person do require." This applies to house lots. The residence of William Carpenter appears by the description given in his will and by tradition to have been located in the "Ring" directly east of the meeting house. At a meeting the same year (1644) it was ordered "for the time past, and time to

come, that all workmen that have worked or shall work in any common work or for any particular person shall have for their wages for each day's work as follows. For each laborer from the first day of November until the first day of February, eighteen pence per day, and for the rest of the year twenty pence per day, except in harvest, for six oxen and one man seven shillings and six pence per day, and for eight oxen eight shillings." The price fixed for wheat was four shillings and six pence per bushel. Wampum was fixed at eight for a penny. About 1642 William Carpenter was appointed captain for one or more years by the General Court of Massachusetts at Boston. This appointment was made necessary by the attempt of Samuel Gorton and his followers to seize portions of the lands included in the Providence Plantations, claiming them as their own by right of purchase from the Indians. In 1643-44 troops were sent from Massachusetts to arrest Gorton and his followers, but being resisted by them the troops were ordered to open fire which brought them to submission, and they were taken to Boston and imprisoned. William Carpenter married Abigail ———, and they had seven children. John, William, Joseph, Hannah, Abiah, Abigail and Samuel.

(II) Joseph Carpenter, son of William and Abigail Carpenter, was born in England, probably about 1633. He accompanied his parents to America, he being then five years of age. He was one of the founders of the first Baptist church in Massachusetts, in 1663. The Rev. Mr. Miles formed the fourth Baptist church in America at Swansea, Massachusetts, consisting of seven members, among whom was Joseph Carpenter, who contributed to the building of the house, in consequence of which he was fined five

105

pounds and prohibited from worship for the space of one month. The variance that appeared in their religious belief did not disturb his business relations with the family or settlers of Rehoboth as he was one of the company of the North Purchase and drew one share. He moved from Rehoboth to Swansea in 1661-62, soon after his father died. The Plymouth Colony Records say that on "May 25, 1657, Joseph Carpenter had eight acres of land granted him, adjoining the lot he now liveth on, which was given to John Titus." His will was dated May 3, 1676, he gave land to his three sons, Joseph, Benjamin and John; he also gave to them his rights in the common of Rehoboth, likewise his rights in Swansea. He married, May 25, 1655, Margaret Sutton, daughter of John Sutton. Children. 1 Joseph, born August 15, 1656, died February 26, 1718, he was a wheelwright, resided in Rehoboth and Swansea, he married, February 23, 1681, Mary ———, who died in 1717. 2 Benjamin, of whom further. 3 Abigail, born March 15, 1659. 4 Esther, born March 10, 1661. 5 Martha, born 1662, died March 22, 1735, at Swansea, Massachusetts. 6 and 7 John and Hannah, twins, born January 21, 1671-72, in Swansea. 8 Solomon, born April 27, 1673, died October 25, 1674, at Swansea. 9 Margaret, born May 4, 1675, married, January 4, 1695, Thomas Chaffee. Joseph Carpenter was buried May 6, 1675, two days after the birth of his youngest child, and his remains were interred near the one hundred acre cove in Barrington. His wife was buried in the East Providence burial ground. The stone is marked "M C D V, 1700, A G 65." The letters on this stone are very plain.

(III) Benjamin Carpenter, son of Joseph and Margaret (Sutton) Carpenter, was born January 19, 1658, and died May 22, 1727. He married (first) 1678-79 Re-

new Weeks, born in 1660, died July 29, 1703, daughter of William and Elizabeth Weeks, of Dorchester, Massachusetts. He married (second) November 27, 1706, Martha Toogood. She was living in 1727. Children of first wife. 1 Benjamin, born January 27, 1680, moved to Ashford, Connecticut, about the year 1733-34; a farmer; married, January 23, 1706, Mary Barney. 2 Jotham, of whom further. 3 Renew, born April 14, 1684, married, at Swansea, December 4, 1703, John West. 4 Elizabeth, born February 28, 1685-86, married ——— Winslow, of Swansea. 5 Hannah, born May 3, 1688, died October 2, 1768, married, October 23, 1725, David Thurston. 6 Jane, born March 31, 1690, died June 15, 1690. 7 John, born March 25, 1691-92, died in 1766, resided in Mansfield and Stafford, Connecticut, married (first) September 12, 1717, Sarah Thurston, who died October 24, 1744, aged fifty-three years, married (second) Martha H ———, of Windham; married (third) March 19, 1748, Hannah Martin, of Warwick, Rhode Island. 8 Submit, born June 22, 1693, died February 9, 1741, at Swansea. 9 Job, born March 16, 1695; married (first) Anne ———; married (second) December 17, 1764, Barbara Miller; resided in Rehoboth and Swansea. 10 Kesiah, born March 26, 1697, married Thomas Horton, published April 29, 1721, at Swansea. 11 Hezekiah, born March 27, 1699, died March 19, 1750; he gave a lot of land to the First Baptist Church of Newport, Rhode Island, in 1738, the lot was seventy-three by sixty-four and was situate on what is now West Broadway. The house was sold in 1738 and a new house erected on the same site, this was taken down and a new house erected in 1741. He was known as "Colonel Hezekiah." 12 Edward, born December 8, 1700, died December 12, 1778, at Swansea; married, August 12, 1724, Elizabeth Wilson, born

July 8, 1706, died April 24, 1791, daughter of Benjamin and Elizabeth Wilson, of Rehoboth

(IV) Jotham Carpenter, son of Benjamin and Renew (Weeks) Carpenter, was born in Rehoboth, Massachusetts, June 1, 1682, and died in 1760. According to "Savage" he was baptized at Dorchester, Massachusetts, June 1, 1683. Administration papers were taken out on Jotham Carpenter's estate as residing in Rehoboth by his son, Jotham Carpenter, of Rehoboth, at the probate office at Norton, Massachusetts dated August 14, 1760, by George Leonard, Jr, register. He married (first) July 10, 1707, Desire Martin, who died September 12, 1727. He married (second) June 6, 1728, Isabel Sherman. Children of first wife 1 Jotham, born August 1, 1708, died May 10, 1777, resided in Cumberland, Rhode Island, was constable of Rehoboth in 1735, served as deacon in the Baptist church in Rehoboth for a number of years, and from his removal to Cumberland until his death was deacon of the Baptist church there; he married (first) May 11, 1728, Mehitable Thompson; she died February 10, 1747; married (second) March 17, 1748, Freelove Kingsley, her will was dated October 12, 1801 2. Amos, born September 1, 1710 3 Hannah, born June 6 1712, published to David Round, August 29 1730 4 Renew, born June 6, 1714, married April 26 1733, Jabez Round (see Round II) 5 Desire, born June 3, 1716, married, April 15, 1738, Hezekiah Hix 6 Hezekiah, born January 6, 1725, married (first) August 16, 1745, at Johnson, Rhode Island, Phoebe Bowen, married (second) Prudence Johnson of Hopkinton, married (third) July 2 1769, Joanna Aldrich, of Mendon, he moved to Hopkinton from Johnson after his third marriage; he was a soldier of the Revolution

TINKHAM, Ebenezer,

Representative Citizen

The American families thus far traced descend from the first settler of the name in this country

(I) Sergeant Ephraim Tinkham came from Ashburham near Plymouth, England. He came no doubt under contract, in the service of Thomas Hatherly to pay his passage. In 1634 a transfer placed him in the service of John Winslow, the town of Duxbury granting him land, namely thirty-five acres. He became a proprietor, August 2, 1646, held offices of trust and honor, was prominent in public life both in civil and military service, was also selectman and sergeant, and in 1670 was admitted a freeman. In 1668, Ephraim Tinkham, Edward Gray and William Crowell comprised a commission to settle the bounds of the governor's lands at Plainsdealing. By deed of October 27, 1647, he and his wife sold to Henry Thompson a third part of a lot of land with dwelling and other buildings which belonged to Peter Brown. In 1662 he and twenty-five other men purchased the Indians the land territory which comprises the town of Middleborough, and here he made and built his home. He married, in 1647 or 1648, Mary, daughter of Peter Brown. Her father was a "Mayflower" passenger. His will of date January 17, 1683, was proven June 5, 1685, and bequeaths to wife Mary, and to children Ephraim, Ebenezer, Peter, Hezekiah John, Isaac, Mary Tomson. Children, born at Plymouth or Duxbury, Massachusetts Ephraim, mentioned below, Ebenezer, September 30, 1651. Peter, December 25, 1653; Hezekiah, February 8, 1656, John, June 7, 1658, Mary, August 5, 1661, John, November 15, 1663, Isaac, April 11, 1666

(II) Ephraim (2) Tinkham, eldest

child of Sergeant Ephraim (1) and Mary (Brown) Tinkham, was born August 1, 1649, in Duxbury, and died October 13, 1714, in Middleborough He was constable in 1681, was propounded for a freeman in 1682, and settled in Middleborough, Massachusetts By inheritance his father's house in Middleborough became his home He married, in 1678, Esther Wright, born in 1649, and died March 28, 1717 She was a granddaughter of Francis Cook, "Mayflower" passenger in 1620, and a great-granddaughter of Alexander Carpenter Children, born in Middleborough, Massachusetts: John, August 23, 1680, Jeremiah, mentioned below, Ephraim, born October 7, 1682, and died July 11, 1713, Isaac, June, 1685, Samuel, March 19, 1688

(III) Jeremiah Tinkham, son of Ephraim (2) and Esther (Wright) Tinkham, was born February 13, 1681, and died April 5, 1715 He married Joanna Powell, and resided in Middleborough, Massachusetts Among their children was Ebenezer, mentioned below.

(IV) Ebenezer Tinkham, son of Jeremiah and Joanna (Powell) Tinkham, was born December 16, 1714, and died November 17, 1801 He married Hannah Shaw, and among their children was Isaac, mentioned below

(V) Isaac Tinkham, son of Ebenezer and Hannah (Shaw) Tinkham, was born November 26, 1741, and died April 18, 1818 He married Lucretia Hammond, of Dartmouth, Massachusetts Children, born in Middleborough, Massachusetts 1 Elias, September 1, 1767 2 Betsey, born July 7, 1769, married Jeptha Whitman, April 14, 1790 3 Isaac, born April 29, 1773, died April 5, 1821; he served as a private in Captain Abishai Tinkham's company, Colonel Ebenezer Sproutts' regiment, entered service, May 6, discharged May 9, entered service Sep-

tember 6, discharged September 12, service nine days; company marched from Middleborough to Dartmouth on two alarms in 1778; muster rolls, "Massachusetts Soldiers and Sailors," volume xv, page 768. 4. Ebenezer, mentioned below 5 Ruth, born October 5, 1779, married Josiah Barrows, April 5, 1801 6 Nathaniel, born July 21, 1783, died April 14, 1856 7 Hannah, born December 4, 1789, died December 27, 1864

(VI) Ebenezer (2) Tinkham, son of Isaac and Lucretia (Hammond) Tinkham, was born December 13, 1777, in Middleboro, Massachusetts, and died March 11, 1856 He married, June 3, 1800, Hannah Morrison, daughter of William Morrison, of Middleboro. Children: Calvin, born March 16, 1801, married Harriet Harlow, Betsey, June 8, 1803, married Jacob Thomas, Sally, March 13, 1805, married Levi Morse; Hannah, August 30, 1808, married Jacob Bennett, Ebenezer, mentioned below; Elias, April 9, 1816, died April 30, 1817; William, April 13, 1818, died November 10, 1887; Abisha, April 23, 1820, married Hannah Harvey

(VII) Ebenezer (3) Tinkham, son of Ebenezer (2) and Hannah (Morrison) Tinkham, was born February 11, 1813, in Middleboro, Massachusetts, and died September 25, 1892, in Attleboro, Massachusetts He was located in Norton, his business for the most of his active life being the machinist's trade For a period of his life he lived in Attleboro and later in Pawtucket, Rhode Island Ebenezer Tinkham married (first) April 10, 1843, Adeline Arnold, born July 6, 1811, daughter of Lemuel and Ann (Hodges) Arnold, of Norton, Massachusetts. Children: Abbie Morrison, born March 8, 1844, married (first) Edward G Anthony, (second) William Sawyer, Frederick Wallace, December 24, 1845, married Ellen Plympton; Howard Arnold, September 21, 1847, married Elizabeth A Arnold, Annie Carpenter, June 20, 1857, married Charles R Bates Ebenezer Tinkham, the father, married (second) Alice Gruninger

(The Morrison Line)

(I) The founder of this family was William Morrison, of Plymouth county, Massachusetts He was a son of Robert Morrison. He settled in the town of Bridgewater, Massachusetts, in 1740. He died in prison during the French war, June 12, 1758 On November 10, 1748, he married Sarah Montgomery She married (second) William Strowbridge, Jr, of Middleboro Children William, mentioned below, Robert, born January 26, 1751, married Dorcas Staples, Alexander, baptized August 25, 1752, John, baptized December 22, 1754, James, born February 28, 1757

(II) William (2) Morrison, son of William (1) and Sarah (Montgomery) Morrison, was born August 16, 1749 He married, about 1773, Hannah Benton, born January 7, 1752, died March 13, 1825 Until 1805 they lived in Middleboro, when they removed to Farmington, Maine, where he died August 29, 1826 Children: William, born May 26, 1774, died January, 1788, Sally, February 11, 1776, married Adam Keith; Robert, February 19, 1778; Hannah, mentioned below, Betsey, April 28, 1782, John, March 3, 1784, Jane, January 31, 1786

(III) Hannah Morrison, daughter of William (2) and Hannah (Benton) Morrison, was born December 11, 1779 She married in Middleboro, Massachusetts, June 3, 1800, Ebenezer Tinkham (see Tinkham VI)

(The Arnold Line)

The origin of the Arnold family is among the ancient princes of Wales

They trace from Gnir, a paternal descendant of Cadwalader, King of the Britons From this ancestry came Roger Arnold, of Llanthony, in Monmouthshire He was the first of the family to adopt a surname Roger Arnold, Esq, married Joan, daughter of Sir Thomas Gamage, Knight Lord of Coytey Mr Arnold's descent was twelfth generation in direct line from Gnir, King of Gwentland.

(I) Joseph Arnold, the American ancestor, was born in England about 1625, and settled early in Braintree, Massachusetts He resided in the eastern part of Braintree, now the city of Quincy, on Quincy avenue To his youngest son, Ephraim, he deeded the homestead, November 25, 1696 He married at Braintree, June 8, 1648, Rebecca Curtis, who died August 14, 1693 Children William, born March 16, 1649, died young, John, April 3, 1650, died young, Joseph, October 8, 1652, died young, John, April 29, 1655, Samuel, August 7, 1658, died same day, Ephraim, mentioned below

(II) Ephraim Arnold, son of Joseph and Rebecca (Curtis) Arnold, was born in Braintree, Massachusetts, June 11, 1664, lived also in Boston He married Mary ———, and their children were Samuel, mentioned below, Mary, born October 1, 1690, married Benjamin Hammond; Ephraim, July 21, 1695, Rebecca, married, December 11, 1722, Jonathan French

(III) Samuel Arnold, son of Ephraim and Mary Arnold, was born January 7, 1689, in Braintree He was drowned in the Neponset river, February 9, 1743 He married Sarah Webb, daughter of Christopher and Mary (Bass) Webb She was born December 18, 1688 Children, born in Braintree Samuel, May 16, 1713, died young, Mary, December 22, 1714, married John Spear, Sarah, September 14, 1716, married Benjamin Hunt, Joseph,

October 11, 1718, married Mary Butts, John, October 4, 1720, died February 11, 1738, Moses, June 11, 1722, Abigail, February 12 1725, married Samuel Savel, Nathaniel, October 18, 1726, Deborah, November 14, 1729, died December 14, 1792, David, mentioned below

(IV) David Arnold, son of Samuel and Sarah (Webb) Arnold, was born July 25, 1732, in Braintree, Massachusetts, and settled near the Taunton line of the town of Norton, Massachusetts. He owned a place near Burts brook, Norton. He was a Revolutionary soldier, lieutenant in Captain Benjamin Morey's company, Colonel John Daggett's regiment, and served under various enlistments. He died in Norton in 1810. He married Phebe Pratt, of Taunton, Massachusetts, intentions entered in Norton, December 9, 1756. Children, born in Norton. David, December 23, 1757, Phebe, April 1, 1760, John, May 23, 1763, Samuel, January 13, 1766, Asa, February 3, 1768, Salmon, 1771, William, March 28, 1774, Lemuel, mentioned below, Sally, 1778

(V) Lemuel Arnold, son of Lieutenant David and Phebe (Pratt) Arnold, was born September 15, 1776, and died February 13, 1861. He married Ann Hodges, of Norton, May 18, 1801. She was the daughter of Captain James and Mary (Briggs) Hodges, born April 22, 1777, and died February 7, 1854. Captain James Hodges, son of Nathan and Experience (Williams) Hodges, of Taunton, was born April 22, 1737, in Norton, Massachusetts. His parents were married December 12, 1728, in Norton. Captain Hodges first enlisted as a private in Captain Robert Crossman's Minute-Men Company. He served under various enlistments. Children of Lemuel and Ann (Hodges) Arnold. Nancy, born July 23, 1802, Lemuel, December 27, 1803, Mary P., September 25, 1805, Laban, November 7, 1807,

Adeline, mentioned below, William Earle, April 19, 1813, Samuel, September 17, 1815, Charles G., September 19, 1817, Edwin Howard, January 11, 1819, David Augustus, May 11, 1823

(VI) Adeline Arnold, daughter of Lemuel and Ann (Hodges) Arnold, married in Norton, Massachusetts, April 10, 1843, Ebenezer Tinkham (see Tinkham VII).

GOOCH,

And Allied Families

John Keene, the immigrant ancestor, was born in England, in 1578. In the early records his name is spelled Keen, Kean, Kein, and in all other ways that the name might be spelled. He came in the ship "Confidence," from Southampton, England, sailing April 11, 1638, with his wife Martha, and children, John, Eliza, Martha, Josiah and Sarah. He settled in Hingham, Massachusetts, where he afterward kept a tavern. Children. John, Eliza, Martha, Josiah, mentioned below, Sarah

(II) Josiah Keene, son of John Keene, was born in London, England, about 1620, and came to America with his parents. From Boston he went with his parents to Hingham and later he settled in Marshfield, Massachusetts, near Duxbury. He married (first) at Marshfield, Abigail Little or Littell; (second) in 1665, Hannah Dingley, daughter of John Dingley. He served on the grand jury from Duxbury, in 1689. The town confirmed to him a tract of thirty acres, February 24, 1696-97, some land that his son Josiah, Jr., had bought of Francis West on Pudding Brook, adjoining land of Josiah Keene, Sr. He died soon after this date. Children of first wife. Josiah, mentioned below, a daughter, died young. Children of second wife. John, born 1667, ancestor of the famous shipbuilders; Mathew,

Ephraim, Hannah, married Isaac Oldham, Elizabeth, Abigail, Sarah

(III) Josiah (2) Keene, son of Josiah
(1) Keene, was born in Marshfield, about
1660. He had land laid out to him, February 21, 1690, in Duxbury, and was then
doubtless of age. Soon afterward he
bought nine acres on Pudding Brook,
Duxbury. Thirty acres were laid out to
him by the town of Duxbury, February
24, 1696-97, as mentioned above. He was
a grand juror in 1703, when he was still
called "Jr." He married, about 1681,
Lydia Baker. Children, born in Duxbury:
Benjamin, born July 26, 1682, Josiah, Jr.,
September 27, 1683, died young, Abigail,
April 7, 1686, Eleanor, Lydia, Josiah,
soldier, went to the West Indies; Nathaniel, born November 11, 1692, Bethia,
Samuel, Isaac, Hezekiah, mentioned below.

(IV) Hezekiah Keene, son of Josiah
(2) Keene, was born in Duxbury, August
8, 1702, and died December 27, 1770. He
married Alice Howland, daughter of
Prince Howland, granddaughter of
Arthur Howland, and great-granddaughter of Arthur Howland, immigrant, whose
brother John came in the "Mayflower."
She was born October 30, 1709, died October 13, 1785. Children, born in Duxbury: Prince, mentioned below, Charles,
Mark, Robert, Alice, Diana, Bethia, Hezekiah, Jr., Daniel, born December 30, 1748,
settled in Bristol, Maine, Mary, William.

(V) Prince Keene, son of Hezekiah
Keene, was born in Duxbury or vicinity.
He was of Duxbury, March 7, 1758, when
he married at Pembroke, Elizabeth Ford.
Children: Benjamin Prince, mentioned
below; Deborah, baptized December 27,
1761.

(VI) Benjamin Prince Keene, son of
Prince Keene, was born in Pembroke,
September 5, 1759. He married Mary
Gardner. They settled in Kinderhook,

New York, but later removed to Apple-
ton, Maine. Children: Caleb G., born at
Kinderhook, September 1, 1787, Elizabeth
Ford, June 12, 1789; Robert Stien, men-
tioned below; Maria Antoinette, born
February 9, 1794, Benjamin, born Octo-
ber 9, 1796, died March 4, 1876, Charles
Augustus, born March 1, 1801.

(VII) Robert Stien Keene, son of Benjamin Prince Keene, was born at Kinderhook, New York, March 12, 1792. He
came to Appleton, Maine, with his parents, and lived there the remainder of his
life, dying there August 21, 1870. He was
a farmer and owned extensive tracts of
land. He married, December 12, 1822, at
Appleton, Isabel Davis, born April 5,
1804, died April 30, 1896 daughter of
John and Mary (Martin) Davis, granddaughter of John and Sarah (Bradford)
Davis (see Bradford VI), of Friendship,
Maine. Children: 1 Caleb Gardner, born
October 12, 1823, died September 23,
1824. 2 William G., born December 28,
1824, died January 17, 1866, married,
March 6, 1853, Mercy Jameson. 3 Eliza
Ford, mentioned below. 4 Albert Gard-
ner, born September 18, 1828, died in
Worcester, Massachusetts, September 6,
1851. 5 Theresa Antoinette, born Octo-
ber 10, 1830, married Benjamin Jacobs,
December 25, 1853, and died at Milwau-
kee, Wisconsin, February 13, 1904. 6
Sarah Bradford, born August 25, 1832,
died August 8, 1916, married, October 9,
1853, Thomas H. Hunt, of Camden,
Maine. 7 Isabel Davis, born June 21,
1834, married, September 7, 1864, Daniel
B. Ball, and died in Wilcox, Nebraska,
September 11, 1901. 8 Edwin S., born
October 31, 1836, died at Appleton, June
25, 1883, married (first) June 2, 1861,
Marietta Johnson, (second) September 6,
1868, Martha Wentworth. 9 Robert
Stien, born April 1, 1839, died March 12,
1908, in Appleton, married (first) Sep-

tember 10, 1876, Mary B. Wentworth, and (second) June 4, 1892, Cora E. Thompson. 10 Edward, born July 29, 1841, died March 14, 1842 11 Ormond, born March 21, 1843, died at Boston, September 29, 1866.

(VIII) Eliza Ford Keene, daughter of Robert Stien and Isabel (Davis) Keene, was born January 22, 1827 She married, October 19, 1851, James Murray Smith, who was born at Aberdeen, Scotland, son of John and Anne (Denny) Smith. His father was a soldier in the British army and came with his command to Halifax, Nova Scotia, remaining there after his discharge and locating finally in Cape Breton, where he spent the remainder of his life. James Murray Smith learned the printer's trade at Halifax and worked as a journeyman printer in Halifax, and in the offices of various newspapers in Boston and New York City For many years he was employed in the composing room of the Boston "Herald." He died in 1876, and was buried at Appleton, Maine, by the side of his wife, who died October 24, 1866 Children of James M and Eliza Ford (Keene) Smith Annie Isabel Smith, died at the age of twenty-seven years; Mary Theresa Smith, died at the age of twenty-two years, Wallace B. Smith, resides at Minneapolis, Minnesota; Sarah Eliza Smith, married Wilzue Whitson, and resides in Neola, Iowa; and Carrie Hunt Smith, mentioned below

(IX) Carrie Hunt Smith, daughter of James M and Eliza Ford (Keene) Smith, was born in Boston, October 12, 1861 She received her education in the public schools in Nova Scotia After the death of her parents she went to live with an uncle and aunt, Philip and Agnes Smith, in Nova Scotia She returned to Boston, after a few years, and married, August 14, 1895, John Brackett Gooch, who was born in Lyman, Maine, April 1, 1854, son

of Charles and Asenath (Perkins) Gooch He died December 24, 1898. Their only child, Helen Agnes Gooch, born May 25, 1897, is now a student in the Massachusetts State Normal School at Bridgewater. Mrs Gooch resides in Whitman, and is a member of Deborah Sampson Chapter, Daughters of the American Revolution of Brockton

Colonel Caleb Gardner, Revolutionary ancestor of Mrs. Carrie H Gooch, or Whitman, lived in Newport, Rhode Island, and was a soldier in the Revolutionary War He married, in August, 1752, Eleanor Phillips, at Trinity Church, Newport He died October 23, 1801, and she died November 26, 1803 Both died in Providence and are buried in Swan Point Cemetery, of that city. Children, born at Newport John, born September 8, 1753, died May 27, 1754; Elizabeth, March 29, 1755; John, September 10, 1756, died July 11, 1757; Eleanor, April 7, 1759; Mary, September 1, 1761, married Benjamin Prince Keene (see Keene VI)

(The Bradford Line)

The Bradford family history dates back in England to the beginning of surnames One of the first martyrs burned at the stake during the reign of Bloody Mary was John Bradford, prebend of St Paul's, and a celebrated preacher, born in Manchester, in 1510, executed July 1, 1555; a friend of Rogers, Hooper, Latimer, Cranmer and Ridley, who also perished in the same manner The coat-of-arms is described Argent on a fesse, three stags' heads erased or

The ancestry of Governor Bradford has not been traced further than his grandfather, though the evidence shows that he belonged to the ancient Bradford family in England

(I) William Bradford, grandfather of Governor William Bradford, lived at Austerfield, County Nottingham, England, and in 1575, he and John Hanson were the only subsidiaries located there. William Bradford was taxed twenty shillings on land, John Hanson the same on goods. His grandson, William Bradford, lived with him after the death of his son, William Bradford. The date of his burial at Austerfield was January 10, 1595-96. Children: William, mentioned below; Thomas; Robert, baptized June 25, 1561 (with him Governor Bradford lived after his grandfather died), Elizabeth, baptized July 16, 1570.

(II) William (2) Bradford, son of William (1) Bradford, was born at Austerfield, about 1560, and died July 15, 1591, married Alice Hanson. Children, born at Austerfield: Margaret, baptized March 8, 1585, died young; Alice, baptized October 30, 1587; William, mentioned below.

(III) Governor William (3) Bradford, son of William (2) Bradford, was born at Austerfield and baptized March 19, 1590. After his father and grandfather died, he went to live with his uncle, Robert Bradford, at Scrooby, and he joined the church where John Robinson preached. Though he had little schooling he became proficient in Dutch, Latin, French and Greek, and even studied Hebrew so that he could read the Bible in the original form. He went to Holland with the Pilgrims. He learned the trade of fustian or friece weaving. He married, at Amsterdam, Holland, December 9, 1613, Dorothea May, who was then sixteen. They came in the "Mayflower," but before landing finally, his wife fell overboard and was drowned, December 9, 1620. Soon after the death of Carver, William Bradford succeeded him as governor of Plymouth and continued by annual reëlection as governor, except in 1633, 1634, 1635, 1638 and 1644, until he died. He wrote a history of the colony and the original manu-script may be seen in the State Library, Boston. A complete history of Bradford's life would require a volume by itself and include the history of the Colony of Plymouth. He married (second) Alice (Carpenter) Southworth, widow of Edward Southworth, and daughter of Alexander Carpenter. She died March 26, 1670, and he died May 9, 1657. Child by first wife: John, of Duxbury. Children by second wife: William, mentioned below; Mercy, Joseph, mentioned below.

(IV) Major William (3) Bradford, son of Governor William (3) Bradford, was born June 16, 1624, at Plymouth, and died February 20, 1703. He removed to Kingston, Massachusetts. He was assistant deputy governor and in 1687 one of Governor Andros's council. He became the chief military officer of the colony. His will is dated January 29, 1703. He married (first) Alice Richards, who died at Plymouth, December 12, 1671, a daughter of Thomas and Wealthy Richards, of Weymouth. He married (second) Widow Wiswell, (third) Mary Holmes, widow, who died June 6, 1714-15, widow of Rev. John Holmes, of Duxbury, and daughter of John Atwood. Children by first wife: John, born February 20, 1653; William, March 11, 1655; Thomas, of Norwich; Alice, Hannah, Mercy, Melatiah, Mary, Sarah; Samuel, 1668. By second wife: Joseph, of Norwich. By third wife: Israel, mentioned below; David, Ephraim, Hezekiah.

(V) Israel Bradford, son of Major William (4) Bradford, was born at Kingston, about 1680. He married Sarah Bartlett, of Duxbury. Children, born at Kingston: Ruth, December 11, 1703, died young; Bathsheba, November 8, 1704; Benjamin, October 17, 1705; Abner, December 25, 1707; Joshua, mentioned below; Ichabod, September 22, 1713; Elisha, March 26, 1718.

(VI) Joshua Bradford, son of Israel Bradford, was born at Kingston, June 23, 1710 He married Hannah Bradford, daughter of Elisha Bradford, mentioned below They moved to Medumcook, later called Friendship, Maine, where he was killed by Indians, May 27, 1756, and his children carried to Canada, where they remained until Quebec was taken They then returned to their old home Children Cornelius, born December 10, 1737, Sarah, born October 16, 1739, married John Davis, and their son, John Davis, Jr, married Mary Martin and had Isabel Davis, who married Robert Stien Keene (see Keene VII), Rachel, born January 28, 1741, Mary and Melatiah, March 16, 1744, Joshua, April 2, 1746, Hannah, March 9, 1748, Joseph, March 19, 1751, Benjamin, May 28, 1753, Elisha, October 15, 1755, Winslow, 1757

(IV) Joseph Bradford, son of Governor William (3) Bradford, was born in 1630 He married Jael, daughter of Rev Peter Hobart, of Hingham, May 25, 1664. She died in 1730, aged eighty-eight years They lived at Kingston on the Jones river, half a mile from its mouth Children Elisha, mentioned below, Joseph, born April 18, 1665

(V) Elisha Bradford, son of Joseph Bradford, was born in 1664 He married (first) Hannah Cole, (second) Bathsheba Le Brocke, September 7, 1718 His widow married (second) Joshua Oldham, of Pembroke Children by second wife Hannah, born April 10, 1720, married Joshua Bradford (VI), mentioned above, Joseph, December 17, 1721, Nehemiah, July 27, 1724, Laurana, March 26, 1726, Mary, August 1, 1727, Elisha, October 6, 1729, Lois, January 30, 1731, Deborah, November 18, 1732, married Jonathan Sampson, Jr, and became mother of Deborah Sampson, who was famous because, disguised as a man, she served as a soldier

in the Revolution, Allis, November 3, 1734; Asenath, September 15, 1736, Carpenter, February 7, 1739, Abigail, June 20, 1741, Chloe, April 6, 1743

JACKSON, Willard Everett,
Business Man

Abraham Jackson, the immigrant ancestor, came to Plymouth in the third ship "Ann" in 1623, at the age of thirteen years, with Secretary Morton, to whom he was apprenticed, and whose daughter Remember he married, November 18, 1657 Her father was a historical character, financial agent of the Pilgrims in Holland, and is said by one writer to have purchased the "Mayflower" for them, Remember was born to his second wife, Hannah, former widow of Richard Templar, of Charlestown, and daughter of Richard Pritchard, at Plymouth in 1637, and she died July 24, 1707 She was granddaughter of George and Ann (Carpenter) Morton and of Alexander Carpenter George Morton or Mount wrote a history of Plymouth colony, called "Mount's Relation" Abraham Jackson died October 4, 1714 Children Lydia, born November 19, 1658, Abraham, Nathaniel, Eleazer, mentioned below, John

(II) Eleazer Jackson, son of Abraham Jackson, was born in October, 1669 He married, in 1690, Hannah Ransom, daughter of Robert and Anna Ransom, of Plymouth and Sandwich, Massachusetts Children, born at Plymouth John, born 1692, Eleazer, 1694, Joanna, 1696, Mercy, 1697, Hannah, 1698, Mary, 1701, Abigail, 1702, Deborah, 1704, Content, 1705, Susanna, 1706, Ransom, 1708, Benjamin, 1710; Experience, 1713, Ephraim, mentioned below

(III) Ephraim Jackson, son of Eleazer Jackson, was born in Plymouth, September 10, 1714, resided in Wrentham and Bridgewater; married, in 1736, Lydia Leach, granddaughter of Giles and Anna (Nokes) Leach, of Bridgewater Among his children was Ephraim, mentioned below

(IV) Lieutenant Ephraim (2) Jackson, son of Ephraim (1) Jackson, was born in 1739 He married (first) in 1765, Bathsheba Trask, daughter of John and Penelope (White) Trask, granddaughter of William and Ann (White) Trask, great-granddaughter of William and Ann (Putnam) Trask, the first settlers Captain William Trask commanded a company in the Pequot war, he was a settler in Salem in 1628 Ann (White) Trask was a daughter of Joseph and Lydia (Rogers) White, of Mendon, granddaughter of Thomas White, pioneer, of Weymouth Ann (Putnam) Trask was a daughter of Thomas and Ann (Holyoke) Putnam, granddaughter of John and Priscilla Putnam, the pioneers, whose ancestry in England has been traced for many generations Lydia (Rogers) White was a daughter of Deacon John and Judith Rogers, who came from England Ephraim Jackson married (second) in 1784, Hannah Delano His first wife died December 24, 1782 He died at North Bridgewater, May 29, 1814 His grave, near the Brockton fair grounds in the old cemetery, is marked by the Sons of the Revolution He served in the French and Indian war in Captain Simeon Cary's company, Colonel Thomas Doty's regiment, March 13 to December 11, 1758, and in the Revolutionary War in Captain Daniel Lothrop's company, Colonel John Bailey's regiment, in 1775 Children by first wife, born at North Bridgewater: Asa, born December 5, 1765; Oliver, mentioned below, Caleb, September 3, 1769, Lydia, February 26, 1771, Bathsheba, July 28, 1772, George Washing-

ton, October 19, 1776, Rhoda, January 16, 1778, Calvin, June 17, 1779, Clarissa, December 20, 1780 By second wife Barnard, Lucy and Polly

(V) Captain Oliver Jackson, son of Ephraim Jackson, was born at North Bridgewater, March 18, 1767, died March 19, 1845 He married, May 6, 1807, Olive Gurney, born December 1, 1786, daughter of Captain Zachariah and Matilda (Packard) Gurney, granddaughter of Lieutenant Zachariah and Mary Gurney, great-granddaughter of Zachariah and Sarah (Jackson) Gurney, of Weymouth and Abington Zachariah Gurney, father of last mentioned Zachariah, married Mary Benson, daughter of Joseph Benson, granddaughter of John Benson, who came from Gonsham, Oxfordshire, England, in 1638, and lived at Hingham and Hull, had wife Mary Matilda (Packard) Gurney was a daughter of William and Sarah (Richards) Packard, of Bridgewater, granddaughter of David and Hannah (Ames) Packard, great-granddaughter of Zaccheus and Sarah (Howard) Packard, and great-great-granddaughter of Samuel Packard, who came from Windham, near Hingham, England, in 1638, moving afterward to Bridgewater Sarah (Richards) Packard, born 1730, died January 4, 1806, was a daughter of Benjamin and Mehitable (Alden) Richards, of Plymouth and Bridgewater, granddaughter of Joseph and Sarah Richards, and great-granddaughter of William and Grace Richards, who came from England to Plymouth, later to Scituate Joseph Richards was in King Philip's war, settled in Weymouth Mehitable (Alden) Richards was a daughter of Isaac and Mehitable (Allen) Alden, granddaughter of Joseph and Mary (Simmons) Alden, great-granddaughter of John and Priscilla (Molines) Alden, who came in the "Mayflower" Mehitable (Allen) Alden was a daughter of Samuel and Sarah (Partridge) Allen, granddaughter of Samuel and Ann Allen, pioneers Sarah (Partridge) Allen was a daughter of George and Sarah (Tracy) Partridge, granddaughter of Stephen and Tryphosa Tracy, who came in the ship "Ann" in 1623 Hannah (Ames) Packard was a daughter of John and Sarah (Willis) Ames, granddaughter of William and Hannah Ames, of Duxbury, and great-granddaughter of Richard Ames, or Bruton, Somersetshire, England Sarah (Howard) Packard was a daughter of John and Martha (Hayward) Howard, mentioned elsewhere in this work Sarah (Jackson) Gurney was a daughter of Edmund and Mary Jackson, granddaughter of Edmund and Eliabeth (Pilkinton) Jackson, of Boston Children of Oliver Jackson, born at North Bridgewater Benjamin Franklin, mentioned below, Henry, born July 26, 1811, Alpheus Gurney, June 11, 1813; Eliza, August 21, 1817; Oliver, October 16, 1819, Thomas, September 21, 1822, Olive, November 14, 1825.

(V) Benjamin Franklin Jackson, son of Captain Oliver Jackson was born at North Bridgewater, October 1, 1808 He married there, September 26, 1834, Rebecca Snell, daughter of Alvin Snell Children, born at North Bridgewater Andrew, born November 30, 1838, Laban, October 23, 1840, Oliver, November 15, 1843, Alvin, January 8, 1847, Willard Everett, mentioned below

(VI) Willard Everett Jackson, son of Benjamin Franklin Jackson, was born in North Bridgewater, May 4, 1851 He resides on Summer street, Brockton, and is one of the leading contractors of the city, a progressive and enterprising citizen He married, July 21, 1875, at West Bridgewater, Mary Jane Copeland, born there April 29, 1856, a daughter of Lawrence and Mary Lucella (Snell) Copeland

(see Copeland VI) Mrs Jackson is quite an active member of the Old Bridgewater Historical Society and of Deborah Sampson Chapter, Daughters of the American Revolution, of Brockton, and she is also a member of the Alden Kindred of America and of the Congregational Church They had one son, Willard Franklin, born May 2, 1876, in Brockton, and educated there in the public schools and in the Massachusetts Institute of Technology, Boston, now an architect in Brockton; married Lillian Buck, who was born in Easton, a daughter of Franklin and Ellen (Stearns) Buck Children Robert Copeland, Helen Stearns and Virginia

(The Copeland Line).

(1) Lawrence Copeland, the immigrant ancestor, was born in Scotland, it is said, in 1599. The Scotch family of Copeland has been located in Durfriesshire since before the year 1400 He came to this country about the time that Cromwell sent over his Scotch prisoners of war and may have been one of them He settled in Braintree, where he married, soon afterward, December 12, 1651, Lydia Townsend, who died January 8, 1688 He died December 30, 1699, aged one hundred years, according to Marshall's diary and other testimony, as well as the town record One statement of a contemporary makes him even older, but even if born in 1599, he was over fifty when he married his wife Lydia and seventy-five years old when his youngest child was born, a fact that supports the tradition that a first wife came with him He was a farmer and a quiet citizen Children by wife Lydia at Braintree · Thomas, born December 3, 1652, died young, Thomas, February 8, 1655, William, mentioned below; John, February 10, 1659, Lydia, May 31, 1661; Ephraim, January 17.

116

1665, Hannah, February 25, 1668; Richard July 11, 1672; Abigail, 1674.

(II) William Copeland, son of Lawrence Copeland, was born at Braintree, November 15, 1656, and died there October 30, 1716. He was a farmer. William Copeland is on record as dissenting from the vote of the town to pay the minister's salary in full, 1690-91, was fence viewer in 1696, and signed the agreement of the proprietors of Braintree, January 10, 1697-98, to defend the title of the proprietors of Braintree to their land. He married, April 13, 1694, Mary (Bass) Webb, widow of Christopher Webb, Jr., and daughter of John and Ruth (Alden) Bass. Her mother Ruth was a daughter of John and Priscilla (Molines) Alden, the Mayflower Pilgrims, and all her descendants are eligible to the Mayflower Society (see Alden in this work). Mary Bass descended from Samuel Bass, of Boston and Braintree, deacon, made freeman May 10, 1634, deputy to the General Court in 1643, deacon, died December 30, 1694, aged ninety-four years, when his descendants numbered one hundred and sixty-two persons. Children of William Copeland, born at Braintree William, born March 7, 1695; Ephraim, February 1, 1697; Ebenezer, February 16, 1698; Jonathan, mentioned below; David, April 15, 1704; Joseph, May 18, 1706; Benjamin, October 5, 1708; Moses, May 28, 1710; Mary, May 28, 1713.

(III) Jonathan Copeland, son of William Copeland, was born August 31, 1701, in Braintree, settled in Bridgewater, where he died September 11, 1790. He was a farmer, currier and tanner and tradition says his tannery was in West Bridgewater. He married, January 14, 1723, Betty Snell, daughter of Thomas Snell, born 1671, and granddaughter of Thomas Snell, the immigrant (see Snell

I) Children of Jonathan Copeland, all born at Bridgewater Abigail, born December 9, 1724; Betty, April 17, 1726; Jonathan, August 9, 1728; Mary, March 26, 1731; Joseph, April 28, 1734; Hannah, May 13, 1737; Elijah, June 3, 1739; Daniel, September 13, 1741; Sarah, February 13, 1744-45; Ebenezer, mentioned below; Betty, September 23, 1750.

(IV) Ebenezer Copeland, son of Jonathan Copeland, was born at Bridgewater, July 27, 1746; died at Foxborough, May 27, 1830. He married (first) in Norton, Massachusetts, March 18, 1771, Abbie Godfrey, who was born there May 10, 1752; died in 1800, daughter of Lieutenant James and Mary Godfrey (see Godfrey). Children of Ebenezer Copeland Betty; Ebenezer mentioned below; James, January 28, 1775; Lydia, Molly, died in infancy; Molly, Rachel, Oakes, September 22, 1794; Ruth, James. He married (second) at Foxborough, Massachusetts, Bridget (Greatrocks) Wood, of Stoughtonham, widow of Dr Joshua Wood. She died December 24, 1831.

(V) Ebenezer (2) Copeland, son of Ebenezer (1) Copeland, was born in Bridgewater, June 21, 1773, lived and died there. He married (first) July 1, 1798, Mehitable Snell, who died March 11, 1800, aged twenty-five years. He married (second) at Norton, May 17, 1801, Hannah Godfrey, born May 9, 1778, daughter of Samuel and Mary (Hodges) Godfrey (see Godfrey V). Child by first wife Mehitable S, born January 2, 1799. Children by second wife James, February 5, 1802, Rachel, September 1, 1803; Mary Hodges, November 19, 1804; Abby G, October 9, 1806, Ruth, July 27, 1808, married Ephraim Brett; Hannah G, June 13, 1810; child, November 2, 1812, died in infancy, Lawrence, mentioned below; Betsey, May 17, 1819.

(VI) Lawrence (2) Copeland, son of

Ebenezer (2) Copeland, was born at Bridgewater, March 27, 1815 He attended school in what is now West Bridgewater, and lived there until 1855, when he moved to Brockton, where he was successfully engaged in agricultural pursuits, and where he resided to the end of his life He died May 19, 1892, and was buried in Pine Hill Cemetery, West Bridgewater, in the family lot He was a Republican in politics, and a member of the Congregational church of West Bridgewater He married Mary Lucella Snell, daughter of John Eliot Snell (see Snell VI) Children Grace Greenwood, born November 10, 1852, married Dennis Tribou, Arthur Grenville, June 12, 1854, died February 20, 1865, Mary Jane, April 29, 1856, married Willard F Jackson (see Jackson VI), Anna Snell, September 23, 1858, married Fred H Rhue, of Vermont, and they reside in Brockton on the Copeland homestead

(The Snell Line)

(I) Thomas Snell came from England and about 1665 settled in what was afterward known as West Bridgewater, Massachusetts He was a nephew of Samuel Edson, one of the first settlers of Bridgewater He prospered and became one of the largest landowners in the town From him Snell's Plain, Snell's Meadow and other localities take their names He married Martha Harris, daughter of Arthur Harris Their children Thomas, born 1671, Josiah, mentioned below, Samuel, 1676, Amos, 1678, John, 1680, Joseph 1683, Ann, 1685, Mary, 1689, Martha, 1692

(II) Josiah Snell, son of Thomas Snell, was born in Bridgewater in 1674, and died there in 1753 He married, in 1699, Anna, daughter of Zechariah Alden, of Duxbury She died in 1705 She was a granddaughter of John and Elizabeth (Averill) Alden, and great-granddaugh-

ter of John and Priscilla (Molines) Alden, who came in the "Mayflower" Children of Josiah Snell, born at Bridgewater Josiah, mentioned below, Abigail, 1702, Zechariah, 1704

(III) Josiah (2) Snell, son of Josiah (1) Snell, was born in Bridgewater in 1701 He married, in 1728, Abigail Fobes, daughter of John Fobes Children, born at Bridgewater Josiah, born 1730, Anna, 1732, Elijah, mentioned below, Mary, 1736, Abigail, 1739, Rhoda, 1743, Nathan, 1748

(IV) Deacon Elijah Snell, son of Josiah (2) Snell, was born in Bridgewater in 1734 He was deacon of the church, and soldier in the Revolution He was first lieutenant of Captain Eliakim Howard's company, Third Plymouth County regiment, commissioned March 2 1776, and was also in Colonel Edward Mitchell's company in 1776 and in 1780 in the Rhode Island campaigns (page 591, volume xiv "Massachusetts Soldiers and Sailors of the Revolutionary War") He married (first) in 1760, Susanna, daughter of Seth Howard, (second) Ann Reynolds, widow of Jonas Reynolds and daughter of Luke Perkins, of Bridgewater Children, born at Bridgewater Huldah, born 1762, Bezer, 1764, Calvin, 1766, Susanna 1770, Elijah, 1772, Mehitable and Parnell, twins, 1774, Abigail, 1776, Ann, 1778, Polly, 1780, John Eliot, mentioned below, Lucinda, 1789

(V) John Eliot Snell, son of Deacon Elijah Snell, was born in 1783, in Bridgewater, and married Annie LaFollet, of Maine Their children were Ann, Samantha, Susan, Josiah, who died young, Lloyd, Mary Lucella, mentioned below, Abbie, Josiah, Seneca, who died young, Henry, Eunice, and Jerusha

(VI) Mary Lucella Snell, daughter of John Eliot Snell, married Lawrence Copeland (see Copeland VI)

(The Godfrey Line)

(I) Richard Godfrey, American immigrant, located in Taunton, now Raynham, as early as 1652, and was a landowner there, died in Taunton, 1691   He lived near the iron works   His will mentions his children   His wife was a daughter of John Turner   Children   Richard, mentioned below; John; Robert; Jane, married John Cobb; Alice, married Peter Holbrook; Susanna, married Edward Kettle

(II) Richard (2) Godfrey, son of Richard (1) Godfrey, married Mary Richmond, daughter of John Richmond, of Taunton   Children   Alice, born August 20, 1679; Richard, mentioned below; Mary, May, 1682; Abigail, November 5, 1684; Joanna, July 30 1686; Sarah, May 15, 1689; John, October 31, 1691, captain, father of the distinguished Brigadier-General George Godfrey, of Revolutionary War fame; Joseph, March 1, 1695

(III) Richard (3) Godfrey, son of Richard (2) Godfrey, was born at Taunton, March 1, 1681, married, December 15, 1709, Bathsheba Walker   Children, born at Raynham   Richard, born March 23, 1711; Bathsheba, May 24, 1713; James, mentioned below; Mary, married Colonel Thomas Gilbert

(IV) Lieutenant James Godfrey, son of Richard (3) Godfrey, was born in Raynham or vicinity about 1715   He married Mary ——   Children, born in Norton   Bathsheba born May 9, 1738; Mary, May 4, 1740; James, March 19 1742; Gershom, February 29, 1744; Samuel, mentioned below; Rachel, September 2, 1748; Abbie, May 10 1752, married Ebenezer Copeland (see Copeland IV)

(V) Samuel Godfrey, son of Lieutenant James Godfrey, was born at Norton, July 7, 1746   He married there, December 29, 1774, Mary Hodges, daughter of Isaac Hodges (see Hodges IV)   He lived in West Bridgewater   His daughter Hannah, born May 9, 1778 (gravestone), married Ebenezer Copeland, Jr (see Copeland V)

(The Hodges Line)

(I) William Hodges, the pioneer, was born in England and came to Salem, Massachusetts, where he was a juror as early as March 27, 1638, thence he went to Taunton and his name appears there on the second list of proprietors of the town   He was reported among the men able to bear arms in 1643, and was admitted a freeman of the colony, June 5, 1651, and on the same day elected constable of Taunton   He served on the grand jury, June 2, 1652, and on a coroner's jury, August 2, 1653, at Plymouth   He was one of the original owners of the Taunton Iron Works, subscribing twenty pounds for a whole share   He was well-to-do for his day   He married Mary Andrews, daughter of Henry Andrews, one of the original purchasers of the town of Taunton and one of the first seven freemen there one of the first two deputies to the General Court in 1639 and deputy also in 1643, 1644, 1647 and 1649, dying in 1653   Mary (Andrews) Hodges was born about 1628, she married (second) April 2, 1654, Peter Pitts, of Taunton   Children, born in Taunton   John, born 1650, Henry, mentioned below

(II) Henry Hodges, son of William Hodges, was born in 1652 at Taunton, and died there September 30, 1717, aged sixty-five years   He married, December 17, 1674, at Taunton   Esther Gallop, daughter of John and Sarah (Lake) Gallop   She was born July 31, 1653   He was a leading man of the town, holding town offices for a long period; captain of the military company; deacon and presiding elder of the church and at times occupying the pulpit with Rev Samuel Danforth, the pastor   He owned much

real estate and settled many estates
From his prominence as a lot-layer in
allotting the common lands it is presumed
that he was a surveyor. He was on a
coroner's jury at Plymouth, October 30,
1678, on a grand jury, June 6, 1683 constable, selectman for twenty-eight years,
1687 to 1701, 1703 to 1709, 1711 to 1716,
member of the town council in 1689-90,
and deputy to the General Court five
years, 1704, 1713, 1715, 1716 and 1717
His name appears in the roster of the
Third Squadron, April 8, 1682, ordered
to bring arms to church on Sundays; he
was ensign of the first military company
in March, 1690, when the town was
greatly excited over the question of captaincy of the company. Before 1703 the
second military company was organized
and he became its first captain, retaining
his commission until 1714. He was a
subscriber to the fund for the Canada Expedition in 1690. When the North Precinct of Taunton was established he donated land as an inducement for a minister to settle in the new parish. He was
a shareholder in the Taunton Iron Works
He died September 30, 1717, and his
gravestone is standing. Children, born in
Taunton. Mary, born February 3 1676,
Esther, February 17 1677-78, William,
March 18, 1679-80, Charity, April 2, 1682;
John, 1684, Henry, 1685-86; Joseph, mentioned below; Benjamin, about 1691,
Ephraim, about 1693, Elizabeth, Abigail

(III) Major Joseph Hodges, son of
Captain Henry Hodges, was born in
Taunton, about 1688, and died in 1745,
soon after his return from the capture of
Louisburg, Cape Breton. He was very
prominent in the civil and ecclesiastical
councils of Bristol county. Soon after
his first marriage he settled in the south-
erly part of Norton, near the Taunton
line at Crooked Meadow, where his grandson, Seth Hodges, lived as late as 1844

There he built a saw mill on Cedar Swamp
Brook. He was assessor of Norton, 1723,
1724, 1725 and 1727, selectman, 1729,
1730, 1733, 1734, 1741 and 1742, deputy
to the General Court in 1737, deacon of
the church from 1736 until he died, ensign as early as 1729, captain, 1737, and
he commanded a company in the old
French and Indian war, was major of the
Bristol county regiment which took part
in the siege of Louisburg in 1745, dying
on the journey home or soon afterward
His will was dated February 26, 1744-45,
mentioning among other personal effects
a silver-hilted sword. He married (first)
March 11, 1712-13, in Taunton, Bethiah,
born 1692, died between 1731 and 1738,
daughter of Thomas and Mary (Macy)
Williams. He married (second) October 26, 1738, in Barrington, Rhode Island.
Mary (Toogood) Barney, daughter of
Nathaniel and Elizabeth Toogood. She
was born in 1696, at Swansea, married
(first) December 10, 1710, Joshua Kent
(second) January 22, 1729-30, Joseph
Barney, of Rehoboth. She died May 20,
1782, at Rehoboth, and was buried in
Barrington. Children, all by his first
wife, born in Norton. Joseph, born April
25, 1714, Charity, March 30, 1716, Timothy, October 11, 1718, Jonathan, February 26, 1721-22. Bethia, November 30,
1723, Mary, July 2, 1726, Isaac, mentioned below, Mehitable, October 24,
1731

(IV) Isaac Hodges, son of Major Joseph Hodges, was born at Norton, February 4, 1728-29. He married, January
31, 1751, Mary Pratt. Children, born at
Norton. Isaac, born March 27, 1752, died
young, Jesse, October 3, 1755. Isaac, August 25, 1757; Lucelde, May 27, 1760,
Mary, married, December 29, 1774, Samuel Godfrey (see Godfrey V), Anne, November 21, 1763, Darius, October 2, 1765,
Rachel March 11, 1768, Seth July 1, 1770

COLE, James,

Public Official

The surname Cole is derived from an ancient personal name of unknown antiquity. Coel, as the name was formerly spelled, was the founder of Colchester, England, and was one of the early kings of Britain. Justice Cole lived in the days of King Arthur. Another Cole defeated Swayne, the Danish chieftain, at Pinhoe, in the year 1001. William Cole and wife Isabella are mentioned in the Assize Roll of County Cornwell in the year 1201, showing that Cole was at that time in use as a surname.

Various branches of the English Cole family bear coats-of-arms, all indicating relationship by the similarity with the device. The Hertfordshire branch, to which the American family is believed to belong, bears Party per pale or and argent, a bull passant within a bordure sable, on a chief of the third three bezants. Crest: A demi-dragon vert bearing in his dexter paw a javelin armed or, feathered argent.

(1) James Cole was living in Highgate, a suburb of London, England, in 1616. According to tradition he was very fond of flowers. He married, in 1624, Mary Lobel daughter of the noted botanist and physician, Mathieu Lobel, who was born in 1538, at Lille, France, son of Jean de Lonel, a distinguished lawyer. Dr. Mathieu Lobel was a physician at Montpelier, Germany, Italy and Switzerland. He practiced medicine at Antwerp and was physician to William of Orange, at London, where he was physician to James I., he was author of books on medicinal plants. The plant lobelia is named for him. He died at Highgate, March 2, 1616. In 1632 James Cole, wife and two children, came to Saco, Maine, and in the following year located at Plymouth, Mas-

sachusetts, where he was admitted a freeman in the same year. He was a mariner. In 1634 his name appears on the tax list and he received a grant of land. His house was on the site of the present Baptist church. He was the first settler on what is still known as Cole's Hill, where the first burying ground of the Pilgrims is located. He had various other grants of land, was surveyor of highways in 1641-42, 1651-52, constable in 1641-44, and served in the Pequot war. Soon after his arrival at Plymouth he opened the first inn, which was kept by himself and son James until 1698. This was probably the first public house in New England. Children: James, born 1626, in England; Hugh, mentioned below; John, November 21, 1636; Mary, 1639, married (first) John Almy, (second) John Pococke.

(II) Hugh Cole, second son of James and Mary (Lobel) Cole, born 1627, probably in London, England, came to America with his parents in 1632, and with them probably went to Plymouth, of which he was made a freeman in 1657. At the opening of King Philip's war in 1675 two of the sons of Mr. Cole were made prisoners by the Indians. Philip ordered them to be set at liberty, because their father had been his friend. He sent word to Hugh Cole that for safety he should remove his family to Rhode Island, which he did. Perhaps in an hour after he left his house was in flames. He lived for a time at Portsmouth, Rhode Island. According to Savage, Mr. Cole was a sergeant in the war. He removed to Swansea in 1677, and built a house within a few rods of the present home of Miss Abby Cole, and this land on the Kickemuit river has never passed out of the possession of the Cole family, being now owned by the lady named. He was selectman of Swansea, and for a number of years deputy to the General Court. He

ENCYCLOPEDIA OF BIOGRAPHY

died in Swansea, January 22, 1699 He
married (first) January 8, 1654, Mary,
born August 17, 1635, in Scituate, daughter of Richard and Ann (Shelly) Foxwell,
of Barnstable, Massachusetts, her father
having come from England with Governor Winthrop in 1631 and settled in
Scituate He married (second) January
1, 1689, Elizabeth, widow of Jacob Cook,
former widow of William Shurtliffe, and
daughter of Thomas and Ann Lettuce, of
Plymouth She died in Swansea, Massachusetts, October 31, 1693, and he married (third) January 30, 1694, Mary,
widow of Deacon Ephraim Morton, former widow of William Harlow, and
daughter of Robert and Judith Shelly Of
his ten children the first three were born
in Plymouth and the others in Swansea
They were James, born November 3,
1655, Hugh, March 6, 1658; John, May
15, 1660, Martha, April 16, 1662, Anna,
December 14, 1664, Ruth, January 8,
1666, Joseph May 18, 1668, Ebenezer,
1671; Mary, 1676, Benjamin, mentioned
below

(III) Benjamin Cole, youngest child of
Hugh and Mary (Foxwell) Cole, was
born 1678, in Swansea, where he lived,
and was a husbandman He was a deacon in the church from 1718 until the time
of his death, September 29, 1748 The
house he built in 1701 is still standing
He married, June 27, 1701, Hannah,
daughter of Caleb and Elizabeth (Bullock) Eddy She died May 15, 1768, and
both were interred in the Kickemuit burying ground Children Hopestill, born
October 9 1703, Jonathan, October 4,
1704, Benjamin, mentioned below, Fox-
til, September, 1708, Isaiah, March 4,
1710, Ebenezer, March 29, 1712, Andrew,
May 28, 1714, Hannah, January 14, 1716

(IV) Benjamin (2) Cole, son of Benjamin (1) and Hannah (Eddy) Cole, was
born October 31, 1706, in Swansea, and

died December 20, 1776 He married
(first) November 19, 1730, Elizabeth,
daughter of Thomas and Hope (Huckins)
Nelson, of Middleboro, Massachusetts
She died March 25, 1748, and he married
(second) September 22, 1749, Hannah,
widow of Job Luther, and daughter of
Richard and Mary Harding Children
Isaiah, mentioned below, Hope, born
1733, Lois, 1735, Hannah, 1736, Andrew,
Lillis, 1745, Elizabeth, Benjamin, July 7,
1750, Job, March 28, 1753, Parker, January 13, 1756, Richard, 1758, Ebenezer,
1760.

(V) Isaiah Cole, eldest child of Benjamin (2) and Elizabeth (Nelson) Cole,
born 1731, in Swansea, was a shipwright
and lived in Warren, Rhode Island, until
after the Revolution, when he removed to
Middleboro, Massachusetts He was a
soldier in the Revolution, but of the several Isaiahs' and Josiahs' services, there
being some confliction between the two
names, there is too much uncertainty
to attempt to assign to each his share
He died November 9, 1811, at Middleboro
His widow died February 8, 1827, at the
home of her daughter Abigail, in Warren,
Rhode Island Children Thomas, born
November 29, 1751, Elizabeth, April 25,
1753, Andrew, January 10, 1755; James,
June 1, 1757, Nathaniel, mentioned below, Abigail, May 26, 1763, Mary, October 27, 1765; Samuel, March 3, 1769

(VI) Captain Nathaniel Cole, fourth
son of Isaiah Cole, was born November
20, 1759, in Warren, Rhode Island, and
was a ship carpenter by trade He was
a patriot of the Revolution, served in Captain Amos Washburn's company, Colonel
Ebenezer Sprout's regiment, May 6, 1778,
also Captain Elisha Haskell's company,
Colonel Benjamin Hawe's (Howe's) regiment, July 29, 1778, to September 11,
1778 After the close of the war, Mr
Cole removed to Middleboro, Massachu-

122

setts, having purchased a farm upon which he lived. He was captain of the Second Company of Middleboro militia from May 7, 1805 to 1809. Subsequently he purchased a farm between Windsor and Hartland, Vermont. He died January 12, 1846, at the home of his daughter, Abigail, in Hartland. He married, October 17, 1784, Nancy Anthony, born January 24, 1762, in Swansea, Massachusetts, died December 8, 1828. Children: James, mentioned below; Judith, born July 24, 1788; William, April 6, 1790; Samuel, April 10, 1792; Thomas, January 10, 1794; Abigail, September 4, 1796.

(VII) James (2) Cole, eldest child of Captain Nathaniel and Nancy (Anthony) Cole, born November 20, 1785, in Warren, was a master millwright, and died at Middleboro, Massachusetts, October 16, 1871. He owned and lived upon a farm at Assawampsett, some four miles from the farm of his father. His children, all born in Middleboro, were: Abigail, born September 4, 1814; Andrew, September 1, 1816; Mary Ann, November 23, 1817; James, mentioned below; Harrison G. D., November 4, 1820; Luther, May 20, 1822; Nathaniel, May 3, 1824; Robert Vaughn, July 14, 1826; Judith Jacobs, August 10, 1828; Ellersener Thayer, March 26, 1832.

(VIII) James (3) Cole, second son of James (2) Cole was born April 7, 1819, in Middleboro, and died there December 8, 1910. The paternal residence in which he was born stood on the site of the present railroad station at Lakeville. Mr. Cole received only an ordinary education, but he was a man of versatile genius, and was justly popular and widely known in Plymouth county, where he served as deputy sheriff from 1869 until his death. There was never a more popular officer, and he found it easy to conduct the duties of his office, because of his innate kindness and sympathy with the misfortunes of others. It was rarely necessary for him to use handcuffs in handling those in his custody, owing to his well-known good nature, as well as great strength. For more than half a century he was a dealer in horses, was a lover of and expert judge of horses, known among breeders of all parts of the United States. Among the first to import blooded horses from Vermont and the West, he realized handsome returns from his enterprise. His rigid honesty, kindly nature and energetic character gained him a multitude of friends and admirers, and he prospered in life. From its organization until his death he was director of the Middleboro Savings Bank, and he was a keen judge of real estate values, and settled many estates. His judgment was often sought as an appraiser and his decisions were fair, wise and always accepted. For fifty years he was an auctioneer, and the scene of his activities was extensive, as were those activities. In 1869 he became affiliated with the Masonic fraternity, continuing to the end of his life a faithful and useful member. His chief diversion was playing checkers, in which he became highly skilled, winning many victories over professional players. In early life Mr. Cole acted in politics as a Democrat, and about the beginning of the Civil War he espoused the cause of Republican principles, to which he thenceforward adhered. It was said of him: "He was a good neighbor, a generous friend of the needy, an indulgent husband and loving father, and a valued and esteemed citizen."

He married Beulah Ann Macomber, born September 16, 1824, died June 20, 1885, in Middleboro, buried in Central Cemetery of that town. She was a daughter of Joseph and Beulah (Thomas) Macomber, of Middleboro (see Macomber VII). Children: Charlotte Elizabeth and Emily Frances, mentioned below.

(IX) Charlotte Elizabeth Cole, married, December 8, 1864, Rufus Henry Ellis, son of Rufus and Lydia (Sears) Ellis, who was born 1840, in Sandwich, Massachusetts, and received his educational training in Paul Wing's School for Boys at Sandwich, and at the Pierce Academy, Middleboro, Massachusetts Early in life he went to sea and made several voyages in coasting vessels He soon abandoned this life and became an apprentice to a tinner in New Bedford, where he continued until the completion of his trade Going to Middleboro, he was long employed by George H Doane, continuing in the same shop fifty-five years While in New Bedford he was a member of the volunteer fire department, and when the city of New Bedford replaced its hand implements for steam, Mr Ellis was instrumental in bringing "Old Six" to Middleboro, where he was also a member of the fire department He was a member of the Veteran Firemen's Association His record of employment in one place is probably without parallel He died March 22, 1916, in Middleboro He was a trustee of the Middleboro Savings Bank, and was highly estemed as a citizen Mrs Ellis is a charter member of the Middleboro Woman's Club and of Nemasket Chapter, Daughters of the American Revolution

(IX) Emily Frances Cole married Lance de Jongh, a well known writer and public speaker, who died at Wickford, Rhode Island, April 10, 1908 His death was superinduced by his efforts to extinguish a fire in his room Mr de Jongh was a native of Newport, son of William and Amelia (Tower) de Jongh, of South Carolina In the early seventies he went to Middleboro, where he resided for a time, prominent in local political circles, and an old school Democrat He was one of the oldest newspaper men in Rhode Island,

and for years had been the south county correspondent of the Associated Press He was a Civil War veteran, serving as a captain's clerk on the United States Steamer "Brandywine," and was a member of the Grand Army of the Republic post at Wickford His remains were buried in the Cole family lot at Central Cemetery Besides his wife, his only known living relative is Charlemagne Tower, former United States ambassador to Germany

(The Macomber Line)

"The evidence is convincing," says Everett S Stackpole, in his "Macomber Genealogy," that "William and John Macomber came from Devonshire, England, or vicinity, along with the other settlers of Plymouth and Bristol Counties, Mass " The tradition is current in almost all the branches of the Macomber family that their first American ancestors were of Scotch origin In 1904 Dove, Lockhart & Smart, lawyers of Edinburgh, wrote to Charles Sumner Macomber, lawyer of Ida Grove, Iowa "Judging from your name we should say you were undoubtedly a Scot by origin The name 'Macomber,' in its various forms, 'McCoombe,' 'McCumber,' 'Macomber,' 'McComish,' 'McCombie,' is well known here As you are no doubt aware it is claimed (and the claim we believe is generally well admitted) that the Macombers are a branch of the clan McIntosh—also sometimes called the Shaws The branch was founded by Shaw McDuff, second son of the fifth Earl of Fife "

(I) John Macomber was admitted a freeman and enrolled in the militia of Taunton in 1643 In 1659 he was granted permission to build a mill in Taunton There were then four persons in his family, and there is no record of more In 1680 he was in a military company A

124

deed shows that he was living in 1687, and another deed shows that he died before 1690 He was a carpenter by trade, was twice married, the name of his first wife not ascertained He married (second) January 7, 1686, Mary Babcock His property was equally divided between a daughter, Mary Staples, and a son, John Macomber.

(II) John (2) Macomber, son of John (1) Macomber, signed a deed with his father in 1672, showing that he was then of age He served in military companies in 1680 and 1700 and also in Queen Anne's War in 1691 His will is dated January 22, 1722, and was probated October 21, 1725 In it he named his wife, four sons, and grandchildren Abiel, William, Anna and Sarah He married, July 16, 1678, Ann, daughter of William and Ann (Hailstone) Evans, of Taunton His four sons, who lived in Taunton, were Thomas, born July 30, 1679, John, mentioned below; William, January 31, 1684, Samuel married Sarah Pierce

(III) John (3) Macomber, son of John (2) and Ann (Evans) Macomber, born March 8, 1681, died December 14, 1747, in Taunton He was a soldier of Queen Anne's War in 1701 and 1711 On January 5, 1732, he deeded one-third of his farm to his sons, Nathaniel and Josiah His son, Elijah, inherited the homestead in East Taunton He married (first) March 17, 1707, Elizabeth Williams, born April 18, 1686, in Taunton, daughter of Nathaniel and Elizabeth (Rogers) Williams, granddaughter of Richard Williams (q v) She was also a granddaughter of John and Ann (Churchman) Rogers, and great-granddaughter of Thomas Rogers, of the "Mayflower" colony She died May 2, 1732, and he married (second) in Raynham, July 12, 1733, Lydia (born King), widow of Nathaniel Williams She survived him and died March 31,

1748 Children: Nathaniel, born February 9, 1709, Josiah, February 19, 1711, John, February 10, 1713, Elizabeth, March 15, 1715, James, September 12, 1717, Elijah, October 25, 1718, Mary, July 30, 1721, Abiah, June 8, 1724, Annah, January 2, 1726, Joseph, mentioned below

(IV) Joseph Macomber, youngest child of John (3) Macomber, born March 28, 1732, in Taunton, resided in what is now Lakeville, on a neck of land between two lakes, known as Assawampsett Neck, then in Middleboro His house is still standing He served as a soldier of both the French and Revolutionary wars; was a corporal in Captain Thomas Cobb's company, Colonel John Winslow's regiment, for the defense of the eastern frontiers, mustered at Castle Island, June 21, 1754 A muster roll dated January 31, 1759, shows him as first lieutenant, Captain Job Winslow's company, Colonel Jedediah Preble's regiment, regiment raised by Massachusetts for the reduction of Canada; served March 13 to November 13, 1758, and credited with fifteen days' travel home He was lieutenant in Captain John Taplin's company from March 31, 1759, to December 31, 1760, at Fort Cumberland, roll dated Boston, December 31, 1760 He was lieutenant in Captain Abiel Pierce's company of minute-men, serving two days at the Lexington Alarm, at the outbreak of the Revolution He was sergeant in Captain Levi Rounseville's company, Colonel D Brewer's regiment, from May 5, 1775, serving three months, four days. He was commissioned January 8, 1776, as lieutenant in Captain Edward Seagrovy's company of the Thirteenth Regiment, commanded by Colonel Joseph Reed He married, March 16, 1761, Thankful Canedy, daughter of Captain William and Elizabeth (Eaton) Canedy, descended through Elizabeth

Eaton from Francis Eaton, Samuel Fuller and John Billington of the "Mayflower" immigrants. Dr. Samuel Fuller's third wife, Bridget Lee, was the mother of Samuel (2) Fuller, born 1625 in Plymouth. He was one of the twenty-six original proprietors of Middleboro, was pastor of the church there, where he died August 17, 1695. He married Elizabeth Brewster, and their third daughter, Elizabeth, born 1666, married Samuel (2) Eaton. The last named was born 1665, in Plymouth, son of Samuel Eaton, who came with his parents, Francis and Sarah Eaton, when an infant, on the "Mayflower." Samuel (1) Eaton lived in Duxbury, Plymouth and Middleboro, dying 1684, in the latter town. His second wife, Martha (Billington) Eaton, was a daughter of Francis and Christian (Penn) Billington, and granddaughter of John and Helen Billington, who came on the "Mayflower" to Plymouth. Joseph Macomber's children: Joseph, mentioned below; Thankful, born January 21, 1764; Betsey, March 24, 1765; Nathan, February 2, 1767; Frederick, December 29, 1768; Elijah, October 14, 1770; Judith, August 24, 1772; Olive, March 20, 1774; Lurana, February 19, 1778; Hannah, May 23, 1780.

(V) Joseph (2) Macomber, eldest child of Joseph (1) and Thankful (Canedy) Macomber, was born September 8, 1762, in Middleboro, and lived on the paternal homestead, where he died July 3, 1800. Before he was eighteen years old he entered the Revolutionary army, first in Captain Amos Washburn's company, Colonel Ebenezer White's regiment, from August 1 to 9, 1780, company marched to Rhode Island on an alarm. He was also in Captain Henry Pierce's company, Colonel Theophilus Cotton's regiment, from March 8 to 31, 1781, serving twenty-six days at Rhode Island, company raised by order of Governor Hancock to serve forty

days unless sooner discharged. He married (published October 23, 1792, in Middleboro) Alethea Robinson, daughter of Josiah and Theodora (Godfrey) Robinson, born about 1768, died 1836. Children: Joseph, mentioned below; Josiah Robinson, born February 20, 1795; Elizabeth, August 22, 1797.

(VI) Joseph (3) Macomber, eldest child of Joseph (2) and Alethea (Robinson) Macomber, born August 14, 1793, in Middleboro, died there April 22, 1862. He married (first) March 7, 1819, Lois, daughter of Edward and Lucy Sherman, born August 9, 1798, died October 25, 1820. He married (second) October 5, 1823, Beulah Thomas, daughter of Churchill and Hannah C (Cushman) Thomas, born November 23, 1801, died July 18, 1892 (see Thomas VII). Child of first marriage: Lois Sherman, born August 12, 1820, children of second marriage Beulah Ann, mentioned below; Clarinda Adams, born October 3, 1826; Hannah Cushman, July 14, 1829; Elizabeth Clark, April 2, 1832.

(VII) Beulah Ann Macomber, daughter of Joseph (3) Macomber, and his second wife, Beulah (Thomas) Macomber, born September 16, 1824, became the wife of James (3) Cole, of Middleboro (see Cole VIII)

(The Thomas Line)

(I) William Thomas, said to have been of Welsh descent, and one of the merchant adventurers of London, came from Yarmouth, England, in the "Marye and Ann" in 1637, and settled in Marshfield, Massachusetts, with his son Nathaniel. He was assistant deputy governor in 1642-50, member of the council of war in 1643, and died in August, 1651, aged seventy-eight years.

(II) Nathaniel Thomas, son of William Thomas, born in 1606, came over with his father, bringing with him his wife and son William. He commanded one of the watches against the Indians in 1643, was one of the volunteers of the Pequot expedition in 1643, was commissioned ensign of the Marshfield company of the Colonial troops and later captain, and in 1654 succeeded Miles Standish in command. He had children besides William. Nathaniel, born 1643; Mary, married Captain Symon Ray; Elizabeth; Dorothy, died young; Jeremiah, mentioned below; Dorothy.

(III) Jeremiah Thomas, son of Nathaniel Thomas, was born 1658-59, and died February 2, 1736. He married Mary, and had children. Nathaniel, born January 2, 1686; Sarah, December 25, 1687; Jeremiah, February 14, 1689; Elizabeth, November 19, 1690; Mary, June 5, 1692; Lydia, March 26, 1694; Thankful, June 30, 1695; Jedediah, mentioned below; Bethiah, March 27, 1701; Ebenezer, November 1, 1703; Priscilla, October 13, 1705; Sophia, 1707.

(IV) Jedediah Thomas, third son of Jeremiah and Mary Thomas, born August 17, 1698, in Middleboro, married, March 12, 1723, Lois Nelson, born April 19, 1704, daughter of Thomas and Hope (Huckins) Nelson, granddaughter of William Nelson, founder of the family in the Plymouth colony; also granddaughter of Joseph Huckins and great-granddaughter of Thomas Huckins, who was commander of the Ancient and Honorable Artillery Company of Boston. Children: Hope, born November 16, 1724; Jedediah, mentioned below; Elizabeth, February 10, 1729; Lois, April 4, 1732; Abiah, August 3, 1737; Joanna, April 6, 1739; Isaac, May 28, 1742.

(V) Jedediah (2) Thomas, son of Jedediah (1) and Lois (Nelson) Thomas, born February 19, 1727, in Middleboro, served in the Revolution. He married in Middleboro, December 28, 1749, Keziah Churchill, born about 1730, probably daughter of Benjamin and Mary (Shaw) Churchill, or of John and Bethiah (Spooner) Churchill, of Plymouth. Only three children are recorded, family records supply others. Mary, born May 3, 1751; Martha, February 15, 1753; Nelson, January 25, 1759; Churchill, mentioned below; Keziah, February 11, 1765. Jedediah Thomas, of Middleboro, was a private in Captain Nehemiah Allen's company, Colonel Jeremiah Hall's regiment, marched December 8, 1776, service ninety-two days, company marched to Bristol, Rhode Island, December 8, 1776; also private in Captain Nathaniel Wood's company, Colonel Ebenezer Sprout's regiment, entered service May 6, 1778, discharged May 9, 1778, service three days, company marched on two alarms at Dartmouth, one in May and one in September, 1778.

(VI) Churchill Thomas, son of Jedediah (2) and Keziah (Churchill) Thomas, was born November 30, 1761, in Middleboro, and died there December 31, 1809, aged forty-eight years. He was a private in Captain John Barrow's company, Colonel Abijah Stearns' regiment of guards, entered service April 14, 1778, discharged July 2, 1778, service two months and twenty-one days at and about Boston; also private in Captain Nathaniel Wood's company, Colonel Ebenezer Sprout's regiment, entered service September 6, 1778, discharged September 12, 1778, service six days, company marched on two alarms at Dartmouth, one in May, one in September, 1778, service six days, roll dated Middleboro, also private in Captain William Tupper's company, Colonel Nathan Sparhawk's regiment, entered service September 28, 1778, discharged December 14, 1778, service two months and sixteen days, at Boston, roll sworn to at Middleboro, also a private in Captain Edward Hammond's company, Colonel Samuel Fisher's regiment, enlisted August 13, 1779, discharged September 13, 1779, service one month, four days, at Rhode Island, travel eighty miles, including company detached from militia to serve for one month in a regiment under Samuel Fisher's command, also a private in Captain Jonah Washburn's company, Colonel Ebenezer White's regiment, marched August 1, 1780, discharged August 9, 1780, service nine days, company marched to Rhode Island on the alarm of August 1, 1780, roll sworn to at Middleboro, also a private in Captain Henry Pierce's company, Colonel Theophilus Cotton's regiment, enlisted March 8, 1781, discharged March 31, 1781, service twenty-six days to Rhode Island, including travel sixty-five miles, out and home, company raised by order of his excellency, John Hancock to serve for forty days, unless sooner discharged   Churchill Thomas married Hannah C Cushman, born November 8, 1761, in Duxbury, daughter of Joseph and Elizabeth (Sampson) Cushman, born August 23, 1772   Children   Harvey Cushman, born November 18, 1788; Elizabeth Sampson, July 4, 1794, Abigail Soule, September 14, 1796, Alfred, July 16, 1799, Beulah, mentioned below

(VII) Beulah Thomas, daughter of Churchill and Hannah C (Cushman) Thomas, was born November 23, 1801, and became the wife of Joseph (3) Macomber, of Middleboro (see Macomber VI)

HILL, Christopher,

Carpenter, Builder

This name was often spelled Hilles, and that form is still used by a large number of the descendants bearing the name   It has been traced to a somewhat remote

period in England, having been found nearly two hundred years before the Puritan emigration   It has been borne by numerous prominent citizens of the American colonies and of the United States, and is still among the most widely distributed names known in the history of the country   An examination of the records relative to the early history of the Hills in America discloses the fact that there were several immigrants of this name who arrived from England prior to 1650, namely   William and John Hill, of Dorchester, Massachusetts, John Hill, of Dover, New Hampshire who was accompanied by at least one brother and perhaps more, Jonathan Hill, of Rhode Island, and Peter Hill, of Saco, Maine   It is probable that William and John Hill, of Dorchester, were brothers, although there does not seem to be any documentary proof of the fact

(I) Jonathan Hill was one of the numerous pioneers of this family in New England before 1660   But little is known of him   He lived at Warwick, Portsmouth, and perhaps elsewhere in Rhode Island, and died in 1690   Children   Robert, married Mary Pearce; Jonathan, mentioned below; Henry, born June 2, 1661, in Warwick, resided at East Greenwich   And others

(II) Jonathan (2) Hill, son of Jonathan (1) Hill, was born 1657, and lived on Prudence Island (Portsmouth), where he died February 5, 1731   He bought land at Cowesit for fifty pounds, on July 6, 1703, became a large landholder, and the inventory of his estate made September 15, 1731, amounted to £791, 3s and 6d   He had children   Jonathan, Caleb, Mary, Patience, Rebecca, Thomas, Ebenezer and Sarah

(III) Thomas Hill, son of Jonathan (2) Hill was born in 1692, and lived in North Kingstown   In 1721 he was living in Swansea, Massachusetts, and received on January 16 of that year, from his father, a deed of one hundred and five acres in Warwick, to which town he removed. He married in North Kingstown, September 16, 1716, Elizabeth Allen, probably a daughter of John and Sarah Allen, of that town.

(IV) Thomas (2) Hill, son of Thomas (1) and Elizabeth (Allen) Hill, was born about 1720, and lived in North Kingstown, where he married, in 1743, Mary Berry On the Scituate records her name appears as Alice He lived in North Kingstown until after 1749, and was living in Scituate in 1754 His children on North Kingstown town records were Jonathan, born September 1, 1744, Benjamin, mentioned below, Thomas, December 29, 1747; John, March 2, 1749, in Scituate Elizabeth, March 14, 1751, Rebecca, June 11, 1754, Anne, July 27, 1756; Henry, February 1, 1759

(V) Benjamin Hill, second son of Thomas (2) and Mary (Berry) Hill, was born March 28, 1746, in North Kingstown, and lived in Foster, Rhode Island, where his children are recorded. He married, December 7, 1768, in Scituate, Hannah Potter, daughter of Christian and Elizabeth Potter, and their children recorded in Foster were Christopher, mentioned below; George, born December 5, 1771, Sarah, September 8, 1773, Elizabeth, March 9, 1775, Benjamin, January 7, 1777, Alice, October 24, 1778; Miles, August 25, 1780; Richard, January 2, 1782, Anna, April 15, 1784; Thomas Tibbetts, December 30, 1786

(VI) Christopher Hill, eldest child of Benjamin and Hannah (Potter) Hill, was born February 14, 1770, in Foster, where he was a blacksmith and farmer. He reared a large family, all of whom were given good educational opportunities. He married, in Foster, April 2, 1795, Mary

Elizabeth Whipple, of Warwick, and their children were Holden, Benjamin, Thomas, Christopher, Amy, who married Stephen Browning, and Patience, who married Thomas Remington

(VII) Christopher (2) Hill, son of Christopher (1) and Mary E (Whipple) Hill, was born July 27, 1800, in Foster, and died in Fall River, Massachusetts, in November, 1872 He was educated in Warwick, Rhode Island, attending school three months in the year, until he was eighteen years of age He learned the carpenter's trade, and settled in Fall River, where he was engaged in building operations throughout his active life He was an attendant of the Congregational church, an upright and respected citizen, a Republican in political principle, and ever ready to foster any plan designed to benefit the community in which he lived He married in Warwick, Hannah Cook Durfee, born May 8, 1808, in Fall River, died there July 24, 1884, daughter of Stephen and Mehitable Durfee, of that city (see Durfee VI) Children Mary Elizabeth, born August 8, 1829, died aged seventeen years, Almy A, born February 4, 1832, died aged seven years; Mehitable Durfee, born November 2, 1835, married in Fall River, December 16, 1869, Robert S Dunning, the noted painter of fruits, who was born January 3, 1829, in Brunswick, Maine, son of Joseph and Rebecca (Spear) Dunning, resides in Fall River; Lucy Chaloner, born September 20, 1839, in Warwick, is a practicing physician in Fall River

(The Durfee Line).

The family of Durfee has been a rather prolific one, and still has many representatives in Rhode Island and Southeastern Massachusetts, where it was very early located Its representatives have been active in every walk of life, and have borne their share in the development of modern civilization

(I) Thomas Durfee, born in 1643 in England, came thence to Rhode Island at an early day, settling there while the Warwick charter of 1643 was still in force He was married (first) in Portsmouth, about 1664, and had the following children born in Portsmouth Robert, March 10, 1665, Richard, Thomas, William, Ann and Benjamin He married (second) Deliverance (Hall) Trip, daughter of William and Mary Hall, and widow of Abiel Trip She died in 1721, the mother of two children by her marriage with Mr Durfee

(II) Benjamin Durfee, son of Thomas Durfee, inherited from his father, in addition to what he had previously given him, large tracts of land within the present limits of Fall River He subsequently acquired more by purchase, and became one of the largest land owners in this section of the country He was a man of great energy, of character, quick of comprehension and intelligent, and held in high estimation in the community in which he lived At his death, in 1754, he left a large estate, some of which long remained in the family, if it has not to the present time, but like most large properties much of it has changed hands, and is now owned by others not of the same name He received by deed of gift from his father, Thomas Durfee, the land from Rodman street on the north to Osborn street on the south, and extending from the shore to East Rod Way This land was purchased of William Manchester in 1680, and was given to Benjamin Durfee in 1709 The latter gave the same land to his son, Captain William Durfee, and, by will, William Durfee gave the south half to his nephew, Richard Durfee, the son of his brother Richard, and James Durfee, the son of his brother Ben-

jamin; the north half he gave to his relative, William Borden James Durfee sold his portion to David Durfee, the father of Hon David Durfee, of Tiverton, who in time gave it to his son, Captain William Durfee, and he, dying in 1816, left it to his children They sold it to Oliver Chace, and it has since been laid out and much of it sold for building lots, upon which may be found some of the finest residences in Fall River Benjamin Durfee married, in 1699, Prudence Earle, daughter of William and Prudence Earle, granddaughter of Ralph and Joan (Sawyer) Earle Children James, born August 28, 1701, Ann, January 17, 1703, Hope, January 7, 1705, William, December 7, 1707, Benjamin, January 5, 1709, Mercy, January 30, 1711, Lusannah, January 28, 1713, Martha, July 13, 1719, Thomas, mentioned below, Richard, mentioned below

(III) Thomas (2) Durfee, fourth son of Benjamin and Prudence (Earle) Durfee, was born November 5, 1721, in Tiverton, and inherited a large estate from his father, residing on the present site of the County House in Fall River Upon the division of her father's estate his wife inherited an interest in the Fall River water power Mr Durfee's farm extended from the Taunton river to North Watuppa pond, and the southern boundary was near the present armory in Fall River He long represented a constituency in both the lower house and senate of the Massachusetts General Court, was six years a member of the Governor's Council, and was active and influential throughout his life in the community At the funeral of Governor John Hancock, in 1793, he was one of the honorary pallbearers Because of a physical infirmity he was not fit for active military service, but commanded a militia company in Freetown in 1776 He married in Tiverton, August 9, 1747, Patience Borden, of that town, born 1731, daughter of Joseph and Abigail (Russell) Borden, died in Freetown in July, 1802 Freetown then included the family residence Mrs Durfee was descended from one of the prominent and oldest families of Massachusetts, founded by Richard Borden, who was of the ninth recorded English generation, born in the parish of Hedcorn, Kent, England, where he was baptized February 22, 1596, son of Matthew and Joan Borden, and died May 25, 1671, in Portsmouth, Rhode Island He married in Hedcorn Church, September 28, 1625, Joan Fowle, who accompanied him to America in 1637-38, and died July 15, 1688, in Portsmouth Children of Thomas (2) and Patience (Borden) Durfee Hope, born September 29, 1748, Joseph, mentioned below, Nathan, April 5, 1752, Benjamin, May, 1754, Prudence, September 6, 1756, Abigail, August, 1759, Charles, November 20, 1761, Susannah, November, 1764, Nathan, March 23, 1766; James, March 25, 1768; Thomas, January 22, 1771; Samuel, August 25, 1773

(IV) Joseph Durfee, eldest son of Thomas (2) and Patience (Borden) Durfee, was born April 27, 1750, in Tiverton, lived many years in that town, and in his old age removed to Assonet Village, in the town of Freetown, where he died December 10, 1841, in his ninety-second year. With his wife he helped organize the First Congregational Church in what is now Fall River, in 1816 In 1775 he was commissioned a captain, and raised a company of minute-men, which was stationed at Fall River about fifteen months Subsequently, with sixty men, he marched to New York and joined the regiment of Colonel Thomas Carpenter, participating in the battle of White Plains In November, 1776, he marched his company back to Tiverton and joined Colonel John

Cook's regiment, which covered the retreat of the Continentals from Rhode Island Before January, 1777, he was commissioned major in Colonel John Hathaway's regiment, and was stationed some six months at Little Compton Early in 1778, with twenty men, he was stationed at Fall River, and in May of that year, when the British forces landed at Fall River, and began burning mills and other buildings, he rallied the citizens with his men and drove the British off, with considerable loss in killed and wounded In August, 1778, he joined General Sullivan's expedition to Rhode Island, as major of Colonel Whitney's regiment In the autumn of that year he was stationed three months at Pawtucket, and early in 1779 he was commissioned lieutenant-colonel in Cornell's brigade, and remained at Tiverton until the British evacuated Rhode Island In October following he was stationed at Newport, where he remained until December In 1782 he was promoted colonel He represented Tiverton in the General Assembly, the town being then a part of Massachusetts, and was ever an influential citizen He married (first) September 24, 1772, Elizabeth Turner, of Tiverton, born 1754, daughter of Dr John and Patience (Gardner) Turner, died May 19, 1817 He married (second) January 29, 1819, Mrs Elizabeth Nicholls Children: Charlotte, born July 15, 1773; Gardner, April 2, 1775, George Washington, April 27, 1777, Rhobe (Phebe), September 23, 1779, Susannah, March 9, 1783, Mehitable, mentioned below; Amelia, July 30, 1787, Aaron, December 17, 1789, Elizabeth, January 19, 1792, Patience, September 5, 1794, Abigail, February 24, 1799

(V) Mehitable Durfee, fourth daughter of Joseph and Elizabeth (Turner) Durfee, was born June 15, 1785, in Tiverton, died in Fall River, September 4, 1857, became the wife of Stephen Durfee, of that city (see Durfee V).

(III) Richard Durfee, youngest child of Benjamin and Prudence (Earle) Durfee, was born November 9, 1723, and married in Plymouth, Massachusetts (Assonet record), August 30, 1749, Rebecca Cole, of Plymouth, born there 1727, daughter of Ephraim (2) and Sarah Cole, granddaughter of Ephraim (1) and Rebecca (Gray) Cole. She owned the house built by her father on Leyden street, Plymouth, which she sold to John Churchill. Children: Ephraim, died in infancy, Sarah, died in infancy, Richard, mentioned below, Rebecca, born August 25, 1765.

(IV) Richard (2) Durfee, only surviving son of Richard (1) and Rebecca (Cole) Durfee, was born September 8, 1758, in what is now Fall River, than a part of Tiverton, and resided in Tiverton, near the south line of Freetown. He was a deacon of the church, and very active in the Revolutionary War. He enlisted first in Captain Loring Peck's company, of Colonel Lippitt's (Rhode Island) regiment, in 1776, and was on the payroll, showing a service of two months and fourteen days, for which he received £4, 18s and 8d, at the rate of two pounds per month. He was again in the service in 1777, and received for travel from Charlestown to Smithfield and to Cumberland from Peekskill, two pounds, one shilling and six pence, roll dated Cranston, January 18, 1777. He was appointed a lieutenant and later captain of the Third Company of Militia of the town of Tiverton, which company was attached to a regiment commanded by Colonel John Cook, and in August, 1778, was paid for five days, at the rate of three pounds per day. This regiment formed a part of the army of General Sullivan. The records

of the United States Pension Office show that he made application for a pension, September 8, 1832, at which time he was seventy-four years old, and was residing in Tiverton. The pension was allowed for fourteen months and fifteen days' active service as a private, and eleven months and fifteen days as captain of Rhode Island troops in the Revolutionary War. The First Congregational Church of Fall River was organized at the house of Captain Durfee, January 9, 1816. Among the five persons who established this organization were Colonel Joseph Durfee and wife Elizabeth, Richard Durfee, and Esther, wife of Charles Durfee, Esq. Thomas R. Durfee, son of Charles and Wealthy Durfee, subsequently became a member. In 1823 Captain Richard Durfee was elected deacon of the church.

He married in Freetown, June 20, 1779, Patience Borden, born August 4, 1762, died November 2, 1836, in Tiverton, daughter of Stephen and Mary (Gray) Borden, of Fall River. The Borden family, like that of Durfee, was very early established in this country, and was of very ancient lineage in England, having been established at the time of the Conquest, coming from Normandy, where the family had previously existed. Richard Borden was born in the parish of Hedcorn, Kent, England, baptized there February 22, 1596, son of Matthew and Joan Borden, and died at Portsmouth, Rhode Island, May 25, 1671. He married in Hedcorn Church, September 28, 1625, Joan Fowle, moved in 1628 to the neighboring parish of Cranbrook, and came to America in 1638, settling at Portsmouth. He was a surveyor and acquired large tracts of land in Rhode Island and New Jersey, was a freeman of Portsmouth, March 16, 1641, and filled many official positions there, including that of deputy from Portsmouth to the General Assembly in 1667 and 1670. His fourth son, John Borden, born September, 1640, in Portsmouth, died there June 4, 1716. He married, December 25, 1670, Mary Earle, born in Portsmouth 1655, died there in 1734, daughter of William and Mary (Walker) Earle. Their third son was Joseph Borden, born December 3, 1680, married Sarah Brownell, of Portsmouth. Their eldest son was Stephen Borden, born August 10, 1705, in what is now Fall River, died August 30, 1738. He married, February 3, 1726, Penelope Read, born October 12, 1703, in Dartmouth, daughter of John (3) and Mary (Pierce) Read. John (3) Read was for some thirty years town clerk of Freetown. He was a son of John (2) Read and his wife Anna, and grandson of John (1) Read, of Newport, Rhode Island. John (2) Read was a cord-wainer by trade and operated a tannery, which was continued by his descendants through four generations, and became a large establishment at Troy, now Fall River. Stephen (2) Borden, eldest son of Stephen (1) and Penelope (Read) Borden, was born October 28, 1728, and died August 15, 1802. He married, October 8, 1748, Mary Gray, born October 14, 1733, in Tiverton, daughter of Timothy and Sarah (Bennett) Gray. They were the parents of Patience Borden, who became the wife of Captain Richard Durfee, of Fall River. Children: William, born December 8, 1780; Stephen, mentioned below; Sarah, April 11, 1785; Philip, June 14, 1787; Benjamin, January 28, 1792; Lydia, February 16, 1794; Susannah, March 1, 1796; John, May 6, 1798; Patience, August 28, 1801, died December 23, 1824; Richard, July 15, 1803; Thomas, April 24, 1805, died September 7, 1805.

(V) Stephen Durfee, second son of Richard (2) and Patience (Borden) Durfee, was born April 11, 1782, in Tiverton, and died at sea, April 25, 1812. He mar-

ried in Tiverton, in April, 1802, Mehitable Durfee, born June 15, 1785, in Tiverton, died in Fall River, September 4, 1857, daughter of Joseph and Elizabeth (Turner) Durfee. She married (second) Elisha C Fuller, of Fall River. Children: William Henry, born November 3, 1804; Leonard B, September 8, 1806; Hannah Cook, mentioned below; Philip, July 9, 1810.

(VI) Hannah Cook Durfee, only daughter of Stephen and Mehitable (Durfee) Durfee, was born May 8, 1808, in Fall River, and became the wife of Christopher (2) Hill, of Warwick, Rhode Island. (See Hill VII.)

ALVORD, Clinton,
Manufacturer

Among the founders of industries of importance in Worcester, Massachusetts, is Clinton Alvord, manufacturer of carpet looms From a small beginning he has built up an extensive and profitable business Mr Alvord comes of old Puritan stock, and his ancestry has been traced for many generations in England. The surname Alvord is identical with Alford and there are many other variations such as Alfred, Alvard, Alvart, Allard, Alved, Alvord, Allvard, Alluard, Olford, Olverd, Olvord, etc The principal seat of the family in England was in County Somerset, where Alvords were located about the time the surname came into use in England It was originally a place name, meaning a ford across a river Robertus Dominus de Aldford was governor of a military station, Aldford Castle, commanding an old ford across the River Dee above Chester The Alvord family had something to do with this fort in ancient times They were owners of land in Somersetshire as early as 1550 The coat-of-arms is described On a wreath of the colors a boar's head couped or, in the mouth a broken spear argent

An excellent genealogy of the family has been published and its author gives special credit to Mr Clinton Alvord for assistance rendered in compiling the work

(I) John Alvord, the English progenitor, was born about 1475, and died at Whitestaunton, Somersetshire He was a witness to the will of John Batley or Bailey, July 4, 1530 He had a son Alexander, mentioned below

(II) Rev Alexander Alvord, son of John Alvord, was born about 1500 He was living at Whitestaunton in 1550 and 1558. His will is dated there, December 22, 1576 The will of his widow, Agnes Alvord, in 1577 mentions children Mary, Alice, Elinor, Salaman, William, John, Bartholomew and Bridget   She was buried at West Moncton, Somersetshire, 1578   Descendants are numerous in Whitestaunton

(III) This generation is in doubt One of the sons of the Rev Alexander Alvord was father of Thomas, mentioned below, however He was also the father of Richard and John Alvord, of Whitestaunton

(IV) Thomas Alvord, grandson of the Rev Alexander Alvord, married, May 11, 1618, Joanna Hawkins at Ashill, Somersetshire   She died a widow at Whitestaunton, May 27, 1636 Children: 1 Benedict, one of the brothers who came to Windsor, Connecticut , was witness to a deed from Richard Sanderwick, of Broadway, Somersetshire, to Nicholas Nurton, of Weymouth, Massachusetts, February 20, 1639, married Jane Nurton at Windsor, November 26, 1640, he died at Windsor, Connecticut, April 23, 1683 2 Alexander, mentioned below 3 Joanna, baptized at Whitestaunton, December 8, 1622 ; married at Windsor, Connecticut, May 6, 1646, Ambrose Fowler, who

removed to Westfield, Massachusetts, about 1671, and she died there, May 22, 1684, leaving seven children

(V) Alexander (2) Alvord, son of Thomas Alvord, was baptized probably at Bridport, County Dorset, England, October 15, 1627 He went to Windsor, Connecticut, as early as 1645, when is mentioned his purchase of a house lot there In 1660 he had a pew in Windsor church among the short seats, for which he paid seven shillings Various grants of land were made to him and he has been described by an early writer as "an early settler and possessed of large means for the times." He moved to Northampton, Massachusetts, in 1661 He subscribed to the fund for Harvard College in 1672 In King Philip's War, in 1676, in Northampton, Massachusetts, his buildings were burned by the Indians, and in the same year he received a war grant of land in compensation In 1668 he was among the signers of a petition against imposts, and in 1671 of another to the Massachusetts General Court for the formation of a society at Northfield, Massachusetts He was admitted to the Northampton church soon after 1672, and his wife, Mary Alvord, joined the same church in 1661, being one of the original members of the society He took the oath of allegiance at Northampton, February 8, 1678 He married, at Windsor, Connecticut, October 29 1646, Mary Vore, daughter of Richard and Ann Vore She died at Northampton, Massachusetts, prior to 1686 He died there, October 3, 1687 Children Abigail, born October 6, 1647, John, August 12, 1649; Mary, July 6, 1651, Thomas mentioned below ; Elizabeth, November 12, 1655; Benjamin, February 11, 1658; Sarah, June 24, 1660, Jeremiah, May 9, 1663, Ebenezer, December 25, 1665, Jonathan, April 6, 1669; Child, born and died in 1671

(VI) Thomas (2) Alvord, son of Alexander (2) Alvord, was born at Windsor, Connecticut, October 27, 1653. He removed to Northampton with his father in 1661. He also took the prescribed oath of allegiance, February 8, 1678, and he received one of the early grants of land there. His house lot butted on the north of Round Hill, Northampton, and was of about four acres. At one time he owned the land which is now the site of the Court House in Northampton. He was a tailor by trade. He served under Captain William Turner in King Philip's War and took part at Turner's Falls in the fight known as the Falls Fight. For his service his son received from the General Court of Massachusetts a grant of land in Fallstown in 1734 (Bernardston). Northampton was an Alvord town and the tablets in the Memorial Hall show the name in all but one of the Indian wars, while there are more soldiers by the name of Alvord upon the rolls than of any other name. Thomas Alvord married, March 23, 1681, at Northampton, Joanna Taylor, born in Northampton, September 27, 1655, died there, February 28, 1727-28, daughter of John and Thankful (Woodward) Taylor. Children, born in Northampton: John, August 10, 1682, Thomas February 28, 1684; John, mentioned below; Josiah, February 7, 1688, died December 13, 1691. John Taylor was killed by the Indians in Easthampton while he was going with other settlers to rescue those who had been captured at the massacre of Pascommuck.

(VII) John (2) Alvord, son of Thomas (2) Alvord, was born at Northampton, Massachusetts, October 19, 1685, and died at South Hadley, Massachusetts, November 21, 1757. His gravestone was still standing, in 1908, in South Hadley, being the oldest Alvord gravestone in the Connecticut Valley. He was a saddler by

trade. He was elected constable of Northampton in 1729, was one of the first assessors of South Precinct, Hadley, March 12, 1733; was on the committee to arrange for visiting ministers and delegates, August 10, 1733, for the ordination of the Rev. Grindell Rawson, in 1741 he was one of a committee that sought the resignation of this minister. His house was west of the road north of Brewster's, on the Connecticut river. He married, at Northampton, December 29, 1708, Dorcas Lyman, born in Northampton, August 11, 1690, died at South Hadley, November 15, 1770, daughter of John and Mindwell Sheldon (Pomeroy) Lyman. Children, the first nine born at Northampton, the others at South Hadley: John, born October 29, 1711; Mindwell, August 4, 1713, Esther, Saul, April 23, 1717, Elijah, mentioned below; Dorcas, March 28, 1720, Gad, died 1723, Gad, born 1726, Job, 1729, Nathan, Gideon, June 12, 1734.

(VIII) Elijah Alvord, son of John (2) Alvord, was born at Northampton, Massachusetts, January 17, 1718-19, and died at Greenfield, Massachusetts, about 1788. He conducted a warehouse near the mouth of Stony Brook, kept the first inn in 1755, and in 1770 Noah Goodman succeeded him as tavern keeper, in 1755 it was voted by the town that he might agree with several persons to cross their lands with lumber in the Falls Field and Taylor's Field, South Hadley, to carry lumber around that had been loaded down the river, he was also a trader, licensed in 1761 to sell tea, coffee and china-ware at South Hadley; he was selectman in 1761. In 1771 he moved to Wilmington, Vermont, in 1775 he was appointed on a standing committee that the people might be informed of the doings of the Friends of Liberty; he represented the town in the first State Legislature in 1778, and the first town meeting of Wilmington was held in his house, January 19, 1778 Later he returned to Massachusetts, residing at Greenfield, but his death occurred shortly afterward Caleb Alvord, his son was appointed to administer his estate, May 15, 1788. Elijah Alvord was a soldier in the Revolution in Captain Caleb Chapin's company He married Hannah Judd, born at Northampton, 1720, died at Greenfield, November 28, 1798, daughter of Thomas and Hannah (Bascom) Judd Children, born at South Hadley Caleb, mentioned below, Hannah, born 1754

(IX) Caleb Alvord, son of Elijah Alvord, was born at South Hadley, Massachusetts, October 5, 1751, and died at Greenfield, Massachusetts, December 22, 1819 He resided in the towns of Wilmington, Vermont, and Greenfield and Bernardston, Massachusetts. In 1778 he was elected the first town clerk of Wilmington, from 1785 to 1792 he kept the tavern at Greenfield, he was selectman of Bernardston, 1793-99, and was representative from that town to the General Court, he was selectman of Greenfield, in 1797 He married, at Wilmington, Vermont, December 26, 1776, Mary Murdock, born in Wilmington, January 15, 1751, died at Greenfield, March 26, 1836, daughter of Samuel and Mary (Huntington) Murdock Children, the two eldest born at Wilmington, the youngest at Bernardston and the others in Greenfield Elijah, mentioned below; Caleb, born May 3, 1779, Pliny, March 13, 1781; Melinda, June 12, 1783, Lucinda, twin of Melinda, Melinda, May 13, 1785, Alpheus, January 17, 1787, Alfred, February 15, 1789, Mary, April 17, 1791, Fanny, September 12, 1793

(X) Elijah (2) Alvord, son of Caleb Alvord, was born at Wilmington, Vermont, November 18, 1777, and died at Greenfield, Massachusetts, September 8, 1840 He read law in Greenfield was

admitted to the bar in 1802 and became a lawyer of note During the last twenty years of his life he was clerk of courts and register of probate for Franklin county and held both offices at the time of his death He represented the town in the General Courts many terms, and was delegate to the Constitutional Convention in 1820 He was influential in securing the division of the county and in having Greenfield designated as the Shire town. A portrait of him by Harding is in the possession of his grandson, Clinton Alvord, of Worcester. He married, November 12, 1805, at Greenfield, Sabra Wells, born at Greenfield, February 3 1785, died there, March 21, 1867, daughter of Colonel Daniel and Rhoda (Newton) Wells Colonel Daniel Wells enlisted in the Revolutionary War at the age of fourteen, and was afterward an officer in the State militia, advancing to the rank of lieutenant-colonel He was town clerk and treasurer of Greenfield, Massachusetts, from 1793 to 1809 He was the head of the first water company in Greenfield, and in 1798 paid the second largest United States direct tax in that place Rhoda (Newton) Wells was a descendant of the Rev Roger Newton, of Farmington, Connecticut, and his wife, Mary, daughter of Rev. Thomas Hooker, who left Cambridge with his congregation and was the founder of Hartford, Connecticut Sabra Wells' great-grandmother was Mary Waite, daughter of the noted Indian fighter, Benjamin Waite, who was killed at Deerfield by the Indians, February 29, 1704 Mary was captured by the Indians when six years of age, September 19, 1677, and taken to Canada with her mother and two younger sisters and rescued the next winter by her father Children of Mr and Mrs Alvord, born at Greenfield Sarah Wells, August 23, 1806, James Church, April 14, 1808, Mary Upham, August 10,

1810, Martha, September 18, 1815, died in infancy; Daniel Wells, mentioned below.

(XI) Daniel Wells Alvord, son of Elijah (2) Alvord, was born at Greenfield, Massachusetts, October 21, 1816, and died at Spring Hill, Virginia, August 3, 1871. He prepared for college at Phillips Academy, Exeter, New Hampshire, and graduated from Union College in 1838. He read law in the office of Chief Justice Daniel Wells, of Greenfield, and at the Dane Law School of Harvard University. He was admitted to the bar in 1841 and practiced in Greenfield for many years. He was offered a seat on the Superior Court bench of Massachusetts, but declined the honor. From 1848 to 1853 he was commissioner of insolvency for Franklin county; represented the town of Montague (in which he did not reside) in the Constitutional Convention of 1853; was senator from Franklin county in 1854; was elected district attorney for the Northwest Judicial District in 1856 and held that office until January, 1863; in August, 1862, was appointed by President Lincoln collector of internal revenue for the Ninth District of Massachusetts and held the office until 1869 when he removed to Spring Hill, Fairfax county, Virginia, where his death occurred. He was prominent in the anti-slavery movement, in which he was influenced and introduced by his elder brother, James Church Alvord, who was elected to Congress from Greenfield in 1838, when only thirty-one years of age, the youngest man in that house, and the first man elected to Congress on a distinctly anti-slavery platform. A fine portrait is in the possession of his nephew, Clinton Alvord, of Worcester. Wendell Phillips, while in London, England, hearing of the death of James C. Alvord wrote: "His services to the cause of Anti-Slavery in the Massachusetts Legislature cannot be too highly

estimated. The right to trial by jury to persons claimed as slaves was gained almost without opposition; not only because his arguments were unanswerable, but because it was he who argued them."

Daniel Wells Alvord married (first) at Greenfield, May 10, 1843, Caroline Matilda Clapp, born in New York City, February 1, 1824, died at Greenfield, Massachusetts, September 17, 1846, daughter of Henry Wells and Eliza (Baldwin) Clapp. He married (second) at Northampton, June 7, 1859, Caroline Betts Dewey, born at Northampton, March 26, 1827, died at Hamilton, Massachusetts, April 4, 1893, daughter of Judge Charles Augustus and Caroline (Clinton) Dewey (see Dewey) and granddaughter of General James Clinton and a niece of DeWitt Clinton. A portrait of her Grandmother Clinton is in the possession of Clinton Alvord, of Worcester. She was a niece of Judge Samuel R. Betts, of New York. Children of first wife: Henry Elijah, mentioned below; Wells, born October 9, 1845, died October 12, 1845; Caroline Matilda Clapp, mentioned below. Children of second wife: Charles Dewey, born March 26, 1860, died at Atlanta, Georgia, November 27, 1888; James Church, mentioned below; Mary, born October 9, 1863, died at Spring Hill, Virginia, March 5, 1870, Clinton, mentioned below; Clarence Walworth, mentioned below.

(XII) Henry Elijah Alvord, eldest son of Daniel Wells and Caroline Matilda (Clapp) Alvord, was born in Greenfield, Massachusetts, March 11, 1844. He married, September 6, 1866, Martha Swink, daughter of William and Margaret Lindsay Swink, of Spring Hill, Virginia. He served in the Seventh Rhode Island Cavalry and in the Second Massachusetts Cavalry through the Civil War, rising from private to major, was afterward commissioned captain in the Tenth Regi-

ment, United States Cavalry For a number of years Major Alvord was connected
with the work of agricultural colleges
He was for a time president of the Association of American Agricultural Colleges
and Experiment Stations In 1895 he
organized and became chief of the dairy
division of the United States Department
of Agriculture, in which post he served
until his death on October 1, 1904.

(XII) Caroline Matilda Clapp Alvord,
daughter of Daniel Wells and Caroline
Matilda (Clapp) Alvord, was born in
Greenfield, Massachusetts, September 17,
1846 She was one of the early missionary teachers to the Freedmen representing
Greenfield in 1866, in the first Freedman
school established in Fairfax county, Virginia She was married, September 13,
1867, to Franklin Sherman, of Ash Grove,
Virginia The latter served in the Union
army during the Civil War, being lieutenant, captain and adjutant in the Tenth
Michigan Cavalry She is the mother of
twelve children, ten of whom are living

(XII) James Church Alvord, son of
Daniel Wells and Caroline Betts (Dewey)
Alvord, was born in Greenfield, Massachusetts, January 24, 1862 He married
Lucy Fairbanks, daughter of Henry and
Annie (Hayes) Fairbanks, of St Johns-
bury Vermont, June 8, 1898 He is a
minister of the Congregational church,
and is an author and playwright of note

(XII) Clinton Alvord, son of Daniel
Wells and Caroline Betts (Dewey) Alvord, was born at Greenfield, Massachusetts, November 9, 1865 He attended the
public schools of Northampton and prepared for college in Williston Seminary
at Easthampton, entering the Worcester
Polytechnic Institute, from which he was
graduated with the degree of Bachelor of
Science in the class of 1886 For a number of years he was employed as draughts-
man for Crompton & Knowles, manufac-

turers of looms, Worcester Here he became interested in textile machinery and
devoted his attention to designing looms
and devising improvements. From time
to time he has had patents issued and
many of them have proved valuable in the
business in which he has been engaged
He has been especially successful in designing looms for the manufacture of pile
carpets, and since 1902 has been engaged
in the manufacture of tapestry and velvet
carpet machinery, improved printing
drums, setting frames and other apparatus
used in carpet mills His business is
located in the same building in which he
started in 1902—Nos 5-9 Summer street,
Worcester Beginning on a small scale
he has extended his business year by year
until he has fifty or more skilled mechanics employed, utilizing ten thousand
feet of floor space For some years the
business was conducted under his own
name In 1904 it was incorporated under
the name of the Worcester Loom Works,
of which he is president manager and
principal owner The product of his shop
goes to all parts of the country, especially
to New England and the Middle States
In politics Mr Alvord is a staunch Republican, a firm believer in the American
system of protection to industry through
tariff laws He is a vigorous writer and
speaker, and in various campaigns he
has taken an active part in the discussion
of issues in the press He is a member
of the Worcester Economic Club, the
Worcester Congregational Club, and is
especially interested in social and economic problems He is an active member
of the Central Congregational Church, and
he is the founder and leader of the Go-to-
Church Band, which was started in February, 1910, in Central Congregational
Church, the object being to gain the persistent and willing attendance of young
people and children at the preaching

service, they trying to make perfect records in attendance. The movement has spread to over four hundred churches in thirty-four states, also into Canada, in fourteen denominations, and with over twenty-seven thousand members. The Band makes church going a contest against failure for four months, and the members try to be present at preaching service at least once each Sunday for the term. The junior department is composed of those thirteen years of age and younger, and the senior department, the especial Alvord feature, is the unique and most valuable part of the movement because by means of it the children graduate naturally into the adult portion of the audience.

Mr. Alvord married, at Worcester, April 20, 1893, Mary Sanford Newton, born at Stafford Springs, Connecticut, October 16, 1865, daughter of Simeon and Clarissa Sanford (Packard) Newton. Mr. Newton was cashier of the Stafford Springs Bank for many years, and Mrs. Newton was the daughter of "Priest" Levi Packard, pastor of the Congregational church of Spencer, Massachusetts, for twenty-seven years. She is a graduate of the Worcester High School. Children, born at Worcester: Charles Clinton, mentioned below; Newton, born August 18, 1902, died August 24, 1903; Eleanor, born March 18, 1905.

(XII) Clarence Walworth Alvord, youngest son of Daniel Wells and Caroline Betts (Dewey) Alvord, was born at Greenfield, Massachusetts, May 21, 1868. He married (first) Mrs. Jane Parrott Blanchard, September, 1893. He married (second) Idress Head, of St. Louis, Missouri. He is a professor of history in the University of Illinois, is an authority on the French occupation of the Middle West prior to the Revolutionary War, and has been vice-president of the Historical Society of the Mississippi Valley.

(XIII) Charles Clinton Alvord, son of Clinton Alvord, was born in Worcester, Massachusetts, December 19, 1896. He attended the public schools of Worcester and is now (1917) a student in the Worcester Polytechnic Institute, of the class of 1918. He is a member of the Worcester Stamp Club, and the Wireless Club of the institute. His principal pleasures are tennis playing and operating his amateur wireless plant. In 1909, when twelve years of age, he talked to and shook hands with a man whose grandmother was killed by the Indians in Deerfield, Massachusetts. This fact shows the comparative youthfulness of this country.

BULLOCK, Augustus George,
Man of Affairs.

This name was originally Balloch, which is from a Gaelic word "bealach" meaning an outlet of a lake or glen. So when surnames were first chosen, he who lived near such an outlet became Balloch; in time Bulloch and Bullock. The Scotch family are descendants of Donald Balloch MacDonald, chief of Clan Ronald, brother to Donald, Lord of the Isles, a descendant of Prince Somerled, of Argyle. The prominent South Carolina family founded by Rev. James, spell the name Bulloch. The New England family use both Bullock and Bulloch, the branch herein recorded using the former. Some of the prominent men of the family are: Alexander H. Bullock, one time governor of Massachusetts; Stephen Bullock, a member of Congress during Jefferson's administration, his son, Dr. Samuel Bullock, a member of the Massachusetts Legislature; Richard Bullock, a merchant of wealth and high standing in Providence, Rhode Island; Nathaniel Bullock, lieutenant-governor of Rhode Island in 1842; Jonathan R. Bullock, lieutenant-governor of Rhode Island in 1860.

(I) The American ancestor was Richard Bullock, born in the county of Essex, England, 1622, died in Rehoboth, Massachusetts, November 22, 1667 Two brothers came to America with him, one of them settling in Virginia Richard Bullock was in Rehoboth, Massachusetts, as early as 1643, remained one year only, but not long afterward returned He was made a freeman, May, 1646, but the colonial records do not show his residence at that time In 1656 he removed to Newtown, Long Island, but soon returned to Rehoboth, where he resided until his death He was one of the fifty-eight landed proprietors of Rehoboth On June 22, 1658, at a "Town meeting lawfully warned" he drew lot No. 19 and also bought the governor's lot valued at two hundred pounds His name appears on the records of the town as early as 1643 and he came there it is said with Roger Williams The town record recites "30th of ye 11 month, 1650, quoted to agree with Richard Bullock to perform the office of town clerk, to give him 16s a year and to be paid for births, burials and marriages besides " He married (first) August 4, 1647, Elizabeth, daughter of Richard Ingraham, of Rehoboth She died January 7, 1659, and he married (second) Elizabeth Billington Children of first marriage Samuel, mentioned below; Elizabeth, born October 9, 1650, Mary, February 16, 1652, Mehitable, April 4, 1655, Abigail, August 29, 1657, Hopestill, December 26, 1658, children of second marriage Israel, born July 15, 1661; Mary, March 13, 1663; John, May 19, 1664; Richard, March 15, 1667

(II) Samuel Bullock, eldest son of Richard and Elizabeth (Ingraham) Bullock, was born August 19, 1648, in Rehoboth, and died there March 10, 1718 He was among the proprietors of the town in 1689, was an extensive farmer, and a contributor to the fund raised for the defence during King Philip's War, in 1675. He married (first) November 12, 1673, Mary Thurber, who died in October, 1674 He married (second) May 26, 1675, Thankful Rouse There was one child of the first marriage: Mary, born October 5, 1674 Children of the second marriage Ebenezer, mentioned below, Thankful, born June 26, 1681, Samuel, November 7, 1683; Israel, April 9, 1687, Daniel, 1689, Richard, July 1, 1692; Seth, September 26, 1693

(III) Ebenezer Bullock, son of Samuel and Thankful (Rouse) Bullock, was born February 22, 1676, at Rehoboth, Massachusetts He married, March 29, 1698, Sarah Moulton, and they resided at Rehoboth Children Mary, born June 6, 1699; Mehitable, April 1, 1701; Samuel, November 17, 1703; Hugh, mentioned below; Aaron, 1707; Squier, March 4, 1709; Miriam, September 30, 1711, Thankful, May 23, 1714, Katherine, died in December, 1717, James, born August 21, 1716.

(IV) Hugh Bullock, second son of Ebenezer and Sarah (Moulton) Bullock, was born April 1, 1706, at Rehoboth, died February 3, 1771 He resided in his native place. He married (first) 1733, Anna Cole, of Swansey, now Warren, Rhode Island, and (second) Mehitable, surname unknown Children James, born December 17, 1734, Alethea, March 12, 1736; Ebenezer, June 30, 1739, Sarah, August 17, 1741, Moulton, November 5, 1743, Prudence, May 6, 1746, Hugh, further mention, Barnet, June 20, 1753

(V) Hugh (2) Bullock, son of Hugh (1) and Anna (Cole) Bullock, was born in Rehoboth, Massachusetts, August 12, 1751, died March 2, 1837 His brother Moulton removed to Royalston, Massachusetts, before the Revolution and settled there Moulton's farm was owned in 1865 by Jason Fisher. Hugh Bullock went to Royalston during the Revolution. His farm was north of his brother's. After his sons were grown up and engaged in other business he built a house on the common, west of his son Barnet's house, and he died there in 1837. This house was occupied in 1865 by C. H. Newton. Hugh Bullock was one of the company that started for Saratoga to repel the invasion of Burgoyne. He was in Captain Peter Woodbury's company, Colonel Job Cushing's regiment, which reinforced General Stark at Bennington, Vermont. Mr Bullock married Rebecca Davis, born in 1759, died in 1809. Children: Rufus, of further mention; Calvin; Moulton, born 1787, died 1865; Barnet, born 1798, died 1884; Candace, was living in Royalston in 1865.

Christopher, Ebenezer, Nathan and David Bullock also settled in Royalston about this time. The history of Royalston states that they were cousins of Hugh and Deacon Moulton Bullock. They were all stalwart men, David being the tallest in the town. Their stay in town was short. When they had their places well cleared and were in the full vigor of manhood they went westward, following the tide of settlers from the Atlantic States inland after the Revolution.

(VI) Rufus Bullock, son of Hugh (2) and Rebecca (Davis) Bullock, was born at Royalston, Massachusetts, September 23, 1779. He was perhaps the most distinguished man who spent his life in the town of Royalston, and he died there, January 10, 1858. With small means he laid the foundation of a good education and became an acceptable school teacher before he was of age. He taught school several winters and worked out at farming during the summers. He was clerk in the country store and finally opened a store on his own account on the common. The business prospered and he led the

life of a country merchant the remainder of his days, accumulating a fortune for his day and enjoying to a remarkable degree the respect and confidence of the people of the vicinity. Mr Bullock made it a rule to expand his business as his means increased, never going beyond, but always using fully what he had. He always gave every detail of his varied business interests his personal supervision. He began to manufacture at his mill in South Royalston, which was very successful. He always conducted a farm and took time to work in the fields himself, notwithstanding the demands of his store and factory. He seemed to find recreation in the variety of his interests.

Mr Bullock often served the town in public office. He was town clerk in 1812-13, and selectman in 1811-12-13. He represented Royalston and his district for five years in the General Court. He was in the Senate, 1831-32. He was delegate to the constitutional conventions in 1820 and 1852, and was once chosen a presidential elector. He left $5,000 in his will to the Congregational church, in which he always took a profound interest; he gave $2,500 to the Baptist Society; a similar amount to the Second Congregational Church at South Royalston, and $5,000 to the town of Royalston for schools. A significant proviso of the last named bequest was that the town keep the cemetery in repair or forfeit the money. The condition of the old graveyards of Massachusetts at times has been a reproach to civilization in this State. Mr Bullock's bequest will doubtless save the graves of Royalston from desecration and neglect. Mr Bullock was a trustee of Amherst College and presented the telescope for the observatory.

He married, May 4, 1808, Sarah Davis, of Rindge, New Hampshire. The history of Royalston says of her: "She still survives (1865) and lives among us, the same industrious and cheerful matron of the olden type, whose wisdom and energy helped to build the house, and who is still spared to enjoy it, when builded, and still to attract the children and the children's children to the ancient homestead." Of Mr Bullock it says "He was a patriot of the early type—a gentleman of the olden school—a friend to be trusted, a man whose principles bore the test of intimate acquaintance and inspection, and whose influence, unobtrusive yet potent, has been eminently useful." Children Maria Louisa, born October 14, 1809, Emily, September 10, 1811, married W D Ripley, died May 1, 1904, Rebecca, born April 28, 1814, married Nelson Wheeler, Alexander Hamilton, of further mention, Charles Augustus, born in 1818, died August 25, 1850; Rufus Henry, born January 9, 1821, died in 1855

(VII) Governor Alexander Hamilton Bullock, son of Rufus and Sarah (Davis) Bullock, was born at Royalston, Massachusetts, March 2, 1816, and died January 17, 1882. He entered Amherst College in 1832, was a diligent student, and at his graduation in 1836 delivered the salutatory oration In the catalogue of his contemporaries at college are found the names of Rev Richard S Storrs, Rev Henry Ward Beecher, Bishop Huntington, and other famous men After being graduated he taught school for a short time at Princeton, New Jersey, and then, partly at the wish of his father and partly on account of his own inclination, entered the Harvard Law School After leaving the law school he spent one year in the office of the well known lawyer, Emory Washburn, of Worcester, where he gained a good knowledge of the details of legal practice, and in 1841 was admitted to the bar Senator Hoar said of Mr Bullock "He disliked personal contro-

versy While he possessed talents which would have rendered him a brilliant and persuasive advocate, the rough contests of the court house could never have been congenial to him He was associated with Judge Thomas as junior counsel in one important capital trial, in which he is said to have made an eloquent opening argument He had a considerable clientage for a young man, to whom he was a safe and trustworthy adviser But he soon established a large business as agent of important insurance companies and withdrew himself altogether from the practice of law "

From early manhood Mr Bullock took a decided interest in politics The prominence of his father in political circles may have increased a natural taste for public life He was particularly well versed in constitutional law and that fact, together with the well defined convictions he held, gave him in debate and administration great advantages He was originally a Whig Step by step he advanced to the highest position in the commonwealth He was a member of the House of Representatives for eight years, first in 1845, last in 1865 In 1862-63-64-65, during the Civil War, all legislative positions were of extraordinary importance and involved great responsibility, and during these four years he was Speaker of the House of Representatives. He was exceedingly popular among his colleagues. He was a State Senator in 1849, judge of the Worcester County Court of Insolvency for two years, 1856-58, having served as commissioner of insolvency since 1853, mayor of Worcester in 1859 The greatest event of his public career was his service as Governor of the Commonwealth, 1866-67-68. At his first election he received nearly fifty thousand votes more than his opponent Governor Bullock had many opportunities to serve in

high positions in the national government. Among other places that he declined was the mission to England offered him by President Hayes.

In financial, humane and all reformatory movements, Governor Bullock was active and efficient. He was president of the State Mutual Life Assurance Company and the Worcester County Institution of Savings; director of the Worcester National Bank; chairman of the finance committee of the trustees of Amherst College, a life member of the New England Historic-Genealogical Society, and a member of the Massachusetts Historical Society and of the American Antiquarian Society. While editor and publisher of "The Daily Aegis," now "The Gazette," he displayed marked ability as a writer and newspaper man. He received the honorary degree of Doctor of Laws from Amherst and Harvard colleges. He was a great friend of learning, interested in all educational institutions.

In 1869 he visited Europe with his family. Upon his return the following year he was received with a public demonstration to welcome him home and give evidence of the respect and love of his townsmen. Governor Bullock was an orator of great power. A volume of his addresses was published. Senator Hoar, who made a special study of orators, said of Governor Bullock's speeches: "Above all, he possessed, beyond any of his living contemporaries, that rare gift of eloquence which always has been and always will be a passport to the favor of the people where speech is free." His eulogy of President Lincoln in Worcester in 1865 was one of many notable public addresses that he delivered. He delivered the commemorative oration at the centennial of the incorporation of his native town of Royalston.

Governor Bullock married, in 1844, El-vira Hazard, daughter of Colonel A. G. Hazard, of Enfield, Connecticut, founder of the Hazard Gunpowder Manufacturing Company. Children: Augustus George, mentioned below; Isabel, married Helson S. Bartlett, of Boston; Fanny, married Dr. William H. Workman, of Worcester.

(VIII) Augustus George Bullock, son of Governor Alexander Hamilton and Elvira (Hazard) Bullock, was born June 2, 1847, at Enfield, Connecticut. His life has been spent from infancy, however, in the city of Worcester. He attended the Highland Military Academy and was graduated from there in 1862. After two years of preparation under Professor F. G. Cutler he entered college in 1864. Professor Cutler, his tutor, was afterward professor of English literature at Harvard. In 1868 Mr. Bullock was graduated from Harvard College. Soon afterward he commenced the study of law in the offices of the late Judge Thomas L. Nelson and the late Senator George F. Hoar. He was admitted to the bar and entered upon the practice of his profession. His career as a lawyer closed with his election to the presidency of the State Mutual Life Assurance Company, from which office he retired January 18, 1910, and is now chairman of the board and senior vice-president. His predecessor in the presidency was Philip L. Moen, who completed the year to which Mr. Bullock's father had been elected in January, 1882, his death two weeks later making a vacancy. In the following year A. G. Bullock was elected. This company began its business in Worcester in 1845. Its first president, John Davis, its third president, Alexander H. Bullock, and its vice-president, Emory Washburn, were at various times elected Governor of the Commonwealth. The second president of the company, Isaac Davis, was almost as prominent in public affairs as his uncle who preceded him He was president twenty-nine years A vice-president and one of the organizers was John Milton Earle, who was editor of "The Spy" for so many years The company has among its assets one of the attractive office buildings of Boston and the most valuable office building by far in Worcester Mr Bullock's other interests are extensive He is president of the Norwich & Worcester Railroad Company; director of the Worcester Consolidated Street Railroad Company; president of the Worcester Railways and Investment Company, trustee and member of the board of investment of the Worcester County Institution for Savings; director of the Providence & Worcester Railroad Company, director of the Boston & Albany Railroad Company, director of the Worcester Gaslight Company, director of the Worcester Trust Company, director of the State Street Trust Company of Boston, director of the American Trust Company of Boston, and trustee of the New England Investment and Security Company He was a commissioner-at-large to the Columbian Exposition at Chicago in 1893, appointed by the President of the United States He has been chairman of the directors of the Public Library, and was formerly a trustee of the State Lunatic Hospital at Worcester; is a member of the American Antiquarian Society and of the Worcester Society of Antiquity He is a member of the Tatnuck Country Club, Worcester Club, University Club of New York, Somerset Club of Boston, Union Club of Boston, the Colonial Society of Massachusetts, and a life member of the Royal Society of Arts, England He attends the First Unitarian Church, and is a Republican He resides at No 48 Elm street, the house built by Governor Bullock By a singular coincidence the former residence of Governor Lincoln is directly

across Elm street Mr Bullock has a country home near Mount Wachusett, in the town of Princeton He married, October 4, 1871, Mary Chandler, daughter of Dr George and Josephine (Rose) Chandler, of Worcester Children

1 Chandler Bullock, born August 24, 1872, in Worcester He attended the public schools of his native city until 1886, spent three years at the high school, then one year in the private school of Charles F Fish, where he was prepared for entrance to college, and from which he was graduated in 1890 He matriculated at Harvard University, was graduated in the class of 1894 with the degree of Bachelor of Arts, then became a student in the law school of the same university, and was graduated from this department in the class of 1897 with the degree of Bachelor of Laws He at once became identified with the legal profession, was admitted to the Worcester county bar, and practiced in the office of the Hon Herbert Parker, at Worcester, for a period of several years In 1910 he was elected general counsel for the State Mutual Life Assurance Company He is a trustee of the Worcester Public Library, and vice-president and director of the Worcester Chamber of Commerce He is a director of the Merchants' National Bank, a trustee of the Worcester Five Cents Savings Bank and a director of the Bancroft Realty Company, which owns the Bancroft Hotel in Worcester While at Harvard he was a member of the "Institute of 1770," and the Hasty Pudding Club, and his present social affiliation is with University Club of New York City, National Association of Life Insurance Underwriters, and member of the Council; Worcester Club, Tatnuck Country Club; Bohemian Club, Worcester Shakespeare Club, Massachusetts Republican Club, in which he is a member of the election committee; and a number of others His religious affiliation is with All Saints Episcopal Church He married October 17, 1900, Mabel Richardson, daughter of George and Anna Ruth (Woodcock) Richardson, of Worcester (see Richardson VIII) Children Margaret, born December 21, 1901, Jo-

sephine Rose, June 21, 1904, Noeline, December 25, 1910

2. Alexander Hamilton Bullock, born November 7, 1874, in Worcester. He was educated in the public schools and at the Dalzell Private School at Worcester, graduating in the class of 1892. Having matriculated at Harvard College, he was graduated from that institution in the class of 1896, with the degree of Bachelor of Arts. He then read law in the office of Kent & Dewey, in Worcester. At the present time he is a director of the Worcester National Bank, a trustee of the People's Savings Bank and a member of the law firm of Thayer, Bullock & Thayer. He married, June 4, 1902, Mrs. Florence (Armsby) McClellan, a daughter of George and Emma (Banister) Armsby, of Worcester. She has one daughter, Beulah, by her first marriage.

3. Augustus George Bullock, born April 20, 1880, died April 29, 1880.

4. Rockwood Hoar Bullock, born August 21, 1881, at Worcester. He was educated at the Dalzell Private School, and after his graduation from this institution became a student at St. Mark's Private School at Southboro, Massachusetts, and was graduated in the class of 1899. Entering Harvard University, he was graduated in 1903, the degree of Bachelor of Arts being conferred upon him. After his graduation he associated with the Worcester Consolidated Street Railway Company as clerk and shophand for two years, later becoming roadmaster, positions he filled from 1903 to 1908. In February, 1908, he opened a general insurance office in the Exchange Building, where he represents The Massachusetts Bonding Insurance Company, Hartford Fire Insurance Company, Hartford Steam Boiler Inspection & Insurance Company, Fidelity & Casualty Company of New York, State Mutual Life Insurance Company, as well as other insurance companies. He is a director of the Mechanics' National Bank of Worcester, director of the Worcester Electric Light Company of Worcester, and a member of the Worcester Club, Quinsigamond Boat Club, Tatnuck Country Club, Worcester Tennis Club. While at Harvard he was a member of the Delta Kappa Epsilon fraternity,

Hasty Pudding Club, "Institute of 1770," and the Owl Club. He married, June 8, 1905, Elizabeth Bliss Dewey, daughter of Francis Henshaw and Lizzie Davis (Bliss) Dewey, of Worcester. Children: A George (2nd), born February 10, 1909, Francis D., February 21, 1911, Elizabeth Chandler, March 7, 1914.

(The Richardson Line)

The great part of the members of this family in New England are descended from three Richardson brothers, who were among the original settlers of Woburn, Massachusetts. They were men of substance and influence, and their descendants are very numerous, many of whom have taken leading places in the direction of business and public events in their different days and generations.

(1) Thomas Richardson was born in England, and had brothers Samuel and Ezekiel, who also came to New England. He was probably the youngest of the brothers, and probably came over in 1635. He was admitted a freeman at Charlestown, Massachusetts, May 2, 1638, was one of seven chosen by the town of Charlestown to commence the settlement of Woburn. His wife was admitted to the church at Charlestown February 21, 1636, and that is the earliest record of the family. He had land assigned him at Malden, and died August 28, 1651. He joined the church in February, 1638, and held various town offices. The Christian name of his wife was Mary, and she married (second) Michael Bacon, said to have come from Ireland, and one of the original inhabitants of Woburn in 1641. She died May 19, 1670. Children: Mary, baptized November 17, 1638, married, May 15, 1655, John Baldwin, of Billerica, Sarah, November 22, 1640, married, March 22, 1660, Michael Bacon; Isaac, born May 14, 1643, married Deborah Fuller; Thomas, October 4, 1645, Ruth, April 14, 1647,

Phebe, January 24, 1649, Nathaniel, mentioned below

(II) Nathaniel Richardson, youngest son of Thomas and Mary Richardson, was born January 2, 1651, in Woburn, where he lived, and was made freeman, 1690 He was a soldier in King Philip's War, in Captain Prentiss' troop of horse, and was wounded in the Swamp Fight, December 19, 1675 He died in Woburn, December 4, 1710, and was survived by his wife Mary, who died December 22, 1719 Children Nathaniel, born August 27, 1673, James, mentioned below, Mary, March 10, 1680, Joshua, June 3, 1681, Martha, 1683, John, January 25, 1685, Thomas, April 15, 1687, Hannah, May 6, 1689, Samuel, September 24, 1691, Phinehas, February, 1694, Phebe, March 4, 1696, Amos, August 10, 1698, Benjamin, August 27, 1700

(III) James Richardson, second son of Nathaniel and Mary Richardson, was born February 26, 1676, in Woburn, was captain of the militia, a soldier in the expedition against the Indians in Maine, and resided in that part of Woburn which is now Winchester, where he died March 23, 1722 The inventory of his real estate amounted to £1,214, 6s, and personal property £366, 9s and 7d Against this were debts of £930 His land was willed to his two sons, William and James He married (first) in 1698, Rebecca Eaton, of Reading, daughter of Joshua and Rebecca (Kendall) Eaton, died in Winchester, 1699 He married (second) in Woburn, December 22, 1699, Elizabeth Arnold, born June 17, 1679, in Reading, daughter of William Arnold, of that town, died November 3, 1744, in Woburn There was one child of the first marriage William, born 1699 Children of second marriage James, died young, James, mentioned below, Josiah, born May 16, 1705, Elizabeth, 1708, Rebecca,

July 14, 1710, Catherine, died young, Catherine, February 6, 1715

(IV) James (2) Richardson, third son of James (1) Richardson, and second child of his second wife, Elizabeth (Arnold) Richardson, was born March 14, 1704, in Woburn, and lived in that town until about 1735, when he removed to Leominster, Massachusetts, then a part of Lancaster His home was in the northern part of Leominster, at the corner of Harvard and Lunenburg roads Here he cleared up new land, and developed a farm, was surveyor of highways in 1745, and died in 1748 He married, September 24, 1728, Sarah Fowle, born July 29, 1703, in Woburn, daughter of Captain James and Mary (Richardson) Fowle, the last named a daughter of Joseph Richardson, and granddaughter of Samuel Richardson, a brother of Thomas Richardson, immigrant ancestor of this line Children James, born December 25, 1729, William, mentioned below, Sarah, December 12, 1732, Luke, August 15, 1734, Esther, 1736, John, July 18, 1741, Josiah, 1742-43, Joseph, 1744

(V) Colonel William Richardson, second son of James (2) and Sarah (Fowle) Richardson, was born May 6, 1731, and resided in that part of Lancaster which is now a part of Princeton, Massachusetts He was active in procuring the charter of the town of Princeton, and was instructed by the General Court to call its first town meeting The town was incorporated, April 24, 1771 Colonel William Richardson was a commander of the militia, was representative from Lancaster ten years, in the period from 1741 to 1751, town clerk of Princeton in 1768 and 1774 In the latter year he was also selectman and assessor He was long a magistrate, was a farmer, a tailor, and merchant, died December 30, 1814 He married, about 1754, Esther Joslin, born in March, 1729, in Lancaster, daughter of John Joslin, granddaughter of Peter Joslin, an early settler of that town. Children Esther, born March 12, 1755, William, January 28, 1757, Abigail, December 28, 1758, Samuel, June 27, 1760, Peter, July 2, 1762; John, mentioned below, Elizabeth, August 31, 1766, Josiah, April 23, 1770.

(VI) John Richardson, fourth son of Colonel William and Esther (Joslin) Richardson, was born April 14, 1764, in Lancaster. He entered Harvard College in 1792. Ill health prevented his graduation, but he was for many years a teacher in Ohio, New Jersey and Massachusetts. He opened the first grammar school on Cape Cod, at Centerville, in the town of Barnstable, Massachusetts, where he died in January, 1842. He married, April 4, 1799, Hannah Lewis, of Barnstable, a descendant of George Lewis, who was early at Plymouth, later in Scituate, and settled in Barnstable in 1639. He was from East Greenwich, County Kent, England. Hannah (Lewis) Richardson died in June, 1861. Children Edward Lewis, born June 20, 1800, John, July 22, 1801, Ephraim, March 31, 1803, Asenath Lewis, February 12, 1806; Josiah, mentioned below, Catherine, June 18, 1811, William, July 24, 1814; Hannah Lewis, August 24, 1816.

(VII) Captain Josiah Richardson, fourth son of John and Hannah (Lewis) Richardson, was born September 2, 1808, in Centerville, and was a shipmaster and merchant. He was lost with his ship "Staffordshire" off Cape Sable, Nova Scotia, December 30, 1853. He married (first) in 1831, Abigail Scudder, who died February 15, 1834. He married (second) November 7, 1837, his cousin, Sophia Howe, born October 20, 1816, in Princeton, Massachusetts, daughter of Israel and Sally (Richardson) Howe, died Octo-

ber 16, 1842. He married (third) October 25, 1843, Harriet Elvira Goodnow, born July 23, 1817, in Princeton, daughter of Edward and Rebecca (Beaman) Goodnow. There was one child of the first marriage William Richardson, died two days old, and three days before his mother. Children of second marriage Abigail Scudder, born 1838, married Lloyd Bion Kimball, whom she survived, Sophia Howe, died one month old. Children of third marriage. Josiah and Edward (twins), died in early childhood; Augusta E., died seven months old; George, mentioned below, Josiah, born April 9, 1854, died 1861.

(VIII) George Richardson, fourth son of Captain Josiah Richardson, and fourth child of his third wife, Harriet E. (Goodnow) Richardson, was born January 17, 1850, in Shrewsbury, Massachusetts, where he spent his early childhood. After an attendance on the public schools of that town, he was a student at Leicester Academy and Phillips Andover Academy, class of 1868, scientific department. He began his business life as an errand boy in the hardware store of C. Foster, in Worcester. In 1876 he acquired partnership interests in association with T. A. Clark, Eben Sawyer and Edward W. Ball. He married, April 28, 1875, Anna Ruth Woodcock, daughter of Theodore Earle and Ellen Orne (Caldwell) Woodcock. Children 1. Mabel, married Chandler Bullock (see Bullock IX). 2. Harriet F., wife of Arthur E. Nye, has a daughter, Anne Elizabeth Nye (see Nye VIII).

NYE, Arthur Eggleston,
Business Man

The name Nye was first found in the middle of the thirteenth century in the Sjelland section of Denmark. In Danish the name signifies new, or newcomer, used as a prefix The name was not adopted as a surname until after the family settled in England, on the adoption of surnames The coat-of-arms is as follows: Azure a crescent increscent argent Crest Two horns couped counterchanged azure and argent

(I) Lave was a son of a descendant of Harold Blautand, who died in 985, through his daughter, who married one of the most famous of the Swedish heroes, Styrbiorn, son of Olaf, King of Sweden He became a man of prominence, and in 1316 was bishop of Roskilde.

(II) Sven was heir of Lave in 1346.

(III) Marten was declared heir of Sven in 1363

(IV) Nils was mentioned in 1418 as owning land in Tudse.

(V) Bertolf, mentioned in 1466 as son of Nils, had sons James and Randolf. James had a duel and was obliged to flee to England, accompanied by his youngest brother, mentioned below

(VI) Randolf Nye settled in Sussex, England, in 1527, and held land in Uckfield His heir was William, mentioned below.

(VII) William Nye married Agnes, daughter of Ralph Tregian, of County Hertford He studied for the ministry and became rector of the parish church of Ballance-Horned, before his father's death He had a son Ralph.

(VIII) Ralph Nye became heir to his father in Uckfield and Ballance in 1556 He married, June 18, 1555, Margaret Merynge, of St Mary, Woolchurch Children Thomas, mentioned below; Edmundus, lived in Somersetshire, and was buried there March 9, 1594; Ralph, married, August 30, 1584, Joan Wilkshire; Anne, married, August 6, 1616, Nicholas Stuart; Mary, married, April 24, 1621, John Bannister

(IX) Thomas Nye, son of Ralph Nye,

married, September 9, 1583, at St Andrew, Hubbard, Katherine Poulsden, of London, daughter of the late Mr Poulsden, of Horley, County Surrey, England He sold to his wife's brother, William Poulsden, a tenement built with a croft adjoining, containing sixteen and a half acres, in Bidlenden, County Kent, England For this he received an annuity of four shillings arising from said lands Children Henry, graduate at Oxford, 1611, and in 1615 was vicar of Cobham, Surrey, rector of Clapham, Sussex, in 1630, Philip, a graduate of Oxford, 1619, rector of St Michael's, Cornhill, and Acton, Middlesex, a celebrated preacher in Cromwell's time; John, Thomas, mentioned below

(X) Thomas (2) Nye, son of Thomas (1) Nye, was a haberdasher of Bidlenden, County Kent, England On July 4, 1637, he granted to his youngest son Thomas land in Bidlenden, and stated in the deed "my oldest son Benjamin having gone to New England" He married, June 10, 1619, Agnes Nye, aged thirty-nine, widow of Henry Nye Children Benjamin, mentioned below; Thomas, born September 16, 1623.

(I) Benjamin Nye, son of Thomas (2) Nye, was born May 4, 1620, at Bidlenden, County Kent, England He came in the ship "Abigail" to Lynn, Massachusetts, and settled in 1637, in Sandwich, Massachusetts. He was on the list of those able to bear arms in 1643 In 1654 he was one of a number to contribute towards building a mill, and in 1655 he contributed for building a meeting house He took the oath of fidelity in 1657, and held many important positions in public affairs He was supervisor of highways in 1655, on the grand jury in 1658, and at other times; constable in 1661-73; collector of taxes, 1674 He received in 1669 twelve acres of land from the town, because he built a

ENCYCLOPEDIA OF BIOGRAPHY

mill at the little pond, and was granted
other land afterward. The town voted,
August 8, 1675, to give permission to
Benjamin Nye to build a fulling mill on
Spring Hill river. It is said that the
ruins of the old saw mill are still extant
at Spring Hill, just west of East Sandwich. He married, in Sandwich, October
19, 1640, Katherine, daughter of Rev.
Thomas Tupper, who came over on the
same ship. Children: Mary, married,
June 1, 1670, Jacob Burgess; John, Ebenezer, Jonathan, born November 29, 1649;
Mercy, April 4, 1652, Caleb, Nathan,
mentioned below; Benjamin, killed by Indians at the battle of Rehoboth, in King
Philip's war, March 26, 1676.

(II) Nathan Nye, fifth son of Benjamin and Katherine (Tupper) Nye, resided
in Sandwich, where he subscribed to the
oath of fidelity in 1678, and shared in the
common land in 1702. He made his will,
September 18, 1741, added a codicil, November 28, 1744, was signed with his
mark, and proved May 13, 1747. He had
wife Mary, and children: Remember,
born February 28, 1687; Temperance,
April 7, 1689; Thankful, August 11, 1691;
Content, September 25, 1693; Jemima,
February 20, 1695; Lemuel, March 21,
1699; Deborah, April 8, 1700; Maria,
April 2, 1702; Caleb, mentioned below;
Nathan, September 28, 1708.

(III) Caleb Nye, second son of Nathan and Mary Nye, was born June 28,
1704, in Sandwich, and lived in that town
until 1736, when he removed to Barnstable, Massachusetts. He probably died
there in 1787, as his will was proved June
5, of that year. He married, October 28,
1731, Hannah, daughter of Benjamin and
Lydia (Crocker) Bodfish, born February
12, 1712, in Barnstable, died March 7,
1779. Children: Silas, died young; Joseph, born April 18, 1735; Benjamin, mentioned below; Simon, July 18, 1737, Eben-

ezer, February 2, 1739; Caleb and Joshua
(twins), April, 1742; Silas, 1744; Hannah,
1750; Prince, 1752; Azubah, about 1756.

(IV) Captain Benjamin (2) Nye, third
son of Caleb and Hannah (Bodfish) Nye,
was born April 18, 1735 in Sandwich,
and settled in the town of Barre, Massachusetts. During the Revolution he
served through many enlistments, credited to the Rutland district. He was a second lieutenant in Captain John Oliver's
company, Colonel Nathan Sparhawk's
regiment, and also in Captain John Black's
company, under the same colonel, Seventh Worcester County Regiment, list
dated Petersham, March 24, 1776, and he
was commissioned April 5, of that year.
He was captain of the First Company of
Worcester County Militia, commissioned
May 14, 1777 and from August 21 to 25
of that year he was captain of a company
in Colonel Sparhawk's regiment raised to
reinforce General Stark at Bennington,
service ten days, including travel home,
ninety-six miles. From September 26 to
October 18, 1777, he commanded a company under Major Jonas Wilder, raised
to serve thirty days in reinforcement of
the northern army. His service, including travel home, was twenty-nine days.
He was captain of a company under Colonel Sparhawk from September 17 to December 12, 1778, at Dorchester. and was
chosen by ballot in the House of Representatives, January 30, 1779, as second
major of Colonel Jonathan Grout's (Seventh Worcester County) Regiment, commissioned on the same day. He died in
Barre, May 27, 1816. His wife, Susan
(Phinney) Nye, born 1735, survived him
more than six years, and died September
16, 1822. Children: Lydia, married Jonathan Tilly, of Barre, Benjamin, mentioned
below; Nathan, Rebecca, married, January 13, 1791, Joseph Barnaby, of New
Braintree, John

149

(V) Benjamin (3) Nye, eldest son of Captain Benjamin (2) and Susan (Phinney) Nye, was born 1769, in Barre, where he passed his life, and died February 28, 1847. He married Bathsheba, daughter of Nehemiah Allen, born 1768-69, died July 26, 1865, in Hardwick, Massachusetts Children Allen, born March 10, 1796, Nancy, September 21, 1798, died young, Ansel, February 16, 1800; Francis, May 12, 1802; John, July 12, 1804, Willard, September 30, 1806; Lyman, mentioned below; Nancy A, May 25, 1814.

(VI) Lyman Nye, sixth son of Benjamin (3) and Bathsheba (Allen) Nye, was born August 7, 1809, in Barre, where he lived, and married (intentions published May 1, 1832) Ursula C Daniels, who died February 24, 1833, in Barre, perhaps a daughter of Captain Joseph and Eliza (Daniels) Hubbardston

(VII) Samuel Daniels Nye, only known son of Lyman and Ursula C (Daniels) Nye, was born February 17, 1833, in Barre, and lived in Worcester, Massachusetts, until 1897, when he removed to Chestnut Hill, same State He married, March 12, 1857, Susan W, daughter of Elijah P and Mary Ann (Williams) Brigham, born June 29, 1836, in Charlestown, Massachusetts, died October 20, 1899 Children Walter Brigham, born February 11, 1862, Mary Eggleston, died two years old; Henry Pearson, May 26, 1870, resides in Worcester, Susie Chollar, died eight months old; Arthur Eggleston, mentioned below

(VIII) Arthur Eggleston Nye, youngest child of Samuel Daniels and Susan W (Brigham) Nye, was born November 7, 1878, in Worcester, Massachusetts, where his life has been chiefly spent. His education was obtained by attendance at the public schools of his home city, including the high school In 1908 he became junior

partner of the J. Russell Marble Company, dealers in paints and oils, and had had a successful business experience

He married, October 17, 1908, Harriet E, daughter of George and Anna R (Woodcock) Richardson, of Worcester (see Richardson VIII) They have one daughter, Anne Elizabeth Nye

---

DEWEY Family.

This name is borne by a large number of the American people, and includes many noted in military, naval, religious and civil affairs, from the Atlantic to the Pacific Its representatives were numerous among the pioneers of many towns in the United States, and they and their progeny have maintained the good standing of the name The name is said to be of French origin, and has been traced to the advent of William the Conqueror in England, in 1066.

(I) Thomas Dewey came from Sandwich, County Kent, England, and was one of the original grantees of Dorchester, Massachusetts He was here as early as 1633, however, was a witness in that year to the non-cupative will of John Russell, of Dorchester, and was admitted a freeman of the colony, May 14, 1634 He sold his lands at Dorchester, August 12, 1635, and removed with other Dorchester men to Windsor, Connecticut, where he was one of the earliest settlers In 1640 he was granted land at Windsor, his home lot in Windsor was the first north of the Palisade, and extended from the main street eastward to the Connecticut river He was juryman in 1642-43-44-45 He died intestate, and the inventory of his estate was filed May 19, 1648, amounting to two hundred and thirteen pounds His estate was divided by the court, June 6, 1650. He married, March 22, 1639, at Windsor, Frances Clark, widow of Joseph

Clark She married (third) as his second wife, George Phelps and died September 27, 1690 Children of Thomas and Frances Dewey Thomas, born February 16, 1640, Josiah baptized October 10, 1641; Anna, October 15, 1643, Israel, born September 23, 1645, Jedediah, mentioned below

(II) Ensign Jedediah Dewey, youngest child of Thomas and Frances (Clark) Dewey, was born December 15, 1647, in Windsor, and died May, 1718, in Westfield, Massachusetts The lands in Windsor belonging to him were sold in his twenty-first year, and that same year he is mentioned at Westfield, which was then being settled under the direction of a committee appointed by the town of Springfield for the purpose On August 27, 1668, he was granted fifteen or sixteen acres of land, and about two years later, in 1670, he received another grant of six acres At this time he probably moved In 1672, he with his two brothers, Thomas and Josiah, with Joseph Whiting, erected a "saw and corn-mill' on a brook then called Two Mile Brook They were granted forty acres of land for the use of the mills, and were to give to the town one-twelfth of the corn which they ground During King Philip's war the settlers of Westfield remained most of the time inside the "Compact Dwelling," which they had been ordered to form for protection against the Indians, and it was not until 1687 that they began to receive grants of land and to build houses outside the two-mile limit thus enclosed In February of the latter year, Jedediah Dewey, with other proprietors, received a grant of twenty acres without the meeting house He served in the various town offices of the period; selectman in 1678-86-95-97-99; mentioned as ensign in 1686; was made a freeman January 1, 1680, joined the church September 28, 1680 By trade

he was a wheelwright He was the only one of the sons of Thomas Dewey to make a will, which was proved May 25, 1718 He married, about 1670, Sarah Orton, daughter of Thomas and Margaret (Pell) Orton Thomas Orton was probably the son of Thomas Orton, of Charlestown, Massachusetts Sarah Orton was baptized August 22, 1652, at Windsor, and joined the Westfield church March 24, 1680 She died in Westfield, November 20, 1711 Children, born in Westfield Sarah, March 28, 1672, Margaret, January 10, 1674, Jedediah, June 14, 1676, Daniel, March 9, 1680, Thomas, June 29, 1682, Joseph, May 10, 1684; Hannah, March 14, 1686, Mary, March 1, 1690, James, mentioned below, Abigail, November 17, 1694

(III) James Dewey, fifth son of Ensign Jedediah and Sarah (Orton) Dewey, was born April 3, 1692, in Westfield, and died June 24, 1756, at Sheffield, Massachusetts He was by trade a wheelwright, and lived near the east end of Silver street, in Westfield, where he served in various town offices, such as selectman and town treasurer He joined the church at Westfield, April 30, 1727, and in 1741 was chosen deacon On November 9, 1746, he resigned and was dismissed to the Sheffield church Here also he held town offices, as selectman and moderator at town meetings On November 22, 1745, he, then of Westfield, deeded to Joseph Clark, of that place, for £320, a hundred and twenty rods in the town plot and on February 12, 1748, then being of Sheffield, he bought thirty acres there of Phineas Smith On February 16, 1753, he bought fifty-five acres of Samuel Churchill, and on October 31, 1754, deeded all his claims to land in Westfield to Samuel Fowler, of that place He married (first) May 15, 1718, at Westfield, Elizabeth Ashley, daughter of David and Mary (Dewey) Ashley Mary Dewey was a daughter of

Thomas Dewey, who was a son of Thomas Dewey, the immigrant, mentioned above Elizabeth Ashley was born at Westfield, March 3, 1698, and died there September 25, 1727, aged thirty-nine years She joined the church, April 30, 1727 He married (second) December 30, 1738, Joanna (Kellogg) Taylor, daughter of John and Ruth Kellogg, and widow of Samuel Taylor, whom she married, December 17, 1719, at Hadley, Massachusetts Samuel Taylor was son of John and Mary (Sheldon) Taylor, born December 3, 1688, died 1735 Joanna (Kellogg) Taylor was born June 12, 1694, at Hadley, and died at Sheffield, December 1, 1762, aged sixty-nine years Her children by Samuel Taylor were Samuel, born October 30, 1721, Joanna, October 9, 1723, married Stephen Dewey, Jonathan, November 21, 1726, Ruth, 1728, married Daniel Dewey, mentioned below, Paul, died July 29, 1747, at Westfield; Silas Children of James and Elizabeth Dewey Stephen, born March 13, 1719, Elizabeth, September 29, 1722, Anna, August 30, 1724, Keziah, October 20, 1726, Daniel, mentioned below, James, August 14, 1731, Josiah, January 29 died March 17, 1733; Mary, April 6, 1735, Josiah, September 8, 1737

(IV) Captain Daniel Dewey, second son of James and Elizabeth (Ashley) Dewey, was born March 10, 1729 in Westfield and died April 1, 1776, at Sheffield, where he was a farmer He served in the war of the Revolution In July, 1771, he was commissioned lieutenant in the South Company in Sheffield, was chosen captain of the first company, being chosen by the company, and accepted by the council of Massachusetts He married (first) May 25, 1751, Ruth Taylor, daughter of Samuel and Joanna (Kellogg) Taylor, born 1728, at Hadley, Massachusetts,

died March 4, 1760, aged thirty-one years He married (second) May 26, 1761, Abigail (Saxton) Huggins, widow of John Huggins, and daughter of James and Adalene (Gilbert) Saxton Children of first marriage: Paul, born March 13, 1752, Eleanor, October 6, 1754, Ruth, February 26, 1760 Of second marriage Phebe, September 6, 1763, Daniel, mentioned below, James, died in infancy, Abigail, died in infancy

(V) Daniel (2) Dewey, son of Captain Daniel (1) Dewey, and child of his second wife, Abigail (Saxton-Huggins) Dewey, was born January 29, 1766, at Sheffield, and died at Williamstown, Massachusetts, May 26, 1815, aged forty-nine years He attended Yale College for two years, and in 1792 received the degree of Master of Arts He lived in Williamstown, where he built a house about eighty rods east of the old College Chapel, owned in 1876 by Hon Joseph White He was a trustee of Williams College almost from its founding until his death In 1809-12 he was a member of the Governor's Council, and in 1813 elected a member of Congress He resigned to become judge of the Supreme Judicial Court of Massachusetts in February, 1814, and held this office until his death Although he lived at a time when party prejudices were very deep and bitter, no one ever said anything against his name He was happy in all social and domestic life Chief Justice Parker said of him "He is almost the only man in an elevated rank and of unalterable political opinions, that has been at no time calumniated" On his monument is this inscription "In memory of the Hon Daniel Dewey, departed this life on the 26th of May, A D 1815, in the 50th year of his age He had held several important offices, and at the time of his death was one of the justices of the supreme judicial court of this commonwealth." He married, May 6, 1792, Maria Noble, daughter of Hon David and Abigail (Bennett) Noble, born October 7, 1770, in Milford, Connecticut, died at Williamstown, March 13, 1813, aged forty-two years Children Charles Augustus, mentioned below; Daniel, born June 20, 1795, died November 5, 1797, Caroline Abigail, mentioned below, Daniel Noble, mentioned below, Edward, born October 3. 1805, died May 7, 1828.

(VI) Hon Charles Augustus Dewey, LL D, son of Daniel (2) and Maria (Noble) Dewey, was born March 13, 1793, at Williamstown, and died at Northampton, Massachusetts, August 22, 1866 He was graduated from Williams College in 1811, and studied law in his father's office From 1814 to 1826 he practiced law in his native town, and from 1826 to 1837 at Northampton. From 1830 to 1837 he was district attorney for the western district of Massachusetts, and from 1837 until his death he was one of the justices of the Supreme Judicial Court of Massachusetts. He served in the House and Senate of Massachusetts In 1840 he received the degree of Doctor of Laws from Harvard University He was very prominent both as a lawyer and magistrate Over fourteen hundred of his written opinions are to be found in the Massachusetts reports and are authority in the courts throughout the United States For forty-two years he was a trustee of Williams College His homestead is now owned by Smith College He married (first) May 16, 1820, Frances Aurelia Henshaw, daughter of Hon Samuel and Martha (Hunt) Henshaw, of Northampton where she was born She died at Williamstown, July 20, 1821 He married (second) July 28, 1824 Caroline Hannah Clinton, daughter of General James and Mary (Little) Clinton, of Newburgh, New York, and sister of Governor DeWitt Clinton She was born January 31, 1800, and died May

28, 1864 Child by first wife 1 Francis Henshaw, mentioned below Children by second wife 2 James Clinton, born November 25, 1825, at Williamstown, died December 3, 1832 3 Caroline Betts, born March 26, 1827, at Northampton, died April 4, 1893, at Hamilton, Massachusetts, married, June 7, 1857, Hon Daniel Wells Alvord, of Greenfield, Massachusetts, children Charles Dewey, born March 26, 1860, James Church, January 24, 1862, Mary Wells, March 9, 1863, died March 5, 1890; Clinton, November 9, 1865, Clarence Walworth, May 21, 1868 4 Charles Augustus, born December 29, 1830, died March 22, 1908; graduate of Williams College, 1850, was a member of Kappa Alpha Society, a lawyer in New York City, Davenport, Iowa, and Milford, Massachusetts; judge of the southern Worcester district court, married March 12 1867 Marietta Thayer, child Maria Thayer, born August 8, 1872, married Charles Cole, and has one child, Charles Dewey Cole, born July 1, 1901 5 Edward James, born November 5, 1832, died May 4, 1836 6 Mary Clinton, born November 5, 1832, twin of Edward James, married Hon Hamilton B Staples, of Worcester, district attorney and justice of the Superior Court of Massachusetts, she died March 14, 1902, children Charles D Staples, born September 2, died October 2, 1869, Francis Hamilton Staples, born April 22, 1871 7 Henry Clinton, born December 8, 1834, died April 18, 1836 8 Maria Noble, born September 15, 1837, died September 27, 1911 9 Dr George Clinton, born December 6, 1840, died April 7, 1864

(VI) Caroline Abigail Dewey, sister of Hon Charles Augustus Dewey, was born April 8, 1798, at Williamstown, married, November 4, 1816, Samuel Rosseter Betts, son of Uriah and Susan (Rosseter) Betts, born June 8, 1787, at Richmond, Massa-

153

chusetts, died November 2, 1868, at New Haven, Connecticut. Judge Betts graduated at Williams College in 1816 and practiced law at Monticello and Bloomington, New York He was a member of Congress and prominent in public affairs, appointed judge of the New York State Circuit Court in 1823 and judge of the District Court of the United States in 1826, serving for forty-one years Children 1 Maria Caroline, born August 15, 1818; married James Whiting Metcalf, and lived in New Haven 2 Charles Dewey, born July 6, 1820, graduate of Williams College, clerk of the United States Court 3 Frances Julia, born November 28, 1822, married William Hillhouse, lived at New Haven 4 Colonel George Frederic, born July 11, 1827, died January 18, 1898; graduate of Williams College, 1844, lieutenant-colonel of the Ninth New York Regiment in the Civil War, married Ellen Porter 5 Emily, born October 7, 1830, lived in New York City, died at New Haven February, 1916, unmarried

(VI) Daniel Noble Dewey, son of Daniel (2) Dewey, and brother of Hon Charles Augustus Dewey, was born April 4, 1800, at Williamstown and died there January 13, 1859 Graduating from Williams College in 1820, of which he became treasurer, he read law in the office of Elijah H Ellis, of Northampton and practiced law afterward in his native place He represented his district in the General Court, served in the Executive Council and from 1848 until he died was judge of probate of Berkshire county. He married, May 9, 1827, Eliza Hannah Hubbell, daughter of Lyman and Louisa (Rossiter) Hubbell She was born May 28, 1806, died November 22, 1887, at Newton, Massachusetts Children 1 Maria Louisa, born October 4, 1829, married, March 10, 1853, Joseph Henry Gray, of Boston 2 Eliza Hubbell, born July 22,

1832, died April, 1833 3 Daniel, mentioned below 4 Lyman H., born July 26, 1836, died May, 1886; lawyer in New York City, married, September 4, 1865, Susan E Sherman 5 Frances Eliza born June 26, 1839, married John L Bailey, who resided in Newton and was in business in Boston; children Lucy Sawyer Bailey, Anna Gray Bailey, Isabel Dewey Bailey and Edward Sawyer Bailey. 6 Edward, born October 3, 1841; wholesale grocer in Milwaukee; married Minette Crosby Sloan, children Francis Edward, born November 29, 1873, Eliza Angeline, born April 29, 1876, Minette Alice, October 2, 1881, Sevan, October 18, 1889

(VII) Hon Francis Henshaw Dewey, only child of Hon Charles Augustus and Frances Aurelia (Henshaw) Dewey, was born July 12, 1821, in Williamstown and died December 16, 1887, at Worcester. He was graduated from Williams College in 1840, and afterward studied at the Yale and Harvard law schools He was a member of Kappa Alpha Society In 1842 he went to Worcester as a student, and in 1843 became a partner of Hon Emory Washburn. Later he was in partnership with Hon Hartley Williams and others In 1869 he was appointed judge of the Superior Court of Massachusetts, and he continued on the bench until his resignation If he had been willing to accept the promotion he would have been appointed a judge of the Supreme Court of the State From 1869 until his death he was a trustee of Williams College, and at the time of his death he was president of the board of trustees of the Free Public Library of Worcester; also president of the board of trustees of the Old Men's Home, president of the Norwich & Worcester Railroad, president of the Mechanics' Savings Bank president of the Rural Cemetery Corporation, president of the Worcester County Horticultural So-

ciety, a trustee of the Washburn Memorial Hospital, a trustee of the Young Men's Christian Association, director of the Mechanics' National Bank, and a director and one of the heaviest stockholders in the Washburn & Moen Manufacturing Company. In addition to his large and varied business interests, he attended to an extensive, important and lucrative practice, and stood among the foremost in his profession. He served the city in both branches of the City Council, and was State Senator for two terms. While a member of the State Senate in 1869 he proposed and secured the passage of the law making Christmas a legal holiday in Massachusetts. In politics he was a Republican of great influence, but he declined to follow a public career.

Judge Dewey married (first) November 2, 1846, Frances Amelia Clarke, only daughter of John and Prudence (Graves) Clarke, of Northampton. She was born in 1826, and died March 13, 1851. Her father John Clarke, founded Clarke Institute for Deaf Mutes. Judge Dewey married (second) April 26 1853, Sarah Barker Tufts, of Dudley, Massachusetts, only daughter of Hon George A and Azuba Boyden (Fales) Tufts born January 31, 1825, at Dudley, died August 24 1906 Child by first wife 1 Fanny, born September 17, died September 18, 1849 Children by second wife 2 Fanny Clarke, born February 1, died July 28 1854 3 Caroline Clinton, born December 18, 1854, married, June 14, 1877 Dr Charles I Nichols, died December 23, 1878, leaving daughter, Caroline Dewey, born December 22, 1878, who married, June 1, 1905, George A. Gaskill (see Gaskill) 4 Francis Henshaw, mentioned below 5 John Clarke, mentioned below. 6 George Tufts, mentioned below 7 Sarah Frances, born September 15, 1860, married Dr. Oliver Hurd Everett, September 15, 1885,

she died June 7, 1892 8 Charles Augustus, born and died in April, 1863

(VII) Daniel Dewey, son of Daniel Noble and Eliza Hannah (Hubbell) Dewey, was born March 3, 1834 He was graduated from Williams College in 1855, and was treasurer of the college for some years. He studied law, and after practicing for a time, he engaged in business in Boston For many years he was a partner in the firm of Dewey, Gould & Dike, wool merchants, at 169 Congress street, established in 1867 by Joseph Henry Gray and Daniel Dewey. The business was removed to 600 Atlantic avenue and in 1902 to Summer street The building consists of seven floors and has a capacity for storing three million pounds of wool They employ twenty-five people Mr Dewey resided in Newton, where he died August 10, 1907 He married, April 29, 1864, Mary Adaline Adams, who died July 30, 1915 Children 1 Sarah Bradstreet, born July 5, 1865, married John Clarke Dewey, mentioned below 2 Daniel, 2nd, born September 29. 1868 3 Percy, born May 26, 1879; educated under governess and private tutors after which he attended Newton High School, matriculated at Harvard College, graduating 1901 with the degree of Bachelor of Arts; several times he visited Europe, both for pleasure and business, in 1902 he entered the employ of his father as office boy, and after one year was assigned to traveling salesman all over the West, as buyer; upon the death of his father in 1907 he became a junior partner of the firm, the other two partners being Joseph Wing and Charles P Nunn, he is a member of the University Club, Harvard Club, Oakley Country Club, he married Jane Swift who was educated in the Belmont High School, graduating with the class of 1899 4 Marjorie, twin sister to Percy, born May 26, 1879, married William Gibbons Morse, and has children Lucy, Marjorie, William, Barbara

(VIII) Francis Henshaw (2) Dewey, son of Hon Francis Henshaw (1) and Sarah Barker (Tufts) Dewey, was born March 23, 1856, in Worcester His early education was received in private school and in the public schools of Worcester, and he fitted for college at Fay School and St Mark's School, Southborough, Massachusetts He was graduated from Williams College in the class of 1876, ranking among the first six and winning membership in the Phi Beta Kappa In 1879 he received the degree of Master of Arts from his *alma mater* After reading law for a time in the office of Staples & Goulding in Worcester, he entered Harvard Law School, from which he was graduated in 1878 He was admitted to the bar in 1879, and since then has practiced in Worcester. His legal work has been largely in the service of important corporations with which he is connected. His career as a banker, trustee, manager and executive of railway and industrial corporations has demonstrated not only his natural aptitude for great and involved financial undertakings, but his high abilities and legal acumen Year by year his activity and influence in steam and electric railway circles have extended In the beginning of his career many of the trusts and offices of his father were transferred gradually to the young solicitor In 1880 he took charge of the legal business, and was elected a trustee of the Worcester Mechanics Savings Bank and solicitor of the Mechanics National Bank, and has continued the principal figure in the management of these large banking institutions to the present time. Since April, 1888, he has been president of the Mechanics National Bank of Worcester There is no more important figure in banking circles in the city or county and not

many perhaps in the State Mr Dewey was elected a director of the Worcester Consolidated Street Railway Company in 1893, and since 1898 he has been president During his administration of this company and others in control of the street railways of Worcester and its suburbs, the system has been extended from a total of forty miles of track to nearly two hundred miles, connecting forty cities and town, provided with thoroughly modern plants and equipment, giving excellent service to nearly sixty million passengers annually and making a creditable financial showing He is president also of the New England Investment and Security Company, a corporation owning various street railways and railway corporations. He is also president of the allied corporations under the same financial management—the Springfield Railways Company, the Springfield Street Railway Company, the Interstate Consolidated Railway Company, the Milford, Attleborough & Woonsocket Street Railway Company, the Attleborough Branch Railroad Company, the Worcester & Webster Street Railway Company, the Webster & Dudley Street Railway Company. He is vice-president of the Worcester Railways and Investment Company, a holding corporation He represents large interests in the New York, New Haven & Hartford Railroad Company, and is a director of the Fitchburg Railroad Company, now operated under lease by the Boston & Maine system, the Norwich & Worcester Railroad operated by the New Haven road, and the New London Northern Railroad Company leased to the Central Vermont Railroad Company Mr. Dewey is also a director of the New England Telephone and Telegraph Company, of the Massachusetts Bonding and Insurance Company, and vice-president of the Morris Plan Com-

pany, a banking institution, and of the Worcester Gaslight Company Years ago he was active in providing for the city an adequate hotel and theatre, and for many years he was in control of the corporations owning the Bay State House and the Worcester Theatre He was an executor of the great estate of the late Stephen Salisbury, and is a trustee and vice-president of the Worcester Art Museum, the principal legatee of the Salisbury estate.

But banks, street railways and large estates have not commanded Mr Dewey's services to the exclusion of public duties, charities and social organizations He is a trustee, treasurer and vice-president of Clarke University and Clarke College He is a director of the Associated Charities, and for many years has served the city as chairman of the commissioners of the City Hospital Funds He is also a trustee of the Memorial Hospital, and has taken an active part in the upbuilding and extension of that institution He is president of the Home for Aged Men, and trustee of the Massachusetts School for Feeble-Minded In religion Mr Dewey is a Unitarian, and since his marriage he has been an active member and generous supporter of the First Unitarian Church of Worcester He has been superintendent of the Sunday school and chairman of the parish committee

For a number of years Mr Dewey was a director of the Worcester Board of Trade, and he has given strong support and encouragement to many other kindred organizations He is a member and on the council of the American Antiquarian Society, one of the oldest and most honorable learned societies of the United States, having its library in Worcester, the home of its founder He is a member of the Society of Antiquity, of the Colonial Society of Massachusetts, St Wulstan Society of Worcester, an organization in

charge of funds for the promotion of art In 1897 he was elected vice-president of the Worcester Bar Association, which office he held for many years He is a member of the famous old Worcester Fire Society In college he joined the Kappa Alpha fraternity. Among the clubs to which he belongs are the following University and Williams College clubs of New York City, the Union of Boston, the Point Judith Country Club (of which he is president) of Narragansett Pier, Rhode Island (where Mr Dewey has a summer home), the Worcester Country, the Worcester, the Tatnuck Country Club of Worcester, the Worcester Automobile Club, and the Quinsigamond Boat Club Mr Dewey's office is in the Central Exchange Building, of which his wife is the owner. He has a beautiful city residence at 71 Elm street, Worcester

He married, December 12, 1878, Lizzie Davis Bliss, who was born March 12, 1856 daughter of Harrison and Sarah H (Howe) Bliss (see Bliss) Her father was associated in business enterprises for many years with Mr Dewey's father. Children 1 Elizabeth Bliss, born July 19, 1883; married Rockwood Hoar Bullock (see Bullock) 2 Francis Henshaw, mentioned below

(VIII) John Clarke Dewey, son of Hon Francis Henshaw (1) and Sarah Barker (Tufts) Dewey, was born May 19, 1857, in Worcester, where he received his early education in private and public schools, graduating from the Classical High School in 1873 He prepared for college, at St Marks School, Southborough, and entered Williams College, and joined Kappa Alpha Society In 1878 he was graduated with the degree of Bachelor of Arts, receiving the degree of Master of Arts in 1881 He studied law in the office of Thomas H Dodge, a patent lawyer, of Worcester, and was admitted to the bar in 1881 From the beginning of his practice he has specialized in patent law, a field of wide range in the industrial city of Worcester, and he has taken rank among the leaders of this branch of his profession Early in his career he was admitted to practice in the United States courts He is a member of the Worcester County Bar Association, and of the Massachusetts Bar Association He is a communicant of All Saints (Protestant Episcopal) Church In politics he has always been a Republican He resides in Worcester and is a member of various clubs, including the Worcester Club, the Worcester Country Club, Tatnuck Country Club, Quinsigamond Boat Club, University Club of New York, and the Union Club of Boston Mr Dewey married, June 12, 1888, Sarah Bradstreet Dewey, daughter of Daniel and Mary A (Adams) Dewey, of Newton, mentioned above Children John Clarke, mentioned below, Daniel, born October 12, 1899, a student at St Mark's School

(VIII) George Tufts Dewey, third son of Hon Francis Henshaw (1) and Sarah Barker (Tufts) Dewey, was born September 12, 1858, in Worcester, Massachusetts After courses of study in Worcester public and private schools, and at Fay School, Southborough Massachusetts, he entered Mt Pleasant Institute, Amherst, Massachusetts, in 1870, continuing until graduation in 1875, when he entered Williams College, and graduated with honors in 1879, receiving the degree of Bachelor of Arts and in 1882 of Master of Arts He was also a member of the Kappa Alpha Society Choosing the profession of law, he began study in Worcester under the direction of Bacon & Hopkins, eminent lawyers of the Worcester bar, continuing his studies in the offices of that firm during the years 1879-81 In 1881 he entered Harvard Law School and finished his law

studies with the class of 1882 He was admitted to the bar of Worcester county in the latter year, and has continued the practice of law in Worcester to the present time He is learned in the law, skillful in its application, and gives to its problems the closest study From 1883 until 1907 he was in partnership with Thomas G Kent, under the firm name of Kent & Dewey, and during his legal career he has made a special study of the law of corporations. He has held the position of general counsel for the Washburn & Moen Manufacturing Company, the Wright Wire Company, the Worcester Electric Light Company, the Graton & Knight Manufacturing Company, and many other large Worcester corporations, and in addition to his corporation clientele has a large private practice He is a member of the American Bar, the Massachusetts State Bar and Worcester County Bar Associations, and is held in high esteem by his contemporaries of the profession

In the business world of his native city, Mr Dewey also ranks high, and has been connected officially with corporations of Worcester whose fame is world-wide He was for many years an active director of the Washburn & Moen Manufacturing Company, director and treasurer of the Wright Wire Company, director of the Worcester Electric Light Company, director and vice-president of the Graton & Knight Manufacturing Company, director and treasurer of the Worcester Cold Storage and Warehouse Company, director of the Columbian National Life Insurance Company, and many other important business corporations The duties of his official positions with these corporations, his responsibility as general legal counsel to many of them, and the exactions of a large private clientele, would fill the life of most men to the exclusion of all else, but Mr. Dewey has neglected none of the

duties of citizenship and has gone far beyond business and professional life in his activities Broad in his sympathy and generous in his impulse, he has proven his interest in the moral and material welfare by giving largely of his time and ability to institutions, religious, philanthropic and social He is a member of the Protestant Episcopal church, and of the vestry of All Saints Parish; and was president of the Boys' Club of Worcester for many years, and a director of the Young Men's Christian Association, member of the Worcester, Tatnuck Country, Economic, Twentieth Century, Worcester Country, Quinsigamond Boat and Republican clubs of Worcester, the Williams College Club of New York; the Williams College Club of Massachusetts His college fraternity is Kappa Alpha

Mr Dewey married, June 28, 1898, Mary Linwood Nichols, daughter of Dr Lemuel Bliss and Lydia Carter (Anthony) Nichols, of Worcester Children 1 Mary Linwood, born in Florence, Italy, educated in private schools, Worcester, Massachusetts, then attended for three years Miss Porter's Private School, Farmington, Connecticut 2 George Tufts, Jr, born in Worcester, Massachusetts, attended private schools in his native city, and in 1913 became a student in a private school in Pomfret, Connecticut, class of 1919. 3 Charles Nichols, born in Worcester, Massachusetts, attended private schools in his native city, then became a student in "The Fay School," Southboro, Massachusetts, and in February, 1917, was an honor student. The summer home of the family is at Lake Sunapee, New Hampshire

(IX) Francis Henshaw (3) Dewey, son of Francis Henshaw (2) and Lizzie Davis (Bliss) Dewey, was born May 19, 1887, in Worcester After a period in private schools, he attended the Worcester

public schools and graduated in 1904 from the Classical High School, completing his preparation for college in the Hackley School at Tarrytown, New York He entered Williams College, from which he was graduated in 1909 with the degree of Bachelor of Arts He joined the Kappa Alpha fraternity His professional training was received in Harvard Law School, from which he was graduated in 1912 Since then he has been associated in business with his father in Worcester. He succeeded his father as solicitor of the Mechanics' National Bank He is an active member and one of the assessors of the First Unitarian Church He is a member of the Worcester Club, the Tatnuck Country Club, the Quinsigamond Boat Club, the Worcester Tennis Club, the Economic Club of Worcester, the University Club and Williams College Club of New York, and the Point Judith Club of Narragansett Pier He married, February 1, 1913, Dorothy P Bowen, daughter of Henry and Belle (Flagg) Bowen, of Providence, Rhode Island Mrs Dewey is a graduate of the Lincoln School of Providence They have two children Elizabeth Bowen, born November 2, 1913, and Frances, born December 11, 1916.

(IX) John Clarke (2) Dewey, son of John Clarke (1) and Sarah Bradstreet (Dewey) Dewey, was born October 14, 1890, in Worcester. He first attended a private school, in 1913 he entered St Mark's School, from which he graduated, class of 1909, and during his course of study there he was prominent in athletics, playing end in baseball club, 1908, and outfield on hockey track, 1909, in the latter named year he became a student at Williams College, from which institution he was graduated, class of 1913, and during this period he was captain of the track team and a member of the Gargoyle

159

Society, and of the Kappa Alpha Society
In the same year of his graduation he
went to Europe, and traveled through
England, France, Germany, Italy, Switzerland and Austria Upon his return in
the same year, 1913, he served as a clerk
for six months in the Bank of Manhattan,
New York City, resigning in order to accept a position as clerk with Spencer,
Trask Company, bankers and brokers, in
which capacity he served until August,
1914, and in September, 1914, he moved to
Boston, Massachusetts, with the above
named company, and was promoted to
the position of bond salesman He is a
member of the Tatnuck Country Club of
Worcester, the Oakley Country Club of
Boston, and Williams Club of New York
City Mr Dewey married, September 30,
1916, Marjorie Dunster Talbot, daughter
of Dr George Henry and Jessie (Randall) Talbot, of Newtonville They reside at No 224 Rawson Road, Brookline,
Massachusetts

(The Bliss Line)

Thomas Bliss was the last English ancestor of the Bliss family of Worcester,
resided at Belstone, and was a man of
property He was a Puritan and his
wealth and prominence perhaps invited
the persecution he suffered and through
which he lost both his wealth and his
health On account of his religious and
political views he was imprisoned His
children, of whom Thomas and George
emigrated to America to escape persecution, were Jonathan, mentioned below,
Thomas, died 1640, Elizabeth, married
Sir John Calcliffe, of Belstone, George,
born 1591, died August 31, 1667, Mary
(Polly)

(II) Jonathan Bliss, son of Thomas
Bliss, was born about 1580, at Belstone,
and died in 1636 On account of his non-
conformist views he was persecuted and

virtually driven out of England, suffering
heavy fines and eventually dying from a
fever contracted in prison Four children
are said to have died in infancy, two
grew up They were Thomas, mentioned below, and Mary

(III) Thomas (2) Bliss, son of Jonathan Bliss was born in Belstone, England On the death of his father, in 1636,
he removed to Boston, thence to Braintree, thence to Hartford, Connecticut,
thence back to Weymouth, Massachusetts, and in 1643, with others, he helped
make the settlement at Rehoboth He
was a freeman at Cambridge, May 18,
1642, and in Plymouth colony, January 4,
1645, in June of the latter year he drew
a lot of land at the Great Plain, Seekonk.
In 1646 he was fence viewer; in 1647 surveyor of highways, two important offices
in the Colonial days He died at Rehoboth, June, 1649, and is buried in the
graveyard at Seekonk, Massachusetts,
now Rumford, East Providence, Rhode
Island His will was proved June 8, 1649.
He married a Miss Ide, and their children
were Jonathan, mentioned below, a
daughter, married Thomas Williams,
Mary, married Nathaniel Harmon, of
Braintree, Nathaniel, possibly of Springfield, seems to have left no descendants in
male line

(IV) Jonathan (2) Bliss, son of
Thomas (2) Bliss, was born about 1625,
in England, and died in 1687 He was a
blacksmith by trade, and in 1655 was
made a freeman of the Plymouth colony
He was "way warden" at the town meeting in Rehoboth, May 24, 1652, and May
17, 1655, was on the grand jury On February 22, 1658, he was made a freeman in
Rehoboth, drew land, June 22, 1658, and
was one of the eighty who made what is
called the North Purchase The inventory of his estate was sworn to May 23,
1687, the magistrate being the famous

governor, Sir Edmund Andros The Christian name of his wife was Miriam, and their children were Ephraim, mentioned below, Rachel, born December 1, 1651, married, October 28, 1674, Thomas Manning, of Swansea, Massachusetts, Jonathan, March 4, 1653, died same year; Mary, September 31 (sic), 1655; Elizabeth, January 29, 1657, married, June 25, 1684, James Thurber, Samuel, June 24, 1660, died August 28, 1720; Martha, April, 1663, Jonathan (sometimes recorded Timothy), September 17, 1666, died October 16, 1719, Dorothy, January 27, 1668, married, June 26, 1690, James Carpenter; Bethia, August, 1671, married, April 15, 1695, Daniel Carpenter, born October 8, 1669, son of William and Miriam (Searles) Carpenter, of Rehoboth, she died February 27, 1703

(V) Ephraim Bliss, son of Jonathan (2) and Miriam Bliss, was born February 5, 1649, in Rehoboth, and resided at Braintree, Quincy, Scituate, Rehoboth, and Providence, Rhode Island Children Jonathan, mentioned below, Mary, Thomas; Ephraim, married Mary ———, born 1702, died November 14, 1730, and resided in Rehoboth, Daniel

(VI) Jonathan (3) Bliss, son of Ephraim Bliss, was born 1673, in Braintree All his children died young without issue except John They were Hannah, Thomas, Mary, John (mentioned below), Nathaniel and Ephraim

(VII) John Bliss, son of Jonathan (3) Bliss, was born 1711, in Rehoboth, and died 1752 He married on Thanksgiving Day, 1735, Rebecca Whitaker She was a very capable and energetic manager, history tells us, who, with great prudence and thrift, cared for her property after the death of her husband Their children were Nathan, mentioned below, Elizabeth, born April 5, 1738, Anne, April 1, 1740, William, June 6, 1742, died 1822,

Rebecca, December 20, 1744, John, August 21, 1747, died March 12, 1825, Abigail, April 28, 1750, Keziah, November 26, 1752, died 1794.

(VIII) Nathan Bliss, son of John and Rebecca (Whitaker) Bliss, was born December 19, 1736; he was a farmer and died December 3, 1820 He married, December 26, 1760, Joanna Bowen, who died March 10, 1823 Children 1 Nathan, mentioned below 2 Abel, born December 22, 1763, was a farmer at Rehoboth, captain in the militia; he married (first) Olive Briggs, of Dighton, who died May 17 1823, (second) Hannah Horton, who died March 7, 1859, aged sixty-six years, he died November 13, 1843, without issue 3 Olive, born October 2, 1765, married, January 4, 1786, Samuel Goff 4 Joanna, born July 25, 1767, married, January 18, 1787, Shubael Horton 5 Sylvanus, born July 9, 1769, died June 23, 1859 6 Rebecca, born July 12, 1771, married, May 23, 1793, Sylvester Goff, of Rehoboth 7 John, born September 1, 1773, died August 29, 1859 8. Thomas, born October 17, 1775, died 1855 9 Anna, born September 17, 1777 10 Cromwell, born March 17, 1779, died February 7, 1848 11 Ezra, born June 17, 1780, died May 11, 1857.

(IX) Nathan (2) Bliss, son of Nathan (1) and Joanna (Bowen) Bliss, was born December 19, 1761, in Rehoboth, and died at Royalston, Massachusetts, January 31, 1852 He was a farmer, and removed to Royalston between 1770 and 1775 He married, at Dighton, Ruth Briggs, born there December 22, 1765, died at Royalston, November 28, 1862 Children Annie, living at Royalston, unmarried, Abel, mentioned below, Ruth, born 1795, died 1856, married James Buffum, who lived in Keene, New Hampshire, Sally, born 1806, married Benjamin Buffum, of Royalston

(X) Abel Bliss, son of Nathan (2) and Ruth (Briggs) Bliss, born August 23, 1785, at Royalston, was a shoemaker, and died July 4, 1852 He married Nicena Ballou, born March 6, 1788, died April 7 1847 Children Nathan, born September, 1808, married, 1832, Emily Lovett, Abel Ballou, February 21, 1811, died August 4, 1852, Harrison, mentioned below Russell, December 5, 1815, married, March 8, 1835, Mary May died June 15, 1852, James, July 16, 1818, married Julia Drury, died January 16, 1842, Nicena J , December 12, 1823, died January 7, 1845, unmarried, Olive Lucian, July 3, 1825, married, May 9, 1847, Charles C Balch, carpenter, resided at Shirley, Massachusetts

(XI) Harrison Bliss, son of Abel and Nicena (Ballou) Bliss, was born October 9, 1812, in Royalston, and died July 7, 1882 What education he received was obtained in the school of his native place, and at the age of eighteen he started out to make his own living He landed at Worcester, as he used to say, with just seventeen cents in his pockets In 1830 he secured his first position, under Dr Oliver Fiske, at the very place where he afterward purchased one of the finest houses in the city He worked for four years in the Worcester Post Office when Deacon James Wilson was postmaster, in the present Union Block, and under Jubal Harrington in the old Central Exchange Building In association with Deacon Alexander Harris he opened a store in the Salisbury Block in Lincoln Square, dealing in groceries and in flour Later he took Joseph E Gregory as a partner In 1850 he sold his interest in this store, and later opened a flour store in partnership with T and J Sutton, under the name of Bliss, Sutton & Company, on Mechanic street, and in 1857 sold out to his partners From that time until his death he was occupied with his real estate

and banking business Mr Bliss was president of the New Bedford & Taunton branch of the Boston, Clinton & Fitchburg Railroad Company, and vice-president of the Framingham & Lowell branch, both of which are now operated by the New York, New Haven & Hartford Railroad Company He and the late Hon Francis H Dewey founded the Mechanics' National Bank in 1848, and from 1860 to his death, in 1882, Mr Bliss was president He was interested in the Mechanics' Savings Bank from its organization in 1851, was on the board of investment, and was president from 1864 to his death Mr Bliss was also largely interested in the old Music Hall Company, the successor of which owns the Worcester Theatre He was interested largely in the Bay State House Corporation In 1855, 1865 and 1874 he was a representative to the General Court, was alderman in 1861, 1863, 1864, 1865, 1875 and 1876

He married, April 5, 1836, Sarah H Howe, daughter of William Howe, of Worcester A brother of his wife, Rev William Howe, of Cambridge, Massachusetts, lived to be a centenarian Her father was a contractor He had the contract for the building of the Worcester turnpike over which for some distance the cars of the Boston & Worcester Electric Railroad run He lost money and was ruined by the contract Mrs Bliss died July 24, 1882, a few weeks after her husband She was a very capable woman and famous for her charities Their children were 1 Harrison, Jr , born July 30, 1843, married, November 6, 1864, Amy Brown, of Dighton, died May 12, 1868 2 Sarah H , born September 22, 1845, died November 18, 1849 3 William Howe, born September 23, 1850, died May 16, 1911 4 Pamelia Washburn, born May 21, 1854, died September 9, 1854 5 Lizzie Davis, mentioned below

(XII) Lizzie Davis Bliss, youngest child of Harrison and Sarah H. (Howe) Bliss, was born March 12, 1856, and married, at Worcester, December 12, 1878, Francis Henshaw Dewey (see Dewey). They have one son and one daughter.

(The Ballou Line)

(I) Maturin Ballou was born in Devonshire, England, between 1610 and 1620, and came to America previous to 1645, the exact date and place of landing being unknown. He is first mentioned as a co-proprietor of Providence Plantations, Rhode Island, January 19, 1646-47. He was admitted a freeman there, May 18, 1658, together with Robert Pike, who became his father-in-law, and with whom he was intimately associated all his life. Their home lots stood adjacent, in the north part of Providence as originally settled. Various parcels of land are recorded to have been subsequently assigned to him, but nothing definite concerning his character and standing is known. He died between February 24, 1661, when he had land assigned to him, and January 31, 1663. His wife was Hannah, daughter of Robert and Catherine Pike, whom he married between 1646 and 1649, probably in Providence, Rhode Island. She died at the age of eighty-eight years. Children, born in Providence: John, 1650, James, mentioned below; Peter, 1654; Hannah, 1656; Nathaniel, died in early manhood; Samuel, 1660, drowned June 10, 1669.

(II) James Ballou, son of Maturin and Hannah (Pike) Ballou, was born in Providence, in 1652. Soon after his marriage, in 1683, he settled in Loquasquissuck, originally a part of Providence, now Lincoln. It is supposed that he began preparations to settle there some time before, and his original log house was erected before 1685. His second home, a framed

house, stood near the same site, and the well still remains. On October 22, 1707, his mother and sister Hannah deeded to him all the property which had come to them from his father, and this, with his own inheritance of lands from his father, made him owner of several hundred acres, together with his homestead. To this he added other tracts by purchase until he became owner of about a thousand acres. His most important acquisitions were in what was then Dedham and Wrentham, most of which became the north section of Cumberland, Rhode Island. His first purchase in this locality was made early in 1690, the grantor being William Avery, of Dedham. In 1706 he added to this enough to make several farms which he afterwards conveyed to his three sons— James, Nathaniel and Obadiah. This division was made April 11, 1713. In July, 1726, he made a gift deed to his youngest son, Nehemiah, of lands situated in Gloucester, Rhode Island, and the same time to Samuel his home farm. His will was made April 20, 1734, and in 1741 he appears to have made another arrangement of his affairs in relation to his personal estate, which he distributed among his children. The exact date of his death is not known, but it is supposed to have been soon after the settlement of his affairs. He was a man of superior ability, enterprise and judgment. He married, July 23, 1683, Susanna, daughter of Valentine and Mary Whitman, born February 28, 1658, at Providence, died probably in 1725. Children: James, mentioned below; Nathaniel, born April 9, 1687; Obadiah, September 6, 1689; Samuel, January 23, 1693; Susanna, January 3, 1696; Bathsheba, February 15, 1698; Nehemiah, January 20, 1702.

(III) James (2) Ballou, eldest child of James (1) and Susanna (Whitman) Ballou, was born November 1, 1684, in

163

that part of Providence which was later Smithfield, and now Lincoln, and resided in Wrentham, Massachusetts, on land that is now a part of Cumberland, Rhode Island He married, about 1712, Catherine, daughter of Elisha and Susanna (Carpenter) Arnold, born February 8, 1690. Children: Sarah, born November 15, 1713, Ariel, November 18, 1715, Bathsheba, November 26, 1717, Martha, October 6, 1720, James, December 10, 1723, Elisha, November 15, 1726, Priscilla, November 6, 1731

(IV) James (3) Ballou, second son of James (2) and Catherine (Arnold) Ballou, was born December 10, 1723, in Wrentham, near Cumberland, Rhode Island, and died January 21, 1812 He was made a freeman of Cumberland, April 19, 1749, in 1774 moved to Richmond. New Hampshire, with other Rhode Island associates, and with other Ballous settled on what has since been known as Ballou Hill The town was divided in factions later owing to a schism in the Baptist church caused by "the New Lights," in which James Ballou was interested but later abandoned His wife, Tamasin (Cook) Ballou, died April 25, 1804, and he married (second) June 19, 1806, Huldah Carpenter, widow of Joseph Carpenter Children Seth, born February 20, 1748, married Margaret Hilton, Olive, May 13, 1751, married Preserved Whipple, Silas, February 24, 1753, married, April 17, 1774 Hannah Hilton, Susanna, June 16, 1755, married, June 4, 1775, Nathan Harkness; Oziel, July 11, 1757, married, December 7, 1790, Hannah Robinson, Tamasin, June 29, 1759, married, February 15, 1778, Ebenezer Swan, James, April 25, 1761, married, November 5, 1786, Mehitable Ingalls, Russell, mentioned below; Aaron, September 25, 1766, married, September 8, 1786, Catherine Bowen, Daniel, May 26, 1768, married, April 8, 1787, Mary

Hix, Priscilla, January 3, 1772, married, February 28, 1790, Nathan Bullock

(V) Russell Ballou, fifth son of James (3) and Tamasin (Cook) Ballou, was born July 11, 1763, at Cumberland, and died at Swansea, New Hampshire, November 10, 1847 In 1804 he removed to Royalston, Massachusetts He married (first) Henrietta Aldrich, of Cambridge, Massachusetts, who was born August 20, 1764, certified (married) February 23, 1783 All their children were born in Richmond, New Hampshire She died June 8, 1827, aged sixty-seven, and he married (second) Mrs Beebe Mellen, of Swansea, New Hampshire, widow of Joel Mellen, she died 1854 His children were Betsey, born October 6, 1783, married, November 18, 1802, Royal Blanding; Amey, October 27, 1785, married Stephen Parks, Nicena, mentioned below; Asquire, May 8, 1792, married, May 29, 1816, Arathusa Maynard; Russell, September 9, 1794, married, January 29, 1816, Lucy D Norton, Luther, September 7, 1797, married, December 3, 1818, Clarissa Davis, Priscilla, June 25, 1800, died May 8, 1814, Olive, August 29, 1803, married, 1829, Jacob Boyce; Russell, died in infancy

(V) Nicena Ballou, daughter of Russell and Henrietta (Aldrich) Ballou, was born March 6, 1788, and married, 1806, Abel Bliss (see Bliss X)

BLISS, George Rolland,
Merchant.

The Bliss family, one of the oldest in this country, is described on preceding pages of this work The first known English ancestor was Thomas Bliss, who with his son, Jonathan Bliss, suffered great persecution in England because of their Puritan principles Thomas (2) Bliss, son of Jonathan Bliss, born in England, settled in Rehoboth, Massachusetts, where

he died in 1649 His wife was a member of the Ide family, which was conspicuous in the early days of Rehoboth and Attleboro They were the parents of Jonathan (2) Bliss, who was an active citizen of Rehoboth, and one of the founders of Attleboro He married Miriam Harmon, probably a daughter of Francis Harmon, who was born in 1592, and came to Boston in the ship "Love," in 1637 The eldest child of this marriage, Ephraim Bliss, was a native of Rehoboth, and lived in various places, lastly at Providence, Rhode Island Jonathan (3) Bliss, son of Ephraim Bliss, born at Rehoboth, 1672-73, had a large family, but only one son who left issue, namely, John Bliss, born at Rehoboth in 1711, and died in 1752 He married (intentions published in Rehoboth, December 6, 1735) Rebecca Whittaker, born August 3, 1712, in Rohoboth, daughter of John and Mehitable Whittaker She survived him and is described as a very capable and energetic manager, who cared well for the estate of her deceased husband and her children. The eldest of these was Nathan Bliss, born at Rehoboth in 1736 He married, December 26 1760, Joanna Bowen, born October 27, 1737, in Rehoboth, died March 10, 1823, daughter of Jabez and Johannah (Salisbury) Bowen Their eldest son, Nathan (2) Bliss, was born in Rehoboth in 1761, settled in Royalston, Massachusetts, where he died in 1852 He married Ruth Briggs, and their eldest son was Abel Bliss, born in Royalston, 1785, who married Nicena Ballou, daughter of Russell Ballou (see Ballou V)

(XI) Abel Ballou Bliss, second son of Abel and Nicena (Ballou) Bliss, was born February 21, 1811, in Royalston, Massachusetts When a young man he went to Worcester, Massachusetts, where he was successfully engaged in business until 1845, when he removed to the town of

Gill, Franklin county, Massachusetts, and there engaged in farming until his death, August 4 1852 He married (first) April 6, 1835, Rebecca S Flint, who died December 29, 1835 He married (second) in September, 1837, Mary Ann Stillman, who died August 13, 1843 He married (third) May 28, 1845, Rhoda Allen Deane, born April 16, 1808, in Burlington, Otsego county, New York, daughter of Jeremiah and Rhoda Deane There was one child of the first wife, Rebecca Flint, born December 27 1835, died in 1852 Children of second wife Frances Eugenie, born June 17, 1838, married Norman Carl, and died in Chicago, Illinois, 1863; Abel Harrison, born March 31, 1840; Mary Elizabeth, born and died in 1843 Children of third wife George Rolland, mentioned below; Mary Ann, born November 6, 1847, died 1851; Maria Rheda, born November 30, 1848, married Augustus W Holton, William Amburt born July 4, 1851, James Oliver, born November 24, 1852

(XII) George Rolland Bliss, second son of Abel Ballou Bliss and eldest child of his third wife, Rhoda Allen (Deane) Bliss, was born July 17, 1846, in Gill, Massachusetts Here his boyhood days were passed and advantage taken of the limited school privileges which the town afforded These were supplemented later with a course at Williston Seminary, Easthampton, Massachusetts, from which institution he graduated in 1869 The early death of his father, at the age of forty-one, left the family with limited resources, and the education of George R Bliss was acquired solely by his own efforts and its expenses met by his own earnings received from teaching district schools and conducting school boarding clubs Following his graduation from Williston Seminary, he became a clerk for A P Ware & Company of Worcester, with whom he continued three and one-half years The following year he became junior partner of Henry Valentine & Company, dealers in clothing and furnishings, with a store on Main street, Worcester This association continued until 1876, and in 1877 he established his present business, that of a dealer in hats, caps and gentlemen's furnishings, at No 522 Main street The business has experienced a steady growth, requiring several removals and enlargements In 1892 it was removed to larger quarters at the corner of Main and Austin streets, Worcester In 1902 the adjoining store was leased, giving an additional space of 25x90 feet in area In 1899 Mr Bliss admitted his son, Walter Stoughton Bliss, as a partner, and the business has since been conducted under the name of George R Bliss & Son, carrying a stock of clothing, hats, caps, and all the accessory of furnishings which men wear From the modest beginning of 1877, the house has by honorable dealing and never a compromise of a business obligation, steadily grown during this period of forty years and is to-day one of the prominent clothing houses of the city While advancing his business by energy and sound management, Mr Bliss has always been active in furthering the public interests He is a member of the Economic Club, of the Congregational Club, the Worcester County Musical Association, of which he has been treasurer since 1896, also member of the Old South Church since 1871 He married, February 28, 1871, Anna E Stoughton, daughter of Samuel and Eliza (Spaulding) Stoughton, of Gill, Massachusetts (see Stoughton VII) Mr and Mrs Bliss have been extensive travelers both in their own country and in foreign lands

(XIII) Walter Stoughton Bliss, eldest child of George Rolland and Anna E

(Stoughton) Bliss, was born May 21, 1872, in Worcester He attended the public and high schools of his native city, graduating in 1890 After a course of one ane one-half years in Hinman's Business College, he became associated with his father's business, in which he became a partner in 1899 He is interested in and a lover of music and has been tenor and director of music in various Worcester churches for a period of fifteen years He is an active member of the various Masonic fraternities and past master of Morning Star Lodge. He is also a member of Kiwanis, an active business men s club He married, May 21, 1901, Winnie Meyers, daughter of Deacon Albert F and Charlotte Eugenie (Rawson) Meyers, of Worcester, and they are the parents of three daughters Dorothy May, Virginia and Louise Marietta

(XIII) George Rolland (2) Bliss, second son of George Rolland (1) and Anna E (Stoughton) Bliss, was born August 16, 1874, in Worcester, Massachusetts He graduated from the Worcester Classical High School in 1892 and entered Amherst College, from which he received the degree of A B in 1896 For seven years he was a traveling salesman, representing the Royal Worcester Corset Company, and was subsequently, for three years, sales manager of that company In 1907 he became treasurer of the O C White Company of Worcester, manufacturers of adjustable electric lighting fixtures and other metal specialties Mr Bliss is affiliated with the Masonic fraternity, and is a member of various organizations and clubs

(XIII) Edith Georgianna Bliss, only daughter of George Rolland (1) and Anna E (Stoughton) Bliss, was born December 24, 1878, in Worcester, Massachusetts After graduating at the high school of that city, she was a student for two years

166

at Mt Holyoke College She was married, September 16, 1902, to William Dexter White, assistant manager of the Holyoke Machine Company, a son of William W. White.

(The Stoughton Line)

The name of Stoughton is very ancient in England In the time of King Stephen (1135-54) Goodwin de Stocton resided at Stoughton in Surrey In the eighth year of King Edward I, Henry de Stoughton received one hundred and sixty-eight acres there The mansion known as "Stoughton Place" was located in the center of the manor The site is now a plowed field, but is still called Stoughton Garden

(I) Thomas Stoughton resided at Stoughton in Surrey

(II) Gilbert Stoughton, son of Thomas Stoughton, married Mary, daughter of Edward Banbesey

(III) Lawrence Stoughton, son of Gilbert Stoughton, married Ann, daughter of ——— Comb, of Ford, in County Sussex His will, made May 10, 1571, was proved April 28, 1572.

(IV) Thomas (2) Stoughton, son of Lawrence Stoughton, born 1521, died 1575 He married Elizabeth, daughter of Edmund Lewkenor

(V) Lawrence (2) Stoughton, son of Thomas (2) and Elizabeth Stoughton, born 1554, died at Stoughton in 1615 He married Rose, daughter of Richard Ive, citizen of London

(I) American Generations William Stoughton, son of Israel Stoughton, of Dorchester, at one time a Massachusetts judge, who condemned many people of witchcraft, was a bachelor, and left no progeny.

(II) Rev Thomas Stoughton, born about 1575-78, was a clergyman, and was presented with the "living" of Coggeshall,

December 12, 1600, but was deprived of it for non-conformity in 1606 He married (first) a Montpeson of County Wilts He came to America in Winthrop's fleet in the ship "Mary and John," in 1630 On October 19 of that year he desired to become a freeman of the town of Dorchester, and was admitted May 18 following He was appointed a constable by the court, September 3, 1630, and misunderstanding his powers under the Colonial jurisdiction, he performed a marriage service for Clement Briggs and Joan Allen. For this indiscretion he was fined five pounds, but the fine was later remitted He was a member of the company which settled Windsor, Connecticut, and had a grant of fifty-two acres, comprising a house lot and meadow in that town, January 11, 1640. He also had a grant over the Great river, fifty rods in breadth, and extending three miles eastward, also a grant 'toward Pine Meadow" of sixty-nine acres He was ensign in 1636, was often representative between 1639 and 1648, lieutenant in 1640, and died March 25, 1661. He married, as second wife Margaret (Barrett) Huntington, widow of Simon Huntington, who died on the voyage to America Little is known concerning their children

(II) Thomas (2) Stoughton, son of Rev Thomas (1) Stoughton, born in England was one of the original proprietors of Hartford, Connecticut, and built the house known as "Stoughton" or the Stone Fort He died September 15, 1684. and the inventory of his estate amounted to £909, 8s He married, November 30, 1655, Mary, daughter of William Wadsworth, and they had children John, born June 20, 1657; Mary, January 1, 1659, Elizabeth, baptized November 18, 1660, Thomas, mentioned below, Samuel, born September 8, 1665, Israel, February 8, 1667, Rebecca, June 19, 1673

167

(III) Thomas (3) Stoughton, second son of Thomas (2) and Mary (Wadsworth) Stoughton, born November 21, 1663, in East Windsor, settled at Stoughton Brook, now in South Windsor, where he died January 14, 1749 He was an active and useful citizen, was made ensign of the North Company of the Windsor train band in September, 1689, was later lieutenant, and made captain in May, 1698, of the train band on the east side of the Great river He was deputy to the General Court in 1699, 1725-26, 1729 and 1733 He married (first) December 31, 1691, Dorothy, daughter of Lieutenant John and Helena (Wakeman) Talcott, of Hartford, born February 26, 1666, died March 28, 1696 He married (second) May 19, 1697, Abigail, daughter of Richard and Elizabeth (Tuthill) Edwards, and widow of Benjamin Lathrop, born 1671, died January 23, 1754 Child of first marriage Mary, born January 4, 1693, of second marriage Thomas, born April 9, 1698, Daniel, August 13, 1699, Benjamin, April 28, 1701, Timothy, mentioned below, Abigail, December 21, 1704; David, September 9, 1706, Mabel, August 19, 1708; Jonathan, October 7, 1710, Elizabeth, December 20, 1712, Isaac, November 2 1714

(IV) Timothy Stoughton, fourth son of Thomas (3) and Abigail (Edwards) Stoughton was born June 27, 1703, in Windsor, and moved about the world to many places From 1733 to 1745 he lived in Hartford, in 1751 was a resident of Somerset county, New Jersey, and in 1763 of Frederick county, Maryland He married, June 27, 1733, Hannah daughter of Thomas and Sarah (Foote) Olcott, of Hartford, born August 4, 1707, died 1739-40 Children Jonathan, born April 20, 1735, John, 1738, Samuel, mentioned below

(V) Samuel Stoughton, son of Timothy

and Hannah (Olcott) Stoughton, was born in December, 1739, in Windsor, and lived for some years in Greenfield, Massachusetts, whence he removed, about 1774, to Northfield, same State, and later to Gill, Franklin county, Massachusetts, where he established a home, and died December 25, 1814 His homestead continued in possession of his descendants for several generations He was a soldier of the Revolution, serving first as a lieutenant in Captain Timothy Childs' (Third) company, Colonel David Fields' (Third Hampshire County) regiment of Massachusetts militia, commissioned May 3, 1776 He was second lieutenant in Captain Abel Dinsmoor's company, Colonel Benjamin Ruggles Woodbridge's regiment engaged August 17, discharged October 20, 1777, after service of two months and eight days, including four days' (seventy miles) travel home This company was raised for service in the Northern army till November 30, 1777, roll sworn to in Hampshire county In the pay abstract of officers for rations dated in camp at Scarsdale (near White Plains, New York), December 7, 1777, Samuel Stoughton was allowed seventy-three rations from August 17 to October 28, 1777 He married (first) January 12, 1769, in Greenfield, Mary, daughter of Ebenezer Severance She died December 31 of the same year, and he married (second) December 5, 1770, Sarah, daughter of Seth Munn, born December 5, 1751, probably in Northfield Child of the first marriage Mary, born December 1, 1769 Children of second marriage Sarah, born April 8, 1772, Samuel, September 19, 1773, Timothy, died young, Timothy, baptized November 12, 1780; Fanny, August 3, 1783, Asa, mentioned below, Ira, March 7, 1788; Nancy, February 9, 1791 The first three are recorded in Greenfield, and all are recorded in Northfield

(VI) Asa Stoughton, fourth son of Samuel and Sarah (Munn) Stoughton, was born February 15, 1786, according to the "History of Northfield," August 29, 1785, according to the records of the town of Gill, and lived in the latter town. He married (intentions entered August 28, 1811, in Gill) Anna Stevens, a native of Warwick, Massachusetts. Children: Mary Ann, born December 31, 1812; Samuel, mentioned below; Charles, October 17, 1816; Asa Olcott, August 23, 1819; George Harvey, October 27, 1821; Nancy P., January 23, 1824. The last named graduated from Mt Holyoke College in 1842.

(VII) Samuel (2) Stoughton, eldest son of Asa and Anna (Stevens) Stoughton, was born February 10, 1815, in Gill, Massachusetts, and was a farmer and broom manufacturer in that town. He was a very active church worker, was blessed with great musical talent, both as a singer and instrumental performer, and was organist of the Gill Congregational Church many years. He married (intentions entered May 29, 1842, at Gill) Hannah Eliza Spaulding, born February 1, 1823, in Jaffrey, New Hampshire, daughter of Deacon Abel and Lucy P. (Pierce) Spaulding of that town, formerly of Townsend, Massachusetts. Children: Anna Eliza, mentioned below; Sarah Josephine, born in Gill, June 10, 1848.

(VIII) Anna Eliza Stoughton, elder daughter of Samuel (2) and Hannah Eliza (Spaulding) Stoughton, born March 26, 1844, in Gill, was a student under Professor Wright, and later at Powers' Institute, Bernardston, Massachusetts, graduating in the class of 1863. Entering Mt Holyoke College at South Hadley, Massachusetts, she graduated in the class of 1867, and for three years was teacher of mathematics in Westerly Institute at

Westerly, Rhode Island. She married, February 28, 1871, at the parental home in Gill, George Rolland Bliss, of Worcester (see Bliss XII).

NICHOLS, Charles Lemuel,

Physician.

This name has been traced in England to Nicholas de Albioni, alias Nigell or Nicholl, and came to England in the time of Edward the Confessor.

(I) Thomas Nichols was a resident of Amesbury, Massachusetts, as early as 1665. He had a seat in the meeting house there, was made townsman in 1667, owned land there in 1670; subscribed to the oath of allegiance in 1677, was a member of the train band in 1680, and was probably living in 1708, but died before 1720. Thomas Nichols married Mary ——, and had among their children John. mentioned below.

(II) John Nichols, son of Thomas and Mary Nichols, was born about 1678, and lived in Amesbury, where he was a "snow shoe man" in 1708. He married, January 1, 1702 in Salisbury, Massachusetts, Abigail Sargent, of Gloucester, probably daughter of William and Mary (Duncan) Sargent, born about 1683. Children: Mary, born October 19, 1702, married, May 24, 1721; James Dow, John, July 12, 1704; William, January 21, 1706; Jacob, January 16, 1708; Joseph, September 2, 1709; Daniel, mentioned below Moses, February 25, 1715; Anna, January 30, 1718; Aaron, October 2, 1719; Humphrey April 18, 1723; Thomas, January 18, 1725; Abigail, March 18, 1727.

(III) Daniel Nichols, fifth son of John and Abigail (Sargent) Nichols, was born in Amesbury, Massachusetts, September 30, 1712. He continued to reside in his native town, and died there, March 29, 1804. He married, August 31, 1737, in

Amesbury, Elizabeth Sawyer, born about 1718, died February 7, 1803, in Amesbury, daughter of Benjamin and Elizabeth (Jameson) Sawyer, formerly of Newbury, later of Amesbury Children Enoch, mentioned below, Moses, born June 1, 1743, Elizabeth, November 5, 1745, Eunice, July 11, 1748, Daniel, October 11, 1750, Sarah, July 12, 1753; Stephen, baptized November 23, 1755; Mary, born April 9, 1758, died young; Mary, November 1, 1761

(IV) Enoch Nichols, eldest child of Daniel and Elizabeth (Sawyer) Nichols, was born June 22, 1740, in Amesbury, Massachusetts, where he died October 11, 1830 He married there, August 18, 1762, Anna Chase, born July 29, 1745, in Haverhill, Massachusetts, died October 6, 1819, in Amesbury, daughter of Ezra and Judith (Davis) Chase, of Haverhill Children Ezra, mentioned below, Moses, born March 4, 1766, Anna, died young, Elizabeth, baptized August 13, 1773, died young, Enoch, April 5 1775, died young, Anna, born July 22, 1779, Elizabeth, November 21, 1781, Enoch, July 2, 1784, Mary Chase, June 27, 1793.

(V) Ezra Nichols, eldest child of Enoch and Anna (Chase) Nichols, was born in Amesbury, Massachusetts, January 26, 1764 He resided in Canaan, New Hampshire He married (first) Elizabeth Hazeltine born at Bradford, New Hampshire, June 11, 1773, died March 6, 1793, at Canaan, New Hampshire, daughter of Timothy and Ruth (Stickney) Hazeltine Had one son Ezra, mentioned below

(VI) Dr Ezra (2) Nichols, son of Ezra (1) and Elizabeth (Hazeltine) Nichols, was born in Canaan, New Hampshire, October 16, 1790 He moved to Bradford, New Hampshire where he practiced his profession of medicine, and later removed to Newton Lower Falls, Massachusetts where he died September 29,

1848 He married, at Seabrook, New Hampshire, Waity Gray Smith, and they were the parents of six children Elizabeth Hazeltine, Lemuel Bliss, mentioned below, Abby Smith, Ezra Addison, Jabez Smith, and John Smith

(VII) Dr Lemuel Bliss Nichols, eldest son of Dr. Ezra (2) and Waity Gray (Smith) Nichols, was born at Bradford, New Hampshire, October 6, 1816. At the age of two years his parents moved to Newton Lower Falls, Massachusetts, in which town he obtained his education by attendance at the public and high schools, then entered Brown University, at Providence, Rhode Island, from which institution he was graduated with the class of 1842, receiving the degree of A B His father, though a physician of considerable skill and attainments, had destined him for a farmer's life, but literary tastes and hereditary instincts prevailed, and for four years following his graduation from Brown University he taught in the public schools of Providence, attaining the rank of principal of the Arnold Street Grammar School, and he was instrumental in raising the standard of the Providence schools in general In consequence of sickness in his family, he became acquainted with the homeopathic practice of medicine and studied its principles with Drs Okie and Preston, of Providence After the required amount of study, one year being spent at the Harvard Medical School, he received his degree of a regular physician at the Philadelphia College of Medicine, in 1848 In the following year he came to Worcester, Massachusetts, where he practiced as homeopathic physician until the time of his death September 28, 1883 Although slight in form and delicate in appearance, in consequence of his sedentary life, he possessed a wonderful constitution and great powers of endurance. His quiet confidence and

ready sympathy won him a large place in the public heart and gave him an extensive practice from the beginning, and his death left a wide circle of friends and patients to deplore their loss It was his custom to avoid all public office and to confine himself strictly to the limits of his profession by steady, conscientious effort He was one of the founders of the Worcester County Homeopathic Medical Society, and was its first president, serving from 1866 to 1868 Dr Nichols was a devout and active member of All Saints Episcopal Church, and served as warden for more than sixteen years, during which time he acted as both junior and senior warden He was liberal in his Christian ideas and generous to the call for any worthy charity, whether in the church or outside, and he was also a great lover of music He was a member of the Order of Ancient Free and Accepted Masons, in which he attained the thirty-second degree, affiliated with Athelstan Lodge, Quinsigamond Chapter, and Knights Templar Perhaps the most noticeable characteristic of Dr Nichols, aside from his prominence as a physician, was his unusual linguistic attainments His was indeed a rare knowledge of the many languages, speaking no less than six different languages fluently, and reading with ease the ancient Arabic, Syriac, Sanskrit, Hebrew, Greek, Latin, Italian, French, German, Spanish and many others His love for languages hardly outshone his desire for collecting antiques, China, books, art, and among his extensive collection, which was considered unusual for this period, were to be found china that was once the property of Emperor Napoleon, as well as some of the treasures of Louis Philippe, all of which are still in the possession of surviving members of his family His love for the humane treatment of horses and

other beasts was secondary only to his desire to administer to his fellow man

The following was taken from the Worcester "Daily Spy"

One who was once a patient and friend of Dr L B Nichols, and lived in your city, would like to add a few words of tribute to his memory, as the news comes of his death The writer knew him in the earlier days of his practice in Worcester, while a homeopathic physician could not hope for the good opinion of so many as in these later days when homeopathy is a success He was an earnest believer in its merits, an enthusiast in its practice, and to many a patient gave his service free He was devoted to his family and for their comfort and health spared nothing In their love and esteem he found ample reward He was an earnest churchman, present whenever professional calls did not make it necessary to be absent All Saints Church in those days was not in its present prosperous condition, worshipping in a beautiful structure, but few in numbers, with little enthusiasm, but his influence was always felt He did what he could Though a man tenacious of ideas he considered right, he never obtruded them With much illness in his family at times, he went abroad with a cheerful face, often studying some book as he took a long drive in order to keep up his knowledge of some scientific or classical subject He had a pride in all that advanced the interests of the city, and one of his hopes was that his son might succeed him His wish has been gratified, and the boy, so dutiful and kind in early days, has become honored and successful Thinking of his death we regret the loss to those who knew and loved him best where not only there, but in the church he loved so well he will long be remembered and missed —E H W , Ashburnham, Massachusetts

Dr Nichols married, in North Providence, Rhode Island, December 5, 1843, Lydia Carter Anthony, born May 13, 1824 died June 4, 1888, daughter of James and Sarah Porter (Williams) Anthony, of North Providence, Rhode Island, the former named having been a prominent manufacturer of Greystone Village, North Providence Children Sarah G , born March 14, 1845, died October 25, 1850, Corinne L , born November 7, 1846,

Annie L, born September 24, 1848, Charles Lemuel, mentioned below, William A, born July 1, 1853, died August 23, 1853; Abbie C, born November 28, 1855, died September 15, 1856, Lydia Anthony, mentioned below, Mary Linwood, Mrs. George Tufts Dewey (see Dewey)

(VIII) Dr Charles Lemuel Nichols, eldest son of Dr Lemuel Bliss and Lydia Carter (Anthony) Nichols, was born in Worcester, Massachusetts, May 29, 1851. He prepared for college at the Highland Military Academy, and then entered Brown University, Providence, from which he was graduated in 1872, with the degree of A B, and received the degree of A M, 1875 Immediately after graduation he became instructor in chemistry at Brown University, and in 1873 entered Harvard Medical School, from which he was graduated M D in 1875 In the following year he was an interne in the Homeopathic Hospital at Ward's Island, New York, as chief assistant under Dr Talcott He began the practice of his profession at Worcester in 1877, and has since continued with gratifying success He was instructor in medical history at Boston University School of Medicine from 1885 to 1900 He has been a member of the consulting board of the State Insane Hospital at Westboro since 1894, and was one of the founders of the Worcester County Homeopathic Dispensary Association He is a member of the American Institute of Homeopathy; of the Massachusetts Homeopathic State Medical Society, of which he was president in 1884, of the Worcester County Homeopathic Society, of which he was president, of the American Antiquarian Society, of which he is recording secretary, Massachusetts Historical Society; Worcester Club; Tatnuck Country Club; Worcester Fire Society; St Wolston Society; Bohemian Club of Worcester;

Quinsigamond Boat Club of Worcester, University Club of Boston, Colonial Society of Boston; Hughes Club of Boston; and the Odd Volume Club of Boston, founded in 1887 He is a member of the management of the John Carter Brown Library at Brown University, Providence, Rhode Island He is a trustee of the Mechanics' Savings Bank of Worcester, and since 1903 he has been president of the Associated Charities of Worcester Dr Nichols is interested in literary work, and is the author of a "Bibliography of Worcester," published in 1899, "Library of Rameses, the Great" (1909), for which work Dr. Nichols took the portraits himself in Egypt, "Life and Writings of Isaiah Thomas" (1912), and an 'Almanac Reproduction" (1916) for the American Antiquity Society of Worcester, Massachusetts

Dr Nichols married (first) June 14, 1877, Caroline Clinton Dewey (see Dewey), who died December 23, 1878, leaving a daughter, Caroline Dewey, born December 22, 1878 She attended Miss Lewisson's School at Worcester and Miss Porter's School at Farmington, Connecticut She married George Anthony Gaskill (see Gaskill), son of Judge Francis A and Katherine Mortimer (Whittaker) Gaskill, of Worcester, Massachusetts, and has children Charles Francis, born November 15, 1906, George Anthony, February 9, 1909, Katherine Mortimer, December 5, 1913, they reside in Worcester Dr Nichols married (second) November 26, 1884, Mary Jarette Brayton, of Fall River, Massachusetts, daughter of John Summerfield and Sarah (Tinkham) Brayton, formerly of Middleboro, Massachusetts She died April 2, 1910. Children. 1 Charles Lemuel, born November 29, 1886, graduated A B at Harvard University in 1910, and has a fire insurance office in Worcester 2 Harriet

Brayton, born September 6, 1891, educated in private schools at Worcester and Farmington, resides with her father. 3 Brayton, born December 28, 1892, attended Pomfret School at Pomfret, Connecticut, and graduated in the class of 1915 at Harvard University receiving the degree of A. B., he then entered the Worcester office of Jackson & Curtis, brokers, and during his service there he enlisted in Battery A, of Boston, and with them saw border service on the American and Mexican frontier at El Paso during the disturbing period from June to November, 1916 and upon his return to Boston was mustered out of the service, and at once took up a course of medical studies in that city. During the years 1905-07 Dr Nichols and his family resided in Germany and Switzerland.

(VIII) Lydia Anthony Nichols, daughter of Dr Lemuel Bliss and Lydia Carter (Anthony) Nichols was born May 5, 1857, in Worcester, Massachusetts, and died April 6, 1903. She married, June 19, 1883, Reuben Tyler Palmer, born December 3, 1857, died December 13, 1913, son of Reuben T. and Lavinia (Hill) Palmer, who were the parents of five children. Ida became the wife of Dr ———— Allen, of New London; Emma, unmarried; Reuben Tyler and Tyler Reuben, twins, and Lavinia, became the wife of Frederick Mercer, of New London, and they have one child, Eleanor Mercer. Children of Mr and Mrs Palmer: 1 Charles Tyler, born June 17, 1884, in Worcester; attended private and high schools at New London, St Paul's School, Garden City, and died at the age of eighteen years. 2 Marguerite Linwood, born February 9, 1886, attended a private school in New London, then a school at Briarcliff-on-the-Hudson, she married, June 1, 1909, Nelson McStea Whitney, born February 4 1886, son of George Quintard and Sarah

Elise (McStea) Whitney, of New Orleans, Louisianna, and their children are Morgan Linwood, born April 5, 1910, and Elise, born March 23, 1914. 3 Harold Nichols, born September 27, 1887, married, May, 1916, Mary C. Elliot, of New York. 4 Reuben Tyler (3rd), born February 26, 1899; attended private and public schools of New London, the Worcester Academy, from which he graduated with honor, one of the three speakers of his class, 1917, and then entered Brown University, class of 1920.

CLOYES, Joseph C.,
Civil War Soldier, Respected Citizen

John Cloyes, the pioneer ancestor of the Cloyes family, was a mariner; his name is found upon the records of Watertown, Massachusetts, as early as 1631 The early settlers of the Cloyes family spelled their name Clayes, sometimes Cloise. Whether it is written Clayes or Cloyes, it undoubtedly is the same family. After his house was burned in Watertown, he probably removed to Charlestown, where a deed was given by John Cloyes and wife Jane for a barn and land in Watertown, May 3, 1656 July 25, 1660, he sold his Charlestown lands and removed to Falmouth, Maine, and was killed by the Indians, in 1676. He married (first) Abigail ————, (second) Jane ————, (third) widow of Julian Sparwell, born 1620, she did not die until after 1667, as her name is in a court record of that year. But little seems to be known of the immigrant ancestor. Children of John Cloyes: 1 John, born in Watertown, Massachusetts, August 26, 1638; settled in Wells, Maine. 2 Peter, born in Watertown, May 27, 1640. 3 Nathaniel, born in Watertown, March 6, 1642-43, married Sarah Mills, settled in Wells, Maine, was in Charlestown,

1698 4 Abigail, married Jenkin Williams 5 Sarah, married Peter Housing 6 Thomas, married Susannah Lewis, and was in Saco, 1671, in Falmouth, 1674, in Wells, 1681, killed by the Indians, 1690 7 Mary, born July 1, 1657 8 Martha, born in Charlestown, October 13, 1659

(II) Peter Cloyes, son of John Cloyes, born May 27, 1640, died July 18, 1708, also settled in Maine, and was in Wells as early as 1663 From there he moved to Salem Village, now Danvers, Massachusetts, located permanently in Framingham, Massachusetts, 1693, on what is now known as the Barton place He was always interested in public affairs When the first town meeting of Framingham was held, in August, 1700, Peter Cloyes was elected town treasurer The first meeting house was framed in 1698, but was not completed until 1701 Peter Cloyes was one of the number elected to "gather ten pounds in money by way of rate" for finishing of the meeting house, to employ a carpenter and see that the money was spent to the best advantage When the first minister, Rev John Swift, was called to the parish, Mr Cloyes was one of the men selected to extend the call in behalf of the rest of the inhabitants Rev Mr Swift left a record, dated October 8, 1701, in which he gave the names of the first eighteen members of the church Peter Cloyes's name was included in the list

Peter Cloyes married (first) Hannah ———, who died about 1680, (second) Sarah Towne Bridges, born in 1638, daughter of William and Joanna Blessing Towne, who came to New England from Yarmouth, Norfolk county, England, about 1639 She was the widow of Edmund Bridges, son of Captain Benjamin and his wife Alice Sarah Towne Cloyes was the sister of Rebecca Towne Nourse The story of the Salem Witch-

craft and that of Rebecca Nourse are both familiar tragedies in colonial history Possibly the story of her sister Sarah is less known Rebecca Towne, wife of Francis Nourse, and Sarah Towne Cloyes were among the first victims in Salem to be accused of witchcraft They were committed to the Boston prison, March 1, 1692 At the first trial of Mrs Nourse, who was a member of the Salem church and seems to have been a woman of culture, the evidence was so weak that she was not convicted; at a second trial she was also acquited, but at a third trial she was convicted and sentenced to be hung as a witch, because she had not given the magistrate the proper answer to his questions It was afterwards learned that owing to deafness she had failed to comprehend the questions The sentence was carried out in spite of the forty neighbors who gave their signatures to a declaration that "they had known her for many years and had observed her life and conversation to be according to new profession" She was executed July 19, 1692 Sarah Cloyes was also convicted, received the death sentence, and was committed to the jail in Ipswich to await execution Her husband, Peter Cloyes, was allowed to visit her, and in some unknown way she managed to make her escape and was concealed by her friends until she came to Framingham in 1693 and settled in the part of the town that has since been known in Framingham history as Salem End Sarah Towne Cloyes died in 1703

The third wife of Peter Cloyes was Widow Susana Beers, daughter of Robert Harrington, of Watertown, and this marriage was also her third, she having married (first) February 9, 1671-72, John Cutting, of Watertown, (second) Ehezer Beers, of Watertown, (third) Peter Cloyes There seems to have been no record made of the birth of the children of Peter Cloyes, but his will and deeds give the following list 1 Hannah, born about 1665; married, 1686, Daniel Ellist, and lived in Framingham and Oxford 2 Sarah, born about 1667, married, in Salem Village, March 13, 1688, John Cunnabel, lived in Boston, died before 1700, had children Deborah, Hannah, and probably John, Elizabeth, Susanna and Robert 3 Mary, married (second) Joseph Trumbull 4 James 5 Peter 6 Abigail, married ——— Waters, and died before 1708, leaving daughter Abigail 7 Hepzibah, married, February 3, 1708, E Tenezer Harrington 8 Alice, married, before July 15, 1708, ——— Bridges

(III) James Cloyes, son of Peter Cloyes As the birth of the children of Peter Cloyes was not recorded, there is of course no authority record of his birth, neither is there any date of his marriage recorded, and only the Christian name of his wife (Mary) given in the town history In the Framingham tax list dated June 27, 1710, his name appears At this time the town was divided into two constable wards On the basis of each mans' proportion to a tax of £10 to procure a stock of ammunition, James Cloyes's tax amounted to two shillings and two pence During Ralle's war, which lasted from 1722 to 1726, Framingham furnished its quota, and we find in the list the name of James Cloyes as it appears on the muster roll of Captain Isaac Clark's company of troopers out from August 21 to September 18, 1725 At this period the first meeting house built in 1701 was becoming almost too dilapidated for use, and when the second meeting house was under consideration, the town voted at a meeting held April 19, 1725, to raise £100 for that purpose, James Cloyes was one of the committee chosen to agree with a workman to build the house The controversy over where this house should

be built extended over a period of ten years One of the sites selected did not meet the approval of one of the leading citizens of the town, so he confiscated the timbers and built a barn for himself The General Court was called upon to settle the dispute, but it was not until March 25, 1734, that an amicable settlement was made The house was built the following year James Cloyes served as a member of the board of selectmen for five years, from 1730 to 1735 Children of James and Mary Cloyes 1 Esther, born April 27, 1702, married, June 17, 1725, Captain Daniel Howe, of Shrewsbury; she died July 27, 1759 2 Keziah, born December 8, 1705, married, 1727, William Goddard, of Shrewsbury 3 John, born September 25, 1707, died 1794 4 James, born June 10, 1710, died January, 1798 5 Mary, born October 12, 1712, married Deacon Jonathan Morse 6 Hannah, born April 4, 1717, married, 1735, Josiah Wilson, of Hopkinton

(IV) James (2) Cloyes, son of James (1) and Mary Cloyes, was born in Framingham, June 10, 1710, died in January, 1798 James, like his father and grandfather before him, was a part of the church life in Framingham When the second minister, Rev Mathew Bridge, accepted the call to preside over the parish, James Cloyes, Jr, was appointed one of a committee to take care of the meeting house upon the ordination day, which occurred February 19, 1746 He was also prominent in the secular affairs of the town, having served five years upon the board of selectmen, and in 1770 was appointed one of the overseers of the work house and the poor

In 1745 James Cloyes was a member of Ephraim Baker's company, Sir William Pepperell's regiment, in the Louisburg expedition Again, in the last

French and Indian war, we find his name enrolled upon the alarm list in Captain Jeremiah Belvernap's company, April 26, 1757 Less than a month after the tea was thrown overboard in Boston Harbor, the selectmen espousing the cause of Boston called a town meeting (January 10, 1774) to see if the town would come into any determination relating to the matter whereby to contribute their mite with other towns in the province James Cloyes's signature was attached to the warrant

It was a nephew of this James Cloyes who was killed by lightning out of a clear sky, June 3, 1773 A local school mistress has bequeathed to us a poem of forty-eight verses which gives a vivid description of scene and which has become historic "The Lord gave forth his thundering voice which proved the death of Rice and Cloyes Thus in the twinkling of an eye, they passed into eternity" Another verse of the poem is inscribed upon the gravestone of one of the men "My trembling heart with grief o'erflows, While I record the death of those, Who died by thunder sent from heaven, In seventeen hundred and seventy-seven" At this date the family must have spelled their name Cloyes, as Miss Lydia Learned spelled it thus in her poem

He married (first) July 24, 1735, Lydia Eames, who died November 8, 1736, (second) May 28, 1740, Abigail Gleason, born November 13, 1717, daughter of Captain John and Abigail Learned Gleason, a descendant of Thomas Gleason, the immigrant ancestor, who settled in Watertown in 1652 She died in April, 1798. Children of James and Abigail Gleason Cloyes 1 Peter, born October 30, 1736 (son of Lydia), died young 2 Josiah, born September 30, 1741, died May 13, 1858 3 James, born February 13, 1742-43, died December 9, 1809 4

Elijah, born September 5, 1744, died at White Plains, 1776 5 Lydia, born August 7, 1746, married Simon Fozer 6. Abigail, born August 7, 1752, married John Mayhew 7 Peter, born March 28, 1754

(V) James (3) Cloyes, son of James (2) and Abigail Gleason Cloyes, born February 3, 1742-43, died December 9, 1809 This James, like all his ancestors, was loyal not only to his native town, but also to his country, and was ever ready when the call came for military service November 8, 1774, the town voted to accept the resolve of the Provincial Congress, passed October 26, 1774, which provided for the enlistment and equipment of companies which should hold themselves in readiness to march at a minute's notice Two companies of minute-men were formed in Framingham, Massachusetts, at this time, and James Cloyes was one of the first to enlist The company was duly organized December 2, 1774 On that memorable call, April 19, 1775, the Framingham men followed the British as far as Cambridge and spent the night there On the muster roll of a minute company belonging to Framingham, under the command of Captain Simon Edgell, who marched on the alarm on the 19th of April, 1775, to Concord and Cambridge, we find the name of James Cloyes, Jr, and in 1777 he was a member of the committee of correspondence At a town meeting held May 22, 1780, he was one of a committee of fifteen to examine the new Constitution, or "Frame of Government" In 1807, when the American frigate, "Chesapeake," was attacked by the British frigate "Leopard," because the commander, Commodore Barron, of the American ship, would not allow the British commander to search the "Chesapeake" for deserters, detachments from the militia companies were

ENCYCLOPEDIA OF BIOGRAPHY

called at short notice, and, as in the Revolution, enrolled as minute-men   Sergeant James Cloyes and seven men were
detached from Captain Benjamin Wheeler's company   Like all his forebears, he
was also interested in the affairs of the
town, and served four years as a member of the board of selectmen, in 1772-73,
and again in 1780-81   He married Mehitable Gates, daughter of Oldham and
Mehitable Trowbridge Gates, of Framingham   They removed to Spencer,
where she was born June 3, 1746, died
November 2, 1822   She traced her ancestry back to Stephen Gates, the immigrant, who came to Hingham in 1638
Children of James and Mehitable (Gates)
Cloyes   1 Ruth, born December 24
1767, married, December, 1790, died
young   2 James, born July 31, 1773, died
September 18, 1777   3-4 Ezra and Micajah, twins, born December 23, 1776, Ezra
married Lydia Hill, of Buffalo, New York,
died 1840, Micajah married, January 26,
1800, Dolly Morse, settled at Eaton,
Madison county, New York where he
died, August, 1852   She died at Morris-
ville, Madison county, New York, September 3, 1863   5 James, born July 30,
1781   6 Elijah, born December 15 1783,
married Asenath Morse, died February
25, 1863   7 Jonas, born April 14, 1788

(VI) Jonas Cloyes, son of James (3)
and Mehitable (Gates) Cloyes, was born
in Framingham, April 14, 1788, died February 26 1856, and is buried in Edgell
Grove cemetery   He was a granite worker, and many of the old mill stones used
in the water power mills were made by
the Cloyes family   One of the natural as
well as curious objects of the town was
the old House Rock   It was composed of
two granite slabs thirty feet in length,
which in the subsidence after an up-
heaval, met on the upper edge at an angle
which formed a peaked roof, the edges

resting on the ground   The walls were
blackened with smoke, as it was probably
often used as a temporary lodging place
for strolling Indians   The slabs were
flawless, and finally furnished the material for mill stones which were hewn
into shape by Jonas Cloyes about 1822 or
a little later   Mr Cloyes was also a land
surveyor, and when the town in 1850
granted the sum of $75 to pay for a new
survey of the town and procuring a map
of same, Colonel Jonas Cloyes and Warren Nixon were employed to make the
surveys   The map is said to be both
accurate and complete   Mr Cloyes was
also interested in the uplift of the town,
and realized the advantages to be derived
from good and accessible literature   The
first library of the town had its beginning
about 1785   The book fund was the proceeds of the sale of the last of the common lands   But little is known of its history   It was reorganized in 1815 under
the name of the Social Library, by several
of the leading citizens of the town,
among them was Jonas Cloyes   This
library was in existence for several years,
and might well be called the progenitor
of the present beautiful public library of
stone, which was built as a memorial to
the soldiers who gave their lives in the
Civil War   Efficiency seems to have been
the slogan of the Cloyes family, and it
was surely recognized by the Framingham citizens, as each generation served
the term as one of its selectmen ; Jonas
Cloyes served in that capacity from 1818
to 1821   He was also, like his ancestors,
ready and willing to serve his country
Was commissioned lieutenant-colonel of
the Fourth Regiment, First Brigade.
Third Division, Massachusetts Militia,
June 29, 1816   The old brick house on
the Worcester turnpike was built by him
He married, June 28, 1822, Susan Morse,
who died April 18, 1870   She was the

N E—7—12   177

daughter of Asa and Susannah Eames Morse, and traced her ancestry back to Joseph Morse and his wife Dolly, who came from Ipswich, England, to America, and settled in Ipswich, Massachusetts, about 1636 Children of Jonas and Susan (Morse) Cloyes: 1 Addison D, born October 8, 1823, died in Southboro, Massachusetts 2 Frederick, born 1825, went to Grand Rapids, Michigan 3 Franklin, born April 6, 1827, died February 6, 1854, in Framingham 4. James G, born November 30, 1829, went to Grand Rapids, Michigan 5 Charles, born March 5, 1831, went to Chicago, Illinois, and died in Washington, D C 6 George, born December 28, 1832, went to Albany, New York, and is now living in Somerville, Massachusetts 7 Henry C., born February 21, 1834, died in Grand Rapids, Michigan 8 Joseph C, born November 12, 1835.

(VII) Joseph C Cloyes, son of Jonas and Susan (Morse) Cloyes, was born November 12, 1835, in Framingham, Massachusetts He died very suddenly, on August 7, 1917, seated in his chair, on his porch There was no premonition, and his devoted wife, on returning to his side after a moment's absence, found that he had passed away.

His education was obtained in the public schools of the town When he grew to manhood he became engaged in the same business that his father had followed, that of a granite worker He opened up the granite quarries, which were operated by him for many years Many hands were employed in preparing the stone for building purposes, street curbing and for various other uses For several years he was engaged with David Fiske in the general mercantile business at Framingham Center, which was conducted under the name of Fiske & Cloyes, and later under the firm name of Cloyes

& Bean After Mr Cloyes sold out his interests and gave his entire attention to his granite works He continued in the business until failing eyesight compelled him to turn the business over to his foreman In 1900 he became totally blind, and for seventeen years had seen the world only through the eyes of a devoted wife, who always took good care that the lenses were rose colored She brought so much sunshine into his life that from his appearance one would never notice his great affliction, as he simply radiated cheerfulness and contentment Mr Cloyes was one of those cultured, courteous gentlemen of the old school, with the winning personality which makes and holds many friends

Although of a quiet retiring nature and fond of the home life, he was always interested in town affairs, and served his native town in the same capacity as each of his ancestral line had served, since Peter Cloyes was elected as one of the selectmen at Framingham's first town meeting in 1700 His term of office was from 1874 to 1881 And, like all his forebears, he faithfully served his country When Lincoln sent out his call for volunteers in the great crisis of 1861, Joseph C Cloyes enlisted for nine months' service. He was enrolled in Company F, Forty-fifth Regiment, Massachusetts Volunteer Infantry, under command of Captain Daland and Colonel Charles R. Codman, and saw active service in several battles Mr Cloyes served the full term of enlistment He was a member of General J G Foster Post, No 163, Grand Army of the Republic, of Framingham, in which he had held minor offices He was also a member of Middlesex Lodge, Ancient Free and Accepted Masons, and one of the oldest Masons in Middlesex county, having been a member of the fraternity for over sixty years Middlesex Lodge is very

178

proud of its history Its charter bears the signature of Paul Revere, who was grand master of the Grand Lodge of Massachusetts at the time of its organization in 1795, and had for its first worshipful master the gallant Captain Jonathan Maynard, of Revolutionary fame Mr Cloyes had always been intensely interested in the history of his town, and a few years ago was made a life guest of Framingham Chapter, Daughters of the American Revolution Mr Cloyes was the last of his line in the town of Framingham He married, December 5, 1866, Belinda A Nichols They had no children

(The Nichols Line).

Joseph Nichols's family was in Framingham previous to 1730 He was a tavern keeper in 1752 He was active in military affairs, and served in the company of militia under command of Captain Henry Eames, April 26, 1757, in the last French and Indian war His name again appears in 1758, in Captain Taplin's company, out from March 3 to December 5 He married Martha How, daughter of Samuel and Abigail Mixter How, of Sudbury, and granddaughter of the Samuel How who gave the new grant of land to his son John, upon which he built the Red House Tavern, made famous by the poet Longfellow in his "Tales of the Wayside Inn" Children of Joseph and Martha (How) Nichols John, born April 7, 1731, Joseph, born October 8, 1738, Alpheus, born November 5, 1742, Martha, born October 31, 1746, married Nathan Goddard, Mitty, born 1752, died in Utica, New York

Joseph Nichols, son of Joseph and Martha (How) Nichols, was born October 8, 1738, went to Fitzwilliam, New Hampshire, about 1781, and probably died there He was considered one of the prominent men of Framingham, serving on many of

the special committees previous to the American Revolution In 1771 he served the town as one of the wardens, and as selectman in 1778. He was also much interested in the betterment of the schools of Framingham At the age of thirty-seven he was mentioned as the youngest of the political leaders, and was active in everything pertaining to the war of the Revolution He was ready to serve his country when the first call came, and was one of the minute-men in Captain Simon Edgell's company, which marched on the alarm on the 19th of April, 1775 He was also one of the men who enlisted as sergeant for eight months' service in Captain Thomas Durry's company, Colonel John Nixon's regiment, company return dated September 30, 1775 He must have continued in service, as there was an order for bounty coat or its equivalent in money, dated Camp Winterhill, December 22, 1775 He married Sarah Hemenway, daughter of Ralph and Sarah (Haven) Hemenway, and a direct descendant of Ralph Hemenway, the pioneer Children of Joseph and Sarah Nichols Mary born October 16, 1762, married, July, 1784, Nathan Newton Joseph, born March 17, 1764, Benjamin Goddard, born August 18, 1765, How, born May 27, 1767, John, born July 17, 1769, Mitty, born January 21, 1771, Daniel, born December 15, 1772, Sarah, born January 1, 1775, Laban Wheaton, born March 30, 1777, Nabby, baptized October 17, 1779, Alph, born December 11, 1780, Patty, born December 12, 1782

John Nichols, son of Sergeant Joseph and Sarah (Hemenway) Nichols, was born July 17, 1769 He was a farmer and settled in Southboro, Massachusetts, where he built a saw and grist mill He spent the remainder of his life and died in Southboro The mill property, which was formerly owned by his grandson, D

179

Clinton Nichols, is now included in the Metropolitan water system of Boston The marriage intentions of John Nichols and Hannah Nixon were published in Southboro, April 11, 1790 Hannah Nixon, born September 21, 1772, was the daughter of Colonel Thomas and Bethiah (Stearns) Nixon Colonel Thomas, brother of General John Nixon, died on a voyage from Boston to Portsmouth, August 12, 1800 Like his brother, he was imbued with the military spirit He enlisted in Captain Nervel's company, and was at Crown Point, March, 1755, to January, 1756, lieutenant in same company in General Amherst's campaign, 1759 He was elected captain in the second company of minute-men of Framingham, 1774, resigned, and served as lieutenant in his brother's Sudbury company, April 19, 1775, lieutenant-colonel in brother's brigade In 1780 was in command of the Sixth Massachusetts Regiment Obtained a furlough from General Gates, December 20, 1780 He retained his commission until the close of the war, when he received an honorable discharge Children of John and Hannah (Nixon) Nichols Betsey, born July 30, 1791, Richard, born May 20, 1792, Laura, born January 15, 1794, Betsey (2nd), born October 4, 1795; Horace, born February 1, 1798, Oren, born May 25, 1801, Hiram, born April 1, 1803, Harriet, born November 9, 1804, Tryphena, born December 18, 1805, Sophia, born April 16, 1807, Otis, born December 29, 1810. Hannah Nixon Nichols died in 1810, and John married (second) Mrs. Polly Nichols, daughter of Jonathan Leland, of Sherborn

Oren Nichols, son of John and Hannah Nixon Nichols, was born in Southboro, Massachusetts, May 25, 1801, and died there in 1876 He was by trade a cabinet maker, and while a young man went to Lowell, Massachusetts, where he followed his trade, and later engaged in business After spending several years in Lowell, he returned to Southboro and continued the saw and grist mill business which was established by his father and known as the Nichols Mills, he also managed the farm Mr Nichols was a well known and respected citizen, a man of temperate and quiet habits and very devoted to his home, He married Mary A. Woodbury, of Pelham, New Hampshire, daughter of John and Hannah (Gibson) Woodbury She was a member of the Congregational church, and very devoted to both the home and church life Children of Oren and Mary A (Woodbury) Nichols were Georgiana, who died young, George W was a Civil War soldier, and died during the war, D Clinton, resides in Southboro, Belinda A, born October 27, 1838. Belinda A. Nichols, born in Lowell, Massachusetts, daughter of Oren and Mary A (Woodbury) Nichols, married Joseph C Cloyes, December 5, 1866 They celebrated their silver wedding anniversary in 1891, and in 1916 they kept open house at their home on Salem End road, in commemoration of the golden anniversary of their marriage Mrs. Cloyes is a woman of culture and refinement, and since her husband was stricken with blindness, was his constant and devoted companion, and has endeared herself to all by her noble Christian qualities. Previous to her husband's misfortune she was a member of the Framingham Woman's Club, and Orient Chapter, O E S, of which Mr. Cloyes was also formerly a member. She is a charter member of Framingham Chapter, Daughters of the American Revolution, being eligible to membership in the organization through the military record of her great-grandfather, Joseph Nichols, and obtaining membership through the service of the brave and efficient officer, Colonel Thomas Nixon.

ANTHONY, Harold H.,

Business Man

Conspicuous in public affairs in the colonial period, the Anthonys have since sustained the family name and reputation in the annals of American history. They, too, have given to science and other fields in educational lines men of distinction, and as well to the business life of the country some of its leading and most successful business spirits

(I) William Anthony, the first known of the family, was born in Cologne, Germany, in 1495 He came to London, England, as chief engraver of the mint and seals to King Edward VI, and also served in that same capacity to Queen Mary and Queen Elizabeth He was the father of three sons, namely Thomas, Derick and Francis.

(II) Francis Anthony, youngest son of William Anthony, married Judith Roby daughter of William Roby, of London He, like his father, was an eminent goldsmith in the city of London, and had employment of considerable value in the jewel office under Queen Elizabeth He was the father of one son, Francis, mentioned below

(III) Dr Francis (2) Anthony, son of Francis (1) and Judith (Roby) Anthony, was born in London, April 16, 1551 The "Biographa Britannica" says he was a very learned physician and chemist Having been thoroughly trained in the first rudiments of learning at home, he was about the year 1569 sent to the University at Cambridge, where he studied with great diligence and success, and some time in the year 1574 took the degree of Master of Arts It appears from his own writings that he applied himself for the many years that he studied in the university, to the theory and practice of chemistry He left Cambridge at the age of forty

years, and began soon after to publish to the world the effects of his chemical studies, and in the year 1598 sent abroad his first treatise concerning the excellency of a medicine drawn from gold He commenced medical practice in London without a license from the College of Physicians, and after six months was called before the president and censors of the college, A D 1600 He was interdicted from practice and for disregarding this injunction was fined five pounds and committed to prison, whence he was released by a warrant of the Lord Chief Justice He continued to practice in defiance of the college, and performed numerous cures on distinguished persons and further proceedings were threatened, but not carried out, probably because he had powerful friends at court His practice consisted chiefly, if not entirely, in the prescription and sale of a secret remedy called *Aurum Potabile*, or potable gold He was obnoxious to the college not only because he practiced without a license, but because he kept the composition of his remedy a secret, and put it forward as a panacea for all diseases The career of Dr Anthony and his conflict with the College of Physicians illustrates the condition of the medical profession in the seventeenth century From the sale of his remedy he derived a considerable fortune Dr Anthony was a man of high character and very liberal to the poor He died in his seventy-fourth year, and was buried in the Church of St Bartholomew the Great, where a handsome monument is erected to his memory Dr Anthony was twice married, by his first wife, Susan Howe, were born three children, two sons and one daughter, namely John, Charles and Frances John and Charles became physicians, and Frances married Abraham Vicars, of St Olave, Old Jewry, London, in 1608 Dr An-

181

thony married (second) September 23, 1609, Elizabeth Lante, or Trinity, Menaries, London, widow of Thomas Lante

✓ (IV) John Anthony, son of Dr Francis (2) and Susan (Howe) Anthony, was born in 1585, and died in 1655 He was graduated at Pembroke College, M B, in 1613, M D, in 1619, was admitted licentiate of the College of Physicians of London in 1625; served in the civil war on the Parliamentary side as surgeon to Colonel Sandays, was author of a devotional work, "The Comfort of the Soul," laid down by way of meditation, in 1654

(V) John (2) Anthony (or Anthonie, as he wrote it), son of Dr John (1) Anthony, and the first American ancestor, was born in 1607 He was a resident of the village of Hampstead, near London, England, and came to New England in the barque "Hercules," April 16, 1634 He is of record in 1640 at Portsmouth, Rhode Island, and was made a freeman there the 14th of the 7th month, 1640 He became a corporal in a military company, and had land assigned to him at the "Wadding River" in 1644 He had authority granted him May 25, 1655, to keep a house of entertainment in Portsmouth He was commissioner in 1661, and deputy from 1666 to 1672 He married Susanna Potter, and both he and his wife died in 1675 Their children were John, born in 1642, Susanna, born in 1644, Elizabeth, born in 1646, Joseph, born in 1648, and Abraham, born in 1650

(VI) Abraham Anthony, son of John (2) and Susanna (Potter) Anthony, was born in 1650, in Portsmouth, Rhode Island, and married, December 26, 1671, Alice Wodell, daughter of William and Mary Wodell, of Portsmouth He was made a freeman in 1672 He was deputy much of the time from 1703 to 1711, and in 1709-10 was speaker of the House of Deputies He died October 10, 1727, and

his widow passed away in 1734 Their children were John, born in 1672, Susanna and Mary, twins, born in 1674, William, born in 1675; Susanna (2), born in 1677, Mary (2), born in 1680; Abraham, born in 1682, Thomas, born in 1684; Alice and James, twins, born in 1686, Amy, born in 1688, Isaac, born in 1690 and Jacob, born in 1693

(VII) William (2) Anthony, son of Abraham and Alice (Wodell) Anthony, was born October 31, 1675, and married, March 14, 1694, Mary Coggeshall, who was born September 18, 1675, daughter of John and Elizabeth (Timberlake) Coggeshall, granddaughter of Major John Coggeshall, and great-granddaughter of John Coggeshall, who was the first president of the Colony of Rhode Island William Anthony was of Portsmouth, Rhode Island, and of Swansea, Massachusetts He died December 28, 1744, his wife passing away in 1739 Their children were William, born in 1695, died in infancy, Abraham, born 1696, Elizabeth, born in 1698, Mary, born in 1699, died in infancy, John, born in 1700, died in infancy; Alice, born in 1705, Anne, born in 1707; John and Amey, twins, born in 1708, William, born in 1709, James, born in 1712, Job, born in 1714; Benjamin, born in 1716, and Daniel, born in 1720

(VIII) John (3) Anthony, son of William and Mary (Coggeshall) Anthony, was born November 16, 1708, and married, December 16, 1733, Lydia Luther, who was born September 19, 1714, daughter of Hezekiah and Martha Luther, of Swansea Their children were William, born in 1734; Job, born in 1736, Avis, born in 1739, Edward, born in 1741, Israel, born in 1743; Sarah, born in 1747, Elizabeth, born in 1748; Lydia, born in 1750, John, born in 1752; Gardner, born in 1754, and Jonathan, born in 1757

(IX) John (4) Anthony, son of John

(3) and Lydia (Luther) Anthony, was born July 1, 1752, and died July 11, 1793. He married Sarah Baker, who was born September 18, 1748, and their children were Lydia, born September 19, 1772, Israel, born February 20, 1775, who died in infancy, Israel (2), born April 28, 1777; Elizabeth, born November 13, 1779, who died in infancy; Edward, born February 26, 1781, Moses, born April 12, 1782; Sarah, born May 3, 1784; and Elizabeth (2), born January 28, 1796

(X) Edward Anthony, son of John (4) and Sarah (Baker) Anthony, was born February 26, 1781, and died December 5, 1869 He married Persis Butterworth, who was born September 3, 1786, and died May 9, 1857 Their children were John, born October 23, 1807, mentioned below; and Moses, born December 22, 1809, who married Elizabeth Welsh, and they had three children

(XI) Rev John (5) Anthony, son of Edward and Persis (Butterworth) Anthony, was born October 23, 1807 He was a minister of the Gospel He married, October 18, 1829, Maria Bloomfield Davis, who was born August 24, 1805, daughter of David and Sarah (Simmons) Davis, of Somerset, Massachusetts To Rev John and Maria B. (Davis) Anthony were born the following children John Nelson, born October 18, 1831, died September 28, 1832, John Nelson (2), born October 11, 1832, died August 9, 1861, Edward Francis, born December 30, 1835, married Mary B Kimball, David Mason, born September 24, 1835, mentioned below, Charles Wesley, born November 10, 1838, died March 3, 1898; George Moses, born July 21, 1839, Mary Elizabeth, born May 7, 1840, died August 31, 1841, and Enoch Bower, born March 24, 1843, died January 25, 1899

(XII) David Mason Anthony, son of Rev John (5) and Maria B (Davis) An-

thony, was born September 24, 1835, on Pearl street, Fall River, Massachusetts, and at the age of four years, with his parents, removed to Somerset, Massachusetts, which was his mother's native town Under the private tutelage of his father and in the district schools he acquired his early educational training, which was rather meagre with the majority of the boys of that day At the age of eight years he returned to Fall River, and worked in the Robeson Print Works as tier boy, working from five o'clock in the morning until seven-thirty at night, for which services he received five dollars per month After working there for two years he returned to Somerset, where he spent about one year, again returning to Fall River, in which city he resided on Hartwell street until twelve years of age, when he removed to No 368 North Main street, which location was thereafter his home, and where all his children were born, and upon which land he later built his handsome brick residence, in which he passed away November 6, 1915

At the age of fourteen years he went to work for a Mr Sweet on a milk farm, working thirteen hours per day, at the remunerative salary of seven dollars per month During the two years spent on this farm he acquired a practical training in agricultural pursuits, and at the age of sixteen years he conducted his grandfather's farm on shares for one season He then became apprenticed to the mason's trade, at which he served four years In 1856 he shipped "before the mast" on a voyage to Cuba, the vessel going from there to Mobile and from there to New York, where he disembarked This ended his seagoing career In 1857 he bought out a meat market in City Hall, Fall River, which was his beginning in that line of business, in which he ever after continued and in which he met with such marked success In 1869 he formed a partnership with his brother, Charles W Anthony, and Gustavus F Swift, which was incorporated as Swift & Company in April, 1889, and which has developed into the highly successful and world-renowned meat packing and provision corporation of to-day In 1871, Mr Anthony erected a large and commodious packing house on Davol street, Fall River, where he successfully conducted business for many years under the firm name of D M Anthony, this firm being widely known throughout Southern Massachusetts and Rhode Island Mr Anthony was of material assistance to the Swifts in the early days of their business which has since grown to such wonderful proportions, and at the time of his death and for many years prior was a director of Swift & Company, the Chicago corporation besides holding the same office in several of the less prominent of the Swift concerns He was also widely known in Boston financial circles, as a result of his extensive business connections, and was for a number of years a director of the Federal Trust Company of that city He was also at various times connected with other financial and business interests, in connection with which his advice and counsel proved valuable

On June 3, 1863, Mr Anthony was united in marriage to Ruth Ann Horton, who was born May 15, 1839, daughter of Mason and Sarah Ann (Baker) Horton, and to this union were born three children, namely 1 Ella Martin, born January 19, 1867, married, October 25, 1890, Frank Horton 2 David Mason. Jr, born June 6, 1869 3 Harold Horton, born November 28, 1876. The mother of these children passed away April 18, 1879, and Mr Anthony married (second) in January, 1882, Abbie Carll Webb, of Maine, who passed away May 30, 1898

Mr Anthony was absolutely simple, modest, courteous, and without pretense He was content to do his share in accomplishing results, and leave to others whatever of fame or glory might result from having accomplished them. 'To be, and not be seen, was this man's wisdom." He was a man of great energy, splendid executive ability, indomitable perseverance, great business foresight, and had the rare faculty of bringing things to pass" on a large scale and in accordance with well-thought-out plans A man little given to display, he went along in the even tenor of his way unassumingly, quietly, but showing the force of his character in everything to which he gave his attention Through his keen foresight and business sagacity he accumulated a fortune He was a man of fixed ideas, conservative, indepedent in action, doing what he thought was right and not afraid to speak his mind when he considered it necessary In political sentiment he was a Republican, but took no active part in party affairs Throughout his life, from early boyhood, Mr Anthony was fond of out-door pursuits, living as much as possible in the open He took great pleasure in his farm at South Swansea, which he kept well stocked and in a high state of cultivation, and where he devoted much of his time, especially during his latter years, and on the day when his last illness first required him to take to bed, he had been all day at the farm and about the beach, in very good spirits and apparent good health He had been failing for several months, however, before his death, which occurred November 6, 1915, at the advanced age of eighty years In his death Fall River sustained the loss of one of its most prominent as well as one of its most successful business men and useful citizens

(XIII) Harold Horton Anthony, youngest son of David Mason and Ruth Ann (Horton) Anthony, was born in Fall

River, Massachusetts, November 28, 1876. His educational training was acquired in the schools of his native city, graduating from the B. M. C. Durfee High School of Fall River in 1895. After leaving school he immediately became connected with his father in the meat and provision business, with which business he has since been prominently identified and since his father's death has acted as trustee of the latter's estate.

On January 5, 1898, Mr. Anthony was united in marriage to Caroline Goodwin Cook, daughter of Edward C. and Susan (Goodwin) Cook of Unionville, Connecticut, and they are the parents of one daughter, Ruth Goodwin Anthony who was born May 17, 1902.

BUFFINTON, Waldo A. and Frank,

Men of High Character

The Buffinton family is one of the leading families of Fall River, Somerset, and the old town of Swansea, Massachusetts. For generations they were faithful members of the Society of Friends, and in the early days suffered the persecutions inflicted upon all Quakers. Bovington and Buffington are variations in the spelling.

(I) Thomas Buffinton, the American immigrant is said to have come from Scotland. Soon after 1650 he was located at Salem, Massachusetts, where he married, December 30, 1671, Sarah Southwick, a daughter of John and Sarah Southwick, and granddaughter of the pioneer ancestors, Lawrence and Cassandra Southwick, who became Quakers and were fined, whipped and imprisoned for adhering to their religious faith, despoiled of their property, and finally banished. Thomas Buffinton was also a Friend, but seems to have escaped trouble with the Puritan authorities. The commoners records indicate that he was living as late as 1723. Children: Thomas, born March 1,

1673; James, Benjamin, mentioned below; Joseph, of Swansea; Abigail, July 25, 1695; Hannah, May 11, 1701, and perhaps others.

(II) Benjamin, son of Thomas Buffinton, was born at Salem, July 24, 1675. He and his wife Hannah were Quakers, and like many others in Salem felt constrained to depart. In 1698 he went South as a Quaker missionary. They located in Swansea about 1700. About fifty Quaker families went from Salem to this section and bought homesteads, paying the Indians as well as the proprietors. Descendants still have the deed showing the purchase of three hundred acres from one Marcy. His homestead has remained in the possession of the family to the present time. The records of the branch that has remained on the original homestead have been kept by the family, and from this record were obtained the dates in the early generations of the family as herein given. Children: Benjamin, born at Salem, May 9, 1699 died young; Benjamin, mentioned below; William, born at Swansea, October 9, 1703; Esther, married Stephen Chase; Hannah married Silas Chase. Jonathan married Sarah Luther.

(III) Benjamin (2), son of Benjamin (1) Buffinton, was born at Swansea, April 9, 1701 and died April 9, 1760, and was buried in the Friends' graveyard at Swansea. He married Isabel, daughter of Joseph and Sarah Chase, who died April 6, 1791, at Swansea. She was born July 6, 1705 at Swansea. He was a member of the Swansea monthly meeting to the end of his life. Children born at Swansea: Benjamin, born November 7, 1737; Moses, mentioned below; Stephen, February 25, 1743; Elizabeth, August 21, 1746; Hannah, July 30, 1749.

(IV) Moses, son of Benjamin (2) Buffinton, was born at Swansea, May 8, 1741. He married (first) Isabel Baker, born July

4, 1741, daughter of Daniel and Sarah (Chace) Baker, (second) Patience Chace. He also lived in Swansea. He died April 7, 1817, his first wife, Isabel, died May 4, 1781, and both are buried in the Friends' burying ground at Swansea. Excepting Daniel and Aaron, all his children were born in Swansea. Children by first wife: Benjamin, born November 1, 1762, Sarah, September 25, 1764; Rebecca, August 24, 1768; Ama, July 25, 1770, Daniel, mentioned below, Moses, married Sarah Chase; Aaron, July 21, 1776, died November 15, 1777, Bethany, July 28, 1778, died August 31, 1779. Aaron, April 24, 1780. Children by second wife: Eber, born December 6, 1783; Mary, September 21, 1786, Elizabeth, June 8, 1788, married Nathan Chase.

(V) Daniel, son of Moses Buffinton, was born at Dighton, January 7 1773. He died January 17, 1844. He followed farming in Somerset until 1803. when he removed to Fall River, locating on a place owned by Samuel Rodman, of New Bedford, comprising four hundred and fifty acres, extending from the Taunton river to the North Pond. He was a member of the Society of Friends. He married (first) Rebecca Earle, daughter of Caleb Earle of Somerset, and (second) Ruth Hart. Children by first wife: 1 Daniel, married (first) Hannah Buffinton, (second) Eliza Gray. 2 Caleb, never married. 3 Oliver, mentioned below. Children by his second wife. 4 Benjamin, married Eliza Carr 5 Edward, married Sarah Ann Hathaway, of Northbridge, Massachusetts. 6 Ruth, married (first) Edward Holder, of Bolton, Massachusetts, and (second) James Brownell, having one daughter by her second husband, Mary Ella Brownell, who married James C. O. Davol, and had two children Edward and Bradford Davol. 7 Henry Slade, married Amanda Palmer.

(VI) Oliver, son of Daniel Buffinton, was born at Fall River, August 19, 1805, and was educated there in the public schools. He was the first birthright member of the Society of Friends, born in Fall River. During his youth he worked with his father on the farm. He became associated with Israel Buffington in the manufacture of cotton in Fall River, and was afterward on his own account a manufacturer of cotton yarn, cotton batting and other specialties. From 1857 to 1868, a period of eleven years, he was superintendent of the Oak Grove Cemetery in Fall River. Afterward he retired and spent his last years in his home on Hanover street, cultivating his garden and living to a good old age. He died there January 20, 1885, in the eightieth year of his age.

He married Elizabeth Mason Reynolds who was born at Wickford, Rhode Island April 23, 1805 died April 29, 1892, daughter of Abel and Elizabeth (Mason) Reynolds. Children 1 Mary Elizabeth born April 4, 1830, mentioned below. 2 William Henry, born February 14, 1832, died January 24, 1857, a farmer, unmarried 3 Waldo Ames, mentioned below 4 Lydia Ann, born February 24, 1840. died October 7, 1841. 5 Frank, mentioned below.

(VII) Waldo Ames, son of Oliver Buffinton, was born at Fall River, March 20, 1838 He was educated in the public schools of his native town, and early in life entered the employ of the New York, New Haven & Hartford Railroad Company, formerly the Old Colony, at Fall River, as clerk, and rose to positions of large responsibility and trust in the service of this corporation. For many years he had charge of the transportation of freight in Fall River by rail and steamboat. In politics he was a sterling Republican. He was a highly useful, upright and honorable man He died March 14, 1916. He married, in 1868, Mary Elizabeth Almy. Children, born in Fall River 1 William Henry, born April 29, 1869, married Sarah Sabrina Holway, of Chatham Massachusetts. 2. Gertrude, died aged two years. 3 Annie Elizabeth, born June 28, 1879, married Fergus Ferguson, and has a son, William Buffinton Ferguson

(VII) Frank Buffinton, brother of Waldo Ames Buffinton, was born in Fall River, July 8, 1846, and died in Fall River, March 18, 1916. From 1860 until his death he had been engaged in business as a florist in Fall River in partnership with his sister, Mary E Buffinton, and their lives had much in common To-gether they attended the public schools in youth, and established the business, which at length became the oldest establishment in the city in this line, and one of the most extensive. This business requires a thorough knowledge of flowers, of the market and the public taste, a high degree of artistic instinct and great resourcefulness The firm maintained the highest standards of honor in all their transactions, their goods were always perfect and they attracted and held the best trade of this section Mr Buffinton was a Republican in politics, but not a seeker of office In religion he was a member of the Church of the New Jerusalem

Perhaps no better comment can be made, in concluding this account of the family, than the following editorial from the "Fall River News" of March 20, 1916

Seldom has an occurrence of local events so startled this community as that of the deaths of the brothers Waldo and Frank Buffinton within four days of one another, and with scarcely the slightest forewarning in either case, indeed none at all in the first.

Both were taken from the midst of their active participation in life's duties Since they ceased to be members of their father's family, they had lived along side of one another on the same parcel of ground, which was their ancestral inheritance Few men were better known than they in the community or more implicitly trusted or more highly respected. Their lives of activity were different but both were brought into contact with many men by their business interests and responsibilities Both were men of unbending integrity, of large intelligence, of wide sympathy with that which was good Both were loyal to the churches of their parents, which was their church, that of the New Jerusalem, and both of them have been almost together, translated to the City of Peace

They were members of one of the oldest of the Fall River families When their father, Oliver Buffington, was born, there were very few houses on the whole tract north of the Quequechan river When he located his home on Hanover street there were almost no residences in all that section east of Rock street, even if on that street All the immediate district in which they lived was a part of the Buffinton homestead.

The life work of the elder brother, to whom the call home came first, was that of handling the railroad freight entering and leaving Fall River In this business he was both skillful and faithful in a high degree

The work of the younger, as everybody knows was with flowers his knowledge of which was extraordinary his love of which was a passion of his life Through them he has ministered to most of our oldest families as well as to many of the more recent comers In this way he came into close touch and into most friendly relations with a multitude of people The story of the sudden ending of the life of the beloved florist and the expert decorator of churches, halls and homes, is told in another column

Either event would have touched the community widely The concurrence of both within four days, and circumstances in some respects so similar, is most unusual and startling A great volume of Fall River history was carried in the minds of these men and of their now doubly bereaved sister Miss Mary Elizabeth Buffinton Their sudden departure is a loss that can never be made up

To Miss Buffinton, the sister, older than either and to the other members of the family group, so suddenly stricken the sympathy of their friends and neighbors goes out, expressed or unexpressed, it is deeply felt

ROUNSEVILLE, Cyrus C,

Manufacturer, Financier

The Rounsville or Rounseville family is said to have been of French-Huguenot stock, driven by religious persecution to England, but the family was well established in England at the time the first immigrant came to America

(I) Philip Rounseville, the first of the family in this country, son of William, was born in Honiton, Devonshire, England, about 1680 He was a cloth dresser or fuller by trade, and came to New England when a young man, settling in Freetown, near Assonet village, following his trade there in the employ of Captain Josiah Winslow From a letter that has been preserved, dated December 25 1704, from his father to him, we have the approximate date of his arrival in this country He afterward moved to the site of the Malachi Howland house, built a dam, and engaged in business in a mill of his own About 1721 he moved to another location near Hunting House Brook, in Middleborough, and afterward to that part of Tiverton which was later East Freetown He there purchased a large tract of land and built the mill dam at Freetown village, where his sons afterward erected a blast furnace a saw mill, grist mill, and finally a sash door and blind factory He married, about 1705 Mary Howland, daughter of Samuel and Mary Howland and granddaughter of Henry Howland, who came to Plymouth as early as 1624 a brother of Arthur Howland and of John Howland, who came in the "Mayflower" Henry Howland and wife, Mary (Newland), came from England and settled in Plymouth, about 1624 He later went to Duxbury, where he died July 17, 1671, his wife, Mary, dying June 17, 1674 He joined the Society of Friends about 1657, and was

not a little persecuted on this account Perhaps none of the colonists have a better record for intelligence, thrift, uprightness and faith in the Divine One than he In 1652, with others, he purchased a large tract of land in Dartmouth, and in 1659 he was one of the twenty-seven purchasers of what is now Freetown, and in the division of 1660 received for his share the sixth lot, which was afterward inherited by his son, Samuel Howland, father of the wife of Philip Rounseville Mr Rounseville died November 6, 1763, his wife, Mary, died May 8, 1744 Their children were William, born October 10, 1705, married Elizabeth Macomber, of Taunton, John, born in 1706, married (first) Sarah Holloway, and (second) Sarah Spooner, Philip, mentioned below, and Mary, born March 3, 1711, married Henry Hoskins, Jr, of Taunton

(II) Philip (2) Rounseville, son of Philip (1) and Mary (Howland) Rounseville, was born about 1708 He married Hannah Jenney, and they resided in Freetown, where the following children were born to them : Hannah born May 2, 1749, and Philip, mentioned below

(III) Philip (3) Rounseville, son of Philip (2) and Hannah (Jenney) Rounseville, was born July 2, 1750, in Freetown He was a soldier in the Revolution from Freetown, born about 1780, being a member of Captain Joseph Norton's company, Colonel John Hathaway's regiment, in the Rhode Island campaign (See "Massachusetts Soldiers and Sailors in the Revolution," p 611, vol xiii) He married, in 1775, Mercy Cole, daughter of Abial and Anna (Pierce) Cole, granddaughter of Ebenezer Pierce and wife, Mary (Hoskins), great-granddaughter of Isaac Pierce, Jr, and wife, Judith (Booth), great-great-granddaughter of Isaac Pierce, who was a soldier in the Narragansett War, and received a grant of land for his services, and died in Lakeville, Massachusetts, in 1732, and great-great-great-granddaughter of Abraham Pierce, who is of record at Plymouth in 1623, and who served as a soldier under Captain Miles Standish To Philip and Mercy (Cole) Rounseville were born the following children Gamaliel, born October 12, 1776, Philip, born February 7, 1779, who never married, Abial, born September 6, 1780, Hannah, born April 12, 1783, who married Bradford Rounseville, Ebenezer, born September 21, 1785, who married Sally Rounseville, Lydia, born December 3, 1787, who never married, Phebe, Benjamin, born November 28, 1789, who married Ann Gifford, Joseph, born March 25, 1792, who married Delia Lawrence, Phylena, born August 12, 1794, who married Jonathan Washburn, of Dartmouth; Alden, born October 26, 1797, who married Cornelia Ashley, of Freetown, and Robert G, who married, in 1827, Mrs Delia, widow of Joseph Rounseville

(IV) Abial Rounseville, son of Philip (3) and Mercy (Cole) Rounseville, was born September 6, 1780, at Freetown He was a farmer by occupation in his native town He married, July 20, 1803, Betsey Ashley, of Freetown, where the following children were born to them Amos; Clarinda, who married Pardon Gifford, and died in Mattapoisett, Macomber, died in 1854, Mercy, who married Stephen Nye, of Fall River; Abial, who went West when a young man, and all trace of him has been lost, Sophronia, who married Hosea Presho, of Raynham; Betsey, who married Elbridge Werden, and died in Providence, Cyrus Cole, mentioned below, and Ebenezer, a sea faring man, engaged in the whaling industry, who died in the Sandwich Islands

(V) Cyrus Cole Rounseville, son of Abial and Betsey (Ashley) Rounseville,

was born in Freetown, March 6, 1820. Early in life he went to sea from New Bedford on a whaling vessel, and continued in the whaling industry until his death In the course of time he rose to the rank of first officer of his vessel, and on his last voyage was taken ill and placed in a hospital on the Island of Mauritius, in the Indian ocean, and died there October 18, 1853, in the thirty-fourth years of his age, where his remains are buried He married, September 1, 1844, Irene P Ashley, who was born at Lakeville, Massachusetts, March 18, 1828, daughter of James Emerson and Orinda (Haffards) Ashley Her father was a farmer in Freetown, born January 31, 1806, and died August 4, 1883, her mother was born July 14, 1802, and died October 22, 1868 After the death of her husband, Mrs Rounseville continued to reside for a few years in Acushnet, then removed to East Freetown, where her parents were living Subsequently she married (second) Aaron S Drake, of Stoughton, Massachusetts, by whom she had one daughter, Carrie W., who became the wife of Josiah Brown, of Fall River Mrs Rounseville spent her last years in the family of her son, the only child by her first marriage, Cyrus Cole Rounseville, Jr, mentioned below, at whose home in Fall River she passed away April 24, 1909, at the age of eighty-one years

(VI) Cyrus Cole Rounseville, only child of Cyrus Cole and Irene P (Ashley) Rounseville, was born at Acushnet, Massachusetts, December 8, 1852, and upon the death of his father, when he was but a mere child, he was taken by his widowed mother to live at East Freetown His early educational training was obtained in the district schools, and when older he attended Bryant & Stratton's Commercial School at Boston, from which he was graduated He started his business career when seventeen years of age, in Fall River, as clerk in the freight office of the Narragansett Steamship Company, then owned by James Fisk, of New York, and during the two years he was with this company acquired valuable training and experience In January, 1872, he accepted a position as clerk in the office of the Granite Mills, and during the twelve years in this office he earned the respect and confidence of his employers, and was from time to time promoted and given additional responsibilities, finally being recommended by them to the important and responsible position of treasurer of the Shove Mills, to succeed George Albert Chace, assuming that office August 10, 1884, having been treasurer and business manager since that time, as well as being a director of the corporation In the administration of the financial affairs of this corporation, which he has served for more than thirty years, Mr Rounseville has displayed the highest order of ability, and to his energy, industry and thoroughness must be ascribed in large measure the growth, prosperity and importance of the Shove Mills. Now one of the oldest treasurers in the textile industry of the city and State, in point of service, Mr. Rounseville has good reason to take pride and satisfaction in his long and successful career He is widely known, not only among his business associates in Fall River and elsewhere in textile circles, but among all classes of people in the city, and, wherever he is known, he is honored and respected for his high personal character

Mr Rounseville has not only been an important factor in the development and management of the Shove Mills, but has been interested in other Fall River enterprises, being vice-president of the Union Savings Bank, and has taken an important part in the management of that highly successful financial institution, he is also

vice-president since 1887 of the Troy Co-Operative Bank, which was organized in 1880, and of which he was one of the incorporators and the first secretary, serving in that capacity from 1880 until his his promotion to the vice-presidency in 1887 For a period of fifteen years he served as secretary of the Cotton Manufacturers' Association, from 1885 to 1900, and was also a member of the executive committee of that organization He was also an active member of the selling committee of that association, which was formed in 1898 for the purpose of selling the product manufactured by the various mills of Fall River, and was one of its first trustees

In political faith, Mr Rounseville has always been a stalwart adherent of the principles of the Republican party, and at times has been active in public affairs, always keenly interested in the city, State and national governments For three years from 1883 to 1885 he represented his ward in the common council of the city of Fall River, early taking a position of leadership in that body, and during his last year served as president He has also been active in religious circles, being a leading and zealous member of the Unitarian church, having served as chairman of the standing committee of the church, and as superintendent of the Sunday school

Mr Rounseville married November 8, 1893, in Fall River, Mary O Pitman, who was born in that city, daughter of John H Pitman, and granddaughter of Charles Pitman, who was the first postmaster of Fall River Mr and Mrs Rounseville have two children Marion Pitman, who was born August 31, 1894, and Cyrus Cole, Jr, who was born January 28, 1898, a graduate of the Moses Brown Preparatory School, of Providence, in the class of 1916, and now a student of Dartmouth College, class of 1920

ENCYCLOPEDIA OF BIOGRAPHY

HEMENWAY-WEEKS

The Hemenways are of an old New
England family Upon the early records
we find the signatures spelled in various ways—Henenway, Hemingway, Hem-
mingway, Heneway, Hinningway Ralph,
the founder of one branch, was in Roxbury, Massachusetts, as early as 1633;
was a member of the church, freeman in
1634 He died in 1678 He married, July
5, 1634, Elizabeth Hews, and their children were Mary, born April 4, 1635, died
young, Samuel, born June, 1636, settled
in New Haven, Connecticut, married
Sarah Cooper, Ruth, born September 21,
1638, unmarried, died 1684, John, born
April 27, 1641, settled in Roxbury, Massachusetts, married Mary Trescott, Joshua,
baptized April 9, 1643; Elizabeth, born
May 31, 1645, married a Bolbrook; Mary,
born April 7, 1647, died young
(II) Joshua, son of Ralph and Elizabeth (Hews) Hemenway, was baptized
April 9, 1643, lived in Roxbury and probably died there, October 29, 1716 He
married (first) Joanna Evans, January 16,
1667-68; (second) Mary ——, who died
May 5, 1703, (third) April 5, 1704, Elizabeth, daughter of William Weeks, born
1655, died September 20, 1737 Children
Joshua, born September 15, 1668, Joanna,
baptized October 2, 1670, married Edward
Ainsworth; Ralph, baptized May 18, 1673,
died June 1, 1699, Ichabod; Elizabeth,
married —— Stanhope, Samuel, baptized September 30, 1683, John, Ebenezer, baptized April 29, 1688
(III) Ebenezer, son of Joshua Hemenway, baptized April 29, 1688, died 1755.
He was a weaver by trade There seems
to be no record of his settlement in Framingham, Massachusetts, but his brother
Joshua settled there in 1692-93, and Ebenezer was a citizen of the town prior to
1710, as his name appears upon a tax list
to procure a stock of ammunition dated

June 27, 1710 He married (first) May
17, 1711, Hannah Winch, born June 16,
1687-88, died April 27, 1737, she was the
daughter of Samuel and Hannah (Gibbs)
Winch Samuel Winch was one of the
petitioners for the incorporation of the
town of Framingham, and at the first
town meeting in 1700 was elected one of
the surveyors of the highways He married (second) February 23, 1738, Thame-
zin, daughter of Benjamin Nurse; she
died about 1767 Children of Ebenezer
and Hannah (Winch) Hemenway were
Ebenezer, born October 24 1712, Samuel
Hemenway, lived in Attleboro, Keziah,
baptized August 4, 1717, married Jeremiah Pike, Daniel, born February 2, 1719,
settled in Marlboro, in 1745 removed to
Shrewsbury, where he died November 15,
1794, Jacob, born March 20, 1721-22, settled in Worcester, where he died; Samuel, born August 3, 1724, married Hannah
Rice, daughter of Richard, died June 18,
1806; Elizabeth, born June 19, 1727, married, 1747, Benjamin Robins, of Stur-
bridge
(IV) Ebenezer (2), son of Ebenezer
(1) and Hannah (Winch) Hemenway, was
born in Framingham, Massachusetts, October 24, 1712, and died in 1781 During
the last French and Indian War his name
appears on the list of Framingham men
who served as soldiers in Colonel Joseph
Buckminster's company of militia, April
26, 1757, Hezekiah Stone, clerk. He married Mary Eve There is a tradition in
the Hemenway family that during infancy
she was captured by Indians and re-
deemed in girlhood She died November
29, 1805, aged ninety-three Children of
Ebenezer and Mary (Eve) Hemenway
1 Mary, born November 4, 1734, blind,
died unmarried, February 18, 1821 2
Hannah, born March 26, 1737, died young
3 Hannah, married Charles Dougherty,
who was very active during the war of

191

the American Revolution; was a minute-man in Captain Micajah Gleason's company at Concord, April 19, 1775, quartermaster in Colonel Jonathan Brewer's company at the battle of Bunker Hill, and with General John Nixon at the battles of Stillwater and Saratoga, made lieutenant and served until the end of the war 4 Ebenezer, born May 6, 1740 5 Adam, may have settled in Shrewsbury or Boylston 6 Samuel 7 Jacob, died December 19, 1822, married (first) an Eaton, (second) Sybil Walker

(V) Ebenezer (3), son of Ebenezer (2) and Mary (Eve) Hemenway, was born May 6, 1740, and died December 11, 1831 He saw much service in several wars. In the last French and Indian War he was in the same company with his father, Colonel Joseph Buckminster's, April 26, 1757, and in 1761, after the capture of Montreal and the surrender of the Province of Canada to the British crown, he was enrolled as sergeant in Captain John Nixon's company (Massachusetts) and was in service from April 18, 1761, to July 28, 1762 He was also prominent in the war of the American Revolution In 1774 was clerk in the second company of minute-men, as clerk under Captain Thomas Nixon The company went in for active drill at once The name of Ebenezer Hemenway, clerk, also appears upon the muster roll of minute-men from Framingham under command of Captain Micajah Gleason at Concord and Cambridge, April 19, 1775. He was in Captain Gleason's company when he shot a British soldier named Thomas Sowers, near Merriams Corner, and took his gun, which he brought home with him. August 22, 1776 Twelve men from Framingham enlisted for the defence of Boston and were assigned to Captain Caleb Brook's company, in Colonel Dike's regiment Ebenezer Hemenway was one of the twelve and served until December 1, 1776 Again, when Framingham sent

twelve men with Captain John Gleason to North Kingston, Rhode Island, April 12, 1777, Ebenezer Hemenway was one of them, and served two months and eight days in Colonel Josiah Whitney's regiment His name also appears upon the muster roll of Captain Joseph Winch's company, in Colonel Samuel Ballard's regiment of Massachusetts State Militia from August 16 to December 10, 1777 He was a member of the North Company, serving as ensign with Captain Lawson Buckminster in May, 1779, Colonel Abner Perry's regiment From July 5 to November 30, 1781, he was in Captain John Hayward s company He rose to the rank of lieutenant; his name was on the pension list in 1801. Ebenezer Hemenway married Bathshebah Stone Hemenway, widow of John, born September 20, 1739, died July 19, 1828. She was the daughter of Samuel and Rebecca (Clark) Stone The Stone family was among the early New England settlers, and like many others settled in Watertown, Massachusetts, before coming to Framingham She traced her ancestry back to the immigrants, Gregory and wife Lydia, who came from England in 1635. Samuel Stone was a Revolutionary soldier, and marched to the alarm on the 19th of April, 1775, to Concord and Cambridge, also served in the Northern Department from August 14 to December 10, 1777, was a member of the company engaged in the battles under General Gates which led to the surrender of Burgoyne, and was present at the surrender Ebenezer Hemenway was also of this company

Children of Ebenezer and Bathshebah (Stone) Hemenway 1 Fanny, born November 2, 1764; married Josiah Warren 2 Levinah, born April 1, 1767, married Elijah Clayes 3 Olive, born April 1, 1769, died March 30, 1787 4 Josiah, born June 26, 1771 5 Sally, born March 1, 1774; married Abel Eaton, sergeant in

the Framingham artillery company, 1814
6 Adam, born March 15, 1777; married
Catherine Patterson, died December 31,
1864   7 Samuel, born August 8, 1779
physician, removed to Dummerston, Vermont, married Rebecca Stone, died November 20, 1834   8 Bathshebah, died
young   9 Lucy, born January 24, 1784,
married Thomas Larrabee

(VI) Josiah, son of Lieutenant Ebenezer (3) and Bathshebah (Stone) Hemenway, born June 26, 1771, died January 28,
1848   He married, February, 1793, Mary
Parkhurst, born November 15, 1771, died
December 31, 1858   She was the daughter of Josiah and Elizabeth Parkhurst,
who settled in Framingham, Massachusetts, in 1762   She was a lineal descendant of George Parkhurst and wife Lu-
sanna, who were in Watertown as early
as 1643, removed to Boston, 1645   Children of Josiah and Mary (Parkhurst)
Hemenway   1 Dexter born August 22,
1794, married, November 23, 1820 Ann
Manson daughter of Loring Manson   2
Windson, born September 13, 1796, died
December 2, 1862, married, May 8, 1823,
Sophronia, daughter of Deacon Enoch
Belknap, a descendant of Abraham and
wife Mary, of Lynn, 1637   3 Adam born
March 12, 1800   4 Willard, born Octo-
ber 17, 1802, married, April 21, 1831,
Jerusha H Parmenter, of Sudbury   5
Josiah, born June 27, 1804, died young
6 Eliza, born February 24, 1806   mar-
ried William Moulton, son of Lieutenant
Winsor Moulton, of Sudbury   7 Josiah,
born May 1, 1808, died April 14, 1883;
married, November 25, 1839, Ann Maria
Eames, daughter of Lorell and Lucy
Eames   both were direct descendants of
Thomas Eames, the pioneer ancestor,
who came to America as early as 1634 The
Eames came from a little town near Stratford-on-Avon, England   The name is a
prominent one in the annals of Framingham history, partly because of the Eames

massacre which took place during King
Philip's War, also because Lucy Eames
and her sister Hitty were the pioneer
straw bonnet workers, and were really
the founders of what later developed into
one of the largest straw goods industries
in New England   (See history of Eames
family)   8 Fisher, born February 22,
1811, married, May 14, 1835, Elizabeth
J Fitch, lived in Hopkinton, Massachusetts   9 John, born April 8, 1813, married, April 1, 1839, Susan Coolidge, daughter of Peter and Mary Monroe Coolidge,
and a descendant of John, the emigrant
ancestor, who came from Cottenham,
England, in 1630   10 Ebenezer Thomas
Sovvers, born February 18, 1817, lived
in Hopkinton and Worcester, Massachusetts

(VII) Adam son of Josiah and Mary
(Parkhurst) Hemenway, was born in
Framingham, March 12, 1800, died October 23 1890, and is buried in Edgell
Grove Cemetery   He lived in the north
part of Framingham, and was by trade a
carpenter   Many of the houses at the
center were built by him   He was also
a large landowner   Adam Hemenway
was a man of quiet and domestic tastes
of temperate habits, and of liberal religious views, voted the Democratic
ticket   He was for many years a member
of the Masonic fraternity   He was one
of the grand old men of the town in which
he lived for ninety years, respected for his
upright character   He married, November 29, 1830, Deborah Brown Sanger, born
in Framingham, March 28 1807, daughter
of Daniel and Betsey Goodnow (Sudbury) Sanger   Daniel Sanger kept a
tavern opposite where St Stephen's Catholic Church now stands, at South Framingham   The nearby land was used as a
muster field, 1820-30   Her grandfather,
Daniel Sanger, was also proprietor of the
noted Sanger Tavern   During the War
of the American Revolution he was a

member of the committee of correspondence, 1779, and was one of the original members of the Framingham Artillery Company, organized March, 1799, also served as a member of the board of selectmen for several years. Mrs. Hemenway was a member of the Unitarian church, died in Framingham, October 4, 1887, and is buried in Edgell Grove Cemetery. Children of Adam and Deborah Brown (Sanger) Hemenway: 1. Maria Frances, born August 31, 1831, died November 23, 1914; married Dr. George A. Hoyt, born September 13, 1825, son of Dr. Enos Hoyt, of Sanbornton, New Hampshire, and Grace R. Crosby. He was a graduate of Dartmouth College, 1847, and from Harvard Medical School, 1851, died October 15, 1857, in Framingham, where he was in practice. 2. Martha Olivia, born December 8, 1840, married, August 20, 1863, George H. Weeks.

Mrs. Weeks is a highly cultured woman, with deep sympathies, is greatly interested in the work and charities of the Unitarian church, of which she is a member. She is also interested in the work of the Framingham Hospital and the Edgell Grove Cemetery Association. She is at present (1917) the president of the latter organization, organized May 1, 1849, which for sixty-eight years has held an annual May festival. For many years Mrs. Weeks has been one of the leaders in this worthy organization, managed entirely by ladies, which has expended several thousand dollars in beautifying Edgell Grove and Church Hill cemeteries. She is also a charter member of Framingham Chapter, Daughters of the American Revolution, being eligible through the military service of several Revolutionary ancestors, but coming into membership through the service of her great-grandfather, Ebenezer Hemenway (see Ebenezer V).

George H. Weeks was born in Wayne, Maine, July 1, 1822, son of John and Sarah Weeks. The Weeks family is of ancient English origin; and as early as 1598 were settled in Gloucester and Devon. Leonard Weeks, son of John, baptized at Crompton Martin, England, August 7, 1593, came to America, and his name first appears as witness to a bond upon the public records in New York county, Maine. This Leonard Weeks, or Wyke, was probably the founder of the Maine branch of the Weeks family. George H. Weeks left his home in Maine when a young man and came to Boston, Massachusetts, and engaged in the wholesale grocery business in latter years conducted under the firm name of Weeks & Company, which he continued until his death, May 28, 1895. He made his home in Framingham Center, and is buried there in Edgell Grove Cemetery. Two children were born to Mr. and Mrs. (Martha Olivia Hemenway) Weeks: 1. Harry Winthrop, born May 30, 1864, in Framingham Center. His education was obtained in the public schools of his home town, and at a boys' school in Southboro, Massachusetts. After leaving school he was engaged for a time as salesman in the shoe trade, later in the wholesale grocery business in Boston succeeding his father, which he still conducts (1917). He resides in Framingham Center, occupying the beautiful old colonial mansion which was the home of his father. He married Edith Sturtevant, of Framingham, Massachusetts, no issue. 2. George H., Jr., died in infancy.

_____

ANGELL, Nedabiah,
Exemplary Citizen.

The origin of Angell as a surname is uncertain. Some authorities claim that it is derived from Angel, a town in

France, and some claim it is from the Greek word meaning "messenger." In very ancient times it was used in connection with the Christian name as a descriptive term applied to character, and later to show that the family was of extraordinary beauty. In the Bysantine Empire in 1185, Konstantinos Angelos was a young man of noble family who received his name for that reason.

(I) Thomas Angell was born in England about 1618. There is a tradition that he was the son of Henry Angell, of Liverpool, England, and that at the age of twelve he went to London to seek his fortune. In 1631 he came with Roger Williams in the ship 'Lion" from London to Boston, and he was then regarded as a servant or apprentice of Williams. He went with Williams to Salem, remaining until 1636. He removed with him to Providence, Rhode Island. In the Rhode Island Historical Society's rooms is shown the plat of land grants to the early settlers of Rhode Island. Thomas Angell's grant was the first one north of the one on which the First Baptist Church now stands, it comprised a strip one hundred and seven feet wide, fronting on what was then Towne street, now North Main street, extending east to a point near Prospect street, containing five and one-half acres. This was in 1638. Later Thomas and Angell streets were named for him. On the reverse side is a rough drawing of the part of plat on which Thomas Angell's grant laid. In 1652 and 1653 Thomas Angell was elected a commissioner, and in 1655 constable, which office he held for many years. He was, as were all the inhabitants of Providence of that day, a farmer. He was about seventy-six years old at the time of his death, and his will, dated May 3, 1685, was proved September 18, 1685. The will of his wife Alice was dated October 2, 1694,

proved the January following. Children John, mentioned below, James, married Abigail Dexter, Amphillis, married Edward Smith, Mary, married Richard Arnold, Deborah, married Richard Seabury, Alice, married Eleazer Whipple, Margaret, married Jonathan Whipple.

(II) John, eldest child of Thomas and Alice Angell, was born in Providence, Rhode Island, and died there July 27, 1720. For a few years he lived on the Daniel Jenckes farm, five miles from Providence, towards Lime Rock, on the Lewisquisit road. He removed to Providence, where he continued farming, and was a freeman, October 16, 1670. He married, 1669, Ruth Field, daughter of John Field. Children Thomas, born March 25, 1672, John, Daniel, mentioned below; Hope, 1682; James.

(III) Daniel, third son of John and Ruth (Field) Angell, was born May 2, 1680, in Providence, in which town he made his home, and died June 16, 1750. He is described as a man of large frame and possessed of great physical strength. He was prosperous and was often in the public service. Being naturally left-handed, by constant practice he became ambidextrous, and was noted as a hunter. He made frequent trips to Boston with team to market. On one of these trips he was challenged by a British officer, and finally, losing patience, agreed to fight a duel. However, when the time came to begin he laid out the offender with one blow of his left fist, and was thereafter suffered to go his way in peace. He left farms and other property to each of his sons, and made liberal gifts to his daughters. He married, May 2, 1702, in Providence, Hannah Winsor, granddaughter of Roger Williams. Children Samuel, born December 12, 1707, John, October 18, 1709, Nedabiah, mentioned below, Joshua, February 26, 1714, Mary, January 4, 1716, Job, January 1, 1718, Daniel, October 27, 1720, Ezekiel, 1722, Waite, and Mercy

(IV) Nedabiah, third son of Daniel and Hannah (Winsor) Angell, was born April 29, 1712, and died April 19, 1786 He resided in North Providence, in what is now Smithfield, where he owned and tilled a farm, and also followed his trade of blacksmith He was an industrious and intelligent citizen, his wife a very capable woman, and they reared a good family Many of their descendants are now located in the west He married (first) June 22, 1740, Mary, daughter of Joshua and Mary (Barber) Winsor, born September 2, 1718, died June 9, 1758 He married (second) November 25, 1759, Bethiah (Luther) Hammond, widow of Nathan Hammond, born 1727, died May 6, 1820, probably a descendant of the Rehoboth family of Luther Children Zilpha, born December 25, 1742, Jesse, mentioned below; Jabez, October 19, 1746, Hannah, December 14, 1750, Eseck, September 12, 1752, Mercy, January 9, 1761

(V) Jesse, eldest son of Nedabiah and Mary (Winsor) Angell, was born January 6, 1745, died January 20, 1830, aged eighty-five He resided in Smithfield, where he married Amey, daughter of Nathan Hammond, of that town, who died June 27, 1834, in her eightieth year He went to sea in early life, and became a master mariner, and after several voyages he settled on a farm in the southwestern part of the town of Scituate, Rhode Island He had been successful as a mariner, was a prudent and prosperous farmer and good citizen, a soldier of the Revolution Children George, born January 16, 1774, Sarah, September 15, 1775, Jesse, September 16, 1780, died at sea, Amey, August 2, 1782, Anstross, April 13, 1786, Samuel, December 31, 1787, Nedabiah, February 11, 1791, Na-

than, November 2, 1792, Mary, November 22, 1794

(VI) Nedabiah (2), fourth son of Jesse and Amey (Hammond) Angell, born February 11, 1791, made his home for some years at Chepatchet, where he kept a hotel, was some time a resident of Providence In 1853 they removed to Cranston, into (what was then) the Jeremiah Fenner house, opposite Fenner's Ledge, and died April 7, 1855 He was a carpenter by trade His body was laid to rest in Chepatchet He married (first) Lucy Colwell, born September 1, 1798, died July 15, 1844 He married (second) January 27, 1848 in Providence, Amanda M Goff, born June 16, 1809, in Rehoboth, daughter of Joseph (2) and Bathsheba (Williams) Goff She died May 3, 1894, in Rehoboth, and was buried in Swan Point Cemetery, Providence Children of first marriage George, born September 5, 1820, died August 29, 1909, Joseph C, born August 14, 1823, died March 7, 1828, Charles F, born April 30, 1829, died June 26, 1904, Edward H, born April 7, 1835, died November 11, 1836 Child of second marriage Lucy Amanda, mentioned below

(VII) Lucy Amanda Angell, only child of the second marriage of Nedabiah Angell, was born August 7, 1849, in Providence, and received instruction in the schools of Johnston, Rhode Island, North Providence, Rhode Island, and Pierce Academy, Middleboro, Massachusetts Since 1874 her home has been in Rehoboth, where the last twenty years of her mother's long life was made happy and comfortable by her filial care and devotion She is a member of Lydia Cobb Chapter, Daughters of the American Revolution, of Taunton, the Roger Williams Family Association of Providence and the Rehoboth Auxiliary of Taunton, Division of American Red Cross

ENCYCLOPEDIA OF BIOGRAPHY

(The Williams Line)

Genealogists and historians have spent much time in the effort to learn the origin of Emanuel (Immanuel, Amanuel, etc) Williams, of Taunton It is possible that he was a son of John Williams, of Scituate and Barnstable, Massachusetts, who was divorced from his wife Sarah in 1673, but it seems more probable that he was a grandson of Richard Williams, a pioneer of Taunton, whose history is told at some length elsewhere No wills are on record now in Taunton to show anything concerning the parentage of Emanuel Joseph Williams, son of Richard, died August 17, 1692, in Taunton He married, November 28, 1667, Elizabeth, daughter of George Watson Several children are found of record It is quite possible that Emanuel, born about 1673-74, was a son of Joseph and Elizabeth

(I) It is certain that Emanuel Williams was born between 1670 and 1680, and died about 1719 His home was in Taunton, and there he married, about 1703, Abigail Makepeace, born November 25, 1686, died 1724, daughter of William and Abigail (Tisdale) Makepeace Thomas Makepeace, born about 1592, probably came from Bristol, England, and was in Dorchester, Massachusetts, in 1635 Two years later he was in Boston, where a house lot was granted to him, in the present Hanover street, near Court In 1638 he was a member of the Ancient and Honorable Artillery Company For £100 he received a deed dated August 1, 1638, conveying a house in Boston, one hundred acres of upland in Muddy River (Brookline), ten acres of meadow, woodlands, two gardens, and one-half acre on Fort Hill In 1641 he owned lands in Dorchester, where he then resided, and was one of the original supporters of free schools He sold seven acres to Roger Williams, of Dorchester, January 13, 1649,

for £21 July 11, of the same year he sold nine acres in Dorchester He was among the patentees of Dover, was in the Narragansett expedition of 1654, and died early in 1667 His property was inventoried at £297 7s 1d, including a dwelling and ground valued at £180 His second wife, a widow, Elizabeth Mellowes, was dismissed from the First Church of Boston to the Dorchester church July 25, 1641 She survived him Their second son, William (2) Makepeace, married, May 23, 1661, Ann Johnson He was interested in Block Island, and may have lived there a short time He settled on the Taunton river and bought land April 8, 1661, for £30, at "Quequechan," now Freetown This he sold in 1672, and purchased another tract nearby in February, 1679 He was drowned August 9, 1681, in the Taunton river, and his estate was valued at £180 4s 6d His eldest child was William (3) Makepeace, born 1662-63, lived in Freetown, was constable in 1685, and member of town council in 1691 He moved to Taunton about 1703, and his will was made November 16, 1736 He married, December 2, 1685, Abigail Tisdale They were the parents of Abigail Makepeace, wife of Emanuel Williams, as above noted She received fifty acres from her father, June 10, 1703 Abigail Tisdale was a daughter of John (2) Tisdale, who was a son of John and Sarah Tisdale John (2) Tisdale married, November 23, 1664, Hannah Rogers a granddaughter of Thomas Rogers, who came in the "Mayflower" to Plymouth His son, John Rogers, married, April 16, 1639, in Weymouth, Massachusetts, Ann Churchman, probably a daughter of Hugh Churchman, of Plymouth They were the parents of Hannah Rogers, wife of John (2) Tisdale, and grandparents of Abigail Makepeace, wife of Emanuel Williams Children of the latter couple

197

John, born 1704, Gershom, mentioned below, Anna, 1708, Lydia, 1710, Phebe, 1712, Simeon, 1716

(II) Gershom, second son of Emanuel and Abigail (Makepeace) Williams, was born 1706, in Taunton, and died there October 8, 1775 He married in Dighton, August 2, 1729, Abigail, daughter of Samuel Waldron, of that town She died April 6, 1789 His will, made September 9, proved November 17, 1775, mentions all his children except the youngest They were all born in Dighton, viz: Gershom, February 23, 1731, married Abigail Talbut, of Dighton, no children; Abigail, mentioned below; Simeon, March 21, 1735, Hannah, June 16, 1737, married William Holloway, Jr, Ruth, March 14, 1740, died June 25, 1751; Lemuel, August 3, 1742, married (first) Molly Jones, of Dighton, (second) Abigail Briggs, George, September 28, 1744, married Marcy Paull, David, mentioned below, John, July 16, 1749, Jonathan, August 21, 1751, Ruth, October 10, 1753, married Daniel Hayford

(III) Abigail, eldest daughter of Gershom and Abigail (Waldron) Williams, born February 1, 1733, in Dighton, was married, December 20, 1753 (as his second wife) to John Briggs, of Berkeley, Massachusetts, born 1720, died March 11, 1790

(IV) Abigail, second daughter of John and Abigail (Williams) Briggs, was born January 4, 1761, in Dighton, and was married, January 15, 1793, to Simeon Webster, of Dighton

(III) David, fifth son of Gershom and Abigail (Waldron) Williams, was born October 24, 1746, in Dighton, and was a soldier of the Revolution He served thirty-seven days in Captain Robert Davis' company, Colonel Freeman's regiment, company raised for a secret expedition to Rhode Island, roll sworn to in Suffolk, December 4, 1777 He was a

member of the Bristol county brigade, commanded by Brigadier-General George Godfrey, was a private in Captain Elijah Walker's company, Colonel John Hatch's regiment, marched to Tiverton on an alarm of August 2, 1780, served three days He married, January 1, 1771, Lois Webster, born 1746, daughter of Stephen and Bathsheba (Bryant) Webster, of Dighton Children Nancy, born November 12, 1771, died June 30, 1832, Lydia, August 18, 1773, died September 29, 1850, David, June 14, 1775, died December 22, 1830, Gershom, December 19, 1776, died May 24, 1851, Bathsheba, mentioned below, Eleanor, December 14, 1780, died March 6, 1862

(IV) Bathsheba, third daughter of David and Lois (Webster) Williams, was born November 30, 1778, in Dighton, and became the wife of Joseph (2) Goff, of Rehoboth (see Goff III)

Stephen Webster, of Dighton, born about 1720, lived in Dighton and Berkeley, Massachusetts, and was sergeant of militia He married Bathsheba Bryant, daughter of Stephen (3) and Sarah (Magoon) Bryant, of Dighton (see Bryant III). He served twenty-nine days in the Revolutionary forces, a private in Captain James Briggs' company, which marched October 2, 1777, under Colonel Freeman, on a secret expedition to Rhode Island, was discharged October 29, 1777

(The Bryant Line)

(I) Stephen Bryant was a resident of Duxbury, Massachusetts, as early as 1643, and was in Plymouth in 1650 He married Abigail, daughter of John Shaw Children John, born April 7, 1650; Mary, May 29, 1654, Stephen, mentioned below; Sarah, November 28, 1659, Lydia, October 23, 1662; Elizabeth, October 17, 1665

(II) Stephen (2), second son of Stephen (1) and Abigail (Shaw) Bryant, was born February 2, 1658, in Plymouth, and lived in Middleboro, Massachusetts, with his wife Elizabeth. She died and he married (second) September 9, 1702, in Plymouth, Bathsheba Briggs. Children: Stephen, mentioned below; David, born 1687; William, 1692; Hannah; Ichabod, 1699; Timothy, 1702.

(III) Stephen (3), eldest child of Stephen (2) and Elizabeth Bryant, was born 1684, in Middleboro, and married in Duxbury, November 23, 1710, Sarah Magoon.

(IV) Bathsheba, daughter of Stephen (3) and Sarah (Magoon) Bryant, married Stephen Webster, of Dighton (see Williams III)

(The Goff Line).

The name Goff has an historic identity with the early settling of New England. One Thomas Goff, a wealthy merchant of London, England, Matthew Craddock, John Endicott, Sir Richard Saltonstall, and others, were among the principal actors in laying the foundation of the Massachusetts Bay Colony. "By mutual agreement among themselves they were formed into a body politic and confirmed or rather so constituted by the royal charter." The first governor chosen was Matthew Craddock, the first deputy governor Thomas Goff, both of whom were sworn, March 23, 1628. Edward or Edmund Goff, of Cambridge, and a proprietor of Watertown, and John Goff, of Newbury, a proprietor, were other pioneers of the name in New England. The vital records of Rehoboth, the mother town of many in its region both in Massachusetts and Rhode Island, begin with the families of Richard, Samuel and Robert Goff, following later with that of William Goff, beginning with the early years of the eighteenth century. From this source spring many of the name both in Massachusetts and Rhode Island.

(I) Richard Goff, of Barrington, and Martha Toogood, of the same town, daughter of Nathaniel and Martha Toogood, were married, July 19, 1722, and their children of Rehoboth town record were: Sarah, born October 19, 1723; Joseph, mentioned below; Squire, June 18, 1727; Bethia, January 31, 1730; Rachel, July 28, 1731; Rebecca, May 11, 1733; Dorothy, August 4, 1735; Richard, July 31, 1741.

(II) Joseph Goff, son of Richard and Martha (Toogood) Goff, was born December 12, 1725. He utilized the water power of the village tributary to Palmer's river for sawing lumber and other mill purposes prior to the year 1764, and his son Richard, and the latter's sons, Nelson and Darius, used the same stream for power in their manufacturing projects. Joseph Goff married, October 1, 1748, Patience Thurber, daughter of Jonathan and Mehitable (Bullock) Thurber. Children, of Rehoboth town record: Richard, born February 21, 1750, Sarah, June 19, 1751, Patience, June 20, 1753, Huldah, February 19, 1755, Experience, April 27, 1759, Dorcas, March 17, 1763, Hannah, January 20, 1765, Joseph, mentioned below, Mehitable, October 20, 1773, Rebecca, January 29, 1776.

(III) Joseph (2), son of Joseph (1) and Patience (Thurber) Goff, was born November 8, 1771, and married (first) Bathsheba Williams, born November 30, 1778, died March 7, 1814, daughter of David and Lois (Webster) Williams, of Dighton (see Williams III). He married (second) Abigail Webster. Children of first marriage: Bathsheba Williams, born July 1, 1801, Joseph, February 21, 1803, Rebeckah, May 17, 1805, William Leonard, August 16, 1807; Amanda M., mentioned below, Ida Madison, January 13, 1811, of second marriage: Abby Lucena, born February 13, 1818; Simeon

Webster, March 22, 1820, Appollas Leonard, September 5, 1826; Mary Ann, December 2, 1828.

(IV) Amanda M., third daughter of Joseph (2) and Bathsheba (Williams) Goff, born June 16, 1809, became the wife of Nedabiah Angell, of Providence (see Angell VI).

LINCOLN, Frederick W.,

Business Man.

Hingham, Massachusetts, is distinguished as the home of all the first settlers of the surname Lincoln. From these pioneers are descended all the Colonial families of the name, including President Lincoln, more than one governor and men of note in all walks of life. The surname was variously spelled Linkhorn, Linkeln, Lincon, and was common in old Hingham, in England, for more than a century before immigrant ancestors made their home in Massachusetts. The origin or meaning of the name has been a theme of discussion. Some have maintained that it is a relic of the Anglo-Saxon-Norman Conquest period, when, near some waterfall (Anglo-Saxon "lin") (a colony Roman "colonia") was founded, thus giving Lincolonia or finally Lincolnshire. Eight of the name were among the first settlers of Hingham, coming thither from Wymondham, County Norfolk, England. Three brothers, Daniel, Samuel and Thomas, came with their mother Joan. There were no less than four named Thomas Lincoln, adults and heads of families, all doubtless related. They were distinguished on the records and in local speech by their trades. They were known as Thomas, the miller; Thomas, the cooper; Thomas, the husbandman; and Thomas, the weaver. There were also Stephen Lincoln who came with his wife and son Stephen, from Wymond,

England, in 1638. This name is spelled also Windham and Wymondham.

(I) Thomas Lincoln, the miller, was born 1603, in Norfolk county, England, came to Hingham, Massachusetts, in 1635, was one of the proprietors the same year, drew a house-lot of five acres at Hingham, July 3, 1636, on what is now South street, near Main, and later drew lots for planting. Before 1650, he had removed to Taunton, Massachusetts, and had built a grist mill there on Mill river at a point in the very heart of the present city, near the street leading from the railroad station to City Square. It is said that King Philip and his chiefs once met the colonists in conference in this mill. He served in Taunton on the jury in 1650; was highway surveyor there in 1650 and the largest land owner. He became one of the stockholders in the famous Taunton iron works, established October, 1652, as a stock company. Among other stockholders were Richard Williams, Richard Stacy and George Watson. These works were operated until 1883 and the dam and foundation still mark one of the most interesting sites in the history of American industry. Thomas Lincoln gave land in Hingham to his son Thomas, who sold it October 11, 1662, specifying the history of the transactions. His will was dated August 23, 1683, when he stated his age as about eighty years. The will was proved March 5, 1684. He married (first) in England, wife's name unknown, and (second) December 10, 1665, Elizabeth (Harvey) Street, widow of Francis Street. Children: Samuel, baptized 1637, in Hingham, Massachusetts; Thomas, mentioned below; John, February, 1639, married Edith Macomber, Mary, October 6, 1642, married (first) William Hack, (second) Richard Stevens, Sarah, December, 1645, married Joseph Wills, of Taunton, and settled in Scituate.

(II) Thomas (2) Lincoln, son of Thomas (1) Lincoln, was baptized in February, 1638, in Hingham, and settled in Taunton, where he made a will, May 4, 1694 He married, in 1651, Mary Austin, daughter of Jonah and Constance (Kent) Austin, died about 1694 Jonah Austin was mayor of the borough of Tenterden, England, sailed from Sandwich in the ship "Hercules" in 1633, with his wife Constance, and located first at Cambridge, Massachusetts, where he sold land in 1638, was at Hingham, Massachusetts, as early as 1635 His land there was sold in 1650 About the same time he purchased fifty-one acres in Taunton, became interested as a shareholder in the famous iron works in that town, and died there July 30, 1683 His wife died April 22, 1667. Children of Thomas (2) Lincoln Mary, born May 12, 1652; Thomas, died young, Sarah, died young, Thomas, mentioned below, Samuel, March 18, 1658, Jonah and Sarah (twins), July 7, 1660, Hannah, March 15, 1663, Constant, May 16, 1665, Mercy, April 3, 1670, Ephraim, died April 9, 1673.

(III) Thomas (3) Lincoln, second son of Thomas (2) and Mary (Austin) Lincoln, was born April 21, 1656, and died in 1720 He married (first) Mary Stacy, daughter of Richard Stacy, who appears in the list of those able to bear arms at Taunton in 1643 Richard Stacy was surveyor of highways and often a member of the jury, was one of the original shareholders of the iron works, and died in 1687 His wife's name was Abigail Thomas Lincoln married (second) November 14, 1689, Susanna, daughter of Samuel Smith. Children Thomas, mentioned below, Benjamin, born 1681, William, 1682, Jonathan, died January 5, 1773, Silas, Nathan; Tabitha, Hannah, born 1692, Constant, 1696; Lydia

(IV) Thomas (4) Lincoln, eldest son of Thomas (3) and Mary (Stacy) Lincoln, was born about 1680, in Taunton, and married Rebecca Walker, born about 1693, fifth daughter of James and Bathsheba (Brooks) Walker, of Taunton

(V) Isaac Lincoln, son of Thomas (4) and Rebecca (Walker) Lincoln, was born 1710-11, in Taunton, and married, July 6, 1736, Mary Sanford, of Berkley, Massachusetts probably the daughter of Eben and Mary (Woodward) Sanford, of Newport, Rhode Island, born about 1719.

(VI) Isaac (2) Lincoln, son of Isaac (1) and Mary (Sanford) Lincoln, was born 1738, and married, in 1759, Lydia Drake, born 1739, died 1825, probably of the Weymouth family of Drake No record of her birth or parentage has been discovered Isaac (2) Lincoln died 1808 Children Isaac, born 1760, Lott, 1762 Sanford, mentioned below, Mercy, 1768; Cecilia, 1771

(VII) Sanford Lincoln, third son of Isaac (2) and Lydia (Drake) Lincoln, was born 1765, in Taunton, died 1825, and was buried at Briggs Corner, in the town of Attleboro He married, 1786, Sybil Williams, born February 19, 1768, died March, 1843, daughter of Rufus and Mercy (Shaw) Williams, of Attleboro (see Williams VI)

(VIII) Williams Sanford Lincoln, son of Sanford and Sybil (Williams) Lincoln, was born 1793 and made his home in Attleboro, where he was engaged in agriculture, and died July 31, 1844. He was married, June 20, 1819, in Attleboro, by Rev Richard Cavigue, to Louisa Tifft, born November 14, 1799, in Attleboro, daughter of Stephen and Lois (Guild) Tifft, died February 9, 1877 (see Tifft VI).

(IX) Williams Sanford (2) Lincoln, son of Williams Sanford (1) and Louisa (Tifft) Lincoln, was born in October, 1827, in Mansfield, Massachusetts He was a jeweler by trade, and a well known resident of Attleboro, where he was one of its leading and progressive citizens. He died from the effects of injuries received in a railroad accident, January 3, 1884, and was buried in Attleboro. He married, June 13, 1852, Ann Sophia Bliss, born August 26, 1826, in Attleboro, daughter of Martin and Sophia (Wright-ington) Bliss, of that town, and she died in Attleboro, January 29, 1866 (see Bliss X). They were the parents of two children. Frederick William, and Annabell Sanford, born December 26, 1858, living in Attleboro, unmarried.

(X) Frederick William Lincoln, only son of Williams Sanford (2) and Ann Sophia (Bliss) Lincoln, was born July 2, 1853, in Attleboro, and has continued to make his home in that town to the present time. Its public schools supplied his education, and he early turned his attention to the manufacture of jewelry, learning the business with his father, and in 1876 became interested in the electro plating business, in the establishment conducted under the firm name of Nerney & Lincoln. This business was successfully conducted for a period of twelve years, at the end of which time the business was sold, he and Mr. Nerney going into the C. A. Wetherell & Company, jewelry manufacturers, in which concern they had had an interest for some time. In 1890, Mr. Lincoln disposed of his interests in C. A. Wetherell & Company, and took a special course in the School for Christian Workers, now known as the International Young Men's Christian Association College, at Springfield, Massachusetts, where he spent about a year in preparing himself to take up that line of work. Upon returning to Attleboro, on account of the illness of his former partners, Mr. Lincoln took the management of the C. A. Wetherell & Company concern, continuing in

that capacity for about two years. In March, 1897, Mr. Lincoln bought an interest in the J. M. Fisher Company, jewelry manufacturers, and upon the incorporation of this concern, in 1911, he was made treasurer of the company, continuing in that capacity until 1914, when he retired from active business cares. He is one of the best known and most progressive citizens of Attleboro, and takes much interest in the growth and progress of its institutions. While a most public-spirited citizen, his chief interest is in his home and family. He is blessed with an artistic taste and temperament, as shown in his home and garden. Many of the surroundings were constructed from his own designs. Mr. Lincoln is one of the most active and useful members of the Methodist Episcopal church, in which he has served as trustee and superintendent of the Sunday school, and is active in all the works of the organization. Most temperate in his life and habits—he is popular and appreciated as a good citizen.

He married, in Attleboro, June 26, 1876, Ermina Chester Shaw, born January 27, 1856, in Fair Haven, Massachusetts, daughter of William Penn and Susan E. (Blossom) Shaw (see Shaw VIII). Mrs. Lincoln is, like her husband, a valued member of the Methodist Episcopal church, and a useful member of society. She is descended from some of the oldest families in New England. Children: 1. Ermina Chester, born in Attleboro, December 6, 1881, was educated in the public and high schools; became active in Sunday school work, and was connected with the State Sunday School Association of Pennsylvania, as primary secretary. She married William T. Cooper, of Chattanooga, Tennessee, and they now reside in Philadelphia, Pennsylvania, where he is engaged in the practice of law; they are the parents of one daughter: Helen

Margaret Cooper, born August 3, 1913 2
Helen Bliss, born August 7, 1885, resides
with her parents, was educated in the
public and high schools of Attleboro.

In the ancient town of Taunton there
are still representatives of the famous
Cromwell-Williams line of the family
bearing the latter name. Reference is
made to some of the posterity of Richard
Williams, who, with Oliver Cromwell,
the "Lord Protector," sprang from the
same ancestor, William Cromwell, a son
of Robert Cromwell, of Carleton-upon-
Trent, a Lancastrian, who was killed at
the battle of Towton, in 1461. Many
years ago the statement was made, and
afterward vehemently doubted, that the
family of Richard Williams, of Taunton,
was connected by ties of blood with that
of Oliver Cromwell. This fact was established by the wonderful patience and perseverance, and at considerable expense,
of the late Hon. Joseph Hartwell Williams, of Augusta, Maine, a former governor of Maine, a direct descendant of
Richard Williams of Taunton. The following is an account of this connection
taken from the New England Historical
and Genealogical Register of April, 1897,
abridged by the late Josiah H. Drum-
mond, LL. D., of Portland, Maine.

The Cromwell line dates from Alden
de Cromwell, who lived in the time of
William the Conqueror. His son was
Hugh de Cromwell, and from him descended ten Ralph de Cromwells in as
many successive generations; but the
tenth Ralph died without issue. The
seventh Ralph de Cromwell married, in
1351, Amicia, daughter of Robert Berer,
M. P. for Notts, besides the eighth Ralph,
they had several other sons, among whom
was Ulker Cromwell of Hucknall Tor-
kard, Notts. Ulker had Richard, and he,

John of Cromwell House, Carleton-upon-
Trent, Notts, and he, Robert, the names
of the wives are not given.
(I) Robert Cromwell, of Carleton-
upon-Trent, was a Lancastrian. He was
killed at the battle of Towton, in 1461.
His lease of Cromwell House was seized
by Sir Humphrey Bourchier, Yorkist,
who was the husband of Joan Stanhope,
the granddaughter of the ninth Ralph,
through his daughter Matilda, wife of Sir
Richard Stanhope. Ralph left a son William, the ancestor of Robert Cromwell,
and a daughter Margaret, the ancestor
of both Oliver Cromwell and Richard
Williams, of Taunton.
(II) William Cromwell, of the prebend
of Palace Hall, Norwalk, Notts, settled in
Putney, Surrey, 1452. He married Margaret Smyth, daughter of John Smyth, of
Norwalk, Notts, and had John. Margaret
Cromwell married William Smyth (son
of John). They had son, Richard Smyth,
and daughter, Joan Smyth.
(III) John Cromwell, son of William
Cromwell, married his cousin, Joan
Smyth. He was a Lancastrian, and his
lands at Putney were seized by Archbishop Bourchier Lord of the Manor of
Wimbledon, and his lease of Palace Hall,
Norwalk, Notts remised by Lord Chan-
cellor Bourchier. They had among
other children, Walter Cromwell. Richard Smyth, of Rockhampton, Putney, by
wife, Isabella, had daughter Margaret
Smyth, who married John Williams,
fourth in descent from Howell Williams,
the head of the Williams line.
(IV) Walter Cromwell married, in
1474, the daughter of Glossop of Wirks-
worth, Derbyshire, in 1472 he claimed
and was admitted to two virgates (thirty
acres) of land at Putney, in 1499 Archbishop Morton, Lord of Wimbledon
Manor, gave him six virgates (ninety
acres) of land in Putney as a solatium for

the property taken from his father by the Bourchier Yorkists He died in 1516, leaving among other children Katherine Cromwell

(V) Katherine Cromwell married Morgan Williams, fifth in descent from Howell Williams, and had a son Richard Williams, born about 1495

(VI) Sir Richard Williams, alias Cromwell, married, in 1518, Frances Murfyn He died at Stepney in 1547 and was buried in Gt St Helen's Church, London. He left son, Henry Cromwell, alias Williams

(VII) Sir Henry Cromwell, alias Williams (called "The Golden Knight"), of Hinchenbrook, married Joan, daughter of Sir Ralph Warren, Lord Mayor of London, and they had Sir Oliver, Robert, Henry, Richard, Philip, Joan, Elizabeth and Frances

(VIII) Robert Cromwell, of Huntingdon, brewer, married Elizabeth Stewart, widow of William Lynn, of Bassingbourn and their fifth child was Oliver Cromwell, the "Lord Protector." Robert's sister, Elizabeth Cromwell, married William Hampden, of Great Hampden, Bucks, and among their children were John Hampden, "The Patriot," and Richard Hampden

Governor Williams, through his assistants, traced the Williams line back to Howell Williams, Lord of Ribour

(I) Howell Williams, Lord of Ribour, married Wenllon, daughter and heiress of Llyne ap Jevan, of Rady, and had son, Morgan Williams

(II) Morgan Williams, of Lanishen, Glamorgan, married Joan Batton, daughter of Thomas Batton, of Glamorgan, and they had Thomas and Jevan Jevan Williams married Margaret, daughter of Jenkin Kemeys, of Bagwye Man They had son, William Williams, of Lanishen, bailiff for Henry VIII, who (wife not

known) was the father of Morgan Williams, of Lanishen, Glamorgan, and later of Putney, Wansworth and Greenwich, for Henry VII and Henry VIII, and the husband in 1494 of Katherine Cromwell —see ante Cromwell, No 5, et seq

(III) Thomas Williams, of Lanishen, Glamorgan, died at St Helen's, Bishopgate, London, was buried in the church there, "with his brass on stone"

(IV) John Williams, steward of Wimbledon Manor, Surrey, married Margaret Smyth, daughter of Richard Smyth, and granddaughter of Margaret Cromwell (see ante Cromwell, Nos 1, 2) He died at Mortlake in 1502, and she in 1501 They had two sons, John and Richard John Williams, born in 1485, married Joan Wykys, daughter of Henry Wykys, of Bolleys Park, Chertney, and sister of Elizabeth Wykys, who married Thomas Cromwell (brother of Katherine), secretary to Henry VIII, Lord Cromwell of Oakham, Earl of Essex

(V) Richard Williams was born in Rockhampton in 1487 He settled at Monmouth and Dixxon, Mon., where he died in 1559 He was twice married. The name of his first wife is not known She is credited with one daughter, Joan His second wife, Christian, had two daughters, Reece and Ruth, and one son, John

(VI) John Williams, of Huntingdon, near Wotton under Edge, Gloucester, died in 1579, leaving son William No other particulars of this family are given

(VII) William Williams, of Huntingdon, married (first) November 15, 1585, Jane Shepherd She died about 1600, a child of hers having been baptized December 2, 1599 He married (second) December 4, 1603, Jane Woodward She died February 2, 1614, and he in 1618. The first child of his second marriage, born in January, 1606, was Richard Williams, of Taunton Of the change of his name by Sir Richard Williams, Governor Williams said "Oliver Cromwell in the male line of Morgan Williams of Glamorganshire His great-grandfather, Sir Richard Williams, assumed the name of 'Cromwell,' it is true, but not until in mature years he had distinguished himself in the public service (temp Henry VIII), under the patronage of his uncle, Thomas Cromwell (Vicar General, 1535), whom he proposed to honor by the adoption of his name In fact, ever afterwards Sir Richard used to sign himself, 'Richard Cromwell, alias Williams,' and his sons and grandsons, and Oliver Cromwell himself, in his youth (1620), used to sign in the same manner In important grants from the crown to Sir Richard (29 and 31, Henry VIII), the grantee's name appears in both forms, 'Cromwell, alias Williams' and 'Williams, alias Cromwell'" It is not believed that, in the light of Governor Williams' researches, the relationship of Richard Williams, of Taunton, and the Cromwell family will again be questioned.

(I) Richard Williams, son of William Williams, of Huntingdon, and his wife, Jane (Woodward) Williams, born in January, 1606, married in December, England, February 11, 1632, Frances Dighton, daughter of Dr John Dighton, and for whom the town of Dighton, Massachusetts, was named Richard Williams came to America and was among the first purchasers of Taunton He was a man of good abilities, was deputy to the General Court of Plymouth Colony from 1645 to 1665; selectman in 1666 and 1667, and was one of the proprietors of the "New Purchase," now Dighton, was a member and deacon of the First Church He died in the year 1693, aged eighty-seven The children born to Richard and his wife Frances (Dighton) Williams, the eldest two being born while the parents

were living in Gloucester, in the parish of Whitcombe Magna, were John, mentioned below, Elizabeth, baptized February 7, 1636; Samuel, Joseph, married (first) November 28, 1667, Elizabeth Watson, (second) Abigail Newland; Nathaniel, married, in 1668, Elizabeth Rogers; Thomas, Benjamin, married Rebecca Macy; Elizabeth, born about 1647, Hannah, married John Parmenter

(II) John Williams, son of Richard Williams, born March 27, 1634, in Taunton, married Jane Bassett, of Dighton, Massachusetts, daughter of William Bassett, who came to Plymouth in 1621, and his wife, Elizabeth, said to have been a Tilden

(III) Benjamin Williams, son of John and Jane (Bassett) Williams, was born 1654, and died November 1, 1726. He married, March 18, 1690, Rebecca Macy, born April 3, 1658, daughter of Captain George Macy, of Taunton Children Rebecca, born November 27, 1690, Josiah, November 7, 1692; Benjamin, mentioned below, John, March 27, 1699

(IV) Benjamin (2) Williams, second son of Benjamin (1) and Rebecca (Macy) Williams, was born July 31, 1695, in Taunton, lived in that part of the town now Norton, where he died April 1, 1775 He married, December 22, 1720, Susannah Howard, born August 8, 1698, in Bridgewater, Massachusetts, daughter of Major Jonathan and Sarah (Dean) Howard

(V) Rufus Williams, son of Benjamin (2) and Susannah (Howard) Williams, was born 1723, and died January 25, 1769 He married Mercy Shaw

(VI) Sybil Williams, daughter of Rufus and Mercy (Shaw) Williams, was born February 19, 1768, and died March, 1843 She married, in 1786, Sanford Lincoln, of Attleboro (see Lincoln VII)

(The Tifft Line)

This family was very early established in Rhode Island, where descendants are still numerous, and where the name, as originally spelled Tefft, is still used very largely.

(I) John Tefft, a native of England, was for a short time a resident of Boston, in Massachusetts, whence he removed to Portsmouth, later to Kingstown, Rhode Island, and died January 8, 1676. He was a freeman in 1655, and at the town meeting, November 30, 1657, was granted planting land on Hog Island. In May, 1671, he was among the freemen of Kingstown, and was probably for some years before that, as he sold land in Portsmouth, November 22, 1662. His will was made November 30, 1670. He married Mary Barbour, who died in 1679. Children: Samuel, mentioned below; Joshua, of Kingstown; Tabitha, born 1653, married George Gardiner.

(II) Samuel Tifft, son of John and Mary (Barbour) Tefft, resided in Providence and South Kingstown, was a freeman in 1667, taxed three shillings and one and one-half pence, July 1, 1679, in Providence. In Kingstown, September 6, 1687, he was taxed nine shillings and four and one-half pence. In association with twenty-six others, he purchased a tract of Narragansett lands, known as Swamptown, June 28, 1709. His will, made March 16, was proved December 20, 1725, and the inventory of his estate, amounting to £1010 2s. and 8d., included large tracts of land, much live stock, tools and other personal property. He married Elizabeth Jencks, born 1658, died 1740, daughter of Joseph and Esther (Ballard) Jencks, and sister of Governor Joseph Jencks, one of the most distinguished citizens of Rhode Island. At her death she left an estate of £401 12s. Children: John, of South Kingstown; Samuel, of

the same town; Peter, mentioned below; Sarah, married Ebenezer Witten; Elizabeth, married Solomon Carpenter; Esther, married Thomas Mumford; Mary, married —————— Newton; Tabitha, Mercy, and Susanna, wife of Peter Crandon.

(III) Peter Tifft, third son of Samuel and Elizabeth (Jencks) Tifft, resided in Westerly, Rhode Island, and Stonington, Connecticut, where his youngest child was born, and where he died about 1725. His wife's baptismal name was Mary, and they had children, all born in Westerly, except the last: Peter, June 19, 1699; Samuel, mentioned below; John, December 27, 1706; Joseph, January 8, 1710; Daniel, April 10, 1712; Samuel, February 14, 1715; Jonathan, October 18, 1718.

(IV) Samuel (2) Tifft, second son of Peter and Mary Tifft, was born February 24, 1705, in Westerly, and was deceased at the time of his son's marriage, in November, 1773. He married, May 5, 1753, at Stonington, Mary Ellis, of Preston, Connecticut.

(V) John Tifft, son of Samuel (2) and Mary (Ellis) Tifft, was born about 1754, and lived in Westerly, Rhode Island. He married, November 24, 1773, a widow, Mary Lewis. Children: Joseph, born October 17, 1774; Peleg, May 18, 1777; David, March 21, 1779; Stephen, mentioned below; Lewis, November 11, 1783; Fannie, March 27, 1788; Annie, July 9, 1790.

(VI) Stephen Tifft, fourth son of John and Mary (Lewis) Tifft, was born April 9, 1781, in Westerly, and lived in Smithfield, Rhode Island, and North Attleboro, Massachusetts. He married Lois Guild, daughter of Ebenezer and Mary (Lane) Guild, of Attleboro.

(VII) Louisa Tifft, daughter of Stephen and Lois (Guild) Tifft, became the wife of Williams Sanford (1) Lincoln, of Attleboro (see Lincoln VIII).

The Bliss family seems to be descended from the Norman family of Blois, gradually modified to Bloys, Blyse, Blysse, Blisse, and in America finally to Bliss, dated back to the time of the Norman Conquest. The name is not common in England. The coat-of-arms borne by the Bliss and Bloys families is the same. Sable, a bend vaire, between two fleur-delis or. Crest. A hand holding a bundle of arrows. Motto *Semper sursum*. The ancient traditions of the Bliss family represent them as living in the south of England and belonging to the class known as English yeomanry or farmers, though at various times some of the family were knights or gentry. They owned the houses and lands they occupied, were freeholders and entitled to vote for members of Parliament. In the early days, of course, they were faithful Roman Catholics, but later after England had become Protestant they became Puritans and became involved in the contentions between Charles I and Parliament. The Blisses who settled in New England in 1636 had dwelt in Daventry, Northamptonshire, England, for one hundred and fifty years before the emigration. Daventry is twelve miles from Ecton, from which came the ancestors of Benjamin Franklin, and twenty-five miles from Stratford-on-Avon, where Shakespeare was born, and close by the battlefield of Naseby, where the forces of Cromwell crushed the army of Charles I. The early Daventry ancestors of the Bliss emigrants were mercers or linen drapers, and since 1475 they were blacksmiths. The religious controversies of the times leading up to the overthrow of King Charles were partly responsible for the departure of the Blisses, who were non-conformists, but the hunger for land had probably more to do with the emigration.

(I) Thomas Bliss, the progenitor, lived in Belstone Parish, Devonshire, England. Very little is known of him except that he was a wealthy landowner, that he belonged to the class stigmatized as Puritans on account of the purity and simplicity of their forms of worship, that he was persecuted by the civil and religious authorities under the direction of Archbishop Laud, and that he was maltreated, impoverished and imprisoned and finally ruined in health, as well as financially, by the many indignities and hardships forced on him by the intolerant church party in power. He is supposed to have been born about 1550 or 1560. The date of his death was 1635 or about that year. When the Parliament of 1628 assembled, Puritans or Roundheads, as the Cavaliers called them, accompanied the members to London. Two of the sons of Thomas Bliss, Jonathan and Thomas, rode from Devonshire on iron grey horses, and remained for some time in the city—long enough at least for the king's officers and spies to learn their names and condition, and whence they came; and from that time forth with others who had gone to London on the same errand, they were marked for destruction. They were soon fined a thousand pounds for non-conformity and thrown into prison, where they remained many weeks. Even old Mr. Thomas Bliss, their father, was dragged through the streets with the greatest indignity. On another occasion the officers of the high commission seized all their horses and sheep, except one poor ewe that in its fright ran into the house and took refuge under a bed. At another time three brothers, with twelve other Puritans, were led through the market place in Okehampton with ropes around their necks, and fined heavily, and Jonathan and his father were thrown into prison, where the sufferings of the son eventually caused his death The family was unable to secure the release of both Jonathan and his father, so the younger man had to remain in prison and at Exeter he suffered thirty-five lashes with a three-corded whip, which tore his back in a cruel manner Before Jonathan was released the estate had to be sold The father and mother went to live with their daughter who had married a man of the Established Church, Sir John Calchffe The remnant of the estate was divided among the three sons who were advised to go to America where they might escape persecution Thomas and George feared to wait for Jonathan, who was still very ill, and left England in the fall of 1635 with their families Thomas Bliss, son of Jonathan Bliss, and grandson of Thomas (1) Bliss, remained with his father, who finally died, and the son then came to join his uncles and settled near Thomas At various times their sister sent from England boxes of shoes, clothing and articles that could not be procured in the colonies, and it is through her letters, long preserved, but now lost, that knowledge of the Devonshire family was preserved Children: Jonathan, mentioned below; Thomas, born in England, about 1585, at Belstone, Elizabeth, married Sir John Calchffe, of Belstone, George, born 1591, settled at Lynn and Sandwich, Massachusetts, and Newport, Rhode Island, Mary or Polly

(II) Jonathan Bliss, son of Thomas Bliss, of Belstone, was born about 1580, at Belstone, died in England, 1635-36 On account of his non-conformity he was persecuted, and suffered heavy fines, eventually dying at an early age, from a fever contracted in prison Four children are said to have died in infancy, and two grew up Thomas, mentioned below, Mary

(III) Thomas (2) Bliss, son of Jona-

than Bliss, of Belstone, England, was born there, and on the death of his father, in 1636, he went to Boston, Massachusetts, and from there to Braintree, same State He next went to Hartford, Connecticut, and finally to Weymouth, Massachusetts, whence, in 1643, he joined in making a settlement at Rehoboth He was made freeman at Cambridge, May 18, 1642, and in Plymouth Colony, January 4, 1645 In June, 1645, he drew land at the Great Plain, Seekonk, in 1646 he was fence viewer, surveyor of highways in 1647 He died at Rehoboth, in June, 1649, and is buried in the graveyard at Seekonk, Massachusetts, now Rumford, East Providence, Rhode Island His will was proved June 8, 1649 His wife's name was Ide Children: Jonathan, mentioned below, daughter, married Thomas Williams, Mary, married Nathaniel Harmon, of Braintree, Nathaniel, seems to have left no descendants of the Bliss name

(IV) Jonathan (2) Bliss, son of Thomas (2) and Ide Bliss, was born about 1625, in England, and in 1655 was made freeman of the Plymouth colony He was "way wardon" at the town meeting in Rehoboth, May 24, 1652, and May 17, 1655, was on the grand jury He was a blacksmith, was made a freeman in Rehoboth, February 22, 1658, drew land June 22, 1658, and was one of the eighty who made what is known as the North Purchase He married, 1648-49, Miriam Harmon, probably a daughter of Francis Harmon, born 1592, and came to Boston in the ship "Love" in 1635 Jonathan Bliss died in 1687 The inventory of his estate was sworn to May 23, 1687, the magistrate was the famous governor, Sir Edmund Andros Children: Ephraim, born 1649, Rachel, December 1, 1651; Jonathan, March 4, 1653, died same year; Mary, September 31 (sic), 1655, Elizabeth, January 20, 1657; Samuel, June 24, 1660; Martha, April, 1663; Jonathan, mentioned below (sometimes recorded Timothy), Dorothy, January 17, 1668; Bethia, August, 1671

(V) Jonathan (3) Bliss, fourth son of Jonathan (2) and Miriam (Harmon) Bliss, was born September 17, 1666, and died October 16, 1719. His name was sometimes recorded Timothy. He was a man of standing and influence in Rehoboth and held various town offices. It is said that he gave the land for the old cemetery about two miles south of Rehoboth Village, whereon a church was built. He married (first) June 23, 1691, Miriam Carpenter, born October 26, 1674, died May 21, 1706, daughter of William and Miriam (Searles) Carpenter. Her brother Daniel married Bethia Bliss, her husband's sister. Jonathan Bliss married (second) April 10, 1711, Mary French, of Rehoboth, who married (second) as third wife, Peter Hunt, and died December 10, 1754, aged seventy years. Children of first wife. Jonathan, born June 5, 1692, died May 3, 1770; Jacob, March 21, 1694; Ephraim, December 28, 1695, died young; Elisha, October 4, 1697; Ephraim, mentioned below; Daniel, January 21, 1702; Noah, May 18, 1704, died September 20, 1704; Miriam, August 9, 1705. Children of second wife. Mary, born November 23, 1712; Hannah, January 7, 1715; Bethiah, May 10, 1716; Rachel, August 10, 1719.

(VI) Lieutenant Ephraim Bliss, fifth son of Jonathan (3) and Miriam (Carpenter) Bliss, born August 15, 1699, lived in Rehoboth, and married, December 5, 1723, Rachel Carpenter, born May 19, 1699, daughter of Abiah and Mehitable (Read) Carpenter. Children: Ephraim, born January 2, 1725, died young; Ephraim and Noah (twins), June 3, 1726; Rachel, March 6, 1728; Abiah, January

26, 1730; Jonathan, September 8, 1731, died young; Lydia, July 3, 1733; Keziah, February 7, 1735; Hannah, February 16, 1737; Jonathan, mentioned below; Abadial, December 15, 1740; Benjamin, December 24, 1743.

(VII) Captain Jonathan (4) Bliss, sixth son of Lieutenant Ephraim and Rachel (Carpenter) Bliss, born January, 1739, lived in Rehoboth, and died January 24, 1800. He married, December 27, 1759, Lydia Wheeler, born October 17, 1737, died April 11, 1803, daughter of Squier and Lydia (Bowen) Wheeler Children: Keziah, born October 10, 1760; James, January 18, 1762; Jonathan, December 6, 1763, died young; Chloe, March 4, 1765; Jonathan, mentioned below; Lucy, June 23, 1769; Asahel, September 6, 1771; Shubael, October 30, 1773; Lydia, December 29, 1776; Zenas, November 12, 1779; Nancy, May 15, 1784

(VIII) Jonathan (5) Bliss, third son of Captain Jonathan (4) and Lydia (Wheeler) Bliss, born April 3, 1767, resided in Rehoboth, and died March 19, 1799. He married, March 19, 1792, Hannah Kent, born August 11, 1769, daughter of Elijah and Hannah (Perrin) Kent (see Kent V). She married (second) Otis Capron, of Attleboro, Massachusetts, and died May 27, 1836. Children of Jonathan (5) Bliss. Jonathan, born February 15, 1793, died September 2, 1872; Martin, mentioned below; Zeba, August 20, 1796, died July 29, 1858; George, February 3, 1799, died March 3, 1851.

(IX) Martin Bliss, second son of Jonathan (5) and Hannah (Kent) Bliss, was born October 24, 1794, died March 29, 1864 in Attleboro. He married, August 26, 1819, Sophia Wrightington, daughter of Robert and Hannah Wrightington, born March 18, 1796, died June 4, 1880, in Attleboro. Children William M, born August 2, 1821; Sophia Capron, October

26, 1822, died 1823, Rodolphus, May 26, 1824; Ann Sophia, mentioned below; Francis LaFayette, September 6, 1829, died 1836.

(X) Ann Sophia Bliss, second daughter of Martin and Sophia (Wrightington) Bliss, born August 26, 1826, became the wife of Williams S. Lincoln, of Attleboro (see Lincoln IX)

(The Shaw Line).

(I) Anthony Shaw was early in Boston, Massachusetts, whence he removed to Portsmouth, Rhode Island, and later to Little Compton, same colony, where he died August 21, 1705 The inventory of his estate tooted two hundred and thirteen pounds, twelve shilling, two pence, including a negro man valued at thirty pounds, and silver money amounting to nine pounds On April 20, 1665, he bought ten acres of land in Portsmouth, for forty pounds, including a house and three hundred good boards He married Alice, daughter of John Stonard, of Boston where their first three children were born, namely William, January 21, 1654, died February 10 following; William, February 24, 1655; Elizabeth, May 21, 1656 The others, born in Rhode Island, were Israel, mentioned below; Ruth, wife of John Cook; Grace, wife of Joseph Church

(II) Israel Shaw, third son of Anthony and Alice (Stonard) Shaw, lived in Little Compton, and married, in 1689, a daughter of Peter Tallman, of Portsmouth Her baptismal name is not preserved He sold two parcels of land in Portsmouth, February 11, 1707, to his brother-in-law, John Cook, of Tiverton, and in the bargain were included buildings and orchards, and a share in Hog Island The consideration was two hundred and ten pounds and ten shillings Children Wilham, born November 7, 1690 Mary, February 17, 1692, Anthony, January 29, 1694, Alice, No-

vember 17, 1695, Israel, mentioned below; Hannah, March 7, 1699, Jeremiah, June 6, 1700, Ruth, February 10, 1702, Peter, October 6, 1704, Elizabeth, February 7, 1706; Grace, October 20, 1707, Comfort, August 9, 1709, Deborah, July 15, 1711

(III) Israel (2) Shaw, third son of Israel (1) Shaw, was born August 28, 1697, in Little Compton, and lived in that town He married, August 10, 1721, Abigail Palmer, born April 5, 1702, in Little Compton, died 1790, daughter of William and Mary (Richmond) Palmer. Children Lemuel, born September 6, 1722, Blake, February 21, 1724, Parthenia, March 19, 1725, Eunice, October 7, 1728, Lois, died young, Lillis, March 26, 1733, Merebah, November 2, 1736, Israel, May 28, 1739, Lois, January 7, 1742, Seth, mentioned below

(IV) Seth Shaw, youngest child of Israel (2) and Abigail (Palmer) Shaw, was born November 6, 1745, in Little Compton, and died there, January 17, 1835 He was a soldier of the Revolution in Colonel Crary's regiment, in 1776, as evidenced by a payroll showing him entitled to six pounds, five shillings and seven pence He married (first) in 1768, Elizabeth, surname unknown He married (second) November 5, 1772, Priscilla Church, daughter of William and Parnel Church He married (third) November 24, 1776, Mary Davenport, of Tiverton, daughter of John and Elizabeth Davenport, of that town, born May 1, 1741 (see Davenport III) There was one child of the first marriage Elizabeth, born November 9, 1769; and one of the second Lemuel, March 23, 1774 Children of third marriage Seth, born July 2, 1778; Priscilla, September 22, 1780, Timothy, mentioned below

(V) Timothy Shaw, youngest child of Seth and Mary (Davenport) Shaw, was born April 4, 1782, in Little Compton, and

210

died there about November 1, 1835. He married, March 4, 1804, Clarissa Allen, born June 6, 1784, in Middletown, Rhode Island, daughter of William and Lucy (Little) Allen (see Allen V), died about the same time as her husband, according to Little Compton Congregational church records. Children: Seth, mentioned below; Mary Taylor, born March 12, 1807; Allen, June 24, 1809; Major Willis, September 16, 1811; William Pitt, February 15, 1814; Bradford Cornhill, July 15, 1817; Abigail Palmer, July 4, 1822; Ann Elizabeth, March 28, 1826.

(VI) Seth (2) Shaw, eldest child of Timothy and Clarissa (Allen) Shaw, was born May 18, 1805, in Little Compton, and married there, September 12, 1830, Clarissa Westgate, of Tiverton, perhaps a daughter of Jonathan and Dorcas (Austin) Westgate, Friends of that town.

(VII) William Penn Shaw, son of Seth (2) and Clarissa (Westgate) Shaw, was born in Little Compton, and was a butcher. He early lived in Fair Haven, Massachusetts, and when about twenty-six years of age located at Attleboro, where he resided until his death, which occurred October 14, 1879. He married Susan E. Blossom (see Blossom VII) and their children were 1 Horace B. born August 8, 1854, lives in Attleboro, where he was formerly engaged in the livery business. He married (first) Carrie A. Everett, and (second) Cora B. Mathews, and has one daughter by his first marriage, Gertrude Everett Shaw. 2. Ermina Chester, mentioned below. 3. Sarah Alice, who died at the age of seven years. 4. Joseph Blossom, born in June, 1859, died February 8, 1913. He married (first) Emily Bicknell, and (second) Margaret Crawford, and his children by the first marriage are Mabel B., who married Ernest J. Qvarnstrom, of Attleboro; Emily B. and Jesse Allen Shaw.

(VIII) Ermina Chester Shaw, daughter of William Penn and Susan E. (Blossom) Shaw, was born January 27, 1856, in Fair Haven, Massachusetts, became the wife of Frederick William Lincoln, of Attleboro (see Lincoln X).

(The Kent Line)

Between 1633 and 1644 there came from England to New England three families bearing the surname Kent, who became the progenitors of three distinct lines. The first account of the Kent family occurs in the account of settlement of Ipswich, Massachusetts, in 1635. Under date of May 2, 1643, the town records of Dedham state that "Joshuah Kent is admitted Townsman & hath libertie to purchase Edward Culvers Lott." The records of the First Church of Dedham say that "Joshua Kent went for England with our testimonial but to returne again 11m, 1644, md he returned 1645." "md ye said Joshuah Kent, having brought ov'r 2 of his brothers & placed them in ye country, yet with his wife returned to England 10m 1647." "md ye said Joshuah Kent upon ye trobles arising againe in England & wares ther 1648 he returned with his wife againe about ye 8m yt year." His brothers were named John and Joseph, and the three brothers were the founders of the Dedham line. The Kent English ancestry has not been traced, and it is not known what relationship existed, if any, between the Kents of Newbury, Gloucester and Dedham, Massachusetts. One of the most ancient coat-of-arms of the Kent family is Gules, a chief argent.

(I) Joseph Kent, of Braintree, on March 19, 1653, testified in a law suit between the Widow Wilson and Thomas Faxon, both of Braintree, and in his testimony gave his age as sixteen years. It is well known that in 1644 Joseph, with his brother John, was brought from England by their brother Joshua, of Dedham, but their parentage or English birthplace is as yet unascertained The fact that Joseph was but seven years of age, and his brother John but a little older, when brought from England, would indicate that they were left at least motherless, and perhaps orphans when very young Joshua and John Kent settled in Dedham, while Joseph Kent, the ancestor of the line of Kents here following was placed, it would seem, in the custody of his aunt, Elizabeth Hardier, of Braintree, and here he continued to reside until arriving at man's estate, when he married Susannah George, daughter of Peter George About 1660 Joseph Kent became a resident of Block Island, Rhode Island, which at this time was settled almost wholly by Braintree people In May, 1664, the first assembly of Rhode Island established by the charter convened at Newport The affairs of Block Island were arranged and settled at this first session, and Joseph Kent with two others were the "messengers" or deputies from the island On December 15, 1673, he was admitted an inhabitant of Swansea, and his name frequently appears in the records of the town after that date In the court orders of Swansea he was mentioned to be propounded a freeman, June 7, 1681, and on June 6, 1682, he was made a freeman On July 7, 1681, he with others was appointed on a committee by the town of Swansea in the town s behalf for the regulation of differences in the division of Swansea lands Another court record of the town reads "In reference unto sixteen or seventeen bushells of corne taken from Joseph Kent of Swansea and improved for the reliefe of some souldiers in the time of the late Indian wars the Courtt have ordered that it or the value thereof to be repayed by the Treasurer." Joseph Kent was doubtless a farmer, and like thousands of others of the Pilgrims and Puritans who settled New England, he seems to have been an honest, an industrious and a God-fearing man Possessing neither much of wealth or of education, their strong right arms and their fear of God became their best and only assets, the former assuring them a living wrung from the woods and the soil and the latter an honest and a sufficient government in a New World Children of Joseph and Susannah (George) Kent Joseph, mentioned below, Samuel, born 1668, died 1737, Joshua, 1672, died August 11, 1675; Susannah, September 25, 1687, died August 10, 1774

(II) Joseph (2) Kent, eldest child of Joseph (1) and Susannah (George) Kent, was born 1665, on Block Island, Rhode Island, and died in Rumford, March 30, 1735 He seems to have been brought up in Swansea, where he lived many years, going from there to Rehoboth, where the last of his children were born While a resident of Swansea he was ensign and representative to the General Court, and in July, 1696, was a grand juryman at Bristol, Rhode Island He married, November 11, 1690, Dorothy Brown, daughter of James Brown, granddaughter of John Brown She was born October 29, 1666, in Swansea, and died in Rumford, June 2, 1710 Her mother was Lydia (Howland) Brown, daughter of John Howland and his wife, Elizabeth (Tilley) Howland, who came in the "Mayflower." Hon John Brown from 1637 to 1653 was governor's assistant in Plymouth Colony, and long a leading man of affairs, while his son James carried the last message to King Philip before the outbreak of war Children of Joseph (2) Kent Lydia, born March 15, 1692, Joseph, August 19, 1693; Dorothy, August 13, 1695; John, mentioned below, Susanna, 1698, died young, Hezekiah, February 6, 1699, Susannah,

March 1, 1701, Mary, March 3, 1703, James, August 20, 1707 (III) John Kent, second son of Joseph (2) and Dorothy (Brown) Kent, was born August 9, 1697, in Rehoboth, Massachusetts, died November 1, 1780. All his life he seems to have been a husbandman, minding his own affairs and holding or seeking no public office In the inventory of his estate, which totalled some two thousand pounds, he is styled "gentleman." He married, November 20, 1725, Rachel Carpenter, daughter of Nathaniel Carpenter, son of William (2) Carpenter, son of William (1) Carpenter The Carpenter line has been traced into England for nine generations preceding this William (1) The mother of Rachel Carpenter was Mary Preston, daughter of Daniel Preston, son of Daniel Preston, son of William Preston Rachel Carpenter was born March 29, 1705, in Attleboro, Massachusetts, and died in Rehoboth about 1770 Children Elijah, mentioned below; Dorothy, born March 4, 1729, John, April 8, 1732, died May 26, 1736, Nathaniel, November 12, 1734, died May 10, 1756; Joseph, February 3, 1736, died January 8, 1804; John, May 9, 1739, Mary, August 18, 1741, died February 7, 1766, Ezekiel, June 22, 1744, Remember, July 28, 1746, died December 17, 1773, Rebecca, August 18, 1750, died September 19, 1750

(IV) Elijah Kent, eldest child of John and Rachel (Carpenter) Kent, born December 30, 1727, in Rehoboth, was received into the church there with his wife, May 19, 1754, and died September 22, 1815 He married (intentions published March 3, 1753) Hannah Perrin, born February 23, 1729, in Rehoboth, daughter of Daniel and Abigail (Carpenter) Perrin Children Remember, born January 7, 1754, Lydia, March 16, 1756, Hannah, September 12, 1759, died young, Hannah, mentioned below.

(V) Hannah Kent, youngest child of Elijah and Hannah (Perrin) Kent, was born August 11, 1769, and became the wife of Jonathan (5) Bliss, of Rehoboth (see Bliss VIII)

(The Davenport Line).

There were several immigrants in America in the days of its early settlement bearing this name, and the ancestry of the Connecticut branch has been traced in England for many generations

(1) Thomas Davenport was a member of the Dorchester church, November 20, 1640, was a freeman, May 18, 1642, and served the town as constable in 1670. He purchased a house and lands, November 25, 1653, and his residence was on the east slope of Mount Bowdoin, near the corner of the present Union avenue and Bowdoin street, Dorchester He purchased additional lands, February 5, 1665 After his death, which occurred November 9, 1685, an inventory of his estate was made, amounting to £332, 16s and 8d His wife Mary joined the Dorchester church, March 8, 1644 She survived him nearly six years, dying October 4, 1691 Children Sarah, born December 28, 1643; Thomas, baptized March 2, 1645, Mary, January 21, 1649, Charles, September 7, 1652, Abigail, July 8, 1655, Mehitable, born February 14, 1657, Jonathan, mentioned below, Ebenezer, April 26, 1661, John, October 20, 1664

(II) Jonathan Davenport, third son of Thomas and Mary Davenport, was born in 1659, and died January 11, 1729 He married, December 1, 1680, Hannah Warren, born 1660, died January 14, 1729, in Little Compton Children Thomas, born December 10, 1681; Jonathan, November 3, 1684, died October 14, 1751, Hannah, December 23, 1686, Simeon, December 27, 1688, died December 8, 1763, Ebenezer, September 2, 1691, died August 4, 1776; John, mentioned below, Joseph,

March 25, 1696, died September 2, 1760, Benjamin, October 6, 1698, Sarah, December 10, 1700

(III) John Davenport, fifth son of Jonathan and Hannah (Warren) Davenport, was born January 12, 1694, in Little Compton, and died April 20, 1741. He married in Little Compton, June 15, 1726, Elizabeth Taylor, born January 4, 1701, daughter of Peter and Elizabeth Taylor Children Noah, born May 7, 1727, died March 5, 1818, Sarah, October 27, 1729, Jonathan, January 22, 1733, John; Ephraim, July 2, 1736, Phebe, May 19, 1739, Mary, mentioned below

(IV) Mary Davenport, youngest child of John and Elizabeth (Taylor) Davenport, was born May 1, 1741, in Tiverton, eleven days after the death of her father, and was married by Rev Othniel Campbell, November 24 1776, to Seth Shaw, of Little Compton (see Shaw IV)

(The Allen Line)

This is one of the names most frequently met in the United States, and is represented by many distinct families Its use arises from the Christian name, which is very ancient In the roll of Battle Abbey, Fitz-Aleyne (son of Allen) appears, and the name comes down through the ages to the present Alan, constable of Scotland and Lord of Galloway and Cunningham, died in 1234 One of the first using Allen as a surname was Thomas Allen, sheriff of London, in 1414 Sir John Allen was mayor of London in 1524, Sir William Allen in 1571, and Sir Thomas Alleyn in 1659 Edward Allen (1566-1626), distinguished actor and friend of Shakespeare and Ben Johnson, founded in 1619 Dulwich College, with the stipulation that the master and secretary must always bear the name of Allen, and this curious condition has been easily fulfilled through the plentitude of scholars of the

name There are no less than fifty-five coats-of-arms of separate and distinct families of Allen in the United Kingdom, besides twenty others of different spellings There were more than a score of emigrants of this surname, from almost as many different families, who left England before 1650 to settle in New England The name in early times was spelled Allin, Alline, Alling, Allyn Allein and Allen, but the last is the orthography almost universally used at the present day It is found not only in the industrial but in the professional life of people who have stood for all that is noblest and best It has been identified with the formative period of New England history, and from that region has sent out worthy representatives

(I) William Allen, by tradition a native of Wales, came to this country in 1660, and is of record at Portsmouth (Prudence Island), Rhode Island, in 1683 He purchased a large tract of land, which included the subsequent village of Drownville (now West Barrington), built a house, and was resident of that place prior to 1670 Both he and his wife Elizabeth died in the year 1685 Children Mary, William, mentioned below; Thomas, or Swansea, Massachusetts, John, of North Kingstown, Rhode Island, Matthew, of Portsmouth, Warwick and North Kingstown, Mercy, Sarah, and Benjamin, of Rehoboth, Massachusetts

(II) William (2) Allen, eldest son of William (1) and Elizabeth Allen, lived in Portsmouth, which town he represented in the General Court in 1705 He was fined six shillings and eight pence, December 13, 1687, for refusing to take the oath as a grand juror This indicates that he was a Quaker, as was presumably his father, and suggests that the family may be connected with the ancient Allen family of Sandwich and Dartmouth William Allen had three sons, of whom the name of only one is preserved.

(III) John Allen, son of William (2) Allen, was born December 27, 1691, in Portsmouth, where he resided, and died November 6, 1783, in his ninety-second year. His wife's name was Elizabeth. He may have lived in other towns, and was in Middletown in 1734, when one child is recorded there.

(IV) Peleg Allen, son of John and Elizabeth Allen, was born March 21, 1734, in Middletown, where he made his home, and married there, December 29, 1759 Elizabeth Cornell, born May 17, 1740, in Portsmouth, daughter of William Cornell. Two children are recorded in Portsmouth, and others in Middletown, namely: William, mentioned below; Thomas Cornell born December 14, 1762; Hannah, October 16, 1765; Elizabeth, February 27, 1768; Susannah, March 11, 1770; Abigail, August 1, 1772; Martha, July 22, 1775; Rachel, March 20, 1778; Anne, March 4, 1781; Phebe, April 3, 1783.

(V) William (3) Allen, eldest child of Peleg and Elizabeth (Cornell) Allen, was born April 17, 1760, in Portsmouth, and lived in Middletown, where he was married, August 12 1781, by Rev. Jonathan Ellis, to Lucy Little, born August 23 1761, in Little Compton, Rhode Island, daughter of Fobes (2) and Sarah (Wilcox) Little, of that town (see Little V). Children: Ruth, born November 2, 1782; Clarissa, mentioned below; Nancy, August 11, 1787; Selma, January 9, 1790; George, September 22, 1792; William, May 15 1794; Mary, June 4, 1797; Hannah, April 11, 1799; Peleg, April 6, 1803; Thomas Cornell, September 29, 1807.

(VI) Clarissa Allen, second daughter of William (3) and Lucy (Little) Allen, was born June 6, 1784, in Middletown, and was married in Little Compton, March 4, 1804, to Timothy Shaw, of Tiverton (see Shaw V).

(The Blossom Line)

The Blossom family of Fair Haven and New Bedford is one of the oldest in New England, dating back to the days of the Pilgrim Fathers.

(I) Thomas Blossom, born in 1580, in England, was one of the Pilgrims who came from Leyden, Holland, to Plymouth, Massachusetts, but being on board of the "Speedwell" was disappointed of passage with the "Mayflower," from England, and soon went back to encourage emigration of the residue. A son who came and returned with him died before December, 1625, and two other children had been born in the interval. In 1629 he came again, probably in the "Mayflower." He was a deacon of the church, and died in the summer of 1632. His widow Ann married (second) October 17, 1633, and in 1639 they removed to Barnstable. Children of Thomas and Ann Blossom: Elizabeth, born 1620; Thomas, 1622; Peter, mentioned below.

(II) Peter Blossom, son of Thomas and Ann Blossom, born about 1632, was a landowner and farmer in Barnstable, and died in July, 1706. He married, at Barnstable, January 21, 1663, Sarah Bodfish. Children: Mercy, born April 9 1664, died in 1670; Thomas, December 20, 1667; Sarah, 1669, died in 1671; Joseph, mentioned below. Thankful, 1675; Mercy, August 1678; Jabez, February 16, 1680.

(III) Joseph Blossom, second son of Peter and Sarah (Bodfish) Blossom, was born December 10, 1673, and married (first) June 17, 1696, Mary Pinchon; (second) in 1708, Mary ———; and (third) in 1720, Mehetabel ———. Children: Joseph, born March 14, 1704; Mary, December 11, 1709; Thankful, March 25, 1711; Benjamin, mentioned below.

(IV) Benjamin Blossom, youngest child of Joseph and Mehetabel Blossom, born March, 1721, died October 25, 1797, and was buried in the cemetery at Acushnet

He married, October 31, 1751, Bathsheba
Percival, born December 21, 1725. Children: Benjamin, born August 18, 1753;
Ansel, April 6, 1755, Mary, March 2, 1758,
Samuel, May 26, 1760, Joseph, mentioned
below; Elisha, August 23, 1767, was killed in a naval engagement in the War of
1812.

(V) Joseph (2) Blossom, fourth son of
Benjamin and Bathsheba (Percival) Blossom, was born December 4, 1763, and married Elizabeth Hathaway.

(VI) Joseph (3) Blossom, son of Joseph (2) and Elizabeth (Hathaway) Blossom, was born in 1793, and married Betsey Copeland.

(VII) Susan E. Blossom, daughter of
Joseph (3) and Betsey (Copeland) Blos-
som, became the wife of William Penn
Shaw (see Shaw VII).

(The Little Line).

(I) Thomas Little, a native of England,
the first of the name in New England, a
lawyer by profession, located in Plymouth, Massachusetts, in 1630, and died in
Scituate, same colony, March 12, 1672. In
1650 he settled in Marshfield, and owned
one thousand acres of land in the section
now called Sea View. In 1643 he was a
member of the Plymouth Military Company. He married, in Plymouth, April 19,
1633, Anne Warren, born 1611, in England, died 1675, a daughter of Richard
Warren, one of the "Mayflower" passengers, and signer of the Compact made November 11, 1620, in the cabin of that vessel, while lying in Provincetown Harbor.
Children: Thomas, Samuel, Ephraim,
Isaac, Hannah, Mary, Ruth and Patience.

(II) Ephraim Little, son of Thomas
and Anne (Warren) Little, was born May
17, 1650, in Marshfield, represented that
town in the General Court in 1697, 1699,
and 1705, and died November 24, 1717, in
Scituate. He married, November 22, 1672,

Mary Sturtevant, born December 7, 1651,
in Plymouth, died February 10, 1718,
daughter of Samuel and Ann Sturtevant,
of Plymouth. Children: Ann, born August 23, 1673, Ruth, died young; Ephraim, September 27, 1676, David, March
17 1681, John, mentioned below; Mary,
July 7, 1685, Ruth, November 23, 1686.

(III) John Little, third son of Ephraim and Mary (Sturtevant) Little, was
born March 17, 1683, in Marshfield, where
he made his home, and died February 26,
1767. The house which he built in 1720
is still standing, and owned by one of his
descendants. He was representative to
the General Court in 1728, 1737, 1745,
1750-51 and 1755. By his will he gave to
each of his daughters a negro slave
woman, and to each of his sons a farm.
He married, April 8, 1708, Constance
Fobes, born 1686, in Little Compton,
Rhode Island, daughter of Lieutenant
William and Martha (Peabody) Fobes,
granddaughter of William and Elizabeth
(Alden) Peabody, the last named a
daughter of John and Priscilla (Mullins)
Alden, of the "Mayflower." Two children are recorded in Little Compton
Fobes, mentioned below, and Joseph, born
May 6, 1719.

(IV) Fobes Little, son of John and
Constance (Fobes) Little, was born
March 9, 1712, graduated from Harvard
College in 1734, and died in Little Comp-
ton, 1795. He married, in 1738, in Little
Compton, Sarah, whose surname is not
preserved.

(V) Fobes (2) Little, son of Fobes (1)
and Sarah Little, was born about 1738,
and married, in Little Compton, July 28,
1758, Sarah Wilcox, born July 16, 1740,
in that town, daughter of Ephraim and
Mary (Pierce) Wilcox, granddaughter of
Edward Wilcox. Children: Lucy, mentioned below; Nathaniel, born March 16,
1764; William, January 3, 1768; Eph-

raim, 1770, Nancy, October 20, 1772; Mary, January 17, 1775, Sarah, July 4, 1779; Fobes, October 11, 1781, Thomas, August 17, 1784

(VI) Lucy Little, eldest child of Fobes (2) and Sarah (Wilcox) Little, was born August 23, 1761, in Little Compton, and married in Middletown, Rhode Island, August 12, 1781, to William Allen, of that town (see Allen V).

SWEENEY, George A,

Merchant, Public Official

Mary E. Bowman, daughter of David Sands and Anna (Burdick) Bowman, was married, July 9, 1872, to George A Sweeney, who was born in Searsport, Maine, son of John and Lady Katherine (Collins) Sweeney Children 1 Katherine C, married Walter F King, of Attleboro, and they have two children Walter F, Jr, and Elizabeth Brewster King 2 Anna Gertrude, married Willard M Whitman, and they reside at Swampscot, Massachusetts, the parents of one child, Evlyn Whitman 3 George A, Jr, married Grace Brett, who died February 9, 1916, leaving one child, Elsie Brett Sweeney 4 Mary Elizabeth, married Edmund Reeves, Jr, and they reside in Attleboro, Massachusetts

George A Sweeney was born of farming parents, in the little seacoast town of Searsport, Maine As the result of an early call to obtain his livelihood, he sailed away upon a sea voyage Four of his brothers having been lost at sea while engaged in the merchant marine service, however, had a depressing effect upon him and he forsook the sea, and being a youth of studious habits, he turned his attention to work more congenial to his temperament, and for a time was engaged in teaching school The opportunities in a small seacoast town were few, so he

thought of the Old Bay State, conceiving the idea that here were greater chances of advancement At an early age he reached the town of Attleboro, Massachusetts, but as he did not immediately find employment as a teacher, he turned his attention to what first came to his mind, which proved to be the trade of tinsmithing A strong characteristic of his was faithfulness and a dogged persistence to acquire a thorough knowledge of whatever he undertook to do He worked at this time at Leach's store on Park street; later he purchased the store now occupied by the Nahum Perry Company, on Railroad avenue, after a few years he moved into the store since known as Sweeney's Emporium The tinsmith trade was finally abandoned and he started a housefurnishing business, which, with his energy, shrewdness and industry, he developed until it stands to-day a large and high-grade business Since his death the affairs of the firm have been well conducted by his son, George A Sweeney Jr

At one time Mr Sweeney's sole interest in local affairs was his service in the fire department, which he served faithfully, becoming assistant engineer His interest ever remained unabated, but the excitement at the time of a fire proved too much for his health, obliging him to resign, although he still delighted in the upbuilding of the town's fire department

His marriage with Mary Elizabeth Bowman occurred soon after his establishment of the housefurnishing business Mr Sweeney strongly believed that a man's place was in the home circle, and in his later years he devotedly gave of himself to his family They had a summer home at West Falmouth Massachusetts, where he was a summer visitor for many years and became well known throughout the district

His tenacity of purpose and his successful business qualities were fully in play and benefited the town during the years he was a member of the Board of Selectmen. His applied work was seen in the abolition of grade crossings, policy in street improvements, and in the upbuilding of various town departments. In fact, in all the big local enterprises he accomplished fine work, as the changes came to a village, conservative, provincial and more or less active, developing to a city's population. After completing a term as postmaster, he was elected in 1898 to the Board of Selectmen. Many times he presided as chairman during the fifteen years he was returned to the board. Mr. Sweeney was a member of Orient Lodge, Independent Order of Odd Fellows, Attleboro Lodge, Benevolent and Protective Order of Elks, Pythagoras Lodge, Knights of Pythias, Pennington Lodge Ancient Order of United Workmen; and the Royal Arcanum.

Mr. Sweeney passed away at the age of sixty-one years, from an acute attack of heart trouble, his illness covering a period of several months. His passing took from the town one who for a long period of years held a unique place in the political and business life of the community. There was a prayer service in his late home, No. 52 Holman street, after which the body was escorted to the Second Congregational Church, where the services were public. The Odd Fellows were in charge. The honorary pall bearers were composed of the heads of all different town departments, namely Selectmen, Millard F. Ashley, assessors, Walter J. Newman, schools, Benjamin P. King, water department, Harry P. Kent, library trustees, Dr. Charles S. Holden, sewer commissioners, Hugh A. Smith, town clerk, Frank I. Babcock, overseers of the poor, Joseph V. Curran, board of

health, Stephen J. Foley, police, Charles E. Wilbur; fire department, Hiram R. Packard; board of trade, Frank I. Mossberg. There were bearers chosen from each lodge of which Mr. Sweeney was a member. The flag on the common was placed at half mast, and the selectmen issued a request that all stores should be closed between the hours of three and four on the afternoon of Mr. Sweeney's funeral.

Mrs. Mary Elizabeth (Bowman) Sweeney was born in the town of Falmouth, county of Barnstable, State of Massachusetts, daughter of David Sands and Anna Goodson (Burdick) Bowman, granddaughter of David and Lois (Hatch) Bowman, and great-granddaughter of Joseph and Rose Hatch. Joseph Hatch was a Revolutionary soldier serving his country in the capacity of private soldier, sergeant and secret service man. He enlisted from Falmouth in a company commanded by Captain Ward Swift, of Sandwich. He served in a secret expedition to Rhode Island, October, 1777; afterwards he was sergeant under Captain Joseph Palmer, Colonel Freeman's regiment, and served in that capacity at Falmouth and Dartmouth, September, 1778, also at Dartmouth, February 4, April 2 and May 16, 1779, roll sworn to in Barnstable county. She is also a direct descendant of Captain Ichabod Burdick, of the Rhode Island Artillery in the Revolutionary War.

Mrs. Sweeney is a member of All Saints' Episcopal Church, and has rendered faithful service in the various church departments. During the years 1911 and 1912, Mrs. Sweeney was regent of Attleboro Chapter, Daughters of the American Revolution, of which she is a valued member. She has for many years been a member of the Eaterio, a literary club, and is also a member of Attleboro Woman's Club.

CUSHMAN, Everett Morton,

Representative Citizen

The Cushman family of Taunton, here briefly reviewed, is a branch of the family bearing the name of ancient Plymouth, which with its allied connections is one of the historic families of New England Its progenitor, though of short life in New England, was one of the leading spirits in all the preliminary movements in both England and Holland incident to the coming of the "Mayflower" Pilgrims to New England, where his descendants soon allied themselves with those of the "Mayflower" passengers

(I) Robert Cushman, a wool carder of Canterbury, England, was associated with William Brewster as agent of the Leyden church in negotiations for removal, and came to New England in the "Fortune" in 1621, bringing with him his only son, Thomas He returned to England on business of the colony, and died there in 1626, leaving his son Thomas in the care of Governor Bradford It is well known that Robert Cushman was among the eighteen or twenty persons left at Plymouth when the 'Mayflower" made her final departure from England When the Pilgrims came to Southampton from Holland he was there, having gone ahead of them to England, and he was among them when they set sail from that port, only to put back into Dartmouth They started again, and again returned, this time going into Plymouth, whence they made their final departure Robert Cushman was, therefore, a passenger on the "Mayflower" from the time she left Southampton until she left Plymouth Governor Bradford says, "He" (meaning Christopher Martin) "was Governor in the bigger ship, and Master Cushman, Assistant" At the bottom of one of the panels of the Forefathers' Monument at

Plymouth is this statement "Robert Cushman, who chartered the May Flower and was active and prominent in securing the success of the Pilgrim Enterprise, came in the Fortune, 1621 " He married as his second wife, at Leyden, Holland, June 3, 1617, Mary, widow of Thomas Chingleton, of Sandwich, England An extended account of the succeeding generations of this family is given elsewhere in this work, including Thomas, who accompanied his father to Plymouth in 1621 in the ship "Fortune," and became an important man here in church and colony He was chosen and ordained elder of the Plymouth church in 1649, and was forty-three years in that office He married Mary Allerton, of the "Mayflower," and their son, Thomas (2) Cushman, lived to be eighty-nine years of age. He was the father of Benjamin Cushman, who lived on a part of his father's farm, in a home on the south side of or near to Colchester brook. He married Sarah Eaton, and their eldest child, Jabez Cushman, was the father of Zebedee Cushman, who was a private in Captain William Crow Colton's company, Colonel Josiah Whitney's regiment from July 29 to September 13, 1778, serving one month and sixteen days in Rhode Island He also served as a private in Captain William Tupper's company, Colonel Ebenezer White's regiment, which marched to Rhode Island on the alarm of August 1, 1780, discharged August 8, roll sworn to at Middleboro He married Sarah Padelford, of Taunton

(VII) Alvah Cushman, youngest child of Zebedee and Sarah (Padelford) Cushman, was born October 10, 1797, in Taunton, where he made his home He married, November 27, 1818, Sally Leonard, daughter of William Leonard. She was a strong and forceful character, and her influence was a potent factor in the upbringing of her children These children were David, born July 15, 1820; Horatio Leonard, October 22, 1826; Sally M , July 29, 1830, Christianna L., January 7, 1832; William, August 28, 1834, Harriet F , October 14, 1837, William H , mentioned below

(VIII) William H Cushman, youngest child of Alvah and Sally (Leonard) Cushman, was born November 2, 1839, in Taunton, and spent his entire life in his native place For many years he was a nail maker with his brother David, and was well known and beloved by all He was a member of Alfred Baylies Lodge, Ancient Free and Accepted Masons, and held office in it for many years He married Joanna Harlow, born October 12, 1840, daughter of John B and Rebecca (Reed) Paine, the mother being a daughter of Levi and Lucy (Doten) Reed, of Plymouth Mrs Cushman is now a resident of New Bedford Children Henry Presbrey, born October 8, 1860, died March 9, 1861; Herbert Elsworth, born January 1, 1862, Albert Francis, born March 21, 1864, died November 17, 1884; William Alvah, born March 30, 1871, resides in New Bedford, and is connected with the Southern Massachusetts Telephone Company; Jennie Edith, born January 12, 1874, married, September 8, 1897, Lewis Bright Barker, now of Central Falls, Rhode Island, and they have one son, Winston Cushman, born December 25, 1899, Everett Morton, mentioned below; Grace Reed, born January 31, 1881, died August 29, 1882; Bessie May, born February 24, 1883, married, July 6, 1910, Francis N Smith, and resides in New Bedford

(IX) Everett Morton Cushman, fifth son of William H and Joanna Harlow (Paine) Cushman, was born February 16, 1876, and resides in New Bedford, where he is superintendent of the Holmes Manu-

facturing Company He married, July 19, 1905, Adelaide Louise Miner, daughter of Howard and Josephine (Hutchens) Miner (see Miner VIII) They have one son, Robert Miner, born October 16, 1906 Mrs Cushman is a member of Fort Phenix Chapter, Daughters of the American Revolution, of New Bedford, of which she is auditor, and is quite active in the Young Women's Christian Association of that city

(The Miner Line)

The origin and early ancestry of the Miner family in England is as follows Edward III , of England, going to war against the French, marched through "Somersetshire, came to Mendippe hills, where lived Henry Miner, who with all carefulness and loyalty, having convened his domestic and menial servants armed with battle axes, proffered himself and them to his master's service, making up a complete hundred " For this service he was granted the coat-of-arms Gules a fesse between three plates argent

(I) Henry Miner, mentioned above, died in 1359. Children Henry, Edward, Thomas, George

(II) Henry (2) Miner, son of Henry (1) Miner, married Henrietta Hicks, daughter of Edward Hicks, of Gloucester Children William; Henry, who served in 1384 under Richard II

(III) William Miner, son of Henry (2) Miner, married ―――― Hobbs, of Wiltshire Children Thomas , George, lived in Shropshire

(IV) Thomas Miner, son of William Miner, lived in Herefordshire, in 1399, married a daughter of Cotton Gresslap, of Staffordshire Children Lodowick, George, Mary

(V) Lodowick Miner, son of Thomas Miner, married Anne Dyer, daughter of Thomas Dyer, of Staughton, Hunting-

donshire Children Thomas, mentioned
below, George and Arthur (twins), born
1438, served in the house of Austria
(VI) Thomas (2) Miner, son of Lodowick Miner, was born in 1436 He married Bridget, daughter of Sir George
Hervie, of St Martin's, County Middlesex He died in 1480, leaving two children to the tutorage of the mother, but
she resigned them to her father and
turned to monastic life in Dutford
(VII) William (2) Miner, son of
Thomas (2) Miner, married Isabella Har-
cope de Folibay, and lived to revenge the
death of the two young princes slain in
the Tower by their uncle, Richard III
Children William, George, Thomas,
Robert, Nathaniel, John, and four others
(VIII) William (3) Miner, son of Wil-
liam (2) Miner, was buried at Chew
Magna, February 23, 1585 Children
Clement, Elizabeth
(IX) Clement Miner, son of William
(3) Miner, died March 31, 1640, at Chew
Magna Children: Clement, married
Sarah Pope; Thomas, mentioned below,
Elizabeth, Mary (This English line was
prepared while the American ancestor
was living)
(I) Thomas (3) Miner, son of Clement
Miner, was the American ancestor of the
family He was born in Chew Magna,
County Somerset, England, April 23,
1608, and died in Quiambaugh, a part of
Stonington, Connecticut, October 23,
1690 He came to this country in 1630,
in the ship "Arabella," and settled in
Charlestown, Massachusetts He served
in the colonial wars In 1636 he removed
to Hingham, Massachusetts, where he remained until 1646, when he settled in
Pequot, now New London, Connecticut
In 1652 he settled in Stonington, where
he resided the remainder of his life He
was one of the committee chosen to determine the boundary lines between Con-

necticut and Rhode Island He married,
April 23, 1634, in Charlestown, Grace,
daughter of Walter Palmer She survived him only a few weeks, dying the
same year, 1690. Children John, born
1636, in Charlestown In Hingham
Clement, baptized March 4, 1638;
Thomas, baptized May 10, 1640, Ephraim, mentioned below, Joseph, baptized
August 25, 1644 In New London· Ma-
nasseh, April 23, 1647, Ann, April 28,
1649, Maria, 1650, Samuel, March 4,
1652, served in King Philip's war In
Stonington Hannah, September 15, 1655
(II) Ephraim Miner, son of Thomas
(3) and Grace (Palmer) Miner, was born
in Hingham, Massachusetts, where he
was baptized May 1, 1642, and died May
16, 1724, aged eighty-two years He went
with his parents to New London, and to
Quiambaugh (Stonington), in 1653, and
the place on which they settled in this
town has remained in the family until the
present time He served in King Philip s
war, 1675 He was buried in Taughwonk
He married, January 20, 1666, Hannah
Avery, who died August 22, 1721 Children, born at Stonington· Ephraim, June
22, 1668, Thomas, December 17, 1669,
Hannah, April 21, 1671, Rebecca, September, 1672, Elizabeth, April, 1674,
Samuel, December, 1676, Deborah, April
15, 1678, Samuel, August, 1681, James,
mentioned below, Grace, September,
1683, John, April 19, 1685, son and daughter, born and died March 21, 1687
(III) James Miner, fifth son of Ephraim and Hannah (Avery) Miner, was
born in November, 1682, in Stonington,
and married there, February 22, 1705,
Abigail Eldredge Children James, born
October 28, 1707; Charles, mentioned below, Jerviah, October 8, 1711; Daniel,
January 24, 1713, Abigail, August 18,
1715
(IV) Charles Miner, second son of

James and Abigail (Eldredge) Miner, was born March 14, 1709, in Stonington, and married there, December 9, 1740, Mary, widow of Isaac Wheeler, and daughter of Thomas and Mary (Miner) Wheeler Children · Charles, born October 3, 1741 ; Thomas, mentioned below, Christopher, March 16, 1745 ; Mary, August 1, 1746 ; Daniel, June 21, 1749 ; Abigail, November 8, 1756

(V) Thomas (4) Miner, second son of Charles and Mary (Wheeler) Miner, was born March 11, 1743, in Stonington, and there married (first) September 8, 1765, Mary Page, born January 30, 1749, daughter of Joseph (2) and Mary (Hewitt) Page, of Stonington. He married (second) Lydia York, born December 28, 1760, daughter of John and Anna (Brown) York, of Stonington (see York V) There was a Thomas Miner, who served nine days in a New London company on the Lexington Alarm of April 19, 1775 He may have been the Thomas Miner who was killed in the engagement with the English at Groton, September 6, 1781 Children of first marriage · Persis, born December 20, 1766, Priscilla, April 26, 1769, Asher, January 30, 1772, Adam, July 5, 1774 ; Roswell, August 29, 1776, Sally, May 6, 1779 ; Phebe, November 5, 1781, Betsey, August 23, 1783 Of second marriage Oliver, December 14, 1791, Abby, 1800, Ezra D , mentioned below , Lawrence, 1803

(VI) Deacon Ezra D Miner, sixth son of Thomas (4) Miner, and third child of his second wife, Lydia (York) Miner, was born March 12, 1802, in Stonington, and lived in that town, where he died He married Desire Hewitt, born September 27, 1803, in Stonington, daughter of Benjamin and Desire (Babcock) Hewitt, of that town (see Hewitt VI) Children · Susan, Emily, Mary, Howard

(VII) Howard Miner, only son of Deacon Ezra D and Desire (Hewitt) Miner, was born June 5, 1833, in North Stonington, where he grew to manhood, and soon after attaining his majority settled in Dane county, Wisconsin, where he followed farming for several years Returning to New England he was for some years superintendent of the Robert Knight farm in the town of Warwick, Kent county, Rhode Island After he retired he made his home in New Bedford, Massachusetts, where he died September 22, 1914 He served as a soldier in the Civil War, being a member of Company E, Twenty-first Connecticut Regiment, in which he won promotion to the rank of sergeant He married in Wisconsin, July 19, 1865, Josephine Hutchens, born February 22, 1844, at Bath, New York, lived with George and Phebe Buten Children George, died in infancy, Howard, died young, Ezra, resides in East Greenwich, Rhode Island, married Jennie Adams, of Natick, Rhode Island , Emogene, married Frank Gray, of Koshkonong, Wisconsin , Adelaide Louise, mentioned below

(VIII) Adelaide Louise Miner, youngest child of Howard and Josephine (Hutchens) Miner, became the wife of Everett Morton Cushman, of New Bedford (see Cushman IX)

(The York Line)

(I) James York was born in 1614, and died in 1683, aged sixty-nine years He came to this country in 1635, when he was twenty-one years of age, in the ship "Philip," which sailed June 20, 1635, from Gravesend, England, for Virginia If they landed in Virginia, James York did not remain there long He doubtless came north soon after his arrival, and the first record found of him is in Braintree, Massachusetts In 1660 he settled in Stonington, Connecticut, when it was under the jurisdiction of Massachusetts and called Southerton He settled on grants of land which included the present farm of Gideon P Chesebrough, east of Anguilla or Wequetequock brook, also the farm of Erastus D Miner and the Simon Rhodes place, he built a house on the north side of the Indian path, now known as the old Post road, and there he lived the remainder of his life His wife Joannah, whom he married about 1637, died in 1685 Children Abigail, born about 1638 or 1639, James, mentioned below

(II) James (2) York, son of James (1) and Joannah York, was born June 14, 1648, and died October 26, 1676 He doubtless came to Stonington with his father when a boy, as his name is mentioned in several records before 1672 In that year he sold his estate in Boston, where he had been engaged in business, and settled in Stonington On January 15, 1667, one hundred acres of land were laid out to him, and he also received land for services in the Indian wars He was made freeman in Connecticut in 1673 He married, in Stonington, January 19, 1669, Deborah Bell, daughter of Thomas and Anne Bell She married (second) March 12, 1679, Henry Elliot, and had seven children Children of James and Deborah (Bell) York Deborah Bell, born January 8, 1670, died February 21, 1672; James, born December 17, 1672, William, July 26, 1674; Thomas, mentioned below

(III) Thomas York, youngest child of James (2) and Deborah (Bell) York, was born October 17, 1676, in Stonington, where he made his home, and married, January 3, 1704, Mary Brown, born there May 26, 1683, daughter of Thomas and Hannah (Collins) Brown Children William, born October 3, 1705, Mary, October 17, 1710, Thankful, April 23, 1712; Thomas, January 24, 1714, John, mentioned below, Joseph, January 22, 1718,

Deborah, January 13, 1720, Collins, 1722, Bell, 1725

(IV) John York, third son of Thomas and Mary (Brown) York, was born March 16, 1716, in Stonington, and married, July 30, 1743, Anna Brown, of that town Children John, born July 30, 1744, Anna, died young Anna, born July 17, 1755, Lucy, August 31, 1758, Lydia, mentioned below, Martha, April 17, 1762

(V) Lydia York, third daughter of John and Anna (Brown) York, was born December 28, 1760, in Stonington, and became the wife of Thomas (2) Miner, of that town (see Miner V)

(The Hewitt Line)

(I) Thomas Hewitt was in Stonington, Connecticut, as early as 1651, and was in command of a vessel owned by Thomas Miner, in 1656 He purchased land on the east side of Mystic river, where the Elm Grove Cemetery of Stonington is now located In 1662 he sailed for the West Indies with a cargo of live stock, and was never heard from again He married, April 26, 1659, Hannah, daughter of Walter Palmer, who came from Nottingham, England, resided for some time in Charlestown, Massachusetts, was later in Rehoboth, and finally purchased about twelve hundred acres in what is now Stonington, on which he resided until his death, November 19, 1661 His second wife, Rebecca (Short) Palmer, was the mother of Hannah, wife of Thomas Hewitt She married (second) December 27, 1671, Roger Sterry, and (third) as his second wife, John Fish Thomas Hewitt left two sons, Thomas, born May 20, 1660, and Benjamin, mentioned below

(II) Benjamin Hewitt, second son of Thomas and Hannah (Palmer) Hewitt, was born in 1662, in Stonington, and married there, September 24, 1683, Marie

223

Fanning, daughter of Edmund and Ellen Fanning Children Benjamin, born 1688, Israel, 1691, and Tabitha, all baptized July 24, 1692, Mary, baptized August 12, 1694, Joseph, December 13, 1696, Elkanah, mentioned below, Hannah, June 29, 1701, Henry, July 30, 1704, Content, April 3, 1708

(III) Elkanah Hewitt, third son of Benjamin and Marie (Fanning) Hewitt, was baptized May 7, 1699, in Stonington, where he lived, and married, in 1722, Temperance Keeney Children Elkanah, born May 10, 1723, Thankful, February 23, 1726, Sarah, March 26, 1729, Henry, mentioned below, Arthur, August 8, 1732, Tabitha, December 7, 1735, Jonas, November 2, 1737, Simeon, March 9, 1739

(IV) Henry Hewitt, second son of Elkanah and Temperance (Keeney) Hewitt, was born August 10, 1730, in Stonington, where he made his home He married (first) Sarah Keeney. He married (second) January 2, 1772, Phebe Prentice, born February 22, 1738, in Stonington, daughter of Deacon Samuel and Abigail (Billings) Prentice He married (third) Mrs Content Wheeler Palmer Children Joseph and Benjamin (twins), born August 8, 1774, Amos, November 14, 1776, Phebe, December 9, 1778, Prentice, married Peggy Brown

(V) Benjamin (2) Hewitt, son of Henry and Phebe (Prentice) Hewitt, was born August 8, 1774, in Stonington, and married Desire Babcock Children Desire, died young, Sarah, born January 17, 1802, Desire, mentioned below, Phebe, August 24, 1806, Emmilla, June 19, 1808, Benjamin Babcock, October 11, 1811, Joseph Denison, November 15, 1815, Mary Louise, April 13, 1818, Francis M, March 25, 1820

(VI) Desire Hewitt, third daughter of Benjamin (2) and Desire (Babcock) Hewitt, was born September 27, 1803, in

Stonington, and was married, October 9, 1823, to Deacon Ezra D Miner, of that town (see Miner VI).

MUNRO, William R,

Financier.

There seems to have been several of this name in and about Bristol, Rhode Island, probably brothers, including John, Thomas, William and George

(I) George Monroe lived in Bristol, Rhode Island, where he died September 9, 1744 The records are silent as to his birth, but he was probably born about 1655-58 His wife Mary was born 1670, as shown by the Bristol records, and died November 8, 1760, in that town. Children William, born December 24, 1701, Sarah, February 23, 1706, Benjamin, April 26, 1711, Simeon, mentioned below, Thomas, October 21, 1715

(II) Simeon Munroe, third son of George and Mary Monroe, was born July 30, 1713, in Bristol, in which town he made his home, and died May 23, 1789 He married (first) December 19, 1732, Rebecca Wardwell, born March 22, 1715, died September 28, 1761, daughter of James and Sarah Wardwell He married (second) January 31, 1762, Mrs Rachel Walker Children of first marriage Dorcas, born April 2, 1734, Rebecca April 30, 1736, Mary, November 20, 1738, William, March 30, 1741, Simeon, March 11, 1744, Achibald, mentioned below, Sarah, October 16, 1749

(III) Archibald Munroe, third son of Simeon and Rebecca (Wardwell) Munroe, was born November 11, 1746, in Bristol, where his home was, and where he died January 15, 1812 He married, November 28, 1769, Rebecca, daughter of Richard and Lucretia (Diman) Smith, born July 1, 1750, died November 3, 1827 Children Josiah, mentioned below,

Mary, September 24, 1779; George, January 7, 1782, Rebecca, February 2, 1784, Jeremiah, March 3, 1791.

(IV) Josiah Munroe, eldest child of Archibald and Rebecca (Smith) Munroe, was born April 5, 1771, in Bristol, and lived in that town and in Warren, Rhode Island. His wife's baptismal name was Sarah, and the following children are recorded in Warren: Rebecca, born September 28, 1794; Sarah, March 28, 1798, Mary Mason, June 11, 1799; Josiah Smith, September 24, 1805. It appears that Josiah Munroe had a second wife, Rebecca (Harding) Munroe, and John H. was probably their child.

(V) John H. Munroe, son of Josiah Munroe, as shown by family records, was born November 22, 1810, in Bristol, Rhode Island, and lived in that town, in Warren and in Fall River, Massachusetts. He was a tailor by trade, and conducted a mercantile business in Fall River, where he died March 24, 1876. He married Susan Ware.

(VI) Josiah (2) Munroe, son of John H. and Susan (Ware) Munroe, was born August 11, 1842, in Warren, Rhode Island, came to Fall River, Massachusetts, in his youth, and ever after made this city his home. Learning the tailor's trade with his father, he followed that as an occupation and business throughout life, and with that success that made him comfortable. He was for many years located in business on North Main street, nearly opposite the "Wilbur House," later removing to Bedford street, near Rock. He understood his trade thoroughly, was a good workman, and as a man and citizen was respected and esteemed. Mr. Munroe was a charter member of Fall River Lodge, Independent Order of Odd Fellows. He died of heart disease, July 6, 1904, at his home on Belmont street, Fall River, aged sixty-one

years, eleven months. He married, 1862, Helen J. Robertson, of Fall River, who survives him. She is a daughter of William S. and Harriet (Palmer) Robertson, the former from Renfrew, Scotland, the latter of Westport Harbor (see Palmer X). Children: William R., mentioned below; Josiah Frank, of Fall River; Harriet C., wife of George R. Mason, of Fall River, and they have one child, William Mason; Charlotte B., of Fall River; Mary A. T., who graduated from the Fall River High School in 1900, with high honors, winning the Davis medal for proficiency in study, and died October 27, 1902, at the age of twenty years.

(VII) William R. Munroe, eldest child of Josiah (2) and Helen J. (Robertson) Munroe, was born 1863, in Fall River, and in 1883 received the degree of B. M. from the B. M. C. Durfee High School. A short time after his graduation he traveled through various parts of the Middle West, locating in Florence, Kansas. Here he was first employed unloading brick near the railroad station, and by his industry and thrift came to be agent for the Atchison, Topeka & Santa Fe railroad, a position which he held for twenty-three years. During that time he had been transferred to the Carbondale agency for the same railroad, but returned to Florence. Eight years ago Mr. Munroe retired from active participation in railroad affairs and devoted his energies to the organization of the Florence State Bank, and has been largely instrumental in making that institution one of the strong banks of Marion county, Kansas. In 1915 he was elected president of the Railroad Building Loan and Savings Association, of Newton, Kansas, one of the largest home building institutions in the West. Mr. Munroe married (first) Adina Belle Reid, (second) Elizabeth Playford

The name Palmer was originally a common title of those who had returned from the Holy Land, and brought back, as a token and remembrance of their pilgrimage, a palm branch. Thus in Marmion, Canto I, xxiii:

From Salem first, and last from Rome
Here is a holy Palmer come,

Certain returned Crusaders, as a recognition of their merit, were knighted and allowed to assume this title as a surname. It is a common name in England, and there were several representatives of it in New England previous to 1635.

(I) William Palmer, the first American immigrant of the name, came to this country in the ship 'Fortune" with his son William in 1621, and was followed two years later by his wife Frances in the ship "Anne." He settled in Plymouth. His land was in what was later set off as Duxbury. There he lived and died. His will was dated December 4, 1636, and proved March 5 following, it mentions "young wife Rebecca." By his second wife he had a son Henry and a daughter Bridget. His land in Duxbury was sold in 1638 to John Bissell.

(II) William (2) Palmer, son of William (1) Palmer, was born in England, and died in Plymouth before his father. He married, in Scituate, March 27, 1633, Elizabeth Hodgkins. After his death his widow married (second) John Willis. She sued the executors of the will of William (1) Palmer, because she had been the wife of William (2) Palmer, for a share in the former's estate, but it was denied her.

(III) William (3) Palmer, son of William (2) and Elizabeth (Hodgkins) Palmer, was born June 27, 1634. He married a daughter of Robert Paddock, of Plymouth, who died early. He settled in Dartmouth, of which he was one of the first

purchasers, and died in 1679, previous to June 3d. He left a widow, whose name was Susannah, a tradition makes her a Hathaway, at any rate, Arthur Hathaway was joined with her in the administration of her husband's estate. He left children, including William, mentioned below, and John.

(IV) William (4) Palmer, son of William (3) and Susannah Palmer, born 1663, lived in Little Compton, Rhode Island, where he married, in 1685, Mary Richmond, born 1668, probably daughter of Edward and Amy (Bull) Richmond. Children: William, born January 17, 1686; Elizabeth, November 12, 1687, married Henry (2) Head (see Head II), Joseph, June 19, 1689; Susanna, October 24, 1692; John, mentioned below; Thomas, January 7, 1697; Mary, January 10, 1699; Benjamin, November 3, 1700; Abigail, April 5, 1702; Patience, February 19, 1704; Sylvanus, May 2, 1706; Peleg, March 18, 1708.

(V) John Palmer, third son of William (4) and Mary (Richmond) Palmer, was born November 19, 1694, in Little Compton, and lived in that town and in Dartmouth, Massachusetts. He married, February 23, 1716, in Little Compton, Alice Shaw, born there November 17, 1695, daughter of Israel Shaw. Children: Peleg, born November 21, 1716; Bathsheba, June 4, 1718; Judith, March 28, 1719; Dudley, September 13, 1720; Alice, January 15, 1722, died young; Elizabeth, October 1, 1723; Alice, October 15, 1725; Benjamin, February 4, 1728; John, mentioned below; Perez, 1733.

(VI) John (2) Palmer, fourth son of John (1) and Alice (Shaw) Palmer, was born September 22, 1731, in Little Compton, and there married, November 7, 1767, Mary Stoddard, of that town, born October 4, 1732, daughter of Jonathan and Mary (Dring) Stoddard.

(VII) John (3) Palmer, son of John

(2) and Mary (Stoddard) Palmer, resided in Little Compton, and married Margaret, daughter of William and Sarah (Brownell) Macomber, of Westport, Massachusetts In 1806 John Palmer, Jr, deeded to his sons, Gideon and Dudley, his farm, and they in the same year leased it to their father

(VIII) Gideon Palmer, son of John (3) and Margaret (Macomber) Palmer, was born in Westport, October 4, 1774, and married in Little Compton, in 1806, Lois Head, born there April 9, 1787, daughter of Daniel and Hannah (Davenport) Head (see Head VI) Children Betsey, mentioned below, Deborah Ann, born February 13, 1810, married Philip Grinnell, of Westport; Gideon, February 3, 1812, died in Fall River, Cordelia, April 25, 1814, married a Brightman, Almira, April 21, 1816, Thomas Davenport, October 10, 1818, was lost at sea, Lorinda, January 19, 1821, Harriet, mentioned below, George Seabury, born February 28, 1825, and Julia Ann, born August 4, 1826, who died aged ten years Gideon Palmer, the father, died July 4, 1840, in Fall River, and his widow passed away June 13, 1860, at Westport.

(IX) Betsey Palmer, eldest child of Gideon and Lois (Head) Palmer, was born December 6, 1806, and married Edward Jennings, of Fall River

(IX) Harriet Palmer, daughter of Gideon and Lois (Head) Palmer, born February 10, 1823, married William S Robertson, who came from Renfrew, Scotland

(X) Helen J Robertson, daughter of William S and Harriet (Palmer) Robertson, was married, in 1862, to Josiah (2) Munroe, of Fall River, Massachusetts (see Munroe VI)

(The Head Line)

(I) Henry Head, born 1647, as shown by the records of Little Compton, Rhode Island, died in that town, July 1, 1716 He was representative to the Plymouth Court in 1683, and for several years afterward, and on the consolidation of the Massachusetts Bay and Plymouth colonies, he was representative to the General Court at Boston in 1692 He married in 1677, Elizabeth Pabodie, born 1654, died June, 1748, according to the records of Little Compton She was a daughter of William Pabodie, and his wife Elizabeth, daughter of John Alden, of the Mayflower Colony Children Jonathan, born 1678, Henry, mentioned below; Ebenezer, 1682, Mary, 1684, Innocent, 1686, Benjamin, 1687, died August 6, 1717

(II) Henry (2) Head, second son of Henry (1) and Elizabeth (Pabodie) Head, was born 1680, and died March 4, 1755 He married, June 29, 1708, Elizabeth Palmer, born November 12, 1687, daughter of William (4) and Mary (Richmond) Palmer, of Little Compton (see Palmer IV) Children Henry, mentioned below, Abigail, born December 24, 1710, Mary, April 16, 1712, Innocent, March 13, 1713, Lovet, September 27, 1714, Elizabeth, March 21, 1716, Benjamin, September 17, 1718, died March, 1796, William, July 12, 1721, Deborah, January 16, 1725, Amey, May 15, 1727

(III) Henry (3) Head, eldest child of Henry (2) and Elizabeth (Palmer) Head, was born November 7, 1709, in Little Compton He married, in June, 1730, Anna Paddock, born in Swansea, Massachusetts Children Jonathan, mentioned below, Joseph, born September 11, 1733, John, August 5, 1736, Deborah, April 13, 1739

(IV) Jonathan Head, eldest son of Henry (3) and Anna (Paddock) Head, was born May 31, 1731, in Little Compton, and settled in Dartmouth, Massachusetts, where he was probably a farmer He was a soldier of the Revolution, served as a private in Captain William Hicks'

(Dartmouth) company, Colonel Pope's regiment, marched December 7, 1777, served sixteen days He married in Little Compton, October 21, 1760, Ruth Little, born in that town, April 2, 1742, daughter of Forbes and Sarah Little, granddaughter of John and Constance (Fobes) Little, and great-granddaughter of William and Martha (Pabodie) Fobes, daughter of William Pabodie. Children Joseph, born February 14, 1762, Forbes, April 9, 1763, Daniel, mentioned below, Lydia, December 19, 1769, Jonathan, May 1, 1774, Ruth, October 10, 1776

(V) Daniel Head, third son of Jonathan and Ruth (Little) Head, was born March 29, 1765, in Dartmouth, and lived in Little Compton, where he was married, January 1, 1787, by Adam Simmons, justice, to Hannah Davenport, born April 26, 1764, died March 17, 1844, daughter of Thomas and Deborah (Simmons) Davenport, of that town (see Davenport VI) Deborah Simmons, wife of Thomas (3) Davenport, was the daughter of John and Comfort (Shaw) Simmons, the last named a daughter of Israel Shaw. John Simmons was a son of William and Abigail (Church) Simmons, the last named a daughter of Joseph and Mary (Butler) Church. Joseph Church was a son of Richard Church, whose wife, Mary (Warren) Church, was a daughter of Richard Warren, of the "Mayflower" William Pabodie, who married Elizabeth Alden, had a daughter, Martha Pabodie, who became the wife of William Fobes (or Forbes), whose daughter, Constance Fobes or Forbes, married John Little, and was the mother of Forbes Little, who is supposed to have married Sarah Wilcox, and was the father of Ruth Little, wife of Jonathan Head, of Dartmouth Thus there are two lines of descent from John Alden and Priscilla Mullins Daniel and Hannah (Davenport) Head had chil-

dren Lois, mentioned below, Sarah, born November 30, 1789, married Humphrey Brownell; Abel, November 30, 1791; Deborah, October 28, 1794, Ruth, February 10, 1797, Lydia, November 10, 1798; Betsey, October 17, 1800, Hannah Phillips, April 4, 1803

(VI) Lois Head, eldest child of Daniel and Hannah (Davenport) Head, was born April 9, 1787, in Little Compton, and married, 1806, Gideon Palmer, of Westport, Massachusetts (see Palmer VIII)

(The Davenport Line)

(I) Thomas Davenport was a member of the Dorchester church, November 20, 1640, was a freeman, May 18, 1642, and served the town as constable in 1670 He purchased a house and lands, November 25, 1653, and his residence was on the east slope of Mount Bowdoin, near the corner of the present Union avenue and Bowdoin street, Dorchester He purchased additional lands, February 5, 1665 After his death, which occurred November 9, 1685, an inventory of his estate was made, amounting to 332 pounds, 16 shillings and 8 pence His wife Mary joined the Dorchester church, March 8, 1644 She survived him nearly six years, dying October 4, 1691 Children · Sarah, born December 28, 1643, Thomas, baptized March 2, 1645, Mary, January 21, 1649; Charles, September 7, 1652; Abigail, July 8, 1655, Mehitable, born February 14, 1657, Jonathan, mentioned below, Ebenzer, April 26, 1661, John, October 20, 1664

(II) Jonathan Davenport, third son of Thomas and Mary Davenport, was born March 6, 1659, in Dorchester, and settled in Little Compton, Rhode Island He married there, December 1, 1680, Hannah Warren Children Thomas, mentioned below, Jonathan, born November 3, 1684, died October 14, 1751; Hannah,

December 23, 1686, Simeon, December 27, 1688, died December 8, 1763, Ebenezer, September 2, 1691, died August 4, 1776; John, January 12, 1694, died April 20, 1741, Joseph, March 25, 1696, died September 2, 1760, Benjamin, October 6, 1698, Sarah, December 10, 1700

(III) Thomas (2) Davenport, eldest child of Jonathan and Hannah (Warren) Davenport, was born December 10, 1681, and married (first) June 20, 1704, Catharine Woodworth, born 1673, died June 1, 1729, daughter of Walter Woodworth. He married (second) Mary Pittman Children of first marriage Eliphalet, mentioned below, Mary, born February 8, 1707, Ephraim, December 25, 1708; Deborah, December 12, 1710, Hannah, October 27, 1712, Oliver, February 5, 1714 Of second marriage Gideon, June 7, 1738, Susannah, January 24, 1740

(IV) Eliphalet Davenport, eldest child of Thomas (2) and Catharine (Woodworth) Davenport, was born May 7, 1705, and married (first) Hannah Phillips, born 1707, died January 9, 1738 He married (second) Ann Devol Children of first marriage Catharine, born 1729, died 1806, Deedy, 1727, died young, Deedy, 1732, Thomas, mentioned below Of second marriage Hannah, born 1742, Phebe, 1744, Eliphalet, 1748, died January 21, 1812; Jonathan, 1750; Judith, 1753; Ruth, 1755, Caleb, 1757

(V) Thomas (3) Davenport, son of Eliphalet and Hannah (Phillips) Davenport, was born May 15, 1735, in Little Compton, and died October 28, 1820 He married, December 3, 1761, Deborah Simmons, born October 13, 1736, died January 8, 1809, daughter of John and Comfort (Shaw) Simmons, of Little Compton (see Simmons VI) Children Hannah, mentioned below; Deborah, born February, 1767, Lois, August, 1768

(VI) Hannah Davenport, eldest child

of Thomas (3) and Deborah (Simmons) Davenport, was born April 26, 1764, in Little Compton, and married there, January 1, 1787, Daniel Head (see Head V)

(The Simmons Line)

(I) Moses Simonson, or Symonson, a native of Leyden, Holland, came to Plymouth, Massachusetts, in the ship "Fortune," in 1621, and settled at Duxbury, near Plymouth His father was a communicant of the Dutch church at Leyden, and Moses was one of the "purchasers," which entitled him to admission to the Plymouth church in this country, where his children were baptized He was made a freeman in 1634, and served three years later as a juryman In 1638 he received a grant of land in addition to one previously made He had sons, Moses and Thomas

(II) Moses (2) Simmons, son of Moses (1) Simonson, or Simmons, as the name very quickly was rendered by the English-speaking people, resided in Duxbury, where he died in 1689 He had a wife Sarah and children John, Aaron, Mary, Elizabeth and Sarah, all of whom married and reared families

(III) John Simmons, son of Moses (2) and Sarah Simmons, married, about 1670, Mercy Pabodie, born January 2, 1649, daughter of William and Elizabeth (Alden) Pabodie The last named was a daughter of John and Priscilla (Mullens) Alden, of the "Mayflower," and their descendants are all eligible to the Society of Mayflower Descendants Children John, born February 22, 1671 William, mentioned below; Isaac, January 28, 1674, Martha November 1677

(IV) William Simmons, second son of John and Mercy (Pabodie) Simmons, was born September 24, 1672, in Duxbury, and joined the movement from that town which was largely instrumental in the settlement of Little Compton, then in Massachusetts, now a part of Rhode Island. He married, in 1696, Abigail, born 1680, daughter of Joseph and Mary (Tucker) Church. She died July 4, 1720, and was survived for about forty-five years by her husband, who died in 1765. Children: Mercy, born July 1, 1697, William, September 30, 1699; Lydia, December 15, 1700, Joseph, March 4, 1702, John, mentioned below, Abigail, July 14, 1706. Rebecca, May 8, 1708, Mary, October 15, 1709, Benjamin, February 21, 1713, Ichabod, January 6, 1715, Peleg, December 21, 1716. Sarah, August 26, 1718.

(V) John Simmons, third son of William and Abigail (Church) Simmons, was born August 14, 1704, and died in Little Compton, March 8, 1774. He married Comfort Shaw, born August 9, 1709, died May, 1785, daughter of Israel Shaw. Children: Phebe, born December 28, 1728, died April 24, 1730; Sarah, January 26, 1730, Zarah, October 13, 1731, Ichabod, November 28, 1732, died February 8, 1756, Deborah, mentioned below, Ezekiel July 25, 1740; John, August 26, 1741, Comfort, October 28, 1743; Elizabeth, October 14, 1745, died 1747; Rachel, November 30, 1751; Lydia, March 1, 1753.

(VI) Deborah Simmons, fourth daughter of John and Comfort (Shaw) Simmons, was born October 13, 1736, died January 8, 1809, and married, December 3, 1761, Thomas (3) Davenport (see Davenport V)

GUITERAS,

And Allied Families

The first of the direct line of whom we have authentic information, Mateo Guiteras, was a native of the town of Canet Le Mar, and a member of a family long established and prominent in the Province of Catalonia, in Spain. Canet Le

Mar is to-day a town of note in Catalonia, which borders on the historic and famous province of Toledo, and in the time of Mateo Guiteras was a flourishing center of trade.

Guiteras Arms, Spain—Vert. five greyhounds' heads, erased proper, vulned, and distilling drops of blood gules, posed two, one and two.

Of the character of Mateo Guiteras and of his immediate family, we can only form a vague yet satisfying opinion, from the career and subsequent achievements of his son, Ramon Guiteras. From the position which the latter occupied in Cuba, it is entirely lawful to assume that he came of a strong, progressive, and intellectually as well as practically able stock. Mateo Guiteras passed his entire life in Spain, where he died.

He married Maria de Molines, also a member of an honorable and historically noted family, and a native of Canet Le Mar. They were the parents of Ramon Guiteras, mentioned below.

De Molines Arms—Azure a cross moline or quarter pierced of the field
Crest—A Saracen's head affrontee couped below the shoulders proper, wreathed about the temples
Supporters—Two lions collared and ducally crowned
Motto—Vivere sat vincere

(II) Ramon Guiteras, son of Mateo and Maria (de Molines) Guiteras, was born in the town of Canet Le Mar, Province of Catalonia, Spain, where he spent the early portion of his life. In young manhood he left Spain, however, and went to Cuba, where he later became a noted merchant. He was representative of a type of dynamic, forceful, tirelessly energetic business man, characteristic more of the twentieth century than indigenous to Spain and the Spanish provinces of his day. Ramon Guiteras was

the founder of many notable enterprises, among them a flour mill, a bakery, and an extensive coffee estate In the course of a long and successful business career he amassed a considerable fortune, and died possessed of much valuable property.

He married Gertrudis Font, a native of Canet Le Mar, who accompanied him to Cuba They resided at Matanzas, Cuba, where their son, Ramon (2), was born

Font Arms Catalonia Spain—Azure a fountain composed of a basin standing in another basin, spouting four jets of water all argent

(III) Ramon (2) Guiteras, son of Ramon (1) and Gertrudis (Font) Guiteras, was born at Matanzas, Cuba, August 4, 1811 At the age of four years he was taken by his father to Spain, on account of political uprisings in Cuba. On his return to Cuba he received an excellent and comprehensive educational training, and became especially proficient in languages, developing great linguistic ability Ramon Guiteras subsequently traveled extensively in Europe, spending four years at Barcelona, Spain, and in America

He married, in Bristol, Rhode Island, September 27, 1853, Elizabeth Manchester Wardwell, daughter of Benjamin (3) and Elizabeth (Manchester) Wardwell (See Wardwell VI) After his marriage, Ramon Guiteras made his home in Bristol, retaining, however, a few of his interests in Cuba, a small portion of the original estate of his father He died February 13, 1873 The children of Ramon (2) and Elizabeth Manchester (Wardwell) Guiteras were 1 Gertrude Elizabeth Guiteras, born March 2, 1855, who resides in Bristol, Rhode Island 2 Ramon Guiteras, M D, of whom further

(IV) Ramon (3) Guiteras, M. D., was born in Bristol, Rhode Island, August 17, 1858, the son of Ramon (2) and Elizabeth

Manchester (Wardwell) Guiteras, he was a grandson of Benjamin (3) Wardwell, and in honor of his grandfather bore the name Ramon Benjamin Guiteras in early life He received his elementary education in the schools of Bristol, and after attending the Alexander Military Institute at White Plains, New York, for one year, became a student in Mowry & Goff's English and Classical School in Providence, where he prepared for college in part Completing his preparation at Joshua Kendall's school at Cambridge, he matriculated at Harvard At the end of a two-year course he went to Europe, where he devoted a year and a half to acquiring a knowledge of Spanish and French In 1880 he returned to America and entered the Harvard Medical School, from which he was graduated in 1883 with the degree of Doctor of Medicine. He then went to Vienna, Austria, studying medicine there in the university, which at that time was the finest in the world. This was followed by a period of six months at the University of Berlin, at the end of which time he returned to New York, where he took the naval medical examination for the post of assistant surgeon. He passed this severe test with the highest honors in the class, and immediately on receiving his appointment resigned, having taken it merely to test his ability Dr Guiteras then entered Blackwell's Island Hospital, where he spent a year and a half At the end of this time he established himself in general practice in New York City. At a later date, however, he confined his work solely to kidney and intestinal diseases, and is to-day one of the foremost and most notable surgeons in this branch of medical science in the United States

Dr. Guiteras is very prominent in the medical profession in New York He is a member of the Columbus Hospital staff

231

and is secretary of the Pan-American Medical Association, and member of the New York Medical Association, and of the American Medical Association. He is well known in club life in New York City, and is a member of the Players' Club, the New York Athletic Club, the Harvard Club and the Union Club.

Dr Guiteras is a lover of outdoor sport, a hunter of great skill, and has twice been into the interior of Africa for big game On his first trip, from which he returned about 1900, he was accompanied by Dr Louis Livingston Semon, well known surgeon of New York, and his wife. Two years later he made another trip, this time returning with handsome trophies.

Dr Guiteras is unmarried, and makes his home in New York. His office is located at No 80 Madison avenue, New York City

(The Wardwell Line)

Arms—Argent on a bend between six martlets sable three bezants

Crest—A lion's gamb holding a spear, tasseled or

Motto—*Avito viret honore*

The surname Wardwell had its origin in the medieval institution of 'watch and ward," which at one time flourished in England Early ancestors of the family in England may actually have been those who kept the "watch and ward," or guardians of the peace and safety of the towns of the realm, or they may merely have been residents in the vicinity of the watch towers The family in England attained high rank and great power and influence in the early part of the dominion of the Normans in England, and is traced in a direct line to a member of the train of William the Conqueror, who in return for his services was given extensive estates under the feudal system in Westmoreland When the adoption of sur-

names spread among the upper classes, this noble, following an almost universal custom assumed the name of Wardell, or Wardwell, from an old watch tower or watch hill which stood on his estate on the northern borders of Westmoreland Here signals were given to Moothy Beacon on any inroad of the fierce Scotch tribes of the borderland The Wardwell family maintained its prestige and prominence in England through intervening centuries down to the period of colonial immigration

In the early part of the colonial period the American branch of the family was planted in New England by one William Wardwell, or Wardell The family early assumed a place of distinction and prominence among our early colonial families, and to the present day has not relinquished but has added to the prestige of a time-honored name The Wardwells of New England have played a notable part in the development of its life The name is found with frequency and in the high places in the annals of our military and naval achievements, and in the history of the professions, business, finance, and the industries Bristol, Rhode Island, has been the home of the branch of the Wardwell family herein under consideration for two and a half centuries From this branch sprang the following men whose names are notable in the history of Rhode Island affairs Benjamin Wardwell, Colonel Samuel Wardwell, Colonel Hezekiah Church Wardwell, Hon William T C Wardwell, and Hon Samuel D Wardwell

(I) William Wardwell or Wardell, immigrant ancestor and American progenitor, was a descendant of the ancient Norman family above mentioned He emigrated from England early in the third decade of the seventeenth century, and is first of record in the New England colo-

nies in 1634, when his name appears on
the records of the church at Boston; on
February 9 of that year he became a member of the church, about a year after his
arrival in Boston. William Wardwell
was later one of those who with their
families were turned out of the old Boston Second Church with Wheelwright,
and accompanied him to Exeter, New
Hampshire, before going to Ipswich,
Massachusetts, where they finally settled.
He returned to Boston, however, where
his first wife was buried and where he
married his second wife, who assisted him
in conducting the old Hollis Inn.

He married (first) Alice ——; (second) December 5, 1657, Elizabeth widow
of John Gillet or Jillett. Among his children was Uzal, mentioned below.

(II) Uzal Wardwell, son of William
and Alice Wardwell, was born April 7,
1639, and died October 25, 1732. He married (first) in Ipswich, Massachusetts,
May 3, 1664, Mary Ring, widow of Daniel
Ring, and daughter of Robert and Mary
(Bordman) Kinsman, of Ipswich, where
she died. He married (second) Grace
—— who died May 9, 1741, it is possible that this marriage was recorded some-
where between Ipswich and Bristol,
Rhode Island, and that the first three
children were born there; nothing has
been found on the identity of Grace, second wife of Uzal Wardwell. His will,
dated January 10, 1728, mentions wife
Grace, daughters Mary Barker, Grace
Giddens, Sarah Bosworth Alice Gladding, Abigail Greene, Hannah Crompton;
sons Uzal, James, Joseph, William, Benjamin. The will of Mrs Grace Wardwell,
dated October 19, 1733 mentions her eldest son Uzal, daughter Grace Giddens,
sons James and Joseph; Benjamin, deceased.

Children of the first marriage: 1 Abi-
gail, born October 27, 1665, married John
Green 2 Hannah, born 1667, married
—— Crompton 3 Alice, born Decem-
ber 27, 1670, married, October 31, 1693,
John Gladding, Jr
Children of the second marriage 4
Mary 5 Uzal 6 Grace, married Joseph
Giddens (Giddings), and died May 1,
1768, aged ninety years 7 Sarah, born in
1682, in Bristol, Rhode Island; married
Nathaniel Bosworth, Jr 8 James, born
June 30, 1684 in Bristol 9. Joseph, born
July 30, 1686, in Bristol 10 Benjamin, of
whom further 11 William, born May
3, 1693, in Bristol 12 Rebecca, twin of
William

(III) Benjamin Wardwell, son of Uzal
and Grace Wardwell, was born April 19,
1688, and died in June, 1739 He married
(first) Mary ——, who died May 2,
1733. He married (second) January 17,
1734, Mrs. Elizabeth Holmes, of Norton,
Massachusetts, who died June 6, 1737
Children of the first marriage 1 Mary,
married, in 1731, Nathaniel Turner 2
Uzal, married in November, 1739, Sarah
Lindsey, who died in 1745, at Cape
Breton, and he died there September 17,
1745 3 Jonathan, died in May 1745, at
Cape Breton. 4 Benjamin, died in June,
1739, lost at sea 5 Benjamin, of whom
further 6 Isaac, born in 1730, married
in September, 1756, Sarah Waldron, and
died May 7, 1810, at Bristol. 7 Olive,
married, June 19, 1753, John Goddard, of
Newport, Rhode Island

(IV) William (2) Wardwell, son of
Benjamin and Mary Wardwell, was born
in 1722, at Bristol, Rhode Island He was
a large landowner and prominent member
of the community William Wardwell
married, September 26, 1742, Mary Howland, daughter of Samuel Howland, and
granddaughter of Jabez Howland, son of
John Howland, the Pilgrim Their children, all born in Bristol, were 1 William, born January 8, 1743-44 2 Abigail,

baptized June 9, 1745 3 Mary, born October 25, 1747 4 William, born January 28, 1749-50 5 Benjamin, of whom further 6 Sarah, born March 3, 1754 7 Martha, born June 29, 1755 8 Samuel, born May 25, 1760

(V) Benjamin (2) Wardwell, son of William (2) and Mary (Howland) Wardwell, was born in Bristol, Rhode Island, and baptized there, February 9, 1753 He was a lifelong resident of the town, and a highly respected and prosperous citizen

He married (first) June 8, 1773, Sarah Smith, who died November 20, 1779 He married (second) November 19, 1780, Katherine Glover, daughter of Captain Joseph and Elizabeth (Bass) Glover, of Braintree, Massachusetts, who died January 14, 1803 He married (third) January 15, 1804, Mrs Huldah (Goff) Wheeler, daughter of Joseph and Patience Goff.

Children of the first marriage 1 William, born April 19, 1776; died April 21, of the same year 2 Lucretia, born May 30, 1777, married, June 17, 1798, John Sabin, and died September 11, 1811 3 Sarah, born November 11, 1779, married Nathaniel Church, and died February 21, 1861

Children of the second marriage 4 Polly, born October 4, 1781, died December 12, 1781 5 Polly, born August 30, 1783, died September 23, 1783 6 Benjamin, of whom further 7 Polly, born August 13, 1785, died September 22, 1787 8 William, born October 4, 1786, died September 22, 1787 9 Henry, born April 7, 1789, died October 12, 1789 10 Polly, born October 24, 1791 11 Katherine Glover, born July 8, 1793, died April 1, 1863 12 Francis, born in September, 1794, died July 25, 1796

(VI) Benjamin (3) Wardwell, son of Benjamin (2) and Katherine (Glover) Wardwell, was born August 24, 1784, in

the town of Bristol, Rhode Island He received his education in the public schools of his native town, and early in life entered the leather business He subsequently engaged in the grocery business, and for more than fifty years conducted an establishment in a building which formerly stood on the east side of Thames street, south of State street, Bristol. He was a leader in business life in the town, and was highly successful in business affairs, strictly upright and fair in all his dealings, he was recognized as a man of sterling worth, and was highly respected in Bristol, where he died September 12, 1871, at the venerable age of eighty-seven years Benjamin Wardwell was a member of the Congregational Church of Bristol, and a strict observer of the Sabbath, a man of deep religious convictions, bound up in his church

Benjamin (3) Wardwell married, January 14, 1807, Elizabeth Manchester, of Little Compton, Rhode Island, where she was born, daughter of Zebedee and Deborah Manchester She was baptized in the Congregational Church of Bristol July 31, 1810. Children:

1 Henry, of whom further
2 Benjamin, born August 9, 1809, died May 31, 1885, married, February 2, 1836, Eliza Cook, who was born February 18, 1810, and died April 27, 1860, they were the parents of one daughter 1 Eleanor, born in December, 1840, married, in 1869, Joseph Burr Bartram
3 George, born September 2, 1810; died October 11, 1810
4 A son, born September 12, 1812, died same day
5 A daughter, twin of the son, died same day
6 Jeremiah, born December 7, 1813 died in December, 1881; married (first) June 19, 1844, Mary Jane Sturgis, daughter of Lathrop L Sturgis, of New York, she died October 3, 1860; he married (second) November 18, 1865, Mrs Eliza B Ingraham, daughter of William Fel-

lows, of Staten Island, New York; children of first marriage 1 William Henry, born March 29, 1846, married, in December, 1881, Virginia Sniffin 11 Theodore Sturgis, born June 13, 1848 111 Richard Patrick, born April 17, 1852, married Anna Oaks Woodworth 1v Mary, born April 16, 1855, died July 22, 1855 v Helen, born September 6, 1857, married William Brown Glover v1 Jane Elizabeth, born August 17, 1859, married Charles Potter, who died in November, 1904

7 Elizabeth Manchester, born March 7, 1816, died January 18, 1826

8 A daughter, born September 2, 1817, died September 4, 1817

9 A daughter, twin, died September 12, 1817

10 Adam Manchester, born November 6, 1818, baptized March 29, 1819, died January 23, 1827

11 George William, born March 14 1821, died August 16, 1821

12 Catherine Glover, born May 28, 1822, died October 31, 1894

13 Marianne, born October 6, 1825

14 Elizabeth Manchester, born November 6, 1827, married, September 27, 1853, Ramon Guiteras, of Matanzas, Cuba, who was born August 4, 1811, and died February 13, 1873, at the age of four years Ramon Guiteras was taken by his father to Spain on account of political troubles, he later returned to Cuba, where he was given an excellent education at Matanzas, Cuba, and became an able linguist, speaking several languages, he traveled extensively on the continent and in America, and spent four years at Barcelona, Spain Ramon Guiteras disposed of practically all his holdings in Cuba, although retaining a few interests there, he resided in Bristol, Rhode Island, after his marriage; children 1 Gertrude Elizabeth Guiteras, born March 2, 1855 Miss Guiteras resides at the family home in Bristol, Rhode Island She is prominent in the life of Bristol, and well known for her charitable activities She is a woman of great culture and refinement, widely traveled, and possesses the broad tolerance and sympathy of the true cosmopolitan 11 Ramon Guiteras, M D, born August 17, 1858, a specialist of note in New York City (q v)

(VII) Henry Wardwell, son of Benjamin (3) Wardwell and Elizabeth (Manchester) Wardwell, was born March 17, 1808, in Bristol, Rhode Island, and died October 2 1875 He was reared and educated in his native city, attending the school of Mr Alden, who was considered one of the best masters of that day In his seventeenth year Mr Wardwell secured employment as clerk with Benjamin Hall, of Bristol, his store being located on the corner of Thames and State streets, and when twenty-five years of age he bought the business from Mr Hall, who retired at that time He handled groceries and the produce of the farmer, which he sent to the West Indies This business he conducted for twenty-eight years, or until he was fifty-three years of age He made his start by buying potatoes and onions, consigning this produce to steamers engaged in the coastwise trade, the cargoes were disposed of in Cuban ports, and the proceeds used to purchase molasses, which was brought to Bristol, to Mr Wardwell, who disposed of it in Rhode Island markets During this time Mr Wardwell became interested in from ten to fourteen vessels, and continued to engage in the West Indies trade and whaling business for many years He was a man of great energy and fine business ability, self-made in the best sense of the word, and honorable and just in all his dealings Shortly after the close of the Civil War he was compelled to retire from active business life, by failing health He was at one time director in the old Pocanock Cotton Mill, and filled the same post in the Eagle, Freeman's and First National Banks for more than thirty years, he was also a trustee of the Bristol Institution for Savings, from the time of its founding until his death

Although he eschewed public life entirely, Mr Wardwell was deeply interested in the welfare of Bristol, and was

235

prominent in its life He was highly respected in business and in social circles, and was an earnest worker in behalf of the Congregational church, of which he was treasurer for many years He was a gifted singer, and for more than thirty years was director of the choir of the Congregational church His political affiliation was with the Republican party

Henry Wardwell married, November 11, 1835 Sarah Luther Lindsay, who died November 8, 1890, daughter of Thomas and Rhoda Lindsay They were the parents of eight children as follows 1 Benjamin, born May 6, 1836, died the same day 2 Sophia Lindsay, born May 3, 1838, unmarried, resides in Bristol 3 Annie Elizabeth, born August 9, 1840; died November 18, 1866 4 Sarah Frances, born January 25, 1843; married William H Bourne, now deceased; she is residing in Bristol 5 Harriet Parker, born July 4, 1845, unmarried; residing in Bristol 6 Isabella Mein, born January 12, 1848, unmarried, residing in Bristol 7 Henry Adam, born August 26, 1850; died February 18, 1853 8 Henry Irenius, born July 15, 1853; died June 29, 1854

(The Manchester Line)

Manchester Arms—Quarterly, first and fourth argent, three lozenges conjoined in fess gules within a bordure sable Second and third, or an eagle displayed vert, beaked and membered gules
Crest—A griffin's head couped wings expanded or, gorged with a collar argent charged with three lozenges gules
Supporters—Dexter a heraldic antelope or armed, tufted and hoofed argent. Sinister a griffin or, gorged with a collar, as the crest
Motto—Disponendo me, non mutando me (By disposing of me, not changing me)

I homas Manchester, the immigrant ancestor of this notable Rhode Island family, was born in England and was a resident of New Haven, Connecticut, in the year following the planting of the colony,

1639. Afterward, however, he settled at Portsmouth, Rhode Island, where he is first mentioned in the land records January 25, 1655, when he and his wife sold to Thomas Wood twelve acres of land He married Margaret, daughter of John Wood, who under her father's will received eight pounds, which it was ordered, March 17, 1655, John Wood pay to his sister, Margaret Manchester Eight acres of land were granted at Portsmouth, to Thomas Manchester, December 10, 1657, and July 6, 1658, he sold to Richard Sisson one-three-hundredth right in Canonicut and Dutch Islands He and his wife testified June 7, 1686, that they heard and saw Ichabod Sheffield married by William Baulstone many years before. He deeded to his son John, July 9. 1691, his mansion house and all lands at Portsmouth, except the piece at the lower end of the ground, in possession of his son Thomas, one-half to be his at the death of the grantor and the other half after the death of the grantor's wife, mother of the grantee, provided he pay to the sons Thomas, William and Stephen ten shillings each, to Job twenty shillings, and daughters Mary and Elizabeth ten shillings each. He also deeded to his son John all his personal property, including cattle, chattels, implements, bonds, sums of money and whatever belonged to him at the time of his decease. Thomas Manchester died in 1691, and his wife in 1693

Their children were 1 Thomas, born about 1650, died after 1718, prominent citizen of Portsmouth, Rhode Island 2 William, born in 1654, died in 1718 married Mary Cook, daughter of John and Mary (Borden) Cook; William Manchester, then of Puncatest and seven others, bought of Governor Josiah Winslow lands at Pocasset for £100 There were thirty shares, of which he had five March 2, 1692, he was an inhabitant of Tiverton,

Rhode Island, when that town was organized 3 John, freeman in 1677, died in 1708 4 George, admitted a freeman in 1684. 5 Stephen, freeman in 1684, died in 1719, married (first) Elizabeth Wodell, daughter of Gershom and Mary (Tripp) Wodell, (second) Damaris ———, who died in 1719, he was a resident of Tiverton at the time of the founding of the town 6. Job, died in 1713, married Hannah ——— 7 Mary 8 Elizabeth.

For more than two hundred years the Manchester family has been identified with Tiverton and the surrounding towns of Newport county, Rhode Island Elizabeth Manchester, who became the wife of Benjamin (3) Wardwell, of Bristol, Rhode Island, was a member of this old family She was the daughter of Zebedee and Deborah Manchester, and granddaughter of Archer and Elizabeth Manchester, of Little Compton

Elizabeth Manchester was born in the town of Little Compton, Rhode Island, and was baptized July 31, 1810, in the Congregational church of Bristol, daughter of Zebedee and Deborah (Briggs) Manchester She married January 14, 1807, Benjamin (3) Wardwell (See Wardwell VI)

Briggs Arms—Argent three escutcheons gules, each charged with a bend of the field

Crest—An arm vambraced, and hand holding a bow and arrow proper

(The Howland Line)

The original, highly ornamented, water color painting of the Howland escutcheon from which copies of the arms used in this country have been made, is said to have been brought to America shortly after the arrival of the "Mayflower." In 1865 this painting was in the possession of Rev T Howland White, of Shelbourne, Nova Scotia, a grandson of Gideon White, whose wife was Joanna,

daughter of John Howland, son of the Pilgrim The arms bear the following inscription

He beareth sable, two bars argent, on a chief of the second three lions rampant of the first and for his crest on a wreath of his colors a lion passant sable, ducally gorged or By the name of Howland

The original Howlands in America were Arthur, Henry and John The last named was of the "Mayflower" number, and is the progenitor of the line herein under consideration. The progeny of these three Howlands is a large and prominent one in New England, and from the earliest years of the struggle of Plymouth Colony for a foothold in the New World has played an important part in our life and affairs

(I) Humphrey Howland, the first of the line of whom we have definite information, was the father of the American immigrants, and was a citizen and draper of London His will, proved July 10, 1646, bequeathed to sons George, of St Dunstan's in the East, London, Arthur, Henry and John The last three were to receive under his will, dated May 28, 1646, £8 4s 4d out of the debt "due the testator (Humphrey) by Mr Buck, of Salem, Massachusetts." Annie Howland, widow of Humphrey Howland, was executrix of the estate She was buried at Barking, County Essex, England, December 20, 1653 The sons Arthur, Henry and John, were in Scrooby, England, and were members of the band of Puritans who left England because of religious intolerance and sought freedom in Amsterdam, Holland, where they remained a year, subsequently removing to Leyden, whence they emigrated to the New World

(II) John Howland, son of Humphrey and Annie Howland, held to the original faith of the Puritans, and was an officer of Rev John Cotton's church, and a staunch adherent of the orthodox faith until his death, while Arthur and Henry were Quakers John Howland's was the thirteenth name on the list of forty-one signers of the "Compact" in the cabin of the "Mayflower," in "Cape Cod Harbor," November 21, 1620 At this time he was twenty-eight years of age and according to Prince was a member of Governor Carver's family How this came about is not known, but it is probable that Carver saw elements in his character which led him to supply young Howland's wants for the journey to America, and to cause him to be considered one of the family That he possessed sound judgment and business capacity is shown by the active duties which he assumed and the trust which was reposed in him in all the early labors of establishing a settlement While the "Mayflower" was yet in Cape Cod Harbor, ten of "her principal" men were "sente out" in a boat manned by eight sailors, to select a place for landing, among them was John Howland A storm drove them into Plymouth Harbor and Plymouth was selected as the place of settlement

The first mention of John Howland in the old Plymouth Colony records is on a list of freemen, and in an enumeration of the members of the Governor's "councill" of seven, of which he is the third In 1633 or 1634 he was an assessor, was selectman of Plymouth in 1666, and was chosen deputy of the same town, in 1652-56-58-61-62-66-67-70 He was elected to public office for the last time on June 2, 1670, at which time he was nearly eighty years of age Besides these public positions of honor and trust, he was very often selected to lay out and appraise land to run highways, to settle disputes, and to serve on committees of every description He was not only full of zeal

for the temporal welfare of the colony, but gave powerful encouragement to a high standard of morals and religion, so much so that he is recorded as "a godly man and an ancient professor in the ways of Christ " It is shown that he was active in Christian work, for Governor Bradford notes that he became "a profitable member both in Church and Commonwealth," and it appears that at the ordination of John Cotton, Jr , in 1667, John Howland "was appointed by the church to join in the imposition of hands." He lived at what was called Rocky Nook, where he died February 23, 1672-73.

John Howland married Elizabeth Tilley, daughter of John Tilley, and ward of Governor Carver, into whose family she was taken at the death of her father, when she was about fourteen years of age She died December 21, 1687, aged eighty years, in Swanzey, Massachusetts, at the home of her daughter, Lydia Brown, and was the last but three of the "Mayflower" passengers to die Their children were 1 Desire, born October 13, 1623, in Barnstable, married, in 1643, Captain John Gorham 2 John, born in Plymouth, February 24, 1627 3 Jabez, of whom further 4 Hope, born August 30, 1629, died January 8, 1684, married, in 1646, John Chipman 5 Elizabeth, married (first) September 13, 1649, Ephraim Hicks, of Plymouth, who died December 2, 1649, married (second) July 10, 1651, John Dickarson, of Plymouth. 6 Lydia, married James Brown, and settled in Swanzey 7 Ruth, married, November 17, 1664, Thomas Cushman 8 Hannah, married, July 6, 1661, Jonathan Bosworth 9 Joseph, died in January, 1704 10 Isaac, born November 16, 1649, died March 9, 1724, married Elizabeth Vaughn born in 1652, died October 29, 1727

(III) Jabez Howland, son of John and Elizabeth (Tilley) Howland, was born in Plymouth, Massachusetts, in 1628 He resided in Plymouth during the early part of his life, and took an active part in public life, holding various civil offices He served as a lieutenant under Captain Benjamin Church in King Philip's War, and proved his bravery under a test made by Church for that purpose He was a blacksmith and cooper, doing a very large business in both these trades, which were of large importance in early colonial days He removed to Bristol, Rhode Island, where he settled, and conducted a blacksmith establishment His residence was on Hope street, where he kept a hotel Jabez Howland was first town clerk of Bristol, and subsequently became prominent in the affairs of the town He was selectman, assessor, and deputy to the General Court He was active in the construction of the First Congregational Church of Bristol His will, dated July 14, 1708, was proved April 21, 1712, and disposed of an estate valued at £600 He was one of the most influential citizens of early Bristol, highly esteemed

He married Bethiah Thatcher, daughter of Anthony Thatcher, and granddaughter of Anthony Thatcher, who came from Sarum, England, with his second wife, Elizabeth Jones, in the ship ' James," in April, 1635 The vessel was wrecked off Cape Ann, August 16 of that year, and he was made administrator of the estate of Joseph Avery, one of the victims of the disaster The General Court gave to Anthony Thatcher the island on which the vessel was wrecked He was a tailor by trade, and settled first in Marblehead, whence he removed to Yarmouth, on Cape Cod, and gave allegiance to the Plymouth Colony, January 7, 1639 He was deputy to the General Court, a magistrate, and was licensed to marry persons

Thatcher Arms—Gules a cross moline argent, on a chief or three grasshoppers proper
Crest—A Saxon sword or seax proper

Children of Jabez and Bethiah (Thatcher) Howland 1 Jabez, born November 15, 1670 2 John, born March 15, 1673 3 Bethiah, born August 6, 1674 4 Josiah, born October 6, 1676 5 John, born September 26, 1679, recorded in Bristol, Rhode Island 8 Judah, born May 7, 1683 9 Seth, born January 5, 1684-85 10 Samuel, of whom further 11 Experience, born May 19, 1687 12 Joseph, born October 14, 1692.

(IV) Samuel Howland, son of Jabez and Bethiah (Thatcher) Howland, was born in Bristol, Rhode Island, May 16, 1686 He married, May 6, 1708, Abigail Cary, born August 31, 1784, daughter of John and Abigail (Allen) Cary, she died August 16, 1737 Samuel Howland was a lifelong resident of Bristol, prominent in its affairs, and the owner of considerable property Children 1 Samuel, born April 3, 1709 2 Abigail, born October 18, 1710 3 John, born September 27, 1713 4 Tabitha, born November 13, 1715 5 Seth, born July 9, 1719 6 Phebe, born September 9, 1721; married John Wardwell 7 Mary, of whom further

Abigail Allen, mother of Abigail (Cary) Howland, was the daughter of Samuel Allen, who came from Bridgewater, England, with his wife Anne, and settled in Braintree, Massachusetts The wife died in 1641, and he married (second) Margaret Lamb, who was the mother of Abigail Allen, wife of John Cary John Cary, ancestor of Abigail (Cary) Howland, was born about 1610, and resided near Bristol, Somersetshire, England, whence he came about 1634 to America, and settled in Duxbury, Massachusetts, where he had a farm He was one of the proprietors of Bridgewater, Massachusetts, and one of its first settlers, locating in what is now West Bridgewater, one-quarter of a mile east of the present town house Bridgewater was incorporated as a town in 1656, and John Cary was its first town clerk, filling that office for several years He married, in 1644, Elizabeth, daughter of Francis and Elizabeth Godfrey His eldest child, John (2) Cary, was born November 4, 1645, in Duxbury, Massachusetts, resided in Bridgewater until 1680, when he removed to Bristol, Rhode Island, and died there July 14, 1721, his estate valued at £700 The deed of his first land in Bristol was dated September 14, 1680, and he was present at the first town meeting of that town, prominent in town affairs, and deacon of the church from its organization until his death He was one of the first "raters" or assessors, secretary of the county, clerk of the peace, and representative in the General Assembly in 1694 He married in Bridgewater, December 7, 1670, Abigail, daughter of Samuel Allen and his second wife, Margaret Lamb, who at the time of her marriage to Samuel Allen was a widow, maiden name French His second daughter became the wife of Samuel Howland, as previously noted

(V) Mary Howland, daughter of Samuel and Abigail (Cary) Howland, was born in Bristol, Rhode Island, March 18, 1720 She married, September 26, 1742, William (2) Wardwell, of Bristol, descendant in the fourth American generation of William Wardwell, founder of the line in New England (See Wardwell IV)

(The Tilley Line).

The surname Tilley is found in England as early as the Norman Conquest, and appears in the "Domesday Book" The name was common also in France and Holland at an early date, and is doubtless the Norman-French origin, as Lower states that there is a village of Tilly in the Department of Calvados, in Normandy The name is spelled in ancient records Tillie, Tilly, Teley, Tiley, Tilee and Tely We have at the present time the surname Tylee, probably of the same stock

Tilley Arms—Argent a wivern with wings endorsed sable charged on the breast with an annulet or

Crest—The head of a battle-ax issuing from the wreath

Edward and John Tilley were among the passengers of the "Mayflower" Edward and his wife Ann both died in the spring of 1620-21 John brought his wife and daughter Elizabeth, and he and his wife also died early in 1621 The only descendants of these Pilgrim Tilleys are through Elizabeth Tilley, who became the wife of John Howland No person can claim descent through these ancestors in the male line There was another John Tilley in Dorchester who came in 1628; died without issue William Tilley, of Barnstable and Boston, came from Little Minories, England, in the ship "Abigail," in June, 1636, left a daughter Sarah, but no sons Others of the name came later

(I) John Tilley, immigrant ancestor, came to the American colonies in December, 1620, a passenger, with his wife and daughter Elizabeth, in the ship "Mayflower" Both John Tilley and his wife died early in 1621

(II) Elizabeth Tilley, daughter of John Tilley, was born in England, accompanied her parents to New England After the death of her parents she became the ward of Governor John Carver, when she was about fourteen years of age She married John Howland, who was also a passenger on the "Mayflower" Elizabeth (Tilley) Howland died December 21, 1687, aged eighty years (See Howland II)

(The Glover Line)

Glover Arms—Sable a fesse embattled ermine between three crescents argent

Crest—Out of a mural crown a demi-lion rampant holding between the paws a crescent

The surname Glover, since the founding of the New England Colonies a notable one in America, was anciently spelled Glofre, and Golofre Glove as a surname appeared in the middle of the fourteenth century, and was shortly followed by Glover, under which form the name is found in all English-speaking countries to-day It is of the occupative class Through successive centuries, among the men who have brought honor to the name and made it historical, we find gentlemen, heralds, and heraldic writers, vicars, church wardens, heretics, authors, knights, attorneys-at-law, poets, merchants, members of parliament, philanthropists and public benefactors The American branch of the family has contributed many notable figures, and ranks to-day among the foremost of American colonial families

Several immigrants of the name settled in New England in the first half of the colonial period Their progeny is large and widespread In the records of the ancient town of Salem, New England, there appears the following "John Glover married to Mary Guppy, by Major Hathorn, the 2d January, 1660." This appears to be the earliest mention of this founder John Glover died in May, 1695 and his will was proved on May 13th of that year He is believed to have been a son of Charles Glover, who came from England, in 1630, and united with the First Church in Salem, in full communion, June 10, 1649, there is, however, no satisfactory proof of the relationship beyond the supposition This is in a large measure due to the faulty records of New England in the early days The Glover family has been especially prominent in Massachusetts A member of the Braintree branch of the family was Captain Joseph Glover, who was prominent in the military affairs of the town, and one of its

leading citizens He married Elizabeth Bass, who was also a member of a long established Braintree family, and they were the parents of Katherine Glover Katherine Glover married, November 19, 1780, Benjamin (2) Wardwell, of Bristol, Rhode Island (See Wardwell V)

Bass Arms—Sable a bordure argent
Crest—Out of a ducal coronet two wings proper

PECK, Albert Henry,
Highly Regarded Citizen

This name is of great antiquity, and is local in its derivation signifying "at the peck," that is, "at the hill top " It is found in Belton, Yorkshire, England at an early date, and from there scattered not only over England but into every civilized country A branch settled in Hesden and Wakefield, Yorkshire, whose descendants removed to Beccles, County Suffolk, and were the ancestors of Joseph Peck, of Hingham, County Norfolk, the progenitor of the Peck family in America, of which the late Albert H Peck, of Rhode Island, was a descendant in the seventh American generation

Arms—Argent on a chevron engrailed gules, three crosses formed of the first
Crest—A cubit arm erect, habited azure, cuff argent, hand proper, holding on one stalk enfiled with a scroll three roses gules leaved vert

The above arms of the Peck family are quartered with those of the Brunning and Hesselden families

The pedigree of the English family, extending from the founder to the American progenitor covers a period of twenty generations, and is as follows

I John Peck, of Belton, Yorkshire, married a daughter of ——— Melgrave II Thomas Peck married a daughter of ——— Middleton, of Middleton III

Robert Peck, of Belton, married ———— Tunstall IV. Robert (2) Peck, of Belton, married ———— Musgrave. V John (2) Peck, of Belton, married ———— Watford VI. Thomas (2) Peck, of Belton married ———— Blaxton, of Blaxton Children Thomas, mentioned below, Joseph, settled in Northamptonshire VII. Thomas (3) Peck, of Belton, married ———— Littleton VIII. John (3) Peck, of Belton, married ———— Carre IX John (4) Peck, of Belton, married ———— Flemming X. John (5) Peck married ———— Wembourne Their children 1 John, whose daughter, his sole heir, married John Ratcliffe, thus taking the estate of Belton out of the direct line 2 Richard, mentioned below XI Richard Peck married ———— Brunnung XII. Richard (2) Peck, of Hesden, married ———— Savill XIII. Thomas (4) Peck, of Hesden. married ———— Bradley XIV Richard (3) Peck, of Hesden and Wakefield, Yorkshire, married a Hesselden Children John, mentioned below, Richard, died young Thomas XV John (6) Peck married Isabel Lacie, of Brombleton, and and was a lawyer Children Richard, mentioned below, Thomas, Catherine, Robert, John, Margaret XVI Richard (4) Peck was of Wakefield, and married Joan, daughter of John Harrington, Esq Children Richard, mentioned below, Margaret, Isabel, Joan, Judith, Elizabeth XVII Richard (5) Peck married Alice, daughter of Sir Peter Middleton Children John. mentioned below, Margaret, Ann, Elizabeth Isabel XVIII John (7) Peck, of Wakefield, married Joan daughter of John Aune, of Trickley. Children Richard, married Anne Holtham, John, Thomas, Ralph, Nicholas, Francis Robert mentioned below

(XIX) Robert (3) Peck was of Beccles County Suffolk, England He married (first) ———— Norton, (second) ————

Waters Children 1 John 2 Robert, mentioned below 3 Thomas 4 Joan 5 Olivia 6 Margaret 7 Anne.

(XX) Robert (4) Peck was born and resided all his life in Beccles, where he died in 1593, at the age of forty-seven years. He married Helen, daughter of Nicholas Babbs, of Guilford, England Their children were 1 Richard, died without issue, in 1615, aged forty-one. 2 Nicholas, born in 1576, married Rachel Yonge, 1610. 3. Robert, born in 1580; took degree at Magdalen College, Cambridge, A B, 1599, A M, 1603; inducted over parish of Hingham, England, January 8, 1605. 4 Joseph, mentioned below 5 Margaret. 6. Martha. 7. Samuel, died 1619

(The Peck Family in America.)

(I) Joseph Peck, immigrant ancestor of the American family, was born in Beccles, County Suffolk, England, the son of Robert (4) and Helen (Babbs) Peck He was of the twenty-first generation from the founder of the line, John Peck, of Belton, Yorkshire In 1638 he and other Puritans, with his brother, the Rev Robert Peck, their pastor, fled from the persecutions of their church in England, and came to America They set sail in the ship "Diligent," of Ipswich, John Martin, master The records of Hingham, Massachusetts, state "Mr Joseph Peck and his wife, with three sons and a daughter and two men servants and three maid servants came from Old Hingham and settled at New Hingham" From the number of his servants it is judged that Joseph Peck was a man of considerable wealth and position in England prior to his coming to the New World He later became one of the leading citizens of the community He was granted a house lot of seven acres adjoining that of his brother He remained at Hingham seven years, and then removed to Seekonk, Rhode Island At

Hingham he was deputy to the General Court in 1639. He took an active and influential part in the affairs of the town, was selectman, justice of the peace, assessor, etc. In 1641 he became one of the principal purchasers of the Indians of that tract of land called Seekonk, afterwards the town of Rehoboth, including the present towns of Rehoboth, Massachusetts, and Seekonk, and Pawtucket, Rhode Island. Joseph Peck removed to his new home in 1645. An incident of the trip is found on the town records of Rehoboth: "Mr Joseph Peck and three others at Hingham, being about to remove to Seaconk, riding thither they sheltered themselves and their horses in an Indian wigwam, which by some occasion took fire, and, although there were four in it and labored to their utmost, burnt three of their horses to death, and all their goods, to the value of fifty pounds." He was appointed to assist in matters of controversy at court, and in 1650 was authorized to perform marriages. He was second on the tax list. In some instances land granted to him is still owned by his descendants. His house was upon the plain in the northerly part of the "Ring of the Town," near the junction of the present Pawtucket with the old Boston and Bristol road, not far from the Boston & Providence railroad station.

He died December 23, 1633. His will was proved March 3, 1663-64. His sons united in the amplification of the written will which was made on his death-bed and the court accepted it as a part of the will.

Joseph Peck married (first) in Hingham, England, May 21, 1617, Rebecca Clark, she died and was buried there, October 24, 1637. The name of his second wife is unknown. His children were: 1 Anna, baptized in Hingham, England, March 12, 1618, buried there July 27, 1636. 2 Rebecca, baptized there, May 25,

1620, married ——— Hubbard. 3 Joseph, baptized August 23, 1623. 4 John, born about 1626. 5 Nicholas, baptized April 9, 1630. 6 Simon, baptized in Hingham, Massachusetts, on February 3, 1638-39. 7 Nathaniel, mentioned below. 8 Israel, baptized March 11, 1644, died young 9-10 Samuel and Israel, baptized July 19, 1646.

(II) Nathaniel Peck, son of Joseph Peck, was born in Hingham, Massachusetts, and baptized there October 31, 1641. He died early in life, and was buried August 12, 1676. He removed to Seekonk with his father and family, and there settled upon the lands given him and his brother Israel, in what is now the town of Barrington, Rhode Island, near what was later the residence of Leander R. Peck. These lands were a part of those purchased by the proprietors of Osamequin and his son Wamsetta. They had been known by the name of Poppanomscut, alias Phebe's Neck, Sowames or Sowamsit, and are now partly in Bristol, Warren, Swansea, Rehoboth, and Barrington. The lands given to Nathaniel and Israel by their father remained undivided, the most of them at least, until after the son of Nathaniel came of age. After the decease of Nathaniel they are referred to as the lands of Israel and the heirs of Nathaniel, and afterwards, as the lands of Nathaniel and his uncle Israel.

Nathaniel Peck married Deliverance ———, who was buried May 1, 1675. He had three children, and left at his decease, as appears by the Massachusetts Colonial records, two children, a son and a daughter. Two of his children were: 1 Nathaniel, mentioned below. 2 Elisha, born April 19, 1675, died April 30, 1675.

(III) Lieutenant Nathaniel (2) Peck, son of Nathaniel (1) and Deliverance Peck, was born on July 26, 1670, and died August 5, 1751. He settled on the lands left him by his father, and became one of

243

the prominent men of the town, filling
various public offices. For several years
he is called Lieutenant Nathaniel on the
records of the town, and then deacon.
He married (first) March 8, 1695-96,
Christian Allen, of Swansea, who died
June 8, 1702, he married (second) Judith
Smith, of Rehoboth, Massachusetts, who
died November 10, 1743. Their children
were 1. Ebenezer, born April 24, 1697.
2. Thomas, born October 4, 1700. 3.
Daniel, born July 28, 1706. 4. David,
born November, 1707, mentioned below.
5. Abigail, born July 12, 1709. 6. Bathsheba, born January 15, 1711. 7. Soloman,
born November 11, 1712. 8. Child, born
July 1, 1714, name unknown. 9. John,
born February 29, 1716.

(IV) David Peck, son of Lieutenant
Nathaniel (2) and Judith (Smith) Peck,
was born in November, 1707, and married,
September 20, 1744, Sarah Humphrey. He
settled upon a part of the homestead,
which in 1863 was occupied by Sebea
Peck, his grandson. David Peck died
March 4, 1771. Children 1. David, born
August 18, 1746. 2. Ezra, born July 3,
1748. 3. Sarah, born March 19, 1749-50
4. John, born March 8, 1751-52. 5. Ezra
(2), born October 5, 1753. 6. Rachel,
born October 20, 1754. 7. Lewis, born
October 18, 1757. 8. Joel, mentioned below. 9. Lewis (2), born August 20, 1761.
10. John, born May 12, 1763. 11 Noah,
born March 31, 1765, later in life settled
in Vermont. 12. Sarah, born March 7,
1767.

Three of the sons of David Peck served
in the American Revolution. David Peck
was a member of Captain Thomas Allin's
company. Lewis Peck enlisted in the
militia guard of Barrington, serving from
April 5 to May 20, 1778. Joel Peck also
served in the conflict, and is mentioned
at length below

(V) Joel Peck, son of David and Sarah
(Humphrey) Peck, was born August 28,

1759, and resided in Barrington during his
entire life. He married Lucy Fish, daughter of Daniel Fish, of Seekonk, Rhode
Island. He inherited and resided upon
the homestead, which had been in the
family since the first American generation. The house in which he lived is
still standing, and is regarded as a land-
mark of the early architecture of the town
of Barrington, Rhode Island. Joel Peck
served with valor in the American Revolution, enlisting with other soldiers from
Barrington, in Captain Thomas Allin's
company. He died on November 11, 1833,
and his widow became a United States
pensioner. Joel Peck was a highly respected citizen of Barrington, and was
prominent in local affairs. His widow
died on March 2, 1864, at the advanced
age of ninety years. Their children were
1. Horatio, born December 3, 1793. 2
Elnathan, born January 27, 1796. 3. Bela
mentioned below. 4. Wealthy, born September 22, 1800. 5. Sebea, born January
25, 1803. 6. Fanny, born September 6,
1805. 7. Bethia, born August 4, 1808,
married Benjamin B. Medbury. 8. Clarissa, born December 13, 1812, married
Robert T. Smith, son of Ebenezer Smith,
of Barrington, Rhode Island, she was living in 1904 at the age of ninety-two years.
She was presented with a souvenir spoon
by the National Chapter of the Daughters
of the American Revolution, as a true
daughter of the Revolution

(VI) Bela Peck, son of Joel and Lucy
(Fish) Peck, was born in Barrington,
Rhode Island, January 29, 1798. He re-
moved later in life to East Providence,
Rhode Island, where he died. He mar-
ried, March 18, 1821, Lemira A Peck,
daughter of Ambrose Peck, of Seekonk,
Rhode Island. Their children were 1
Alpheus M, born December 20, 1821. 2
Edwin F., born December 8, 1823. 3. Al-
bert H, born January 10, 1827, mentioned
below. 4. Susan A., born August 29, 1829,

married George Bowen and lived in Edgewood, Rhode Island 5 Albert H (2), born June 14, 1833 6. Horace T, born March 28, 1836, died young 7 Horace T (2), born April 2, 1839 8 Amy Ann, born March 19, 1842.

(VII) Albert Henry Peck, son of Bela and Lemira A (Peck) Peck, was born in the town of Seekonk, Massachusetts (now East Providence, Rhode Island) He received his early educational training in the local schools of the town Mr. Peck was of that sturdy, upright and able type of men who form the backbone of the nation, the able and rugged stock which formed and has continued to be the basis of America's greatness He was a farmer, and extensive agriculturist, a prominent and influential citizen in the community, and a man highly respected and loved by a host of friends and acquaintances

In 1863 Mr Peck purchased the farm of George K Viall, which he made his home and on which he continued to reside for the remainder of his life This land was formerly owned by Perez Richmond, and prior to his time by Thomas Medbury, who owned and occupied it as far back as the time of the American Revolution At the time when he purchased it, the farm was in poor condition, and consisted largely of twenty acres, part of which was woodland, and a farm house He immediately set to work to reclaim the land, succeeding gradually in bringing it up to a standard of modern efficiency and usefulness, which is not surpassed by any farm of the kind in the neighboring countryside He also added to the original purchase, until the farm to-day consists of sixty acres, a handsome residence and well kept lawns and orchards, and may be justly termed a monument to Mr Peck's untiring work and genius as a farmer.

Mr Peck was prominently identified with the local interests of the community of Barrington, and held several important public offices He was for a number of years a member of the town council of Barrington, and was also a surveyor of highways He contributed to the support of the Congregational Church of Barrington, which he attended, and of which his family are members

Mr Peck married, May 29, 1863, Mary Elizabeth Medbury, daughter of Benjamin B and Bethia (Peck) Medbury, of Barrington, Rhode Island Their children are

1 Mabel F, born March 20, 1867, married, June 14, 1894, Edward D Anthony, son of Charles F and Harriet A (Davis) Anthony, Mr Anthony is purchasing agent and chief clerk of the Providence Engineering Corporation, Providence, Rhode Island, they are the parents of one daughter 1 Marian Elizabeth, born March 1, 1896, who is now attending Brown University, Providence, and resides at the dormitory on Cushing street

2 Clarence I, born April 9, 1872; married Bessie McLane, daughter of William and Mary (Lindley) McLane; children 1 Frances Elizabeth, born July 25, 1908, 11 Albert H, born February 14, 1913 Clarence I Peck is a successful market gardener, and conducts his father's farm at Peck's Corner, Barrington, Rhode Island

3 Ethel G, born August 25, 1879, married Findlay B Beard, son of William S and Nina (Stout) Beard, their children are 1 Virginia Burns, born July 20, 1910, 11 Madeline Peck, born January 14, 1917. Mr Beard is a rigging and erecting engineer and is located at No 530 South Main street, Providence, where he conducts an extensive business

Albert Henry Peck died in Barrington, Rhode Island, November 17 1909 He is survived by Mrs. Peck, who resides at the homestead in Barrington, Rhode Island.

LONG, John Davis,

Governor, Cabinet Official.

The youngest chief executive the State of Massachusetts ever had, and one of her "favorite sons," Mr Long was best known to his countrymen as Secretary of the Navy under President McKinley and as the man who stood at the head of the Navy Department during the war with Spain He was continued in President McKinley's second cabinet, and for a year under President Roosevelt, who, in accepting Secretary Long's resignation in 1902, wrote "It has never been my good fortune to be associated with any public man more single-minded in his devotion to the public interest" His service to his State was as one of her most eminent lawyers, as legislator and speaker of the House, as Lieutenant-Governor and Governor, and as Congressman, to the nation as Secretary of the Navy under two Presidents, and to the navy as its persistent friend, champion and historian To him is due the first real expansion in ships and men, the agitation which finally resulted in the privilege of promotion of enlisted men to commissioned rank, and the placing of thousands of navy yard employes under the civil service rules, who had previously been subject to removal and appointment with every change of administration During his five years as Secretary of the Navy, the department spent more money under Secretary Long's direction than had been appropriated for the navy in any ten years previous, the enlisted force also growing from 12,500 to 24,000, while the Marine Corps more than doubled He was the original "apostle of preparedness," and had his ideas and plans received the proper support from Congress, and had the Secretaries of the Navy who have followed him been in like sympathy,

the present agitation would have been unnecessary and impossible A biographer wrote of him during his lifetime

As a man of letters Governor Long has achieved a reputation Some years ago he produced a scholarly translation in blank verse of Virgil's Aeneid, published in 1879, in Boston, which has found many admirers Among his other literary productions may be mentioned his "Afterdinner Speeches," "The Republican Party, Its History, Principles and Policies," and "The New American Navy" His inaugural addresses were masterpieces of art, and the same can be said of his speeches on the floor of Congress, all of them polished, forceful and to the point Mr Long is a very fluent speaker, and, without oratorical display, he always succeeds in winning the attention of the auditors It is what he says, more than how he says it, that has won him his great popularity on the platform Amid professional and official duties he also has written several poems and essays which reflect credit upon his heart and brain

He was not a native son of Massachusetts, but of Maine, his Massachusetts residence beginning in 1863 as a young lawyer in the city of Boston, but Massachusetts quickly adopted him and was proud to claim him as her own He traced his ancestry to an early settler of North Carolina, James Long, to Thomas Clarke, one of the Pilgrims, to Richard Warren, of the "Mayflower," and to Dolor Davis, who came in 1634

(I) James Long, an early settler in North Carolina, was a resident of Perquimans precinct, Albemarle county, at the time of his death in 1682, and his will mentions sons, James, Thomas and Giles

(II) James (2), son of James (1) Long, died in Tyrrell county, North Carolina, November 15, 1711 From his will we learn that the Christian name of his wife was Elizabeth, and that he had sons James, Thomas and John, and daughters, Mary and Elizabeth He was a man of prominence in the administrative affairs

246

of the colony, and a member of the House of Burgesses.

(III) James (3), son of James (2) and Elizabeth Long, was of Chowan, Tyrrell county, North Carolina, and died there, September 1, 1734. His will, which was probated at the April term of court in the following year, mentions eldest son James, second son Giles, brothers, Thomas, John and Andrew, son Joshua, and daughter Elizabeth.

(IV) Giles, second son of James (3) Long, died in 1782, leaving a son Miles. The "North Carolina Historical and Genealogical Register" fails to mention any other child of Giles Long.

(V) Miles, son of Giles Long, came from North Carolina, and lived in Plymouth, Massachusetts. He married, in Plymouth, in 1770, Thankful Clark, born 1750, and lived in Plymouth. She survived him, and afterward married Ezra Holmes. Children of Miles and Thankful (Clark) Long: Thomas, born August, 1771. Betsey, married John Clark.

Thankful Clark, wife of Miles Long, was a daughter of Israel Clark, born 1720, lived in Plymouth, who married Deborah Pope, of Sandwich. Israel Clark was son of Josiah Clark, born 1690, lived in Plymouth, and married Thankful Tupper. Josiah Clark, son of Thomas Clark, was born and lived in Plymouth, and was called "Silver-headed Thomas," because, having been scalped by the Indians when a boy, he wore a silver plate; married Elizabeth Crow. Thomas Clark was son of James Clark, born in Plymouth, in 1636, married, 1657, Abigail Lothrop, who was born 1639, daughter of Rev. John Lothrop, who came over in the "Griffin" in 1635, and was the first minister in Barnstable, where his house still stands, and is used as a public library. James was a son of Thomas Clark, the Pilgrim, who came to Plymouth in the

"Ann," in 1623. He lived in Plymouth, where he married Susannah Ring, and his gravestone still stands on Burial Hill, Plymouth.

(VI) Thomas son of Miles and Thankful (Clark) Long, was born in Plymouth, Massachusetts, in 1771 and died in Buckfield, in 1806. He married, November 8, 1795, Bathsheba Churchill, born May 26, 1766, died in Buckfield, July 27, 1853. Children: 1 Betsey, born about 1796; married Isaac Ellis. 2 Thomas, born about 1798. 3 Zadoc, born July 28, 1800. 4 Sally, born about 1802, married Lucius Loring. 5 George Washington, died in infancy. 6 Bathsheba, married Isaac Bearse. 7 Harriet, died in infancy. 8 Miles, married Ann Bridgham. 9 Thankful, died in infancy. 10 Washington, born about 1811. 11 Harriet. 12 Thankful C., married William W. Bacon.

Bathsheba Churchill, wife of Thomas Long, was a daughter of Zadoc Churchill, born 1747, son of Stephen Churchill, born 1717, son of Stephen Churchill, born 1685; son of Eleazer Churchill, born 1652, son of John Churchill, who came from England to Plymouth, Massachusetts, 1643 and married, 1644, Hannah, daughter of William Pontus. Zadoc Churchill married Bathsheba Rider, born 1750, concerning whose ancestry authorities are at variance. One writer says Richard Warren, of the "Mayflower," 1620, son of Christopher, of Kent county, England, married Widow Elizabeth Marsh, who came over in the "Ann," 1623, Robert Bartlett, who came in the "Ann," had Sarah Bartlett, who married, 1656, Samuel Rider (second wife); had Samuel Rider, born 1657, married, 1680, Lydia Tilden, had Joseph Rider, born 1691, married, 1740, Elizabeth Crossman, (second wife), had Bathsheba Rider, born 1650, married Zadoc Churchill.

On the other hand, Mr Bowman, secretary of the Society of Mayflower Descendants, says that James Chilton, of the "Mayflower," 1620, had a daughter Mary, who married John Winslow (brother of Governor Winslow), and had Mary Winslow, who married, 1650, Edward Gray, of Plymouth, and had Desire Gray, born 1651, married Nathaniel Southworth, son of Alice Southworth, second wife of Governor Bradford, and had Mary Southworth, born 1676, married Joseph Rider, and had Joseph Rider, Jr, who married (second wife) Elizabeth Crossman, and had Bathsheba Rider, born 1750, married Zadoc Churchill, and had Bathsheba Churchill, who married Thomas Long

(VII) Zadoc, son of Thomas and Bathsheba (Churchill) Long, was born in Middleboro, Massachusetts, July 28, 1800, and died in Winchenden, Massachusetts, February 3, 1873 He was a man of considerable prominence in his native State, and in 1638 was the Whig candidate for Congress He received a plurality, but not a majority of votes, hence failed of election He was also presidential elector and justice of the peace He married, August 31, 1824, at New Gloucester, Maine, Julia Temple Davis, born in Falmouth, Maine, February 17, 1807, died in Buckfield, Maine, September 19, 1869 Children 1 Julia Davis, born August 16, 1825, died October 31, 1882, married Nelson D. White. 2. Persis Seaver, born February 14, 1828, died April 27, 1893; married Percival W. Bartlett. 3. Zadoc, Jr, born April 26, 1834, died September 14, 1866, married Ruth A Strout 4. John Davis, born October 27, 1838

Julia Temple Davis, wife of Zadoc Long, was a descendant in the seventh generation of Dolor Davis, born in Kent, England, about 1600, and came to Boston in May, 1634, with Simon Willard He settled in Cambridge, then in Duxbury,

about 1643, then at Barnstable, where he died in 1673. Meantime he lived in Concord from 1655 to 1666, where his sons settled and lived Dolor married, about 1624, Margery Willard, born in 1602, daughter of Richard Willard, of Horsemonden, Kent, England She died in Concord, Massachusetts, after 1655 and before 1666 Their son Samuel married, January 11, 1665, at Lynn, Massachusetts, Mary Meads (or Meadows), who died in Concord, 1710 Their son Simon, known as Lieutenant Simon, born 1683, died in Holden, married, 1713, Dorothy ——, who died at Holden, 1776 Their son Simon, born 1714, died 1754, he lived in Rutland, Massachusetts, and married Hannah Gates, of Stow, who died in 1761 She was a descendant of Stephen Gates, one of the early settlers of Hingham Their son, Deacon David, born 1740, lived at Paxton, and married Abigail Brown, 1764 Their son Simon, born in Paxton, September 2, 1765, died in Falmouth, Maine, March 17, 1810 He married, 1802, at West Boylston, Widow Persis Seaver, maiden name Temple, born 1766, at Shrewsbury, a descendant of the Temple family. Their daughter, Julia Temple Davis married Zadoc Long August 31, 1824

(VIII) John Davis Long, son of Zadoc and Julia Temple (Davis) Long, was born in Buckfield, Oxford county, Maine, October 27, 1838, died at Hingham, Massachusetts, August 28, 1915. He acquired his earlier literary education in public schools and the academy at Hebron, in the latter fitting for college under the principalship of Mark H Dunnell, afterward a member of Congress from Minnesota He entered Harvard, taking the academic course, graduated Bachelor of Arts 1857, second in his class, and wrote the class ode, which was sung on commencement day. For two years after

leaving college he was principal of the
Westford Academy, and at the end of
that time entered Harvard Law School
He also studied law in the office of Sidney Bartlett and Peleg W Chandler, of
the Boston bar In 1861 he was admitted
to practice, and the same year began his
professional career in Buckfield He remained there six months, then came to
Boston, and became partner with Stillman B Allen Alfred Hemenway was
afterward a partner, a relation which was
maintained until November, 1879, when
Mr Long was elected Governor of Massachusetts

Soon after he had become a member of
the Boston bar, Governor Long took up
his residence in Hingham In 1875 he
was elected representative from the Second Plymouth District to the General
Court, was reelected at the end of his first
term, and twice afterward, during the
legislative sessions of 1876-77-80 he was
speaker of the house, and the unanimous
choice of the house in 1877 At the Republican State Convention in Worcester
in 1877 he was mentioned for the gov-
ernorship but his name was withdrawn.
At the convention of the next year he received two hundred and sixty-six votes
in his candidacy for the gubernatorial
office, but when his name was presented
for the lieutenant-governorship he was
nominated by a large majority and elected to that office In 1879 he was nominated and elected Governor, succeeding
Governor Talbot In the campaign of
that year his Democratic opponent was
General Benjamin F Butler, with John
Quincy Adams and Rev Dr Eddy as
nominees of minor political factions. In
1880 he was the unanimous choice of the
convention, and at the polls in November
he received a vote as gratifying as it was
unprecedented in a gubernatorial contest
in this State in any other than a presi-

dential year In November, 1881, he was
reëlected for another term, and served in
all three years In 1884 he was elected
representative in Congress, and twice
reëlected, serving during the Forty-
eighth, Forty-ninth and Fiftieth sessions
of that body

On March 6, 1897, he was appointed
Secretary of the Navy in President Mc-
Kinley's cabinet, and retired from that
office May 1, 1902 At the close of the
last session of his six years in Congress,
Governor Long returned to Boston and
resumed his law practice, and with the
exception of the years in the President's
cabinet was not particularly identified
with the public service In addition to
an extensive law practice conducted with
his partner of earlier years, Alfred Hemenway, Mr Long had large business
interests and was one of Boston's leading financiers. He was president of the
Puritan Trust Company, director of the
United States and Chelsea Trust Companies and trustee of the Five Cent Savings Bank For several years he was a
member of the State House construction
commission. He was president of the
board of overseers of Harvard College,
member of the Massachusetts Total Ab-
stinence Society, president of Wentworth
Institute, trustee of Thayer Academy,
trustee of Howard Seminary, president
Harvard College Alumni Association,
president of the Massachusetts Club,
president of the Unitarian Club, the Men's
Union, Mayflower and Boston Author's
Club In religious faith he was a Unitarian The Zadoc Long Free Library
at Buckfield, Maine, was presented to the
town by Governor Long in 1901 as a
memorial of his father.

In 1880 Governor Long was honored
by his *alma mater* with the degree of Doctor of Laws, and later with the same degree by Tufts College On September 13,

1870, he married (first) Mary Woodward Glover, born in Roxbury, June 29, 1845, died in Boston, February 16, 1882; married (second) May 22, 1885, Agnes Peirce, born at North Attleboro, Massachusetts, January 3, 1860.

Mary Woodward Glover, first wife of Governor John Davis Long, was a daughter of George Stephen Glover, born in Dorchester, Massachusetts, in 1816, and married, about 1841, Helen Paul, of Sherborn. George Stephen Glover was a son of Captain Stephen Glover, born in Dorchester, January 9, 1729, died October 11, 1811, master mariner and deep sea navigator, married (first) Elizabeth, daughter of Thomas and Elizabeth (Clough) Glover, married (second) October 15, 1759, Jerusha Billings, born in Dorchester, September 22, 1743, died in Quincy, April 2, 1807, daughter of John and Miriam (Davenport) Billings. Captain Elisha Glover was son of John Glover, born in Dorchester, September 18, 1687, died in Braintree (Quincy) July 6, 1768, was land holder; married (first) January 1, 1714, Mary Horton, of Milton, died December 19, 1776. John Glover was a son of Nathaniel Glover, born in Dorchester, January 30, 1653, died there January 6, 1723-24; married, 1672-73, Hannah Hinckley, of Barnstable, born April 1, 1650, died in Dorchester, April 30, 1730, fourth daughter of Governor Thomas Hinckley by his first wife, Mary Richards. Nathaniel was son of Mr. Nathaniel Glover, born 1630-31, died in Dorchester, May 21, 1657, married, March 22, 1652, Mary Smith, born at Toxeth Park Mary (Smith) Glover married (second) March 2, 1659-60, Thomas Hinckley, of Barnstable, afterward governor of Plymouth colony. Nathaniel Glover was fourth son of John Glover, Esq., of Prescott, England, and of Dorchester and Boston, New England, born in Rainhill

parish, Prescott, Lancashire, England, August 12, 1600, died in Boston, December 11, 1653.

Agnes Peirce second wife of Governor John Davis Long, was born January 1, 1860, daughter of Rev. Joseph D Peirce, born November 15, 1815, died in North Attleboro, Massachusetts, November 16, 1880, married, November 30, 1858, Martha S Price, born 1830, died 1885, daughter of George Price Rev Joseph D Peirce was son of John Peirce, born Scituate, Massachusetts, October 29, 1776, died at sea, May 16, 1816 married, November 10, 1810, Mercy Merritt, born January 24, 1784, died April 4, 1838 John Peirce was son of Seth B Peirce, born September 7, 1728, died December 9 1810, married, September 6, 1766, Jemina Turner, died April 19, 1814 Seth B Peirce was son of Thomas Peirce, born November 14, 1692, died before March 28, 1786. Thomas Peirce was son of Captain Benjamin Peirce, born 1646, died 1730, married (first) February 5, 1678, Martha, daughter of James Adams, married (second) July 21, 1718, Mrs. Elizabeth (Adams) Perry Captain Benjamin Peirce was son of Captain Michael Peirce, born about 1615, in England, came to America about 1645, and was first of Hingham and afterward of Scituate. He was killed in battle while leading his company against King Philip's savage warriors, on Sunday, March 26, 1676 His first wife died in 1662, and he married (second) Widow Anna James

Jemina Turner, above named, was a descendant of Elder William Brewster, of the "Mayflower" She was a daughter of Richard Turner, son of John Turner, who was son of John Turner and Mary Brewster who was daughter of Jonathan Brewster, son of William Brewster.

John Davis Long and his first wife, Mary Woodward Glover, were the parents of three children I Margaret, born in Hingham, January 26, 1872, died same day 2 Margaret, born in Boston, October 24, 1873 3 Helen, born in Hingham, June 26, 1875, died October 4, 1901 By his second wife, Agnes (Peirce) Long, who survives him, he had an only son Peirce, born at North Attleboro, December 29, 1887

DANIELSON, John W.,

Financier, Industrial Leader

To understand the meaning to a man of the honor of his family—to know the general status in a democracy of families of old and honorable lineage, is to know and understand the meaning and brightness of the national honor. For this can never be any brighter than the honor of the family. This statement is nowhere more clearly and conclusively proved than in the Roman civilization, in which the dominant unit was the family, and in which the parent was given the power to slay any of his sons who brought disgrace to the family name. To-day the weapon which the community uses to punish the crime of staining family honor is public opinion. Public opinion, the moral law love of country, home and God, are what have made the aristocracy of America, not an aristocracy of wealth, nor noble blood in the ordinary interpretation of the word, but an aristocracy of right and of noble deeds

In the foremost ranks of this aristocracy in the State of Connecticut, is the Danielson family, which holds a place of honor and respect in the community eclipsed by none The Danielson family is of Scotch origin, and was established in America in the middle part of the seventeenth century. Since the time of its founding the family has been prominent and active in the service of the country,

and has furnished its sons liberally in times of peace and war Its members have from time to time been distinguished in military service, and have rendered valuable services in official life The borough of Danielson, in the State of Connecticut the home of several generations of Danielsons, was named in their honor, and is to-day a silent monument to them, mute evidence of the high place which they have always held in the hearts and minds of the community

Danielson Arms—Argent a bend sable

(I) Sergeant James Danielson, progenitor of the family in America, was a native of Scotland, whence he emigrated to the New World, settling on Block Island, now the town of New Shoreham Rhode Island among the earliest residents of that place Early land records show him to have been a man of considerable fortune He assumed a prominent place in the town Between the years 1688 and 1705 he purchased several large tracts of land in Block Island, and was admitted a freeman of Rhode Island at the May session of the General Assembly in 1696 In 1700, he was elected sergeant of the town of New Shoreham In September, 1696, he agreed to raise £100 to pay for making a suitable harbor In the same year he served as a soldier in the expedition against Quebec, under General Wolfe, and participated in the engagement on the Heights of Abraham against the French under Montcalm In early life he served almost continuously in the wars against the Indians, and in reward for heroic services received a grant of land in Voluntown, in the eastern part of Connecticut, from the General Assembly His purchases of land were very extensive In 1706 he bought eight hundred acres of land on the Quinebaug river, in what is now the town of Pomfret This included a mansion house and barn The following year he bought a tract of two thousand acres of land lying between the Quinebaug and Assawauga rivers. He is said to have been the first settler south of Lake Mashapaug, at the southern end of which he built a garrison house. This new settlement afterward became the present town of Killingly. James Danielson became one of the most prominent and influential citizens of the community. He presented the town with a burying ground, located between the two rivers above named, and was the first to be buried in it. He died on January 22, 1728, at the age of eighty years. He was twice married, the maiden names of his wives being unknown. His first wife was Abigail. His second wife, Mary Rose, died February 23, 1752, in her eighty-sixth year.

(II) Samuel Danielson, son of Sergeant James and Mary Rose Danielson, was born in 1701. He inherited a large part of his father's extensive property holdings, including his homestead, in what is now the town of Killingly. He succeeded to his father's place in the community, which was much like that of the English country squire. He became a leader in the industrial affairs of the town. Part of the vast Danielson holdings on the Quinebaug river became the site of a manufacturing village named Danielsonville, now known as Danielson. Samuel Danielson married Sarah Douglas, on March 26, 1725. She was born about 1704, and died March 29, 1774, aged seventy-five years.

(III) Colonel William Danielson, son of Samuel and Sarah (Douglas) Danielson, was born August 11, 1729, in the town of Killingly, Connecticut, and resided there all his life, becoming very prominent in the town affairs. He was elected constable and collector of taxes

in 1760. In the same year he was elected lieutenant. In 1774 he became first major of the Eleventh Militia Regiment, and in the following year took one hundred and forty-six men from Killingly to Cambridge, Massachusetts. He became colonel in 1776, and after the close of the Revolutionary War a general of militia. In 1788, Colonel William Danielson was a member of the State Convention called to ratify the National Constitution. He married, October 29, 1758, Sarah Williams, born in 1737, died January 10, 1809. He died in Killingly, August 19, 1798.

(IV) General James Danielson, son of Colonel William and Sarah (Williams) Danielson, was born in Killingly, Connecticut, January 18, 1761, and died there October 25, 1827. He married, on December 3, 1788, Sarah Lord, of Abington, Connecticut. She was born June 17, 1769, and died April 28, 1852.

(V) Hezekiah Lord Danielson, son of General James and Sarah (Lord) Danielson, was born in Danielson Connecticut, December 16, 1802, and resided there all his life. He was prominent in local affairs in the town and was a deacon of the Congregational church. He died in 1881. He married Laura Weaver, of Brooklyn, Connecticut. Their children were: 1 Charlotte Tiffany, born in 1827, married Orville M. Capron, and resides in Danielson. 2 Lucy Storrs, born in 1829, married John Hutchins and resides in Danielson. 3 Elizabeth S., born in 1831, married Charles C. Cundall, and died in Seattle, Washington, July, 1916. 4 John Weaver, mentioned below. 5 Joseph, born in April, 1835, died in 1898. 6 Edward, born in 1837, died in 1882. 7 Daniel, born in 1842, now a resident of Danielson. 8 Henry M., born in 1845, resides in Danielson.

(VI) John Weaver Danielson, son of Hezekiah and Laura (Weaver) Danielson, was born in Danielson, Connecticut, March 30, 1833, and received his early education in the public schools. He later attended the Woodstock Academy, after leaving which he entered the business world as a clerk in the establishment of Edwin Ely. Shortly afterward he was given the position of clerk in the mill office in his native town, of which Amos De Forest Lockwood was agent.

In 1860 he left Connecticut, and went to Lewiston, Maine, in company with Mr. Lockwood, who was superintending the construction and equipment of the Androscoggin Mills there. Mr Danielson remained in Maine for thirteen years. In 1873 he resigned as agent and went to Providence, Rhode Island, where in partnership with Mr Lockwood he engaged in business. Mr Lockwood died in 1884, and in the same year Mr Danielson was elected treasurer of the Quinebaug Company of Danielson, and the Lockwood Company of Waterville, Maine. He rapidly became a power in the line of industry in which he was engaged, and a leader in several enterprises of considerable magnitude. He was treasurer of the Wauregan Mills at Wauregan, Connecticut, the Lewiston Bleachery and Dye Works at Lewiston, Maine, and the Ponemah Mills at Taftsville, Connecticut. In addition to his huge cotton interests in the New England States, he was also a stockholder in several cotton mills in the South. Mr. Danielson was a well-known figure in the financial world. In 1877 he became a member of the corporation of the Providence Institute for Savings, and in 1884 was elected a director of the same institution. He was also a director of the Rhode Island Hospital Trust Company, and a member of its finance committee. from 1887 to 1908 he served as treasurer of the Rhode Island Hospital. He was a deacon of the Central Congre-

gational Church at Providence. From 1886 until the time of his death, Mr Danielson was a member of the Rhode Island Historical Society.

John Weaver Danielson married, on August 24, 1858, Sarah Deming Lockwood, born May 30, 1836, at Slatersville, Rhode Island, the daughter of Amos De Forest and Sarah Fuller (Deming) Lockwood. Mrs Danielson survives her husband and resides at No 160 Waterman street, Providence. Their children were. 1 Edith Lockwood, married Elisha Harris Howard of Providence, children 1. John Danielson Howard, who married Mildred Grandstaff they have one daughter, Catherine Howard, 11 Elisha Harris Howard, Jr , 111 Alice Lockwood Howard, married Raymond E Ostby, of Providence 2 Alice Weaver, the wife of Theodore P Bogert, of Providence, Rhode Island has adopted two children—Alice, who died at the age of one and one-half years, and Edith 3 Amos Lockwood, married Charlotte Ives Goddard, and had one child 1 Henry L Danielson, who died at the age of fourteen years 4 John De Forest, died October 16 1909, married Pauline Root, who now resides in Boston

Mr. Danielson was a member of the Hope and Art clubs, of Providence; of the Arkwright Club of Boston, and of the Oquossoc Angling Association of the Rangely Lakes, Maine. He was a man of sterling worth, and greatly respected and loved in Providence. The following is an excerpt from the resolution passed by the Rhode Island Historical Society at the time of his death

He was conspicuous for his wide activity and success in business and manufacturing interests, and his devotion to the mission of the Christian church. He was wise in counsel, upright in life public spirited as a citizen, and greatly honored by all who knew him

LOCKWOOD, Amos De Forest,
Leader in Industrial Development

Lockwood is an English surname of very ancient origin, and is found in the "Domesday Book," which dates back a period of eight hundred years It is a place name, and the family has several branches in England, Staffordshire, Yorkshire, County Essex, and Northampton The family is a very ancient and honorable one, and entitled to bear arms by royal patent The coat-of-arms of the Lockwoods is derived from the Rev Richard Lockwood, rector of Dingley, County Northampton, in the year 1530

Arms—Argent a fesse between three martlets sable
Crest—On the stump of an oak tree erased proper a martlet sable
Motto—*Tutus in undis*

(I) Robert Lockwood, the immigrant ancestor of the family in America, was a native of England, and emigrated to the colonies in the year 1630 He came first to Watertown, Massachusetts, where he was admitted a freeman on March 9, 1636-37 He was the executor of the estate of one Edmund Lockwood, supposed to have been his brother About 1646 he removed from Watertown, Massachusetts, to Fairfield, Connecticut, where he died intestate, in 1658 Robert Lockwood was admitted a freeman at Fairfield, Connecticut, May 20, 1652 He was appointed sergeant at Fairfield in May, 1657, and is said to have lived for a time in Norwalk, Connecticut In 1660 he deeded to Rev John Bishop the house and lot which he purchased of Elias Bayley, Rev Mr Denton's attorney.

He married Susannah ———, who married (second) Jeffrey Ferris, and died at Greenwich, Connecticut, December 23, 1660 Children 1 Jonathan, born September 10, 1634 2 Deborah, born October 12, 1636 3 Joseph, born August 6,

1638 4 Daniel, born March 21, 1640 5 Ephraim, born December 1, 1641 6 Gershom, mentioned below 7 John 8 Abigail, married John Harlow, of Fairfield, Connecticut 9 Sarah 10 Mary, married Jonathan Heusted

The inventory of the estate of Robert Lockwood, dated September 11, 1658, amounted to £467 63s, taken by Anthony Wilson and John Lockwood On May 13 1654, Susan Lockwood, wife of Robert Lockwood, gave evidence in a witch case at a court held at New Haven, Connecticut, and stated that she was present when goodwife Knapp was hanged for a witch (New Haven Colonial Records)

(II) Lieutenant Gershom Lockwood, son of Robert and Susannah Lockwood, was born in Watertown, Massachusetts, September 6, 1643, and died in Greenwich Fairfield county, Connecticut, March 12, 1718-19 He removed to Greenwich with his father when he was nine years of age He became one of the twenty-seven proprietors of the town of Greenwich, and held many positions of public trust and importance in the town By trade he was a carpenter, and was the principal builder in the town In 1694-95 Gershom Lockwood and his son were taxed on £153 15s He made his will November 22, 1692, and was called at that time, Gershom Lockwood, Senior

Lieutenant Gershom Lockwood married Lady Ann Millington, a daughter of Lord Millington, of England She came to New England in search of her lover, a British army officer Failing to find him, she taught school, and subsequently married Gershom Lockwood, of Greenwich, Connecticut In 1660 her parents sent her from England a large oak chest, ingeniously carved on the outside, and strongly built; tradition says that the case contained half a bushel of guineas, and many fine silk dresses The chest has

254

been handed down through several generations and at last accounts was in the home of Mr Samuel Ferris, in Greenwich, Connecticut. Lieutenant Gershom Lockwood married (second) Elizabeth daughter of John and Elizabeth (Montgomery) Townsend, and the widow of Gideon Wright. The children of Lieutenant and Ann (Millington) Lockwood were 1 Gershom 2 William, died young 3 Joseph 4 Elizabeth, married John Bates. 5. Hannah, born in 1667; married (first) John Burwell, married (second) Thomas Hamord. 6 Sarah, received by her father's will "a certain negro girl being now in my possession." 7. Abraham, twin of Sarah, mentioned below.

(III) Abraham Lockwood, son of Lieutenant Gershom and Ann (Millington) Lockwood, was born about 1669, in Greenwich, Connecticut, and died in June, 1747, at the age of seventy-seven years. He was the first of the line to remove to Rhode Island, and there established the family. He was a resident of Old Warwick, Rhode Island, and a prosperous farmer and landowner there. He married, about 1693, Sarah Westcott, born in 1673 daughter of Amos and Deborah (Stafford) Westcott. Their children were 1 Deborah, married, November 29, 1725, Nathaniel Cole 2 Amos, mentioned below 3 Adam, married, December 24 1734, Sarah Straight. 4 Sarah Lockwood, married, June 6 1728, Abel Potter. 5. Abraham, married Mary ――

(IV) Captain Amos Lockwood, son of Abraham and Sarah (Westcott) Lockwood, was born in Warwick, Rhode Island, about 1695, and died there on March 11, 1772. He was admitted a freeman of the Colony of Rhode Island, April 30, 1723 (Rhode Island Colonial Records, vol 4 p. 327.) Captain Amos Lockwood was prominent in public life in the colony, and held the office of deputy from Warwick, May 1, 1749

He married Sarah Utter, December 23, 1725 She was the daughter of William and Anne (Stone) Utter, of Warwick, Rhode Island, and was born August 1, 1707, died January 4, 1780 Their children were 1 Amos, Jr, born April 25, 1727, married Mary Knight 2 Sarah, born January 26, 1728-29, married Sion Arnold 3 Ann, born December 28, 1730 married Joseph Arnold 4 Benoni, mentioned below 5 Alice, born October 10, 1735; married John Healy 6. Marcy, born November 26, 1737, married Stephen Greene 7 Waite, born September 2, 1742, married William Greene. 8. Phebe. born June 20, 1744 9 Barbary, born April 24, 1747 10 Abraham, born December 26, 1748, married Patience Greene 11 Millacent, born April 25, 1750

(V) Captain Benoni Lockwood, son of Captain Amos and Sarah (Utter) Lockwood, was born November 26, 1733, in Warwick, Rhode Island He removed from Warwick to Cranston, Rhode Island where he became a leading citizen and active in military affairs

He married, April 5, 1772, Phebe Waterman, born April 11, 1748, died October 19, 1808, daughter of Resolved and Sarah (Carr) Waterman She married, after the death of Captain Lockwood, Moses Brown, who died in 1836 Captain Benoni Lockwood died in Cranston, Rhode Island February 19, 1781, aged forty-eight years The children of Captain Benoni and Phebe (Waterman) Lockwood were 1 Sarah, born April 24, 1773, married Bates Harris. 2 Avis, born December 7, 1774. 3 Benoni, mentioned below 4 Phebe, born December 9, 1778

(VI) Benoni (2) Lockwood, son of Captain Benoni (1) and Phebe (Waterman) Lockwood, was born in Cranston Rhode Island, April 2, 1777 During the early years of his life he followed the sea, ranking as captain. He later entered the profession of civil engineering, in which he engaged for the remaining years of his life. He died in Cranston, April 26, 1852. The following mention of him is found in the "History of Warwick, R. I." p. 311:

"Dan'l Arnold left legacies to the Shawomet Baptist Church, which has brought to light the existence of a few members who claimed to be the church, their names are Benoni Lockwood, Amelia Weaver, Lucy A. Lockwood and Eliza I. Lockwood."

Captain Benoni (2) Lockwood married, April 29, 1798, Phebe Greene, daughter of Rhodes and Phebe (Vaughan) Greene. Their children were: 1. Rhodes Greene, died young. 2. Phebe Greene, married Reuben Peckham. 3. Sarah. 4. Mary. 5. Benoni, born April 26, 1805; married Amelia Cooley. 6. Avis Waterman married Rhodes B. Chapman. 7. Amos De Forest, born October 30, 1811, mentioned below. 8. Anna Tucker, born October 13, 1813, married James Dennis. 9. Moses Brown, born August 25, 1815, died May 13, 1872. 10. Dorcas Brown.

(VII) Amos De Forest Lockwood, son of Captain Benoni and Phebe (Greene) Lockwood, was born at Pawtuxet, Rhode Island, October 30, 1811. His education was terminated in his sixteenth year, and at that age he entered the business world in the employ of the firm of Peck & Wilkinson, merchants and manufacturers, of the town of Rehoboth, ten miles from his home, and his occasional visits to his home were made on foot. For two years he served as clerk in the store, and for two years was a mill hand, acquiring a knowledge of the manufacture of cotton fabrics. Thence he became an operative in the employ of Almy, Brown & Slater, at Slatersville, Rhode Island. He found this work congenial and put all his energy

into an exhaustive study of its every phase, familiarizing himself with all the details of the work, and making himself in a short time one of the firm's most valued employes. He later became superintendent of the mill before he had attained his majority, and three years later was made resident agent. After eight years of faithful service in this capacity he became one of a company formed to rent and operate the property, which was successfully carried forward for a period of ten years.

Mr. Lockwood remained a resident of Slatersville twenty-one years, and his influence upon the community was most salutary. He had early formed religious connections under the care of Rev. Thomas Vernon at Rehoboth, and his life and conduct were calculated to inspire noble motives in others. When the lease of the Slatersville property expired, Mr. Lockwood became interested in the Quinebaug Mills of Danielson, Connecticut, and was one of the original proprietors of the Wauregan Mills in Plainfield, same State, which were begun under his supervision and managed by him several years. After residing in Danielson five years he went to Lawrence, Massachusetts, in 1855, and rearranged the Pacific Mills of that State. Three years later, in 1858, as mechanical engineer, he took charge of extensive operations for Boston capitalists at Lewiston, Maine, and in other places in that State and Northeastern Massachusetts. He still resided in Danielson until 1860. Under his supervision the Androscoggin Mills at Lewiston were built, equipped, and put in operation, and for several years he was resident agent. He resided twelve years in Lewiston, where the operations under his charge were very profitable, and he acquired a great variety of business interests. He was elected treasurer of Bowdoin College, and about the same time became a corporate member of the American Board of Commissioners for Foreign Missions, both of which positions he filled during his life

In the spring of 1874 a corporation was formed to engage in manufacturing at Waterville, Maine, and Mr Lockwood was chosen treasurer of the company, which took his name, and the Lockwood Mills, erected according to his plan, were operated with great success and profit In 1873 he returned to Rhode Island, and continued thereafter to reside in Providence At the time of his decease he was president of the Saco water power machine shop at Biddeford, Maine The minutes of the directors relating to his death speak of him as one who had been associated with them from the beginning of the enterprise, and one who was interested and active in its success, and whose loss could not be measured, and 'to the managers a personal loss which cannot be filled " The institutions, corporations and associations of various kinds with which he was identified numbered nearly one hundred His memorialist says "It seems amazing that one man has done so much and done it so well, and, yet, as one has said, 'was never in a hurry'." Mr Lockwood was one of the early presidents of the Congregation Club of Rhode Island, which passed appropriate resolutions following his death, of which the following is the closing paragraph

Resolved That in the death of Amos D Lockwood we have suffered no common loss He was identified with the industries of our State, with its soundest business enterprises, with its charitable institutions and with its religious life In all these departments his influence was felt in a marked degree, and always on the side of right By his death we have lost a leader or industry, who was an ornament to our community, a counselor whose advice was always wise, a man whose uprightness and integrity stood

firm as the everlasting hills, a friend whose kindliness endeared him to all who knew him, a Christian whose daily life exemplified the faith which he professed

Mr Lockwood lived in the times of the greatest development in the American industries, and he contributed no small share not only to the material development of the region in which he lived, but also to its moral and social uplifting He assisted in planting the cotton industry in the South, where it has grown to large volume The directors of the Pacelet Manufacturing Company at Spartanburg, South Carolina, passed proper resolutions upon his death, which follow

Resolved, That we have heard, with much regret, of the death of Amos D Lockwood, for whom we had the highest respect and regard

Resolved, That in him was found a true friend not only of our company but also of the entire South While his death will be a great loss to the many enterprises with which he was connected, the entire manufacturing interest of the South is no less a sufferer By his works he showed great faith in the future of this country Full of energy and experience he commanded our respect and confidence. Frank and candid, useful in every way, full of honors, a Christian gentleman, we saw in him a man as he should be His life was worth living

A man of strong convictions, he was of most kindly nature, and to him the home circle was very dear He was a child when among children; was very fond of music and gifted with a sweet voice, which retained its strength and purity to the last He was never too busy or too weary to listen to singing, or join in it Particularly marked in his observance of the Sabbath, he could ill bear the presence in his family of any one who intruded themes of business on sacred time He never would permit repairs on mills under his control on that day Having been asked his opinion in regard to Sabbath work in manufacturing establishments,

Mr Lockwood closed his letter in reply with the following words ' My habit from the commencement of my business life has been to work only six days in a week, and to have those under me do the same, and never have I departed from this custom except when property has been in danger from fire or flood " Kind, charitable, as he was in respect to the opinions and practices of others, his convictions were an abiding law to himself This appears, also in his staunch adherence to the cause of temperance

Mr Lockwood was one of the early presidents of the Congregational Club of Rhode Island As an expression of a sense of bereavement and an estimate of his character, at a meeting held February 11, 1884, the following resolutions, offered by Hon. Rowland Hazard, were unanimously adopted

Whereas, It has pleased Almighty God to remove from us, by sudden death. our well-beloved friend and associate, Amos D Lockwood a former President of the Club, a valued member of the Congregational Church, and a citizen of this Commonwealth, known and respected of all men for his sagacity. for his prudence, for his kindly courtesy, for his sterling integrity, and for his Christian character: and.

Whereas. We desire to give some expression however inadequate, to the feelings which we share in common with this whole community. it is therefore,

Resolved, That in the death of Amos D. Lockwood we have suffered no common loss He was identified with the industries of our State, with its soundest business institutions, and with its religious life In all these departments his influence was felt in a marked degree and always on the side of the right By his death we have lost a leader of industry, who was an ornament to our community, a counselor whose advice was always wise, a man whose uprightness and integrity stood firm as the everlasting hills, a friend whose kindliness endeared him to all who knew him a Christian whose daily life exemplified the faith which he professed

Resolved, That when such a man dies, it is the duty of the living to bear testimony to the worth of the dead. We perform this duty with no empty form of words With true and earnest feeling we would say Here was a man of whom we were justly proud, here was a life rounded and filled with duties faithfully performed, here was an example to put to shame our own shortcomings, and to lead us upward to loftier heights of Christian living

Resolved, That we tender our heartfelt sympathies to the afflicted family of our deceased friend Within the sacred circle of private grief we cannot intrude, but the memory of his noble life, the recollection of his kindly deeds, and the record of his Christian example form an heirloom in which we also have a part We ask that those who were near and dear to him will permit us to lay our tribute of respect upon his tomb. Careful of his own reputation as a business man he would not speak ill of others

He married, May 27, 1835, Sarah Fuller Deming, of Boston, born August 24, 1812, died May 23, 1889, daughter of Charles and Mehitable (Fuller) Deming, of Needham Children 1. Sarah Deming, mentioned below 2 De Forest, born 1838, died young 3 Amelia De F, November 29, 1840, died in 1910, unmarried 4 Mary, August 8, 1847, died young

(VIII) Sarah Deming, eldest child of Amos De Forest and Sarah F. (Deming) Lockwood, was born May 30, 1836, in Slatersville, and became the wife of John W Danielson (see Danielson VI).

WATERMAN, John O,
Man of Great Enterprise

(I) Richard Waterman, the American ancestor. was born in England about the year 1590 He came to New England in 1629, not a decade later than the Pilgrims of the Mayflower," and like them he settled in Massachusetts But the good people of Salem banished him from their midst for religious heresy as they did Roger Williams, he removed to Providence in March 1638, and became the founder of one of the oldest families of

Rhode Island, one allied with several other of the historic families of that State

Waterman Arms—Or a Buck's head caboshed gules

Richard Waterman, after coming to Rhode Island, first settled in Providence, there residing many years, and also made his residence in Newport He was one of the seven to whom Roger Williams deeded land in Providence, and in 1639 was one of the twelve original members of the first Baptist church in America In 1640 he was one of the signers to an agreement for a form of government, was made a freeman in 1655, and was successively commissioner, juryman and warden, also holding a colonel's rank in the militia Died 1673 Married Bethia ———, died 1680 Issue 1 Nathaniel Waterman, married Susanna Carden 2 Resolved Waterman, mentioned below 3 Mehetable Waterman, married Captain Arthur Fenner 4 Waite Waterman, married Henry Brown

(II) Resolved Waterman, son of Richard and Bethia Waterman was born in 1638 He only lived to attain the age of thirty-two years, but he had risen to the distinction of deputy to the General Court in 1667, being then twenty-nine, and gave great promise of a life of usefulness and honor Died 1670

Married, in 1659, Mercy Williams, born in Providence, Rhode Island, July 15, 1640, died 1707, daughter of Roger Williams, born 1599, died 1683 and his wife, Mary Barnard Mrs Waterman married (second) Samuel Winsor Issue 1 Richard Waterman, born January, 1660, died September 28, 1848, married Anne Waterman, daughter of Nathaniel and Susanna Waterman 2 Mercy Waterman, born in 1663, died February 19, 1756, married Tristan Derby 3 John Waterman, of Warwick, born 1664 or 1666, died August

28, 1748, married Anne Olney, daughter of Thomas and Elizabeth (Marsh) Olney 4 Resolved Waterman, mention below 5 Waite Waterman, born about 1668, married John Rhodes, of Pawtucket, Rhode Island

(III) Ensign Resolved Waterman, was born in 1667, and in 1689 settled in the now town of Greenville, Rhode Island He served as ensign of militia for many years, and in 1715 represented the town in the General Assembly Died January 13, 1719 Married (first) Anne Harris, born November 12, 1673, daughter of Andrew Harris and granddaughter of William Harris Married (second) Mercy ———, died 1759 Issue (by first wife) 1 Resolved Waterman, mentioned below 2 Mercy Waterman 3 Joseph Waterman Issue (by second wife) 4 Waite Waterman 5 John Waterman 6 Hannah Waterman

(IV) Colonel Resolved Waterman, son of Ensign Resolved Waterman and his first wife, Anne Harris, was born at Smithfield, Rhode Island, March 12, 1703 He built the Greenville Tavern in 1733 and was a man of importance, the records naming him as "Esq." He represented Smithfield in the General Assembly in May and July, 1739, in May and October, 1740, in May and October, 1741 died July 15, 1746 Married, September 20, 1722, Lydia Mathewson born June 7, 1701 Issue 1 Captain Andrew Waterman, born 1724, died March 6, 1812, a very prominent man of his day Married (first) Sarah Wilkinson, of Scituate Married (second) Margaret Foster, daughter of John and Hannah Foster 2 Resolved Waterman, died 1772, proprietor of the Greenville Tavern for many years, major and colonel of militia 3 Stephen Waterman, died young 4 John Waterman, mentioned below 5 Annie Waterman, born December 12, 1729 6 Ste-

phen Waterman, born May 12, 1737 7
Lydia Waterman, born 1733 8 William
Waterman, born 1736 9 Annie Water-
man, born September 11, 1740

(V) Captain John Waterman, son of
Colonel Resolved and Lydia (Mathewson) Waterman, was born in 1728 He
became a ship owner and sea captain, sailing his own ships to China and other
foreign countries He was known as
"Paper Mill John," from the fact that he
built one of the first paper mills in America He was an early and extensive manufacturer not only of paper, but operated
a fulling mill, a woolen cloth finishing
mill, and a chocolate factory In 1769
he engaged in printing and publishing
His enterprises brought him great gain,
and he was rated among the wealthiest
men in the State, part of his wealth consisting of slaves His wealth was inherited by his only son, his daughters
only being given their wedding outfits
Died February 7, 1777

Married, January 17, 1750, Mary Olney
born 1731, died September 5, 1763, daughter of Captain Jonathan and Elizabeth
(Smith) Olney, her father the founder of
Olneyville, Rhode Island, her mother a
daughter of Christopher Smith Mrs
Waterman was a granddaughter of James
and Hallelujah (Brown) Olney, and a
great-granddaughter of Daniel Brown,
son of Chad Brown Issue 1 Lydia
Waterman, born March 12, 1751, married Daniel Waterman 2 Betsey Waterman born October 18 1753; married
———— White 3 Nancy Waterman, born
May 1, 1756, married (first) ————
Nichols, (second) ———— Winsor 4
John Olney Waterman, mentioned below 5 Mary Waterman, born 1760, died
1762 6 Mary Waterman, born September 5, 1763, married ———— Phillips

(VI) John Olney Waterman, son of
Captain John and Mary (Olney) Water-

man, was born May 28, 1758 He inherited
and spent his father's large estate in his
short life of thirty-eight years He became a member of St John s Lodge, No
1, Free and Accepted Masons, in 1779,
as soon as he was eligible (twenty-one
years), his name being the ninety-third
to be enrolled a member of that, the oldest
lodge in Rhode Island Died February
18, 1796

Married Sally Franklin, born February,
1762, a woman of strong character, a great
beauty and a belle, daughter of Captain
Asa and Sarah (Paine) Franklin Captain Franklin, related to the Benjamin
Franklin family, was a captain in the
French and Indian War, ensign of the
First Light Infantry in Providence county, ensign in June, 1769, of the Second
Company, Providence Militia, ensign
May, 1770, ensign in August, 1774, of
Providence County Light Infantry, lieutenant in May, 1789, September, 1790
May, 1791, June, 1792, May, 1793, his
military service long and honorable Issue
1 Mary Waterman, born February 18,
1784; married Nathan Searle, son of Ed-
ward Searle, of Scituate, Rhode Island
2 John Waterman, mentioned below 3
Sarah Waterman, born February 25, 1788,
died unmarried, 1808 4 Henry Waterman, born December 21, 1789, married
Mary, daughter of Benoni Searle 5
George Waterman, born August 19, 1793
died in California, where he is buried,
April 26, 1850, married (first) Patience
Brownell, (second) Brittannia Franklin
Baxter 6 James Franklin Waterman,
born June 27, 1795, died in Kansas, where
he is buried, February 12, 1892, married
Polly Pickering

Mrs Sally Franklin Waterman, widowed at the age of thirty-four years, married
(second) Edward Searle, of Scituate,
Rhode Island Issue 1 Richard Searle,
married Sylvia Peck Being again

widowed, she spent the last twelve years of her life with her son, John Waterman Died June 5, 1842, aged eighty years

(VII) John Waterman, son of John Olney and Sally (Franklin) Waterman, was born in Providence, Rhode Island, March 22, 1786, and lived to the great age of ninety-three years. He was educated in the public schools, and then began learning the carpenter's trade. After a few months he entered the employ of his uncle, Henry P Franklin, a cotton manufacturer, and liked the mills so well that he remained and became an expert not only in cotton mill management, but in building machinery for the mill. In 1808, in partnership with Daniel Wilde, he contracted with Richard Wheatley to run his cotton mill at Canton, Massachusetts. In connection with the mill was a machine shop equipped for repairing and building machinery, which was an important adjunct to the business during the three years the partnership existed. For a time thereafter, Mr. Waterman continued alone in the manufacture of machinery, but in 1812, in association with his uncle, Henry P. Franklin, he built and put in operation the 'Merino Mill,'' in Johnston, Rhode Island. This mill, with a capacity of fifteen hundred spindles, was run for seven years with Mr. Franklin as financial head, Mr. Waterman acting as manufacturing agent. In 1819 Mr. Waterman leased the Union Mills in which he had first learned the business. He suffered considerable loss in the operation of the "Merino Mill," and to finance the Union Mill purchase and outfitting he borrowed $20,000 of Pitcher & Gay, of Pawtucket Four years later, so profitable had the venture been, that after paying Pitcher & Gay he had a handsome balance to his credit For the next three years he was resident agent for the Blackstone Manufacturing Company, but health failing, he

resigned and went south, although there he acted as purchasing agent for the Blackstone Mills and also as salesman For ten years he remained in the south, located at New Orleans, acting as cotton broker for northern mills, associated part of that ten years with Thomas M. Burgess, of Providence. In 1829 he returned to Providence and that year built the 'Eagle Mills'' at Olneyville Mill No. 1 began operations in the spring of 1830, and in 1836 Mill No. 2 was built, Mr. Waterman continuing their operation until his retirement in 1848.

Mr. Waterman was initiated in St. John's Lodge, No. 1, Free and Accepted Masons, May 1, 1822 and raised to the degree of Master Mason the following November. He became a companion of Providence Chapter, No. 1, Royal Arch Masons, February 27, 1823, a cryptic Mason of Providence Council, Royal and Select Masons No. 1, January 29, 1824, and a Sir Knight of St. John's Commandery, No. 1, Knights Templar, February 7, 1825. He was in sympathy with the Baptist church, although not a member, and it was largely through his generosity that the Baptist church in Olneyville was built. Died at his farm in Johnston, Rhode Island, to which he had retired after leaving the business world, October 26 1879.

Married, in Canton Massachusetts, in 1809, Sally Williams, born March 1, 1787, died suddenly April 10, 1862, daughter of Stephen Williams, and a descendant of Roger Williams, through his son Daniel, his son Joseph his son Goliath, his son Stephen. Issue:

1. John Olney Waterman, mentioned below
2. Albert Waterman, married Mary J Cook, of Tiverton Rhode Island, who died March 26, 1906. Issue 1 Byron H. Waterman, married Emilie L. W. Jew-

ett, July 17, 1865 II Ada A Waterman, married D Everett Rounds, of Providence, February 21, 1871; they were the parents of Albert W Rounds, born September 13, 1873, he was educated at the University Grammar School, and later attended Brown University, from which he was graduated with the class of 1895, he then entered Harvard Medical School, taking the degree of Doctor of Medicine in 1898, he later specialized in orthopedic surgery, is now practicing in Providence, Rhode Island, at No 79 Broad street III John Albert Waterman, married Mrs Lissie (Gleason) Pitts, died June 22, 1898. IV Mary Frances Waterman

3 Andrew Searles Waterman, born June 7, 1815, died in New Orleans, June 10, 1852, a graduate of Brown University

4 Sarah A Waterman, born August 31, 1822, died unmarried, June 1, 1886

5 Mary Frances Waterman, born October 12, 1825, died September 1, 1829

6 Henry Francis, born July 31, 1830, died unmarried, September 15, 1859.

All are buried in Swan Point Cemetery, Providence

(VIII) John Olney Waterman, son of John and Sally (Williams) Waterman, was born in Canton, Massachusetts, November 4, 1810. In infancy he was brought to Johnston, Rhode Island, and all his life was a true and loyal son of Rhode Island in all but birth He was educated in the public schools and Plainfield (Connecticut) Academy, early beginning work in the cotton mills He was clerk in the store operated by the Merino Mills in 1727-28-29, leaving in the last year to become agent for the Eagle Mills, owned by his father, at Olneyville He continued in that capacity until 1847, then was engaged to build and operate the first cotton mill in the town of Warren, Rhode Island, for the Warren Manufacturing Company From that time until the present the name of Waterman has been connected with successful cotton manufacturing in Warren From the completion of the first

mill, Mr Waterman maintained official relation with the Warren Manufacturing Company as treasurer and agent, devoting thirty-three years of his life to its affairs, seeing the single mill of 1847 grow to three large mills equipped with 58,000 spindles and 1,400 looms, weaving sheetings, print cloths and jaconets The second mill was built in 1860 from the profits of the first, and the third in 1870 from the profits of the first and second mills, the company later increasing its capital stock to $600,000.

Mr Waterman during his Providence residence served as a member of Common Council from the Sixth Ward, and for many years was a member of the Board of Independent Fire Wards In 1845 he was elected to the Rhode Island Legislature from Providence, and reelected in 1846, serving with honor In 1848 he moved his residence to Warren, Rhode Island, and there his great business ability, his conservative managerial talents and his sagacious financiering, made him a leader In 1855 he was elected a director of the Fireman's Mutual Insurance Company of Providence, in 1860 a director of the newly organized Equitable Fire and Marine Insurance Company, in 1868 a director of the Blackstone Mutual Fire Insurance Company, organized that year, and in 1874 of the newly formed Merchants' Mutual Fire Insurance Company, holding these directorships until his death He was equally prominent in Warren's banking circles, in July, 1855, he aided in organizing the Sowamset State Bank, and was chosen a director, also was made a director of the First National Bank of Warren upon its organization in 1864, and was elected vice-president in 1866, serving until his death; was one of the founders of the Warren Institution for Savings, and in 1870 was chosen a trustee, in 1875 was elected a director of the

Old National Bank of Providence, and later and until his death its honored president. He was identified with other interests and institutions, among them the Providence Board of Trade. He was the friend of every deserving person or enterprise, and freely gave them his aid. In fact, "he represented that class of men whose untiring industry superior natural gifts and strict integrity place them at the head of the great manufacturing interests for which Rhode Island is justly celebrated."

Died at his home in Warren, April 24, 1881 all business in the town being suspended on the day of his funeral, out of respect to his memory

Married (first) in 1838, Caroline Frances Sanford, died 1840, daughter of Joseph C Sanford, of Wickford, Rhode Island. Married (second) June 26, 1849 Susan Johnson Bosworth, born March 22, 1828, died in Warren, March 16, 1897, daughter of Colonel Smith Bosworth of Rehoboth and Providence his wife, Sarah Tripp Mrs. Waterman is buried with her husband in Swan Point Cemetery Providence.

Issue (a daughter and a son)

1. Caroline Frances Waterman born in Warren Rhode Island, July 9, 1850 Married, March 2, 1908 Arthur Henry Arnold, of Providence, who died April 24, 1913

2. John Waterman born in Warren, January 11, 1852 He was educated in a private school in Warren until thirteen years of age, then spent six years in Warren High School, leaving at the age of nineteen to enter the business world in which his forefathers had won such high reputation and such sterling success He inherited their strong business traits, and although but forty-eight years were allotted him, he worthily bore the name and upheld the family reputation Upon the death of his honored father in 1881, he succeeded him as treasurer of the Warren Manufacturing Company, and at the time of his death was a director of three of Warren's four banks and connected

with banks and insurance companies in Providence In 1895 the three mills of the Warren Manufacturing Company were destroyed by fire, and from the ruins arose one magnificent mill with the capacity of the former three, a splendid monument to the Watermans, father and son, to whom the wonderful success of the company was due For many years John Waterman emulated the example of his sire in the interest he took in the George Hail Free Library, and all public affairs of Warren He was a member of the building committee in charge of the erection of the town hall, and at the time of his death chairman of a committee for increasing school facilities He was for many years colonel of the Warren Artillery, and was past master of Washington Lodge, Free and Accepted Masons From boyhood he had been an attendant at St Mark's Episcopal Church, of which he was a confirmed member, had been a member of the church choir, had served as an officer of the Sunday school for thirty-one years, for twenty-four years was a vestryman, and for eleven years junior warden He personally superintended the improvement and enlargement of St Mark's Chapel, a movement he inaugurated and generously supported He possessed the Waterman energy, vacations were almost unknown to him, and although the possessor of great wealth, he was one of the most democratic of men Kindly and genial in nature, he mingled freely with all classes preserving the strictest integrity in his dealings with all, and in all his enterprises exhibiting remarkable persistency and tenacity of purpose, laboring faithfully and unceasingly

Died at his home in Warren, Rhode Island December 21 1900, his funeral being largely attended, business being largely suspended during the services, out of respect to his memory

Married, December 17, 1884, Sarah Franklin Adams, who survived him, and married (second) April 4, 1904 Rev Joseph Hutchinson of Columbus, Ohio, Issue (constituting the tenth generation)

i John Olney Waterman, born September 21 1885

ii Andrew Searles Waterman, born June 30,

1887, married, October 4, 1912, Ruth Townsend, of Providence, born May, 1895
iii Susan Bosworth Waterman, born February 9, 1890; married, June 24, 1914, Henry S. Newcombe, of Marlboro, Massachusetts, born October 11, 1890
iv Albert Franklin Waterman, born December 1, 1891; married Celeste Butts, of East Greenwich, Rhode Island, June 30, 1915
v Henry Everett Waterman, born August 7, 1893
vi Carrie Louise Waterman, born March 5, 1895, died September 21, 1895
vii Byron Adams Waterman, born May 20, 1897

(The Bosworth Line)

Arms—Gules a cross vair between four annulets argent
Crest—A lily proper, slipped and leaved

(I) Edward Bosworth, like Richard Waterman, first settled in Massachusetts, but this branch did not appear in Rhode Island until the seventh American generation Edward Bosworth never reached New England alive, but died at sea as the ship 'Elizabeth and Dorcas,' which sailed for New England in 1634, was approaching Boston harbor He was buried in Boston, and his children founded the family prominent in New England history The widow and children of Edward Bosworth were of Hingham, Massachusetts, in 1635, the mother dying there Died on shipboard, in 1634 Married Mary ———, died May 18, 1648 Issue 1 Edward Bosworth 2 Jonathan Bosworth mentioned below 3 Benjamin Bosworth, born 1613 4 Mary Bosworth, born 1614 5 Nathaniel Bosworth, born 1617

(II) Jonathan Bosworth, son of Edward Bosworth, was born in 1611, but beyond the fact that he was living in Hingham, Massachusetts, with his mother in 1635, nothing is recorded of him further, except that he married and had issue
1 Jonathan Bosworth, mentioned below

(III) Jonathan (2) Bosworth, son of Jonathan (1) Bosworth, married Hannah

Howland, daughter of John and Elizabeth (Tilley) Howland, both her parents coming to New England in 1620 in the 'Mayflower" Issue 1 Jonathan Bosworth mentioned below

(IV) Jonathan (3) Bosworth, son of Jonathan (2) and Hannah (Howland) Bosworth, was born September 22, 1680 Married Sarah Rounds Issue 1 Ichabod Bosworth, mentioned below 2 Christian Bosworth, born at Rehoboth, Massachusetts, May 16, 1708 3 Jonathan Bosworth, born at Rehoboth, February 10, 1711 4 Elisha Bosworth born July 8, 1713

(V) Ichabod Bosworth, son of Jonathan (3) and Sarah (Rounds) Bosworth was born at Swansea, Massachusetts, May 31, 1706 Married (first) January 12, 1726-27, Mary Brown Married (second) in Warren, Rhode Island, November 19 1748, Bethia Wood, of Swansea, Massachusetts Issue (by first wife) 1 Bethia Bosworth 2 Mary Bosworth 3 Ichabod Bosworth 4 Elizabeth Bosworth Issue (by second wife) 5 Peleg Bosworth, mentioned below 6 Joseph Bosworth born April 10, 1756 7 Charity Bosworth, born April 21, 1758 8 John Bosworth, born June 14, 1706

(VI) Peleg Bosworth, son of Ichabod Bosworth and his second wife, Bethia Wood, was born May 6, 1754 He was a soldier of the Revolution, serving as a private in Captain Stephen Bullock's company, Colonel Carpenter's regiment, marching to Bristol, Rhode Island, on the alarm of December 8 1776, serving twelve days to December 20, 1776, also in Captain Israel Hick's company. Colonel John Daggett's regiment, marched January 5, 1778, discharged March 31, 1778, serving two months, twenty-seven days in Rhode Island, also in Lieutenant James Horton's company, Colonel Thomas Carpenter's regiment, enlisted August 2, 1780, discharged August 7, 1780, serving six days on an alarm, marched to Tiverton, Rhode Island. All his service is credited to Massachusetts.

Married, September 1, 1774, Mary (Polly) Smith, born in Rehoboth, Massachusetts, August, 1749, died 1818. Issue: 1 Smith Bosworth, mentioned below.

(VII) Colonel Smith Bosworth, son of Peleg and Mary (Polly) (Smith) Bosworth, was born at Rehoboth, Massachusetts, October 28, 1781. After a limited period of school work, he began the active business of life by completing in Providence, Rhode Island, an apprenticeship at the mason's trade. From a journeyman mason he advanced to contracting, and in partnership with Asa Bosworth erected many of the beautiful homes on the east of the river in Providence, also a number of the city's churches and public buildings. Bosworth & Bosworth were the contractors for St. John's Episcopal Church on North Main street, Providence, and the Beneficent Congregational Church on Broad street, and in 1814 built the mills of the Providence Dyeing, Bleaching and Calendering Company on Sabin street. Two years later, on March 16, 1816, Colonel Bosworth accepted an appointment as agent of the company, and for nineteen years filled that responsible post with efficiency and ability. In 1835 he resigned but until 1841 continued in the company's service as superintendent or general outside manager. His connection with that company brought him wide acquaintance and reputation among business men and under his able management the company experienced great prosperity, becoming one of the largest establishments of its nature in the United States.

Long before Providence became a city, Colonel Bosworth was active in public affairs and held many town offices. After incorporation as a city, he was a member of the Board of Fire Wards, chief engineer of the fire department and street commissioner. His military title came from his service in the Rhode Island State militia, in which he held the rank of colonel for many years. He directed the erection of the earthworks on Fox Point in 1812 and during the Dorr War was captain of the City Guards of Providence. He was a member of St. John's Lodge, No. 1, Free and Accepted Masons, of Providence, and late in life became a member of Beneficent Congregational Church, in which faith and connection he died. He was most generous in his benefactions, kindliness and a keen sense of justice also being marked characteristics. He lived in the love and good will of his fellow citizens, and was highly esteemed as a man of uprightness and integrity. Died in Providence, March 9, 1857.

Married, January 31, 1805, Sarah Tripp, born October 6, 1785, died November 13, 1860, at Warren, Rhode Island, and is buried in North Graveyard, Providence, daughter of Othniel and Sarah Tripp, of Swansea, Massachusetts. Issue (all born in Providence):

1. Thomas Tripp Bosworth, born November 6, 1805, died July 3, 1867, married, November 16, 1834, Mary Greene Case, born September 7, 1816, in Rehoboth, Massachusetts, died February 21, 1897. Issue:

i Sarah Smith Bosworth, born in Rehoboth, Massachusetts, September 13, 1835, married William Abbott Cornell, March 11, 1855, died June 8, 1857.

ii Lydia Horton Bosworth, born in Rehoboth, Massachusetts, October 2, 1837, died March 8, 1839.

iii Esther Bosworth, born in Rehoboth, Massachusetts, October 6, 1839.

iv Isabel Bosworth, born in Raynham, Massachusetts, July 30, 1842, died in Providence, Rhode Island, May 11, 1844.

v Thomas Tripp Bosworth, Jr., born in

Warren, Rhode Island, February 10, 1845, died December 6, 1860.

vi Frank Smith Bosworth, born in Warren, Rhode Island, February 23, 1849, died March 7, 1854

vii Mary Smith Bosworth, born in Warren Rhode Island October 24 1853 married Edward Foster Jarvis, in Quincy Massachusetts, September 3, 1872

viii William Quincy Bosworth, born in North Quincy, Massachusetts, November 28, 1859 died January 16, 1884 unmarried

2 Mary Smith Bosworth, born February 2, 1808 died, unmarried, September 30, 1849

3 Joseph Haile Bosworth, born August 31, 1810, died October 29, 1885, married, September 2, 1850, Mary Easton Rousmaniere, of Newport Issue

i Sarah Elizabeth Bosworth, married (first) George Blackmar (second) Dr Benjamin Burrell, who died in Denver she died in Denver

ii Mary Rousmaniere Bosworth, born January 13, 1855, married John O Darling, of Providence, born December 24, 1852

4 Charles Henry Bosworth, died unmarried

5 Smith Bosworth, Jr, died unmarried

6 Sarah Tripp Bosworth, born January 26, 1821, died, unmarried, September 1, 1849

7 Ann Sophia Bosworth, born December 25, 1822, died October 10 1856, married, November 28, 1849, Stephen A Arnold, of Providence Issue

i Eliza Rhodes Arnold, born August 28, 1850, married, July 12, 1868 Charles A Pierce, of Providence, born December 17, 1849. Issue a Ann Sophia Pierce, married October 8, 1907, Arthur P Billings, of Lunenburg, Massachusetts b Frank Wetherell Pierce

ii Frances Bosworth Arnold married, November 5, 1872, Cyrus Withington Eddy, of Providence, died March 28, 1911. Issue a Sarah Frances Eddy, born July 8, 1873, married, August 8, 1895, John Henry Bartlett b Stephen Tourtelott Eddy, born November 28, 1874, died September 3, 1879 c

Thomas Arnold Eddy, born November 9, 1876, died October 26, 1902 d Albert Henry Eddy, born July 15, 1878, married Annabelle Maud Gillam e William Anthony Eddy, born June 13, 1880, died April 23, 1894 f Charles Andrew Eddy, born August 27, 1882, died May 10, 1894 g Cyrus Tourtelott Eddy, born July, 1884 married Eliza Ruth Anderson h Walter Rhodes Eddy, born June 29 1887, died April 17, 1894 i Mildred Eddy, born November 19, 1891 j Irvin Eddy, born May 4, 1893

8 Susan Johnson Bosworth, born March 22, 1828, died March 16, 1897, married John Olney Waterman (see Waterman IX)

9 Frances Eleanor Bosworth, born September 12, 1829, died, unmarried, February 3, 1842

ARNOLD, Arthur H,
Representative Citizen

Arms—Purple azure and sable three fleurs-de-lis or, ior Ynir gules a chevron ermine, between three pheons or, ior Arnold

Crest—A demi-lion rampant gules, holding between its paws a lozenge or fire ball

Motto—*Mihi gloria cessum*

The family of Arnold had its beginning among the ancient princes of Wales, tracing according to the records in the College of Arms to Ynir, King of Gwentland 1100, a lineal descendant of Ynir, second son of Cadawalder, King of the Britons In the twelfth generation a descendant of Ynir, Roger, adopted the surname Arnold. From Roger Arnold came William and Thomas Arnold, brothers, the American ancestors of the distinguished Arnold family of Rhode Island The descent from Roger Arnold is through his son Thomas Arnold, his son Richard Arnold his son, Richard Arnold, his son Thomas Arnold, his sons William and Thomas Arnold

Thomas Arnold lived for a time at Melcombe Horsey from whence he moved to Cheselbourne, Dorsetshire settling there on an estate previously owned by his father Richard Arnold, who was lord of the manor of Bagbere Thomas Arnold married (first) Alice Gulley, daughter of John Gulley, of Northover, Dorsetshire, who bore him a son, William Arnold, by a second wife he had a son, Thomas Arnold, those two sons bringing the name to the New World

(I) William Arnold, eldest son of Thomas Arnold and his first wife, Alice Gulley, was born in Leamington, England, June 24, 1587, and in 1635 came to New England in the ship Plain Joan, his younger half-brother accompanying him After a short settlement at Hingham, Massachusetts, he moved to Providence, Rhode Island, in 1636, and became one of the twelve associates to whom Roger Williams conveyed the lands granted him by the Indians William Arnold in 1638, was one of the four first settlers of Pawtucket and in 1639 was numbered among the twelve first members of the first Baptist church in America From William Arnold sprang a numerous and influential family distinguished in public, private and business life

Married Christian Peake Issue 1 Stephen Arnold, mentioned below 2 Benjamin Arnold, president of Providence Plantations, 1657, 1660 and 1662, 1663, Governor of the Colony 1663-1678; and others

(II) Stephen Arnold son of William and Christian (Peake) Arnold was born in Leamington, England, December 22, 1622 and in 1635 was brought to New England by his parents He was deputy to the Rhode Island General Court, 1664-1667 inclusive 1670 to 1677 inclusive, 1684, 1685 and 1690 He was assistant 1667, 1678 to 1681 inclusive, 1680, 1681, 1690, 1691, 1696, 1698 Died November 15, 1699

Married, November 24 1646, Sarah Smith, born 1629, died April 15, 1713, daughter of Edward Smith. of Rehoboth, Massachusetts. Issue: 1. Israel Arnold mentioned below; and others

(III) Israel Arnold, son of Stephen and Sarah (Smith) Arnold, was born at Pawtucket, Rhode Island October 30, 1649 Died at Warwick, Rhode Island, September 15. 1716 Married April 16 1677, Mary (Barker) Smith, a widow Issue: 1. William Arnold mentioned below; and others

(IV) William Arnold, son of Israel and Mary (Barker-Smith) Arnold, was born at Warwick, Rhode Island. about 1681 Died at Warwick June 1759 Married about 1705, Deliverance Whipple born February 11, 1679 Issue 1 Caleb Arnold. mentioned below; and others

(V) Caleb Arnold son of William and Deliverance (Whipple) Arnold, was born at Warwick, Rhode Island, about 1725 Died at Pawtucket, Rhode Island, March 13, 1799 Married Susannah Stafford, born March 10, 1722-23, daughter of Joseph and Susannah Stafford. Issue 1 Joseph Arnold, mentioned below

(VI) Captain Joseph Arnold, son of Caleb and Susannah (Stafford) Arnold, was born at Warwick Rhode Island August 13, 1755 He was a soldier of the Revolution. serving with Captain Thomas Holden's company, Colonel James Varnum's regiment, at Bunker Hill, and later came under General Washington's command In June 1777, he was appointed as first lieutenant of Captain Cole's company He was ensign in Colonel Christopher Greene's regiment, which marched to Morristown New Jersey, serving under General Washington in April of that year, marched to Fort Montgomery, joined the main army in Pennsylvania marched to Whitestone, going later into winter quarters at Valley Forge with the army which

267

suffered such hardships. On June 1, 1788, he was appointed captain, was in General Sullivan's expedition, recruited a company of black troops which he commanded and later mustered out of service. By virtue of his rank he was entitled to membership in the Society of the Cincinnati, joining the Rhode Island branch of the Society, December 17, 1783. Died at Warwick, July 20, 1840. Married, September 6, 1788, Sarah Stafford, daughter of Stukley Stafford. Issue. 1 Joseph Franklin Arnold, mentioned below; and others.

(VII) Joseph Franklin Arnold, son of Captain Joseph and Sarah (Stafford) Arnold, was born at Warwick, in 1785. Died in Warwick August 15, 1855. Married. March 24, 1816, Sarah Rice, born April 2, 1795, daughter of William and Sarah Rice, of Cranston, Rhode Island. Issue. 1 Joseph Franklin Arnold mentioned below; and others.

(VIII) Joseph Franklin (2) Arnold, son of Joseph Franklin (1) and Sarah (Rice) Arnold, was born in Warwick, Rhode Island, June 23, 1821. Early in life, after western travel, he settled at New Orleans, Louisiana, then third in commercial importance among the cities of the Union. He there became identified with Mississippi river steamboat navigation, and owned the "Eclipse" and the "Natchez," two boats well known on the river. The Civil War swept away the fortune he had been many years in amassing, and drove him a fugitive to the wilderness, but he finally succeeded in reaching his native State.

He at once began rebuilding his fortunes by establishing a sale and exchange mart in Providence, which he successfully conducted the remainder of his life. Died in Warwick, December 21, 1881. Married. at New Orleans, June 14, 1849. Louisa Constance, born in Demeroringer, France,

April 6, 1831, and died January 6, 1917. Issue. 1. Augustus Franklin Arnold, born August 24, 1850, married, October 28, 1874, Ellen Ward Mills, died May, 1904. Issue. 1 Jeannette Arnold, born April 29, 1877, married, October 8, 1902, Dr. Bradlee Rich. Issue. a Constance Rich, born July 20, 1906. b Arnold Rich, born September 1, 1908. 11 Norman Arnold, born December 28, 1885; married, October 25, 1909, Mary Bullfinch. 2 Sarah Williams Arnold, born in New Orleans, April 15, 1852, died in Lowell, December 4, 1876, married, December 25, 1872, Hiram E. Green. 3 Arthur Henry Arnold, mentioned below. 4 Charles Williams Arnold, born November 10, 1858, died December 4, 1867. 5 Louise Constance Arnold, born December 20, 1860, died August 3, 1862. 6 Annie Louise Arnold, born March 31, 1865, married, August 12, 1885, William H. Gilbert, resides in San Francisco, California. Issue. 1 Louise Gilbert, married, July 7, 1915, Alvin Nathaniel Lofgren, of San Francisco. 7 Caroline Arnold, married, June, 1893, Joseph Gilbert, born July 24, 1852, died March 20, 1917, she resides at Apponaug, Rhode Island. Issue. 1 Constance R. Gilbert, born April 20, 1904.

Joseph Gilbert, connected with the Arnold family of Rhode Island through his marriage in June, 1893, to Miss Caroline Arnold (see Arnold VIII), daughter of Joseph Franklin and Louisa (Constance) Arnold, was born in the town of Woonsocket, Rhode Island, July 24, 1852. He received a liberal education at the public schools of his native place, and after graduating he immediately entered into business, spending the following forty years in the latter town, and in Blackstone, Rhode Island. After several extensive business trips through the southern States, he returned north and settled in 1893 in Apponaug, where he resided the remainder of his life

Although keenly interested in many branches of business, he followed the real estate trade for a great many years He started in a small way in Woonsocket, but soon struck out for larger fields, and opened offices in the old Howard Building, in Providence He soon became known and popular among the business men of the latter city He was naturally affable and friendly, and his ingrained integrity and honesty inspired a trust among his associates seldom encountered in the present day of business He became identified with the many large movements that have played such a prominent part in the development of Providence and its outlying districts, and he also held extensive interests in land located in the surrounding towns and villages Through his energy, perseverance and native ability in his chosen work he rose gradually to an enviable position in the business world

He took a great interest in the town affairs and civic management of Apponaug, though he had not the time at his disposal that he would have wished to devote to it He was the Independent party candidate for the office of town treasurer in the fall of 1916, but was defeated by the Republican candidate

Mr. Gilbert died at his home in Apponaug, March 20, 1917, at the age of sixty-four years

(IX) Arthur Henry Arnold son of Joseph Franklin (2) and Louisa (Constance) Arnold, was born at New Orleans, Louisiana, September 8, 1855 In 1861 he was brought to Warwick by his parents, who were obliged to flee from the south with the outbreak of the Civil War, and there he attended the public schools He made further preparation in the select school of Mrs Graves, the Quakeress, then entered

East Greenwich Seminary under the then principal Rev James T Edwards At an early age he became associated with his father in business in Providence, but in 1869, after a tour of western and southern cities, was prevailed upon to remain in New Orleans, the city of his birth From 1869 until 1872 he was connected with the New Orleans and St Louis Steamboat Company In the same year he came north and entered the employ of the Boston & Providence Railroad Company, advancing through all intermediate grades to that of passenger conductor In 1880 he was made conductor of the Dedham & Boston Express and when the new station at Dedham, Massachusetts, was completed, he had the distinction of running the first train out of the new structure With the passing of the road to the Old Colony Railroad Company, Mr Arnold was transferred to the main line, and was conductor of the Colonial Express on its first trip under the new management Later he was conductor of a train running between Providence, Rhode Island, and Plymouth, Massachusetts In 1910 he retired from the railroad, and devoted the remaining three years of his life to the real estate business

Mr Arnold possessed musical talent of a high order, and while in the south placed himself under capable instructors and thoroughly trained his fine baritone voice in form, shade, expression and sentiment Under Signor Brignoli, the Italian composer and opera tenor, he perfected the cultivation of his voice after returning east, and often held positions in concert and choir work He was strongly urged to go upon the operatic stage professionally, but he could not be induced to do so, although he often appeared as a baritone soloist in concerts, and added greatly to the success of such entertainments

Genial, affable and social by nature, he was yet very strict in the performance of duty He was thoroughly fitted for his work, found it congenial to his tastes and gave to his work his best abilities, becoming a favorite with the traveling public and was highly esteemed by the railroad management He was a popular member of the Masonic order, belonging to Mt Vernon Lodge, No 4, Free and Accepted Masons, Providence Chapter, No 1, Royal Arch Masons, Providence Council, No. 1, Royal and Select Masters; St. John s Commandery, No 1, Knights Templar, Rhode Island Consistory, thirty-second degree, Ancient Accepted Scottish Rite, Palestine Temple, Nobles of the Mystic Shrine He was a member of the Conductors' Relief of Boston, vice-president of the Conductors' and Engineers' Investment Company, member of Rhode Island Society, Sons of the American Revolution, through the service of his great-grandfather, Captain Joseph Arnold, member of the Rhode Island Chapter, Society of Colonial Wars, through the services of his ancestor, Stephen Arnold, of the second American generation Died at his handsome residence, 572 Elmwood avenue, Providence, April 24, 1913

Mr Arnold was thrice married Issue by first wife 1 Louise, married James T Kenyon, of Providence Married (second) Cora Etta Barnes, born November 2, 1869 died July 2, 1906 Married (third) March 2, 1908, Caroline Frances Waterman daughter of John Olney and Susan Johnson (Bosworth) Waterman, of Warren Rhode Island (see Waterman VIII)

Mrs Arnold continues her residence in Providence, is active in all good works, noted for her charity and benevolence, her gracious hospitality and womanly graces She is a member of the Rhode Island Historical Society, Gasper Chapter, Daughters of the American Revolution, through the service of her maternal great-grandfather, Peleg Bosworth, Rhode Island Society of Colonial Dames of America, Rhode Island Society of Colonial Governors; Rhode Island Society of Mayflower Descendants eligible to all these societies through her distinguished maternal and paternal ancestry

---

CHARNLEY, Joseph G,
Highly Regarded Citizen.

All human lives are like the waves of the sea "They flash a few brief moments in the sunlight, marvels of power and beauty, and then are dashed upon the remorseless shores of death and disappear forever As the mighty deep has rolled for ages past and chanted its sublime requiem and will continue to roll during the coming ages until time shall be no more, so will the waves of human life follow each other in countless succession until they mingle at last with the billows of eternity's boundless sea "

Arms—Azure, a bend between three hawks' lures or.
Crest—A griffin passant argent holding in the dexter claw a buckle or

To acquire distinction or great prosperity in the business pursuits which give to the country its financial strength and credit requires ability of as high an order as that which leads to victory on the field of battle This fact is apparent to all who engage in the thoroughfares of trade, commerce and finance Eminent business talent is composed of a combination of high mental and moral attributes It is not simple energy and industry; there must be sound judgment, breadth of capacity rapidity of thought, justice and firmness, the foresight to perceive the course of the drifting tides of business

and the will and ability to control them. The combination of these qualities in the late Joseph Gilchrist Charnley made him in his day one of the most prominent hotel proprietors of the city of Providence, Rhode Island, a man known throughout Central New England in the hotel business, and a figure of prominence in the affairs of the city, where for several decades he carried on his affairs.

Joseph Gilchrist Charnley was a son of William and Dorothy Charnley, and a descendant of an old and honorable English family. William Charnley, the father of Joseph G. Charnley, was connected with the huge cotton industry in England, and was a superintendent in a large mill there. He lived and died in his native land. After his death his widow, Dorothy Charnley, emigrated to America with her three daughters, settling there.

Joseph Gilchrist Charnley was born in Cheshire, England, where the family has been located for several generations, in the opening years of the nineteenth century. He received an excellent education in the public schools of Cheshire, and on reaching a suitable age was apprenticed to learn the trade of block printer. Thinking America a better field for success in this line he left England and came to the United States in his early youth. Arriving here he found employment in his trade difficult to secure and intermittent. After a short period spent at his trade in different cities in the East Mr. Charnley came to Providence, Rhode Island, the city with which he was conspicuously identified until the time of his death. His first venture, which proved highly successful, was the Manufacturers' Hotel, which was situated at what is now No. 20 Market Square. The excellence of the accommodations, service and *cuisine* here brought to the hotel numerous patrons,

and the fact that the stage coach line from Providence to Boston started at his hotel brought to Mr. Charnley a large and prosperous clientele. The financial success of his first venture enabled him, shortly afterwards, to open the Union House on Weybosset street, Providence, and here he initiated a policy like that of the Manufacturers Hotel. The Union House was equally successful and for several years Mr. Charnley conducted both houses. This continued up to the time of his retirement from active business life.

Mr. Charnley was intimately connected with public and fraternal interests in Providence during the period of his active business life. He was a member of the First Light Infantry of Providence, under Colonel Brown. Though he maintained no connection with the organization here he was an officer in the Independent Order of Odd Fellows in England, prior to his immigration to this country. He was a man of magnetic personality, well known, loved and highly respected by a large circle of friends and acquaintances. He drew to his hotels patronage of a high class, and they were frequented by some of the most prominent men of the day, men who have since become famous in various walks of life. A genial host and fine conversationalist, diffusing hospitality broadcast, radiating good cheer, he became a figure of prominence in the social interests of the city. His retirement from business was accepted with genuine regret.

Joseph Gilchrist Charnley married (first) Ann Pearce, of New Bedford, Massachusetts. They were the parents of three children: 1. William Henry, who was born in Taunton, Massachusetts, but in early life removed to Providence, Rhode Island, with which city he was afterward connected; he was prominent in public life in Providence, and was responsible

271

for the preservation to the city of Abbott Park in which he made many improvements, among them the placing of the fountain, he was prominent in club and fraternal life in the city, a member of the old Union Club and several others of importance, he was one of the Grace Church Corporation, he died in Providence, March 18, 1904   2. Ellen S   3 Amelia A

Joseph G Charnley married (second) Isabella Bartlett, who died at the Charnley residence at No 8 Abbott Park Place, Providence, March 21, 1907   After the death of her husband, Mrs Charnley resided in the family home with her three daughters   The children of Joseph G. and Isabella (Bartlett) Charnley were   1 Edward A , died in infancy   2 Isabella J , residing at the family residence in Providence   3. Mary C , residing with her sister   4. Annie L., who died November 4, 1915

Mrs Charnley was the daughter of James and Sarah (Johnston) Bartlett, both of whom were natives of Scotland, later emigrating to America, and settling in Boston, Massachusetts, where Mrs Charnley was born July 8, 1822   The death of Joseph Gilchrist Charnley occurred in his home at No 8 Abbott street, Providence, in the year 1868, in his sixty-second year

(The Bartlett (Bartlet) Line)

The surname Bartlett is of the baptizmal class, and is derived from the nickname Bartle, and its diminutives Bartlot and Bartlet, signifying ' the son of Bartholomew." The variants of the name are very numerous, and from ancient English records it is evident that Bartlet or Bartlot was a very popular nickname   The English family of Bartlett dates back to the time of the Norman Conquest, and the name in England and Scotland is an ancient and honored one, recurring frequently in history and tradition

Arms—Sable three sinister falconers' gloves argent arranged triangularly two above and one below pendant, bands around the wrist and tassels or

---

WARDWELL, Samuel D ,

Enterprising Citizen, Legislator.

Wardwell is an ancient English surname of local origin, derivative from the place name Wardle, a township in the parish of Bunbury, County Chester, England   There is another locality of the name in the parish of Rochdale, County Lancashire   The name was well established in the year 1273, and is found in the Hundred Rolls   The orthography of the name varies greatly, the forms most commonly used being Wardwell, Wardell, Wardill   Wardwell is given in "Burke's Armory," also Wardle and Wortley   All carry the same arms

Arms—Argent, on a bend between six martlets sable three bezants
Crest—A lion's gamb holding a spear proper, tasseled or
Motto—Avito viret honore

The Wardwell family was of Norman-French origin, and was established by one of the followers of the Conqueror, Sir Gilbert Ward, and it is said that he saved the life of Queen Elinor of France and the king said that it was a deed "well done,' hence the name being changed from Ward to Wardwell   On the northern borders of Westmoreland, England, there stands an ancient watch tower where "watch and ward" were kept to prevent sudden incursions of the fierce Scottish tribes of the Borderland   Here signals were given to Moothy Beacon on any suspicion of trouble with the enemy

The American branch of the English

family was established in New England in 1633, and has since the time of its establishment held rank among the first families of the states of Massachusetts and Rhode Island. The Rhode Island Wardwells have played a prominent part in the history of Rhode Island from the early days of the little colony's founding until the present time. The name has been prominently connected with the military history of the State, been ably and honorably represented in the early and latter wars. The principal branch of the Rhode Island Wardwells has been located in the town of Bristol for more than two hundred years. Since the year 1754, when Lieutenant John Wardwell served in one of the four companies which went from the town and county to serve in the expedition against Crown Point, the name has been officially connected with military matters in Bristol. Upon the organization of the Bristol Train of Artillery more than one hundred years ago, Colonel Samuel Wardwell became its commander, and in successive generations up to the present time the name has been officially connected with the body, offices not infrequently descending from father to son. In the last century the family has played a prominent part in the business and industrial life of the section.

(I) William Wardwell, immigrant ancestor and progenitor of the family in America, was born in Lincolnshire, England, in 1604. Whether religious intolerance and persecution in the Mother Country drove him to the New World, or whether he came hither impelled merely by the spirit of adventure, is not known. He arrived in Boston, in the Massachusetts Bay Colony, in 1633. On February 9, of the following year he became a member of the church of Boston, but with his family was later one of those who were turned out of the Old Boston Second

Church with Wheelwright. In company with Wheelwright he went first to Exeter, New Hampshire, where he remained for a period, but later removed to Ipswich, Massachusetts. William Wardwell later returned to Boston, and passed the remainder of his life there, and during his latter years conducted the old Hollis Inn. He married (first) Alice ———, who was buried in Boston. He married (second) in Boston, December 5, 1657, Elizabeth, widow of John Gillet or Jillett. The date of his death is not recorded. Among his children was Uzal, mentioned below.

(II) Uzal Wardwell, son of William and Alice Wardwell, was born in America, probably in Boston, Massachusetts, April 7, 1639, and died October 25, 1732, at the advanced age of ninety-three years. Uzal Wardwell removed to Bristol, Rhode Island, at a date unknown, and established there, in the second American generation, the Rhode Island branch of the Wardwells. During the early portion of his life he was a resident of Ipswich, Massachusetts, whither he accompanied his father.

He married (first) in Ipswich, Massachusetts, May 3, 1664, Mary Ring, widow of Daniel Ring, and daughter of Robert and Mary (Borseman) Kinsman, of Ipswich. She died in Ipswich, and he married (second) Grace ———, who died on May 9, 1741, having survived her husband nine years. His will, dated January 10, 1728, mentioned his wife Grace, daughters Mary Barker, Grace Giddens, Sarah Bosworth, Alice Gladding, Abigail Green, Hannah Crompton, sons Uzal, James, Joseph, William, Benjamin. The will of Mrs. Grace Wardwell, dated October 19, 1733, mentions her son Uzal, daughter Grace Giddens, sons James and Joseph, and Benjamin, deceased. Children of Uzal and Mary (Kinsman-Ring) Wardwell. 1 Abigail, born October 27, 1665,

married John Green 2. Hannah, born in
1667, married a Mr Crompton 3 Alice,
born December 27, 1670, married, October 31, 1693, John Gladding, Jr All of
these children were born in Ipswich
Children of Uzal Wardwell and Grace
Wardwell 1 Mary 2 Uzal 3 Grace,
married Joseph Giddens (Giddings), and
died May 1, 1768, aged ninety years 4
Sarah, born in 1682, in Bristol, Rhode
Island, married Nathaniel Bosworth, Jr.
5 James, born June 30, 1684, in Bristol
6 Joseph, born July 30, 1686, in Bristol
7 Benjamin, mentioned below 8 William, born May 3, 1693, in Bristol 9
Rebecca, twin of William

(III) Benjamin Wardwell, son of Uzal
and Grace Wardwell, was born April 19,
1688, in Bristol, Rhode Island He was
a prosperous farmer He married (first)
Mary ———, who died May 2, 1733, married (second) January 17, 1734, Mrs Elizabeth Holmes, of Norton, Massachusetts,
who died June 6, 1737 Children (by first
wife) 1 Mary, married, in 1731, Nathaniel Turner 2 Uzal, married, in November, 1739 Sarah Lindsey, who died in
1745, at Cape Breton, he died there also,
on September 17, 1745 3 David, died
September 17, 1745 4 Jonathan, died in
May, 1745, at Cape Breton 5 Benjamin,
died in June, 1739, at sea 6 William,
mentioned below 7 Isaac, born in 1730,
married, in September, 1756, Sarah Waldron, and died May 7, 1810, at Bristol 8
Olive, married, June 19, 1753, John Goddard of Newport, Rhode Island Benjamin Wardwell died in June, 1739

(IV) William (2) Wardwell, son of
Benjamin and Mary Wardwell, was born
in Bristol, Rhode Island in 1722 He was
a farmer and prominent citizen of Bristol
He married, September 26, 1742, Mary
Howland, daughter of Samuel Howland
granddaughter of Jabez Howland, and
great-granddaughter of John Howland,
the Pilgrim

Howland Arms—Sable, two bars argent, on a
chief of the second three lions rampant of the
first
Crest—On a wreath of the colors a lion passant sable, ducally gorged or

Children of William (2) and Mary
(Howland) Wardwell 1 William, born
January 8, 1744 2 Abigail, baptized June
9, 1745 3 Mary, born October 25, 1747
4 William, born January 28, 1749-50 5
Benjamin, mentioned below 6 Sarah,
born March 3, 1754 7 Samuel, born May
25, 1760, a sketch of whom follows

(V) Benjamin (2) Wardwell, son of
Benjamin (1) and Mary (Howland)
Wardwell, was born in Bristol, Rhode
Island, and baptized February 9, 1752
He was prominent in local affairs, and
owned much property in the town He
married (first) June 8, 1773, Sarah Smith,
who died November 20, 1779 He married (second) Katherine Glover, daughter of Captain Joseph and Elizabeth
(Bass) Glover, of Braintree, Massachusetts

Glover Arms—Sable, a fesse embattled ermine, between three crescents argent
Crest—Out of a mural crown a demi-lion
rampant, holding between the paws a crescent

Children of Benjamin (2) Wardwell
by first wife 1 William, born April 19,
1776, died April 21, 1776 2 Lucretia,
born May 30, 1777, married, June 17,
1798, John Sabin, died September 11,
1811 3 Sarah, born November 11, 1779,
married Nathaniel Church, and died February 21 1861 Children by second wife
4 Polly, born October 4, 1781, died December 12, 1781 5 Polly, born August
30, 1783, died September 23, 1783. 6
Benjamin, mentioned below. 7 Polly,
born August 13, 1785, died October 7,
1787 8 William, born October 4, 1786,
died September 22, 1787 9 Henry, born
April 7, 1789, died October 12, 1789 10
Polly, born October 24, 1791 11 Kath-

erine Glover, born July 8, 1793, died April 1, 1863   12 Francis, born in September, 1794, died July 25, 1796.

Benjamin (2) Wardwell married (third) January 15, 1804, Mrs Huldah (Goff) Wheeler, daughter of Joseph and Patience Goff

(VI) Benjamin (3) Wardwell, son of Benjamin (2) and Katherine (Glover) Wardwell, was born in Bristol, Rhode Island, August 24, 1784   He was engaged in the leather business in the early years of his life, and later conducted a grocery business in Bristol, in a building which stood on the east side of Thames street, south of State street   His business was a successful and prosperous one, and he continued in the same location for a period of fifty years, up to the time of his retirement from active business life   He was a Christian of the rugged and stern type which characterized the day, a Congregationalist in religious faith, and very devout in his observance of the tenets of that body   He was a man of the highest principles and applied the same standards to his business affairs and dealings as he did to the other relations of life   He was one of the most prominent men of the town, highly honored and respected, although he took no active or official part in public affairs   Benjamin Wardwell was a Whig   He was a fine singer, and sang for years in the choir of the Congregational church

He married, January 14, 1807, Elizabeth Manchester, of Little Compton, Rhode Island, baptized in the Congregational church of Bristol, July 31, 1810, daughter of Zebedee and Deborah (Briggs) Manchester, who was descended from the old Rhode Island family of Sir Walter Gifford

Manchester Arms—Quarterly, 1st and 4th argent, three lozenges conjoined in fess gules, within a bordure sable   2nd and 3rd, or, an eagle displayed vert, beaked and membered gules

Crest—A griffin's head couped, wings expanded or, gorged with a collar argent, charged with three lozenges gules

Supporters—Dexter, a heraldic antelope or, armed tufted and hoofed argent   Sinister, a griffin or, gorged with a collar, as the crest

Motto—*Disponendo me, non mutando me* (By disposing of me, not changing me)

Children of Benjamin (3) and Elizabeth (Manchester) Wardwell

1 Henry, mentioned below

2 Benjamin, born August 9, 1809, died May 31, 1885, married, February 2, 1836, Eliza Cook, born February 18, 1810, died April 27, 1860   they were the parents of one daughter, born in December, 1840, who married, in 1869, Joseph Burr Bartram

3 George, born September 2, 1810, died October 11, 1810

4 A son, born and died September 12, 1812

5 A daughter, twin of the son, died same day

6 Jeremiah, born December 7, 1813, died in December, 1881; married (first) June 19, 1844, Mary Jane Sturgis, daughter of Lathrop L. Sturgis, of New York; she died October 3, 1860; he married (second) November 18, 1865, Mrs Eliza B Ingraham, daughter of William Fellows, of Staten Island, New York   Children of first marriage   i William Henry, born March 29, 1846, married, in December, 1881, Virginia Sniffin; ii Theodore Sturgis, born June 13, 1848, iii Richard Patrick, born April 17, 1852, married Anna Oaks Woodworth   iv Mary, born April 16, 1855, died July 22, 1855, v Helen, born September 6, 1857, married William Brown Glover, vi Jane Elizabeth, born August 17, 1859, married Charles Potter, who died in November, 1904

7 Elizabeth Manchester, born March 7, 1816, died January 18, 1826

8 A daughter, born September 2, 1817, died September 4, 1817

9 A daughter, twin, died September 12, 1817

10 Adam Manchester, born November

275

6, 1818, baptized March 29, 1819, died
January 23, 1827.
11 George Williams, born March 14,
1821, died August 16, 1821
12 Catherine Glover, born May 28,
1822, died October 31, 1894
13. Marianne, born October 6, 1825,
died January 26, 1915
14 Elizabeth Manchester, born November 6, 1827, died December 12, 1905,
married, September 27, 1853, Ramon
Guiteras, of Matanzas, Cuba, born August 4, 1811, died February 13, 1873; at
the age ot four years he was taken to
Spain, whither his father went to avoid
political troubles in Cuba, returning to
Cuba later the boy was educated in Matanzas; he travelled extensively and was
a finished linguist; he was the owner of
much land in Cuba, but atter his marriage
spent all his time in Bristol, Rhode Island;
children 1 Gertrude Elizabeth, born
March 2, 1855, unmarried, resides now in
Bristol, Rhode Island, 11 Ramon, born
August 17, 1858, at Bristol, Rhode Island,
where he attended private and public
schools, after which he attended the Alexander Military Institute at White Plains,
New York, the Mowry and Goff English
and Classical High School at Providence,
the Joshua Kendall School at Cambridgeport, Massachusetts, and Harvard University, which he attended about two
years He then travelled in Europe for
two years studying languages in France
and Spain, and after thoroughly master-
ing both of these languages he returned
to America and entered Harvard Medical
School, where he received his degree of
Doctor of Medicine After this he went
to Vienna and studied medicine for about
a year and a half, and from there entered
a university at Berlin remaining for
about six months Upon his return to
the United States he entered an examination for the navy and passed with the
highest honors of the year, and upon receiving his papers he immediately resigned, his reason being that he did not
wish to enter the navy, but passed the
examination just for experience He then
entered the Charity Hospital at Blackwell's Island and remained there for about
one and a half years, after which he practiced in New York as physician and sur-

geon, and is to-day one of the foremost
specialists for kidney troubles in the
country Dr Ramon Guiteras is very
prominent in social life in New York and
belongs to many clubs, including the following Union Club, New York Athletic
Club, Explorers Club, and the Harvard
Club He is also very fond of and de-
votes a great deal of time to big game
hunting, going to British South Africa
every two years, and he finds this gives
him the rest he requires from his large
practice Since the European war he has
served for several months each year as
surgeon in the French army

The Guiteras (Spain) Arms—Vert, five
greyhounds' heads erased proper, vulned
and distilling drops of blood gules, posed
two, one and two

(VII) Henry Wardwell, son of Benja-
man (3) and Elizabeth (Manchester)
Wardwell, was born March 17, 1808, in
Bristol, Rhode Island He received his
early education in the public schools of
Bristol and later attended the school of
Mr Alden, reputed to have been one of
the finest masters of the day Entering
the business world in his seventeenth
year, Henry Wardwell became a clerk in
the employ of Benjamin Hall, of Bristol,
whose store was located on the corner of
Thames and State streets He found the
business, that of handling of farm products for home and West Indian trade, to
his liking, and during the eight years he
spent as an employee he learned thoroughly all the details of the business,
familiarizing himself with its every phase
At the age of twenty-five years he bought
the business of Mr Hall, and continued
to conduct it successfully until he retired
at the age of fifty-three years, a period of
twenty-eight years He purchased from
farmers in the vicinity whole crops of
potatoes and onions, which he consigned
to vessels in the West Indian trade The
captains of the vessels he used disposed
of their cargoes in West Indian ports, and

with the proceeds bought molasses which they brought back for home consumption Mr Wardwell also became interested in whaling In connection with his West Indian trade he came to have an interest in from ten to fourteen vessels Mr Wardwell was one of the most prominent merchants and business men in the town of Bristol in his time, and was connected in executive capacities with many of its large industrial and financial ventures He was at one time a director in the Pocanock Cotton Mill, and for thirty years was a director in the Eagle National Bank, the Freeman's National Bank, and the First National Bank, of Bristol He was also a trustee of the Bristol Institution for Savings from the time of its organization He was prominent in local affairs though not officially connected with public life He was a man of keen judgment and excellent business sense, a man whose opinion was respected and much sought Of the highest moral principle, unimpeachable integrity, fair in all his dealings, he was honored and loved in Bristol In his work and life he sustained and advanced the honorable traditions of his family, and brought honor on his name He was a member of the Congregational church, and active in its work, serving as treasurer and leader of the choir for nearly thirty years.

Henry Wardwell married May 11, 1835 Sarah Luther Lindsay, daughter of Thomas and Rhoda Lindsay Mrs Wardwell died on November 8, 1890

Lindsay Arms—Gules, a fesse chequy argent and azure, in chief a mullet of the second
Crest—A castle proper
Motto—*Firmus maneo.*

Children of Henry and Sarah Luther (Lindsay) Wardwell 1 Benjamin, born May 6, 1836, died the same day 2 Sophia Lindsay, born May 3, 1838, died April 15,

1916, at Bristol, Rhode Island, unmarried 3 Annie Elizabeth, born August 9, 1840, died November 18 1866 4 Sarah Frances, born January 25, 1843; married William H Bourne, now deceased; she is a resident of Bristol 5 Harriet Parker, born July 4, 1845, unmarried, resides in Bristol 6 Isabella Mein, born January 12, 1848, unmarried, resides in Bristol 7 Henry Adam, born August 26 1850, died February 18, 1853 8 Henry Irenius born July 15, 1853, died June 29, 1854

Henry Wardwell died in Bristol, Rhode Island, October 2, 1875

(V) Colonel Samuel Wardwell, son of William (2) and Mary (Howland) Wardwell, was born in Bristol, Rhode Island, May 25, 1760 He was one of the first men of Bristol, and played a prominent part in public affairs in the town He was representative in the General Assembly of Rhode Island of the town of Bristol, and was also very active in military affairs in the town

He married Elizabeth Church, of Bristol, where she was born August 16, 1766, daughter of Samuel and Ann (Davis) Church Their children were 1 Maria born in 1791, died early in life 2 Hezekiah Church, mentioned below 3 Samuel Church born in 1794, died early in life 4 Mary Ann, born in 1796, married William Coggeshall, of Bristol and Fall River

(VI) Colonel Hezekiah Church Wardwell, son of Colonel Samuel and Elizabeth (Church) Wardwell, was born in Bristol, Rhode Island, in 1792 He learned the trade of carpenter and engaged successfully in it for several years. He later became interested in lumbering and had very large interests in this industry He was prominent publicly in Bristol, and frequently held important offices Colonel Hezekiah Church Wardwell was the representative from Bristol in the Rhode

ENCYCLOPEDIA OF BIOGRAPHY

Island Assembly in 1849-50-51, and in
1849 was inspector of ferries In 1821 he
was commissioned first lieutenant of the
Bristol Train of Artillery, and in May of
the following year received his commission as colonel, which post he held for
several years He was marshal of Bristol
during the Dorr War, with immediate
jurisdiction over the Bristol custom house
and post office Though a Democrat in
political affiliation the issue at stake and
not party lines decided his vote

He married, December 24, 1820, Sally
Gifford, daughter of Ephraim Gifford, and
granddaughter of Captain David Gifford,
of Dartmouth, Massachusetts, an officer
in the American Revolution and representative from Portsmouth in the Colonial Assembly She died February 28,
1870 Their children were 1 Elizabeth
Church, born September 29, 1821, married Thomas J Holmes, children Julia
and Silas 2 Samuel Drury, mentioned
below 3 Ruth Hall, born March 10,
1826, married William Henry Teel, child,
Henry Russell 4 Almira Gifford, born
June 15, 1828, married Benjamin Thomas
Church, no issue, both deceased 5 Augusta, born October 3, 1832, married William Trussell; children Evelyn, married
Frank Morgan, Edward, deceased, Lena
6 William T C, born September 20, 1835,
married Lenora F Gladding

(VII) Samuel Drury Wardwell, son of
Colonel Hezekiah C and Sally (Gifford)
Wardwell, was born in Bristol, Rhode
Island, October 5, 1823 He received an
elementary education in the public schools
of Bristol, and at the age of eleven years
apprenticed himself to his father to learn
the carpenter's trade At the age of
eighteen years he entered the lumber
business of his father This business,
established in 1830 by Colonel Hezekiah
Church Wardwell, proved from the first
a succesful enterprise, and upon the en-

trance into it of Samuel Drury Wardwell
the firm name was changed to Hezekiah
C Wardwell & Son Later William T.
C Wardwell, youngest son of Colonel
Wardwell, was admitted to the business,
and upon the retirement of the elder man
the two sons succeeded to the business
The firm then became known as Wardwell Brothers, and conducted an extensive and prosperous business in lumber,
and carpenters' and builders' supplies,
such as doors, sashes and blinds, lime and
cement, hair, etc After a period of more
than forty years in active business life,
Samuel Drury Wardwell retired from
business, and the firm name was then
changed to the Wardwell Lumber Company, the executive offices being held by
W T C Wardwell, president, and Frederick F Gladding, secretary and treasurer

After his retirement from business,
Samuel Drury Wardwell purchased a
small farm in the country, and turning
to agricultural pursuits, devoted his time
solely to the cultivation of his farm lands
during the remainder of his life He continued to take an active interest in public
affairs, however, and was prominently
connected with political life in the town
In 1890 he was representative of the town
of Bristol in the Rhode Island Legislature He was a member of the Town
Council for six years, during half of that
period serving as its president For several years he served as chief of King
Philip Engine Company, fire department
of Bristol He was a member of the
Methodist Episcopal church

Samuel Drury Wardwell married, July
29, 1880, Annie Elizabeth Blake, who was
born April 3, 1854, daughter of Edward
Allen and Mary (Young) Blake, of Bristol, Rhode Island Mrs Wardwell is a
member of a family of ancient and honorable lineage in New England

Jonathan Blake, progenitor of the Blake

278

family, married Elizabeth Norris, daughter of John Norris Their son, Ebenezer Blake, married ——— Cox Their son, Ebenezer Blake, married Abigail Munroe and had sons William, Richard, Ebenezer, Allen, Samuel, and daughters Abigail and Nancy Samuel Blake married Hannah Case, a French-Huguenot, daughter of Gardner and Janet Belle Case, of Rehoboth Children Edward Allen, Rebecca, Martha Frances, married Colonel Samuel Lindsay Edward Allen Blake married Mary Young, born in Manchester, England, and they had daughters, Eleanor, who married Mark A DeWolf, son of William Bradford DeWolf, grandson of Captain James DeWolf, and Annie Elizabeth, married Samuel D Wardwell, aforementioned

Children of Samuel Drury and Annie Elizabeth (Blake) Wardwell 1 Samuel Church, born October 6, 1884, graduate of Brown University in the class of 1908, senior member of the firm of Wardwell & Goddard, boat builders, member of the Masonic order. Married, October 16, 1915, Edith Burdick, daughter of Benjamin Franklin and Emlie Burdick, resides in Bristol 2 William Allen, born November 17, 1887, graduated from Bristol High School in 1905, and from the Bryant & Stratton Business College in 1906, in charge of the eastern market of the National India Rubber Company, with offices in Boston, Massachusetts; member of the Episcopal church, Free and Accepted Masons and the Independent Order of Odd Fellows Married, October 15, 1914, Helen Luther Waldron, daughter of Colonel Charles and Carolyn (Luther) Waldron, child, Carolyn, born November 12, 1915, resides in Quincy, Massachusetts.

Samuel Drury Wardwell died in Bristol, Rhode Island, May 15, 1906 He was a man highly respected and honored in the business world of Bristol, and was deeply mourned at his death He was universally recognized as a man of the cleanest and most straightforward business principles, upright and honorable He was a public-spirited citizen, and rendered service of much value to the town during his terms in office He was a prominent layman in the Methodist Episcopal church, and gave liberally to its charities and benevolences Samuel Drury Wardwell was a representative of the fine old type of New England merchant which is fast dying out

ALDRICH, Edwin A,
Lawyer, Enterprising Citizen

According to the authority, Bardsley, the name Aldrich is distinctly of baptismal origin, though it is frequently stated to be of local derivation The surname was originally derived from the personal name Alderich, and signifies in its present form "the son of Alderich." The name is a very ancient one, and is found in English record and documents as early as the year 1273.

Arms—Or a fesse vert, a bull passant argent
Crest—A griffin segreant

Several immigrants of the name came to the American colonies in the early part of the colonial period, and their progeny is now to be found in every State in the Union The family of Aldrich herein under consideration is that branch of which the late Edwin Aldrich, of Providence, Rhode Island, one of the most prominent and distinguished members of the Rhode Island bar, financier and business man of note, was a member The Aldrich family in Rhode Island has been prominently identified with Providence and the surrounding country for more than two and a half centuries. It is mainly descended from Joseph and Jacob

Aldrich, sons of the progenitor George Aldrich, and in latter generations has furnished to the professions, business, industrial and public life, men who have left their mark on the times

(I) George Aldrich, immigrant ancestor and founder of the family in America, was a native of Derbyshire, England, and emigrated to the New World in the year 1631 He is first of record in the Massachusetts Bay Colony in that year, and in 1636 he became a freeman at Dorchester. In 1640 he received a grant of land in Boston, and is of record in Braintree, Massachusetts, from 1644 to 1663 George Aldrich was among the pioneer settlers of the town of Mendon, Massachusetts, whither he went in the year 1663, and where he died in 1683

He married, in England, in 1629, Catherine Seald, who accompanied him to America They were the parents of nine children, of whom Jacob, mentioned below, was the youngest

(II) Jacob Aldrich, son of George and Catherine (Seald) Aldrich was born in Braintree, Massachusetts, February 28, 1652. He accompanied his father to Mendon, Massachusetts, and is recorded as assessor there in 1694 During King Philip's War he went to Braintree, returning to Mendon, when hostilities ceased.

He married, November 3, 1675, Huldah Thayer born June 16, 1657, daughter of Ferdinando and Huldah (Hayward) Thayer Jacob Aldrich, like the majority of the men of the period, was a farmer, inheriting land from his father, and acquiring considerable property of his own

(III) Moses Aldrich, son of Jacob and Huldah (Thayer) Aldrich was born in Mendon Massachusetts, April 1, 1690 He married, April 23 1711, Hannah White, born December 9, 16— Among their children was Robert, mentioned below

(IV) Robert Aldrich, son of Moses and Hannah (White) Aldrich, was born December 1, 1719, in Mendon, Massachusetts He removed to Cumberland, Rhode Island, after his marriage, and there established the Rhode Island branch of the family He married, September 7, 1746 Patience Mann

(V) Amos Aldrich, son of Robert and Patience (Mann) Aldrich, was born in Cumberland, Rhode Island, June 11, 1756 He married, in Smithfield, Rhode Island, July 20, 1782, Sally Cook, daughter of Silas Cook, of Warwick, Rhode Island. Amos Aldrich resided in Cumberland all his life, and was a highly respected citizen

(VI) Joseph Cook Aldrich, son of Amos and Sally (Cook) Aldrich, was born in Cumberland, Rhode Island, April 13, 1787. He married Asenath Gaskill, of Blackstone, Massachusetts Their children were 1. Henry, born October 15, 1817 2 Peter G, born August 15, 1819 3 Hannah, born June 20, 1821 4 Elias, born February 14 1823 5 Joseph Barton born December 30, 1824 6 Lucy Barton, born January 2, 1827 7. Jane, born July 10, 1832 8 John born July 10, 1832, twin of Jane 9. Caroline, born July 25 1834 10. Edwin, mentioned below 11 Moses, born December 11, 1839 12. Mary, born May 15, 1842

(VII) Edwin Aldrich, son of Joseph Cook and Asenath (Gaskill) Aldrich, was born in Woonsocket, Rhode Island, October 14, 1836 He attended the elementary and high schools of his native town, and entered Tufts College, where he spent one year. He entered Brown University, in Providence, in his sophomore year, and remained until the end of his junior year, when he was compelled to discontinue his studies by failing health

After a period spent in regaining his health. Mr Aldrich entered the office of Hon Wingate Hayes, of Providence, having formed a decision to enter the legal profession. He next entered the Albany Law School, where he was graduated with the class of 1863 with the degree of Bachelor of Laws. He was admitted to the bar in the same year and commenced the active practice of his profession in the town of Neenah, Wisconsin. He met with a high degree of success and a few months later formed a partnership with Moses Hooper, at Oshkosh, in the same State. He rose rapidly in the legal circles of the State, and came to be known as a lawyer of ability. His practice was very large and lucrative, but in the comparatively undeveloped territory which Wisconsin then was, did not offer sufficient possibilities of advancement to a man of ambition. Consequently, in 1864 Mr. Aldrich returned to the East, and entered upon the practice of law in Woonsocket, Rhode Island, where he met with ready success, and shortly became known as one of the ablest lawyers in the State. In 1868 he became associated with Leland D. Jenckes, under the firm name of Aldrich & Jenckes, and the partnership continued until the death of the junior partner in 1872, from which time forward Mr. Aldrich practiced alone. In the ensuing period he handled cases which have since occupied places of the utmost importance in Rhode Island legal history. He was acceded to be one of the most skilled attorneys practicing before the bar of the State—of swift keen judgment, analytic and clear mind, broad education, and a forceful and convincing public speaker.

Edwin Aldrich took a prominent part in the public life of the city of Woonsocket, and for a number of years filled various public offices. He was town solicitor before the incorporation of Woonsocket as a city, and in 1867-68-69 represented the city in the Rhode Island Assembly, being elected to office on the Re-

publican ticket. His work in the Legislature was distinguished by the same qualities which marked his work as a lawyer, and brought eminent satisfaction to the city, in whose behalf he was influential in having many beneficial measures passed through the body of which he was a member. In latter years, however, the weight of his other affairs prevented his accepting further nomination for public office. Mr. Aldrich was a well known and influential figure in the financial world of Woonsocket, and also in its business interests. He was a director in the Woonsocket Gas Company for many years and became its president on the death of George A. Buffum, of Providence, continuing in that office until his demise. He was also trustee of the Woonsocket Institution. He was the owner of considerable real estate in the city and vicinity.

Mr. Aldrich was active and prominent in club life in Woonsocket, and was also a member of the Masonic order, for two years filling the honored post of commander of the Woonsocket Commandery, Knights Templar. His death came as a grief to all Woonsocket.

He married, June 17, 1869, Augusta Gaylord, born at Naugatuck, Connecticut, daughter of Luther and Laura (Judd) Gaylord, and granddaughter of Allen Gaylord, founder of the family in America. The Gaylord family is of French origin, and the name is found in French history of a very early date. The family in its principal branches is found in the French provinces of Flanders, Gascony, Guienne and Poitou, and is entitled to bear arms. The name in its original form was Gaillard, and the English branch of the Norman-French Gaillards was founded in England at the time of the Norman Conquest by a knight in the train of the Conqueror.

281

Mrs Aldrich survives her husband, and resides at the family home at No 344 Benefit street, Providence, Rhode Island They were the parents of the following children 1 Florence A, who resides with her mother in Providence 2 Edwin, who died in infancy 3 Alice, who married Lester B Murdock 4. Paul Edwin, married Emma Dexter Thayer 5 Lotta, married John P Sawyer, of Waterbury, Connecticut 6 Katherine, who married Henry J Hart, of New Haven, Connecticut, in 1910, died in April, 1915

Edwin Aldrich died suddenly of heart failure in the Banigan Building in Providence, March t, 1905 The following resolutions, passed by the members of the Woonsocket bar, will give as far as is possible a conception of the honor and respect which was accorded to him in the cities of Woonsocket and Providence

Whereas, The Almighty Judge of the universe has seen fit to bring sorrow upon us by removing from this earthly tribunal to the Supreme Court above our late respected and honored brother, Edwin Aldrich; and,

Whereas, His long and active career as counselor and advocate in this city is well known to us, and his successful and unremitting devotion to his professional duties and the interests of Woonsocket as town solicitor and member of the House of Representatives of the State, has signally distinguished him much beyond the limits of the immediate arena of his lifelong mission performed in this, the city of his birth and affection; and,

Whereas, His brilliancy of mind, keenness of legal sense and genial comradeship have endeared him most to those nearest to him, who have seen and bear witness to the success that has attended in a material way the judicious employment of that peculiar endowment of thrift and industry increasing to the end of his nearly "three-score years and ten," and,

Whereas, His fatherly love and pure devotion to his family and all the bonds of home make it difficult for us to comfort those who are in a sorrow whose boundaries the nature of the mourner and the nearness of the lost one alone determine,

Be It Resolved, That we, the members of the Bar, practicing in the City of Woonsocket, in special session assembled, do hereby extend our heartfelt sympathy, to the wife and family of our late brother in their great affliction and offer this tribute to his masterly ability as a lawyer, to his services as a citizen and his value as a friend and counsellor of many years,

And Furthermore, Be It Resolved, That a copy of these resolutions be communicated to the family of our late brother and printed in the journals of this city, and that the committee on resolutions be instructed to appear before the next session of the district court of the Twelfth Judicial District, to be held on Saturday, March 4, 1905, and in open court move that these resolutions be inscribed on its records.

JOHN J HEFFERNAN,
ERWIN J FRANCE,
GEORGE W. GREENE,
Committee on Resolutions

The following resolutions were adopted by the board of trustees of the Woonsocket Institution for Savings

Edwin Aldrich, Esq, a member of this Board of Trustees, died in Providence, March first, 1905, aged sixty-eight years, and it is hereby

Resolved, That in the death of Mr Aldrich, this Board has lost a cherished friend and associate, he having been a member of the Board for thirty-seven years, and its legal adviser He had always a great interest in the growth and welfare of this Institution, and will be greatly missed as a pleasant associate and a faithful and efficient member of this Board It is therefore,

Resolved, That while deprived of his presence and wise counsels we shall ever hold his name in greatful remembrance as an upright and faithful official,

Resolved, That a copy of these resolutions be sent the family of deceased and that they be spread upon the record of this Board.

COMSTOCK, Andrew,

Man of Affairs, Legislator.

Arms—Or, a sword point downwards, issuing from a crescent, in base gules, between two bears rampant sable

Crest—An elephant rampant proper, issuing out of a baron's coronet.

Motto—*Nid cyfoeth ond boddlondeh* (Not wealth, but contentment)

There is a difference of opinion among authorities as to the origin of the name Comstock. It is held by some to be of German origin, and by others to have been derived from an English source, and to this latter theory the majority incline. The source of the English surname was the place-name Culstock, or Colmstocke, an ancient town of England, which is found mentioned in the 'Domesday Book" in the reign of William the Conqueror. The name is found later in the records of the town of Exeter, in the vicinity of Culstock, in the year 1241, when Petro de Columstock is entered as a witness. The office of prior at Taunton, England, was occupied in 1325 by Richard de Colstoke, and in 1331 by Ralph de Colmstoke, who resigned in 1338. For several centuries the name was found prominently throughout all England, and the family was large in numbers, of high rank and reputation, and held much landed property. Its numbers were much depleted by colonial emigration. The family in America came to occupy a similar position to that of the English family.

The theory of the German origin of the name is based on the following statements, there has been no proof found, however, and research has failed to discover the records mentioned and said to exist in the Muniment Office at Frankfort-on-Main, in Germany. The name in Germany is spelled with a "K," and there is said to exist in the Muniment Office a pedigree of the family of Komstock extending for nine generations previous to the year 1547, when Charles Von Komstohk, a baron of the Roman Empire, was implicated in the Von Benedict treason and escaped into England with several nobles of Austria and Silesia, founding there a branch of the family.

In the opening years of the colonial period there came to the New World one William Comstock, an Englishman, the first of the name to arrive in New England, and the progenitor of the large Comstock race in this country. Since the time of its establishment the family has occupied in its various branches a position of prominence and influence in the affairs of New England, and has made the name known in all fields of endeavor in that section of the country.

(I) William Comstock, immigrant ancestor and founder of the family, was a native of England. He was twice married, and came to America with his second wife, Elizabeth. The date of his arrival in this country is not known, but he is known to have been in Wethersfield, Connecticut, early. According to the historian, Stiles, in his "History of Wethersfield,' William Comstock was doubtless one of the fifty-six men who under the leadership of Captain John Mason captured Pequot Fort, at Mystic, Connecticut, May 26, 1637, and killed about five hundred Indians. During the time of his residence in Wethersfield, Connecticut, he was the owner of land on the Connecticut river, this fact is recorded under the date April 28, 1641. The land was not received by grant, but was purchased by him from Richard Milles. Richard Milles was the plaintiff in an action against William Comstock and John Sadler, charging slander, argued before the court of election at Hartford Connecticut, August 1, 1644; the damages awarded were £200 William Comstock later removed to the town of Pequot, which is now New London, Connecticut. There, with several others, he agreed to accept the judgeship of the court of magistrates of the town in the matter of gifts and grants of rights of land there. He received a grant of land from the town on June 21, 1647, and on December 2, 1651, received a grant at Nahantic (Niantic). At a town meeting,

November 10, 1650, he voted to cooperate with John Winthrop in erecting a corn mill, and in July of the following year he, with other townsmen, worked on a mill dam which is still in use. On February 25, 1662, 'Old goodman Comstock" was chosen sexton, to order the youth in the meeting. The children of William Comstock were 1 John, an influential and prominent member of the community at Saybrook, Connecticut 2 Samuel, mentioned below 3 Daniel, died at New London, in 1683 4 Christopher, died December 28, 1702 5 Elizabeth, died in July, 1659.

(II) Samuel Comstock, son of William Comstock, was probably born in England, and accompanied his father on the voyage to America. The first record of him in New England is found in the Colonial records of Connecticut, on March 1, 1648, on which date he gave recognizance at Hartford for ten days of good behaviour and for satisfying what damage Mr. Robbins should sustain for the want of his servant. This would seem to indicate that he was apprenticed to the said Mr. Robbins. Samuel Comstock left Connecticut and settled in Rhode Island in the year 1653, and was the first of the name to reside in the Colony. In the same year, when relations with the Dutch were strained and war was looming on the horizon, he went on the "Swallow" to Block Island, where the ship's company seized the goods and people under the Dutch Captain Kempo Sybando, bringing the entire outfit back to New London, in all probability to Governor John Winthrop. He purchased his house and lot in Providence on March 1, 1654, of John Smith.

Samuel Comstock married Anne —— who married (second) John Smith, a stone mason of Providence. His death occurred some time previous to March 9 1660, on which date the town council of Providence took action regarding the estates of Samuel Comstock and John Smith, deceased. On May 4, 1661, Anne Smith, of Providence, widow of John Smith, and formerly widow of Samuel Comstock, sold the house and home plot of Samuel Comstock, to Roger Mowry This land was a tract of four acres situated in the northern part of Providence. Anne Smith died after February 10, 1667. Children 1 Samuel, mentioned below 2 Daniel, born May 12, 1656.

(III) Captain Samuel (2) Comstock, son of Samuel (1) and Anne Comstock, was born in Providence, Rhode Island, in 1654. He later rose to prominence in public affairs, and held many of the important offices in the gift of the Colony He was taxed eight pence on July 1, 1679 He served as deputy to the General Assembly of Rhode Island in the years 1669-1702-07-08-11, and on May 6, 1702, was appointed a member of a committee by the Assembly to audit the general treasurer's account and the colony debts In April, 1708, he served on a committee to fix the rates of grain and other articles brought to the treasury He was active in the military affairs of the colony, and held the rank of captain in the militia at the time of his decease. In August, 1710, he ordered Henry Mowry to impress men to go to Port Royal Captain Samuel Comstock was the plaintiff in a long action against the town of Mendon Massachusetts, regarding the ownership of a nine hundred acre tract located on the present boundary of the States of Massachusetts and Rhode Island He received permission from the selectmen of Mendon to cut timber for a saw mill and dam at the falls on the Great river, on November 21, 1698. Among others he received a grant of land on Woonsocket Hill, Rhode Island, on April 14, 1707, and he and Richard Arnold were the first settlers of the place. On May 6, 1707, Ensign Samuel Comstock was appointed to the office of deputy to the General Court from Providence. He was a resident of that part of Providence known as Smithfield. According to a deposition taken on March 22, 1717, he was then sixty-three years of age. He died on May 27, 1727, and his will, dated April 10, 1745, was proved December 8, 1747.

He married, November 22, 1678, Elizabeth Arnold, daughter of Thomas and Phebe (Parkhurst) Arnold. She was born in Watertown, Massachusetts, in 1645, and died October 20, 1747. Children: 1. Samuel, born April 16, 1679, died April 1, 1727, married Anna Inman. 2. Hazadiah, born April 16, 1682, died February 21, 1764, married (first) Catherine Pray; (second) August 10, 1730, Martha Balcom. 3. Thomas, born November 7, 1684, died in 1761, married, July 9, 1713, Mercy Jenckes. 4. Daniel, born July 9, 1686, died December 22, 1768, married (first) ————— —————, (second) August 2, 1750, Elizabeth Buffum. 5. Elizabeth, born December 18, 1690, married, December 1, 1717, John Sayles. 6. John, mentioned below. 7. Ichabod, born June 9, 1696, died January 26, 1775, married (first) September 13, 1722, Zibiah Wilkinson; (second) March 26, 1747, Elizabeth Boyce. 8. Job, born April 4, 1699, married (first) Phebe Jenckes; (second) November 22, 1735, Phebe Balcom.

(IV) John Comstock, son of Samuel (2) and Elizabeth (Arnold) Comstock, was born in Providence, Rhode Island, March 26, 1693. He followed the occupation of blacksmith in his native town all his life. He inherited a large portion of the landed property of his father, and, adding to this through purchase, he increased his holdings greatly becoming one of the largest real estate owners in Provi-

dence and one of the wealthiest men of his time in the colony. He disposed of the greater part of his property in gifts to his sons before his death. His son Samuel received thirty acres, dwelling house and barn; Joseph, seventeen acres and dwelling house; John, a quarter of forge adjoining to corn mill, etc.; Jeremiah, one hundred and fifty acres; to sons John, Jonathan, James, Nathan and Ichabod, "my homestead farm and dwelling house in which I now dwell, about one hundred and seventy acres, and also land in the neck I bought of Sam, an Indian, and other lots." He died in Providence, January 12, 1750, and was buried in the North Burial Ground. Administration on his estate was granted to his sons Samuel and John, February 12, 1750. The inventory of the estate amounted to £1 968 2s.

John Comstock married (first) Esther Jenckes, daughter of William and Patience (Sprague) Jenckes; married (second) Sarah Dexter, born June 27, 1698, died in 1773, daughter of John and Alice (Smith) Dexter. Children: 1. Samuel, born in 1715; died January 16, 1755, married, January 1, 1738, Anne Brown. 2. Joseph, married, June 7, 1747, Anne Comstock. 3. Jeremiah, married, October 25, 1749, Phebe Arnold. 4. John, died in 1813. 5. Jonathan, married, April 9, 1750, Sarah Comstock. 6. James, mentioned below. 7. Ichabod, born in 1734, died December 19, 1800, married, April 11, 1760, Sarah Jenckes. 8. Nathan, born December 5, 1735, died in 1816, married, March 29, 1764, Mary Staples.

(V) James Comstock, son of John Comstock, was born in Providence, Rhode Island December 12, 1733. In 1756 he sold land in Providence, and in the following year became a freeman. In 1774 he was a resident of North Providence, Rhode Island. He owned considerable real estate, and was a well known man in local affairs.

He married, about 1752-53, Esther Comstock, daughter of Thomas and Mary (Jenckes) Comstock, and granddaughter of Samuel (2) Comstock, above mentioned. She died in Providence, March 12, 1808. The children of James and Esther (Comstock) Comstock were: 1. Richard, born April 19, 1754. 2. Amy, born September 21, 1755. 3. Mercy, born July 20, 1757. 4. Woodbury, mentioned below.

(VI) Woodbury Comstock, son of James and Esther (Comstock) Comstock, was born in Providence, Rhode Island, December 9, 1759. He removed to North Providence, and there established himself. He died in North Providence, November 7, 1793. He was a member of the Society of Friends.

Woodbury Comstock married, May 1, 1786, Hannah Read, born October 30, 17—, daughter of John Read. She married (second) Samuel Smith, of Mendon, Massachusetts, and died February 26, 1838. Their children were: 1. Lydia, born November 23, 1786. 2. Amey, born August 19, 1788. 3. Mercy, born April 14, 1791. 4. James, mentioned below.

(VII) James (2) Comstock, son of Woodbury and Hannah (Read) Comstock, was born in North Providence, Rhode Island, February 27, 1793. He removed with his mother, after her second marriage, to that part of Mendon, Massachusetts, which is now called Blackstone. Here he farmed on a large scale and also conducted a retail butcher trade. He died in Blackstone, April 26, 1861. James Comstock was a member of the Society of Friends.

He married, March 9, 1814, Catherine Farnum, of Cheshire, Massachusetts, born November 1, 1793, died July 20, 1867, daughter of Jonathan Farnum, of Cheshire, and a descendant of Ralph Farnum, the progenitor of the Farnum lines of Worcester and the vicinity. Their children were: 1. Woodbury L., born January 26, 1815. 2. Lydia, born December 15, 1816, married Laban Bates. 3. Jonathan Farnum, November 24, 1818, married Mary Hall. 4. Anna Smith, born December 9, 1820, married Albert Gaskill. 5. Andrew, mentioned below. 6-7. James Kelley and Catherine Farnum, twins, born June 29, 1827, the former married Charlotte Kelley Benson and the latter Richard Beede.

(VIII) Andrew Comstock, son of James (2) and Catherine (Farnum) Comstock, was born March 6, 1823, in Blackstone, Massachusetts, and died November 30, 1898. He received his early education in the Friends' School in Providence, and upon leaving this institution entered the business world.

Shortly afterward he entered into partnership with his brother, Jonathan Farnum Comstock, in the wholesale beef and pork business, under the firm name of J. F. & A. Comstock. The business, which was begun on a small scale, rapidly developed to the point where increased quarters were necessary, and in 1857 the establishment was removed to Providence. Here the firm met with success and grew to be one of the foremost of the kind in the surrounding country, ranking high among concerns of like nature, and enjoying a reputation for purity of product and fairness of dealing, which was excelled by none other. Mr. Comstock also was prominent in the organization and management of the firm of Comstock & Company for a period, but withdrew from this to give his attention to his other large interests. He was known throughout the East and Middle West in connection with the wholesale beef and pork provision business, and was president of the G. H.

286

Hammond Company, one of the largest beef houses of Hammond, Indiana, operating plants in Chicago and Omaha He was also a well known figure in the financial circles of Providence, and for several years filled the office of president of the Commercial National Bank of Providence, administering the duties of his incumbency greatly to the advantage of the institution He was also a trustee of the People's Savings Bank and of Brown University

Mr Comstock was a member of the Cranston Street Baptist Church of Providence, and was deeply interested in the work of the parish He contributed often and generously to the support of movements conducted under the auspices of the church, and was prominent in almost every phase of its labors He was one of its deacons for twenty-eight years Although closely in touch with every department of the city life, he never took an active part in politics He was, nevertheless, an excellent citizen, and a man who appreciated the duties and benefits of his citizenship to the fullest extent He at one time served as a member of the Rhode Island Legislature, representing Providence

Andrew Comstock married, on May 24 1856, Juliette Paine, daughter of John Jay and Olive (Hall) Paine, of Smithfield, Rhode Island, and a descendant in the eighth generation of Stephen Paine, the progenitor in America of one of the numerous and distinguished Paine families of New England Mrs Comstock was born December 25, 1825, and died February 3, 1911 She was a Christian gentlewoman of the highest type, and was deeply loved and reverenced by all with whom she came in contact The children of Andrew and Juliette (Paine) Comstock were 1 Frederick Dana, born May 27, 1858, died October 11 1858 2 Frank Paine,

born February 26, 1864, mentioned below 3 Clara Elizabeth, born November 6, 1866, now residing at the old family home, No 550 Broad street, Providence, Rhode Island Miss Comstock was graduated from Brown University in the class of 1895 with the degree of Ph B, two years later receiving the degree of A M She has traveled extensively in this country and Europe Miss Comstock is a member of the Association of Collegiate Alumnæ, the Rhode Island Society for the Collegiate Education of Women, the Rhode Island Women's Club, and vice-president of the Consumers' League of Rhode Island She is also a director of the Federal Hill House Association

(IX) Frank Paine Comstock, son of Andrew and Juliette (Paine) Comstock, was born in Providence, Rhode Island, February 26, 1864 He received his early education at the Mowry & Goff English and Classical School in Providence, and was graduated from that institution in the class of 1881

Upon completing his education he immediately entered the business of J F Comstock & Sons, with which he has since been connected Mr Comstock is now one of the ablest men in the large concern He was also a director for several years of the G H Hammond Company and the Hammond Packing Company He was president of the Providence Ice Company for a number of years He is well known in business life and in club and fraternal circles in Providence, and is a member of the Hope Club, the Squantum Association, the Commercial Club, the Providence Board of Trade and the Churchman's Club He is a member of Grace Episcopal Church, where he is one of the vestry

Frank Paine Comstock married, on May 11, 1887, Laura W Burroughs, daughter of Samuel N and Katherine (Sherman)

Burroughs, of Providence They are the parents of three children 1 Andrew Burroughs, born August 4, 1888; married, June 18, 1914, Marion Hamilton 2 Hope Marguerite, born October 16, 1891 3 Katherine, born March 4, 1900.

DIMAN FAMILY,

Notable in Public Life and the Professions.

The Diman family of Rhode Island has played a distinguished part in the affairs of that region since early in the eighteenth century, and has been resident in New England since early Colonial times It is of French-Huguenot origin, and like so many of the Huguenot families which settled amidst the English speaking communities of the New World, we find its name under a great variety of spellings, such as Diamond, Diament and Diamont, the latter being the form used most frequently by the progenitor of the Rhode Island Dimans

Diman Arms—Argent five fusils in fesse conjoined gules each charged with a fleur-de-lis or
Crest—A demi-lion or, holding in dexter paw a fusil gules charged with a fleur-de-lis of the first

(I) Thomas Diamont was one of the early settlers of Farmington, Connecticut, but removed from there and went to live at Easthampton, Long Island, in the year 1660, and there died in 1682 There are many records concerning him preserved at Easthampton, from which we find that he was a man of considerable prominence in the community We find that on March 1, 1663, he purchased for the sum of fifty pounds housing and fencing land and accommodations of one Richard Smith, and on September 28, 1667, purchased meadow land of Stephen Shamger and Benjamine Haset The following year he contributed land to the community to be used as a

highway, and on March 15, 1679, sold a lot of forty square poles We find also that on July 28, 1682, he made a deed of gift to his son James, in which he mentions several previous deeds and which included a house and barn, thirty-five acres of meadow land, and two-thirds of his commonage and other properties

He married, in 1645, Mary Sheaffe, and they were the parents of six children, three sons and three daughters, as follows: 1 James, who has already been referred to, and who is mentioned below 2 Thomas 3 John 4 Hannah 5 Elizabeth 6 Sarah, married a man by the name of Headley, and made her home in New Jersey

(II) James Diman, eldest son of Thomas and Mary (Sheaffe) Diman (Diamont) was born in the year 1646, at Easthampton, Long Island, and continued to make his home there during his entire life, his death occurring December 13, 1721 Like his father, he conducted many business transactions, and seems to have been active in the community

He married, in 1677, Hannah James, a daughter of the Rev Thomas James, of Charlestown, Massachusetts, and they were the parents of the following children 1 Thomas, mentioned below 2 Nathaniel, who married Lois Hedges in 1721 3 John, born 1690, died 1764 4 Mary

(III) Thomas (2) Diman, eldest son of James and Hannah (James) Diman, was born at Easthampton, Long Island, about the year 1679, and continued to reside in that town until the year 1712 He was the founder of the Diman family in Rhode Island, moving to the town of Bristol there in the aforesaid year

He married, in 1706, Hannah Finney whose death occurred in 1744, and they were the parents of the following children 1 John 2 Rebecca 3 Jonathan,

288

deacon of the First Church of Plymouth, Massachusetts 4 Rev James, born November 29, 1707, pastor of the Second Church at Salem, Massachusetts, where his death occurred October 8, 1788 5 Jeremiah, who is mentioned at length below 6 Phebe, born 1717, and died September 14, 1789 7 Lucretia, born 1719, became wife of Richard Smith, and died January 31, 1790 8 Daniel, died December 16, 1797

(IV) Jeremiah Diman, third son of Thomas (2) and Hannah (Finney) Diman, was born at Easthampton, Long Island, about 1710, and was brought by his parents to Bristol, Rhode Island, when an infant We have a record of him, together with his wife, being admitted to the Congregational church at Bristol in 1741, and he continued to reside in that community until the time of his death, which occurred November 10, 1798

He married, May 13, 1733, Sarah Giddings, who was born about 1709-10, and died October 13, 1790, and they were the parents of the following children: 1. Nathaniel, mentioned below. 2. James, born October 9, 1735. 3. Sarah, born February 5, 1738, and became the wife of John Lawless 4 Jeremiah, born July 13, 1740, and died at Albany, New York, in 1760 while in active service as a soldier in the French War 5 Jonathan, born October 19, 1742 6. Hannah, twin of Jonathan, married, October 29, 1761, George Oxx 7 William, born December 10, 1744 8. Joseph, born about 1746 9 Thomas, born about 1748 10 Benjamin, who served in the Revolutionary War, and rose to the rank of major, and whose death occurred December 31, 1777

(V) Nathaniel Diman, eldest child of Jeremiah and Sarah (Giddings) Diman, was born January 29, 1734, at Bristol, Rhode Island and lived there until the day of his death on May 24 1812 He

married, October 18, 1756, Anna Gallup, a daughter of Samuel and Mary Gallup, and granddaughter of Samuel and Elizabeth Gallup, who were among the first settlers of Bristol A number of children were born to them, the birth of two of them being recorded at Bristol, namely, William, who was born there November 1, 1759, and who was a soldier in the Revolution, and Jeremiah, mentioned below They were the parents of other children as follows 1 Mary, born September 18, 1764, and became the wife of Nathaniel Ingraham 2 Nancy, born in 1775, and was the second wife of Nathaniel Ingraham 3 ———, born in 1775, and became the wife of John Richardson 4 John, who went to sea from Bristol, and was never thereafter heard from

(VI) Deacon Jeremiah (2) Diman, second son of Nathaniel and Anna (Gallup) Diman, was born January 4 1767, at Bristol, Rhode Island, and there died August 10, 1847, after spending his entire life in the community. He engaged in business there as a cooper and gauger, and he was also interested in a number of commercial enterprises and the shipping business. He was a man of deeply religious instincts, and was a deacon of the First Congregational Church there

He was married on November 6, 1794, to Hannah Luther, a daughter of Barnaby Luther, of Swansea, Massachusetts, where she was born about 1770. Her death occurred June 7, 1840, at the age of seventy years. To Jeremiah and Hannah (Luther) Diman two children were born, as follows 1 Byron, mentioned below 2 George Howe, born August 19 1797, and met his death in an accident, December 7, 1815

(VII) Hon Byron Diman eldest son of Deacon Jeremiah (2) and Hannah (Luther) Diman, and the father of Professor Jeremiah Lewis Diman, with whose career this brief notice is especially concerned, was himself one of the most prominent men in the State of Rhode Island during his life, taking a vital part in public affairs and holding the office of Governor He was born August 5, 1795, in his father's home at Bristol, and received an excellent education in private schools there His studies were conducted to a large extent under the tuition of the celebrated educator, the late Bishop Griswold While still a mere youth he entered the office of the Hon James DeWolf, where he gained his first acquaintance with business methods generally, and in whose employ he remained until his death in 1837, continuing with the concern until the settlement of the estate. He was a man of very marked business ability, and at an early age began to associate himself with many important industries in the community, notably those connected with the whale fisheries and the West India trade. He engaged in these enterprises himself, and conducted a very large and successful commercial business. It was at a time when the cotton industry was enjoying its period of most rapid growth, and the young man, perceiving the enormous opportunities in this direction, interested himself therein and became an extensive owner in two large cotton manufacturing concerns in Bristol, and served on their board of directors He was also connected with the Bristol Steam Mill, and was first its treasurer and subsequently its president for a number of years. He was also president of the Bank of Bristol, and a director of the Pokanoket Mill. Indeed, his activities, without question contributed in no small degree to the industrial and financial growth of the community in that day.

The name of the Hon Byron Diman is of course associated with public affairs to an even larger degree than with the busi-

ness world of Bristol, his career in the former direction having been particularly noteworthy as illustrative of his truly great qualities as a man He was politically affiliated with the Whig party, and was a strong advocate of Henry Clay and the policies which that great statesman stood for. While still a young man he was elected to the General Assembly of the State, and served in that body for a large number of years, during which time he made his influence felt mostly potently in the matter of legislation of a reformed character In 1840 he was a delegate to the Harrisburg convention which nominated General William H Harrison for the Presidency He was elected in 1850 to the State Senate and served in that body in that and the two following years He had been a member of the Governor's Council in 1842, during the time when the Dorr Rebellion broke out, and he was one of those who took an active part in suppressing it and restoring peace to the community In 1843 he became Lieutenant-Governor of the State, and in 1846 was elected Governor His administration of this exalted office was so successful and proved him so efficient and disinterested a public officer that there seemed every reason to believe that his career in politics would lead him to even higher posts Great pressure indeed was brought upon him by his colleagues in the Republican party, both to continue as Governor, and also to accept the nomination for United States Senator To all these representations, however, he turned a deaf ear, and after the expiration of his first term as Governor he retired to private life, although he always remained a potent factor in the politics of the State He did hold one official post, in the performance of which he found a scope for his deeply philanthropic instincts, namely, that of Commissioner of the Indigent

Blind, Deaf and Dumb It was Governor Diman who issued the call for the first meeting held in Bristol for the organization of the Republican party, and he was one of those most active in the support of the principles and policies of Abraham Lincoln

Governor Diman was a man of strong religious feeling, and by belief a Congregationalist He did much to advance the cause of that church in Rhode Island, and held for a number of years the presidency of the Catholic Congregational Society At the age of sixty years he withdrew from active business and spent the remainder of his life in a well-earned retirement, devoting much of his attention to social life and reading of which he was very fond Much of his time was spent in his library, and he had been a diligent student all his life, so that few men possessed a wider range of knowledge than he He was a man of profound culture, and in this direction alone exerted a most potent and beneficial influence upon the community He was a deep student of English literature and history and was a notable antiquarian

Governor Diman married (first) June 1, 1823 Abigail Alden Wight, a native of Bristol, Rhode Island, born October 21, 1802, and a daughter of Rev Henry Wight, D D, who for more than forty years was pastor of the Congregational church in that city, and of his wife, Clarissa (Leonard) Wight, of Raynham, Massachusetts To Governor and Mrs Diman the following children were born 1 George Byron, May 16, 1824, died February 4, 1903 2 Clara Anna, born August 8, 1826, died in infancy 3 Clara Anna (2), born April 1, 1828, married, June 30, 1847, A Sidney DeWolf, and died June 9, 1913 4 Jeremiah Lewis Wight, born April 2 1835, who became paymaster in the United States navy, and

served on the gunboat 'Kineo" during a portion of the Civil War, and who was for some twenty-four years United States Consul to Oporto and Lisbon, Portugal, and died in the latter place in September, 1884. 6 Abby Byron, born May 7, 1838, died in infancy

Governor Diman married (second) May 2, 1855, Mrs Elizabeth Ann (Liscome, born October 11, 1816, at Warren, Rhode Island, a daughter of of Thomas Baker and Sarah (Hawkins) Wood One child was born of this union, Elizabeth Byron, June 22, 1857, who married, January 8, 1890, Henry Hyde Cabot, a native of St Louis, born May 11, 1857, a son of Joseph Clarke and Catherine (Wales) Cabot.

(VIII) Rev Jeremiah Lewis Diman, second son of the Hon Byron and Abigail Alden (Wight) Diman, was born May 1, 1831, at Bristol, Rhode Island, and died in Providence, Rhode Island, February 3, 1881 From his earliest youth he displayed the remarkable talents and scholarship which distinguished his career in later life, and while still a boy developed a profound fondness for the study of history His early education was received from private tutors and principally from the Rev James N Sikes, pastor of the Baptist church at Bristol, who was himself a notable scholar Under the preceptorship of this excellent man, the youth pursued his studies to good purpose, and entered Brown University at the age of sixteen years He had already, prior to this time, prepared a number of historical papers, which he entitled "Annals of Bristol," and which, published in "The Phenix," a local periodical, bear eloquent testimony to his scholarship at that early age He left behind a remarkable record at Brown University, from which he was graduated with the class of 1851, and during his after life considered himself deeply indebted to his *alma mater* for the formation of his literary taste It was here that he took up those historical and philosophical studies to which so much of his life was subsequently devoted At college he made so excellent a reputation in these branches that he was selected to deliver the classical oration at the commencement exercises of his class, and selected for his theme on that occasion 'The Living Principle of Literature " It was in college also that he definitely determined upon the ministry as his career in life, and it was at this time that he united with the Congregational church of Bristol Upon completing his studies at Brown University, he went to reside in the family of the Rev Dr Thatcher Thayer, of Newport, under whom he studied philosophy, theology and the classics, for the purpose of preparing himself for his life work In 1852 he entered Andover Theological Seminary at Andover, Massachusetts, where he studied for two years. He had in the meantime, however, decided to complete his preparatory work abroad and chose the German universities for this purpose Accordingly, in 1854 he went to Europe and continued his studies in theology, philosophy and history at the Universities of Halle, Heidelberg and Berlin, under eminent European professors He also devoted some time to the study of art at Munich, after which he returned to the United States in the spring of 1856 Once more he took up his studies at Andover, and was finally graduated from that institution in 1857

His first pastorate was the First Congregational Church at Fall River, Massachusetts, in charge of which he was placed in the same year, and in 1858 he declined an invitation to become a colleague of the celebrated Dr Horace Bushnell, in charge of a Congregational church at Hartford, Connecticut He continued at Fall River

for about four years, and in the latter part of 1860 became pastor of the Harvard Congregational Church of Brookline, Massachusetts His great learning and scholarship had already met with wide recognition, and in 1864 his *alma mater* called him to take the chair of history and political economy there His abilities eminently qualified him for this post, and in 1870 he received the distinction of the degree of Doctor of Divinity from Brown University. Dr Diman's professorial duties were eminently congenial to him, and he entered into them with an enthusiasm and judgment which gained for him a very wide and enviable reputation as an instructor and teacher He greatly enlarged the department of history and political economy at Brown, until indeed it was recognized as the best and most effective of any chair of history in the universities and colleges of the land

Besides his notable work as teacher, Professor Diman became widely known as an author, and contributed largely to many important journals, both in the city of Providence and elsewhere. Among these should be mentioned the ' Providence Journal," the "New York Nation," the "North American Review" and the "Monthly Religious Magazine " In 1873 he was elected a corresponding member of the Massachusetts Historical Society Among the important works from Dr Diman's pen are printed collections of his sermons, among which should be mentioned that delivered by him on October 16, 1867, in the chapel of Brown University, and at the request of the faculty, in commemoration of the Rev Robinson Potter Dunn, D D , who for many years had occupied the seat of rhetoric at that institution , an address delivered July 6, 1879, before the Phi Beta Kappa of Amherst College, entitled "The Method of

Academic Culture," an address delivered in Boston in 1870, entitled "Historical Basis of Belief," an oration before the Phi Beta Kappa Society of Cambridge, Massachusetts, which was afterwards published with the title or 'The Alienation of the Educated Class From Politics," an address delivered at Portsmouth, Rhode Island, July 10, 1877, at the Centennial Celebration of the Capture of General Prescott by Lieutenant-Colonel Barton; an address delivered October 16, 1877, at the request of the municipal authorities of Providence, in commemoration or the life and services of Roger Williams, in Roger Williams Park, an address delivered at the dedication or the Rogers Free Library at Bristol, January 12, 1878. In the year 1879 Dr Diman delivered a course of lectures before Johns Hopkins University upon 'The Thirty Years' War," and in 1880 a course before the Lowell Institute of Boston on 'The Theistic Argument as Affected by Recent Theories " These lectures were edited by Professor George P Fisher, of Yale, after the death of Dr Diman, and published in the year 1881 and in the following year there appeared Professor Diman's "Orations and Essays, With Selected Parish Sermons," in which was included the commemoration address delivered by Professor James O Murray, of Princeton In 1887 there was published his "Memoirs, Compiled From His Letters, Journals, and the Recollections of His Friends," by Caroline Hazard now president of Wellesley College, and in which was included a complete list of his publications

Professor Jeremiah Lewis Diman always remained affiliated with the Congregational church, but he was often called upon to supply pulpits in the Unitarian church Toward the latter part of his life, however, he was an attendant at the services of the Episcopal church in

Providence, and continued to be so until the time of his death While it is not possible to compare directly the various services wrought for the community by different types of men engaged in divergent kinds of work, while the benefits resulting from the achievements of a merchant and artist, ror instance, are incommensurable terms and cannot be submitted to the same standard of measure—yet it is possible by a sort of spiritual calculus to judge of the relative values of such elements, and at least say of them that they are great or small in a general scale of magnitudes And upon such a scale it is obvious that we must rank the work of the educator as very high, as possessing a very large value for the community, of making a great contribution to the general sum of human happiness In this comparison the achievement of a man such as the late Professor Jeremiah Lewis Diman, of Providence, Rhode Island deserves especial consideration and the more so that it partakes of the characters of more than one type of service and may be classified at one and the same time with the more practical and the more idealistic aspects of life

On May 15, 1861, Professor Diman was united in marriage with Emily Gardner Stimson, a native of Providence, born March 4, 1837, a daughter of John Jones and Abby Morton (Clarke) Stimson (see Stimson) Mrs Diman died in Providence, March 21, 1901 To them the following children were born 1 Maria Stimson, February 12, 1862, who met her death in an accident, April 29, 1881 2 John Byron, mentioned below 3 Louise, December 23, 1869 4 Emily, April 8, 1873

(IX) Rev John Byron Diman, only son of the Rev Jeremiah Lewis and Emily Gardner (Stimson) Diman, was born May 24, 1863, at Brookline, Massachusetts, during the time that his father was pastor of the Congregational church there. He was but an infant when his parents removed to Providence, Rhode Island, and it was in this city that his early education was received at the English and Classical School. Here he was prepared for college, and in 1881 matriculated at Brown University, from which he graduated with the class of 1885, taking the degree of Bachelor of Arts. In 1903 he received from Brown University the honorary degree of Master of Arts. He entered Cambridge Episcopal Theological School, and received therefrom the degree of Bachelor of Divinity in 1888, and in 1896 the degree of Master of Arts from Harvard University. He was ordained a deacon of the Episcopal church at Providence in the year 1888, and his first church was St. Columba's Chapel at Middletown, Rhode Island, of which he was placed in charge in 1888, and where he remained until 1892. In that year he resigned to accept a position as teacher in the University Grammar School of Providence, where he remained for three years. In 1896 he founded St. George's School for Boys at Newport, and later removed this institution to Middletown, Rhode Island, and was master of this celebrated school until he resigned from the position, January 1, 1917.

(The Stimson Line)

Although the name Stimson appears to have been of Welsh origin, there is a tradition also of an admixture of Scotch blood, according to documents in the Astor Library, New York City. The first ancestor of the Massachusetts branch of the Stimson family of whom we have knowledge, George Stimson, came to this country from Wales, and settled in Ipswich, Massachusetts. He married Sarah Clarke, an "English lady of some note and a zealous Puritan." Some account of

them may be found in the records of the church in Ipswich. Their son, George (2) Stimson, born in Ipswich, Massachusetts, in 1693, married Margaret Rust. Their son George (3) Stimson, was born in Ipswich, Massachusetts, in 1726, and when he was about eight years old the family removed to Hopkinton, same State. He married, in 1751, Abigail Clarke, and later in life moved to Windham, New York, located in the Catskill Mountains. Their son, Jeremy Stimson, was born in Hopkinton, Massachusetts, in 1751, there lived all his days, and died in 1821. He graduated at Harvard College, entered the Revolutionary army as a surgeon, and had a large medical practice for many years. He married Anna (Nancy) Jones, daughter of Colonel John Jones, 2nd, of Hopkinton. Children: Emily, born March 21, 1781, died January 18, 1808; Jeremy, Jr., born October 17, 1783, was a physician in Dedham, Massachusetts, for many years; Mary Jones, born March 24, 1785, died May 1 1866, was the second wife of the Rev. Pitt Clarke, of Norton; Nancy, born December 18, 1786, became the wife of —— Stone, of Ashland, Massachusetts; Abigail Clarke, born May 1, 1789, died November 24, 1813; John Jones, born June 11, 1798, died in Providence, Rhode Island, January 20, 1860. He moved to Providence about 1824, where he engaged in business as a wine merchant, under the name of Stimson & Hodges. He married in 1828, Abby Morton Clarke, daughter of the Rev. Pitt Clarke, of Norton, and their children were. Frederick Clarke, born December 25, 1830, died March 19, 1836; Maria Rebecca, born July 14, 1832, died August 11, 1856; John Jones, Jr., born January 17, 1835, died June 13, 1836; Emily Gardner, born March 4, 1837, died in Providence, March 21, 1901, aforementioned as the wife of the Rev. Jeremiah Lewis Diman.

294

THAYER, Philo E,

Man of Affairs, Public Official

The English Thayer family from which Thomas Thayer, progenitor of the American branch, was descended, was a distinguished and honorable one in England, and was entitled to bear arms

Arms (registered in the Herald's office in London, England)—Per pale, ermine and gules, three talbots' heads, erased, counterchanged
Crest—A talbot's head, erased, or
Motto—*Foecundi Calices*

The name Thayer is baptismal in its derivation, and is thought by the eminent authority, Bardsley, to have been derived from the Old French popular nickname Thierry, or Thierre Thayer is a modern English modification of the above surname, and though it barely exists, is familiar in America The earliest mention of the name in official documents is in 1605 Anthony Thayer and Martha Bowman, marriage license in London 1753, Bartholomew Penny and Ann Thayer married at St George Chapel, Mayfair In 1756 John Huggins and Hannah There were married at St George s, Hanover Square, London

(I) Thomas Thayer, an Englishman, who settled in Braintree, Massachusetts, during the early days of that colony's history was the progenitor in America of the Thayer family of which the late Philo Elisha Thayer, of Pawtucket, Rhode Island, was descended in the ninth generation In 1630 the two brothers Richard and Thomas Thayer, came from England, and settled in Braintree, Massachusetts, becoming respectively the heads of families of that name which have since spread throughout the New England States, and rank among the most prominent and important in the country Thomas Thayer brought with him his wife, Margery, and

their children Thomas, Ferdinando, mentioned below, Shadrach

(II) Ferdinando Thayer, son of Thomas, the progenitor, and Margery Thayer, was born in England, and came to America with his parents in 1630 He resided at Braintree, Massachusetts, until after the death of his father He then removed to Mendon, Massachusetts, which was settled with a group of colonists from Braintree and Weymouth. He became one of the prominent and influential citizens of the community there, and was a proprietor of the town His home was located a short distance south of the present center of the town on Providence road He held various public offices in the town and Commonwealth, and was regarded as a man of wealth He was an extensive landowner and dealer, acquiring much valuable land through allotment in the division of public lands and much through purchase On January 14, 1652, he married Hannah Hayward, of Braintree, Massachusetts Their children, born in Braintree, were Sarah, born March 12, 1654, Huldah, April 16, 1657, Jonathan, January 18, 1658 David April 20, 1660, Naomi, November 28, 1662 The following children were born in Mendon, and the records of their births were destroyed in the destruction of the birth records of the town during King Philip's War Thomas, Samuel, Isaac, mentioned below, Josiah, Ebenezer Benjamin, David (2), baptized September 17, 1677, died August 29, 1678 Ferdinando Thayer died at Mendon, Massachusetts, March 28, 1713

(III) Isaac Thayer, eighth child of Ferdinando and Hannah (Hayward) Thayer was born in Mendon, Massachusetts, and lived there all his life engaged in agricultural pursuits He married (first) Mercy Ward, February 1, 1691-92 She died December 18, 1700 He

ENCYCLOPEDIA OF BIOGRAPHY

married (second) in 1703, Mary ———
Children by first wife · Mary, born November 2, 1693, Isaac, September 24,
1695, Ebenezer, mentioned below, Comfort, February 19, 1700 Children by second wife Mary, born December 22, 1704;
John, May 6, 1706, Nathaniel, April 20,
1708, Moses, May 10, 1710, Samuel, 1713,
Joseph, 1715, Ichabod, March 17, 1721

(IV) Ebenezer Thayer, third child of
Isaac and Mercy (Ward) Thayer, was
born September 6, 1697, in Mendon, Massachusetts On May 9, 1719, he married
Mary Wheelock, and removed to Bellingham, Massachusetts, where five subsequent generations of the family lived and
where the late Philo Elisha Thayer was
born Their children were Ebenezer,
mentioned below; Huldah, born in March,
1722, Elizabeth, 1724, Micah, 1726, Isaac,
March 11, 1729, Abigail, November 11,
1731, Peter, 1733; Lydia, 1736

(V) Captain Ebenezer (2) Thayer, son
of Ebenezer (1) and Mary (Wheelock)
Thayer, was born in June, 1720. On April 24, 1734, he
married Hannah Greene, of Mendon, and
after his marriage settled in Bellingham,
Massachusetts, where he engaged in farming on an extensive scale His wife died
in 1783 Their children were Hannah,
born December 3, 1735; Ebenezer, mentioned below, Lydia July 31, 1739, Elias,
June 22, 1742, Silas, November 30, 1746,
Huldah, September 19, 1749

(VI) Ebenezer (3) Thayer, son of Captain Ebenezer (2) and Hannah (Greene)
Thayer, was born in Bellingham, Massachusetts, May 21, 1737 He resided there
all his life, a prosperous farmer as his
father and grandfather had been before
him. He married Hannah Thayer, daughter of Uriah and Rachel Thayer Their
children were· Thaddeus, born August
10 1760, Calvin, July 7, 1763, Luther,
October 6, 1766; Irene, September 16,

1770, Ebenezer, mentioned below, Philo,
1779

(VII) Ebenezer (4) Thayer, son of
Ebenezer (3) and Martha (Thayer)
Thayer, was born November 29, 1772, in
Bellingham, Massachusetts He was also
a gentleman farmer He married, June
28, 1798, Sabra Darling Among their
children was Samuel, mentioned below

(VIII) Samuel Thayer, son of Ebenezer (4) and Sabra (Darling) Thayer, was
born April 22, 1804, at the family homestead in Bellingham, Massachusetts He
was a large property owner, and farmer
and broke steers for the Brighton Market
He devoted much time to the raising of
stock, and was noted throughout the
vicinity for the excellence of his stock
He was one of the most prominent and
popular men of the town His death was
caused early in life by an accident received on his farm In 1826, he married
Miranda Sherman, of Foxboro, Massachusetts Their children were: Allen, engaged as a retail grocer in Woonsocket,
Rhode Island, where he died Three
other sons became manufacturers at Pawtucket, Rhode Island, and are now deceased Their daughters Julia Ann, married George F Greene, a brush manufacturer of North Attleboro, Sarah Wil-
ber, married Henry E Craig, of Walpole
Massachusetts The other son of this
marriage, Philo Elisha, is mentioned below

(IX) Philo Elisha Thayer, son of Samuel and Miranda (Sherman) Thayer, was
born at Bellingham, Massachusetts, March
4 1847, of the ninth generation in direct
descent from the progenitor, Thomas
Thayer He died in Pawtucket, Rhode
Island, March 12, 1908, at the age of sixty-one years Philo E Thayer received
his early education in the public school
at Bellingham, where he was born, but
upon the death of his father, his mother

296

decided to leave Bellingham, and he accompanied her to Woonsocket, where he continued his schooling, entering the high school in that city His mother later married Samuel Kelley, a woolen manufacturer, of West Milton, Ohio, and removed there After his graduation from high school, he left West Milton in 1864, and came East to enter the employ of his brother, Ellis Thayer, who was then engaged in the manufacture of brushes in Worcester, Massachusetts After a few months in this work he entered the employ of his brother, Allen Thayer, hereinbefore mentioned as a grocer in Woonsocket, Rhode Island, remaining with him in the capacity of clerk until 1870, when he went into partnership with his other two brothers, Ellis and George Wesley Thayer, who had purchased Thomas Green's brush factory on East avenue, Pawtucket Rhode Island He was made foreman of the factory, but found the work distasteful, and returned to Woonsocket and became a clerk for A B Warfield, who engaged in the grocery business in that city

His brother, George W Thayer died in 1873, and at the request of Ellis Thayer Philo E Thayer returned to Pawtucket, and again assumed the position of foreman in the factory He subsequently purchased his late brother's interest in the factory In 1880 he purchased also the interests of George W Thayer in the business becoming sole owner of the concern, which then became known by the firm name of P F Thayer & Company Mr Thayer was a keen business man, and was backed in his work by knowledge and business methods used by his father and brothers He profited by these and introduced new methods of manufacture improved working conditions, increased the output of the factory, and made the business a success in every way In 1907

the P E Thayer Company was incorporated with Philo E Thayer as president He served in addition to his own business interests in various official and executive capacities in the commercial, financial and political interests of the city of Pawtucket He held large interests in a brush factory in Woonsocket Rhode Island, which he sold in 1893 to his nephew, Walter S Thayer Mr Thayer was a director of the Pawtucket Mutual Fire Insurance Company, the Isaac Shove Insurance Company, and was a director and member of the executive committee of the Oneonta Electric Light and Power Company

On March 7, 1866 Mr Thayer married Georgianna F Arnold, daughter of Ira W and Harriet (Snell) Arnold, formerly of Plainfield, Connecticut and later of Woonsocket, Rhode Island Their children are 1 Annie Louise, who married Dr Frank R Jenks, and they have two sons Richmond Thayer and Harry Arnold 2 Mrs Hattie Miranda Church, mother of one son, Ralph C Fletcher 3 Daughter, who died in infancy unnamed Mrs Thayer survives her husband and resides at No 58 Olive street, Pawtucket

Mr Thayer was very prominent in public affairs in Pawtucket, despite the absorbing interests of his business, and was active in public office. He was elected a member of the Common Council from the Third Ward, and served in that capacity during six terms, was member of the Board of Aldermen for four years, member of the General Assembly for six years Philo E Thayer was later elected to represent the city of Pawtucket in the Rhode Island State Legislature, and while serving in that body was appointed on May 24, 1897, a member of the new State line commission, was also appointed chairman of the Pawtucket commission to abolish grade crossings, was a member of the special committee appointed by the City Council in charge of the "Cotton Centennial" in 1890, and was chairman of the committee on manufactures. This committee had charge of the exhibits of manufactures during the Centennial, and arranged an exhibit which brought wide and favorable comment at the time, because of its educational, manufacturing and agricultural interest. This exhibit showed cotton in the raw state, through every phase of manufacture to the finished cloth.

Mr. Thayer was a man of genial nature, and magnetic personality, and in consequence of these qualities had numerous friends throughout the city and State. He was prominent in club life and in the fraternal bodies of the city. He was a member of the Masonic fraternity, holding all the degrees of the York and Scottish Rites in Free Masonry up to and including the thirty-second degree. He belonged to the Morning Star Lodge, Free and Accepted Masons, Union Chapter, Royal Arch Masons, Pawtucket Council, Royal and Select Masters, Woonsocket Commandery, Knights Templar; Palestine Temple Nobles of the Mystic Shrine, all Consistory Bodies of the Ancient Accepted Scottish Rite. He was also a member of the Independent Order of Odd Fellows, of the Royal Arcanum, of which he was treasurer for twelve years and a past Regent, and Knight of Honor. He was a communicant of the High Street Universalist Church, serving on the board of trustees. He was also a member of the Pawtucket Business Men's Association, the West Side Club of Pawtucket, and the Central Club of Providence.

TEEL, Benjamin G.,

Manufacturer, Enterprising Citizen.

The name Teel is a survival in surname form of the ancient and often used nick-

name meaning "the teal," a small duck. It acquired favor as a surname in the eleventh and twelfth centuries, and it is to be found quite generally throughout the early records of England and the later ones of America since that time.

The names of Matilda Tele and Martin Tele, who was probably her husband or some near relative, are found in the Hundred Rolls of the year 1273, their address being given as County Cambridge. The names of John and Thomas Telcock, this surname gaining its derivation from the same source as the more simple forms and intended to distinguish the masculine gender, are found among the same records. John Teel was prominent in County Somerset during the reign of Edward the Third.

As in many other cases, the style of spelling the above name has changed materially during the many generations it has been in use, although not to the extent that might be supposed. In the modern day we find it in four forms—Teal, Teel, Teale and Teall. The two first mentioned are the most common and the latter ones are used in very rare instances.

Arms—Argent a python reguardant in chief three teals proper.
Crest—A spaniel sejant proper, reposing the dexter foot on an antique shield argent, thereon a teal of the first.

(I) William Teal, the founder of this family in America, settled originally in Malden, Massachusetts, and lived also in Medford and Charlestown. He was a nephew of William Clement, of Newton, and was probably a son or a relative of Nicholas Teal, who lived in Watertown in 1638 and sold lands there September 23, 1645, by wife Elizabeth. Nicholas had son Joseph, born October 24, 1640, and Elizabeth, born June 5, 1643.

William Teal married (first) Mary

———, (second) Hannah Kendrick He had thirteen children, the first five of whom were born in Medford, and the others in Charlestown William was the only one of the sons who remained at Charlestown Children 1 Abigail, born January 1, 1685 2 Benjamin, November 2, 1689. 3 Elizabeth, June 22, 1696 4 Oliver, July 19, 1699; lived at Charlestown, Chelmsford, Dracut, New Haven, and Killingworth, and his son Oliver settled at Hillside, New York. 5 Hannah, July 25, 1707 6 John, September 25, 1708 7 Rachel, August 2, 1709. 8 Esther, September 9, 1711 9 Mary, March 30, 1713 10 William, baptized October 3, 1714 11 Caleb, mentioned below 12 Abigail, baptized June 30, 1723 13 Elizabeth, October 12, 1725.

(II) Caleb Teal, eleventh child of William Teal, was born in the town of Charlestown, in the year 1717, and was baptized there June 23, 1717 He lived in his native town until after his marriage to Grace Robbins (who was admitted to the church in Charlestown, July 23, 1740), on July 11, 1740, when he removed to Providence, Rhode Island, where he died December 1, 1801, at the advanced age of eighty-five years, his wife died on the same day There were five known children, and perhaps other daughters of whom no record has been found 1 Caleb, baptized July 26, 1741, and died March 8, 1748 2 John, May 27, 1744 3 Elizabeth, baptized December 7, 1746 4 Mary, baptized December 23, 1750 5 Caleb, mentioned below

(III) Caleb (2) Teal, son of Caleb (1) and Grace (Robbins) Teal, was born probably in the city of Providence, Rhode Island, about the year 1755 The Rhode Island State census of the year 1774 shows that Caleb, Sr., and his son, John Teal, were the only heads of families in the State bearing that surname According

to the above record, Caleb had two males over sixteen in his family, and John had one son under sixteen and two or three daughters In 1790, sixteen years later, Caleb, Sr, and Caleb, Jr, both had families in Providence, and John had three males over sixteen and three females The Providence vital records, however, do not give the names of any of the Teal children Caleb (2) Teal was a gallant exponent of American liberty, and was one of the first soldiers of the Revolution

(IV) Nathan Roten Teel, son of Caleb (2) Teel, or Teal, was born in Providence, Rhode Island, September 17, 1788, and lived in North Providence, until his death He married, in Providence, September 15, 1811, Betsey Arnold, a daughter of Thomas and Anstiss (Thornton) Arnold, born October 15, 1792, a member of one of the oldest of Rhode Island and New England families She died February 28, 1815, at the age of twenty-four years Her father, Thomas Arnold, was born in the year 1749 and died in 1799. There were two children Daughter, who died in infancy, and Benjamin Gustavus Teel, mentioned below

It is interesting to note that the change of the form of the name occurred in this generation through the simplification of its spelling

(V) Benjamin Gustavus Teel, only son of Nathan Roten and Betsey (Arnold) Teel, and of the fifth generation of this family in America, was born in North Providence, Rhode Island, February 3, 1815 His father died in the year 1815 at the age of twenty-seven years, while on the return voyage from Savannah, Georgia, where he had gone in the hope of regaining his lost health, and his mother passed away shortly after his birth, thus leaving him at this early age an orphan He was taken into the family of his Grandmother Arnold, and there received the best of care The Arnold family was itself in straightened circumstances, however, so that Mr Teel had few opportunities to pursue his education, but when still very young he hired himself out to the farmers in the vicinity, and in this manner supported himself and managed to contribute a small sum to the support of the family which had adopted him Growing older, he began to realize the value placed on skilled labor and he learned the trades of stone-mason and carpenter, following these occupations for some years until he had amassed what seemed a fortune to him in those days, enough money to enter into business for himself He formed a company for the purpose of manufacturing sash, doors and blinds, and, after many reverses and discouragements, fighting his way through all obstacles with sheer pluck and perseverance, he reached a high position in the esteem of his fellow business men in Providence, and attained the business success for which he had worked with such zeal His product was often considered the best manufactured in Providence and was consistently demanded by the builders and contractors with whom he dealt.

Mr Teel also invested greatly in real estate, using the sound common sense for which he was noted in other lines of business, with good success in the latter He was more greatly interested, however, in his manufacturing business than in the latter, which he considered somewhat of a side line, and he continued active in the former until his death

He was a Republican in politics, keenly interested in all affairs of a public nature, but never engaging actively in the management of his community He cared little for the social life of his community, preferring to find his recreation and rest from the turmoil of the business world in the quiet of his home, and for this reason

he never identified himself with clubs, societies or organizations of a similar nature He expended all his available time between his family and his business, and it was a common saying that he could be found either at his office or his home at any hour He was well known for his honesty and sterling character, his early adversities, instead of souring his nature, as is often the case, only made him the more tolerant of the faults of others He made many friends and held them, and he was sincerely respected by all who knew him

Mr Teel passed away in Providence, Rhode Island at his home on Westminster street, February 5, 1872, at the age of fifty-seven years, two days He is buried in the old North burying ground in the latter city.

Benjamin Gustavus Teel married, June 13, 1841, Dorcas Knight Brown, daughter of Richard and Penelope (Farnum) Brown (see Brown VI) Mrs Teel, died at her home on Courtland street, Providence, September 13, 1861, and her remains rest in the North burying ground beside those of her husband There were three children born to this union

1. Martha Brown, born September 4, 1844, in Providence, Rhode Island, received her education in the public schools of that city and under the tutorship of Brown University professors She took up teaching as a career, and in the year 1874 she was appointed principal of the Branch Avenue Grammar School, being the first woman to hold that position in the State She retained that office until her death, November 1, 1900 She was known as a woman of culture and learning, and admirably fitted by nature for the work which she followed with such good success

2. Dorcas Brown, born in Providence, April 4, 1849, was educated in the public schools of the latter city, and made due preparation to follow in the path of her

elder sister She formed a connection as a teacher with the Mount Pleasant Street Grammar School in the year 1870, and later acted in a like capacity on the staff of teachers at both the Academy Avenue Grammar School and the Federal Street School Her length of service extended over a period of more than forty years She was a model teacher, devoted to her profession, highly esteemed by parents and pupils and beloved in her home and by many friends She died April 12, 1910

3 Mary Antiss, born at Providence, Rhode Island, June 7, 1853, received an excellent education at the public schools and at the select school of the Misses Fielding and Chase, pursuing her studies diligently with the intention of following the profession of her sisters Ill health, however, interfered, and she always remained at home, devoting her life to the care of her parents and sisters, all of whom have passed away She occupies the family home on Westminster street.

(The Brown Line)

Arms—Sable three lions in bend, between two bendlets argent

The surname Brown is derived from two separate and distinct sources which will be dealt with in the order of their greater popularity

First in this order is the baptismal class, the original form of which, as also applies to the second in order, was Brun It was first used as a personal name, and meant 'the son of Mount," or Brown It has always been exceedingly high in public favor, the ancient records of England teem with it, and it stands in the present day sixth in point of numbers as it is used by the descendants of the original families It gained favor as a surname in the eleventh or twelfth centuries

Gamel fil Brun gained popularity and prominence in England under the reign of Henry I (1068-1135), and his name is found among those in the "Rotuli Litterarum Clausarum in Turri Londinensi

— Valor Ecclisiasticus " He made his home in Cumberland county Brun Edrith, which gives an idea of the personal use of the name, lived in the county of Salop in the thirteenth century The name of German Bruno is found in Domesday Book, and there are several representatives among the records of the Hundred Rolls of the year 1273, Matilda relicta Brun, of Oxford county, and Brune relicta Johannis, of Cambridge, among others. Reginald fil. Brun is found in the "Rotuli Curiai Register," and records of Willelmus Bronson or Brunson are found as far back as the year 1379 The latter example, Brunson, portrays unusually well the meaning of the name as it was originally understood

Next we have the class gaining their derivation from the continuance as a surname of what was originally used as a nickname The parentage of this class and the one given above have nothing in common—they are applied to two distinct families, and are only related through their common forms This latter class was originally applied as a sobriquet of complexion and held the meaning "the brown " It was extremely common in all early registers The two forms have in modern times lost the individual marks which in early days distinguished them, but in so far as can be ascertained from the records of the middle ages, the first was the more popular

Hugh le Brun lived in County Suffolk in the early part of the thirteenth century The name of Robert le Brun appears among those in the Hundred Rolls of 1273 as living in County Bucks, and Johanna la Brune, another common form of the name, lived in County Oxford Robert Broun was prominent in Somerset county under the reign of Edward III, and Willelmus Broune lived in the same county in the year 1379

The name is found in two different forms in the modern day—Brown, far the more popular, and Browne Brownson and Bronson were derived from the same sources, but were never as commonly used

(I) Chad Brown, the progenitor of the branch of that large family herein treated, was born in England in the early part of the seventeenth century, married there Elizabeth ———, and had a son John, and perhaps other children In the year 1638, with his wife and son John, who was then eight years of age, he took passage on the ship "Martin," bound for Boston, Massachusetts, where it arrived in July of the latter year During the long voyage a fellow passenger died, and shortly after reaching Massachusetts, Mr Brown witnessed the will, this is probably the first public record we have of him in the new land He did not long remain in Massachusetts, probably because of religious views, but soon removed to Providence, Rhode Island, where very shortly he began to show signs of that innate quality of leadership which characterized his nature throughout his long and useful life That same year (1638) he and twelve other inhabitants of Providence Plantations drew up and signed a compact relative to the government of the town, and a short time after acting in the capacity of surveyor, he received an appointment to a committee the duty of which was to compile lists of the home lots of the first settlers of the "Towne Street," and the meadowlands allotted them His own grant fronted on this street, now South Main and Market Square, with the southern boundary to the southward of College and South Main streets A large part of the grounds now occupied by the campus and buildings of Brown University, originally belonged to Mr Brown's tract In

1640 he served on the committee that settled the question of the disputed boundary lines of Providence and its neighbor, Pawtuxet, and that same year he, with Robert Cole, William Harris and John Warner, formed the committee of Providence Colony to report their first written form of government, which was subsequently adopted and enforced until 1644, when Roger Williams returned from England with the first charter Chad Brown was the first of the thirty-nine signers of this agreement In 1642 he was ordained as the first settled pastor of the Baptist church, and a year later he was chosen as a member of the committee formed for the purpose of making peace between the Warwick settlers and the Massachusetts Bay colony Their efforts, however, were unavailing

Chad Brown died in Providence, September 2, 1650, on which date the name of his widow first appears on the tax list as a landholder His children were five in number 1 John, mentioned below 2-3 James and Jeremiah, both of whom removed to Newport, Rhode Island 4 Judah, or Chad, died May 10, 1663, unmarried 5 Daniel

(II) John Brown, son of Chad and Elizabeth Brown, was born in England in the year 1630, and died in Providence, Rhode Island, about 1706 He followed in his father's footsteps, serving his community in various official capacities, and doing a great deal towards the future development of the town He acted several times as juryman, was commissioner on union of towns in 1654, took the oath and became a freeman in 1655 In the year 1659 he became surveyor of highways, and was later moderator, member of the town council, deputy in the Legislature and assistant He took the oath of allegiance May 31, 1666 In the year 1672 he sold the home lot of his father, which had fallen to him through inheritance, to his brother James, of Newport, who resold it the same day to Daniel Abbott Nearly one hundred years later a part of it was repurchased by his great-grandsons, John and Moses Brown, and by them presented to the College of Rhode Island at the time of its removal from Warren to Providence The cornerstone of University Hall, for many years the only building owned by the college was laid in 1770 by John Brown.

John Brown married Mary, a daughter of the Rev Obadiah and Catharine Holmes, of Newport, and to them were born seven children 1 Sarah 2 John, born March 18, 1662 3 James, mentioned below. 4 Obadiah 5 Martha. 6 Mary 7 Deborah.

(III) James Brown, son of John and Mary (Holmes) Brown, was born in Providence, Rhode Island, in the year 1666, and died there October 28, 1732. He engaged actively in the civic affairs of his native place, serving as a member of the town council almost continuously from 1705 to 1725, and from 1714 to 1718 as treasurer He was long pastor or elder of the First Baptist Church, and in 1726 succeeded Rev Ebenezer Jenkes in the ministry, a position greatly prized, which he held until his death One historian remarks, "He was an example of piety and meekness worthy of admiration." He had inherited from his father a large portion of the family estate, including three home lots, dwelling houses and other property, the greater part of which he passed on to his children, for whom he provided well in his will, dated March 3, 1728

He married, December 17, 1691, Mary Harris, daughter of Andrew and Mary (Tew) Harris, granddaughter of William and Susannah (Clarke) Tew, born December 17, 1671, died August 18, 1736 Children 1 John, born October 8, 1695

2 James, March 22, 1698 3 Joseph, mentioned below 4 Martha, October 12, 1703 5 Andrew, September 20, 1706. 6 Mary, April 29, 1708, died February 20, 1729 7 Anna, 1710 8 Obadiah, October 2, 1712 9 Jeremiah, November 25, 1715 10 Elisha, May 23, 1717

(IV) Joseph Brown, son of James and Mary (Harris) Brown, was born in Providence, Rhode Island, May 5, 1701 He followed agricultural occupations from early childhood until his death, his farm covering many acres of the excellent country-side of that region He was energetic and persevering, and prospered more than the usual farmer of the day His first wife, Martha Field, was a daughter of William Field, of Field's Point, and by her he had one child, Gideon, who was born in the year 1726 She died April 19, 1736, at the age of twenty-six years, and he married (second) Abigail Brown, who died May 23, 1784, in her seventy-third year Mr Brown died May 8, 1778. The children by his second wife were 1 Elisha 2 Andrew, mentioned below 3 Joseph

(V) Andrew Brown, son of Joseph and Abigail Brown, was born in the town of North Providence, Rhode Island, July 30, 1750, and died January 8, 1832 He married (first) January 27, 1773, Dorcas Knight, daughter of Richard Knight, and a member of the old Knight family of Cranston, Rhode Island His second wife was Widow Susie Westcott, and his third, whom he married, April 14, 1805, Sarah (Humphrey) Shorey, the widow of Miles Shorey The children by his first wife were as follows 1 Abigail, born September 30, 1773 2 Waite, September 10, 1775. 3 Mary, May 10, 1778. 4 Sarah, May 20, 1780 5 Jeremiah, June 14, 1782 6 Joseph, May 10, 1784 7 Ethan, October 20, 1785 8 Richard, mentioned below

(VI) Richard Brown, son of Andrew

and his first wife, Dorcas (Knight)
Brown, was born in North Providence,
June 17, 1789 He inherited a good portion of his father's estate, which he improved, and throughout life he followed
the occupation of farming. He was prominent and prosperous, and took a keenly
active interest in the public affairs of his
day, serving his community in many civic
offices of importance, for some years acting as representative to the General Assembly of the State of Rhode Island His
wife, Penelope Farnum, whom he married, February 23, 1812, was born April
12, 1793, and died July 24, 1869 She was
a member of the Society of Friends; a
daughter of Joseph and Hannah (Congdon) Farnum Their children, six in number, were 1 Sarah Ann, born February
11, 1813, died March 4, 1815 2 Martha
Ann, born February 16, 1815, died July
15, 1832 3 Dorcas Knight, born March
29, 1818, married Benjamin G Teel, and
died September 13, 1861 (see Teel V)
4 Mary Jane, born April 6, 1821, married
Andrew Winsor, and died February 23,
1904 5. Obadiah, born November 30,
1823, died February 2, 1907 6 Joseph
Farnum, born May 16, 1835, died in February, 1886

Richard Brown passed away March 28,
1840, at the age of fifty-one years, leaving his son Obadiah, who was then a
youth of seventeen years, in charge of the
farm, and at the head of the family homestead

CRANSTON, Francis A,
Financier, Man of Affairs.

Cranston is of Scottish origin, and signifies "belonging to Cranston or Crans-
toun," meaning Cran's estate It is a combination of the genitive case of the word
cran, a nickname for the crane, and the
old English tun

Arms (Samuel C Cranston, Governor of
Rhode Island, 1724)—Gules, three cranes within
a bordure embattled argent.
Crest—A crane passant argent
Motto—*Dum vigilo curo.*

The name Cranston is one of the most
prominent in the history of the State of
Rhode Island, and one of the most distinguished in the early Colonial history
of New England The family is a branch
of the ancient Scottish family of the name,
and was settled in America prior to 1644,
when it first appears in authentic record
The Cranstons furnished Colonial Rhode
Island with two of her strongest and
most able governors, and have since their
time, in every generation, produced men
of mark and influence in every phase of
life. The pedigree of the family prior to
its transplantation in the New World is
given herewith

(I) Lord William Cranston, so created
November 19, 1609, by King James VI
of Scotland, was a noble of prominence
during the reign of the aforementioned
monarch, and was related to the ancient
Earl of Crawford, Bothwell and Traquair
He married Helen, daughter of James
Lindsley, predecessor of the Earl of
Crawford

(II) James Cranston, son of Lord William and Helen (Lindsley) Cranston,
married Elizabeth Stuart, daughter of
Francis Stuart, Earl of Bothwell, who
was a grandson of James V and nephew
of Mary, Queen of Scots

(III) John Cranston, son of James and
Elizabeth (Stuart) Cranston, married
Christian, daughter of Sir Robert Stuart,
predecessor of the Earl of Traquair, also
of the Royal Stuarts

(IV) James (2) Cranston, son of John
and Christian (Stuart) Cranston, was
chaplain to King Charles I of England
and Scotland

The lineage of that branch of the Cranston family of which the late Francis Augustus Cranston, banker of Providence, Rhode Island, was a descendant, from the immigrant ancestor to the present day, is as follows

(V) Governor John (2) Cranston, son of James (2) Cranston, was born in 1625, and emigrated to America, where his name first appears in the Colonial records of Rhode Island in 1644, at which time he was an inhabitant of Portsmouth In the year 1655 he removed from Portsmouth to Newport, becoming one of the most prominent men in the official life of the Colony He was elected attorney-general in 1654 and reëlected the following year He was commissioner from Newport in 1655-56-57-60-64-65-66 and assistant in 1669-70-71 In 1672 he was elected deputy governor, and also in 1673, and again in 1676-77-78 In November, 1678, he was elected governor and filled that office until the March following, when he died (March 12, 1680) Governor Cranston was a man of unusual education for his time, was a physician and surgeon, and bore the title of Doctor of Medicine

He married Mary Clarke, who was born in 1641, and died April 7, 1711, daughter of Jeremiah and Frances (Latham) Clarke

(VI) Governor Samuel Cranston, son of Governor John (2) and Mary (Clarke) Cranston, was born in Newport, Rhode Island, in 1659 He was admitted a freeman in the Colony on May 6, 1684 He is recorded as an assistant in 1696, and is thought to have held that office for several years prior to that date As no record exists between the years 1692 and 1696 this cannot be proved He rose rapidly to a position of prominence in the colony, and in 1698 was elected governor of Rhode Island, succeeding in office his uncle, Governor Walter Clarke He con-

tinued to be elected to the office of chief executive until 1727, during which year he died The period of Governor Samuel Cranston's service in office was twenty-nine years "At no period in our colonial history was there more need of the sterling qualities that distinguished Samuel Cranston than that in which was assigned him the onerous task of administering the Rhode Island Government, and he proved himself the worthy successor of his venerable uncle, Governor Walter Clarke."

Samuel Cranston married (first) Mary Hart, daughter of Thomas and Freeborn (Williams) Hart, and a granddaughter of Roger Williams She died in 1710, aged forty-seven years, and he married (second) Judith Parrett, widow of his brother, Caleb Cranston She died in 1737, aged sixty-seven years

(VII) Thomas Cranston, son of Governor Samuel and Mary (Hart) Cranston, settled in Swansea and died at sea

(VIII) Peleg Cranston, son of Thomas Cranston, was a resident of the town of Foster, Rhode Island

(IX) Samuel (2) Cranston, son of Peleg Cranston, was born and died in Foster, Rhode Island, married Zilpha King

(X) Barzillai Cranston, son of Samuel (2) and Zilpha (King) Cranston, was born in Foster, Rhode Island, March 12, 1793 He removed to Providence, and there engaged in the publishing business, in which he was very successful. He became one of the leading business men of the city of Providence In 1859 he became the first secretary and treasurer of the City Savings Bank

On January 24, 1822, he was married to Irene Guild, daughter of Moses and Abigail (Everett) Guild She was a descendant in the sixth generation of John Guild, who came to America from Scotland about 1636, settling in Dedham,

Massachusetts Their children were 1 James Edward, born November 22, 1822; was a publisher and bookseller in Providence, he was assistant treasurer of the City Savings Bank, and succeeded his father as secretary and treasurer in 1868, married Sarah A Walker, died April 5 1901 2 Charles Guild, born January 17, 1826, died October 6, 1901, was a contractor and builder in the West, where he was engaged in building some of the Western railroads, the New York Central being one 3 Albert B, born May 15, 1828, was a merchant in California 4 George King, born September 8, 1830, was assistant cashier in the Old National Bank, of Providence, and in 1878 became secretary and treasurer of the City Savings Bank, in which position he succeeded his brother, James E Cranston, died January 14, 1899 5 Henry Clay, born August 27, 1832, died May 27, 1896, became one of the most prominent business men of the city of Providence 6 Irene M, born September 1, 1834, married W H Dubosq, of Philadelphia, Pennsylvania 7 Francis Augustus, mentioned below

(XI) Francis Augustus Cranston, son of Barzillai and Irene (Guild) Cranston, was born in Providence, Rhode Island, February 4, 1837, died at his home in Providence, April 10, 1909 He received his education in the private academy of the Misses McNeal, of Providence, and in the public schools of the city, preparing for college in the Providence High School He entered Brown University, where he took a course in chemistry under Professor Chase In May, 1854, he entered the National Bank as a clerk, and after remaining in that office for three years was made bookkeeper, in 1864 he became cashier In the following year the National Bank, then subject to the laws of the State of Rhode Island, was

changed to what is now the Old National Bank, operating under federal law Mr Cranston was elected cashier of the new bank, and continued in that office until January 14, 1902, when he resigned He was a man of considerable ability, and figured prominently in the financial interests of the city and State He prepared the paper for the transforming of the Bank from a State to a National Bank His time of service in this institution was forty-seven years and eight months Mr Cranston was affiliated with the Republican party and a staunch supporter of its principles He was a member of the Unitarian Club, and the Athletic Club of Providence He was a member of the Unitarian (First Congregational) Church of Providence

He married Sarah Hill, daughter of Hiram Hill, of Providence Their children are Frank Hill, Sarah, Louise, Helen

---

BALLARD, Harlan Hoge, A B,
Librarian, Litterateur

This surname is an ancient one in England, Wales and Ireland, and it took root in America with the colonization of New England William Ballard, the first known American ancestor of the line herein followed, was born in 1603, and died in Andover, Massachusetts, July 10, 1689 He arrived in this country from England in the ship "James" in 1635, and was one of the earliest settlers of Andover, where he was admitted a freeman, May 2, 1638 His son, Joseph Ballard, was a resident of Andover, Massachusetts, where his death occurred in 1721 He married (first) Elizabeth Phelps, (second) Mrs Rebecca Horne Josiah Ballard, son of Joseph, was born in Andover, Massachusetts, in 1699, and died there in 1780 He married Mary Chandler Their son, Josiah (2) Ballard, was born in Andover, Massachusetts, in 1721, served in the Revolutionary War, and died in 1799 He married Sarah Carter Their son, William Ballard, was born in Lancaster, Massachusetts, March 23, 1764, settled at Charlemont, Massachusetts, and died in that town, May 25, 1842 He was a captain in the State militia He married Elizabeth Whitney Their son, John Ballard, was born in Charlemont, Massachusetts, October 1, 1790, settled in Athens, Ohio, in 1830, and died August 23, 1880 He married Pamelia Bennett

Rev Addison Ballard, D D., son of John and Pamelia (Bennett) Ballard, was born in Framingham, Massachusetts, October 18, 1822 Williams College conferred upon him the degrees of Bachelor of Arts, Master of Arts and Doctor of Divinity Entering the Congregational ministry he held pastorates in Williamstown, Massachusetts, and Detroit, Michigan He held the professorship of Latin at the Ohio University, and that of rhetoric at Williams College, occupied the chair of astronomy, mathematics and natural philosophy at Marietta College, was a professor of Greek and Latin at Lafayette College, Easton, Pennsylvania, also was Professor of Moral Philosophy and Rhetoric in the same institution, and was Professor of Logic in the New York University One of the principal products of his pen is "Arrows, or the True Aim in Study and Teaching" He married Julia Perkins Pratt, who is widely and favorably known as the author of "Building Stones," "Seven Years from Tonight," "Grandmother's Story," "Hole in the Bag" and "Among the Moths and Butterflies" They were the parents of three children Harlan Hoge, Winifred and Julia Spaulding

Harlan Hoge Ballard was born in Athens, Ohio, May 26, 1853 He was graduated from Williams College, Bachelor of Arts, with the class of 1874, received the degree of Master of Arts in 1877, and shortly after leaving college engaged in educational work For six years, from 1874 to 1880, he was principal of the high school in Lenox, Massachusetts, and from 1880 to 1886 was principal of the Lenox Academy, and while residing in that town he founded the Agassiz Association for the study of nature, which has had over one thousand branches In 1887 he was chosen librarian and curator of the Berkshire Athenaeum and Museum and the following year became secretary of the Berkshire Historical and Scientific Society of Pittsfield He is curator of the Museum of Natural History and Art, presented to the city of Pittsfield by Zenas Crane, Esq , of Dalton He was for several years the editor of "The Swiss Cross" He is the author of "Three Kingdoms," 1882, "World of Matter," 1892, "Open Sesame," 1896, "Virgil's Æneid, translated into English Hexameters," 1902-11, and joint author of "American Plant Book," 1879, "Barnes' Readers," 1883, and "One Thousand Blunders in English," 1884 He is a fellow of the American Association for the Advancement of Science, of the American Library Association, member of the Phi Beta Kappa Society, Royal Arcanum, Country Club and Park Club, Pittsfield, and the National Institute of Social Sciences, and an honorary member of the Supreme Council of the thirty-third degree of Scottish Rite Masonry He is a Republican in politics

Mr Ballard married, August 30, 1879, Lucy Bishop Pike, of Lenox, Massachusetts, daughter of John and Lucy (Bishop) Pike, and granddaughter of Nicholas Pike, who was for many years master of the Newburyport grammar school, and was the author of an arithmetic which was in general use in the public schools of his day On the maternal side she was a granddaughter of Judge Henry Walker Bishop, of Lenox, and great-granddaughter of Hon Nathaniel Bishop, of Richmond, Massachusetts Children of Mr and Mrs Ballard Harlan Hoge, Jr, Elizabeth Bishop, Lucy Bishop and Margaret

CARTER, Franklin,
Educator, Author.

Franklin Carter, sixth president of Williams College (1881-1901), was born in Waterbury, Connecticut, September 30, 1837, son of Preserved Wood and Ruth W. (Holmes) Carter

He fitted for college at Phillips Academy, Andover, Massachusetts, where he completed the course in 1855, being valedictorian of his class. The fall of that year he entered Yale College, but on account of impaired health was compelled to leave at the end of his sophomore year. After three years of rest he resumed college work, entered the junior class at Williams College, and was graduated in 1862 Early in 1863 he was appointed Professor of Latin and French at Williams College, and after eighteen months in Europe assumed the duties, continuing in charge until 1868, when he ceased to teach French He retained the chair of Latin until 1872, when he accepted the professorship of German at Yale University He then spent a year in special study abroad, and occupied the chair until 1881, when he was elected president of Williams College Two years later he also became Professor of Theology in that institution He received the degree of Master of Arts from Williams and from Jefferson in 1864, from Yale in 1874; Doctor of Philosophy from Williams in 1877; and Doctor of Laws

from Union in 1881, from Williams in 1904, from South Carolina College in 1905; and from Yale in 1901 He served as trustee of Andover Theological Seminary, and in Clarke Institute for Deaf Mutes, of which school he was president for twenty-one years He was president of the American Modern Language Association and is a member of various literary and benevolent organizations

Some of his principal writings are. An edition of 'Iphigenie auf Tauris" in Whitney's "German Texts," 1879; "A Biography of Mark Hopkins," in series of "American Leaders," 1892, "The New Translations of Laacoon," "Mr Lettson's Version of Middle German Epic," "Science and Poetry," "Bayard Taylor's Posthumous Books," and various other articles contributed to the "New Englander" "On Begessmann's Views as to the Weak Preterit of the Germanic Verbs," "Did Von Der Kurnberg compose the present form of Nibelungen Lied?" and "On Wilmann's Theory of the Authorship of the Nibelungen Lied" were papers in the "Transactions" of the American Philological Association He has published articles in "Modern Language Transactions" and the "American Journal of Philology." Dr Carter has delivered many addresses before learned societies, and baccalaureate sermons before graduating classes While scholarly in his tastes, he is eminently a man of affairs, and his work for Williams College was one of notable progress During his presidency he added eighty acres to the college domain, secured over a million dollars for endowments, and added seven fine buildings to the equipment; nine new professorships and departments were established, and the older professorships liberally furnished, and the number of students in attendance was largely increased As a teacher, Dr Carter is a thorough master and a born leader As the chief executive officer of the college he is quick in decision and promptly secures desired results He was a member of the Massachusetts State Board of Education, 1896-1900, presidential elector, 1896, director of Berkshire Industrial Farm, Canaan, New Hampshire, president of the Massachusetts Home Missionary Society, 1896-1901, fellow of the American Academy of Arts and Sciences, member of the Modern Language Association of America, of which he was president, 1881-86, member of American Oriental Society, American Philological Association, corresponding member of the Massachusetts Colonial Society, and honorary member of the Mattatuck Historical Society, Waterbury, Connecticut He is a member of the Williams (New York) Club

Dr Carter married (first) February 24, 1863, Sarah Leavenworth Kingsbury, of Waterbury, Connecticut He married (second) February 10, 1908, Mrs Elizabeth (Sabin) Leake, daughter of Dr H L Sabin, of Williamstown, Massachusetts

---

CHAMBERLAIN, Alexander Francis,

Anthropologist

Alexander Francis Chamberlain was born in Kenninghall, Norfolk, England, January 12, 1865, son of George and Maria (Anderton) Chamberlain He was brought by his parents to New York in 1870, whence they removed to Canada in 1873. He was graduated from Toronto University in 1886 with honors in modern language and etomology, and received the degree of Master of Arts from that institution in 1889 From 1887 to 1890 he was fellow in modern languages in University College, Toronto, and during these years made a study of the Missis-

siga Indians of Skugog, and visited British Columbia for field work among the Kootenay Indians From 1890 to 1892 he was fellow in anthropology in Clark University, Worcester, Massachusetts, meantime continuing his studies under Professor Frank Boas He received in 1892 from Clark University the degree of Doctor of Philosophy, this being the first time this degree was granted in anthropology in America, his doctor's dissertation was "The Language of the Mississiga Indians of Skugog."

In 1892 he was appointed lecturer on anthropology in Clark University, and at a time when appointments in that field were rare in our universities and unknown in our colleges, and spent the summer of 1891 among the Kootenay Indians of British Columbia, conducting anthropological investigations under the auspices of the British Association for the Advancement of Science He was promoted to the acting assistant professorship in 1900, to the assistant professorship in 1904 and to the professorship in 1911. He devoted especial attention to American aboriginal anthropology and linguistics, and contributed to the "American Folk Lore Journal," "The Anthropologist," "Dialect Notes," "Modern Language Notes," and the "Proceedings of the Canadian Institute." He compiled a "Dictionary and Grammar of the Kootenay Indian Language," and a "Comparative Glossary of Algonkian Dialects."

Dr Chamberlain was a member of the American Antiquarian Society, was elected secretary of the Anthropological Section of the American Association for the Advancement of Science, in 1894, secretary of the Anthropological Section of the British Association for the Advancement of Science, 1897, was a corresponding member of the Institut de Coimbra, Portugal, Societe de Folk-Lore, Chileno

ENCYCLOPEDIA OF BIOGRAPHY

(Santiago), and Société des American-istes (Paris); honorary member American Folk-Lore Society, vice-president of the Anthropologist Association

Dr. Chamberlain was connected in an editorial capacity with the "Journal of American Folk-Lore" (1900-08), was department editor of the "American Anthropologist," and co-editor of "Journal of Religious Psychology." He was the author of "Child and Childhood in Folk Thought," 1896, "The Child—A Study in the Evolution of Man," 1900, "Poems," 1904, also many essays and papers on anthropology, pedagogy, and other subjects He was a contributor to the "New International Encyclopedia," "Monroe's Cyclopedia of Education," "Encyclopedia Americana," "Handbook of American Indians North of Mexico" (Bureau of Ethnology), "Hastings Encyclopedia of Religion and Ethics," "Encyclopedia Britannica." His bibliography, covering the years 1886-1910, contains no fewer than seven hundred and eleven titles

In municipal affairs he took a considerable interest, and served his fellow citizens in the following offices Alderman-at-large, of Worcester, 1905, chairman of the Democratic City Committee, 1904-05, chairman of the Lincoln Centenary Committee, Worcester, 1909

Dr. Chamberlain was married, in 1898, in Worcester, Massachusetts, to Isabel Cushman, of that city He died April 8, 1914, after a short illness

---

ARMINGTON, Hervey,

Physician, Man of Strong Character

The Armington Arms—Per chevron or and azure, in chief two lions rampant combatant of the second in base a lion rampant of the first

For more than two hundred years the name of Armington has been one of the best known in New England Descendants of the original settler have during that period played prominent parts in public and official life, in military affairs, in the professions, and in business and commercial enterprises The family has flourished in those parts of Massachusetts and Rhode Island, which immediately adjoin each other, and its sons have left the imprint of their lives on the communities wherein they have resided. The name is found frequently in Revolutionary rosters, in connection with both the army and navy, is found in the high places during that period of upbuilding which followed the close of the Revolutionary War, and has continued since that early time to grow in prestige and honor Loyalty, patriotism, able and signal service have brought honor to the house, and placed it high among the families who have done much for our country

It is with the line of descent from the founder, of the late Dr Hervey Armington and his distinguished brother, Asa Watson Armington, a well-known figure in the financial world of Providence in the middle of the nineteenth century, and the late Hon James Hervey Armington, that this article deals.

(I) Joseph Armington, immigrant ancestor and founder of the line in America, was born on the Island of Guernsey, Great Britain. He came from England to the American Colonies in 1714, settling in Boston, Massachusetts, where he remained for a short time. He returned to England on business, and died there in 1715. His wife, a woman of great culture and unusual education for the time, after the death of her husband, established a school in Roxbury, Massachusetts, where she taught French.

(II) Joseph (2) Armington, son of Joseph (1) Armington, the progenitor, was born about the year 1707, on the Island of

310

Guernsey, Great Britain, and accompanied his parents to America. Upon reaching his majority he removed to Rehoboth, Massachusetts, where he established himself, and where he died on August 15, 1746. He followed the trade of brickmaker.

Joseph (2) Armington married, in Rehoboth, Massachusetts, May 27, 1729, Hannah Chaffee, born October 3, 1707, daughter of Jonathan and Hannah (Carpenter) Chaffee. "Hannah, widow of Joseph," died at Rehoboth February 22, 1799. Their children were: 1. Nicholas, born January 12, 1730. 2. Joseph, mentioned below. 3. Josiah, born July 28, 1733. 4. John, born June 12, 1735. 5. Deliverance, born October 24, 1737. 6. Susannah, born January 9, 1739. 7. Hannah, born April 20, 1742. 8. Josiah (2), born April 4, 1744. 9. William, born November 22, 1746.

(III) Joseph (3) Armington, son of Joseph (2) and Hannah (Chaffee) Armington, was born in Rehoboth, Massachusetts, June 4, 1731. He was a prominent citizen of the town, and a farmer, as were most men of the period. He married, April 19, 1760, Esther Walker, of Rehoboth, daughter of Daniel and Hannah (Barstow) Walker. Their children were: 1. Nathan, born November 7, 1761. 2. Susanna, born September 29, 1762. 3. Nancy, born May 14, 1765. 4. Asa, mentioned below. 5. Walker, born March 6, 1769. 6. Benjamin, born August 27, 1771. 7. Joseph, born March 31, 1774. 8. Esther, born March 17, 1777. 9. George, born June 17, 1779. 10. Sylvester Ambrose, born August 19, 1782. 11. Gardner, born July 6, 1785. 12. Hannah B., born August 21, 1787. 13. James Gardner, born September 9, 1789. 14. Daniel, born October 12, 1791.

(IV) Asa Armington, son of Joseph (3) and Esther (Walker) Armington, was born April 19, 1767. He married Bethia Remington, and they were the parents of the following children: 1. Asa Watson, born August 18, 1791, died November 16, 1867. 2. Dr. Hervey Armington, mentioned below. 3. Ira, born April 28, 1795. 4. Polly W., born April 1, 1798. 5. Mary A., born December 31, 1800. 6. Ira (2), born May 1, 1803. 7. Horace W., born September, ——, died and was buried in the Bay of Honduras. 8. Emma B., born January 31, 1808.

(V) Dr. Hervey Armington, son of Asa and Bethia (Remington) Armington, was born July 26, 1793. His death occurred in Providence, Rhode Island, on August 3, 1868. It would be impossible to give a better, more comprehensive, account of his life, one which showed more clearly the regard in which he was held in Providence, the feeling of the public toward the man, and the physician, whom it loved and revered, than the sketch of his life, published in the "Providence Daily Journal" under the date of August 8, 1868.

Dr. Hervey Armington, whose death we have already announced, was one of our oldest physicians and his departure from us deserves something more than a simple record of the fact. Dr. Armington was descended from Joseph Armington who with his family, came to Boston from England in the year 1714. He was born in Barrington, Rhode Island, and his elementary education was obtained in a common country school. He subsequently completed his course of instruction at an academy at Leicester, Massachusetts. During his minority he spent several years in a seafaring life, for which he had a fondness and as second mate, and afterward as chief mate, sailed to Virginia, thence to Brazil, touching at some ports in Portugal. The War of 1812 broke up our commercial marine, dissipated the golden dreams of its peaceful vocation, and led to the opening of a business in a country store. This proving unsuccessful, it was abandoned, and the steps of enterprise were turned to the west. Previous to 1812 young Armington proceeded to Cincinnati, Ohio, taking passage to Philadelphia in a schooner just started as a pioneer in the regular freighting business, thence traveling on foot to Pittsburgh, and from that place descending the Ohio in a skiff built by himself and his traveling companion In Cincinnati he engaged in the study of medicine in the office of Drs. Hough and Whitman and after completing his preparatory course became a student in the Ohio Medical College, at the head of which was the late Daniel Drake, M. D While pursuing his medical studies to support himself and defray his college expenses he set up soda water fountains (the first probably in the west) in Maysville, Chillicothe, St Louis, Louisville, and thus contributing to the cause of temperance by substituting a wholesome and delightful beverage for intoxicating liquors In 1822 he was graduated with the honors of the institution, and after receiving his degree established himself in a settlement (if we mistake not called "Yankeetown") about thirty-seven miles from Cincinnati Here he continued but a single season. Dr Armington remained in the west nearly five years, when he returned to Providence and engaged in the drug business, practicing his profession occasionally He likewise engaged in trade in connection with navigation, but failing of anticipated success he returned to the practice of medicine, which became extensive, and in which he ever afterward continued He was a member of the Rhode Island Medical Society and for nine years its treasurer He was also at one time president of the Providence Association of Physicians, and enjoyed the fullest confidence and respect of his associates His medical practice covered a period of about forty years

Dr Armington was very domestic in his habits and found his chief enjoyment in the bosom of his family, and in the society of friends who always met a cordial welcome at his home Though taking no active part in political affairs, he cherished firmly his early and deliberately formed opinions, which his ballot at the polls undisguisedly expressed For many years Dr Armington was a member of the school committee, and during his entire official connection with that body discharged with scrupulous fidelity the duties assigned to him No one felt deeper interest in the education of the young, or appreciated more accurately the importance of our public school system. Changes bearing an evidence of improvement, either in the construction of school houses or in methods of teaching, received from him a hearty approval He was especially interested in the prosperity of the high school and viewed with unmingled satisfaction the blessing it annually

conferred upon its pupils and through them upon the city To his profession as a physician Dr Armington was faithfully devoted and the numerous families in which he practiced welcomed him in the sick room as a safe adviser and friend. He was prompt to meet all calls for professional services and the cases of his poorest patients, from many of whom no pecuniary compensation was expected or rendered, always received conscientious attention Even after declining health warned him to be sparing of his strength his ready sympathy for the suffering prompted him often to transcend prudence in ministering at the bedside of disease and pain He died with calm and cheerful submission to Divine Will His life was formed under the abiding influence of fundamental Christian principles to which he gave unqualified acceptance To his family and to a wide circle of friends his death came as a deep grief From the medical profession a respected and valued member was removed, while from a still wider circle, those by whom he was honored as a dispenser of healing, had been taken one whose memory was ever fragrant of a kind and willing service He was the last, but one, of a family of eight brothers and sisters He passed away August 3, 1868, leaving behind a record full of usefulness and high worth.

Dr Hervey Armington married on December 25, 1825, Ardelia Allin, born April 21, 1803, daughter of Captain Samuel Pearce and Hannah (Baker) Allin (see Allin) Their children were 1 Samuel Allin, married Sarah Sweet, both deceased 2 Hannah Bethiah, died unmarried 3 Horace Ward, died unmarried 4 Rebecca Baker, died unmarried 5 Emily Louise, died unmarried. 6 Juliana Trowbridge, deceased 7. Jerauld Tibbitts, mentioned below 8. Emma Foster, residing in Providence, Rhode Island, at the old family residence at 108 Williams street 9 Hervey Blanchard, who married Esther Paine, both deceased

(VI) Jerauld Tibbitts Armington, son of Dr Hervey and Ardelia (Allin) Armington, was born in Providence, Rhode Island, on September 14, 1842 He received his education in the private academy of Mr Austin, a prominent educator in Providence at the time. He left school early. From earliest childhood he had had a great fondness for horses, and found his first employment in the thing he loved so well—driving an express wagon for a large company of Providence. In 1862, at the age of about twenty years, young Armington heard the call of the West, and with a company of friends set out on the long and arduous journey across the plains. The journey was made by prairie schooner, and the ultimate destination of the party was Denver, Colorado. Here Mr Armington worked for a period of about three months, at the end of which time he had saved enough money to buy an "outfit," a team of horses, and with these he started in a small way in the business which he later developed to such large proportions. Starting as a contractor, he soon made his way into the field of railroad building. After a period, in which he met with much success in his business, Mr Armington admitted into partnership with him Mr Peter Seims, a man of considerable business talent and practical experience. The name of the firm became Armington & Seims, under which style the business was conducted until the retirement of Mr Armington from business life. The firm was given the contracts for portions of the largest railroads in that section of the West, and became one of the most important of its kind in the immediate vicinity.

Mr. Armington was also keenly interested in mining, and conducted large mining operations in the neighborhood of Denver, and Great Falls, Montana, whither he moved later. He owned extensive property holdings in that latter place, and conducted several large ranches. He spent the greater part of his life and his stay in the west in the State of Montana. He was one of the founders of the town of Great Falls, Montana, and

one of its most prominent public men and business officials. A leader in almost every phase of the community's activities, he was also one of its best beloved friends. The Indians, in that country where the strongest antagonism and resentment against the "whites" was almost universal, loved and honored him, and were his friends. They called him "The Medicine Man," because of his knowledge of the medical profession, gained in his early years from his father. Through his knowledge of medicine he was able to relieve much suffering among the ignorant Indians, and they regarded him as a stanch friend. He was also a champion of their rights among the whites. His gifts for charitable purposes, though unostentatious, were large, and large portions of his land in various parts of the country were given to men who had failed in prospecting or in business and were reduced to the point of necessity. His political affiliation was with the Republican party, and in appreciation of his services to the town, he was elected with an overwhelming majority, a member of the first Senate of the State of Montana, which incumbency he accepted for the purpose of accomplishing needed reforms on behalf of the people. After the expiration of his first term, however, he refused to accept office again, though strongly urged to do so.

Mr Armington was well known in the fraternal life of the town, and was a member of the Great Falls Lodge of the Benevolent and Protective Order of Elks, of Montana. He also belonged to the Montana Pioneer Society. He was a gentleman of the old school, kindly, courteous, honorable, and well loved by the people to whom he gave the greater part of his life. He was popularly known as "Senator" or "Doctor" Armington, and occupied a very prominent and influential place in the hearts and lives of the people of Great Falls Mr Armington was the owner of the township of Armington, near Great Falls

The last years of his life were spent with his sisters in Providence, where he died on December 10, 1916

(The Allin Line)

For a period of more than two and a half centuries the family of Allin has held a position of prominence in New England

Arms—Gules three swords barwise argent points to the sinister, hilts and pommels or, between four mullets, two in chief, and two in base of the third
Crest—On a Bible a hand couped close holding a sword erect

During this time the name has been spelled variously Allin, Allen, Allyn, frequently according to the preference of the man who bore it, and oftentimes as a distinguishing mark, when there was more than one family of the name in a community Faulty spelling in early records is responsible for much difficulty in tracing ancestry in the family In the early years of the colonial period we find many immigrants of the name in New England, the heads of families, and to-day the family is represented in every State in the Union The Rhode Island family of Allin has been established there since the year 1683, and in successive generations has played an active part in the building of the little colony, and the growth of the Commonwealth The name is found with great frequency in the rolls of soldiers serving in the wars of our country, and several of them have achieved fame and distinction on the field of battle. The late Mrs Armington, wife of Dr Hervey Armington, was a descendant of one of the ancient colonial families of Allin, tracing in a direct line to one of the early progenitors She was a daughter of Samuel P Allin, of Providence, Rhode Island, and great-granddaughter of John Allin, of Portsmouth, Rhode Island, where the family was established in the year 1683

John Allin, of Portsmouth, Rhode Island, where he was a prominent citizen, married Susan Goddard Wall, widow of William Wall They were the parents of one child, James, mentioned below

James Allin, of Portsmouth, resided there all his life He married Martha Pearce, daughter of Samuel and Esther (Wyley) Pearce, a member of a long established Rhode Island family Their children were 1 Daniel, who removed to Pomfret, Connecticut 2 Cyrus, of Brownsville, New York 3 John Pearce, of Westmoreland, New York 4 Samuel Pearce, mentioned below 5 Cynthia, of Amsterdam, New York. 6. Matthew, of Canajoharie, New York 7 Caleb, of Brownsville, New York 8 Thomas, of Amsterdam, New York 9 James, of Amsterdam, New York 10. Martha, of Johnstown, New York 11 Susan, of Amsterdam, New York 12 Henry, of Amsterdam, New York 13 Juliana, of Amsterdam, New York

Samuel Pearce Allin, son of James and Martha (Pearce) Allin, of Portsmouth, Rhode Island, was born in that town and grew to manhood there He later removed to Providence, Rhode Island, where he resided for the remainder of his life He married Hannah Baker, and they were the parents of the following children 1 Martha 2 Samuel Pearce 3 Louisa 4. Louisa 5 Ardelia, mentioned below 6 Jeremiah 7 Joseph 8. William

Ardelia Allin, daughter of Captain Samuel Pearce and Hannah (Baker) Allin was born April 21, 1803 She married December 25, 1825, Dr Hervey Armington (See Armington V)

WINSLOW, William Copley,

Archaeologist and Historical Writer.

William Copley Winslow, a recognized authority on New England Colonial history, and of world-wide fame in the field of Egyptological research and exploration, was born January 13, 1840, in Boston, Massachusetts, son of the Rev. Hubbard Winslow, D. D., and Susan W. (Cutler) Winslow, of Pilgrim descent. The father was a widely known minister, author and educator, and succeeded the Rev. Lyman Beecher in the pastorate of the Bowdoin Street Church, Boston, where Lowell Mason, as its director in music, composed his hymns, and set to music, "America," there first sung in public.

William Copley Winslow was prepared for college in the Boston Latin School, and was graduated from Hamilton College, Clinton, New York, in 1862. While in college he edited "The Hamiltonian," and he was associated with Joseph Cook and W. G. Sumner, of Yale College, in founding the "University Quarterly Review." In 1862-63 he served on the editorial staff of the "New York World," and later, with the Rev. Dr. Tyng, was associate editor of the "Christian Times." He was meantime engaged in theological studies, being graduated from the General Theological Seminary (New York) in 1865. For some months thereafter he was in Italy, studying Roman archaeology and arts. From 1867 to late in 1870 he was rector of St. George's Church, at Lee, Massachusetts, removing in the latter year to Boston, and for many years taking charge temporarily or officiating in various churches throughout the State and acting as executive secretary of the Free Church Association.

It is, however, in the field of exploration that Dr. Winslow established his high and lasting reputation. A lover of nature as well as art, early in his ministry he had interested himself in the preservation of the Adirondack forests, which he explored for the maps, and in that interest he wrote many articles for the press. In 1880 he passed four months in Egypt and Syria, and he was present when the Obelisk, now in New York, was taken down at Alexandria; and he was instrumental in procuring for the Boston Museum of Fine Arts the colossal statue of Rameses II., the Syenite granite shafts from Bubastis and Ahnas, the head of Hathor, etc., and he also secured for the museum and for various universities of Massachusetts, New York and elsewhere many fine specimens of ancient history and art. Among the one hundred and twenty papyri sent to this country was what has been considered to be the oldest known fragment of the Gospels—a large part of the First Chapter of St. Mathew. This was found in Oxyrhynchus, one hundred and forty miles south of Cairo, near the famous 'Logia," or "Sayings of Jesus," some experts placing its date at 150 A. D., and others making it fifty or sixty years later. Dr. Winslow placed the oldest fragment of St. Paul (Romans I.) yet discovered in the Simitic Museum at Harvard. At a general meeting of the Egypt Exploration Fund in London, England, in the presence of United States Minister Edward J. Phelps and Miss Amelia B. Edwards, Professor R. S. Poole had said that, with the single exception of Sir Erasmus Wilson, "Dr. Winslow had accomplished more than any other, not merely for the work of the society, but for the cause of Biblical research and the spread of Biblical knowledge in connection with Egyptology throughout the civilized world."

He has been an officer or on the committees of the Institute of Civics, Web-

ENCYCLOPEDIA OF BIOGRAPHY

ster Historical Society, Appalachian Club,
American Oriental Society, Bostonian Society, New England Historic-Genealogical Society, various church societies, and
as an archaeologist is an honorary fellow
of the Royal Archaeological Institute,
honorary member of the British Archaeological Association, honorary correspondent of the Victoria Institute, Royal Society of Arts and Sciences, etc , honorary
member of five New England State and
nineteen other State historical societies,
various Canadian and numerous local societies In 1916 the Society of Oriental
Research (Chicago) created him an honorary fellow He was president of the
New England Alumni Association, Hamilton College, and at the Centennial (1912)
of Hamilton College, Elihu Root was
president and Dr Winslow vice-president. Dr Winslow was for many years
excellent high priest of St. Barnard Commandery in Boston

Among his editorial connections he
was associate editor of the "American
Antiquarian," also of "American Historical Register " he was a regular writer for
"Biblia," prepared from one hundred to
one hundred and fifty articles a year for
the daily and weekly press He has contributed articles upon his favorite subjects to encyclopedias and magazines; he
served on various committees of the Chicago Exposition congresses, and read
papers before their sessions, and he is
now (1917) aiding Professor Petrie and
the Egyptian Research Account Society,
of which he is American vice-president
and honorary treasurer He has written
the following monographs "A Greek
City in Egypt," "The Store City of Pit-
hom," "Tombs at Beni Hasan," "Egypt
at Home," "Explorations at Zoan," "Pilgrim Fathers in Holland," "Governor
Edward Winslow," "Winslow Memorial," "Papyria in the United States," and

"Egyptian Antiquities in American Mu-
seums " Among his honorary degrees are
Master of Arts, Hobart College, 1865,
Doctor of Philosophy, Hamilton College,
1886, L H D, Columbia University,
(Centennial) 1887, S T D, Griswold,
1887, Doctor of Divinity, Amherst Col-
lege, 1887, Doctor of Laws, St Andrew's
University, Scotland, 1888; Doctor of
Civil Laws, King's College University,
Nova Scotia, 1888; Doctor of Science, St
John's College (Centennial), Annapolis,
Maryland

Dr Winslow married (first) June 20,
1867, Harriet S Hayward, daughter of
the Hon Joseph H Hayward, of Boston,
Massachusetts She died September 13,
1915, leaving one child, a daughter He
married (second) May 24, 1917, Elizabeth
Bruce Roelofson, of Boston

DANIELSON, George Whitman,

Journalist, Man of Enterprise

The Danielson family, for a period of
over two hundred years, has ranked
among the most distinguished and honorable in the States of Rhode Island and
Connecticut Its sons have in every generation played a prominent part in the
affairs of the communities in which they
have been residents, and have written the
name of Danielson large upon the records
of these two States

The line of descent to be treated in this
article is that of George Whitman Danielson, editor and publisher, of Providence,
Rhode Island, one of the largest figures
in the field of journalism in New England in the middle and latter half of the
last century He was a descendant in the
sixth generation of the founder, Sergeant
James Danielson.

(I) Sergeant James Danielson, progenitor of the Danielsons in America,
was born in Scotland, and came to Amer-

316

ica in the latter half of the seventeenth century. He was among the first settlers of Block Island, Rhode Island. He became the owner of much land on Block Island, purchasing several tracts between 1688 and 1705 James Danielson became a freeman of the colony of Rhode Island in 1696, when the General Assembly admitted him. In 1700 he was elected town sergeant of New Shoreham, Rhode Island, and in 1704-05 was a member of its town council. James Danielson fought during the earlier years of his life against the Indians, and in reward for his distinguished services received a parcel of land in Voluntown, Connecticut, at the time of the distribution of public lands. Some time during the following period, Mr Danielson left Block Island and took up his residence in Connecticut, attracted thither, it is thought, by the aspect of the land over which he had travelled during his campaigning in the Indian wars. In 1706 he purchased a tract of eight hundred acres of land on the Quinebaug river, with a mansion house and barn, in what afterward became the village of Pomfret. He was a merchant and trader with the Indians, and in 1707 purchased from Major Fitch, who was engaged in similar trade, the neck of land between the Quinebaug and Assawauga rivers, comprising about two thousand acres. He is stated to have been the first white settler south of Lake Mashapaug, and is said to have built a garrison-house at the southern extremity of his land. Sergeant James Danielson became a leader in the affairs of the town which sprang up there, and was one of the most prominent men in that section of the country. The new settlement was afterward named Killingly.

James Danielson was a man of substantial wealth, as is evidenced by the fact that for the eight hundred acre tract of land he paid £155, and for the second tract of two thousand acres he paid £170 He had a residence in each settlement, part of his extensive land holdings are still in the hands of lineal descendants. His death occurred on January 22, 1728 In his declining years he "laid out a burial ground between the rivers for the use of the inhabitants, and was the first to be interred in it." James Danielson married (first) Abigail Rose, March 11, 1685. He married (second) January 22, 1700, Mary Ackers, who died February 23, 1752, aged eighty-six years.

His descendants took an active part in the stirring events of colonial and national history, and among the most prominent may be mentioned: Samuel Danielson, who was moderator of Killingly in 1760, and selectman in 1785, William Danielson, who was constable, collector of taxes and lieutenant in 1760, first major of Colonel Williams' Eleventh Regiment. The same William Danielson took one hundred and forty-six men from Killingly to Cambridge in 1775, became colonel in 1776, and after the Revolution became general of militia. In 1788 he was a member of the State Convention called to ratify the national constitution.

(II) Samuel Danielson, son of Sergeant James and Mary (Ackers) Danielson, was born in 1701. He succeeded to his father's place in the community, and inherited a large part of the property of the elder man. He received the homestead in what is now the town of Killingly, and became one of the most prominent citizens of the place. He was also a leader in the industrial life of the town and had a large interest in the factories, which sprang up along the Quinebaug river. The short swift current of this river furnished excellent water power for the operation of manufacturing plants, and several were established on its banks

ENCYCLOPEDIA OF BIOGRAPHY

So great a share of the property was in the hands of the Danielson family that the manufacturing town which was founded along the river was given the name of Danielsonville, later becoming known as Danielson.

Samuel Danielson married Sarah Douglas, March 26, 1725. She was born about 1704, and died March 29, 1774, aged seventy. He died in 1786. They were the parents of ten children.

(III) Captain Samuel (2) Danielson, son of Samuel (1) and Sarah (Douglas) Danielson, was born in Killingly, Connecticut, in 1741. He was active in the militia, and was one of the men who marched to the relief of Boston at the Lexington Alarm in April, 1775. He died on June 13, 1817. Captain Samuel Danielson married, May 6, 1770, Hannah Whitman, born in Providence, Rhode Island, October 10, 1751, died October 3, 1787, daughter of Jacob and Hannah (Hartshorn) Whitman, and a lineal descendant of John Whitman, the progenitor of the Whitman family in America. John Whitman came to New England from England before December, 1638, when he settled in Weymouth, Massachusetts. The line of descent of the wife of Captain Samuel (2) Danielson, was through, John, the founder; Zachariah, John and Jacob.

(IV) Samuel (3) Danielson, son of Samuel (2) and Hannah (Whitman) Danielson, was born December 30, 1772. He married Sarah Beg, born June 13, 1773, daughter of Adam and Sarah (Robinson) Beg, and resided in Killingly all his life. He died July 24, 1845, and his wife on September 9, 1852. Their children were: 1 Adam. 2 Jacob Whitman, mentioned below. 3 Jane. 4 Samuel Sanford.

(V) Jacob Whitman Danielson, son of Samuel (3) and Sarah (Beg) Danielson,

was born in Killingly, Connecticut, May 9, 1798. He was a lifelong resident of Killingly, and one of the most prominent citizens of the town. He was also a large landowner. He married, September 18, 1827, Lucy Maria Prince, born March 13, 1805, died April 19, 1847, daughter of Abel and Lucy (Cady) Prince. He died November 15, 1856. They were the parents of the following children. 1 George Whitman, mentioned below. 2 Edward Prince, born February 21, 1831; married, January 24, 1861, Mary Etta Johnson, of Putnam, Connecticut, died July 8, 1902. 3 Eliza M., born August 26, 1833, married, February 15, 1871, Dr. John Vedder, died January 7, 1908. 4 Lucy Jane, born March 26, 1838; unmarried, lived in Danielsonville, Connecticut, died May 28, 1908. 5 William J., born May 1, 1843, married, November 1, 1871, Anna Russell Saunders, a resident of Providence, Rhode Island; died January 18, 1916.

(VI) George Whitman Danielson, son of Jacob Whitman and Lucy Maria (Prince) Danielson, was born in Danielson, Connecticut, April 26, 1829. He received his early education in the district schools of his native town, and in the periods not spent in school worked on his father's farm. Finding farming work distasteful, and having an inclination toward the printer's trade, he left his father's farm and entered the printing establishment of E. C. Carter in the village of Danielson, to learn the trade. During the first six months of his apprenticeship he received the munificent compensation of three dollars a month and board. This was increased to ten dollars per month during the second six months. He progressed rapidly in the trade, and soon had a thorough grasp of the technical as well as business details of the printing trade, controlling the greater part of the business of the establishment

318

himself In 1845 he went to Providence, Rhode Island, where he worked as a journeyman printer. He also spent a time in New York City, where he set type on one of the great morning dailies, in this position passing through a test which proved his mettle as perhaps none other could He shortly afterward returned to Providence, still a mere youth, and obtained employment

It was his ambition to publish a paper, and in a very short time after his return from New York he brought out the "Daily Sentinel," a promising sheet, though its editor was at the time under twenty years of age Mr Danielson during the following few years edited the "Daily Transcript" of Providence, gradually gaining for himself a recognized and envied place in the field of journalism in the city, and arousing as is usual bitter enmity, as well as sincere appreciation On July 26, 1848, he became editor and publisher of the "New England Arena," at West Killingly, Connecticut, a paper which he dedicated to the spirit of independence, and which during the entire term of its existence typified the stern independence and incorruptible integrity of Mr Danielson, and his strict adherence to the highest standards in his work At the end of a year Mr Danielson returned to Providence, and in May, 1851, became the reporter of marine news for the "Providence Daily Post" He also filled the post of assistant editor and foreman of the composing room His work in this capacity attracted favorable notice among the ablest journalists of the State, and he was looked upon as a coming man, destined to make a mark

George Whitman Danielson, on March 14, 1859, in company with Albert R Cooke, of Providence, established the "Evening Press" in that city, which immediately secured a large circulation, and

a popularity which promised an excellent future In September, 1862, Mr Danielson disposed of his interests in the new publication to his partner, and accepted at the earnest solicitation of Senator Anthony and Joseph Knowles, the office of business manager and managing editor of the "Providence Journal " He brought to the administration of the duties of this office a freshness of ideas and an efficiency which soon infused into the paper a new life, and established its somewhat declining circulation on a firm and sound basis On January 26, 1863, the "Evening Bulletin" was first put into the hands of the public, furnishing the news and the editorial opinions of "The Journal" at a popular price This paper through the business and editorial genius of Mr Danielson was brought up to a circulation of more than twenty-two thousand copies daily in 1884, and achieved a total circulation in combination with "The Journal," which was exceeded by only a few of the newspapers of the world Mr Danielson, who was the guiding genius of "The Journal" and the "Evening Bulletin," was in absolute charge of every detail of their management, and was responsible for the great impetus in the circulation and financial returns of the two papers which took place in the very beginning of his administration and continued until its close He was eminently fitted for the work which he did by reason of his excellent literary ability and his keen business sense, two qualities which are seldom found in combination He was a man of broad sympathies, and possessed a deep human understanding, a love of all mankind and a catholicity of tastes which was a feature of his editorial work

George Whitman Danielson was prominent in almost every phase of life in Providence, and was identified with many

319

important business interests. He was vice-president and director of the Oakland Beach Association, a director of the Phoenix National Bank of the Richmond Paper Company, the Equitable Mutual Insurance Company, and of the Rhode Island Telephone and Electric Company. He was for many years president of the New England Press Association. He was a charter member of What Cheer Lodge, Free and Accepted Masons, and at the time of his death was a member of the Westfield Congregational Church of Danielsonville.

Mr. Danielson married, on January 25, 1881, Rosa Frances Peckham, of Killingly, daughter of Dr. Fenner Harris and Catherine (Torrey) Peckham. Their children were: 1. Whitman, born December 17, 1881. 2. Rosamond, born November 6, 1884.

George Whitman Danielson died on March 25, 1884, at Providence, Rhode Island. He was a public man whose death to the city of Providence was a loss irreparable. What he meant to a large proportion of the population of the city may best be judged by the following tributes of the press and public organizations at the time of his death.

The Providence Journal. The assemblage of the public was large and notable, representing the weightiest influences in the State in public service and private life, and all the interests which contribute to its greatness and welfare. It was touching alike to see the citizens, venerable with grey hair, and of honored names, taking a last farewell of the face and form of their associate in labor for the public welfare and young men receiving a stimulus to it by the impression of the honor it brings. The feeling of respect and honor was universal, including all classes, friends and former opponents, associates and rivals in business, all uniting in paying the deserved tribute. Of the feeling of his employes and those most intimately associated with him it is unnecessary to speak, and it was deeply manifest in their countenances and mien. In accord-

ance with his wishes, the ship which he commanded was not checked in its course but there was a pause in the full activity of the machinery for the hour of the solemn ceremonies of the burial of the dead captain. And when the time came to

> Free the fettered engine
> And speed the hurrying shaft

and for all the stress of strenuous and unceasing labor to be renewed, the officers and crew in performing their duties through the long night, were compelled by irresistible feeling, as they will be for many nights and days to come, to pause often in their work, however engrossing, to wipe away the unbidden tears, starting at the countless familiar touches recalling his voice and hand, or emanations of his vanished spirit, intensifying the poignant grief and sense of irreparable loss.

The Providence Journal, March 25, 1884. The spontaneous and unanimous tribute of the General Assembly to his worth as a citizen only voiced the sentiment of the people of Rhode Island, to whom his name was a household word, and to whom he has for so many years daily sent, not merely the news of the world, but the utterances of reason philanthropy and religion, whatever was best in current thought or highest in the realm of spiritual hope, promise or attainment. Mr. Danielson possessed certain characteristics which were patent to everybody with whom he came in contact; his keen sagacity, his grasp of mind, his vigor of will, and his almost ever unerring judgment impressed the least capable observer.

The Pawtucket Gazette and Chronicle, March 28, 1884. The most eminent journalist of our State has departed. Heaven designated him for a journalist. With an acute intellect and sagacious judgment he noted the improvements that were making in journalism. It was his ambition to avail himself of every agency that promised to expedite the attainment of news, and of every invention which facilitated its publication.

Hon. Henry Howard. Is it saying too much to assert that, by the death of Mr. Danielson, the State has lost its most influential citizen? I think not. Partly by virtue of his commanding position as conductor of a journal long recognized as a power in the community, partly because of rare union of innate common-sense qualities with that resolute courage which holds all considerations of self-interest in perpetual subordination, and somewhat doubtless, because joined to a pure patriotic, and lofty aim, there was in him a well defined sense of enjoyment in the possession of power, and a manly instinct of leadership— he had attained to an influence commanding in degree and surprisingly diverse and wide in its relations I have known him more or less intimately for upwards of thirty years

Right Rev Thomas F Hendricken, Bishop of Roman Catholic Diocese of Rhode Island, March 30, 1884 I cannot leave the altar without expressing regret for the death of George W Danielson I utter these words of regret, not only for myself, but I speak for the 50,000 Catholics in the diocese Mr Danielson was among the first to introduce into his paper a department in which the interests of Catholics were especially considered, a feature which all the leading journals have since adopted He never took any advantage in matters regarding the church or displayed any measures in his dealings with it. Though never personally acquainted with Mr Danielson, I have received many favors from him for myself and for the church When the cornerstone of the Cathedral was laid, Mr Danielson sent the generous contribution of $100 Many other churches have been recipients of his generosity He was exceptionally an able man He was most gentlemanly in the use of his pen, from which no vulgar expression has ever been seen He was above everything mean, just, as far as he could see, as far as he could be. As a man I hold a deep respect and regard for him, and in his death the Journal, the city, and even the State sustains a great loss.

GREEN, Samuel A , A M , M D , LL. D ,
Physician, Litterateur, Author.

Samuel Abbott Green, A M , M D , LL D , who has gained national distinction as physician, academician, litterateur, historian, antiquary, and whose service in the field as a surgeon during the Civil War merited the military honors bestowed upon him, was born in Groton, Massachusetts, March 16, 1830, son of Dr Joshua and Eliza (Lawrence) Green The Green family genealogy leads di-

rectly back to Percival and Ellen Green, who sailed from London for New England in 1635, and in 1636 were living in Cambridge, Massachusetts Throughout the generations between that of Percival Green and the present, the family appears to have been of high standing and intellectual inclinations , many of its members have been in the church ministry, and Harvard University has been the *alma mater* of the main branch of the Green family for more than three centuries, the Rev. Joseph Green having graduated there in 1695, Joshua Green in 1749; Joshua, his son, in 1784, and Dr Joshua Green, father of Samuel Abbott, in the class of 1818

Samuel Abbott Green, after he had passed through Groton Academy, now Lawrence Academy, entered Harvard College, from which he graduated Bachelor of Arts in the class of 1851 His study of medicine was begun in Boston immediately after graduation, under the preceptorship of Dr J. Mason Warren, and was continued by a course of lectures at Jefferson Medical College in Philadelphia, and at the Harvard Medical School, where he graduated with the Doctor of Medicine degree in 1854, also receiving the Master of Arts degree from the college Further professional study in Paris, Berlin and Vienna was followed in due course of time by the practice of medicine in Boston During the years 1858 and 1861 he served as one of the district physicians for the Boston Dispensary On May 19, 1858, he was appointed by Governor Banks surgeon of the Second Regiment Massachusetts Militia Immediately on the outbreak of the rebellion he was commissioned assistant surgeon of the First Massachusetts Regiment, being the first medical officer of the State to be mustered into the three years' service He was promoted to the surgeoncy of the Twenty-fourth Massachusetts Regiment on September 2, 1861, to which regiment he remained attached until November, 1864, during this period, however, serving on the staffs of various general officers. He had charge of the hospital ship "Recruit" in General Burnside's expedition to North Carolina, and later of the hospital steamer "Cosmopolitan" on the coast of South Carolina, was chief medical officer at Morris Island during the siege of Fort Wagner, in the summer of 1863, was post surgeon at St Augustine and Jacksonville, Florida; thence was sent to Virginia, and was with the army at the capture of Bermuda Hundred, in May, 1864; was acting staff surgeon in Richmond for three months after the surrender of the city, and in 1864 was brevetted lieutenant-colonel for "gallant and distinguished service in the field during the campaign of 1864." In February, 1862, Dr Green established a cemetery on Roanoke Island, one of the first general burial places for Union soldiers during the war

After the war, Dr Green was superintendent of the Boston Dispensary from 1865 to 1872. In 1870 he was appointed by Governor Claflin a member of the commission chosen to care for disabled soldiers. From 1871 to 1882 Dr Green was city physician of Boston; in 1860-62 and 1866-72 he was a member of the school board; from 1868 to 1878 was a trustee of the Boston Public Library, and during the last year of this period served as acting librarian. In 1882 he was mayor of the city of Boston, a post of honor his election to which demonstrated his popularity with the people as well as with those of his own station. In 1885-86 he was a member of the State Board of Health, Lunacy and Charity. Dr. Green was an overseer of Harvard University for twenty-nine years, 1869-80 and 1882-

1900, was a trustee of the Peabody Education Fund from 1883 to the time of its distribution, 1914, and secretary of the board, and from 1885 to 1888 he was the acting general agent, in the place of Dr Curry, who had been appointed Minister to Spain. From 1903 to 1907 he was general agent. In 1878 he was chosen a member of the Board of Experts authorized by Congress to investigate the causes and prevention of yellow fever.

In 1896 the degree of Doctor of Laws was conferred upon him by the University of Nashville. Dr Green was vice-president of the Massachusetts Historical Society nineteen years, and for forty-nine years since 1868 has been librarian of the society. He has been president of the Channing Home, a hospital for consumptives, is a fellow of the Massachusetts Medical Society, and a member of the Boston Society for Medical Improvement, of the American Philosophical Society of Philadelphia, and of the American Antiquarian Society. For two years he was on the examining board of the Annapolis Naval Academy. Other offices of trust and honor have fallen to his charge, including the presidency of the board of trustees of Lawrence Academy, at Groton, his native town. His deep interest in that historic place has been shown in many ways, particularly in the numerous historical essays and books he has written, bearing upon the history of the town. His researches in all historical matters have been so thorough and accurate as to establish his writings permanently as an authority for future historians. Among his contributions to the nation's literature are "My Campaigns in America," translated from the French of Count William de Deux Ponts (Boston, 1868), 'Account of Percival and Ellen Green, and Some of Their Descendants" (1876), "Epitaphs from the Old

Burying Ground in Groton" (1878), "The Early Records of Groton, 1662-1707" (1880); "History of Medicine in Massachusetts" (Boston, 1881), "Groton During the Indian Wars" (1883), "Groton During the Witchcraft Times" (1883), "The Boundary Lines of Old Groton" (1885), "The Geography of Groton," prepared for the use of the Appalachian Mountain Club (1886); "An Historical Sketch of the Town of Groton" (Boston, 1891), "Groton Historical Series" (forty numbers, four volumes, 1884-1891), "Groton During the Revolution" (1900), "Ten Fac-simile Reproductions relating to Old Boston and Neighborhood" (1901), "Three Military Diaries kept by Groton Soldiers in Different Wars" (1901), "Ten Fac-simile Reproductions Relating to New England" (1902); "Ten Fac-simile Reproductions Relating to Various Subjects," "Three Historical Addresses at Groton" (1908), "John Foster, the Earliest American Engraver, and the First Boston Printer" (1909), "Facts Relating to the History of Groton, Massachusetts," volume 1 (1912), volume 11 (1914) In addition to the above mentioned, Dr. Green is the author of numerous other monographs and articles on historical and antiquarian subjects

The Venezuelan Order 'Bust of Bolivar" was bestowed upon Dr. Green by the President of Venezuela in recognition of distinguished service rendered to that nation by the eminent physician

---

ANGELL, Andrew A,

Esteemed Citizen

Authorities differ as to the origin of the name Angell It is claimed by some to be derived from Angel, a town in France, and by others to have come from the Greek word for messenger According to some, it is of baptismal origin, and signi-

fies "Son of Angel." It is known that in early times the word was used as a descriptive term applied to character, and was later used to denote extraordinary beauty Example of this second use is found in the year 1185, when Konstantinos, a noble of the Byzantine Empire, received the name of Angelos by reason of his comeliness It was once a very popular name in England, and was thoroughly hated by the Puritans, who were unable, however, to oust it.

Arms—Or, three fusils in fesse azure over all a baston gules
Crest—Out of a ducal coronet or, a demi pegasus argent, crined gules

The Angell family was established in America in the early part of the seventeenth century by Thomas Angell, a descendant of an old English family, and has been prominent in the affairs of New England in the successive generations since the founder

(I) Thomas Angell, progenitor of the American branch of the family, was born in England, about 1618 There is a tradition that he was the son of Henry Angell, of Liverpool, England, and that at the age of twelve years he came to London to seek his fortune In 1631 he came to America in the ship "Lion," sailing from London He was of the party of Roger Williams, and was then regarded as a servant or apprentice of Williams He arrived in Boston, and went with Roger Williams to Salem, Massachusetts, where he remained until 1636 When religious intolerance and persecution of those of his sect in Massachusetts drove Williams to seek a home elsewhere, Thomas Angell accompanied him, and in 1636 settled in Providence, Rhode Island, where he had granted him the lot fronting on North Main street, where now the First Baptist Church, the High School and Angell

323

street are situated. In 1652 and 1653 he was elected a commissioner, and became one of the most influential citizens in early Providence. In 1655 he was constable, which office he held for many years. He was, as were all the inhabitants of Providence in that day, a farmer. His will was dated May 3, 1685, and proved September 18, 1685. He was about seventy-six years old at the time of his death. His wife bore the name of Alice. Her will is dated October 2, 1694, and was proved in January of the following year.

(II) John Angell, son of Thomas and Alice Angell, was born in Providence, Rhode Island, and died there July 27, 1720. For a few years he lived on the Daniel Jenckes farm, five miles from Providence, toward Lime Rock, on the Lewisquisit road. He removed to Providence, later in life, and there followed the occupation of farmer. John Angell was admitted a free man of Providence, Rhode Island, October 16, 1670. He married, in 1669, Ruth Field, daughter of John Field, of Providence.

(III) Thomas Angell (2), son of John and Ruth (Field) Angell, was born in Providence, Rhode Island, March 25, 1672. He learned the carpenter's trade, which he followed during his entire lifetime, erecting many buildings in Providence in his time the most famous of which is the old Angell Tavern in Scituate, Rhode Island. This tavern, which was built by Thomas Angell in 1710, is located on the old Plainfield turnpike, and was occupied by the family for several generations. This house was used as a general meeting place for the townspeople, and was the scene of public meetings of the town of Scituate for a long period. Thomas Angell was one of the most influential citizens and business men of Providence, widely known and re-

spected. In the capacity of innkeeper he was brought into contact with travelers from all parts of the colonies, and was consequently a man well informed on current issues. He was well educated and a keen business man, as well as a genial host. He died in Scituate, Rhode Island, in 1714, and was buried in the old meeting house lot in South Scituate. Thomas (2) Angell married, April 4, 1700, Sarah Brown, daughter of Daniel and Alice Brown; she was born in 1677, and survived her husband many years.

(IV) Jeremiah Angell, son of Thomas (2) and Sarah (Brown) Angell, was born in Scituate, Rhode Island, June 29, 1706, and died there in 1786. He inherited the Angell tavern from his father, whom he succeeded in the management and proprietorship of the famous inn. He was also a capable business man, and managed his real estate interests very successfully. Jeremiah Angell also inherited his father's farm in South Scituate, which he cultivated, and brought up to a fine standard during his lifetime. He cleared and planted much of this large farm, giving much of his time to the study of his work, which for several generations continued to produce results. One orchard which he planted furnished fruit for four generations. In addition to his duties as innkeeper and his work as a farmer, he found time to make a considerable study of the law. He was constantly sought by the people of the town on legal questions, and was probably the most influential public man in Scituate of his time. He was for several years justice of the peace, and was eminently a peacemaker, doing his best to bring about a settlement between the parties in a law suit, by telling them the law in their case and advising that they settle their differences without recourse to law. Jeremiah Angell died in Scituate, Rhode Island, in 1786, and was buried in the old meeting house lot He married (first) Mary Matthewson, (second) Abigail Downs, (third) Betsey Stone.

(V) Andrew Angell, son of Jeremiah and Mary (Matthewson) Angell, was born in Scituate, Rhode Island, January 3 1742 He was educated to become his father's assistant and successor in his various interests in Scituate, and early rendered valuable services to the elder Mr Angell in the management of the Angell Tavern, to which he succeeded at the death of the elder man He was also a well educated man, of intellectual tastes, refined and cultured, and possessed of unusual ability in business He was a true representative of "mine host" of the old school, hospitable, courteous, genial and accommodating He was an excellent conversationalist, and drew much of his ability in this line from the variety and multitude of the experiences of the travelers who stopped at his house, which in the day was one of the most famous in that section of the country The dangers of navigation or in some cases its total obstruction increased travel greatly on the Providence and Norwich road, and brought to the tavern much patronage, which otherwise would not have reached it Many men of fame in the early history of the country traveled this road, among them General Washington, General Lafayette, and Dr Benjamin Franklin.

Andrew Angell married Tabitha Harris, who was born June 21, 1743 He died June 29, 1792 After his death his widow rented the tavern and resided on the farm in Scituate, where she died

(VI) Charles Angell, son of Andrew and Tabitha (Harris) Angell, was born at the Angell Tavern in Scituate, Rhode Island, in 1775 According to the custom of the family, which had been to give its sons the best advantages possible in education, he was excellently trained He subsequently became one of the leaders of the affairs of the community, as his forebears had been for generations before He was president of the town council, and served for several years in the State Legislature, a strong figure in the affairs of that body, and a valuable man to the section which he represented, both because of his honesty and unimpeachable integrity, and because of his keenness of intellect and talent for legal affairs and public service He was elected to the post of a judge of the Court of Common Pleas He was an able and convincing public speaker, and a contemporary report says ' He talked pointedly and well He spoke of the question before him, upon which he had reflected sufficiently to see clearly the order of his thoughts and to connect them in an unbroken chain, each link representing an idea " Charles Angell conducted the Angell Tavern during the War of 1812, and saw much of the stirring events of that time, learning much of the progress of the war also through the men who came to his tavern Charles Angell died in his forty-sixth year, November 13, 1821

He married Olive Aldrich, daughter of James Aldrich, of Scituate, Rhode Island Their children were 1 Tabitha H born February 12, 1801 ; married Abner Peckham. 2 Andrew A. mentioned below 3 Alice Smith, born in Scituate, Rhode Island, September 21, 1805 married George Aldrich.

(VII) Andrew A Angell, son of Charles and Olive (Aldrich) Angell, was born in South Scituate, Rhode Island, December 7, 1802 He was the fifth generation in the direct line to inherit and occupy the Angell Tavern, but because of the change in the attitude of the public toward inns and the growing strength of the temperance reform, together with the inroads which steam and railroads made on the trade which accrued to the taverns from travel, he was compelled to give up the historic old place Mr Angell thereafter directed his entire time and attention to the management of his farm in South Scituate At the time of his death he gave this farm to his wife, who sold it after his death Thus both the tavern and farm passed out of the control of the Angell family, in whose hands they had been for nearly two centuries Mr Angell died October 15, 1864.

He married Amy Aldrich Their children were 1 James Burrill Angell, the famous educator, president of the University of Michigan 2 Eliza A Angell, deceased, married Jeremiah Adams, deceased 3 Charles Angell, deceased 4 Hannah Angell, who became the wife of James Haydon Coggeshall 5 Caroline F Angell, deceased, married Peter Collier, deceased 6 William T Angell, of Chicago

COVEL, Thomas D,

Active Man of Affairs.

Edward Cowell (so spelled), an inhabitant of Boston in 1645, a cordwainer, was a participant in King Philip's war, and was in command of a squad or company of eighteen men in April, 1675, *en route* from Marlboro to Boston, some three miles from Sudbury they were surprised by the Indians, and in the engagement that followed four of the men were killed On this occasion, said one writer "From all the above-mentioned authorities, the true account in brief seems to be, that the English had no suspicions of the great numbers of the Indians that were gathering about Marlborough and Sudbury, or of the vicinity of any, until early in the morning of the 21st (April), when several deserted houses were burnt with the evi-

dent purpose of drawing out the garrisons into an ambuscade Then Deacon Haines's garrison home was attacked with fury by large numbers, but was successfully defended from six o'clock in the morning until one o'clock p m, when the assault was abandoned Twelve volunteers coming from Concord upon the alarm, to aid the garrison, were lured into the river meadow, and all slain save one Mr Edward Cowell, with a body of eighteen mounted men coming from Brookfield by way of Marlborough, and by a different way from that taken by Captain Wadsworth, became sharply engaged with the outlying part of the enemy, and lost four men killed, one wounded and had five of his horses disabled " Edward Cowell had by his wife Margaret the following children John Joseph, mentioned below; Elizabeth, born August 17, 1653; William, June 28, 1655 He married (second) in Hingham, June 26, 1668, Sarah, born November 19, 1644, daughter of Captain Joshua and Ellen (Ibrook) Hobart, and their children were Sarah, born April 2, 1669; Edward, August 12, 1672

(II) Joseph Cowell, or Covel, second son of Edward and Margaret Cowell, was a cooper of Boston, and married (first) about 1673, Mary, daughter of Richard Carter, widow of William Hunter, (second) Alice Palmer

(III) Joseph (2) Covel, son of Joseph (1) Covel, was born 1694, and died 1733 He resided at Chatham, Massachusetts, and Killingly, Connecticut, and had wife Hannah

(IV) Ebenezer Covel, son of Joseph (2) and Hannah Covel, born November 7, 1727, was a resident of the eastern part of Killingly, Connecticut, and died August 23, 1805 His wife Martha died June 20, 1803 Children Samuel, mentioned below; Sampson, born April 4, 1754; Mary,

September 15, 1756, Ebenezer, January 11, 1759, Tamer, March 8, 1761, Keziah, November 8, 1764, Martha, January 26, 1766, James, April 10, 1768, Hannah, August 27, 1770

(V) Samuel Covel, eldest child of Ebenezer and Martha Covel, was born January 13, 1752, and married Judith Bloss

(VI) Benjamin Covel, son of Samuel and Judith (Bloss) Covel, was born January 15, 1779, in Killingly, Connecticut, and died at Berkley, Massachusetts, March 15 1843, aged sixty-four years He was a farmer and ship carpenter by occupation, and settled at Berkley before marriage He married (first) Polly Newell, by whom he had Samuel and Benjamin, and (second) Susan Tinkham.

(VII) Benjamin (2) Covel, son of Benjamin (1) and Polly (Newell) Covel, was born March 2, 1818, in Berkley, Massachusetts, and died November 16, 1892, in Fall River He was reared to country life, and had such educational privileges as the neighborhood schools afforded. His father being a ship carpenter as well as farmer, it was but natural that the son evinced a taste in mechanical lines, and at eighteen years of age he went to Fall River and began an apprenticeship at the carpenter's and joiner's trade under the direction of Melville Borden, a contractor and builder in wood He remained with Mr Borden for a year and a half, then finished his apprenticeship with Pierce, Mason & Company, continuing in their employ until the summer of 1842 For a short time thereafter—from September until November—he was in the employ, as boss carpenter, of Samuel Sanford, in Boston, having general oversight of all the repairing and the erection of the new tenement houses put up by Mr Sanford Returning to his native town, Berkley, in November, 1842, he there remained until the spring of 1843, when he located in Fall River, associated with James Smith as partner, and began business on his own account and a career which proved successful Among some of the early structures built in Fall River by Mr Covel and his partner were the Pearl street church edifice, and the "Richardson House" and "Wilbur House," and for the following forty years or more, during the active period of Mr Covel's life, he was constantly occupied as a contractor and builder of wood, not only in Fall River, but in all the Fall River region, his field of operation sometimes extending to the cities of Boston and Newport Among some of the Fall River buildings that have stood as monuments, as it were, to his workmanship may be mentioned the Troy buildings, the Durfee block, the residence of William C Davol, Jr, and the residence of Alphonso S Covel At the time of the extension of the Old Colony Railroad from Fall River to Newport, Mr Covel constructed all of the bridges and depots on the line, and for this company he erected at Boston one of the large freight houses Commencing life a poor boy, Mr Covel by his own exertions, unaided and alone rose to position and a comfortable competence; truly was he a self-made man He served efficiently as director and president of the Crescent Mills from their organization to the time of his death, and also was vice-president and trustee of the Union Savings Bank at Fall River A Republican in his political affiliations, he was often called to positions of trust and responsibility and served as delegate to both county and State conventions He married, December 14 1841, Angeline Baker, born January 3, 1821, in Dartmouth, Massachusetts daughter of Halsey and Mercy (Allen) Baker, of Dartmouth (see Baker VI) Children Alphonso S, a sketch of

whom follows, Benjamin F, a sketch of
whom follows, Thomas D, mentioned
below, Ina F, 1860, died aged two years
(VIII) Thomas D. Covel, third son of
Benjamin (2) and Angeline (Baker)
Covel, was born June 21, 1850 In 1873
he engaged in the hardware business with
Arnold B Sanford, under the firm name
of Sanford & Covel, as it was until 1884,
when Mr Osborn bought out Mr Sanford's interest and the name became Covel
& Osborn, so continuing until 1898, when
the business was incorporated as the
Covel & Osborn Company, Mr. Covel becoming treasurer. He was for a number
of years president and director of the National Union Bank, and when it was consolidated with the Massasoit National
Bank and Pocasset National Bank, form-
ing the Massasoit-Pocasset National
Bank, he became a director and vice-
president He is vice-president of the
Davis Mills, a director of the Arkwright
Mills, a director and member of the security committee of the Troy Coöperative
Bank, a trustee of the Union Savings
Bank and a member of the executive
committee He is a member of King
Philip Lodge, Ancient Free and Accepted
Masons; Fall River Chapter, Royal Arch
Masons, Fall River Council, Royal and
Select Masters, Godfrey de Bouillon
Commandery, Knights Templar, the Mas-
sachusetts Consistory, thirty-second de-
gree, Ancient Arabic Order Nobles of the
Mystic Shrine He married, October 31,
1876, Betsey Paine, daughter of Franklin
and Irene (Gardner) Gray, of Fall River
(see Gray VII)

(The Baker Line)

(I) Francis Baker was born in England
in 1611 His last residence in his native
land was at Great St Albans, Hertfordshire, and in 1635 he came over in the
ship "Planter," locating at Yarmouth,

Massachusetts He married Isabel Tarning, of Yarmouth, and died in 1696, the
last of the first comers His children
were Nathaniel, John, Samuel, Daniel,
William and Thomas

(II) Daniel Baker, fourth son of Francis and Isabel (Tarning) Baker, married
May 27, 1674, Elizabeth Chase, daughter
of William Chase, the latter born in Yarmouth, Massachusetts, in 1622 Children
Daniel, born 1675; Samuel, mentioned below Elizabeth, 1696; Hannah, Thankful,
1698; Tabitha, 1700.

(III) Samuel Baker, second son of
Daniel and Elizabeth (Chase) Baker, was
born 1676, and married Patience, surname
unknown Children Shubal, mentioned
below; Susannah, born June 22 1711,
Hezekiah August 4, 1715, Tabitha, March
8, 1718, Desire, February 5, 1720; Elizabeth, September 9 1725, Samuel, June 4
1732

(IV) Shubal Baker, eldest child of
Samuel and Patience Baker, born March
24, 1710, married, in 1733, Lydia Stuart
Children Sylvanus, born March 10, 1734,
Azubah, May 17, 1737, Temperance, June
24, 1739, Shubal, mentioned below, Elizabeth, January 2, 1744, Lydia, October 13,
1746, Ruth, June 25, 1749, Patience, July
19, 1752

(V) Shubal (2) Baker, son of Shubal
(1) and Lydia (Stuart) Baker, born November 11, 1741, married, November 15,
1764 Rebecca Chase, born August 24,
1747, daughter of Richard and Thankful
Chase. Children: Hapsabeth (or Hepsi-
bah), born October 15, 1765, married,
March 23 1786, Zenos Chase, Archelus,
November 26, 1767, married, in 1789, Mehitable Chase, Rebecca, December 19,
1770, married, December 11, 1788, David
Howes, Shubal, July 10, 1772, married,
January 10, 1793, Mercy Smalley; Ezra,
September 5 1775, married Susanna
Gage, Michael, November 6, 1776, died

328

April 7, 1796; Ensign, July 3, 1779, married, December 27, 1800, Sally Nickerson, Temperance, October 15, 1781, married, December 4, 1800, Henry Kelly: Abigail, November 22, 1783. married, April 20, 1807, Edward Sears; Sylvanus, August 24, 1786, married Bethiah Crowell Halsey, mentioned below

(VI) Halsey Baker, youngest child of Shubal (2) and Rebecca (Chase) Baker, born February 27, 1789, married, November 28, 1811, Mercy Allen, born May 25, 1792, daughter of Seth Allen, granddaughter of John Allen (born 1729, died April 29, 1811, married, July 25, 1750, Hannah Paine, born 1732, died April 25, 1808), and great-granddaughter of William and Susannah Allen Children of Halsey and Mercy (Allen) Baker Rebecca, born September 6, 1812, married Alexander Nickerson; Ann, January 14, 1814; Joseph, October 26, 1815; Bethany, October 5, 1817, died November 14, 1830; Susan, January 26, 1819, Angeline, mentioned below; Lydia Ann, June 3, 1823, died November 20, 1830; David Gage, June 24, 1825; Mary Jane, March 23, 1828; Edwin W, December 25, 1829; Lydia Maria; George F

(VII) Angeline Baker, fifth daughter of Halsey and Mercy (Allen) Baker, was born January 3, 1821, and became the wife of Benjamin (2) Covel, of Fall River (see Covel VII)

(The Gray Line)

The Gray family has been prominently identified with the history of Southeastern Massachusetts and Rhode Island for many centuries The line herein traced has been for some time identified with Bristol county, Massachusetts, in the vicinity of Fall River, where worthy representatives are still found

(I) Edward Gray was a merchant in Plymouth, Massachusetts, where he was

settled as early as 1643 On June 3, 1662, he was granted a double share of land, and on June 10, the same year, the house bought of him by the town was to be repaired by order of the court On March 5, 1667, his land at Rocky Nook, Plymouth, was ordered to be laid out and a highway to be made by it He was made freeman, May 29 1670, served on the grand jury in 1671, and was deputy to the General Court in 1676-77-78-79 On March 4, 1674, he was granted one hundred acres at Titicut He was on a committee appointed July 13, 1677, respecting the debts due the colony and to balance accounts between towns concerning the late war He was licensed June 6, 1678, to sell small quantities of liquor to those employed by him in fishing With seven others, March 5, 1680, he bought Pocasset (Tiverton) lands of Governor Josiah Winslow He died in June, 1681, and on June 7, 1681, his widow Dorothy was appointed administratrix of his estate On July 1, 1684, she was granted thirty pounds for her charge as administratrix, and March 8, 1684 she was granted sixty pounds towards bringing up the three youngest children She consented, October 28, 1684, that her husband's lands be divided among the children before her share was set off Edward Gray married (first) January 16, 1651, Mary Winslow, born in 1630, died in 1663, daughter of John and Mary (Chilton) Winslow John Winslow was baptized April 18, 1597, and came to Plymouth in the "Fortune" in 1621, in 1655 he moved to Boston, where he bought a mansion September 19, 1671; his wife Mary drew a share in cattle in 1627 in Plymouth, his will was dated March 12, 1673, and proved May 21, 1674 Mary Chilton was daughter of James Chilton, who came to Plymouth in the "Mayflower," and who signed the compact, James brought with him his wife

Mary, who died a few months after their arrival, he died December 6, 1620 Edward Gray married (second) December 12, 1665, Dorothy, daughter of Thomas and Ann Lettice She married (second) Nathaniel Clarke, and died about 1688 Children of first wife Desire, born November 6, 1651; Mary, September 18, 1653, Elizabeth, February 11, 1658, Sarah, August 12, 1659, John, October 1, 1661 Children by second wife Edward, mentioned below, Susanna, October 15, 1668, Thomas, Samuel, 1672, Hannah, Rebecca, Lydia, Anna

(II) Edward (2) Gray, second son of Edward (1) Gray and eldest child of his second wife, Dorothy (Lettice) Gray, was born January 31, 1667, and settled in Tiverton, Rhode Island There he purchased land, October 7, 1696, for which he paid 230 pounds His will, made December 10, 1722, proved June 7, 1726, disposed of a large amount of lands and cash among his children The inventory of his personal estate amounted to 284 pounds, 9 shillings and 10 pence He married (first) Mary Smith, daughter of Philip and Mary Smith, and (second) Mary Manchester, who died in 1729 Children of first marriage Mary, born May 16, 1691; Edward, mentioned below; Sarah, April 25, 1697, Phebe, September 6, 1699, Peleg, February 1, 1702, Thomas, February 4, 1704, Hannah, November 3, 1707 Children of second marriage: John, August 3, 1712; Lydia, May 12 1714; William, July 17, 1716, Samuel, August 31, 1718

(III) Edward (3) Gray, eldest son of Edward (2) and Mary (Smith) Gray, was born January 10, 1693, in Tiverton, and lived in that town with his wife Rebecca Children, recorded there Daniel, born April 1, 1718, Mary, October 8, 1719; Edward, mentioned below, Philip, January 24, 1723

(IV) Edward (4) Gray, second son of Edward (3) and Rebecca Gray, was born June 12, 1721, in Tiverton where he made his home, and married, January 6, 1745, Sarah Cook She was born November 4, 1723, in Tiverton, daughter of Thomas and Philadelphia Cook Children John, born December 23, 1745, died young, Philip, February 26, 1747, Edward, December 3, 1750, Daniel, March 12, 1752, David, September 3, 1753; Elizabeth, January 21, 1755, Thomas, November 25, 1756, Philadelphia, June 18, 1758; Joseph, mentioned below, Sarah, July 15, 1765, Hannah, November 30, 1766

(V) Joseph Gray, seventh son of Edward (4) and Sarah (Cook) Gray, was born May 26, 1762, in Tiverton, and settled in Swansea, Massachusetts, in that part which is now Somerset He was a soldier of the Revolution, enlisting at the age of seventeen years His name first appears on a list of men enlisted to reinforce the Continental army for eight months, agreeable to the resolve of June 9, 1779, delivered by Justin Ely, commissioner, to Lieutenant Reuben Lilley, at Springfield He was a member of Captain Thompson's company, Colonel Porter's regiment, aged seventeen years, stature five feet six inches, complexion dark, hair brown, engaged for the town of Pelham He also enlisted, August 10, 1779, in Major Oliver's company, Third Massachusetts Regiment, for nine months, discharged May 10, 1780 He married Avis Anthony, and their only child was David, mentioned below

(VI) David Gray, son of Joseph and Avis (Anthony) Gray, lived in what is now the town of Somerset, where he was somewhat prominent in public affairs, and represented the town of Somerset in the State constitutional convention of 1820 He died in that town 1843 He married, August 23, 1823, Betsey Paine Winslow,

born March 21, 1795, in Somerset, daughter of Dr. John and Bethany (Brayton) Winslow, of Swansea (see Winslow VI). Children Horace, died young; Franklin, mentioned below; and Betsey, died young.

(VII) Hon Franklin Gray, son of David and Betsey Paine (Winslow) Gray, was born May 29, 1824, in Somerset, Massachusetts Although the family lived on a farm and agricultural pursuits were the chief field of usefulness for the young of those days, Mr Gray early developed a fondness for navigation and, after acquiring his early educational training in the schools of the neighborhood, when about twenty years of age he took to the sea, making several voyages Upon being married, in 1845, he again took up farming life, and followed the same for several years. The discovery of gold in California aroused his interest, and like many others, in 1849, Mr Gray joined the crowd of travelers to the Pacific coast Two years of that life, however, were enough for him, and he returned to his native State In 1853 he became a resident of Fall River, Massachusetts, where he formed a partnership with the late Edward P Buffinton, the second mayor of that city, engaging in the meat business. In a few years, however, the health of Mr Gray proved unequal to the arduous work which in those days seemed necessary to the success of that business, and he was compelled to retire, much to the regret of not only himself but his partner as well For the restoration of his health, Mr Gray made several trips to the West Indies, and after regaining his broken health, the offer of the inspectorship of the port of Fall River, made in 1861 to him by Charles Almy, then collector of the port, was accepted Mr Gray continued to hold this office until 1866, when Andrew Johnson, who succeeded Abraham Lincoln as President, believing in

the "spoils theory," placed new men in the customs offices. Mr Gray was that year elected city marshal of Fall River, and the following year was made assistant assessor of internal revenues The duties of this position he combined with the work of assessing legacies and successions in Bristol county There was no interruption of this employment until 1873, in which year C B H Fessenden, collector, named Mr Gray as deputy collector of internal revenue, an office which he held until the consolidation of revenue districts In 1867 Mr Gray had received a commission as deputy sheriff of Bristol county, and for twenty-eight consecutive years he filled that position His efficient work in the several ways in which he served the public made possible the election of Mr Gray to two offices in 1877, as a member of the House of Representatives and as a county commissioner The Republican party honored him by repeated nominations, which the citizens of the county ratified at the polls, and for a period of eighteen years he continued to hold the office of county commissioner, most of the time being chairman of the board For many years he also served as justice of the peace Mr Gray was one of the early settlers of Fall River, and is without a peer in the length and variety of the services he rendered the public He had lived to see Fall River grow from the village and town of Troy into the commanding position now occupied by that progressive and industrial city He belonged to the class of octogenarians of whom there are comparatively few in the population of to-day, who are native born Mr Gray was a member of the old Commercial Club, of Fall River, and when the Quequechan Club was organized he was one of the first to join, continuing a member of the latter until 1903 Reading was his favorite pastime, and he was excep-

tionally well informed as a result, retaining a keen interest in public affairs up to
the time of his death, although he had
retired from active business cares in 1895
Mrs. Gray passed away February 21, 1899,
after which time Mr. Gray was tenderly
cared for by his only daughter, Mrs.
Thomas D. Covel, with whom he continued to reside until his death, which
occurred January 5, 1909. His body was
deposited in Oak Grove Cemetery. He
married, November 24, 1845, Irene Gardner, born in what is now Warren, Rhode
Island, daughter of Hezekiah and Almira
(Mason) Gardner (see Gardner VI).
Children. David Franklin, died young,
two children died unnamed in infancy,
and Betsey Paine. The mother was
buried in Oak Grove Cemetery. They
were members of the Unitarian church of
Fall River.

(VIII) Betsey Paine Gray, daughter of
Franklin and Irene (Gardner) Gray, was
married, October 31, 1876, to Thomas D.
Covel of Fall River (see Covel VIII).
Mrs. Covel is a member of the Daughters
of the American Revolution, of Fall River,
a lady of culture, refined mind, and a well
known and esteemed member of society.

(The Winslow Line)

(I) William Winslow, or Wyncelow,
first of the line as traced in England, had
children. John, of London, afterward of
Wyncelow Hall, was living in 1388, married Mary Crouchman, died in 1410, styled
of Crouchman Hall, and William, mentioned below.

(II) William (2) Winslow, son of William (1) Winslow, had a son Thomas,
mentioned below.

(III) Thomas Winslow, son of William (2) Winslow, was of Burton, County
Oxford, having lands also in Essex. He
was living in 1452. He married Cecelia
Tansley, one of two daughters, and the

heiress of an old family. She was called
Lady Agnes. Had a son, William (3).

(IV) William (3) Winslow, son of
Thomas Winslow, was living in 1529.
Children. Kenelm, mentioned below,
Richard, had a grant from Edward VI of
the rectory of Elksley, County Notting-
ham.

(V) Kenelm Winslow, son of William
(3) Winslow, purchased, in 1559, of Sir
Richard Newport, an estate called Newport's Place, in Kempsey, Worcestershire. He had an older and very extensive estate in the same parish called Clerkenleap, sold by his grandson, Richard
Winslow, in 1650. He died in 1607 in the
parish of St Andrew. His wife's name
was Catherine. His will, dated April 14,
1607, and proved November 9 following,
is still preserved at Worcester. Only
son, Edward, mentioned below.

(VI) Edward Winslow, son of Kenelm
Winslow, was born October 17, 1560, in
the parish of Saint Andrew, County
Worcester, England, and died before 1631.
He lived in Kempsey and Droitwich,
County Worcester. He married (first)
Eleanor Pelham, of Droitwich; (second)
at St. Bride's Church, London, November
4, 1594, Magdalene Oliver, the records of
whose family are found in the parish register of St. Peter's, Droitwich. Children:
1 Richard, born about 1586 2 Edward,
October 18, 1595, at Droitwich, governor
of Plymouth Colony, married (first) at
Leyden, May 16, 1618, Elizabeth Barker;
(second) May 12, 1621, Susan (Fuller)
White, who came in the "Mayflower"
with Governor Winslow, widow of William White, and mother of Peregrine
White, the first born in the colony 3
John April 16 1597, died 1674, in Boston, married, October 12, 1624, Mary,
daughter of James and Susanna Chilton,
who came in the "Mayflower." 4 Eleanor, April 22, 1598, at Droitwich, and re-

mained in England 5 Kenelm, mentioned below 6 Gilbert, October 26, 1600, came in the "Mayflower" with Edward, signed the compact, returned to England after 1623, and died there 7 Elizabeth, March 8, 1602, buried January 20, 1604, at St Peter's Church 8 Magdalen, December 26, 1604, at Droitwich, remained in England 9 Josiah, February 11, 1606

(I) Kenelm (2) Winslow, son of Edward Winslow and his second wife, Magdalene (Oliver) Winslow, was born at Droitwich, County Worcester, England, April 29, 1599, baptized at St Peter's Church, May 3, 1599, died at Salem, Massachusetts, September 13, 1672 He was the immigrant ancestor, coming to Plymouth, probably in 1629, with his brother Josiah, and was admitted a freeman, January 1, 1633. In 1640 he was surveyor of the town of Plymouth, and was fined ten shillings for neglecting the highways He removed to Marshfield about 1641, having previously received a grant of land at that place, then called Green's Harbor, March 5, 1638. This grant, originally made to Josiah Winslow, his brother, he shared with Love Brewster His home was "on a gentle eminence by the sea, near the extremity of land lying between Green Harbor and South Rivers This tract of the township was considered the Eden of the region It was beautified with groves of majestic oaks and graceful walnuts with the underground void of shrubbery A few of these groves were standing within the memory of persons living in 1854, but all have fallen beneath the hand of the woodman" The homestead he left to his son Nathaniel Other lands were granted to Kenelm as the common land was divided He was one of the twenty-six original proprietors of Assonet, now Freetown, Massachusetts, purchased of the Indians April 2, 1659

and received the twenty-fourth lot, a portion of which was lately owned by a lineal descendant, having descended by inheritance Kenelm Winslow was a joiner by trade as well as a planter He filled various town offices, was deputy to the General Court from 1642 to 1644 and from 1649 to 1653, eight years in all He had considerable litigation, as the early court records show He died at Salem, whither he had gone on business, apparently after a long illness, for his will was dated five weeks earlier, August 8, 1672, and in it he describes himself as "being very sick and drawing nigh unto death" He may have been visiting his niece, Mrs Elizabeth Corwin, daughter of Edward Winslow He married, in June, 1634, Eleanor Adams, widow of John Adams, of Plymouth She survived him and died at Marshfield, where she was buried December 5, 1681, aged eighty-three Children Kenelm, born about 1636, Eleanor or Ellen, about 1637, Nathaniel, about 1639, Job, mentioned below

(II) Job Winslow, youngest child of Kenelm (2) and Eleanor (Adams) Winslow, was born about 1641, at Marshfield, Massachusetts, and died July 14, 1720, at Freetown, same State He settled at Swansea, Massachusetts, about 1666 At the breaking out of King Philip's war in 1675, in which he served, his house at Swansea, which he had inhabited for eight or nine years, was burned He appears to have been one of the early settlers of Rochester, Massachusetts, as he was there about 1680, but he soon removed to Freetown, for in 1686 he was one of the selectmen of that town He was town clerk and grand juror in 1690, assessor in 1691, 1701-06-11, moderator of town meetings in 1708-11, deputy to the General Court of Massachusetts in 1692 under the charter of William and Mary He was a leading man of the church as well as in town affairs, was a lieutenant in the militia company, and was a shipwright as well as a planter. He married Ruth Cole, who survived him. In his will, dated November 12, 1717, he gave to the town the tract of land now known as the "Winslow Burying Ground," situated about two miles from the Assonet Village. He also mentions his wife Ruth, and all his children, given below, with the exception of Mary, Hope and John, who died young. The dates of birth of the first six children are taken from the record of Swansea; of James, Mary, George, Jonathan and John, from the records of Freetown. Children: William, born November 16, 1674; Oliver, February 20, 1677; Ruth, September 13, 1678; Richard, mentioned below; Hope, May 29, 1681; Job, July 10, 1683; Joseph, 1685; James, May 9, 1687; Mary, April 2, 1689, died young; George, January 2, 1691; Jonathan, November 22, 1692; John, February 20, 1695; Elizabeth, 1697.

(III) Dr. Richard Winslow, third son of Job and Ruth (Cole) Winslow, was born March 6, 1680, in Swansea, and settled in Freetown, where he practiced medicine, and died between August 7, 1727, and April 16, 1728. His wife Harriet survived him, and probably married (second) Captain Josiah Winslow. Children: Richard, born August 19, 1711; Hezekiah, mentioned below; Sarah, May 8, 1716; William, September 24, 1718; Hannah, April 14, 1721; Edward, October 10, 1723.

(IV) Captain Hezekiah Winslow, second son of Dr. Richard and Harriet Winslow, was born December 9, 1713, in Freetown, died in Dartmouth. On May 7, 1766, he signed an indenture, agreeing with his neighbor about a division line which had been long in dispute. He married, May 30, 1737, Elizabeth Paine, born June 15, 1714, daughter of Thomas and Susanna (Haskell) Paine, of Freetown. She received three pounds and ten shil-

lings by her father's will. She was born 1715, and died 1794. Children: John, born October 27, 1737; Ebenezer, mentioned below; Ezra, May 10, 1751; Job, died before July 5, 1785.

(V) Dr. Ebenezer Winslow, second son of Captain Hezekiah and Elizabeth (Paine) Winslow, born August 28, 1742, resided in that part of Swansea which is now Somerset. He married (first) February 27, 1766, in Swansea, Elizabeth Eddy, born October 25, 1745, daughter of Constant and Mary (Winslow) Eddy. He married (second) (published June 24, 1798) Catherine Gardner, of Warren, Rhode Island. Children of first marriage: John, mentioned below; Humphrey, born September 19, 1768; Ebenezer, September 1, 1770; Betty, May 19, 1773; Anne, 1776; Mary, December, 1777; Nancy, about 1779; William, May 11, 1781; Mary, June 6, 1790. Children of second marriage: Edward, Betsey, born October 31, 1802; James, July 14, 1804.

(VI) Dr. John Winslow, eldest child of Ebenezer and Elizabeth (Eddy) Winslow, was born November 28, 1766, resided in Somerset, where he married (first) September 30, 1790, Bethany Brayton, daughter of Samuel Brayton. He married (second) February 17, 1803, Mary Brayton, daughter of Thomas Brayton. Children of first marriage: Daughter, married a Mr. Baker; Betsey Paine, mentioned below; Nathaniel Read, born July 13, 1797. Of second marriage: John William, December 8, 1803; Elizabeth Eddy, March 24, 1805; Charles Brayton, May 13, 1807; Sarah Ann, January 19, 1808; Francis Richmond, December 8, 1809; Francis, December 13, 1813.

(VII) Betsey Paine Winslow, eldest daughter of Dr. John and Bethany (Brayton) Winslow, was born March 21, 1795, in Somerset, and became the wife of David Gray, of that town (see Gray VI).

(The Gardner Line)

The surname Gardner and Gardiner have the same origin, and the spelling Gardener is also found This family in the State of Rhode Island, members of which have been most prominent and influential there from the beginning, is as ancient as are the settlements there

(I) George Gardner, believed to have been the son of Sir Thomas Gardiner, knight, was born in England, in 1601, and died in Kings Town, Rhode Island, in 1679 He was admitted an inhabitant of the Aquidneck, Rhode Island, September 1, 1638, and in 1640 was present at a General Court of Election His name is found on the records often from that time until his death, and it was spelled Gardner, Gardiner and Gardener He married (first) about 1640, Herodias (Long) Wickes, who declared that when she was between thirteen and fourteen years of age she was married in London to John Wickes, without the knowledge of her friends Soon after they reached Rhode Island he deserted her, going to New Amsterdam, or, as she expressed it "to the Dutch," taking with him most of her property, left to her by her mother Her marriage to George Gardner was rather irregular in form, consisting in their going before some Friends and declaring themselves husband and wife She refused to take the usual ceremony, as she was a member of the Society of Friends, and was so bound to her religion that she cheerfully walked from Newport to Boston to receive a whipping at the post because of her religious beliefs, carrying a young child in her arms the whole distance According to her own account, George Gardner neglected to provide for her numerous family adequately It may have been her pressing needs, and it may have been the superior attractions of John Porter, with his great wealth of lands (he

being one of the original Pettaquamscutt purchasers) and his promise to provide for her children, that awakened her religious scruples about the legality of her marriage with George Gardner At any rate, she petitioned the General Assembly for a divorce, which was granted, thus proving the legality of her marriage She then married John Porter, who faithfully kept his promise, giving large farms to each of her sons, and possibly her daughters, for the land of John Watson, who married two of her daughters, joined the Gardner lands George Gardner married for his second wife, Lydia Bolton, daughter of Robert and Susannah Bolton The children by his first wife were Benoni, born about 1645, Henry, about 1647, George, about 1649, William, 1651, Nicholas, 1654, Dorcas, 1656, married John Watson, Rebecca, probably the infant carried by her mother to Boston, in 1658. Children born to the second marriage of George Gardner Samuel, mentioned below, Joseph, Lydia, married Joseph Smith, Mary, Peregrine; Robert; Jeremiah

(II) Samuel Gardner, son of George Gardner and his second wife, Lydia (Bolton) Gardner, lived in Newport, Rhode Island In 1687 he removed to Freetown Massachusetts, and in 1693 he purchased, with Ralph Chapman, a farm at Mattapoisett, now South Swansea, Massachusetts, of Ebenezer Brenton He moved to the latter place, lived there the remainder of his life, died December 8, 1696, and left a widow He married Elizabeth, widow of James Brown, and a daughter of Robert Carr, of Newport Children Elizabeth, born 1684, died September 24, 1754, married, January 16, 1699, Edward Thurston, of Newport, Rhode Island, who died April 27, 1727, Samuel, mentioned below, Martha, November 16, 1686, died October 27, 1763, married, March 23, 1704, Heze-

335

kiah Luther, who died November 2, 1763, oi smallpox, Patience, October 31, 1687, married Thomas Cranston; Sarah, November 1, 1692, married Samuel Lee

(III) Samuel (2) Gardner, eldest son of Samuel (1) and Elizabeth (Carr-Brown) Gardner, was born October 28, 1685, and died February 10, 1773 He was married, December 6, 1707, by Governor Samuel Cranston, to Hannah Smith, born December 20, 1688, died November 16, 1768, daughter of Philip and Mary Smith Children Elizabeth, born November 11, 1708, died January 28, 1788, married, July 4, 1728, Ambrose Barnaby, born April 20, 1706, died April 18, 1775, Mary, October 26, 1710, married, January 31, 1731, Barnard Hill, Samuel, October 30, 1712, died young; Samuel, mentioned below, Peleg, February 22, 1719, Patience, February 17, 1721, married, March 30, 1738, Dr John Turner, Hannah, 1724, died December 24, 1811, married Caleb Turner, who died July 20, 1757, Sarah, 1726, died February 29, 1808, married, April 19, 1744, John Mason, born September 28, 1723, died November 27, 1805, Edward, April 22, 1731, died 1795, married, January 11, 1756, Esther Mason, born September 2, 1735, died 1806; Martha, married, May 10, 1753, Job Mason

(IV) Samuel (3) Gardner, second son of Samuel (2) and Hannah (Smith) Gardner, was born February 17, 1717, and married, October 30, 1740, Content Brayton, born April 3, 1724, daughter of Preserved and Content (Coggeshall) Brayton Children Elizabeth, born June 1, 1741, married, March 18, 1762 Samuel Luther, Anne, February 26, 1743, married, June 10, 1762, Richard Barton, Samuel mentioned below, Israel, April 14, 1747, died young; Israel, March 29, 1748, died October 22, 1783; Parthenia, September 2 1750, William, September 12, 1753, married Zerviah McKoon, Hannah, March 3

1756, died July 16, 1835, married Captain Simeon Cockran; Patience, November 15, 1758, married, May 14, 1778, Dr Jonathan Anthony; Mary, December 25, 1760, died December 18, 1805, married, September 11, 1785, Caleb Mason, Content, July 11, 1764, Stephen, August 4, 1766, died November 26, 1819, married, July 22, 1788, Mary Lee, Parthenia, August 11, 1767, died October 15, 1828, married, February 14, 1790, Elias D Trafton

(V) Samuel (4) Gardner, eldest son of Samuel (3) and Content (Brayton) Gardner, was born March 5, 1745, and died September 20, 1822 He married, December 17, 1767, Elizabeth Anthony, who died February 14, 1816

(VI) Hezekiah Gardner, son oi Samuel (4) and Elizabeth (Anthony) Gardner, married Almira Mason

(VII) Irene Gardner, daughter of Hezekiah and Almira (Mason) Gardner, became the wife of Hon Franklin Gray, of Fall River (see Gray VII)

COVEL, Alphonso S,
Man of Affairs

(VIII) Alphonso Smith Covel, eldest son of Benjamin (2) and Angeline (Baker) Covel, was born in Berkley, Massachusetts, November 22, 1842, and in the public schools of Fall River acquired his early educational training His father being extensively engaged in contracting and building, Alphonso S was brought up in that business, working as his father's clerk when not attending school His business career began in 1863, when he established a grocery business in Fall River, at the corner of Ninth and Pleasant streets, which he conducted for several years In 1871 he discontinued the grocery, and became connected with the cotton manufacturing industry, in which he achieved great success Entering the

Troy Mill office, under his brother-in-law, the late Colonel Thomas J Borden, he acted as clerk and as assistant to the treasurer for several years While connected with this corporation, he had charge of the erection of the Troy Building, and also of the building for the Union Belt Company Upon the organization of the Union Belt Company, in 1871, he was elected treasurer and director, and served as clerk of the corporation and of the board of directors until 1886 In 1871, in company with the late G. M. Haffards, he founded the banking house of Covel & Haffards, and was interested in that house until 1877 He was a director of the Wampanoag Mills from 1871 to 1878, of the Richard Borden Manufacturing Company from 1871 to 1890, of the Barnard Manufacturing Company from 1873 to 1887, and of the Crescent Mills from its organization, in 1881, to the time of its liquidation, in 1893 In each of these mills, he was an original director and one of the incorporators He was one of the incorporators of the Union Savings Bank, of Fall River, in 1869, and served as trustee and as a member of the board of investment until his removal to Boston, in 1887, and still remained a member of the corporation at the time of his death He also served as a director of the National Union Bank of Fall River from 1881 to 1888 He was interested in the Fall River Gas Works from 1884 to 1887, and in the Fall River Machine Company, acting as a director from 1880 to 1887, and clerk of the corporation until 1885 He was treasurer and director of the Merchants' Manufacturing Company from 1885 to 1887, and one of the founders, in 1885, of the Fall River Hospital, the successor of which is the present Union Hospital He was clerk of the American Printing Company from 1880 to 1893, a director from 1880 to 1888, and treasurer from 1888 to

1895 He was also a director of the Fall River Iron Works Company from 1889 to 1895

In 1887 Mr Covel removed from Fall River to Boston, to assume the treasurership of the Tremont and Suffolk Mills, of Lowell, Massachusetts, which, under his able direction, grew from a plant of 30,000 spindles to one of 200,000 spindles, and at the same time nearly wiped out a heavy outstanding indebtedness He also served as a director and temporary treasurer of the Boott Cotton Mills Corporation

From modest beginnings, Mr Covel passed within a comparatively short period to considerable wealth, and as he progressed in business he was given, according to his manifestations of interest, positions of honor in the religious and reform world In early manhood he became a member of the Central Congregational Church of Fall River, and so long as he remained a resident of that city he maintained an active and zealous interest in the affairs of the church and the Sunday school, and also in its Pleasant Street Mission He was treasurer of the church society from 1874 to 1878, and superintendent of the mission school from 1881 to 1887 He was also the first president of the Young People's Society of Christian Endeavor, formed in 1883, serving several years in succession in that capacity Mr Covel was full of the courtesies which harmonize with the character of an interested church member and worker, and helped to win many to church attendance Pastors found in him one of the best of helpers in this respect, one who was also ready with his efforts as well as with his means to assist in all worthy projects which had for their object the best interests of the community Upon removing to Boston, he joined the Old South Church (Congregational), and there, too, he was active and helpful in

337

the work of the church He also held official relations with this society, of which he remained a valued and devoted member until his death, being superintendent of the Sunday school for five years, head usher for a period of twelve years, and for seventeen years also served as deacon of the church He was also deeply interested in Christian work for young men, and was conspicuous in his efforts to sustain Young Men's Christian Association work in Boston, being for three years, from 1892 to 1895, the president of the Boston Young Men's Christian Association In political faith Mr Covel was a stalwart adherent of the principles of the Republican party, and while a resident of Fall River served one term as a member of the Common Council, and as the chairman of the Republican city committee Socially, he was a member of the Home Market Club, and one of its vice-presidents in 1906, a member of the Exchange, Boston Art, and Essex County clubs He was a trustee of the Lowell Textile School for several years, under appointment by the State

On May 19, 1869, Mr Covel was united in marriage at Fall River, Massachusetts, to Sarah Walker Borden, who was born May 14, 1844, youngest child of Colonel Richard Borden and Abby Walker (Durfee) Borden, of that city. To Mr and Mrs Covel were born six children, namely 1 Richard Borden, who died in Fall River, in 1879. 2 Abbie Walker 3. Borden, born at Fall River, Massachusetts, September 19, 1879, married, June 8 1904, in Paris, France, Alice M Kuhn, daughter of Leon S and Theresa E (Prorok) Kuhn, of Paris, France, and to this union have been born four children, namely Elizabeth, born November 6, 1905, in Boston ; Richard Borden, born February 27, 1907, in Brookline ; Thomas Edmonson, born May 26, 1910, in Mexico City,

Mexico, and Peter Covel, born November 23, 1916, in Brookline 4 Gertrude Elliott 5 Florence 6 Helen

Mr. Covel passed away at his residence 617 Commonwealth avenue, Boston, Massachusetts, April 13, 1907, in the sixty fifth year of his age, and his remains were laid to rest in Oak Grove Cemetery, Fall River, Massachusetts

---

COVEL, Benjamin Franklin,

Manufacturer.

(VIII) Benjamin Franklin Covel, second son of Benjamin (2) and Angelina (Baker) Covel, was born August 7, 1849, in Fall River, on the site now occupied by the Durfee Mills office building, where his father built his first house on coming to Fall River After pursuing his education in the public schools, including one year in the high school, Benjamin F Covel was employed for some time as carpenter, after which he was some two or three years in the grocery store of his brother, Alphonso S Covel About the time of attaining his majority, he began to learn the machinist's trade with the firm of Gifford & Houghton, with whom he served an apprenticeship of three years and was one year employed as a journeyman In 1870 he established himself in business, under the name of the Covel Machine Company, which name the establishment continued to bear for nearly fifty years, during which time Mr Covel was sole owner For more than twenty years he made a regular practice of paying the wages of his employees on the tenth of the month, and this was never missed but once, except when that day fell on Sunday, on which occasion he paid the following day, the exception was occasioned by a disarrangement of the time lock on the vault of his bank, but the next day Mr Covel was on hand Since he

338

began paying the wages of his employees each week, he never missed a payday At the beginning the business required only a small number of employees, but these were steadily increased as time went on, and the business was very successfully conducted without the aid of any outside capital It is thus apparent that Mr Covel was a sound and conservative business man and that he contributed in no small degree to the growth and development of Fall River as a manufacturing city Mr Covel was long active in the great Masonic fraternity affiliating with King Philip Lodge, Free and Accepted Masons, Fall River Chapter, Royal Arch Masons, Fall River Council, Royal and Select Masters, and the Godfrey de Bouillon Commandery, Knights Templar He was also a member of Mount Hope Lodge, Independent Order of Odd Fellows While independent of political dictation, in all local matters he adhered to the principles of the Republican party on national questions He married (first) June 10, 1873, Mary, daughter of Charles Almy, she died December 30, 1879, and he married (second) August 25, 1898, Susan Maria, daughter of Wilson and Mary (Allen) Osborne, of Fall River (see Osborne III) There is one daughter of the first marriage, Ina F, born June 7, 1874 Mr Covel died June 29, 1917

(The Osborne Line)

This family has been long established in Rhode Island, and was originally planted probably at New Haven Jeremiah Osborne, of New Haven, represented that town in the legislature in 1672, 1674, and died in 1676 His widow and son Jeremiah, and other heirs, were proprietors of that town in 1685 He had children Rebecca, baptized October 23, 1642, Increase, February 5 1644, Benjamin January 3, 1647, Jeremiah, died young, Mary,

born March 29, 1653, Elizabeth, died young; Jeremiah, November 28, 1656; Joanna, December 8, 1658, William, 1660, Elizabeth December 9, 1665

Jeremiah Osborne, of Newport, Rhode Island, died there in 1709 He married Mercy, daughter of Nathaniel and Sarah Davis, she died February 16, 1733 He bought and sold land in Newport, and was a man of property, as is shown by the inventory of his estate, which amounted to 412 pounds and 3 shillings, including two houses and land, live stock, silver to the value of 22 pounds His children were Robert, born August 11, 1684, Katherine, November 12, 1686, John, October 31, 1689, Jeremiah, died young, Margaret, May 27, 1695, Sarah, May 11, 1701, Jeremiah, June 21, 1706

(1) It is presumable that the family continued to reside in Newport, as there are various references to the name in the records of that town Its vital records are, however, so defective as to give no continuous history of the family It is probable that William Osborne, who begins the line which can be completely traced, was a son of Jeremiah Osborne, born 1706, or of his brother, John, born 1689 The name appears with various spellings, and William Osborne, founder of the family in Tiverton, spelled his name Osband It is found that he was born August 16, 1729, in Newport, and went from that town to Tiverton, living during his minority with Samuel Hicks, of that town All except one of his children used the spelling Osborn William Osborn died October 29, 1810 He married, May 28, 1752, in Tiverton, Elizabeth Shrieve, born August 10, 1731, in that town, died about 1814, daughter of Thomas and Frances (Russell) Shrieve Their children, recorded in Tiverton, are Wilson, born June 3, 1753, died about 1757, Weaver, April 17, 1756, Elizabeth,

339

June 8, 1758, Patience, July 17, 1761, died young, Thomas, mentioned below, William, July 18, 1769

(II) Thomas Osborne, third son of William and Elizabeth (Shrieve) Osborne, was born March 31, 1766, in Tiverton, and died there October 7, 1833 He was a ship cooper by occupation, and also engaged in farming in Tiverton, where he married, in 1797, Ann, daughter of Joseph and Abigail (Borden) Durfee, born March 6, 1775 (see Durfee V and Borden IV) Children William, born November 26, 1798, died January 28, 1829, in Tiverton, married Ruth Hambly, Thomas, December 30, 1800, died March 1, 1884, in Tiverton, married Elizabeth S Hambly, Joseph, August 20, 1803, Ann, December 4, 1805, died 1812, Wilson, mentioned below, Eliza Ann, May 25, 1810, married Rev Alexander Milne, and died August 18, 1887, in Fall River, Patience, August 29, 1812, died 1817, Weaver, May 23, 1815, James Munroe, August 27, 1822

(III) Wilson Osborne, fourth son of Thomas and Ann (Durfee) Osborne, was born April 15, 1808, in Tiverton, where he grew to manhood, and learned the trade of blacksmith This was his principal occupation through life He also lived upon and tilled a tract of seventy acres of land, known as the Cook Farm, in Tiverton There he died August 29, 1873 His body was laid to rest in Oak Grove Cemetery, Fall River He was a member of the Baptist church He became colonel of the Twenty-fifth Regiment of the Rhode Island State Militia in 1838, and thus continued until the disbandment of the same He married, August 19, 1832, in Tiverton, Mary Allen, born May 11, 1810, in that town, daughter of Sion and Elizabeth (Dresser) Allen, of Tiverton (see Allen VIII) She died January 27, 1886, in Fall River, and was buried in Oak Grove Cemetery Like her husband, she

was a faithful member of the Baptist church Children George Allen, mentioned below, Mary Elizabeth, born June 1, 1837, died 1856, Susan Maria, May 9, 1842, married, August 25, 1898, Benjamin F Covel, of Fall River (see Covel VIII)

(IV) George Allen Osborne, only son of Wilson and Mary (Allen) Osborne, was born November 3, 1834, in Tiverton, and made his home in Wheeling, West Virginia, where he died June 10, 1911 He married, October 31, 1867, Mary A. Brockett, of Wheeling, who now resides in that city Children Georgia V, married William Bowers, Mary Elizabeth, married Frank J Gaus, has one child, Helen Osborne, Carrie B, married Dr Harry Hubbard, Beulah, married Edward Horstman, has one child, Jane Frances

(The Durfee Line)

(I) Thomas Durfee, born in England in 1643, came to this country in 1660, and settled in the town of Portsmouth, Rhode Island He married as early as 1664, but the name of his first wife is not recorded He married (second) Deliverance, daughter of William and Mary Hall, and widow of Abial Tripp She died in 1721, surviving him some seven years He died in 1712, aged about seventy There were children of Mr Durfee by the second marriage, the eldest of whom is mentioned below

(II) William Durfee, son of Thomas and Deliverance (Hall-Tripp) Durfee, was born 1673, in Portsmouth, and resided in Tiverton, where he died 1727 He was in Tiverton as early as 1698, in which year the ear mark of his cattle was recorded in the town book His first wife Ann died in Tiverton He had a second wife Mary, who is supposed to have been the mother of his youngest child His children were David, born March 1, 1700, Samuel, mentioned below, Joseph, about 1705, died unmarried in Tiverton, Abigail, about 1710.

(III) Samuel Durfee, second son of William Durfee, born 1702, in Tiverton, resided on Tiverton Heights where he owned a large tract of land, and was a noted deer hunter. While the Revolutionary army was encamped on Tiverton Heights, during the Revolutionary War, his house was the headquarters of the commander, General Sullivan. Samuel Durfee was a justice of the peace in 1742, and represented the town in the General Court in 1751-53-56-57-58-60-63-68-69-70, and died November 8, 1788. By his will two negro slaves were set free, and he bequeathed property and cash to a large number of descendants. He married in Tiverton, February 10, 1732, Mercy Durfee, born January 30, 1711, daughter of Benjamin and Prudence (Earle) Durfee of Tiverton where she died. Children: Prudence, born May 28, 1733; William, January 10, 1735; Mary, March 26, 1736, died young; Hope, May 20, 1738; Joseph, mentioned below; Susannah, July 14, 1741; Ruth, October 26, 1742; Mercy, March 11, 1745.

(IV) Joseph Durfee, second son of Samuel and Mercy (Durfee) Durfee, born August 31, 1739, in Tiverton died in Fall River. He married in Tiverton, February 4, 1770, Abigail Borden, born January 27, 1749, daughter of Samuel and Peace (Mumford) Borden, of Tiverton (see Borden V). Children: Joseph born January 5, 1771; Mercy, October 11, 1772; Ann, mentioned below.

(V) Ann Durfee, second daughter of Joseph and Abigail (Borden) Durfee, born March 6, 1775, became the wife of Thomas Osborne, of Tiverton (see Osborne II).

(IV) Samuel Borden, fourth son of Richard (2) (q v) and Innocent (War-

dell) Borden, was born October 25, 1705, in Tiverton, where he grew up participating in the arduous and rigid labors of a rural section in that day. In winter time, when there was not proper snow for logging, or when the family was not in need of firewood, he was permitted to attend the district school. He was, however, a bright and alert youth, and managed to secure a fair common school education and also mastered some of the higher branches of mathematics. Like his father and grandfather, he became a surveyor, and was highly skilled, with a reputation extending far beyond his native town and colony. He was appointed by Governor Shirley, of Massachusetts, to locate emigrants on lands in Nova Scotia, and spent some years in that province. After his return he cultivated his home farm, and died between September 1 and December 1, 1778. He married, about 1735. Peace Mumford, of Exeter, Rhode Island. Children: Joseph, born October 14, 1736, Perry, November 9, 1739, Benjamin, 1741; Ann, March 8, 1743; Abigail, mentioned below; Edward.

(V) Abigail Borden, second daughter of Samuel and Peace (Mumford) Borden, was married, February 4, 1770, to Joseph Durfee, of Tiverton (see Durfee IV).

This is one of the names most frequently met in the United States and is represented by many distinct families. Its use arises from the Christian name, which is very ancient. In the roll of Battle Abbey Fitz-Aleyne (son of Allen) appears, and the name comes down to the present. Alan, constable, of Scotland and Lord of Galloway and Cunningham, died in 1234. One of the first using Allen as a surname was Thomas Allen, sheriff of London, in 1414. Sir John Allen was mayor of London in 1524, Sir William

Allen in 1571, and Sir Thomas Alleyn in 1658 Edward Allen (1566-1626), a distinguished actor and friend of Shakespeare and Ben Jonson, founded in 1619 Dulwich College, with the stipulation that the master and secretary must always bear the name of Allen, and this curious condition has been easily fulfilled through the plenitude of scholars of the name There are no less than fifty-five coats-of-arms of the separate and distinct families of Allen in the United Kingdom, besides twenty others of different spellings. There were more than a score of emigrants of this surname, from almost as many different families, who left England before 1650 to settle in New England The name in early times was spelled Allin, Alline, Alling, Allyn, Allein and Allen, but the last is the orthography almost universally used at the present day It is found not only in the industrial but in the professional life of people who have stood for all that is noblest and best It has been identified with the formative period of New York history, and from that region has sent out many worthy representatives.

(I) George Allen, probably a son of Ralph Allen, of Thurcaston, Leicestershire, England, was born about 1568, under the reign of Queen Elizabeth He was probably a farmer near Bridgewater in Somersetshire, and was a member of a company which set sail March 20, 1635, and arrived at Boston on May 6 following. For a time he resided in Lynn, Massachusetts, and in 1637 joined with Edmund Freeman and others in the purchase of the town of Sandwich When this town was incorporated Mr Allen was chosen first deputy, the first officer in the town, was a member of the church organized at Sandwich in 1638, and was admitted a freeman in that town June 30 of the following year, and elected constable

at the same time In 1640 he was surveyor of highways, and in 1641 a member of a committee of five to divide the meadow lands, himself receiving six and one-fourth acres In 1646 he built his house, one-fourth mile from the meeting house on the road to the cape, and this stood until 1882 After the purchase of Sandwich, several of his sons removed to that town with their families He died there May 2, 1648, aged eighty years His wife Catherine survived him and married (second) John Collins, with whom she removed to Boston In his will he named five sons Matthew, Henry, Samuel, George, William, and also made provision for his "five least children." He had sons Samuel, George, William, Ralph, Matthew, Henry, Francis, James, Gideon, Thomas, Judah and Caleb

(II) Ralph Allen, fourth son of George and Catherine Allen, was born about 1621, in England, and resided in Sandwich, where he died in 1698 He was called a planter and gave considerable land to his sons, between the years 1663 and 1678 He was among the eleven male members of the church at Sandwich in 1643 This church did not conform to the Puritan standards, being a Baptist church, and its members were cruelly persecuted for half a century by the colonial authorities because of their determination to maintain religious freedom In the year 1658 members of the Allen family paid fines aggregating £250, imposed by the church authorities In 1659 Ralph Allen, with his brothers, was taken from the jail at Boston and whipped through several towns as a punishment for their religious opinions They subsequently became allied with the Friends, or Quakers, and were further persecuted for this In 1655 Ralph Allen contributed ten shillings toward building a new meeting house in Sandwich The family held lands on both sides of Buzzard's Bay, and soon removed from Sandwich because of the persecutions inflicted upon them. Ralph Allen married, in 1643, Esther, daughter of William and Jane Swift, of Sandwich, and their children recorded there are John, Joseph, Increase, Ebenezer, Zachariah, Patience. He also had children, probably of a second marriage, unrecorded, namely: Jedidah, Jonah, Experience, Ephraim, Mary.

(III) Increase Allen, third son of Ralph Allen, was born about 1648, and died in 1723, leaving all his property to his widow. His home was in Dartmouth, where he was an extensive landholder, and he also had land in other towns.

(IV) Increase (2) Allen, son of Increase (1) Allen, was born about 1670, and resided upon the paternal homestead in Dartmouth.

(V) Jedediah Allen, son of Increase (2) Allen, resided in Dartmouth, and was married at the Dartmouth monthly meeting, June 2, 1721, to Penelope, daughter of Othniel Tripp, of Newport. She married (second) Barnabas Howland.

(VI) Othniel Allen, son of Jedediah and Penelope (Tripp) Allen, settled before 1760 in the Quaker settlement at Nine Partners, Dutchess county, New York. He was married, February 10, 1758, at the Dartmouth monthly meeting, to Keziah Stafford. The following children are recorded in the Quaker records of Nine Partners: Ruth, born 2nd month, 5th day, 1760, Jedediah, 3rd month, 5th day, 1762, Sion, mentioned below, George, 8th month, 8th day, 1767, Othniel, 3rd month, 22nd day, 1770, Susanna, 9th month, 6th day, 1773.

(VII) Sion Allen, second son of Othniel and Keziah (Stafford) Allen, was born 7th month, 30th day, 1765, at Nine Partners, and was married in Tiverton, April 10, 1791, by Philip Gray, justice of

the peace, to Elizabeth Dresser, daughter of Amos Dresser, of Freetown. They resided in Tiverton, Rhode Island, where the following children are recorded: Abraham, born January 7, 1793, Susannah, October 27, 1794, George, May 20, 1797, William, December 9, 1799, Harriet, September 26, 1807, Mary, mentioned below, Keziah, January 11, 1813, Sion S., August 21, 1816.

(VIII) Mary Allen, second daughter of Sion and Elizabeth (Dresser) Allen, was born May 11, 1810, in Tiverton, and became the wife of Wilson Osborne, of that town (see Osborne III).

WINSLOW, Samuel Ellsworth,
Manufacturer, Public Official

William Winslow, or Wyncelow, first of the line, as traced in England, had children 1 John, of London, afterward of Wyncelow Hall, was living in 1387-88, married Mary Crouchman, died in 1409-10, styled of Crouchman Hall 2 William, mentioned below.

(II) William (2) Winslow, son of William (1) Winslow, had a son Thomas, mentioned below.

(III) Thomas Winslow, son of William (2) Winslow, was of Burton, County Oxford, having lands also in County Essex. He was living in 1452. He married Cecelia Tansley, one of two daughters and heiress of an old family. She was called Lady Agnes. He had a son William, mentioned below.

(IV) William (3) Winslow, son of Thomas Winslow, was living in 1529. Children: Kenelm, mentioned below, Richard, had a grant from Edward VI of the rectory of Elksley, County Nottingham.

(V) Kenelm Winslow, son of William (3) Winslow, purchased in 1559 of Sir Richard Newport an estate called Newport Place in Kempsey, Worcestershire. He had also an older and very extensive estate in the same parish, called Clerkenleap, sold by his grandson, Richard Winslow, in 1650 He died in 1607 in the parish of St Andrew He married Catherine ———— His will, dated April 14, 1607, and proved November 9 following, is still preserved at Worcester His only son, Edward, is mentioned below

(VI) Edward Winslow, son of Kenelm Winslow, was born October 17, 1560, in the parish of St Andrew, Worcestershire, England, and he died before 1631 He lived in Kempsey and Droitwich, Worcestershire He married (first) Eleanor Pelham, of Droitwich; (second) at St Bride's Church, London, November 4, 1594, Magdalene Oliver, the records of whose family are found in the parish register of St Peter's, Droitwich Children 1 Richard, born about 1585 2 Edward, born October 18, 1595, at Droitwich, governor of Plymouth colony, married (first) at Leyden, Holland, May 16, 1618, Elizabeth Barker; (second) May 12, 1621, Susan (Fuller) White, who came in the "Mayflower" with Governor Winslow; she was widow of William White and mother of Peregrine White, the first born of the Plymouth colony 3 John, born April 16, 1597, died 1674, in Boston; married, October 12, 1624, Mary Chilton, daughter of James and Susanna Chilton, who also came in the "Mayflower." 4 Eleanor, born April 22, 1598, at Droitwich, remained in England 5 Kenelm, mentioned below 6 Gilbert, born October 26, 1600, came in the "Mayflower," signed the compact, returned to England after 1623, and died there 7 Elizabeth, born March 8, 1602, buried January 20, 1604, at St Peter's Church 8 Magdalen, born December 26, 1604, at Droitwich, remained in England 9 Josiah, born February 11, 1606

(VII) Kenelm (2) Winslow, son of Edward Winslow, was born at Droitwich, April 29, 1599, baptized at St Peter's Church, May 3, 1599, died at Salem, Massachusetts, September 13, 1672 He was the immigrant ancestor He came, first to Plymouth in 1629 with his brother Josiah and was admitted a freeman, January 1, 1632-33 He was surveyor of the town of Plymouth in 1640, and was fined five shillings in that year for neglecting to do his part on the highways. He re moved to Marshfield about 1641, having previously received a grant of land there at Green's Harbor, March 5, 1637-38 This grant, originally made to Josiah Winslow, his brother, was shared with Love Brewster The home of Kenelm Winslow was "on a gentle eminence by the sea between Green Harbor and South River This tract of the township was considered the Eden of the region. It was beautified with groves of majestic oaks and graceful walnuts with the underground void of shrubbery A few of these groves were standing within the memory of persons now living (1854) but all have fallen beneath the hand of the woodman." The homestead was left to his son Nathaniel. Other lands were granted to Kenelm Winslow, as from time to time the com mon land was divided He was one of the twenty-six original proprietors of Assonet, now Freetown, Massachusetts purchased of the Indians, April 2, 1659 and received the twenty-fourth lot, a por tion of which was lately owned by a lineal descendant, having remained in the family. Kenelm Winslow was a joiner by trade as well as planter He filled various town offices, was deputy to the General Court from 1642 to 1644 and from 1649 to 1653, eight years in all The court records show that he was somewhat litigious He died at Salem, whither he had gone on business, apparently after a long illness, for his will was dated five weeks earlier, August 8, 1672, and in it he describes himself as "being very sick and drawing nigh unto death." He may have been visiting a niece, Mrs Elizabeth Corwin, daughter of Edward Winslow.

He married, in June, 1634, Eleanor Adams, widow of John Adams, of Plymouth. She survived him and died at Marshfield, where she was buried, December 5, 1681, aged eighty-three years. Children. Kenelm, mentioned below; Eleanor or Ellen, born about 1637; Nathaniel, born about 1639; Job, about 1641.

(VIII) Colonel Kenelm (3) Winslow, son of Kenelm (2) Winslow, was born about 1636, at Plymouth, died November 11, 1715, at Harwich, in his seventy-ninth year, according to his gravestone. He removed to Cape Cod and settled at Yarmouth, afterward Harwich and New Brewster, Massachusetts. His homestead was on the border in the west part of the town in the village called later West Brewster, Satucket or Winslow's Mills. He was mentioned in the Yarmouth records in 1668. Harwich was the "con-stablerick" of Yarmouth. In records he was called "Colonel Winslow, planter or yeoman." He bought large tracts of wild land in what is now Rochester, Massachusetts, and several of his children settled in that town. The water privilege there remains to the present day in possession of his descendants. In 1699 he deeded it to his son, Kenelm, and in 1873 it was owned by William T. Winslow, of West Brewster. Kenelm Winslow bought of George Denison, of Stonington, Connecticut, a thousand acres of land in Windham, later Mansfield, March 11, 1700, for thirty pounds. He gave land, October 7, 1700, to his son Samuel, who sold it to his brother Kenelm, but neither of them lived in Windham. He was fined ten shillings, October 3, 1652, for "riding

a journey on the Lord's Day," yet he rode sixty miles to Scituate on three occasions to have a child baptized in the Second Church there, Kenelm in 1668, Josiah in 1670, and Thomas in 1672. He was prominent in the church and, October 4, 1714, served on the important committee to seat the meeting house.

He married (first) September 23, 1667, Mercy Worden, born 1641, died September 22, 1688, daughter of Peter, Jr, and Mercy Worden, of Yarmouth. Her gravestone is in the Winslow graveyard at Dennis. It is of slate, the oldest stone in this old burying ground, which is located near the road leading from Nebscusset to Satucket, near the Brewster line. He married (second) Damaris ——, who was living as late as March 27, 1729. His will was dated January 10, 1712, proved December 28, 1715. Children: By first wife. Kenelm, baptized August 9, 1668, Josiah, mentioned below; Thomas, baptized March 3, 1672-73; Samuel, born about 1674, Mercy, about 1676, Nathaniel, born 1679, Edward, January 30, 1680-81. By second wife. Damaris, married, July 30, 1713, Jonathan Small; Elizabeth, married, August 9, 1711, Andrew Clark, Eleanor, married, March 25, 1719, Shubael Hamblen; John, born about 1701.

(IX) Captain Josiah Winslow, son of Colonel Kenelm (3) Winslow, was born in Marshfield, November 7, 1669, died at Freetown, Massachusetts, April 3, 1761, and was buried in the South Cemetery at Berkley. He received a quarter of his father's lands by deed of gift, February 27, 1693, and bought more land of his father west of the Taunton river and in Freetown. He lived a mile from Assonet village on the road to Taunton. He was a clothier by trade and operated a fulling mill near the Assonet bridge, where at last accounts one of his Winslow descendants was still in the same line of business.

He was one of the proprietors of the forge at Freetown in 1704. In public affairs he was very active and prominent. He was constable in 1696, highway surveyor in 1699; moderator in 1702-08-12-16; assessor in 1702-03-05-07-10-13-22, selectman in 1702-03-04-09-10; treasurer in 1704, grand juror in 1721, first lieutenant of the Assonet company, commissioned its captain, February 9, 1725. He served on the committee on the new meeting house.

He married (first) (intentions dated June 13, 1695) at Freetown, Margaret Tisdale, of Taunton, born 1676, daughter of James and Mary (Avery) Tisdale, granddaughter of John Tisdale, who was slain by the Indians in King Philip's War, June 7, 1675. His wife died January 12, 1737, aged sixty-one years, and was buried in Berkley South Cemetery. He married (second) November 3, 1737, Hannah Winslow. He married (third) March 2, 1748-49, Hannah Booth, of Middleborough, a widow. He married (fourth) November 30, 1749, Martha Hathaway, of Freetown. He married (fifth) (intention dated September 6, 1750) Mary Jones, of Berkley. His will was dated March 5, 1753, and proved May 5, 1761. Children, born at Freetown: Josiah, born June 9, 1697, Mercy, December 19, 1700, Ebenezer, November 22, 1705, Edward, August 11, 1709, James, mentioned below, Margaret, March 24, 1720, Rachel, February 9, 1722.

(X) Colonel James Winslow, son of Captain Josiah Winslow, was born at Freetown, August 10, 1712, died March 1, 1777, and was buried at Berkley. He succeeded his father in the cloth-dressing business and lived at Freetown, where he erected the house lately occupied by Barnaby Winslow. He was sole executor of his father's will. He was also prominent in civil and military life, and filled the offices of justice of the peace, town

treasurer in 1755, selectman in 1762, lieutenant of the first foot company of militia in Freetown, commissioned June 4, 1762, captain of the Second Regiment of Bristol county, commissioned July 25, 1771. He was run over by an ox-sled on the hill a mile from Assonet and killed. His will was dated June 17, 1776, and proved March 22, 1777. He married, June 8, 1738, Charity Hodges, of Norton, Massachusetts, born March 30, 1716, daughter of Major Joseph and Bethia (Williams) Hodges. Children, born at Freetown: Mehitable, born April 22, 1739, Ephraim, July 7, 1741, Margaret, November 23, 1743, Joseph, March 8, 1745-46, James, September 2, 1748, Shadrach, mentioned below; Bethia, August 29, 1753, Thankful, October 30, 1754, Isaac, June 23, 1759.

(XI) Dr. Shadrach Winslow, son of Colonel James Winslow, was born December 17, 1750, at Freetown, died February 1, 1817, at Foxborough, Massachusetts, where he was buried. He was graduated from Yale College in 1771, and became an eminent physician and surgeon. During the Revolution, he helped to fit out a privateer, on which he sailed as surgeon. On the first voyage, the vessel was seized by the British, off the coast of Spain and he was kept a prisoner for a year in the old Jersey prison ship at Wallabout Bay, Brooklyn. His health was impaired by the confinement. On his return home he practiced his profession at Foxborough. "He was much respected as a physician and man." He practiced through a large circuit, extending fully twenty miles from his home, and was widely known and popular. His college diploma, dated September 11, 1771, has been preserved. He married, March 12, 1783, Elizabeth Robbins, who was born April 29, 1764, at Foxborough, died April 1, 1846, daughter of Eleazer and Mary (Savell) Robbins. Children, born at Foxborough Betsey Peck, born September 29, 1784, Eleazer Robbins, mentioned below, James, May 14, 1788, Isaac, February 21, 1791, Jesse, May 25, 1794, Samuel, August 15, 1797, Thomas Jefferson, June 6, 1800, drowned June 18, 1803, Mary, October 3, 1802, Fanny, March 6, 1805, Joseph, August 28 1807.

(XII) Fleazer Robbins Winslow, son of Dr Shadrach Winslow, was born at Foxborough, March 21, 1786, died August 8, 1863, at Newton Upper Falls, Massachusetts "He was engaged in various manufacturing enterprises and in this pursuit showed great and thorough knowledge He was always philosophical and the testimony of those associated with him was that he had few superiors in general intellectual powers On account of ill health, he lived for a time in the Catskill Mountains, at Hunter, Greene County, and Ramapo, Rockland County, New York, and spent his time in hunting bears and wolves, on which at that time the State paid a bounty During his absence his wife and children in their cabin feared the threatened attack of wild beasts and life proved particularly trying to a woman who had spent her early life in the city Mr Winslow was at one time selectman of Newton"

He married, at Boston, April 21, 1813, Ann Corbett, born there October 2, 1793, and educated there, a daughter of David and Deborah (Cowin) Corbett She died September 18, 1871, at Newton Upper Falls She was a woman of fine character and great piety, a friend of the clergy in that section and one of the first seventeen in the Methodist Episcopal class formed at Newton in 1826 Children Charles, born January 30, 1814, Ann, July 13, 1815, at Hunter, Elizabeth Robbins, October 24, 1816, died young, Clarissa Williams, March 13, 1818, David Corbett, at Hunter, June 9, 1819, father of Charles

Howard Winslow, a prominent New York lawyer, Emeline, November 4, 1820, Seth Collins, January 11, 1822, George, August 11, 1823, John, October 21, 1825, Samuel, mentioned below, Deborah Ann, August 8, 1828, Mary Pratt, April 14, 1830, Elizabeth Robbins, twin of Mary Pratt, Martha Switner, April 14, 1834, at Newton, Harriet F, July 25, 1836

(XIII) Hon Samuel Winslow, son of Fleazer Robbins Winslow, was born February 28, 1827, at Newton, died October 21, 1894, at Worcester He was educated in the public schools of his native town, and in his boyhood was employed in the manufacture of cotton machinery, becoming a foreman over fifty men when a boy of twenty He showed great natural ability and inventive genius He removed to Worcester, April 1, 1855, forming a partnership with Seth C Winslow, his brother, and established a machine shop in the old Merrifield building, Cypress street In 1857 the firm began to manufacture skates, establishing an industry that has continued with increasing success to the present time After the death of his brother, Samuel Winslow continued in business alone In 1886 the business was incorporated as The Samuel Winslow Skate Manufacturing Company, of which corporation Mr Winslow was president and treasurer to the end of his life After occupying the original location for twenty-seven years, the plant was removed to its present location at the corner of Mulberry and Asylum streets Mr Winslow took rank among the leading manufacturers of the city

He took a prominent part also in public affairs In 1848 he served on the prudential committee in charge of the schools in Newton Upper Falls, and was active in promoting the building of the railroad, becoming clerk of the Boston Woonsocket division of the New York & New England Railroad Company He was a member of the Worcester Common Council in 1865-66, and was representative to the General Court from Worcester in 1873 74 In 1885 he was in the Board of Aldermen From 1886 to 1889 he was mayor of Worcester He proved to be an able and popular executive, and he contributed materially to the progress and development of the municipality Not the least of his service to the community was the promotion and building of the first electric suburban railroads that have contributed so materially to the growth and wealth of the city He was president and principal stockholder of the Worcester, Leicester & Spencer Street Railway Company, of the Worcester & Millbury Company and of the State Central & Blackstone Valley Street Railway Company, and was active in building and operating these properties to the time of his death The controversy that followed the organization of the latter company undermined his health The State Central line, organized in January, 1893, built a road from Worcester to Marlborough, with branches to Grafton, Westborough and Hudson, and projected a line to Webster The road from Worcester to Spencer was built and an extension to Southbridge planned The Blackstone Valley Company was organized to build to Bramanville and Northbridge A bitter fight developed between Mr Winslow, aided by Burton W Potter and others on the one hand and by H H Bigelow and his associates on the other Mr Winslow spoke at meetings in all the towns where franchises were wanted and finally won, receiving the franchise in Grafton, the other towns falling into line afterward In building and operating the Spencer and Millbury lines, Mr Winslow was a pioneer in the electric railway business, dis-

playing wonderful executive and business ability He was successively trustee vice-president and president of the Mechanics' Association; director of the Citizens' National Bank, of which he was president from 1889 until he died I politics he was a Republican

The following editorial from th Worcester "Spy" was published at th time of his death

He married, November 1, 1848, at New ton Upper Falls, Mary Weeks Robbin born November 12, 1825, at Union, Maine daughter of David and Lydia A (Maxey Robbins Children 1 Frank Ellery, bor May 16, 1852, died June 12 1905 2 Sam uel Ellsworth, mentioned below

(XIV) Hon Samuel Ellsworth Wins low, junior son of Hon Samuel and Mar Weeks (Robbins) Winslow, was bor April 11, 1862, in Worcester, in whic town he has been a very active citize ever since attaining manhood He wa educated in the public schools, includin the high school, from which he graduate in 1880, as president of his class. H then attended Williston Seminary, o which he was class president, and gradu ated Bachelor of Arts from Harvard in the class of 1885 After several months of travel in Europe, he engaged in business in Worcester, in 1886, with his father, as secretary and clerk of The Samuel Winslow Skate Manufacturing Company After an experience in various departments of the business, he went on the road as a salesman, was also a buyer, traveling throughout the United States He is now president of the company, and active in many of the business enterprises of his home city, being a director of the United States Envelope Company, the State Mutual Life Insurance Company of Worcester, and the Mechanics' National Bank For twenty-two years he has been associated with the Worcester City Hospital, of which he has been twenty-one years a trustee, and is now president of the board He is also a member of the executive committee of the Leicester (Massachusetts) Academy, trustee of Worcester Academy, is a member of the Worcester County Musical Association, and vice-president of the Worcester Agricultural Society In religion a Unitarian, in politics a Republican, Mr Winslow has been very active in public concerns, especially in connection with his party He was an aide-de-camp on the staff of Governor J Q A Brackett, with the rank of colonel in 1890, was chairman of the Republican City Committee of Worcester from 1890 to 1892, and of the State Committee from 1893 to 1894 In 1908 he was a delegate to the National Republican Convention at Chicago, and served as a member of the Sixty-third and Sixty-fourth Congresses, representing the Fourth Massachusetts District He is associated with several clubs, including the Worcester Commonwealth, Automobile, Tatnack Country, Worcester Country, Quinsigamond Boat Club, the Harvard clubs of Boston, Worcester, New York and Washington, the Metropolitan,

Chevy Chase and National Press clubs of Washington, the Worcester Grange and many organizations for social purposes

Mr Winslow married, April 17, 1889, Bertha Lucenia Russell, daughter of Colonel Edward J Russell, and his wife, Lucenia (Prouty) Russell, of Worcester (see Russell VIII) Children 1 Dorothy, married William H Sawyer, Jr 2 Russell, unmarried 3 Samuel, 2nd, died at the age of ten months 4. Samuel E , Jr , now a member of the class of 1918 at Harvard University 5 John, now a student at Worcester Academy, class of 1917 6 Kenelm

(The Russell Line)

(I) John Russell, born about 1597, in England, came in the ship "Defiance" to America, and settled at Cambridge, Massachusetts, October 3, 1635, with his sons, John and Philip He was made a freeman, March 3, 1636, surveyor of farms, 1638, selectman, 1642-43, clerk of writs, 1645, and constable, 1648 With his son he removed to Wethersfield, Connecticut, in 1649, and was a freeman of that town, May 17, 1655 As early as 1660 he was in Hadley, Massachusetts, and was made freeman there, March 26, 1661, and became in the same year clerk of writs for that town. He received grants of land there, and died May 8, 1680 The name of his first wife is unknown, and he married (second) in Wethersfield, Dorothy, widow of Rev Henry Smith, first pastor of the church at Wethersfield His elder son, John Russell, became second pastor of the same church

(II) Philip Russell, son of John Russell, born in England, settled in what is now Hatfield, and, like his father, was a glazier by trade He filled various public offices, and died May 19, 1693 The inventory of his estate amounted to 259 pounds, 6 shillings and 1 pence. He married (first) February 4, 1664, Johanna

349

Smith, daughter of his stepmother He married (second) January 10, 1666, Elizabeth Perry, of Windsor, Connecticut She was killed by Indians, December 19, 1677, and he married (third) December 25, 1679, Mary Church, born 1656, daughter of Edward and Mary Church, of Norwalk, Connecticut, and Hatfield, Massachusetts There was one child of the first marriage, which was buried at the same time as its mother. Children of second marriage: John, born January 2, 1667, Samuel, 1669, Philip, January 24, 1672, died young, Stephen, October 12, 1674 Children of third marriage Samuel, December 30, 1680, Thomas, February 12, 1683, Mary, February 10, 1685, Mary, May 21, 1686, Philip, January 2, 1689, Daniel, mentioned below

(III) Daniel Russell, youngest child of Philip and Mary (Church) Russell, was born October 8, 1691, in Hadley, and was among the first settlers in the town of Sunderland, Massachusetts, where he died June 28, 1737 He married, January 18, 1713, Jerusha Dickinson, born March 20, 1693, daughter of John and Sarah Dickinson, of Hatfield She married (second) October 25, 1744, Simon Cooley Children Jonathan, mentioned below, Mary, born November 1, 1716, Daniel, April 12, 1719, Jerusha, married Ebenezer Clark, of Northampton, Sarah, July 7 1723

(IV) Jonathan Russell, eldest child of Daniel and Jerusha (Dickinson) Russell, born August 2, 1714, lived on the paternal homestead in Sunderland, and died there April 8, 1777. He married, November 10, 1743, Mary Smith, born February 10, 1724, daughter of Nathaniel and Abigail (Allis) Smith, died February 28, 1816 Children Daniel, mentioned below, Jonathan, born April 28, 1746, Martha, July 21, 1748, Mary, April 1, 1750, Philip, March 18, 1752, Israel, baptized June 9, 1754, Sam-

uel, born October 17, 1756, John, April 7, 1759, Spencer, November 21, 1761, Persis, March 3, 1765

(V) Daniel (2) Russell, eldest child of Jonathan and Mary (Smith) Russell, born September 10, 1744, settled in the northern part of Hadley, where he died September 30, 1828 He married, February 6, 1771, his cousin, Lucy Clark, born October 24, 1750, daughter of Jedediah and Sarah (Russell) Clark, died October 2, 1840. Children Daniel, mentioned below, Chester, baptized October 7, 1773, Moses, October 8, 1775; Sarah, July 27, 1777, Elisha, November 28, 1779, Polly, born 1783

(VI) Daniel (3) Russell, eldest child of Daniel (2) and Lucy (Clark) Russell, born in North Hadley, was baptized January 12, 1772, and died August 2, 1847 He was a farmer in his native town, a deacon of the Congregational church of North Amherst, and a Whig in politics He married, May 19, 1798, Sarah, daughter of Francis Newton, born 1769, died October 4, 1844 They were the parents of eight children

(VII) Charles Russell, son of Daniel (3) and Sarah (Newton) Russell, was born 1799, in North Hadley, and was a farmer, carpenter and contractor, a Congregationalist, a Whig in politics, a member of the militia in the War of 1812, but saw no active service He married Cordelia Smith, born 1800, in Hadley, and had children. Charles, Francis, Julia M., George, Eliza, Harriet, Edward Julius, Julius Henry

(VIII) Colonel Edward Julius Russell, son of Charles and Cordelia (Smith) Russell, was born October 23, 1833, in North Hadley, Massachusetts, and there passed his boyhood, beginning his education in the "little old red schoolhouse." After attending Deerfield Academy two terms, he set out to make his own way in the world, at the age of eighteen years, having the permission of his parents and promising to care for himself For some two years he worked as a carpenter in Sunderland, Massachusetts, and for a similar period in Northampton, same State After working a few months in Worcester, he went to North Brookfield, Massachusetts, where he was employed two years He was then appointed manager of a department of the Batchelor Shoe Manufacturing Company, in North Brookfield, and while in this employ volunteered as a soldier of the Civil War In May, 1861, he enlisted in what was afterward called Company F, Tenth Massachusetts Volunteers, mustered into service, July 12, 1861 At this time Mr Russell was made second sergeant, and on March 1, 1862, was promoted first sergeant He was commissioned second lieutenant, July 23, 1862, and was made first lieutenant, September 13, same year, following the battle of Antietam On December 21, following, after the battle of Fredericksburg, he was commissioned captain He participated in all the battles of the Army of the Potomac, except that at Gettysburg, during which time he was in hospital suffering from a sunstroke He was very fortunate in escaping any injuries through his long military career On May 11, 1864, Captain Russell was commissioned by Governor Andrews to raise a company as a nucleus of a regiment of heavy artillery, which was filled two weeks later Before the close of the month he had been elected second lieutenant, first lieutenant and senior first lieutenant, and was soon after promoted and made captain of Company K, Third Massachusetts Heavy Artillery In May, 1865, he was commandant of Fort Stevens, District of Columbia, and during the summer of that year was judge advocate of court-martial. He was mustered out

of the service, October 1, 1865 Returning to the arts of peace he was engaged in business for a short period as a manufacturer of wallets He has been much in the civil service since the war From 1867 to 1886 he was justice of the peace, for two years, beginning 1866, was State constable, and was deputy sheriff for eleven years, beginning 1871 For nearly two years he was master of the House of Correction of Worcester county, and on July 1, 1886, he was appointed by Governor Robinson as warden of the State Prison at Charlestown, Massachusetts After five years he resigned this position, and six months afterward was appointed probation officer at the Worcester Central District Court This position he resigned at the age of seventy-five years, after seventeen years' continuous service. In 1884 he was appointed colonel and aide-de-camp on the staff of Governor George D Robinson, and served in that capacity three years For five years, beginning 1896, Colonel Russell was a trustee of the Worcester Public Library For nine years, by appointment of the Superior Court of Massachusetts, he served as bail commissioner, and for six years was agent of the Society for the Prevention of Cruelty to Children He represented the town of North Brookfield in the State Assembly in 1863, was a member of the Common Council of Worcester in 1895, and of the Board of Aldermen of that city in 1898 For a period of five years he was connected with the Cooperative Bank of Worcester, as director and vice-president, and resigned on account of his long absences during the winter season in Florida For many years he was a member of the Masonic fraternity, affiliating with several of its branches, and was a member of Post No 10, Grand Army of the Republic, of Worcester, and the Massachusetts Commandery of the

Loyal Legion He was a member of the Commonwealth Club of Worcester three years, and while warden of the State Prison was associated with the Boston Art Club While not a member of any church organization, he was a faithful supporter of all moral and religious influences He married at North Brookfield, January 8, 1856, Lucenia Prouty, a native of North Spencer, Massachusetts, daughter of a farmer of that town. She was formerly a member of the Salem Street Congregational Church of Worcester, and later affiliated with the old South Church of that city Children Charles Arthur, died at the age of nine months Bertha Lucenia, mentioned below Colonel Edward J Russell died December 16, 1915, in Worcester

(IX) Bertha Lucenia Russell, only daughter of Colonel Edward Julius and Lucenia (Prouty) Russell, was born September 26, 1867, in North Brookfield, and became the wife of Samuel E Winslow, of Worcester (see Winslow XIV)

UPHAM, Roger Freeman,
Active Man of Affairs

John Upham, the pioneer, was born in England, probably in Somersetshire, and came to America with Rev Joseph Hull in 1635, with wife Elizabeth, aged thirty-two years, Sarah Upham, aged twenty-six, and his children, John, Jr, aged seven; Nathaniel, five, Elizabeth, three He located at Weymouth and was admitted a freeman of the colony, September 2, 1635 In 1636 he drew land there, and from time to time shared in divisions of the common land He was one of a committee of six who acquired the Indian titles of Weymouth land for the settlers He was appointed commissioner (magistrate) to end small causes, was selectman in 1645, 1646 and 1647, and deputy

to the General Court About 1648 he removed to Malden, and was selectman of that town, 1651-53, and also commissioner there He married, in August, 1671, Katherine, widow of Angell Holland He was moderator of town meetings in Malden, 1678-80, deacon of the church twenty-four years He and his son were interested in the settlement of Worcester just before King Philip's War He died February 25, 1681, aged eighty-four years. Children Nathaniel, born May 23, 1629-30, in England, Elizabeth, 1632, Phineas, mentioned below, Mary Priscilla

(II) Lieutenant Phineas Upham, son of John Upham, was born in 1635 in Weymouth, or during the voyage hither, married, April 14 1658, Ruth Wood In 1663 he bought land in Malden and settled there. He drew a lot of fifty acres in Worcester, July 8, 1673, but King Philip's War interrupted the settlement of that town He was a lieutenant of the Malden company and took part in the Great Swamp Fight in King Philip's War, where he was mortally wounded He was taken to Wickford, Rhode Island and later to his home, where he died in October, 1676 The General Court made a special appropriation to pay the cost of his long illness and to aid the widow and seven young children His widow died January 18, 1696-97, aged sixty years Children Phineas, born May 22, 1659 Nathaniel, mentioned below, Ruth, 1664; John, December 9, 1666, Elizabeth Thomas 1668, Richard, 1675

(III) Nathaniel Upham, son of Lieutenant Phineas Upham, was born in Malden in 1661, died November 11, 1717, married Sarah Floyd, who died October 14 1715, aged fifty-three years. He had the rank of sergeant in the Malden company His gravestone is standing Children Nathaniel, born 1685-86, Sarah, 1688-89, Ruth, 1691, Dorothy, Noah,

mentioned below, Joanna, 1699, Lois, 1701, Eunice, 1707

(IV) Noah Upham, son of Nathaniel Upham, was born in Malden in 1694, married Lydia Jenkins, widow of Joseph Lewis, of Swansea. She died October 14, 1762. He lived at Malden until thirty-three years of age, when he settled at Pomfret, Connecticut, buying a farm of one hundred and three acres of Joseph Sessions for five hundred pounds. He died February 8, 1766. Children: Noah, mentioned below, Benjamin, born April 10, 1723, Lydia, January 3, 1725, Mary, October 22, 1730, at Pomfret.

(V) Noah (2) Upham, son of Noah (1) Upham, was born at Malden in 1720, died September 16, 1750. His widow Hannah was appointed administratrix and his father guardian of his children. Children: Joseph, born March 30, 1748, Roger, mentioned below.

(VI) Roger Upham, son of Noah (2) Upham, was born at Mansfield or Pomfret, Connecticut December 18, 1749, married (first) March 26, 1771, Rebecca Freeman, born June 14, 1749, daughter of Prince Freeman. He married (second) Widow (Newell) Solace. He removed to Hanover, New Hampshire thence to Monson, Massachusetts, and in 1808, to Marathon, New York. He died at Cincinnatus, New York, February 17, 1817. Children: John, born November 22, 1772, Roger Freeman, mentioned below, Clarissa, March 18, 1785, Newell Noah, August 5, 1793.

(VII) Roger Freeman Upham, son of Roger Upham, was born in Mansfield, Connecticut, January 3, 1777, married November 25, 1802, Anna Howard, who was born at Ashfield, Connecticut, December 27, 1779, died at Belchertown, Massachusetts, in 1812. He died in Belchertown, March 14, 1858. Children: Howard, born December 17, 1803, mar-

ried Cynthia Freeman Childs, Freeman, mentioned below; Lucius, born July 7, 1807, Amos, born August 2, 1809, married Eloisa Leonard, and lived at Castile, New York; Anna, born February 25, 1811, died at Enfield, Massachusetts, unmarried, Newell, born September 6, 1812, married twice, Whitman, born December 6, 1814, died January 22, 1825, Lathrop, born January 1, 1816, married Calista Livermore, Hannah, born December 17, 1817, married, September 24, 1840, Abijah Childs, Porter, born October 1, 1820, died April 17, 1872, unmarried, Martha, born November 18, 1822, married George L Washburn, of Castile, Emily, born August 25, 1825, married, April 7, 1847, Gilbert McKenny, died January 8, 1883

(VIII) Freeman Upham, son of Roger Freeman Upham, was born at Mansfield April 1, 1805, died February 1, 1876. He settled in Worcester after his marriage and was a prominent contractor and builder. He married Elizabeth Livermore, born June 18, 1809 daughter of David Livermore, of Spencer, Massachusetts. They had one child, Roger Freeman, mentioned below.

(IX) Roger Freeman Upham, son of Freeman Upham, was born at Worcester, Massachusetts, September 13, 1848, died April 10, 1917. Through his mother, Mr Upham was descended from Oliver Watson, a soldier of the Revolution. She was a descendant also of John Livermore, a pioneer of Watertown Massachusetts, 1638, and his son, John Livermore, a lieutenant in King Philip's War, and David Livermore, a soldier in the Revolution from Spencer. Mr Upham attended the public schools at Worcester, Massachusetts, and was salutatorian of the class of 1866 in the Worcester High School. Immediately after graduation he entered the employ of the People's Fire Insurance Company, of Worcester, as entry clerk, and was soon promoted to the position of bookkeeper. A few years later he became assistant secretary, a position he held to the time of the great fire in Boston in 1872, when the company was ruined, and directly after he entered the service of the Worcester Mutual Fire Insurance Company, of which he was assistant secretary for ten years and secretary for thirty-five years, also treasurer for a period of nearly as great length. It is the oldest mutual fire insurance company in the State. It was incorporated by act of the Legislature, February 11, 1823. The incorporators were Aaron Tufts, Nathaniel Jones, Salem Town, Sr., John Shepley, Jonas Sibley, Rufus Bullock, James Humphreys, Dexter Fay, Gideon Delano, Calvin Ammidown, Abraham Lincoln, Charles Parkman, Jacob Fisher, Bezaleel Taft, Jr., Levi Lincoln, Benjamin Adams, Stephen P Gardner, John Hobart, leading men of various towns in the county. Levi Lincoln, who resigned during the first year to become Governor of the Commonwealth, was its first president. He was succeeded by Rejoice Newton. The subsequent presidents have been Frederick William Paine, Anthony Chase, Ebenezer Torrey, John A Fayerweather, Hon Lewis N Gilbert, and Roger F Upham. At the time of his death, Mr. Upham was president and treasurer; Harry Harrison, secretary. The directors in 1917 were Hon Lewis N. Gilbert, of Ware, Arthur F Whitin, of Whitinsville, Roger F Upham; George I Alden, of Worcester, C L. S Hammond, of Clinton, Edmund Mortimer, of Grafton, Lyman A. Ely, deceased, and Harry Harrison, of Worcester The company does a general fire insurance business, having its headquarters in its own building, No 377 Main street, Worcester It has been well man-

aged throughout its long history and has enjoyed a substantial prosperity and growth Mr. Upham was one of the veterans in the fire insurance business of the city and State, and was widely known and highly respected He was president of the Massachusetts Mutual Fire Insurance Union, an organization composed of the managers of the various fire insurance companies of the State, and president of the Worcester Protective Department He was a trustee and vice-president of the Worcester Five Cents Savings Bank, trustee of the Rural Cemetery Corporation, and secretary of the Home for Aged Men In religion he was a Baptist, a deacon at the time of his death, served as vice-chairman of the board of deacons for many years, resigning from the chairmanship four years prior to his death, and also served for forty years as teacher in the Men's Bible Class In politics he was a staunch Republican

Mr. Upham married, June 16, 1873, Clara C Story, born April 2, 1850, daughter of Simeon N Story (see Story VII) They had born to them one daughter, Edith Story, a native of Worcester, educated in the public schools of Worcester, a graduate of Worcester Classical High School, 1901, and entered Wellesley College, class of 1906.

The following is a tribute to the memory of Roger F. Upham, late president and treasurer of the Worcester Mutual Fire Insurance Company.

The death of our President and Treasurer, Roger F Upham, which occurred April 10, 1917, calls for an exceptional testimonial to the faithful and efficient service which he rendered to this company. Entering its service in 1872, as Assistant Secretary, he was elected Secretary in 1880 and elected Treasurer in 1887, serving as Secretary and Treasurer until January, 1914, when he was elected President and Treasurer, which offices he held at the time of his death In 1883, he was elected a Director. He was con-

nected with the Company as an Officer for 45 years and as a Director for 34 years In 1894, he was elected President of the Massachusetts Mutual Fire Insurance Union, and served for three years. He was at the time of his death President of the Worcester Protective Department which maintains the Fire Patrol, and was also identified with banking and charitable institutions. His one great desire was to give his very best to the Company, and he was always loyally devoted to its interests, and under his able leadership the company prospered Certainly no man has been more prominently identified with the interests of Mutual Fire Insurance in this State, or wielded a more powerful influence for good underwriting than he He was recognized as a National figure in his chosen field. His death means a great loss to the community in which he lived His genial, kindly nature and his uniform cordiality will not be forgotten by any who knew him We sincerely mourn his loss and honor the memory of his splendid character We extend to the family our sincere sympathy and desire to spread this testimonial upon the records of the Company
WORCESTER MUTUAL FIRE INSURANCE COMPANY
Worcester, Mass.,
May 9 1917

The following is an appreciation of the character of Roger F Upham, presented to board of directors of the Home for Aged Men April 13, 1917:

The death of Roger F Upham on April 10, removes from this Board one who has served it long and well For more than twenty-four years he held the office of secretary His heart was in his work, and no one could have been more faithful in the performance of his duties or more helpful to this institution It is a sad commentary that he should pass away just at the time that the dream of his life is to be realized by the erection of a new home He met the problems of life with courtesy and kindness, combined with an earnestness and energy that was a constant inspiration to his associates He was a man of the highest ideals, of modest and unassuming manner, always a true and loyal friend and citizen, who won the respect of every one with whom he came in contact He has left a void that it will be hard to fill, but he has left a record of a stainless character and an unselfish service which will long continue as an example

to his fellowmen We deeply mourn his loss and if words fail to adequately express our appreciation of his worth, feelings of esteem and affection for him are imprinted in our hearts and cannot be effaced. Our sincerest sympathy is extended to the members of his family in their even greater bereavement

The following is an appreciation from the church of which he was a member and deacon for so many years

Gone to his reward, one of God's select men. Roger Freeman Upham Throughout the years of a long life, he was obedient to his Lord, and so was he to the very end, answering His summons to the mansions on high on the 10th of April, 1917 He leaves behind to mourn his departure a devoted wife and daughter, together with a great host of friends within and without the church In the world of business he had a large acquaintanceship which strangely enough (save to those who knew him well) constituted itself a body of admiration. Throughout New England Mr Upham was known as "The Dean of Fire Insurance Underwriters " To the men of his line of business, his word was all but law because they loved and honored him But it was within the church that he had made his most profound impression upon men Equally with his home and his business he loved his church, and into the Kingdom represented thereby he poured much of the richest of his life For more than thirty years he has been the teacher of a Bible class for men, and in the church proper had from a youth been honored with official position. In his going, therefore, the First Baptist Church has sustained a very great loss; the Kingdom on earth, a valiant soul

Soldier, well done! The cause of right
    Will ever owe thee debt
Well earned thy rest! For us alone
    Is sorrow and regret.

                (Signed)   RAY W GREENE
                           W R McNUTT,
                                    Committee.
        (The Story Line)

(I) William Story, the immigrant ancestor, was born in England in 1614, of an ancient English family. He was a carpenter by trade, and when he passed the

355

examination for permission to go to New England, April 8, 1637, he was in the employ of Samuel Dix, a carpenter and joiner, from Norwich, England. William Story settled in Ipswich, Massachusetts, of which he was a proprietor as early as 1642. Andrew Story, a relative probably, and also of Ipswich, served in the Pequot War, and had a grant of land there in 1639. William Story was a commoner, subscribed to the Major Denison fund in 1648, was a voter in Ipswich in 1679, when he was called "Sr." In 1664 he owned a share and a half in Plum Island. He sold land in Ipswich, February 12, 1643, and bought land of William Symonds, February 12, 1655, and of John West. He was surveyor of highways in 1662. He owned land in the Chebacco district in 1652. He was given permission to set up a mill there on the Chebacco river in 1671. He signed the loyalist petition in 1668 and also the Proctor petition. His wife Sarah deposed in 1668 that she was forty years old. Children: William, Mary, Samuel, mentioned below; Hannah, born August 19, 1662; Seth, born 1664, soldier in King Philip's War.

(II) Samuel Story, son of William Story, was born about 1660 in Ipswich. About 1722 he removed to Norwich, Connecticut, where he died in 1726, leaving five sons, as shown by the probate records, and a son Ephraim, then deceased. Children by wife Elizabeth, born at Ipswich: Ann, born March 31, 1691; Ephraim, October 22, 1692; John, mentioned below; Solomon, March 13, 1696; Stephen, October 7, 1697; Elizabeth, married —— Nidden; Mary, married —— Andrews; Dorothy, married —— Day; Hannah, married —— Knowlton; Margaret, married —— Choate; Samuel.

(III) John Story, son of Samuel Story, was born at Ipswich, June 19, 1694, and went to Norwich with his father. In 1737

he and his brother Samuel were among the largest taxpayers of Norwich. Children, born at Norwich, except the two eldest, by wife Sarah: John, born at Ipswich, November 22, 1717; Sarah, June 2, 1722, at Ipswich; Henry, August 31, 1724; Ephraim, November 9, 1726; William, December 22, 1728; James, July 16, 1730; Mary, February 4, 1732-33; Solomon, March 26, 1737.

(IV) The Story family was numerous in the vicinity of Norwich. In 1790 the following were heads of families in Norwich and vicinity: Ephraim (two of the name), Henry (two), James, William, Solomon, Mehitable, Jonathan and Ebenezer Story, some of whom are mentioned above and others were grandsons of John Story (III).

(VI) Isaac Story, great-grandson of John Story, was born July 16, 1780, in Norwich or in one of the towns adjacent, set off from that old town. His birth record has not been found there. He made his home in Norwich and followed the trade of sailmaker. He was an influential and prominent citizen, deacon of the Baptist church, and justice of the peace. He married, September 15, 1805, Lucy Roath, born July 11, 1784. The town record of his marriage reads: "Mr. Isaac Story and Miss Roath were married together at Norwich, September 15, 1805, by Rev. Walter King." Children, born at Norwich: Frances Rhoda, born January 1, 1807, died young; Harriet Miriam, January 17, 1809; Frances Rhoda, January 1, 1810; Isaac Hatch, January 3, 1812; Frances, April 4, 1813; Simeon Norman, mentioned below.

(VII) Simeon Norman Story, son of Isaac Story, was born in Norwich, January 24, 1817. He received his education in the public schools of his native town. At the age of fourteen he left home to learn his trade in Worcester in the store of P. & D. Goddard & Company, watch-makers and jewelers After an appren-ticeship of seven years, he started in busi-ness on his own account in partnership with Mr. Dunbar, one of his employers. In 1840 Mr. Story bought out his partner and from that time until 1895 continued with uniform success. Few merchants have been in business for so long a period He was highly respected in business cir-cles and widely known in this section. Thoroughly upright in all his dealings, his name was a household word in the county for three generations When he retired, he sold his stock, but for a time occupied himself at his home by repairing watches and doing other fine work. He died April 12, 1909, at his home in Wor-cester.

He was prominent throughout his life in religious circles Joining the First Baptist Church at the age of fourteen, soon after coming to Worcester, he was baptized by Elder Going in 1831 in the baptismal pool in the Worcester and Providence canal, then located at what is now the corner of Green and Temple streets. He served the church for a long series of years as its treasurer through early and difficult conditions, was deacon for nearly forty years, then made deacon *emeritus*; teacher of the Sunday school for nearly sixty years, and a staunch sup-porter of every interest vital to the wel-fare of the church. "An earnest Bible stu-dent, active in the mid-week and other meetings of the church, ready and prompt in bearing his share of committee work, he could always be relied upon to further the cause of the Redeemer's Kingdom Dr. Lemuel Call Barnes at the funeral service, held in the auditorium of our new church, spoke of the life of our senior deacon as illustrating the 'life abundant' which Jesus promised to his disciples, with its glorious 'crown of victory'"

From 1846 to the time of his death, Mr. Story was a trustee of the Five Cents Savings Bank and during most of that time vice-president. In early life he was a Whig in politics, afterward a Republi-can from the time the Republican party was founded.

He married Eunice Howe, daughter of Levi Howe, of an old Worcester fam-ily. She was born January 20, 1820, died October 8, 1877. Children: 1 Emma M., born June 10, 1839, died July 15, 1902. 2 Mary, born December 10, 1841, died February 12, 1842. 3 Charles, died in in-fancy. 4 Clara C., born April 2, 1850, married Roger F. Upham (see Upham)

CHACE, SLADE,
And Allied Families.

The Chace or Chase family is strictly speaking a Massachusetts-Rhode Island one, springing from the early Roxbury-Yarmouth family, later generations of whom settled in Swansea, Massachusetts, and in the adjoining towns of Rhode Island Both branches of this family have shared largely in the commercial and industrial life of this section of Mas-sachusetts and Rhode Island.

(I) William Chace, born about 1595, in England, with his wife Mary and son William came to America in the ship with Governor Winthrop and his colony in 1630, settling first in Roxbury. He soon became a member of the church of which Rev. John Eliot, the Apostle to the Indians, was pastor. On October 19 1630, he applied for freemanship, and was admitted a freeman, May 14 1634. In 1637 or thereabouts, he became one of the company who made a new settlement at Yarmouth, of which town he was made constable in 1639. He resided at Yar-mouth the remainder of his life, dying in May, 1659. His widow died the follow-

357

ing October Their children were William, mentioned below, Mary, born May,
1637, in Roxbury, and Mary (2), born in
1639, in Yarmouth

(II) William (2) Chace, son of William (1) and Mary Chace, born about
1622, in England, came to America with
his parents, married and was a resident
oi Yarmouth He died February 27, 1685.
His children were William, mentioned
below, Jacob, John, Elizabeth, Abraham,
Joseph, Benjamin and Samuel

(III) William (3) Chace, son of William (2) Chace, was born about 1645, and
married (first) Hannah Sherman, daughter of Philip and Sarah (Odding) Sherman the former of whom was the first
secretary of the Rhode Island Colony, and
one of its most influential settlers (see
Sherman I) William Chace married
(second) December 6, 1732, Priscilla
Perry His children, all born to the first
marriage, were William, Eber, mentioned below, Isaac, Nathaniel, Joseph
and Hezekiah The father's will was
proven August 16, 1737

(IV) Eber Chace, son of William (3)
and Hannah (Sherman) Chace, married
Mary Knowles, and their children were
Patience, who married Esek Luther,
Hannah, who married Stephen Brayton,
Daniel who married Mary Baker, William, who married Mercy Cole, Alice,
who married James Anthony, Mary, who
married Abraham Anthony, and Eber,
mentioned below

(V) Eber (2) Chace, son of Eber (1)
and Mary (Knowles) Chace, married
Sarah Baker, and their children were
Patience, who married Moses Buffinton,
Elizabeth, who married Robert Slade,
Peleg, who married Deborah Tripp,
Obadiah, mentioned below Eber, and
William, who married Sarah Buffinton

(VI) Obadiah Chace, son of Eber (2)
and Sarah (Baker) Chace, was born in

Swansea, Massachusetts, the 2d day of
the 5th month, 1752, and died the 28th
day of the 2d month, 1801, and is buried
in the Friends' Yard in Somerset, Massachusetts He married at the Friends
Meeting, Swansea, Massachusetts, the
15th day of the 12th month 1774, Eunice
Anthony, daughter of Job and Abigail
(Chace) Anthony, and their children
were Sarah, born 1775, Eber, 1778, Abigail, 1780, died in 1847, Anthony, mentioned below, Edmund, 1787, Nathan,
1790, and Lemuel, 1797 Obadiah Chace
the father, lived on Prudence Island, engaged in the produce business, and after
his death his widow continued the same
business with great success.

(VII) Anthony Chace, son of Obadiah
and Eunice (Anthony) Chace, was born
in Swansea, Massachusetts, the 30th day
of the 3d month, 1783, and died the 12th
day of the 3d month, 1861, and is buried
in the Friends' Yard at Somerset, Massachusetts He married in Swansea Friends'
Meeting, the 11th day of the 9th month,
1806, Isabel Buffinton, who was born in
Swansea, the 22d day of the 9th month
1786, and died the 4th day of the 3d
month, 1880, and is buried in the Friends'
Yard at Somerset, beside her husband.
She was the daughter of Benjamin and
Charity (Robinson) Buffinton (see Buffinton V) Anthony Chace and his fam
ily lived for a number of years on the
Gardner farm, near Tourisset, Rhode
Island, where he was successfully en-
gaged in agricultural pursuits His chil
dren were Eunice, born at Dighton
Massachusetts, in 1808, Maria, born at
Dighton, in 1811, and died in 1838, in
Warren, Rhode Island, Ruth Buffinton
born at Dighton, in 1814, Obadiah, men-
tioned below, Benjamin Anthony, born
in Warren, in 1820, and Abigail, born at
Warren, in 1824

(VIII) Rev Obadiah (2) Chace, son

358

of Anthony and Isabel (Buffinton) Chace, was born in Warren, Rhode Island, the 12th day of the 4th month, 1818. His educational training was acquired in the Warren district schools, and at the Friends School, in Providence, Rhode Island He was brought up a farmer and followed that occupation successfully until his retirement from that vocation at the age of sixty-six years At the age of thirty-four years he was approved a minister of the gospel, and served faithfully the Somerset Meeting in that capacity for more than half a century, without salary, and at the same time was a liberal contributor to the support of the church Beginning his work when the church was in a relatively low state of Christian life, he was instrumental, through persevering effort and liberal views, in greatly improving its condition, and during his ministry many were added to the membership Although very active as an agriculturist he was never too busy to attend the mid-week meetings, funerals and other religious occasions of the Friends Society Nothing was allowed to come between him and his religious duties Although living seven and a half miles from the meeting house, he would drive twice and when occasion required thrice and sometimes more times—a week to the place of worship. Nor was his work confined to the home meeting; he made two trips through the West one in 1856, and one in 1872, traveling as far as Kansas and visiting meetings and families of Friends He always preserved an active interest in the affairs of the New England Yearly Meeting, and he visited all the meetings within its limits His liberal views were widely known, and his advocacy of church extension was well known, for he would not exclude any from fellowship on account of minor differences of belief He was wont to quote the words

of William Penn 'The Word of God without me, and the Grace of God within me, is the foundation and declaration of my faith let him find a better who can." He was always young-hearted, and a friend of the young people, with whom he mingled in social gatherings, contributing to their enjoyment by an occasional poem or narrative During his career he wrote many poems for social and literary occasions, the greater number of which were brought together in a bound volume As a citizen, Rev Chace was always actively interested in the public welfare He taught school several winters at Warren Neck, and in other towns in this locality, was a member of the Warren Town Council in 1857 and for several years immediately following, and represented the town for two years in the General Assembly During the Dorr Rebellion, in 1842, he took the side of the party in power A watch was kept along the river that year, when two sailboats anchored in Mount Hope bay The crews, composed of six men, hurried to shore and thence to Massachusetts This aroused suspicion and several citizens, including Rev Chace, after detaching the rudders and sails, scuttled the boats at their anchorage The authorities approved the action The crews later returned, and said they came from Warwick to escape from the State and avoid military service, and were arrested and placed in Bristol jail In political faith, Rev Chace was first a Whig, then a Free Soiler and later from the date of the organization of that party, a Republican He worked persistently for good roads and good schools Desiring a school in his own neighborhood, he built a school house and hired the teacher himself He always interested himself in useful inventions and took great pleasure in the inventions of speedy transit like bicycles and automobiles When eighty-nine years of age he would ride in an automobile and never complain of too great speed whatever it might be

On April 28, 1845, Rev Chace was united in marriage to Esther Taber Freeborn, daughter of Jonathan (2) and Esther (Taber) Freeborn (see Freeborn VI), and their happy wedded life covered a period of over sixty years, their twenty-fifth, fiftieth and sixtieth anniversaries were appropriately celebrated, surrounded by their devoted children and grandchildren Mrs Chace, his constant companion in work and travel, passed away November 20, 1905, aged eighty-two years, and he never recovered from the loss then sustained In 1884, he had retired from active work, and removed to Swansea, Massachusetts After the death of his devoted wife, he became a member of the household of his son, Charles A Chace and there, after a gradual decline, passed away Sunday evening, May 19, 1907, in his ninetieth year Until a very few months before his demise he walked every morning to the railroad station in South Swansea to get his daily paper, and he also attended church quite regularly He kept exceptionally well posted on all current topics, and, with a remarkable memory, recalled historical facts and statistics with wonderful accuracy He was a member of the American Peace Society, and kept fully abreast of the progress of peace and arbitration movements in all parts of the world But, alive as he was to the movements of men, he seemed resigned as he neared the close of life, and, indeed, desired the time when he should be called hence Like the Apostle Paul he could say· "These hands have ministered unto my necessities and I have not been chargeable to any of you," and also that he had "fought a good fight, had finished his course, and had kept the

faith." To the Rev Obadiah and Esther Taber (Freeborn) Chace were born four children, as follows Charles Anthony, mentioned below, Emma Rogers, born May 22, 1853, who married Edgar W Chace, and died January 6, 1906, Walter Freeborn, mentioned below, and George Mahlon, mentioned below.

In 1898, Rev. Chace published a book of poems dedicated as follows

To Augustine Jones, Principal of Friends' School, Providence, R I, where I first learned to frame words in metre, I dedicate this Book.

In the preface he says.

The first that I remember of any serious thought of rhyming was when I was about seventeen years of age A phrenologist examined my head, and said in a very slighting kind of way, "I guess he can't write poetry much" I was rather skeptical in regard to the new science, and so I thought I would try to prove whether it were true The following is the result of my first effort.

The titles of poems in this little volume are "The Seasons," "The Slave's Lament," "Ocean," "Slavery." "Composition,' "Lines Written in an Album," "To My Cousin," "Snow Storm," "A Large Rain," "Dedication of Farmer's Hall," "Lines Found in an Old Note Book," "Welcome," 'Written for the Women's Foreign Missionary Society," "Birthday Party," "Re-Dedication of a Church Built in 1743," "Lines Written for the Ninetieth Birthday of Deacon Peck, of Rehoboth," "Christian Endeavor Social," 'The Clambake of 1872," "Christmas Carol," "Missionary Social," "1845-1895, Fiftieth Wedding Anniversary, Ouadiah Chace and Wife," "For the Experience Social," etc In the last year of his life he wrote the following·

We thank Thee, dear and blessed Lord, For gifts sent down from Heaven,

And ask the fullness of His Grace
For Nineteen Hundred Seven

We prize the fitting words arranged
With wisdom and with care,
And brought so lovingly to view
In Bishop Brooks' Prayer

This little poem was inspired by the
famous prayer of Phillips Brooks which
is as follows

Pray the longest prayers. You cannot think
of a prayer so large that God in answering it
will not wish that you had made it larger. Pray
not for crutches, but for wings. Pray that, whatever comes—trial, doubt, failure or success
hope, joy—it may all work together to make your
soul fit, first to receive, and then to shine forth
with, the light of God

(IX) Charles Anthony Chace, eldest
child of the late Rev. Obadiah (2) and
Esther Taber (Freeborn) Chace, was
born December 22, 1846, in Warren,
Rhode Island, and was educated in the
schools of his native town, and at the
Friends' School, Providence Brought up
on a farm he was taught the fundamental
principles of agriculture, and for three
winters also taught school In 1879 he
moved to the Abner Slade farm which he
conducted successfully until 1900, when
he built his present beautiful and modern
residence at South Swansea For many
years Mr Chace and his sons were extensively engaged in erecting windmills
tanks and silos, and in 1902 they incorporated the New England Tank and Tower
Company, Mr Warren O Chace, the
youngest son, taking charge of their
factory at Everett, Massachusetts Mr
Chace was a Republican previous to 1884,
when he joined the Prohibition party becoming one of its most active and leading members He was chosen a member
of the State Central Committee shortly
afterward, and has continued in that position to the present time He was a delegate

from Massachusetts to the National Convention held in Pittsburgh in 1896, when
Joshua Levering, of Maryland, was nominated for President of the United States,
in 1912, in Atlantic City, when Eugene
Chafin, of Arizona, was nominated, in
1916, in St Paul, when J Frank Hanley,
of Indiana, was nominated He was a
candidate for presidential elector from his
congressional district in 1896 and 1904,
receiving 2994 and 4275 votes, respectively In 1900, 1901, 1902 and 1906 was
the candidate for State Senator from his
district, the votes those years being 263,
409, 459 and 738, respectively showing a
marked increase each year In 1909 as
candidate for State auditor, he received
5,663 votes In 1912, as candidate for
State treasurer, he received 5,708 votes,
which was the largest number received
by any Prohibition candidate that year
For seven years Mr Chace served his
town as a member of the school board,
and he is also a member of the Massachusetts Sunday School Association Mr
and Mrs Chace are both active and devoted members of the Friends' Society,
in the work of which they take an earnest
interest They are also both life members
of the American Peace Society

On September 26, 1872, in the Friends'
Meeting House, Mr Chace was united
in marriage to Adeline Francis Slade,
adopted daughter of the late Abner and
Sarah (Sherman) Slade, of Swansea,
and daughter of William and Hannah
(Wheaton) Cole (See Wheaton, Slade,
Sherman and Mitchell families) To Mr
and Mrs Charles A Chace have been born
the following children Benjamin Slade,
mentioned below, Harold Anthony, born
August 13, 1876, died February 28, 1878,
Arthur Freeborn, mentioned below, Warren Obadiah, mentioned below, and Sarah
Slade born April 22, 1889

(X) Benjamin Slade Chace son of

Charles A and Adeline Francis (Slade) Chace, was born January 11, 1875, and married, June 19, 1895, Carrie Estelle Mosher, and they have had six children, namely Fenton Mosher, born August 11, 1896, Harold Dean, born December 22, 1898; Clyde Fuller, born August 6, 1908, Carol Elisabeth, born February 21, 1910, Beryl, born March 8, 1911, died March 28, 1911, and Russell Slade, born August 9, 1912 Mr Chace lives upon the Abner Slade farm, and is ably managing the extensive work thereon, being extensively engaged in fruit growing.

(X) Arthur Freeborn Chace, M. D., son of Charles A and Adeline Francis (Slade) Chace, was born May 13, 1879, and was educated at Oakwood Seminary, Union Springs, New York; Earlham College, Richmond, Indiana, from which he received the degree of A B, and also graduated from Harvard University with the degree of A B, and from the College of Physicians and Surgeons of New York City with the degree of M D Dr Chace has advanced rapidly in his chosen profession, and is now secretary and assistant-treasurer of the New York Post-Graduate Hospital, and a member of its board of trustees He is also a trustee of Bryn Mawr College He is an expert on tropical diseases, and is consulting physician of the War Department by appointment of the United States government He married November 2, 1911, Kathleen Stirling Fletcher, of New York City, where they reside, and they are the parents of two sons, Arthur Freeborn Jr, born December 12, 1913, and James Fletcher born January 19, 1916.

(X) Warren Obadiah Chace, son of Charles A and Adeline Francis (Slade) Chace, was born June 12, 1882, and married October 2, 1907 M Flossie Mosher, and they have two children Esther Freeborn, born January 22, 1911, and Warren

Fuller, born January 15, 1914 Mr Chace has charge of the factory of the New England Tank and Tower Company, at Everett, Massachusetts, where they reside

(IX) Walter Freeborn Chace, son of Rev Obadiah (2) and Esther Taber (Freeborn) Chace, was born February 28, 1858, and resides at Redlands, California He married, December 24, 1880, Celia Perkins Emery, daughter of Eliphalet Emery, former superintendent of the Durfee Mills, at Fall River, Massachusetts To Mr and Mrs. Chace have been born three children, namely 1 Emery Perkins, born July 31, 1882, who married, April 25, 1905, Elsie M Herbst, born August 30, 1882, and they have four children Emery Philip, born January 29, 1906, died November 6, 1907, Ruth, born July 8, 1907, Chester Fredrick, born August 29, 1908, and Gail Perkins, born February 2, 1910 2 Anthony F, born May 1, 1888 3 Walter Freeborn, Jr, born June 27, 1897

(IX) George Mahlon Chace, son of Rev Obadiah (2) and Esther Taber (Freeborn) Chace, was born April 3 1864, and died September 12, 1907, in Fall River On September 7, 1887, he married Emma F. Slade, daughter of Frank Slade He was foreman for Beattie & Cornell contractors, at Fall River, Massachusetts

(The Sherman Line)

The surname of Sherman in England is of German origin, and at the present time in Germany and adjacent countries the name is found spelled Schurman, Schearman, Scherman It is derived from the occupation of some progenitor, that of cloth dresser or shearer of cloth The family bore the Suffolk coat-of-arms, and probably lived originally in the County of Suffolk, whence they removed to Essex, in the fifteenth century The name is found in England as early as 1420, and through wills and other documents is traced as follows

(I) Thomas Sherman, Gentleman, was born about 1420, resided at Diss and Yaxley, England, died 1493 He had a wife Agnes and a son,

(II) John Sherman, a gentleman of Yaxley, born about 1450, died November, 1504 He married Agnes, daughter of Thomas Fullen They had a son,

(III) Thomas (2) Sherman, born about 1480, died in November, 1551 He resided at Diss, on the river Waveney, between the counties of Norfolk and Suffolk His will mentions property including the manors of Royden and Royden Tuft, with appurtenances, at Royden and Bessingham, and other properties in Norfolk and Suffolk His wife, Jane, who was probably not his first, was a daughter of John Waller, of Wortham, Suffolk Children Thomas, Richard, John, Henry, William, Anthony, Francis, Bartholomew and James

(IV) Henry Sherman, son of Thomas (2) Sherman, was born about 1530, in Yaxley, and is mentioned in his father's will His will, made January 20, 1589, proved July 25, 1590, was made at Colchester, where he lived. His first wife, Agnes (Butler) Sherman, was buried October 11, 1580 He married (second) Margery Wilson, a widow Children Henry, mentioned below, Edmund, married Ann Clere, died 1601, his son, Edmund, was father of Rev John Sherman, of New Haven, Connecticut, where Edmund died in 1641; Dr Robert, of London, Judith, married Nicholas Fynce, and John, died without issue

(V) Henry (2) Sherman son of Henry (1) Sherman, was born about 1555, in Colchester, and resided in Dedham, County Essex, where he made his will August 21, proved September 8, 1610 He married Susan Hills, whose will was made ten days after his, and proved in the following month Six of the

sons mentioned below were living when the father died Henry, born 1571, died 1642, Samuel, mentioned below, Susan, 1575, Edmond or Edward, about 1577, Nathaniel, 1580, died young; Nathaniel, 1582, John, August 17, 1585, Elizabeth, about 1587, Ezekiel, July 25, 1589, Mary, July 27, 1592, Daniel, died 1634 Anne, married Thomas Wilson Phebe, married Simeon Fenn

(VI) Samuel Sherman, son of Henry (2) and Susan (Hills) Sherman, was born 1573, and died in Dedham, in 1615 He married Philippa Ward

(I) Philip Sherman, seventh child of Samuel and Philippa (Ward) Sherman, was born February 5, 1610, in Dedham, and died in March, 1687, in Portsmouth, Rhode Island He came to America when twenty-three years old, and settled at Roxbury, Massachusetts, where he was made freeman, May 14, 1634, standing next on the list after Governor Haynes In 1635 he returned to England for a short time, but was again in Roxbury, November 20, 1637, when he and others were warned to give up all arms because "the opinions and revelations of Mr Wheelwright and Mrs Hutchinson have seduced and led into dangerous errors many of the people here in New England " The church record says he was brought over to "Familism" by Porter, his wife's stepfather In 1636 he was one of the purchasers of the island of Aquidneck now Rhode Island, and on the formation of a government in 1639 became secretary under Governor William Coddington The Massachusetts authorities evidently believed he was still under their jurisdiction, for, on March 12, 1638, though he had summons to appear at the next court, "if they had not yet gone to answer such things as shall be objected " He did not answer this summons, but continued to be a prominent figure in Rhode Island affairs He continued to serve the public, was made freeman, March 16, 1641, was general recorder, 1648 to 1652, and deputy from 1665 to 1667 He was among the sixteen persons who were requested, on April 4, 1676, to be present at the next meeting of the deputies to give advice and help in regard to the Narragansett campaign He was public-spirited and enterprising After his removal to Rhode Island, he left the Congregational church and united with the Society of Friends Tradition affirms that he was "a devout but determined man " The early records prepared by him still remain in Portsmouth, and show him to have been a very neat and expert penman, as well as an educated man His will showed that he was wealthy for the times In 1634 he married Sarah Odding, step-daughter of John Porter, of Roxbury, and his wife, Margaret, who was a Widow Odding at the time of her marriage to Porter Philip Sherman's children Eber, born 1634, lived in Kingstown, Rhode Island, died in 1706, Sarah, 1636, married Thomas Mumford, Peleg, 1638, died 1719, in Kingstown, Rhode Island, Mary, 1639, died young; Edmond, 1641, lived in Portsmouth and Dartmouth, died in 1719, Samson, mentioned below, William, 1643, died young, John, 1644, a farmer and blacksmith in what is now South Dartmouth, died April 16, 1734; Mary, 1645, married Samuel Wilbur, Hannah, 1647, married William Chace (see Chace III), Samuel, 1648 lived in Portsmouth, died October 9, 1717, Benjamin, 1650 lived in Portsmouth; Philippa, October 1, 1652, married Benjamin Chase

(II) Samson Sherman, son of Philip and Sarah (Odding) Sherman, was born 1642, in Portsmouth, where he passed his life, and died June 27, 1718 He married, March 4, 1675, Isabel Tripp, born 1651, daughter of John and Mary (Paine)

Tripp, died 1716 Children Philip, born January 16, 1676, Sarah, September 24, 1677; Alice, January 12, 1680; Samson, January 28, 1682; Abiel, October 15, 1684, Isabel, 1686, Job, mentioned below

(III) Job Sherman, youngest child of Samson and Isabel (Tripp) Sherman, was born November 8, 1687, in Portsmouth, and died November 16, 1747, in that town He married (first) December 23, 1714, Bridget Gardiner, of Kingstown, and (second) in 1732, Amie Spencer of East Greenwich, Rhode Island Children of first marriage Philip, born December 12, 1715, Israel, October 31, 1717, Mary, January 16, 1719, Job, May 2, 1722, Bridget, May 7, 1724, Sarah, October 29, 1726, Alice, April 25, 1728, Mary, October 13, 1730 Children of second marriage Amie, born May 27, 1734, Benjamin, September 14, 1735, Samson, mentioned below; Martha, November 28, 1738, Walter, August 20, 1740, Dorcas, November 2, 1742, Abigail, September 10, 1744

(IV) Samson (2) Sherman, fifth son of Job Sherman, and second son of his second wife, Amie (Spencer) Sherman, was born July 23, 1737, in Portsmouth, where he spent his life, engaged in agriculture, and died January 24, 1801 He married, December 9, 1761, Ruth, daughter of David and Jemima (Tallman) Fish, of Portsmouth Children Walter, born April 4, 1763, married Rebecca Anthony, of Portsmouth, Amy, January 6, 1764, married Daniel Anthony, of Portsmouth, Job, January 21, 1766, married Alice Anthony, Susanna, October 19, 1767, married Peleg Almy, of Portsmouth; Hannah, January 27, 1769, married Jonathan Dennis, of Portsmouth; Anne, November 19, 1770, married Nathan Chase, of Portsmouth; David, June, 1772, married Waite Sherman, of Portsmouth Ruth, October 21, 1773, died in infancy, Ruth, February

20, 1778, married Obadiah Davis, or New Bedford, Massachusetts, Asa, mentioned below, Abigail, April 2, 1782, married Abram Davis, or Fair Haven, Massachusetts, Mary, November 18, 1783, married David Shove, of Berkley Massachusetts

(V) Asa Sherman, fourth son of Samson (2) and Ruth (Fish) Sherman, was born December 22, 1779, in Portsmouth, and died at Fall River, December 29, 1863 His remains were deposited in the Friends' Cemetery at Portsmouth He was a birthright member of the Friends, was a farmer and landowner in Portsmouth He married at the Friends Meeting in Portsmouth, November 11, 1805, Elizabeth Mitchell, born October 17, 1782, in Middletown, Rhode Island, daughter of Richard (2) and Joanna (Lawton) Mitchell, of Middletown (see Mitchell III) Children Ruth, born November 21, 1806, Joanna, July 30, 1808, died at Fall River, September 9, 1863, Sarah, mentioned below, Amy, September 16, 1811, married, October 21, 1839, Mark Anthony, or Taunton, Massachusetts, Richard Mitchell, September 16, 1813; Mary, September 16, 1815, married Hon William L Slade, Asa, December 23, 1817, Daniel, June 25 1820 William, April 9, 1823; Annie July 17, 1826, died at Fall River, January 15, 1849

(VI) Sarah Sherman, daughter or Asa and Elizabeth (Mitchell) Sherman, was born February 20, 1810, and married September 30, 1829, Abner Slade, of Swansea (see Slade VI)

(VII) Adeline Francis Slade, adopted daughter of Abner and Sarah (Sherman) Slade, was born March 29, 1849, and married, September 26 1872, Charles A Chace, or Swansea (see Chace IX)

(The Buffinton Line)

The name Buffinton or Buffington was not a common one nor the family a numer-

ous one in early New England, yet a record or it here reaches back some two hundred and more years to the old historic town of Salem, Massachusetts

(I) Thomas Buffinton (or Buffington), the first of the name found in this country, is of record at Salem, where he spelled his name Bavanton He married there, December 30, 1671, Sarah Southwick, and they had children, namely Thomas, born March 1, 1673, Benjamin born July 24, 1675, and Abigail, born July 25, 1699

(II) Benjamin Buffinton, son of Thomas and Sarah Buffinton, was born July 24, 1675, and married Hannah ———, and they had three children, among whom was Benjamin, Jr, mentioned below

(III) Benjamin (2) Buffinton, son of Benjamin (1) and Hannah Buffinton, was born at Lynn, Massachusetts, the 9th of the 2d month, 1701, and died the 9th of the 4th month, 1760, and was buried in the Friends' Yard at Swansea, Massachusetts, whither he had removed, and where he married Isabel Chace, daughter of Joseph and Sarah Chace She was born 6th of the 5th month, 1705, at Swansea, and died the 6th of the 4th month, 1791, and was buried in the Friends' Yard at Swansea His parents were of the Friends' religious persuasion, and he received his religious instruction in that society His father, removing his family within the bounds of the Swansea monthly meeting, became a member thereof, and there continued to live for the remainder of his days His children, born in Swansea, were Benjamin, born the 7th or the 9th month, 1737, Moses mentioned below, Stephen, born the 25th of the 11th month, 1743, Elizabeth, born the 21st of the 6th month, 1746, and Hannah, born the 30th of the 5th month, 1749

(IV) Moses Buffinton, son of Benjamin (2) and Isabel (Chace) Buffinton, born the 8th of the 3d month, 1741, in

365

Swansea, Massachusetts, married (first) Isabel Baker, born the 4th of the 5th month, 1741, daughter of Daniel and Sarah (Chace) Baker, and (second) Patience Chace. He resided in Swansea, where were born all his children, excepting Daniel and Aaron, and they were born in the town of Dighton, Massachusetts. Mr Buffinton died the 7th of the 4th month, 1817, and he and his wife, Isabel are both buried in the Friends' Yard, at Swansea. Their children were Benjamin, mentioned below; Sarah; Rebecca, Anna, Daniel, Moses, Aaron, who died in infancy, Bethany, who died in infancy, and Aaron (2). The children of Moses Buffinton's second marriage were Eber, Mary, and Elizabeth.

(V) Benjamin (3) Buffinton, son of Moses and Isabel (Baker) Buffinton, was born in Swansea, the 1st day of the 11th month, 1762, and died in Troy (now Fall River), Massachusetts, the 20th of the 2d month, 1843, and is buried at Fall River. He married in Swansea, the 25th of the 10th month, 1785, Charity Robinson, who was born the 26th of the 2d month, 1765, daughter of John and Phebe (Chace) Robinson, and granddaughter of William Robinson. The children of Benjamin and Charity (Robinson) Buffinton were Isabel, mentioned below; Ruth, 1788; Nathan, 1790; Daniel, 1794; Darius, 1796, died in 1828; Mary, 1799; Israel, 1802; Elizabeth, 1805; Phebe, 1807. The mother of these children died in Troy (now Fall River), was the 31st of the 3d month, 1829, and is buried at Somerset, Massachusetts.

(VI) Isabel Buffinton, daughter of Benjamin (3) and Charity (Robinson) Buffinton, was born in Rehoboth, Massachusetts, the 22d of the 9th month, 1786, and married, the 11th of the 9th month, 1806, Anthony Chace, of Swansea (see Chace VII).

(The Freeborn Line).

This name appears in the early Rhode Island records Freeborne and is of undoubted English origin. The family was among the founders of the Aquidneck Colony, and very soon became identified with the Society of Friends, with which it has continued down to the present time.

(I) William Freeborn, born in 1594, sailed in the ship "Francis" from Ipswich, England, April 30, 1634, arriving in due time in Boston, where he subscribed to the freeman's oath, September 3rd of that year. The shipping list gives his age as forty, that of his wife Mary as thirty-three, and mentions two daughters, Mary, aged seven, and Sarah, two years. He was not a member of the First Boston Church, and must have lived outside of that city, though he was there in 1637, when he was disarmed, with many others, on account of their adherence to the teachings of Ann Hutchinson. He was a member of the large body which removed from Boston and settled on the Island of Aquidneck, where he was one of the signers of the covenant at Newport in March, 1637. He was granted lot No 39, was made freeman of the Aquidneck Colony, March 16, 1641. served as constable in 1642. commissioner in 1657, and died at Portsmouth, April 28, 1670. His wife Mary was born in 1601, and died May 3, 1670. Children: Mary, born 1627, married Clement Weeper; Sarah, 1632, married Nathaniel Browning, and died April 23, 1670; Gideon, mentioned below. He also had a daughter, who married a Sweet, as indicated by a legacy to his grandchildren.

(II) Gideon Freeborn, son of William and Mary Freeborn, lived in Portsmouth Rhode Island, where he died February 28, 1720. He was deputy to the General Court from Portsmouth in 1675, 1690, 1703-04 and 1713. In 1687 he was overseer of the poor. He purchased five acres of land in Portsmouth, March 5, 1690, for twelve pounds, and was altogether a very extensive landowner, bequeathing by will lands in Misquamicut, one hundred and eighty acres in East Greenwich, other lands in Potowomut, one hundred and twenty acres in Tiverton to his grandson Gideon Wanton, five hundred acres in Pennsylvania to grandchildren; one hundred acres in Freehold, New Jersey, to his daughter, Comfort, two hundred acres in Warwick and a negro boy to his son, John Freeborn, to daughters nine acres in Coweset, and one hundred acres in the same place to his grandson, Gideon Durfee, one hundred and fifty acres in the same section to his three Cornell grandsons His will also made other legacies in lands, varying in amount from twenty-five to fifty acres, and multitudes of cash legacies running from twenty shillings to twenty-five pounds His will also provided that one cord of wood should be delivered each year for ten years at the Quaker meeting house The inventory of his estate amounted to £676 12s and 2d, including three negroes, a man, woman and boy, valued at £102

He married (first) June 1, 1658, Sarah Brownell, daughter of Thomas Brownell, born 1618-19, in Derbyshire, England, and settled in Portsmouth in 1639. Thomas Brownell married in England, in 1638, and was survived by his wife Ann He died in 1665, and she died before the close of the same year, after having executed an exchange in real estate, according to a contract made by him He was a freeman of Portsmouth in 1655, in the same year was a commissioner, and again in 1661-62-63 In 1664 he was deputy to the General Court Their second daughter Sarah, became the wife of Gideon Freeborn, as above noted She died September 6, 1676, and Gideon Freeborn married (second) June 3, 1678, Mary, widow of

John Lawton, daughter of Matthew and Eleanor Boomer She died in 1715 Children of first marriage Mary, born February 12, 1664, died young; Sarah, January 14, 1667; Ann, March 28, 1669; Martha, August 8, 1671; Susanna, March 24, 1674; Patience, March 4, 1676 Children of second marriage Mary, born August 24, 1679; William, February 3, 1682; Gideon, mentioned below; Thomas, February 5, 1688; Comfort, 1691; Mercy, 1692

(III) Gideon (2) Freeborn, second son of Gideon (1) and Mary (Boomer-Lawton) Freeborn, was born April 29, 1684, in Portsmouth, and was a prominent citizen of that town, which he represented in the General Court in 1716, 1719-20-21-23, 1727-28-29, 1731-32-33, and 1740-41 In 1717 he was assistant to the governor, and in 1734-35 one of the four justices of the Court of Common Pleas for Newport county He was executor of his father's will, and received the homestead farm, besides lands from his grandfather, a negro man, two cows, a pair of oxen horse, fifty sheep, two swine, farm implements, a bed, silver tankard, and other personal property At his death, February 21, 1753, he left a large estate, which was inventoried at £3,324 3s Included in this were six negroes, young and old, varying in value from fifty to four hundred pounds. He married (first) February 1, 1706, Eliza Nichols, born June 14 1688, daughter of Thomas and Hannah Nichols He married (second) August 9, 1733, Bethiah Sherman, born 1699, daughter of Benjamin and Hannah (Mowry) Sherman Benjamin Sherman, born 1650, was the twelfth child of Philip Sherman, who was very prominent in Portsmouth Children of Gideon (2) Freeborn by his first wife were: William, born November 19, 1706, died young; Gideon, October 26, 1708; Susanna, January 7, 1710, Thomas,

October 11, 1711, William, March 1, 1713, Elizabeth, July 22, 1714, Joseph, February 25, 1717, Jonathan, mentioned below, Benjamin, January 29, 1722, and Hannah, May 10, 1726 There was one child of the second marriage, Robert Freeborn, born January 11, 1735

(IV) Jonathan Freeborn sixth son of Gideon (2) and Eliza (Nichols) Freeborn, was born March 4, 1719, in Portsmouth, and received by his father's will farm lands and buildings in that town, also a negro boy, and various items of personal property He married, December 15, 1742, Mary Mott, who was born June 2, 1722, in Portsmouth, daughter of Jacob and Mary (Easton) Mott Children William, born September 8, 1743, died young, Jonathan, July 22, 1744, Elizabeth, August 5, 1717, William, September 12, 1749, Thomas, July 13, 1751, Gideon, June 28, 1753, Susanna, April 7, 1755, Benjamin, mentioned below, Joseph August 6, 1759, Mary, February 23, 1762

(V) Benjamin Freeborn, sixth son of Jonathan and Mary (Mott) Freeborn, was born April 13, 1757, in Portsmouth, and died there April 29, 1838 He married (first) January 5, 1785, Ruth Hall, born December 10, 1762, daughter of George and Charity Hall, of Portsmouth, died April 28, 1785 He married (second) January 2, 1788, Hannah Lawton, born April 15, 1759, in Portsmouth, daughter of Isaac and Mary Lawton, died December 22, 1802 He married (third) Susanna Sherman, daughter of Sampson and Ruth Sherman, born October 7, 1767, died November 30, 1820 She was the mother of his youngest child, Hannah Freeborn, born January 9, 1806 Children of second marriage Samuel, born January 29 1791; Edmond, December 28, 1792, Jonathan, mentioned below; Ruth, October 3, 1795, Elizabeth, April 14, 1797

(VI) Jonathan (2) Freeborn, third son of Benjamin and Hannah (Lawton) Freeborn, was born April 16, 1794, in Portsmouth, and lived for a short time in Portland, Maine He married (first) in November, 1820, Esther Taber She died leaving one child, mentioned below He married (second) Lydia Reid, born March 2, 1802, died February 18, 1842, in Pawtucket, Rhode Island Like her husband she was a member of an old Quaker family Her children were Emily Reid, born July 11, 1825, Charles Scott, August 14, 1827, Eliza Alma, July 23, 1832, Benjamin, January 3 1835

(VII) Esther Taber Freeborn, daughter of Jonathan (2) and Esther (Taber) Freeborn, was born January 15, 1822, in Portland, Maine, and married, April 28, 1845, Rev Obadiah (2) Chace, of Swansea, Massachusetts (see Chace VIII).

(The Slade Line).

The name Slade has an interesting origin Its meaning as a common noun is "a small strip of green plain within a woodland" One of the rhymes about Robin Hood runs

> It had been better of William a Trent
> To have been abed with sorrowe,
> Than to be that day in greenwood slade
> To meet with Little John's arrowe

The name Slade was in use as a surname as early as 1200, and the name of de la Slade occurs in the Hundred Rolls of the thirteenth century The Slade family of Trevennen in Gorran, County of Cornwall, in the time of Queen Elizabeth, had a coat-of-arms, as did the Slade family of Maunsell House, County of Somerset, England

(I) Edward Slade, of whom little seems known more than he was admitted a freeman in Rhode Island in 1658, is said to have been a native of Wales, and that he

lost his life in a voyage from America to
England

(II) William Slade, said to have been
a son of Edward Slade, and to have been
born in Wales, comes of a family which
was long and prominently identified with
Somersetshire, England   He appears at
Newport Rhode Island, in 1659, when he
was admitted a freeman of the colony,
and became an early settler in the Shawomet purchase, included in that part of
Swansea, Massachusetts, which became
the town of Somerset, in 1790   As early
as 1680, when the first record book of the
town begins, Mr Slade was a resident of
Swansea, and the meetings of the proprietors were held at his home after their
discontinuance at Plymouth, in 1677   He
was a large landholder, his domain including the ferry across the Taunton
river, which has ever since been known
as Slade s Ferry, and this ferry remained
in the possession of this family until the
river was bridged in 1876, at which time
it was being operated by William L and
Jonathan Slade   Mr Slade married, about
1684 Sarah Holmes, who was born in
1664, daughter of Rev Obadiah Holmes,
of Rehoboth   Mr Slade died March 30,
1729, aged sixty-seven years, and his
widow died September 10, 1761, in the
ninety-seventh year of her age   Their
children were   Jonathan, who died at the
age of eighteen years, Sarah born in
1687, Mary, born in 1689, William, born
in 1692, Edward, mentioned below, Elizabeth, born in 1695, Hannah, born in
1697, Martha, born in 1699, Phebe, born
in 1701, Jonathan (2), born in 1703, and
Lydia, born in 1706.

(III) Edward (2) Slade, son of Wil-
liam and Sarah (Holmes) Slade, was born
June 14 1694   He married (first) in 1717,
Elizabeth Anthony, and (second) Decem-
ber 6, 1720, Phebe Chace, daughter of
Samuel and Sarah (Sherman) Chace,

granddaughter of William Chace, and
great-granddaughter of William Chace,
the immigrant   His third wife was Deborah Buffum   He died April 5, 1755

(IV) Joseph Slade, son of Edward (2)
and Phebe (Chace) Slade, was born November 16, 1724   He married (first) July
25, 1747, Hannah Chace, (second) Deborah Brayton, (third) Priscilla Borden

(V) Benjamin Slade, son of Joseph
and Hannah (Chace) Slade, was born
June 16, 1753   He married, June 17, 1779,
Elizabeth Robinson, daughter of John and
Phebe (Chace) Robinson, and their children were   Rebecca, born August 5, 1780,
Hannah, born January 1, 1783, married
Oliver Earle; Phebe, born October 20,
1785; Elizabeth, born November 25, 1787;
Susanna, born July 12, 1790; Abner, mentioned below, Ruth Borden, born January 25, 1795, married Moses Buffinton,
and Content, born February 8, 1798

(VI) Abner Slade, son of Benjamin
and Elizabeth (Robinson) Slade, was
born in Swansea, Massachusetts, October 2, 1792, on the homestead of his parents, and his long, useful and honorable
life was passed in this vicinity   He was
reared a farmer and tanner, succeeding
his father in the tanning business, which
he followed the remainder of his life   By
perseverance and the strictest integrity
he built up a fine business which grew to
large proportions   He was methodical,
systematic and industrious, and believed
in giving the most minute detail the same
attention he would give to larger affairs
As a reward of his close application to
business and his untiring energy, Mr
Slade was enabled to retire from active
business activities, in 1856, and thereafter
devoted his time to looking after his various investments, having by that time acquired a handsome competency   Although recognized as an able business
man, and one of the town's substantial

citizens, he could not be persuaded to accept public office, having no desire nor inclination to do so, and no political aspirations. For many years he was a director of the Fall River National Bank, and was interested in the Old Colony Railroad, and to some extent in the Providence & Worcester Railroad. He was also a stockholder in various other corporations and manufactories in Fall River and vicinity.

On September 30, 1829, Mr. Slade married Sarah Sherman, daughter of Asa and Elizabeth (Mitchell) Sherman and a direct descendant of Hon. Philip Sherman who was one of the original purchasers of Rhode Island, and the first secretary of the Colony. (See Sherman and Mitchell families.) She was born February 20, 1810, the third child of ten children born to her parents. The married life of Mr. and Mrs. Slade covered a period of over half a century, and it was one of unusual peace and happiness. They had no children, but adopted a little girl of about two years, Sarah Bowers, upon whom they bestowed a filial love until her death, in her twentieth year. They then adopted Adeline Francis Cole when seven years of age, who was born March 29, 1819, daughter of William and Hannah (Wheaton) Cole. (See Wheaton Family.) To the latter Mr. and Mrs. Slade gave the same tender care and affection that they would have given to a child of their own. She married Charles A. Chace, of Swansea, where they reside (see Chace IX). Mr. Slade passed through the years of life to a hale and ripe old age, in which the powers of thought and consolations of religion held sway until his death, which occurred December 2, 1879, at the age of eighty-seven years.

At a special meeting of the board of directors of the Fall River National Bank December 4, 1879, the following preamble and resolution were passed:

Whereas, It has pleased our Heavenly Father to remove by death our highly respected associate Abner Slade, at the ripe age of eighty-seven years, who has been identified with this bank as director for more than thirty-three years, giving to it his counsel and judgment, a man honored for his sterling integrity and Christian character, therefore,

Resolved. It is not as a mere formality that this board recognize the loss they have sustained, and in token of respect to his memory, and to manifest our sympathy with his family, this board will attend his funeral in a body.

Mr. Slade was an earnest member of the Society of Friends and was held in high esteem by his brethren. The "Friends' Review" gave this notice of him:

Abner Slade, an elder of Swansea Monthly Meeting of Friends deceased twelfth month, second 1879 aged eighty-seven. He was truly a father in Israel. While we deeply feel our loss, and miss his sweet words of counsel, we can but rejoice when we think of his triumphal death, and remember how his countenance beamed with joy when he told us he was going to his home in heaven.

(The Mitchell Line)

(I) Richard Mitchell, the ancestor of a New England family, was a native of Bricktown, in the Isle of Wight, Great Britain, where he was born 1686. There he learned the trade of tailor, and on attaining his majority decided to go into business for himself in his native place. He visited London to obtain the necessary materials, and while there was seized by a press gang and taken on board a man-of-war. Tailors were not then exempted, as were other mechanics, from impressment. The vessel on which he sailed spent some time at Newport Rhode Island, and here Mitchell found opportunity to escape. He made a suit of clothes for the governor's son which so pleased the latter that he secreted Mitchell and kept him in concealment until after the vessel had sailed. Mitchell continued to reside in Newport and be-

came a member of the Society of Friends
He married, in 1708, Elizabeth Tripp of
Dartmouth, Massachusetts, born 1685,
daughter of James and Mercy (Lawton)
Tripp, granddaughter of James and Mary
(Paine) Tripp, and also of George and
Elizabeth (Hazard) Lawton, great-granddaughter of Thomas Hazard, founder of
a noted family of Rhode Island Richard
Mitchell died September 24 1722 at the
age of thirty-six years, and his widow
married (second) April 18, 1734, William
Wood, she died February 13, 1740 Children Elizabeth, born July 13, 1709, married, December 8 1726, Jabez Carpenter
Mary, October 17, 1712, married, May 18,
1732, Caleb Coggeshall, James mentioned below, Richard, September 5
1719, settled in Nantucket, Massachusetts, Joseph, November 25 1720

(II) James Mitchell second son of
Richard and Elizabeth (Tripp) Mitchell,
was born April 20, 1715, in Newport, was
a member of the Society of Friends in
which he was an elder, and died October
5, 1799 He lived for a time at Nantucket,
Massachusetts, where he married Anna
Folger, a daughter of Jethro and Mary
Folger, of Nantucket He moved later
to Middletown, Rhode Island near the
Portsmouth line and there continued to
make his home until his death Children
Mary, born November 10, 1739 married
Mathew Barker, of Newport James, August 31 1743 married Elizabeth Anthony Elizabeth, July 9 1746 married
Giles Hosier, Hepsabeth March 14 1750,
married (first) Peter Chase, (second)
David Buffum, Richard mentioned be-
low

(III) Richard (2) Mitchell youngest
child of James and Anna (Folger)
Mitchell was born November 25, 1754,
in Middletown and lived in that town
near what is known as Mitchell's Lane,
where he died October 26, 1833 He mar-

ried, November 6, 1776, Joanna Lawton,
a native of Portsmouth, daughter of John
and Sarah Lawton, died August 6, 1830
Children Jethro Folger, born March 14,
1778, married Anne Gould, Isaac, August
21, 1779, married Sarah Gould, John,
January 15, 1781, married Katharine
Gould, Elizabeth, mentioned below,
Peter, July 3, 1784 married Mary Wales,
Sarah, May 19, 1787, Joanna, December
3, 1788, married David Rodman, Ann,
August 6, 1791, Richard, February 20,
1813

(IV) Elizabeth Mitchell, eldest daugh-
ter of Richard (2) and Joanna (Lawton)
Mitchell, was born October 17, 1782, in
Middletown, and became the wife of Asa
Sherman of Portsmouth (see Sherman
V)

(The Wheaton Line)

For more than two hundred and seventy
years the Wheatons of Southern Massachusetts and the neighboring towns in
Rhode Island have been a continuous
family in that region of country, and
many of the name and blood have both
at home and in the country-at-large
reached high station in the various walks
of life some becoming men of eminence
and distinction

(I) Robert Wheaton born in 1606, was
of Rehoboth Massachusetts, in 1643-46,
and tradition says, came to New England about 1636, from Swansea, Wales,
settled first at Salem, Massachusetts, but
because he would not take the oath he
was warned out From there he went to
Boston which he was obliged to leave
for the same reason He then settled in
Rehoboth where he was one of the original proprietors A descendant of his is
now living in a house on the original
grant He married Alice Bowen, daughter of Richard Bowen, and his children
were Joseph Samuel, and Jeremiah, born
in Salem Obadiah, John mentioned be-

low, Bethia, Hannah, Mary, Ephraim, and Benjamin

(II) John Wheaton, son of Robert Wheaton, was born April 20, 1650, in Rehoboth, Massachusetts, and married Elizabeth Slade, and their children were James, mentioned below, Israel, Isaac, Mary, Nathaniel, Priscilla, Patience, and Samuel

(III) James Wheaton, son of John Wheaton, was born November 16, 1686, and married, March 15, 1715, Hannah Slade, daughter of William Slade, and their children were: Elizabeth, Hannah, John, James, Jr, Jonathan, Joseph, Jonathan, 2d, mentioned below, and Nathaniel

(IV) Jonathan Wheaton, son of James Wheaton, was born April 10, 1725, in Swansea, Massachusetts, and married, September 19 1751, Phebe Peirce, and their children were John, born 1752, Elizabeth, 1757; Jonathan, 1758, Mial mentioned below, and Phebe, 1767

(V) Mial Wheaton, son of Jonathan Wheaton, was born April 3, 1764, in Swansea, and died there in the eighty-ninth year of his age He was prominent in the town's affairs, and served for nine years as selectman, refusing further service He married Eunice Francis, of Dighton, Massachusetts, who died in the ninety-first year of her age Their children were Mial, mentioned below David, born 1792, Phebe, 1794, James, 1797; Eunice, 1798, William, 1799, Seth, 1801, Betsey, 1804, George, 1806, and John, 1811

(VI) Mial (2) Wheaton son of Mial (1) Wheaton, was born November 6, 1788, in Swansea and died in Somerset Massachusetts at the age of ninety-six years He married Martha Pike daughter of James and Hannah (Cummings) Pike, and their children were Hannah who married William Cole, Hiram, who married Annie Codding, of Dighton

Caleb, died young; Nathan, who married Jane Springer, of New Bedford, where he resides, Phebe, who married Henry Williams, of Dighton, Mary, who married Bradford D Chace, of Somerset; James, living in Swansea; Caroline, died young, William, died in infancy; Sarah, who married Benjamin F Chace, of Swansea, where she resides

---

ESTERBROOK,

And Allied Families

Several immigrants of this name were among the pioneers of New England, and the name appears with a great variety of spellings in early records The forms Easterbrook and Estabrook are in common use at present by various branches of the family The family herein traced cannot be connected by authentic records with the descendants of Rev Joseph Esterbrook of Concord, Massachusetts Tradition says that Thomas Esterbrook was his brother

(I) Thomas Esterbrook was born in England about 1629, and died April 11, 1713, in the eighty-fourth year of his age He was admitted an inhabitant of Swansea, Massachusetts, August 13, 1666, was one of those who signed the agreement between Mr Willett and the church in Swansea February 12, 1669 and was a town officer, elected selectman, June 11, 1681 He was buried in the Kickamuit Cemetery at Warren, Rhode Island He married Sarah, daughter of John and Sarah Woodcock of Rehoboth Children John, born May 2, 1669, Thomas, mentioned below, Elizabeth, December 19 1673, Sara, September 19, 1676

(II) Thomas (2) Esterbrook, son of Thomas (1) and Sarah (Woodcock) Esterbrook was born October 18 1671, and died September 27, 1724 He sold forty acres to the town of Swansea to enlarge the Kickamuit Cemetery in Warren, where he was buried He married before 1703, Elizabeth, daughter of John Thurber, granddaughter of John Thurber, the immigrant, who came from England with his wife Priscilla and settled at Swansea She died September 27 1724 Children Thomas Lois, William, John, Benjamin, Charles and Nathaniel

(III) John Esterbrook son of Thomas (2) and Elizabeth (Thurber) Esterbrook was born about 1720 in Swansea where he lived He married, November 5, 1747 in Rehoboth, Abigail Abell of that town born September 6, 1727, daughter of Joshua and Rebecca (Carpenter) Abell Children Abel, born August 31 1748, Aaron, mentioned below Hannah, married John Norris, of Bristol, Sarah August 2, 1760, Abigail, July 19, 1762

(IV) Aaron Esterbrook, second son of John and Abigail (Abell) Esterbrook was born July 15 1750 in Warren or Swansea, and settled in Bristol, Rhode Island where he was for many years clerk of the market, and died December 26 1841 He married (first) May 28, 1775, Leah, daughter of Samuel and Leah Liscomb born October 27 1757 He married (second) Thankful Davis born September 22 1764, died July 27, 1845 Children of first marriage Abel Crawford, born August 27, 1787, Samuel August 21, 1789 of second marriage John mentioned below, Sarah D November 5, 1802 Aaron April 4 1804 Eliza Ann, July 15 1806

(V) John (2) Esterbrook fourth son of Aaron Esterbrook, and eldest child of his second wife, Thankful (Davis) Esterbrook was born November 25, 1800, in Bristol and died June 24, 1857 He married Caroline F, daughter of John A Kault of Newport, Rhode Island, born 1801-02 died February 19 1884 Children John, born July 25 1825 George

W, mentioned below, Anne G, October 24, 1829, Caroline S, married A Judson Matthews, Stephen G August 12 1835, Harriet, October 3 1837, William H, October 17, 1839 Theodore R, August 25, 1841, Frederick A August 24, 1844

(VI) George W Esterbrook, second son of John (2) and Caroline E (Kault) Esterbrook, was born September 21 1827, and married, December 12, 1850 Catherine daughter of Edward and Lydia Gladding Children Gertrude D, born February 22, 1852, Harriet M, December 11, 1853 Charles F, July 19, 1856, John H, mentioned below, Edward G, September 6 1862

(VII) John Henry Esterbrook second son of George W and Catherine (Gladding) Esterbrook, was born December 29, 1859, and is now a resident of Providence, Rhode Island, employed as salesman by R I Rowe & Company He married, November 2, 1881, Ann Lincoln Tilley, daughter of Stockford Ellery and Phebe Ann (Barker) Tilley, of Bristol Rhode Island (see Tilley V)

(VIII) Clarissa Bird Esterbrook, only child of John Henry and Ann Lincoln (Tilley) Esterbrook was born November 24 1884 and was married in 1904 to Fred G McAdams, cashier of the Staples Coal Company of Fall River, Massachusetts Their home is on Madison street in that city and Mrs McAdams is active in the social life of the city being a member of the Fall River Woman's Club, and of Quequechan Chapter Daughters of the American Revolution

(The Tilley Line)

John Tilley, a resident of England, had two sons William and John The last named was the father of William Tilley born about 1641, who settled in Boston, Massachusetts, where he was an extensive rope maker Three of his cousins

373

William (2), John and James Tilley, sons of William (1) above mentioned, came to Boston to work for William Tilley, the rope maker

(I) One of these, William (2) Tilley, son of William (1) Tilley, and grandson of John Tilley, of England, born about 1685, in Exeter, England, came to Boston, as before stated. There he married, in 1736, Dorcas, whose family name has not been preserved, and moved soon after to Newport, Rhode Island, where he spent the remainder of his life

(II) Deacon William (3) Tilley, son of William (2) and Dorcas Tilley, was born October 19, 1738, in Newport, where his life was spent, and died April 14 1825 He was married three times (first) October 28 1759, to Elizabeth, daughter of Jeremiah and Patience Rogers, born August 7, 1743, in Middletown, Rhode Island, died August 28, 1800 She was the mother of seventeen children

(III) James Tilley, third and eldest surviving son of Deacon William (3) and Elizabeth (Rogers) Tilley, was born September 5, 1765, in Newport, and died there March 2, 1800, in his thirty-fifth year He married (first) Rualmy, daughter of Paul Coffin, born 1765-66, died February 11, 1787, within a few months of the marriage He married (second) Mary, daughter of Charles Barker, born 1765-66, died May 20, 1806 Children Rualmy, William James, Mary, Sarah

(IV) William James Tilley, only son of James and Mary (Barker) Tilley, was born July 9, 1791, in Newport, and died there July 2, 1844 He married (first) Eliza, daughter of John and Jane (Manchester) Stockford, of Warren, Rhode Island, born September 8, 1796, died August 18, 1819 Their only child, Mary Jane, was born July 24, 1817 He married (second) September 1, 1820, Clarissa Bird Ellery, born June 6, 1799, in New-

port, daughter of Christopher (2) and Clarissa (Bird) Ellery, of that city (see Ellery V) She died January 30, 1852 Children Eliza Stockford, born August 2, 1821, and Stockford Ellery, mentioned below

(V) Stockford Ellery Tilley, only son of William James and Clarissa Bird (Ellery) Tilley, was born December 15, 1823 in Newport, and married there, in 1844 Phebe Ann, daughter of Peter Barker, born February 1, 1823 Children Clarissa B., William J, Maria, Herbert, Clarence and Ann Lincoln

(VI) Ann Lincoln Tilley, youngest daughter of Stockford Ellery and Phebe Ann (Barker) Tilley, married John Henry Esterbrook, of Providence (see Esterbrook VII).

(The Ellery Line)

(I) William Ellery appears in Gloucester, Massachusetts, as early as 1663, and resided in the section of that town long known as Ellery's Cove He was made freeman in 1676, served several years as selectman, was representative in 1689, and sergeant of the trainband He was one of the few citizens who owned a sloop, and was probably engaged in the mercantile business He married (first) in Gloucester, October 8, 1663, Hannah, daughter of William and Sarah Vinson, probably born in Salem She died December 24, 1675, and he married (second) June 13, 1676, Mary, daughter of John and Mary (Stevens) Coit, born June 4, 1655 Children William, died young Hannah, born 1667; Benjamin, mentioned below; Susanna, 1673; Mary, 1677 Abigail, 1679; John, June 25, 1681; Nathaniel, 1683; Jemima, 1686; Elinor, 1688, died young; Elinor, 1691; William, 1694; Dependence (son), 1696.

(II) Benjamin Ellery, second son of William and Hannah (Vinson) Ellery, was born September 6, 1669, in Gloucester, and settled in Newport, Rhode Island where he was a wealthy merchant, judge, assistant, speaker of the House of Deputies He was granted a letter of marque by King George of Denmark, consort of Queen Anne, and used an armorial seal which appears on deeds and bonds He died in Newport, July 26, 1746 He married Abigail, daughter of John Wilkins born about 1677, died July 26, 1746, the same day as her husband, in Newport One of the papers of that town in speaking of her death said "She was a Gentlewoman who showed the Character of a Christian in every Branch of Female Life, so that she was cordially respected by all sorts of People, and the Poor do in a particular Manner regret a Loss they must sensibly feel." Children Anstiss, February 19, 1697, Abigail, born February 24 1698, William, mentioned below, Benjamin, March 23, 1705, Mary, August 5 1715

(III) William (2) Ellery, senior son of Benjamin and Abigail (Wilkins) Ellery, was born October 31, 1701, in Newport graduated from Harvard College, 1722, and died March 15, 1764 Like his father he was active in mercantile pursuits, possessed of liberal means, was a deputy, judge, assistant and deputy governor He married, January 3, 1723, Elizabeth, daughter of Colonel Job and Ann (Lawton) Almy, born August 1, 1703, died July 3 1783 Colonel Job Almy was a descendant of William Almy, born 1601, resided in Lynn and Sandwich, Massachusetts, and Portsmouth, Rhode Island His wife's name was Audry, and their eldest child, Christopher Almy, was born 1632, and died January 30, 1713 He married July 9, 1661, Elizabeth Cornell, daughter of Thomas and Rebecca Cornell, and they were the parents of Colonel Job Almy, their eighth son, born October 10, 1675, married in March 1696,

Ann Lawton, born April 25, 1678, died February 12, 1739, daughter of Isaac and Elizabeth (Tallman) Lawton Children of William (2) Ellery Benjamin, born February 25, 1725; William, December 22, 1727, signer of the Declaration of Independence, chief justice of Rhode Island, and a classical scholar, Ann May 6, 1732, Christopher mentioned below

(IV) Christopher Ellery, third son of William (2) and Elizabeth (Almy) Ellery, was born April 22, 1736, in Newport and was one of the wealthiest merchants of that city where he died February 24 1789 He also conducted a mercantile business in Bristol, and was a man of very high character, deputy, assistant and judge He married (first) November 26, 1760, Mary, daughter of Samuel (2) Vernon, an eminent merchant of Newport (see Vernon III) She was born 1743, and died September 2, 1776 He married (second) Rachel King, of Salem Children Elizabeth Almy born March 24, 1764, Christopher, mentioned below Mary, May 15 1772

(V) Christopher (2) Ellery, only son of Christopher (1) and Mary (Vernon) Ellery was born November 1 1768 in Newport graduated at Yale 1787, and was a lawyer, a man of very fine presence and manner He was selectman of Newport for several years, and United States Senator during the first four years of Thomas Jefferson's administration He died December 2, 1840, at his home in Newport He married, October 22 1792, Clarissa, daughter of Dr Nathaniel Bird who was a noted beauty of Newport born November 1, 1768 died April 28, 1811 Children Franklin, born August 19, 1793, Frank July 23 1794, Charles September 11, 1797, Clarissa Bird mentioned below, Cornelia, January 27, 1801, married Albert E Harding, Eugene, May 24, 1802 Christopher, July 31, 1803, Emmeline, January 7, 1805, George Henry, May 15, 1810

(VI) Clarissa Bird Ellery, eldest daughter of Christopher (2) and Clarissa (Bird) Ellery, born June 6, 1799, was married at Newport Third Congregational Church, September 1, 1820 by Rev Dr William Potter, to Major William James Tilley, of that city (see Tilley IV)

Nathaniel Bird, of Newport, was undoubtedly a descendant of Thomas Bird, who was born in England, 1613, and settled in Dorchester, Massachusetts, where he joined the church in 1642 He was a tanner by trade, was made bailiff in 1654 and died June 8, 1667 His widow Ann died August 21, 1673 Their second son James Bird, born about 1647, was a tanner, was ensign, constable, selectman and assessor, and died September 1, 1723, leaving an estate valued at £1,107, 16s 8d , including ninety acres of land He married, April 6, 1669, Mary George, who died January 23, 1673 Their son James (2) Bird, was born October 22, 1671, lived in Dorchester with his wife Miriam, who died May 2, 1723 No marriages are recorded in Dorchester from 1692 to 1695 He was constable in 1720, and died September 15, 1728 Their youngest child was Nathaniel Bird born October 14 1711 No trace of him can be discovered It is assumed that he was the father of Dr Nathaniel Bird, who first appears in Newport Rhode Island, and of whose history very little can be at this time learned He was the father of Mrs Clarissa (Bird) Ellery above mentioned

The name of Vernon has been a prominent and conspicuous one in the history of Rhode Island since the early settlement of that State and particularly so in Newport and vicinity Each generation of this honored family has produced men of

distinction who have made their presence felt in the community

(I) Daniel Vernon, son of Samuel Vernon, was born September 1, 1643, in London, England and is said to have come to this country about the year 1666 His emigration is thought to have been in part determined from the losses his father sustained in the great fire of that year in London, a range of his warehouses along the Thames and the quay having been burned in that disastrous fire Mr Vernon had received a very superior education spoke several languages and was long a tutor in the family of Lodowick Updike, or North Kingstown, Rhode Island In 1683 he was clerk of Kingstown, also constable, in 1686 he was appointed marshal of Kings province and keeper of the prison, in 1687 with Henry Tibbets he was appointed to lay out certain highways in Rochester In 1687 he was also a selectman of Kingstown, which was then known as Rochester On his arrival from England he appears to have first resided at Newport, but shortly after removed to Narragansett where at Tower Hill, September 22, 1679, he married Ann Dyre, a widow daughter of Captain Edward Hutchinson Jr and granddaughter of the celebrated Anne Hutchinson and grandniece of John Dryden She died January 10, 1716, her gravestone is still standing in the family lot at Newport beside that of her husband He died October 28. 1715 Their children were Daniel, born April 6, 1682 died young; Samuel mentioned below, Catherine. October 3, 1686, died unmarried in March 1769

(II) Samuel Vernon son of Daniel and Ann (Hutchinson-Dyre) Vernon born December 6, 1683 became a distinguished citizen of Newport was an assistant from 1729 until his death in 1737 and a judge of the Superior Court of Judicature In

1737 he was one of the commissioners appointed to fix the disputed boundary between Massachusetts and New Hampshire. His constant election to office shows that he was highly esteemed in the community, and he doubtless would have attained still further distinction had not his useful career been arrested by his death, December 5, 1737, while still in the prime of life. He married, April 10, 1707, Elizabeth Fleet, of Long Island, died March 5, 1721, aged thirty-seven years. Their gravestones, bearing the family coat-of-arms, are still in the Newport Cemetery. Children: Ann, born January 23, 1708; Elizabeth, August 4, 1709; Samuel, mentioned below; Esther, August 20, 1713; Daniel, August 20, 1716; Thomas, May 31, 1718; William, January 17, 1719; Mary, December 23, 1721. Of these children, Thomas was a merchant of the firm of Grant & Vernon; was royal postmaster at Newport from 1745 to 1775; register of the court of vice-admiralty twenty years; secretary of the Redwood Library, and senior warden of Trinity Church. He was a Tory, the only one in the family, and suffered about four months' imprisonment on account of his Tory principles. He wrote a journal of his captivity, now in the possession of the Newport Historical Society.

(III) Samuel (2) Vernon, son of Samuel (1) and Elizabeth (Fleet) Vernon,

was born September 6, 1711, and was a prominent Newport merchant, long a member of the house of S. & W. Vernon. He was one of the original applicants for the charter of the Redwood Library; and in 1750 was one of the petitioners to the king to restrain the Legislature from issuing bills of credit. He died July 6, 1792. He married Amey, daughter of Governor Richard Ward, and his children were: Elizabeth, born April 24, 1738; William, August 3, 1739, died in infancy; Samuel, July 12, 1740, died in infancy; Amey, September 12, 1741, died in infancy; Mary, mentioned below; Samuel, February 17, 1744, died December 1, 1809; Amey, July 19, 1746, died in infancy; Amey, November 19, 1747, married Samuel King, the portrait painter; William, July 21, 1749, died in infancy; William Ward, March 7, 1752, died April 10, 1774, in Jamaica, West Indies; Thomas, June 6, 1753, died April 6, 1755; Ann, September 29, 1754, married Dr. David Olyphant, medical director of the armies of the Carolinas, under Generals Gates and Greene during the Revolutionary War.

(IV) Mary Vernon, third daughter of Samuel (2) and Amey (Ward) Vernon, was born February 17, 1743, and married Christopher Ellery, an eminent merchant of Newport and a Revolutionary patriot (see Ellery IV).

INDEX

ADDENDA AND ERRATA

INDEX

Sarah, 265
Smith, Col , 265
Bowen, David, 52
  Richard, 51
  Richard, Dr , 51
  Thomas, 51, 52
Bradford, Elisha, 114
  Israel, 113
  Joseph, 114
  Joshua, 114
  William, 112, 113
Brett Hannah F , 19
  Henry A , 18
  Nathaniel, 17
  Samuel, 17
  Seth, 17
  William, 17, 18
  Zenas, 18
Brown Andrew, 303
  Chad, 302
  James, 303
  John, 302
  Joseph, 303
  Richard, 303
Bryant, Stephen, 198, 199
Buffinton, Benjamin, 185, 365, 366
  Daniel, 186
  Frank, 185, 187
  Mary E , 187
  Moses, 185, 365
  Oliver, 186
  Thomas, 185, 365
  Waldo A , 185 186
Bullock, Alexander H , 142, 145
  Augustus G , 139 143
  Chandler, 144
  Ebenezer, 140
  Hugh, 140
  Mary 144
  Richard, 140
  Rockwood H , 145
  Rufus, 141
  Samuel, 140
Burton, Albert W , 69, 71
  Elliott L 71
  George 70

John, 70
Mary E , 72
William, 70

Canedy, Alexander, 86
  William, 87
  William, Capt , 87
  Zebulon I , 88
Carpenter, Benjamin, 106
  Joseph, 105
  Jotham, 107
  William, 104
Carter, Elizabeth, 309
  Franklin, 308
  Preserved W , 308
  Sarah L , 309
Chace, Adeline F 361
  Anthony, 358
  Arthur F , Dr , 362
  Benjamin S , 361
  Carrie F , 362
  Celia P , 362
  Charles A , 361
  Eber, 358
  Emma F , 362
  Esther T , 360
  George M , 362
  Kathleen S , 362
  M Flossie, 362
  Obadiah, 358
  Obadiah Rev , 358
  Walter F , 362
  Warren O , 362
  William, 357, 358
Chamberlain Alexander F , 309
  George, 309
  Isabel, 310
Charnley Amelia A 272
  Ann, 271
  Annie L , 272
  Ellen S , 272
  Isabella, 272
  Isabella J , 272
  Joseph G , 270, 271
  Mary C , 272
  William, 271

283

CPSIA information can be obtained at www.ICGtesting.com
Printed in the USA
LVOW032357041111

253642LV00005B/1/P

9 781116 127416